NELSON EDUCATION SERIES
IN HUMAN RESOURCE MANAGEMENT

FIFTH EDITION

Strategic Human Resources Planning

NELSON EDUCATION SERIES
IN HUMAN RESOURCE MANAGEMENT

FIFTH EDITION

Strategic Human Resources Planning

Series Editor:
Monica Belcourt
SCHOOL OF HUMAN RESOURCE MANAGEMENT, FACULTY OF LIBERAL ARTS
AND PROFESSIONAL STUDIES, YORK UNIVERSITY

Kenneth J. McBey
YORK UNIVERSITY

Ying Hong
McMASTER UNIVERSITY

Margaret Yap
TED ROGERS SCHOOL OF MANAGEMENT
RYERSON UNIVERSITY

NELSON / EDUCATION

NELSON / EDUCATION

Strategic Human Resources Planning, **Fifth Edition**
by Monica Belcourt, Kenneth J. McBey, Ying Hong, and Margaret Yap

**Vice President, Editorial
Higher Education:**
Anne Williams

Acquisitions Editor:
Alwynn Pinard

Marketing Manager:
Dave Stratton

Developmental Editor:
Lacey McMaster

Permissions Coordinator:
Lynn McLeod

Content Production Manager:
Claire Horsnell

Production Service:
MPS Limited

Copy Editor:
Rodney Rawlings

Proofreader:
Jennifer McIntyre

Indexer:
Edwin Durbin

**Senior Manufacturing
Coordinator:**
Joanne McNeil

Design Director:
Ken Phipps

Managing Designer:
Franca Amore

Interior Design:
Dianna Little

Cover Design:
Martyn Schmoll

Cover and Part Opener Image:
Jupiterimages/Getty Images

Compositor:
MPS Limited

Printer:
Edwards Brothers Malloy

**Library and Archives Canada
Cataloguing in Publication**

Strategic human resources
planning / Monica
Belcourt ... [et al.]. -- 5th ed.

(Nelson Education series in human
resource management)
Fourth ed. by: Monica Belcourt,
Kenneth J. McBey.
Includes bibliographical references
and index.
ISBN 978-0-17-650694-0

1. Manpower planning--
Textbooks. I. Belcourt, Monica,
1946- II. Series: Nelson Education
series in human resource
management
HF5549.5.M3S87 2012
658.3'01   C2012-901697-7

ISBN-13: 978-0-17-650694-0
ISBN-10: 0-17-650694-2

To my son Brooker who provides interesting insights on organizational life.

M.B.

With love to the McBey family.
Nulli Secundus!

K.M.

To my supportive husband Bo.

Y.H.

BRIEF CONTENTS

CONTENTS

ABOUT THE SERIES

More than ever, human resources management (HRM) professionals need the knowledge and skills to design HRM policies and practices that not only meet legal requirements but also are effective in supporting organizational strategy. Increasingly, these professionals turn to published research and books on best practices for assistance in the development of effective HR strategies. The books in the Nelson Series in Human Resources Management are the best sources in Canada for reliable, valid, and current knowledge about practices in HRM.

The texts in this series include:

- *Managing Performance through Training and Development*
- *Management of Occupational Health and Safety*
- *Recruitment and Selection in Canada*
- *Strategic Compensation in Canada*
- *Strategic Human Resources Planning*
- *Research, Measurement, and Evaluation of Human Resources*
- *Industrial Relations in Canada*
- *International Human Resource Management: A Canadian Perspective*

The Nelson Series in Human Resources Management represents a significant development in the field of HRM for many reasons. Each book in the series is the leading Canadian text in its area of specialization. Human resources (HR) professionals in Canada must work with Canadian laws, statistics, policies, and values, and this series serves their needs. It is the only opportunity that students and practitioners have to access a complete set of HRM books, standardized in presentation, which enables them to access information quickly across many HRM disciplines. The books are essential sources of information that meet the requirements for the CCHRA (Canadian Council of Human Resource Associations) National Knowledge exam for the academic portion of the HR certification process. This one-stop resource will prove useful to anyone looking for solutions for the effective management of people.

The publication of this series signals that the field of HRM has advanced to the stage at which theory and applied research guide practice. For the practitioner, the series provides many examples of evidence-based best practices. The books in the series present the best and most current research in the functional areas of HRM. Research is supplemented with examples of the best practices used by Canadian companies that are leaders in HRM. Thus the books serve as an introduction to the functional area for the new student of HR and as a validation source for the more experienced HRM practitioner. Cases, exercises, and references provide opportunities for further discussion and analysis.

As you read and consult the books in this series, I hope you share my excitement at being involved in the development of a profession that has such a significant impact on the workplace.

Monica Belcourt, Ph.D., FCHRP
Series Editor
June 2012

ABOUT THE AUTHORS

Monica Belcourt

Monica Belcourt is the founding director of the School of Human Resources Management at the Faculty of Liberal Arts and Professional Studies at York University. Her writing is grounded in the experience she gained as director of personnel at CP Rail, as director of employee development at the National Film Board, and as a functional HR specialist for other organizations. Dr. Belcourt alternated working in HRM with graduate school, earning an M.A. in psychology, an M.Ed. in adult education, and a Ph.D. in management. In 2010 she was awarded the designation of Fellow Certified Human Resource Professional (FCHRP), a lifetime achievement award in recognition of extraordinary contributions to the profession. She has taught HRM at Concordia University, Université du Québec à Montréal (UQAM), McGill University, and York University. At York, she founded and managed the largest undergraduate program in HRM in Canada and Canada's only executive-style Masters in human resources management. She is the academic editor of the Nelson Series in HRM.

Dr. Belcourt was the founding director of the International Alliance for Human Resources Research (now recreated as HRRI [Human Resources Research Institute] and managed by HRPA), a catalyst for the discovery, dissemination, and application of new knowledge about HRM. Under her leadership, IAHRR launched The Research Forum, a column in *Human Resources Professional*; the Applied Research Stream at the annual HRPAO conference; and the best theses awards program.

Professor Belcourt is active in many professional associations and organizations. She was the president of the Human Resources Professionals Association of Ontario (www.hrpa.org). She is a frequent commentator on HRM issues for CTV's *Canada AM*, CBC, *The Globe and Mail*, Report on Business Television, Workopolis, and other media.

Kenneth McBey

Kenneth McBey is a professor of Human Resources Management at York University. His research and teaching draw on his earlier career as an infantry officer in the Canadian army, where he rose to the rank of Lieutenant-Colonel and commanding officer of the 48th Highlanders of Canada. Throughout his military career, Dr. McBey held a wide variety of command and staff appointments, including those in human resources–related areas such as recruiting, operations and training, and personnel officer (adjutant). This real-life testing of HR theories has proved invaluable to his work in the academic realm. Professor McBey earned an Honours B.A. in political economy and a B.Ed. from the University of Toronto, and an M.B.A. and Ph.D. in management from the Schulich School of Business at York University.

Professor McBey is director of the graduate program in Human Resources Management at York University, where he runs the executive masters in HRM, as well as the brand-new doctorate (Ph.D.) in HRM degrees. He teaches a wide variety of graduate and undergraduate courses, including human resources planning; leadership and management skills; recruitment, selection, and performance appraisal; training and development; staffing organizations; organizational behaviour; and organizational theory. He has been a visiting professor at the graduate programs in human resources and management at the University of Aberdeen, Scotland; the Australian National University, Canberra; and the University of Otago, Dunedin, New Zealand.

Professor McBey is active in a wide variety of community and voluntary associations, and he serves on the boards of several not-for-profit organizations. He was awarded the Queen's Golden Jubilee Medal by the Government of Canada for making a "significant contribution to his fellow citizens, community and to Canada." Among Professor McBey's other honours and awards are the J. Reginald Adams Gold Medal from the University of Toronto, the Canada 125th Anniversary Medal for outstanding service to Canada, the Canadian Forces Decoration (C.D.), and appointment to the Order of St. John by Her Majesty Queen Elizabeth II.

Ying Hong

Ying Hong is an assistant professor in Human Resources & Management at McMaster University. She teaches strategic HR planning and compensation. She researches the strategic role of human resources in businesses and has contributed to journals such as *Journal of Applied Psychology*, books such as the *Sage Handbooks of Human Resource Management*, and periodicals such as the *Financial Post*. Ying holds a Ph.D. in Industrial Relations/Human Resources and an M.S. in I/O Psychology.

Margaret Yap

Margaret Yap is an associate professor in human resources management at the Ted Rogers School of Management at Ryerson University. She teaches undergraduate and graduate courses in human resources management at Ryerson University and at the University of Toronto. Her research interests include human resources management in a global economy and diversity and equity in organizations focusing on ethnicity/race and gender. Prior to joining Ryerson, she was a research director at a nonprofit research and advisory organization and had held numerous human resources management roles at a multinational organization, including a three-year international assignment in Asia/Pacific. She was the director of the Diversity Institute in Management and Technology from 2006 to 2011.

Margaret has received numerous grants to conduct research projects in diversity in organizations and has published several articles on the topic. She holds an undergraduate degree in mathematics from York University and graduate degrees from the Centre of Industrial Relations and Human Resources at the University of Toronto. Her doctoral dissertation was awarded the best Ph.D. dissertation in HR by the International Alliance for Human Resources Research (IAHRR). The award was sponsored by HRSDC. Margaret has also been recently selected as one of the finalists for the HR Academic of the Year Award, one of the HR Summit Awards organized by the HRPA to recognize the very best in human resources management across the country.

PREFACE

The fundamental premise of this text is that different organizational strategies require different human resources management (HRM) policies and practices. *Strategic Human Resources Planning*, Fifth Edition, is designed to help human resources (HR) managers plan and make decisions about the allocation of resources for the effective management of people in organizations, within a given strategy.

HR planning should be more than just demand and supply forecasting; HR professionals should be business partners in strategy formulation and implementation and should be concerned with the implications of strategic decisions on HRM practices. A decision to expand internationally affects selection, compensation, and other functional areas. Strategic decisions to merge or downsize have HR implications beyond simple forecasting. All these strategic options will lead to questions about the best types of compensation, selection, and training to ensure the success of the chosen strategy. This text attempts to answer these questions, without neglecting traditional and important HR forecasting processes. It provides tools for HR planning and forecasting and matches corporate strategies with specific HR practices.

STRUCTURE OF THE TEXT

The text is organized to introduce the reader to the concepts of strategy formulation and implementation, within an HR context. Part 1, written by Ying Hong, a professor of HRM at McMaster University, outlines the fundamental building blocks of strategic HR with an introduction to the concepts and their links to HR planning, how trends and issues are identified, and how organizations determine whether implementation of strategies, policies, and plans are successful. Chapter 1 lays the groundwork by introducing the concepts of both corporate and business strategies. We spend some time explaining strategic choices, because it is imperative that, as HR managers become business partners, they understand commonly used business terms. This will help them to participate fully in strategic discussions and to explain the impact of their HR programs on the organization. *Strategy* seems to imply that only corporate-wide plans are made, and that these are used to manage and control the various units that exist within an organization. But many large organizations operate several businesses, each with its own strategy. For example, Alcan Aluminum Ltd. operates two "divisions" or businesses, one that focuses on primary metals and one that focuses on fabrication. Each has a different business strategy, although the overall corporate strategy is growth. Two types of business-level strategies are discussed. Because most HR professionals are becoming strategic planning partners, and are playing a critical role in the development of mission, vision, and value statements, we have included material on describing and differentiating these concepts. In the HR world, there is a growing understanding that human resources provide a competitive advantage. We describe what this means, and distinguish between tangible and intangible assets. We outline the benefits of strategy formulation. A model of strategic HR planning is introduced in this chapter to orient the reader and to provide the structure for the text.

Chapter 2 continues the introduction to strategy by embedding HRM strategy within an organizational strategic framework. A model of strategic HR planning is introduced in this chapter to orient the reader and to provide the structure for the text. As the field of HR develops, many are claiming that the discipline needs to have a theoretical foundation in order to test and validate new ideas about the best way to manage employees. We introduce three perspectives, which may be in the embryonic stages of testable theories: the resource-based view, the behavioural perspective, and the "theory" of human capital. The rest of the chapter is focused on a description of strategic HR, the reasons HR planning is important, and the ways in which the HR function contributes to the strategic planning process. Finally we conclude with a section that outlines the characteristics of an effective HR strategy.

The environmental factors that influence strategic choice, particularly within an HR context, are discussed in Chapter 3. We look at the sources of information about the environment and the methods HR strategists use to scan the environment. In this chapter, we have introduced new information about the stages of environmental planning. We have listed the sources of information that are useful for environmental scanning. We have added additional material about the methods of forecasting, including scenario planning. There is also a new section on competitive intelligence. We then describe changes in globalization, the labour market, politics and legislation, technology, demography, and culture that will influence the practice of HR. We conclude with a description of how stakeholders influence HR policies.

Part 2 focuses on the more traditional aspects of HR planning: forecasting supply and demand, revised by Margaret Yap, associate professor, Human Resources Management, Ted Rogers School of Management, Ryerson University. A critical component of strategy is matching employee capabilities with organizational objectives. The ability to assess current skills is a fundamental part of strategic planning for human resources. Part II provides a comprehensive set of tools that enables the HR professional to develop the numbers and methods needed to support organizational objectives. The critical role of job analysis within a planning context is discussed in Chapter 4. Time is spent analyzing the challenges of job analysis. This chapter describes how to use Canada's National Occupational Classification system, and discussion of the benefits and limitations of using the "competencies."

Chapter 5 explains the techniques used to forecast demand for human resources. Introduced by a new section on the impending talent shortage, this chapter outlines the categories and benefits of forecasting. A description of the personnel categories used by forecasters is provided. A description of the process for estimating net HR requirements begins by determining HR demand and supply, which allows forecasters to calculate surpluses or shortages. Chapter 6 focuses on the use of methods for analyzing demand and describes various qualitative and quantitative approaches for assessing the demand for HR including index/trend analysis, expert forecasting, the Delphi technique, the nominal group technique, staffing tables, envelope and scenario planning, and regression analysis.

Opening with the very timely analysis of the effect of the abolition of mandatory retirement on the supply of employees, Chapter 7 looks at the methods used for determining supply. These include skills and management inventories, replacement charts, Markov models, linear programming, movement analysis, and the vacancy model. Discussions on absenteeism, retention, and leadership development highlight the need for organizations to monitor these indices as part of effective HR supply and HR planning processes.

Managerial succession planning, discussed in Chapter 8, is an important consideration for ensuring that the organization has a stock of replacements for its managers. Succession management has evolved from replacement planning for individual executives to the development of talent pools for broad leadership roles aligned with the organization's strategies. Development techniques such as promotions, job rotations, special assignments, and mentoring and coaching are described. The role of employees in their own career development is outlined.

Chapter 9 builds on the chapter in the Fourth Edition that was written by an expert in human resources management systems (HRMS), Professor Victor Haines at the Université de Montréal. The focus is on the use of information technology specifically for the HR planning process, rather than a broad range of HR activities. The properties of advanced information technologies are described. Then the use of technology to facilitate different planning activities, such as skills inventories, replacement charts, and succession management, is outlined. Different IT solutions to meet different HR needs are presented including human resources information systems (HRIS), specialty products, and enterprise solutions. Prescriptions for choosing software providers are given. The implementation process is outlined, and issues such as data security are debated. The chapter concludes with descriptions of emerging HR technology solutions.

Part 3 examines the types of strategic orientations that firms may choose. Company-wide strategies, sometimes referred to as corporate strategies, are focused on overall strategy for the company and its businesses or interests. Examples of corporate strategies include decisions to merge or to establish the organization in international markets. Strategies at this level are usually also focused on long-term growth and survival goals. We discuss four major decisions facing organizations: restructuring, international operations, mergers and acquisitions, and outsourcing. HRM issues such as HR planning, compensation, selection, training, performance evaluation, and labour relations are discussed within the overall strategies of restructuring, international initiatives, and mergers. By the end of Part III, readers will understand how specific strategic decisions can be matched with HR policies and practices.

Chapter 10, written by Professor Terry Wagar of Saint Mary's University, discusses restructuring and downsizing. Starting with definitions of these two terms, this chapter presents different strategies for reducing the workforce. The reasons for downsizing are delineated. The consequences of reducing the workforce are explained, including survivor syndrome and the impact on financial indices. We include a debate on ethical considerations of downsizing and an introduction to other impacts of restructuring, including corporate reputation, organizational learning, and employee safety. This chapter offers suggestions for effective downsizing. The chapter concludes with a discussion on the effect of downsizing on such HR issues as the psychological contract and labour relations.

We then turn to an area of increasing importance in the strategies of organizations—growth through international initiatives. Chapter 11's author, Professor Stefan Gröschl of the faculty of management at the ESSEC Business School in Paris, France, discusses the growth option of seeking new customers or markets by locating internationally. HR managers state that globalization of their businesses is the number-one trend affecting their organizations. Operating a business in a foreign country, particularly one that is not North American or European, poses singular problems for the western HR manager. This chapter includes material on how to do so effectively.

In Chapter 12, we examine another high-growth area—mergers and acquisitions (M&As). An acquisition occurs when one company acquires another, whereas a merger is typically seen as two organizations merging to achieve economies of scale. Both acquisitions and mergers lead to issues of integration of common functions, elimination of duplication or underproductive units, and a meshing of cultures and practices. This chapter outlines the benefits of M&As, and compares the alleged benefits against the real effectiveness of this strategy. HR has a significant role to play, as mergers often fail because HR issues are not managed in a timely and effective manner. Prescriptions for doing so are provided.

The hot issue of outsourcing is explored in Chapter 13, with a thorough analysis of the reasons, risks, and benefits of the outsourcing decision. The benefits are not always realized, so the chapter offers suggestions for managing the outsourcing arrangement.

A critical part of strategic planning is the ability to measure results and to determine if goals have been met. Chapter 14, dealing with the evaluation of HR programs and policies, ends the book with content about the importance of measuring the effectiveness of HR. Because HR is a young field, we are prone to adopt emerging trends, and so a new section describes how to distinguish a fad from an effective HR program. This chapter provides a framework for understanding how HR processes, practices, and policies can affect organizational outcomes. The chapter outlines the many ways to evaluate effectiveness, and which areas to measure. The section on the HR scorecard captures the essence of this increasingly popular assessment tool. We include a list of the characteristics of successful measurement.

Features retained from the previous edition of this text include chapter learning outcomes, extensive use of Canadian examples, use of figures and tables to convey information efficiently, margin definitions of key concepts, chapter summaries, and listings of key terms.

New content of the fifth edition includes new chapter opening vignettes, as well as new "HR Planning Today" boxes to put issues in a real-life context, and new "HR Planning Notebook" boxes to highlight key points that flow from the chapter. Most of these cases were prepared by Jennifer Harrison, currently a Ph.D. student in HRM at York University. Jennifer interviewed many of the executives who were part of the MHRM program at York, resulting in current and real-life examples of best practices. End-of-chapter material includes some new discussion questions, exercises, and case studies.

Besides these learning features, a notable feature is a link between the textual material contained in this book and the Required Professional Capabilities (RPCs) necessary to earn a Certified Human Resources Professional (CHRP) designation. As a part of the process needed to earn this Canada-wide designation, granted by the Canadian Council of Human Resources Associations, applicants must take two exams, which cover 203 RPCs, organized into eight subject areas. All RPCs are listed on the Professional Assessment Resource Centre (PARC) website at www.cchra-ccarh.ca/parc/en/section_3/ss33e.asp. New to this edition is matching the RPCs covered in the chapter with the actual RPC numbers on the CCHRA website. Our hope is that this linkage of our content to the RPCs will help students and practitioners preparing for the CHRP examinations.

ADDITIONAL RESOURCES
Ancillaries for Instructors

Nelson Education Teaching Advantage (NETA) Program

The Nelson Education Teaching Advantage (NETA) program delivers research-based resources that promote student engagement and higher-order thinking and enable the success of Canadian students and educators. Recognizing the importance of multiple-choice testing in today's classroom and in response to instructors' concerns, Nelson Education has created the NETA Assessment program, a research-based program that improves the quality of our test banks by ensuring that they measure not just recall (as is typical with test banks) but also higher-level thinking skills. The program was created in partnership with David DiBattista, a 3M National Teaching Fellow, professor of psychology at Brock University, and researcher in the area of multiple-choice testing. All NETA test banks include David DiBattista's guide for instructors, *Multiple Choice Tests: Getting Beyond Remembering*. This guide has been designed to assist you in using Nelson test banks to achieve the desired outcomes in your course.

Instructor's Resource CD (0-17-661744-2)

Key instructor ancillaries are provided on the Instructor's Resource CD, giving instructors the ultimate tool for customizing lectures and presentations. The IRCD includes:

INSTRUCTOR'S MANUAL   The Instructor's Manual to accompany *Strategic Human Resources Planning*, Fifth Edition, has been prepared by Natasha Koziol. This manual contains learning outcomes, chapter summaries, suggested classroom activities, case studies, and additional exercises.

NETA ASSESSMENT   The Test Bank was written by Natasha Koziol, University of Western Ontario. It includes over 400 multiple-choice questions written according to NETA guidelines for effective construction and development of higher-order questions. Also included are true/false and short-answer questions.

Test Bank files are provided both in Word format for easy editing and in PDF format for convenient printing whatever your system. The Computerized Test Bank by ExamView® includes all the questions from the Test Bank. The easy-to-use ExamView software is compatible with Microsoft Windows and Mac platforms. Create tests by selecting questions from the question bank, modifying these questions as desired, and adding new questions you write yourself. You can administer quizzes online and export tests to WebCT, Blackboard, and other formats.

MICROSOFT® POWERPOINT®   Key concepts from *Strategic Human Resources Planning*, Fifth Edition, are presented in PowerPoint format, with generous use of figures and short tables from the text. The PowerPoint presentation was created by Natasha Koziol, University of Western Ontario.

IMAGE LIBRARY   This resource consists of digital copies of figures and short tables used in the book. Instructors may use these jpegs to create their own PowerPoint presentations.

DAYONE   DayOne—Prof InClass is a PowerPoint presentation that you can customize to orient your students to the class and their text at the beginning of the course.

WEBSITE (WWW.HRM.NELSON.COM)   All instructor's resources can be downloaded directly from the book's companion site at www.hrm.nelson.com.

Ancillaries for Students
Website (www.hrm.nelson.com)

The companion website for this fifth edition at www.hrm.nelson.com contains chapter quiz questions, allowing students to self-test their understanding of chapter concepts.

We hope that this book provides an enjoyable learning experience.

Monica Belcourt
Kenneth McBey
Ying Hong
Margaret Yap
June 2012

ACKNOWLEDGMENTS

The authors wish to acknowledge the contributions of two experts in HRM: Professor Terry Wagar of Saint Mary's University and Professor Stefan Gröschl of the ESSEC Business School in Paris, France. Each drew on personal research and experience to write outstanding chapters in their areas of expertise. We thank Professor Wagar for the chapter "Downsizing and Restructuring," and Professor Gröschl for building on the work of professors Xiaoyun Wang, of the University of Manitoba, and Sharon Leiba-O'Sullivan, of the University of Ottawa, for the chapter "Strategic International HRM." We also wish to thank Margaret Yap, Associate Professor, Human Resources Management, Ted Rogers School of Management, Ryerson University, who agreed to do the revisions for Chapters 4, 5, 6, and 7 for this edition. We thank Brooker Belcourt, an investment banker in New York City who specializes in mergers and acquisitions, for his review of Chapter 12, and for some useful insights and statistics. A special thanks to Jennifer Harrison, Ph.D. candidate in HRM at York University, for preparing some of the cases and highlights based on interviews with executives in the MHRM program at York.

The authors wish to thank the following reviewers who made helpful comments for this revision: Gordon Barnard, Durham College; Jerome Collins, St. Clair College; Lisa Gugliemi, Seneca College; Ruthanne Krant, Georgian College; Ted Mock, University of Toronto; David Parkes, Grant MacEwan University; Michelle White, Fanshawe College.

The team at Nelson contributed enormously through their professionalism and dedication. Karina Hope, in particular, has been tremendously helpful in the developmental process for the series. We would also like to thank acquisitions editors Amie Plourde and Alwynn Pinard, developmental editor Lacey McMaster, permissions coordinator Lynn McLeod, and the copy editor, Rodney Rawlings.

We are grateful to our students in the HR graduate program, especially those in the HRM Effectiveness class, for their research projects on strategic issues, and in the undergraduate course Human Resources Planning, for their thoughtful comments about the contents of the book. Above all, we wish to thank our colleagues across Canada who have supported the HRM Series by contributing their research, their experience, and their ideas to enable HRM students to read about the HRM landscape in this country.

Finally, we continue to owe much of our career success to the support of our families. I, Monica, thank Michael, my husband, who has been a constant supporter of my professional career. I, Kenneth, acknowledge the loving support of my family and the active interest and involvement of students in my Human Resources Planning courses for the evolution of this text. I, Ying, thank several outstanding scholars—Drs. Catano, Huselid, Jackson, Lepak, and Liao—who greatly influenced my thinking.

Monica Belcourt
School of Human Resource Management
Faculty of Liberal Arts and Professional Studies
York University

Kenneth McBey
York University

Ying Hong
McMaster University

Margaret Yap
Ted Rogers School of Management
Ryerson University
June 2012

PART 1

Introduction

CHAPTER 1

Strategic Management

CHAPTER LEARNING OUTCOMES

After reading this chapter, you should be able to:

- Discuss why managers need to examine the human resources implications of their organizational strategies.
- Discuss why human resources managers need to understand strategy.
- Understand the various terms used to define strategy and its processes.
- Describe organizational strategies, including restructuring, growth, and maintenance.
- Define business strategy and discuss how it differs from corporate strategy.
- Discuss the steps used in strategic planning.
- List the benefits of strategic planning.

STRATEGIC MANAGEMENT AT THE BAY

Hudson's Bay Company (HBC) is Canada's oldest organization, established in 1670 as a fur trading company. It has survived for over 300 years by adapting its strategy to changing environmental conditions, both threats and opportunities. The following condensed history will demonstrate that it has experienced nearly all of the strategic options described in this chapter.

In 1821, HBC merged with its main rival, The North West Company. The declining demand for fur influenced the decision to change the fur trading posts to retail stores, and HBC launched its department store business in 1913. The company also had a diversification strategy and at various times throughout its history sold liquor, salmon, coffee, tobacco, and real estate. The economic downturn of the 1980s caused HBC to rethink its priorities and, like many other firms, return to its core business. Non-retail businesses were sold off and retail businesses added. The pace of retail acquisition increased with takeovers of Zellers (1978), Simpsons (1978), Fields (1978), Robinson's (1979), Towers/Bonimart (1990), Woodward's (1994), and Kmart Canada (1998) following in the tradition of Cairns (1921), Morgan's (1960), and Freiman's (1971). Even HBC's subsidiaries had to adopt new business-level strategies. For example, when Walmart entered the Canadian retail market in 1994, competing head on with Zellers, the latter had to reposition itself from a low-cost business strategy to a differentiation strategy by selling exclusive and slightly upscale products such as Martha Stewart Everyday. Other retailers, such as Eaton's and Consumer Distributors, did not make good strategic decisions, and went bankrupt.

In 2005, HBC adopted a corporate growth strategy and a business-level strategy of differentiation coupled with low cost by opening new store concepts such as Home Outfitters and DealsOutlet.ca. In 2006, American billionaire Jerry Zucker bought HBC. Thanks to HBC's talent management and succession planning systems in place, HBC was able to quickly generate a new executive team from within. When Zucker died, his estate sold HBC to NRDC (owners of the Lord & Taylor department store). The recent economic recession again forced HBC to focus on its department store and specialty store businesses to drive growth. In 2011, HBC decided to spin off 220 stores of its weakest chain, Zellers Inc., to Target Corp for $1.825 billion. The remaining 50–60 stores will continue to operate as a smaller Zellers chain.

The HBC example highlights the strategic decisions made by organizations in their attempts to survive and become profitable. Each strategic choice has implications for the management of human resources. We start in this chapter by establishing a common understanding of strategy, its importance, and its link to human resources management (HRM).

A NEED FOR STRATEGIC HRM

Read any Canadian newspaper and you will see stories such as these:

- Roots Canada, a Toronto-based fashion company, recently launched a major global expansion and opened more than 40 stores in Asia. The company took the international initiative in response to Asian consumers' growing appreciation of foreign styles.
- Canadian workers are migrating from their home towns to cities where the jobs are located. According to Statistics Canada, more than 12,000 Atlantic Canadians moved to Alberta in the years of 2008 to 2009 to take advantage of the dynamic energy sector, which is having problems finding enough Westerners to fill jobs.

- In response to reduced profits and market share, Research in Motion initiated a "cost optimization program," which includes plans to restructure a number of executive positions, hire app developers in Silicon Valley, and lay off 4,000 of its estimated 19,000-person workforce.
- MagIndustries Corp. has been acquired by Evergreen Industries Group, a Shanghai-based private company, for $115 million, as part of its plan into expand to mining businesses.

The common theme in these stories is the adoption of a strategy that has serious HRM implications. In most cases, unless the HRM strategy, for example internationalization or downsizing, is appropriately formulated and skillfully implemented, the success of the organizational strategy is at risk.

We have written this book to provide answers to questions about the proper alignment of HR policies with organizational strategies. Managers who have implemented any kind of change within their organizations realize the importance of matching HRM practices with organizational goals. There is a growing acknowledgment that the strategic management of people within organizations affects important organizational outcomes such as survival, profitability, customer satisfaction levels, and employee performance. Our goal is to help readers understand strategy and the HRM programs and policies that enable organizations to achieve that strategy. We discuss strategy at some length, because HR professionals have been criticized for not understanding or using the language of business when discussing the value of HR programs. HR managers have to use strategy terms to show how their HR practices support organizational strategies.

Strategy

Strategy is the formulation of organizational objectives, competitive scopes, and action plans for gaining advantage.[1] Strategy is the plan for how the organization intends to achieve its goals. The means it will use, the courses of action it will take, and how it will generally operate and compete constitute the organization's strategy.[2]

We have presented one definition of strategy, but there are many others. A sampling is found in HR Planning Notebook 1.1.

The top management team determines strategy through a process of environmental analysis (which is discussed in Chapter 3) and discussions. The strategy developed by senior management is then approved by the board, and negotiated and revised as they filter throughout the organization. The organization then develops plans, which include HRM programs, to achieve those goals. This does not suggest, however, that strategic planning is a unilateral or one-time process. Various organizational outcomes provide a feedback loop to the strategic planning process led by senior management, who will also continuously monitor the dynamic environment to make adjustments to the strategy.

Strategic planning requires thinking about the future. In a perfect world, some experts believe that the strategic planner would establish an objective for five to ten years and then formulate plans for achieving the goals. However, other experts do not perceive strategy in such a simplistic, linear fashion. They assert that the future is not that predictable. Planning for the long term (i.e., more than ten years) is difficult and would be more appropriately judged as a best guess. For example, the nuclear power industry in Japan could not have

Strategy
The formulation of organizational objectives, scopes, and action plans for gaining advantage

HR Planning Notebook 1.1

DESCRIPTIONS OF STRATEGY

Concepts of strategy can be confusing. Here is a guide to some common terms used throughout the text and in the organizations where you work:

Strategy: A declaration of intent

Strategic intent: A tangible corporate goal; a point of view about the competitive positions a company hopes to build over a decade

Strategic planning: The systematic determination of goals and the plans to achieve them

Strategy formulation: The entire process of conceptualizing the mission of an organization, identifying the strategy, and developing long-range performance goals

Strategy implementation: Those activities that employees and managers of an organization undertake to enact the strategic plan and achieve the performance goals

Objectives: The end, the goals

Plans: The product of strategy, the means to the end

Strategic plan: A written statement that outlines the future goals of an organization, including long-term performance goals

Policies: Broad guidelines to action, which establish the parameters or rules

---

predicted the 2011 Tohoku earthquake and tsunami, nor could financial analysts have predicted the 2008 economic meltdown on Wall Street. Besides catastrophic events, there are more typical shocks to the competitive environment that trigger a change in strategy, such as changing market conditions, new technology, emerging markets, and new moves of competitors etc. Some other organizational events that precede strategic change are outlined in HR Planning Notebook 1.2.

Because of the unpredictability of trigger events, many planners look at a relatively shorter period of time, a more predictable term of three to five years. Because of the uncertainty, their plans are formulated to be somewhat flexible so that they can respond to changes in the environment. Thus, strategic planning must be viewed as a dynamic process, moving, shifting, and evolving as conditions warrant changes. The process of subtly redirecting strategy to accommodate these changes is called logical incrementalism.[3] Rather than calling for a straight path to the goal, this strategy calls for a series of actions to react to changes in competitor actions or new legislation. Another name for this reactive process is **emergent strategy**. This cumulative process can look like a dramatic revolutionary change to those on the outside, but to those on the inside, the strategy has been incrementally implemented.[4] Firms can wait passively for these changes to occur and then react, or they can anticipate these moves and adopt a proactive stance.

Writers on strategy sometimes distinguish between intended strategy and realized strategy. The **intended strategy** is the one that was formulated at the beginning of the period. The **realized strategy** is, of course, what actually happened.

Figure 1.1 illustrates these various concepts of strategy.

You may be asking: Why develop a strategy if the organization must continually change it to accommodate unforeseen changes? Think of strategy as a game plan or a flight plan. A pilot's flight plan looks relatively simple: fly from Ottawa to Edmonton. However, before departure, he or she is aware of the environment

Emergent strategy
The plan that changes incrementally due to environmental changes

Intended strategy
The formulated plan

Realized strategy
The implemented plan

HR Planning Notebook 1.2

TRIGGERING EVENTS TO STIMULATE A CHANGE IN STRATEGY

Here are some common examples of events that trigger a change in strategy within organizations:

- *New CEO:* May ask questions about the assumptions underlying the strategy and challenge the status quo.
- *Threat of a change in ownership:* Similarly to a change in CEO, new owners (or a threat of new ownership) causes a reconsideration of the effectiveness of the strategy.
- *External intervention:* Examples are a customer who accounts for a large portion of sales defecting to another company or lodging a serious complaint about a defect, or a financial backer refusing to invest any more in the organization.
- *Performance gap:* When sales or profit targets are not being met, most organizations will review the strategy.
- *Strategic inflection point:* Rapid changes in technology, customer preferences, or industry regulations will trigger a change in strategy.

Sources: Adapted from S.S. Gordon, W.H. Stewart, R. Sweo, and W.A. Luker, "Convergence versus Strategic Reorientation: The Antecedents of Fast-Paced Organizational Change," *Journal of Management*, vol. 26. no. 5 (2000), pp. 911–945; and T.L. Wheelen and J.D. Hunger, *Concepts in Strategic Management and Business Policy, 11th edition*, 2008, (Toronto: Prentice Hall), p. 19.

FIGURE 1.1

The Reality of the Strategic Process

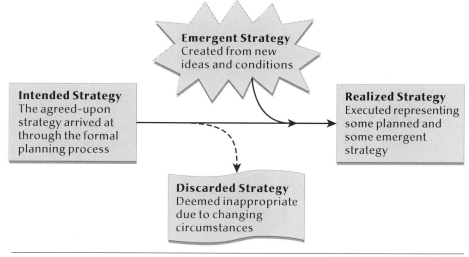

Source: Adapted from work by Henry Mintzberg. Used with permission.

and the capacities (or competencies) of the plane. On the basis of these external and internal factors, the pilot develops a strategy for a safe flight. While on the voyage, however, environmental changes, such as strong winds or a blizzard, may require a change of plans. Even internal factors, such as a passenger suffering a heart attack, may necessitate such a change. But the plane and/or its passengers will somehow, at some time, arrive in Edmonton. This is what is meant by incremental adjustments to the strategy, adjustments that do not require changing the focus of the desired result. There is no strategy so finely crafted that adjustments aren't needed. The general rule is that, unless there is a crisis, it should not be necessary to make quantum leaps in strategies. Thus, these strategies should withstand the test of time and be durable for several years.

A good strategy recognizes the complexity of these realities. To be effective, strategic management anticipates future problems, provides an alignment with external contingencies and internal competencies, recognizes multiple stakeholders, and is concerned with measurable performance[5]—just like the flight plan.

The fundamental premise of this book is that different organizational strategies demand different HR policies and practices. Therefore, before we can discuss HRM strategies, you need to understand the different types of strategies that organizations formulate and implement.

STRATEGIC TYPES

Many executives and senior managers put in an incredible number of hours forging the strategy for the firm, and they believe the strategy they developed, with much sweat and tears, is unique to their organizations. In one sense, pure, unique organizational strategies do exist, because organizations are extremely complex and no two are identical. In another sense, they do not, because it is possible to group strategies into categories or generic types. Just as we can group our friends into personality categories of introvert and extrovert, so we can group organizations by strategy. By virtue of their simplicity, these *typologies*, or classification schemes, aid our understanding. The more we add variables to approximate the reality of an organization, the more unwieldy the typology becomes.[6] Organizational theorists use classification schemes not only to help us understand how organizations work but also to enable us to test the concepts, leading us to better information about how to manage.

These identifiable, basic strategies can be classified into (1) corporate strategies and (2) business strategies.

Corporate Strategies

Corporate strategy
Organizational-level decisions that focus on long-term survival

Company-wide strategies, sometimes referred to as **corporate strategies**, are focused on overall strategy for the company and all of its businesses or interests. Examples of corporate strategies include decisions to compete internationally or to merge with other companies. Strategies at this level are usually focused on long-term growth and survival goals and will include major decisions such as the decision to acquire another company.

Grouped within corporate strategies are three options: restructuring, growth, and stability.

Restructuring Strategies

When an organization is not achieving its goals, whether these are business goals of profitability or social goals of helping rehabilitate prisoners, corporate strategy becomes one of trying to deal with the problem. Restructuring options include turnaround, divestiture, liquidation, and bankruptcy.

TURNAROUND   A **turnaround strategy** (sometimes called a *retrenchment strategy*) is one in which managers try to restore money-losing businesses to healthy profitability or government agencies to viability. Turnaround methods include getting rid of unprofitable products, layoffs, making the organization more efficient, or attempting to reposition it with new products. For example, facing its decreasing market share, which was exacerbated by the massive disruption of BlackBerry service around the world in October 2011, Research in Motion announced that it would adopt a new BBX operating system with new software QNX.[7] See also HR Planning Today 1.1 for a history of the turnaround efforts of McDonald's.

Turnaround strategy
An attempt to increase the viability of an organization

DIVESTITURE   **Divestiture** refers to spinning off a business as a financially and managerially independent company or selling it outright.[8] For example, the private equity fund NRDC acquired the Hudson's Bay Corp. for roughly $1.1 billion in 2008. In 2011, it divested one of HBC's weakest chains, Zellers, which was sold to Target for more than $1.8 billion, much higher than the price NRDC paid for HBC.[9] Quaker Oats, in contrast, sold its Snapple beverage business for $1.4 billion less than it paid for it, because too many new entrants restricted the old oatmeal company's ability to grow into a soft drink powerhouse.

Divestiture
The sale of a division or part of an organization

LIQUIDATION   The least attractive alternative is **liquidation**, in which plants are closed, employees released, and goods auctioned off. There is little return to shareholders under this option. Nevertheless, an early liquidation may allow

Liquidation
The termination of a business and the sale of its assets

HR Planning Today 1.1

Turnaround at McDonald's

The McDonald's burger chain has, for several decades, been a success story. Every year saw increases in outlets, people served, profits, and shareholder value. But in 2003, restaurant sales were down nearly 5 percent and profits were down by 11 percent. McDonald's had since made several attempts to revive its success.

One effort focused on making its food healthier through continuous innovation. It introduced premium salads in 2003, snack wraps in 2006, and real-fruit smoothies and frappés in 2010. Related to these introductions was its switch to trans-fat–free cooking oil for french fries and the use of organic milks. The company also introduced a food and nutrition website, and will create a new mobile app that allows customers to calculate the nutrients in their meal choices.

Another effort attempted to tap regional food interests. It has McArabias (grilled chicken in Arabic bread) in the Middle East, Shogun Burgers (teriyaki pork) in Hong Kong, McShawarmas (kosher meat) in Israel, Bulgogi Burgers in South Korea, and McSpicy Paneer in India.

A third attempt was to diversify; McDonald's added high-margin McCafé coffees in 2009 and Chipotle BBQ in 2011 to broaden its customer base.

Finally, as consumers were facing the economic recession, McDonald's boosted its low-price dollar-menu items, which included a double cheeseburger or a hot fudge sundae.

The company's strategies have, over the long run, proven successful. As of July 2011, sales were at record highs. Its share price has been on a continuous increase from a historic low of $13 a share in 2003 to more than $88 in 2011.

Sources: Adapted from D. Goold, "McDonald's Woes a Matter of Taste," *The Globe and Mail*, November 28, 2002, p. B9; "McDonald's Said Ready for More Restructuring," *The Globe and Mail*, March 24, 2003, p. B1; www.economist.com/blogs/schumpeter/2011/06/fast-food-and-cultural-sensitivity; and company fact sheets, www.mcdonalds.com, retrieved July 26, 2011.

some resources (including human resources) to be salvaged, whereas a bankruptcy does not. Bombay Company, a retailer of home furniture and accessories in the United States and Canada, was liquidated in 2008.

Bankruptcy
A formal procedure in which an appointed trustee in bankruptcy takes possession of a business's assets and disposes of them in an orderly fashion

BANKRUPTCY   **Bankruptcy** occurs when a company can no longer pay its creditors, and, usually, one of them calls a loan. The company ceases to exist, and its assets are divided among its creditors. For example, Borders Group Inc., the second largest bookstore chain in the United States, filed for bankruptcy in 2011, closing 200 of its 642 stores. The company had $1.28 billion of assets and $1.29 billion of debt.[10]

Restructuring strategies, like growth strategies, have profound effects on human resources issues, such as managed turnover, selective layoffs, transfers, increased demands on remaining employees, and renegotiated labour contracts. These issues are described in Chapter 10.

Growth Strategies

Many organizations in the private-sector target growth as their number-one strategy. By this they mean growth in revenues, sales, market share, customers, orders, and so on. To a large extent, the implications of a growth strategy for HR practices are profound. A firm in a growth stage is engaged in job creation, aggressive recruitment and selection, rapidly rising wages, and expanded orientation and training budgets, depending on how the organization chooses to grow.

Growth can be achieved in several ways: incrementally, internationally, or by mergers and acquisitions.

INCREMENTAL GROWTH   Incremental growth can be attained by expanding the client base, increasing the products or services, changing the distribution networks, or using technology. Procter & Gamble uses all these methods:

- Expanding the client base (by introducing skin-care lotion and hair conditioner for babies),

- Increasing the products (by adding Pringles potato chips to a product mix of cleaning and health care products),

- Changing the distribution networks (by adding drugstores to grocery stores), and

- Using technology to manage just-in-time customer purchasing.

INTERNATIONAL GROWTH   Seeking new customers or markets by expanding internationally is another growth option. Operating a business in a foreign country, particularly one that is not in North America or Europe, poses problems for the Western HR manager. The HR implications for an international strategy are described in Chapter 11.

Acquisition
The purchase of one company by another

Merger
Two organizations combine resources and become one

MERGERS AND ACQUISITIONS   Quantum leaps in growth can be achieved through acquisitions, mergers, or joint ventures. An **acquisition** occurs when one company buys another, whereas a **merger** typically is seen as two organizations merging to achieve economies of scale. Acquisitions and mergers have an obvious impact on HR: they eliminate the duplication of functions, meld benefits

HR Planning Today (1.2)

Merger Misery

Minacs Worldwide Inc., a company that operates inbound customer contact centres (i.e., call centres), was a Canadian success story. More and more companies were using its services as they turned to outsourcing their call centres. Minacs had experienced growth rates of 50 percent over five years and, in 2002, employed 4,500 people in 20 countries and generated sales of $250 million. The company expected to double sales and profits very quickly with the purchase of Phoenix Group, a U.S.-based call centre. But the purchase resulted in heavy losses. Although the two cultures seemed similar, the integration proved very difficult and time-consuming due to differences in accounting systems, pricing methods, and efficiency levels. The losses led to layoffs, the consolidation of offices, debt restructuring, and a severe drop in share value. In 2006, Minacs was acquired by TransWorks and has since received several awards for business excellence.

Sources: O. Bertin, "Minacs Worldwide Dials Back in After Disastrous US Purchase," *The Globe and Mail*, March 6, 2003, p. B17; www.minacs.com, retrieved September 30, 2008.

and labour relations practices, and, most importantly, create a common culture. The complexity of merging two companies is outlined in Chapter 12. HR Planning Today 1.2 describes a difficult merger.

Stability Strategies

Some organizations may choose stability over growth. For many reasons, some executives, particularly small business owners in relatively stable markets, wish to maintain the status quo. They do not wish to see their companies grow. The executive team is content to keep market share, doing what it has always been doing. HRM practices remain constant, as they are presumed to be effective for current strategy. Others see this as a temporary strategy ("Pause and proceed with caution") until environmental conditions are more favourable for growth. Or perhaps the organization grew very rapidly, such as Dell did by growing 285 percent in two years, and needed time to handle the growing pains. We have not included chapters on stability strategies, because the HRM issues would, by definition, be subsumed under another generic strategy.

Executives in other companies, recognizing that a current profitable situation will not last forever, choose to milk the investment. This harvest strategy can also be seen as a retrenchment strategy, because no investment or efforts will be made to make the business grow; therefore, the goal will be restructuring.

Businesses can pursue several strategies over time or concurrently. Read in HR Planning Today 1.3 about the strategies implemented by Cara Operations Ltd.

Business Strategies

We discussed corporate strategy as corporate-wide plans used to manage and control the various units that exist within an organization. But many large organizations operate several businesses under the same or different names, and each of these might have its own strategy. For example, Alcan Aluminum Ltd.

HR Planning Today 1.3

Multiple Strategies

The mission statement of Cara Operations Ltd. declares that its aim is to be Canada's leading integrated restaurant company. Cara owns or controls such food outlets as Harvey's, Swiss Chalet, and Milestones Grill and Bar. From 1996 to 2006, Cara's total revenue increased from about $643 million to over $1.44 billion. In 2007, Cara outlets served more than 100 million customers in 726 restaurants. Cara is an example of a company employing multiple corporate strategies—through acquisition, divestiture, and new concept development—to achieve increased sales and profitability.

- *Acquisitions:* Cara began an aggressive acquisitions strategy in 1999 when it bought 61 percent of Kelsey's, a Canadian company that owned 74 restaurants including Kelsey's, Montana's, and Outback. In 2002, Cara bought the Second Cup coffee chain and acquired a 74 percent stake in Milestones, a chain of upscale restaurants.
- *Divestiture:* In 2000, Cara sold its Beaver Food Catering business. In 2001, it sold its healthcare

institutional food services division. In 2006, it sold its airport terminal business as well as Second Cup. It divested the Summit division (distribution company) in 2007. In 2010, it sold its airline catering business, Cara Airline Solutions, to Gategroup, in order to focus its operation on restaurants.

- *Growth:* Cara has divested its non-core businesses and is focused on its restaurants. The divestitures resulted in cash that will be used to expand the number of restaurants. The growth strategy will see a doubling of restaurants (from 726 to more than 1,000) and sales (from $1.5 billion to $3 billion) over the next seven years.
- *Business strategy:* Arjen Melis, president of corporate development at Cara, describes Cara's business strategy as "pursuing a portfolio of distinct brands, each of which targets a differentiated consumer segment."

Sources: Adapted from www.cara.com, retrieved October 7, 2011; "Case Study: Cara Operations Ltd.," *National Post Business*, October 2002, pp. 47–50; interview with Arjen Melis, president of Corporate Development, Cara Operations Limited, May 27, 2008; "Cara Operations Selling Airline Catering Business to Swiss Company Gategroup," *The Canadian Press*, September 15, 2010; "Cara Operations Ltd. Financial Profile," Report on Business Financial Profile, *The Globe and Mail*, April 21, 2011.

Business strategy

Plans to build a competitive focus in one line of business

operates two "divisions" or businesses, one that focuses on primary metals and one that focuses on fabrication. Each has a different business strategy, although the overall corporate strategy is growth.

Business strategy focuses on one line of business (in a diversified company or public organization), while corporate strategy examines questions about which competitive strategy to choose as a multi-business corporation. Corporate strategies focus on long-term survival and growth. Business strategy concerns itself with how to build a strong competitive position. As Thompson and colleagues note, business strategy is the action plan for a single line of business to gain competitive advantage.[11]

Corporate strategies and business strategies are differentiated in the following ways. Corporate strategies are concerned with questions such as these: Should we be in business? What business should we be in? Business strategies are concerned with questions such as these: How should we compete? Should we compete by offering products at prices lower than those of the competition or by offering the best service? Business strategy, on the other hand, is concerned with how to build a competitive position, and with the best way to compete in that line of business. Air Canada was struggling with its business strategy when it attempted to segment the market by creating a series of sub-brands—discount, high-end, and charter. The discount airline Zip was created to compete directly with WestJet. Businesses try to demonstrate to the customer that their product or service is better than their rivals' because they have lower prices or more innovative services.

We will spend some time describing the strategic planning process, because HR professionals are expected to understand the language of business and to be able to discuss HR programs using the terminology of strategic planning. By learning the models and terms used by managers in business, HR managers will be able to propose or defend HR programs in ways that other managers will understand.

THE STRATEGIC PLANNING PROCESS

A strategic plan describes the organization's future direction, performance targets, and approaches to achieve the targets.[12] There are many models or approaches to the development and implement of strategy. Here is a useful framework of the steps that are involved in strategic planning, which is also illustrated visually in Figure 1.2:[13]

1. Establish the mission, vision, and values.
2. Develop objectives.
3. Analyze the external environment.

FIGURE 1.2

The Strategic Planning Process

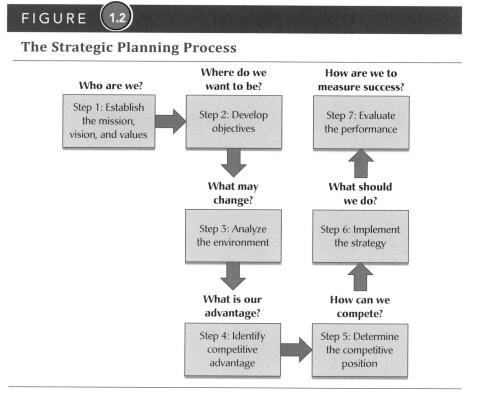

4. Identify the competitive advantage.
5. Determine the competitive position.
6. Implement the strategy.
7. Evaluate the performance.

1. Establish the Mission, Vision, and Values

Mission statement
An articulation of the purpose of the organization and the value it creates for customers

A **mission statement** articulates the purpose for which, or reason why, an organization exists.[14] It also stipulates the value the organization offers for its customers and clients.[15] For example, Walmart exists to provide "everyday low prices for a broad range of goods that are always in stock in convenient geographic locations."

Many believe that conveying a strong sense of mission is the most important role for the CEO. MacMillan Bloedel changed the company's position by articulating this mission statement: "The most respected and environmentally responsible forest company in Canada, and an example for others internationally. The public has granted us a license to operate, and they have a right to expect that we will be responsible guardians of their renewable resource." See HR Planning Today 1.4 to find out if you can recognize some mission statements, and see HR Planning Notebook 1.3 for an exercise to rate your organization's mission statement.

Vision statement
The basic beliefs that govern individual and group behaviour in an organization

A **vision statement** defines the organization's long-term goals. The distinction between a mission statement and a vision statement is that whereas the mission statement answers the questions "Who are we? What do we do? Why are we here?" the vision statement answers the question "Where are we going?"[16] A good vision statement sets a clear and compelling goal that serves to unite an organization's efforts. For example, the vision of Toyota before the financial crisis was to become number-one auto maker in the world. A good vision statement must also challenge and stretch the organization. A classic example is the vision of GE's former CEO Jack Welch, who always mandated each of its business units to become number one or two in its industry.[17]

Values
The basic beliefs that govern individual and group behaviour in an organization

Values are the basic beliefs that govern individual and group behaviour in an organization. While vision and mission statements answer the questions about

---

HR Planning Today 1.4

The "Person on a Bus Test" of Mission Statements

A test of a good mission statement is its ability to pass the "person on a bus test." In other words, could an average person correctly identify the company after reading its mission statement? Can you guess which companies are attached to these mission statements?

1. X will be a world leader in providing innovative physical and electronic delivery solutions, creating value for our customers, employees and all Canadians.

2. Our mission: to inspire and nurture the human spirit—one person, one cup and one neighborhood at a time.

3. To improve the lives of vulnerable people by mobilizing the power of humanity in Canada and around the world.

Answers on page 28.

HR Planning Notebook 1.3

RATE YOUR ORGANIZATION'S MISSION STATEMENT

On a scale of 0–2, with 0 indicating "no," 1 indicating "somewhat," and 2 indicating "yes," evaluate your organization's mission statement using the following questions:

1. Does the statement describe an inspiring purpose that avoids playing to the self-serving interests of stakeholders?

2. Does the statement describe the organization's responsibilities to stakeholders?

3. Does the statement define a business domain and explain why it is attractive?

4. Does the statement describe the strategic positioning that the company prefers in a way that helps to identify the sort of competitive position that it will look for?

5. Does the statement identify values that link with the organization's purpose and act as beliefs with which employees can feel proud?

6. Do the values resonate with and reinforce the organization's strategy?

7. Does the statement describe important behaviours and standards that serve as beacons of the strategy and values?

8. Are the standards described in a way that enables individual employees to judge when they are behaving correctly?

9. Does the statement give a portrait of the company capturing the culture of the organization?

10. Is the statement easy to read?

If the total is ten or less, then work is needed to improve the mission statement. Fifteen or more … great job!

Source: This article was published in *Long Range Planning*, vol. number 30, no. 6, Campbell, A., "Mission Statement," 931–932. Copyright Elsevier 1997.

what must be accomplished, values answer the question "How must we behave?" For example, 3M Company states, "We will grow by helping our customers win— through the ingenuity and responsiveness of people who care."

The mission, vision, and value statements of Cara, a leading food service and restaurant business, are presented in HR Planning Today 1.5.

Sometimes values reflect the founders' ethics; sometimes they are just words on the poster on the wall. In order to develop employee buy-in to values, have them participate in the elaboration of the organization values as described in HR Planning Notebook 1.4. Then these values should be part of every orientation workshop and training course, and be modelled by all employees, especially senior management. The articulation of values serves these important purposes:

• Conveys a sense of identity for employees

• Generates employee commitment to something greater than themselves

• Adds to the stability of the organization as a social system

• Serves as a frame of reference for employees to use to make sense of organizational activities and to use as a guide for appropriate behaviour

HR Planning Today 1.5

Cara's Mission, Vision, and Value Statements

Mission

Enhancing stakeholder value and building leading businesses, by maximizing our resources and living our values and principles.

Vision

To be Canada's leading integrated restaurant company.

Values

Cara's strength is based on our core values or fundamental beliefs of: the importance of our people, self-responsibility, integrity, a passion for winning and quality.

- *People*. Cara's success begins with and endures because of our teammates. We seek out good people, help them grow and improve their skills, appreciate their individuality and contributions, and celebrate their achievements.
- *Self-responsibility*. Teammates take the initiative to do what needs to be done. We take ownership of our work and results, put forth our best effort, and challenge what needs to be challenged. We hold ourselves accountable, and blame no one.
- *Integrity*. We are committed to honesty and doing the right thing. We say what we will do, do what we say, and acknowledge when we are wrong or have made a mistake.
- *Passion for winning*. Winning is much more than luck. It is dedication, desire, enthusiasm for competition, risk and hard work. We set our sights on winning, and are passionate about being first in all we do. Winners attract winners.
- *Quality*. We set high standards, and expect a level of achievement that says "best-in-class," so that it becomes a state of mind and a way of life. We always give our personal best, and continually raise the bar on excellence.

Source: www.cara.com. Reprinted with permission.

2. Develop Objectives

At this stage, the management team develops short-term objectives to realize its high-level mission, vision, and value. Objectives are an expression, in measurable terms, of what an organization intends to achieve.[18] Goals can be

HR Planning Notebook 1.4

CREATING ORGANIZATIONAL VALUES

1. Invite all employees to offer ideas about the current and the desired values for the organization.

2. Record these without judgments, criticisms, or comments.

3. Have the group identify common themes.

4. Discuss and debate these themes, until there is consensus on a short list of core values.

5. Have subgroups take one value, and develop a definition of the value and the employee behaviours related to that value.

6. Have groups present their definitions and behaviours, which may be adopted or revised.

7. Appoint one person from each team to incorporate the revisions into a value statement, which is then combined with all the value statements. These then become the company values.

HR Planning Notebook 1.5

EXAMPLES OF HARD OBJECTIVES

- Profitability
- Growth (increase in sales, assets)
- Shareholder wealth (dividends plus stock price appreciation)
- Market leadership (market share)

- Utilization of resources (return on investment [ROI] or return on equity [ROE])
- Efficiency (cost per unit produced)
- Quality (percentage of waste; percentage defective)

Sources: This article was published in *Long Range Planning*, vol. number 30, no. 6, Campbell, A., "Mission Statement," 931–932, Copyright Elsevier 1997.

classified as hard or soft. Hard goals always include numbers, usually relative to performance last year, or to competition. For example, an organization would not state a goal as "increased profitability"; the statement would be action oriented and specific: "to increase profitability in 2013 by 7 percent over 2012."

HR Planning Notebook 1.5 offers some examples of typical objectives for corporations. Soft goals usually define the targets for the social conduct of the business, and may not always be quantifiable. Soft goals may include being ethical and environmentally responsible, and providing a working environment free of discrimination with opportunities for professional development. One of the most widely applied frameworks for categorizing objectives is the balanced score card model, which divides organizational strategy into four comprehensive perspectives: financial, customer, learning and growth, and internal business process.[19] A merit of this framework is that it forces each organizational member to think about how their actions can contribute to organizational strategy implementation. It has been adopted by many Canadian organizations, such as AT&T Canada, Carlton University, Nova Scotia Power Inc., Ontario Hospitals, Royal Canadian Mounted Police, and St. Michael's Hospital.[20]

3. Analyze the External Environment

To achieve the company objectives, managers must be aware of threats and opportunities in the external environment. By scanning and monitoring technology, laws and regulations, the economy, sociocultural factors, and changing demographics, managers can make reactive and proactive changes to the strategic plan. These will be discussed in detail in Chapter 3.

4. Identify the Competitive Advantage

Besides the external environment, managers also need to consider what **competitive advantage** the organization possesses—that is, what characteristics enable it to generate more value for customers at a lower cost, thereby earning

Competitive advantage
The characteristics of a firm that enable it to earn higher rates of profit than its competitors

higher rates of profit than its competitors.[21] Competitive advantage normally derives from those resources that allow the organization to perform more effectively or efficiently than competitors, which fall into three categories:

- *Tangible assets:* These are future economic resources that have substance and form from which an organization will benefit. Examples are land, inventory, building, location, cash, technology systems.

- *Intangible assets:* These are future economic resources that have been generated from past organizational events. These assets lack substance and form. Examples are human capital, reputation, goodwill, trust, copyright.

- **Capabilities:** These are a complex combination of people and processes that represent the firm's capacity to exploit resources to achieve firms' objectives.[22] Examples are managerial capabilities, innovative capabilities, marketing capabilities, and organizational cultures. These capabilities—the collective skills, abilities, and expertise of an organization—are the outcome of investments in staffing, training, and other HR areas. They are stable over time and are not easy to measure or benchmark; therefore, competitors cannot copy them.[23]

The resource-based view suggests that for these resources and capabilities to provide a sustained competitive advantage, they must meet four criteria:[24]

1. They are *valuable* to the firm's strategy (help generate value/reduce cost).
2. They are *rare* (competitors don't have them).
3. They are *inimitable* (cannot easily be copied by competitors).
4. They are *nonsubstitutable* (cannot be replaced by other substitutes).

The culture at Southwest Airlines meets all these characteristics, as can be seen in HR Planning Today 1.6. Besides culture, many other forms of resources have a potential to meet all four criteria. For example, the innovative capabilities embedded in employees' specialized expertise, knowledge-sharing routines, and incentive systems for innovation are unique to the organization; and customers' trust in the brand name, created by a cumulated history of ethical behaviours of the business and its employees, is not transferable. Some common reasons for these resources and capabilities being a source of sustained competitive advantage are: they are unique, they must be built up over time, they require large-scale investment, and they are socially complex.[25] As you can see, human resources play a key role in creating most capabilities.

Resources and capabilities become **core competencies** when they serve as a firm's competitive advantage. Core competencies distinguish a company competitively and reflect its personality.[26] In other words, a core competency is a competitively important activity that directly contributes to a company's strategy.[27] The core competency of Southwest Airlines is culture and that of Sony is miniaturization. Walmart's core competency is its cross-docking inventory management system, which helps it reduce costs. Kimberly-Clark is the best in the world at producing paper-based consumer products, choosing to specialize in category-killer brands (where the name of the product is synonymous with the name of the category—for example, Kleenex).[28]

Capabilities
A complex combination of people and processes that represent the firm's capacity to exploit resources that have been specially integrated to achieve a desired result

Core competencies
Resources and capabilities that serve as a firm's competitive advantage

HR Planning Today (1.6)

Culture as a Competitive Advantage

Southwest Airlines' strategy is that of low cost/low price/no frills flights, a strategy that has resulted in profits every year since 1974. The organization's culture is its competitive advantage, and possesses all the key characteristics.

Attribute: Valuable

Does the Southwest Airlines culture offer customers something that they value? Yes. The culture results in employees who are productive, flexible, motivated, and willing to accept a low base pay and work long hours. This not only keeps costs down but also improves utilization and on-time delivery performance.

Attribute: Rare

Is Southwest Airlines the only one with this type of culture? If not, is the level of its culture higher than that of competitors? Yes. Each airline has its own culture but only the Southwest culture has inspired employees to care so much about their company that they accept very low base salaries, yet are highly productive and flexible; work almost twice as long and are more motivated than other airline's employees; and would rather support the company than the union. The "family" at Southwest is just not found at other airlines.

Attribute: Imitability

Is it easy for other firms to acquire this culture? No. Duplicating this culture is likely to be difficult. Although others may think that they know what makes Southwest employees so motivated, productive, flexible, and dedicated, that may not be the case. Also, building the Southwest culture may have involved a series of events that are impossible for another firm to re-create.

Attribute: Substitutability

Can another capability offer customers the same value that the "Southwest culture" does? No. In an industry where utilization is critical, it is difficult for another capability to give airlines the value created by a productive, flexible, highly motivated workforce.

Attribute: Able to Appropriate Money

Does Southwest make money from its unique culture? Yes. Southwest's good position in relation to suppliers and customers enables it to appropriate the value from its extraordinary culture. Barring a major change that diminishes the culture or reverses the relationship, Southwest should continue to make money.

Source: Allan Afuah, *Business Models. A Strategic Approach,* © 2004, Table 10.4, p. 207. Reproduced with the permission of The McGraw Hill Companies.

Core competencies can be leveraged. For example, when Amazon.com developed the competency to sell books through the Internet, it leveraged this competency to deliver other consumer products such as CDs. HR managers should be particularly aware of how to contribute to the creation of core competencies.

What if the competencies needed for gaining competitive advantage constantly evolve? In fact, many companies face this difficulty when they continuously compete to seize emerging market opportunity or develop new technology. **Dynamic capabilities**—the ability to adapt and renew competencies in accordance with changing business environment[29]—are particularly important in these situations. Being able to regenerate its competencies responsively, Amazon.com started online bookselling in 1998, more than a decade earlier than Borders. Amazon.com was

Dynamic capabilities
The ability to adapt and renew competencies in accordance with changing business environment

also the first to pioneer digital books with the Kindle e-reader in 2007, three years earlier than Borders. Borders' lack of dynamic capabilities to regenerate itself, in contrast, was one of the main reasons for its bankruptcy.[30]

With the information from external environment and internal competence analysis, managers can summarize the conclusions using a SWOT analysis, which is a tool for analyzing a company's resource capabilities and deficiencies, its market opportunities, and the external threats to its future.[31] SWOT is an acronym for **S**trengths, **W**eaknesses, **O**pportunities, and **T**hreats. A *strength* is something that a company does well or an attribute that makes it more competitive. A *weakness* is something that an organization does poorly, or a condition, such as location, that puts it at a disadvantage relative to competitors.[32] *Opportunities* and *threats* are environmental conditions external to the firm that may be beneficial or harmful. But an organizational strength can be used to combat an external threat. For example, the very capable legal department (a strength) of Texas Instruments was able to collect nearly $700 million in damages and royalties from Korean and Japanese firms that were infringing on its copyright (a threat). Sometimes an external indicator, such as a rising concern with personal health, may be beneficial for one sector (health clubs) and harmful to others (tobacco companies).[33]

5. Determine the Competitive Position

On the basis of the external environment and internal competence, managers then decide the competitive position the company wants to achieve. A company cannot usually compete by being ready to offer any product or service at various prices through multiple channels of distribution. The senior managers must determine who the customers are, where they are located, and what product or service characteristics these customers value. Thus the organization has to create a **value proposition**—a statement of the fundamental benefits it has chosen to offer in the marketplace. The value proposition of TD Bank's Green Line Investor services was very simple: lower-cost transactions than through traditional brokerage channels.

Michael Porter made a major contribution to the field of strategic management by grouping the many ways in which organizations can compete into five generic competitive strategies:[34]

Value proposition

A statement of the fundamental benefits of the products or services being offered in the marketplace

1. *Low-cost provider strategy:* The goal here is to provide a product or service at a price lower than that of competitors while appealing to a broad range of customers. Fast-food businesses use this strategy almost exclusively. A range of customers from toddlers to seniors consumes the cheap hamburger, a good but basic product with few frills. A company competing on this basis searches continually for ways to reduce costs.

2. *Broad differentiation strategy:* An organization employing this strategy seeks to differentiate its products from competitors' products in ways that will appeal to a broad range of buyers. It searches for features that will make its product or service different from that of competitors and that will encourage customers to pay a premium. Thus, Burger King will introduce the Whopper with "frills," for which people will pay an extra dollar. The goal is to provide a unique or superior value to the buyer in terms of product quality, product features, or service.

3. *Best-cost provider strategy:* The goal here is to give customers more value for their money by emphasizing a low-cost product or service and an upscale differentiation. The product has excellent features, including several upscale features that are offered at low cost. East Side Mario's offers hamburgers but presents them on a plate, with extras such as potato salad, served by a waiter in an attractive setting featuring focused lights and art on the walls.

4. *Focused or market niche strategy based on lower cost:* The goal here is to offer a low-cost product to a select group of customers. Red Lobster uses this approach, selling fish and seafood at reasonable prices to a narrow market segment.

5. *Focused or market niche strategy based on differentiation:* Here, the organization tries to offer a niche product or service customized to the tastes and requirements of a very narrow market segment. For example, Bymark Restaurant in Toronto sells a $35 hamburger that uses sirloin meat and truffles.

Under Porter's schema, business strategy concerns itself with the product and market scope. What particular goods and services are to be provided? What distinguishing features or attractive attributes will characterize these products and services? Typical product characteristics are cost, quality, optional features, durability, and reliability. Market dimensions refer to the characteristics of the target market—size, diversity, buying patterns, and geographic regions. The model has been criticized for its overlapping categories. Most textbooks on strategy suggest that there are really only three competitive positions: cost, differentiation, and focus.

6. Implement the Strategy

Strategy implementation is the process of establishing the programs, budgets, and procedures for facilitating the achievement of the strategic goals. If the goal is growth, what are the techniques for achieving this goal? Should a company expand its distribution channels to other regions? Should it attempt to change its culture? **Strategy implementation** is the process by which the strategy is put into action. This process is sometimes called *operational planning.* It consists of programs, budgets, and procedures, such as those for HR. The **program** outlines the steps or activities necessary to accomplish the goal. If the goal is innovation, how can HR recruit, select, train, and create a supportive culture to accomplish it? The role of the HR function in enabling the execution of strategy is discussed in Chapter 2. The budget lists the detailed costs of each program, and defines how the organization is going to allocate its financial resources. Most organizations establish a *hurdle rate,* the percentage of return on investment necessary before a program is implemented. As you will see in Chapter 14 on evaluation, most HR managers are very skilled at preparing a budget for the implementation of a new program, but unable to discuss, in dollars, the rate of return for the program. **Procedures** list the steps required to get the job done. Most HR professionals use procedures—for example, the procedure to recruit a university student—based on experience. But other functional areas would have these procedures established as standard operating practice; these would be applied uniformly across the company, in every site.

Strategic implementation
The process by which a strategy is put into action

Program
The steps or activities necessary to accomplish a goal

Procedures
The steps required to get a job done

7. Evaluate the Performance

Developing a strategy is easy; making it happen is not. The ability to execute strategy is becoming a more important criterion for assessing not only managers but also the whole organization. The successful implementation of a strategy is judged by the ability to meet financial targets such as profits, and the ability to meet benchmarked ratios of efficiency and effectiveness such as R&D expenses to sales, or sales to assets. As you will see in Chapter 14, companies are using the balanced scorecard approach to evaluate other important indicators of success, such as customer satisfaction or employee engagement. These measures are becoming increasingly valuable for their ability to predict financial and operational performance.

Benefits of Strategy Formulation

Working through the strategic planning process has these benefits:

- *Clarity:* There is focused and guided decision making about resource allocations.

- *Coordination:* Everyone is working toward the same goals.

- *Efficiency:* Daily decision making is guided toward the question "Does it fit with our strategy?"

- *Incentives:* Employees understand the behaviours and performance that will be rewarded.

- *Adjustment to change:* If a major change is under consideration, understanding the current strategy is essential.

- *Career development:* Helps potential employees decide if they want to work for the company, if there is a skills fit, and what training and development they will need to undergo.

Organizations that do not see the benefits of strategic planning have succumbed to these errors:

- Relegating the process to official planners, and not involving executives and managers (and even employees), resulting in no buy-in

- Failing to use the plan as the guide to making decisions and evaluating performance

- Failing to align incentives and other HR policies to the achievement of the strategy

An understanding of the strategic planning process is the essential first step to creating an HR strategy that makes sense for the organization. Strategic HR planning complements the traditional approach to HR planning (forecasting supply and demand) but adds more strategic choices. Thus, at the most senior levels of the corporation, HR professionals move from an administrative role to the role of strategic partner. They understand strategies and business needs and create the kind of HR competencies that build competitive advantage.

FIGURE 1.3

An Overview of the Organization of the Textbook

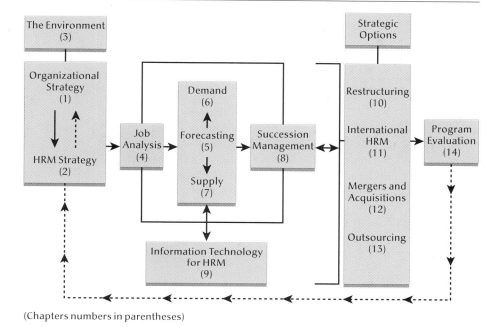

(Chapters numbers in parentheses)

The strategic planning model has dictated the structure of this text. We emphasize aligning HR strategy with business strategy (Chapter 2), monitoring and analyzing external factors (Chapter 3), assessing the strengths and weaknesses of organizations' human resources (Chapters 4–9), determining the HR implications of such corporate strategies as restructuring (Chapter 10), going international (Chapter 11), mergers and acquisitions (Chapter 12), outsourcing (Chapter 13), and assessing the effectiveness of these efforts (Chapter 14). Figure 1.3 graphically summarizes the organization of this book.

SUMMARY

It is important that HR professionals appreciate the role of strategic planning in their organizations and understand the language and terminology of strategic planning. A strategy is a planned process whereby organizations can map out a set of objectives and methods of meeting those objectives. A strategy may be *intended*—formulated at the beginning of the process—or *realized*—what actually happens. The strategy may also be *emergent*; that is, it is changing as necessary to deal with environmental changes. Corporate or company-wide strategies are concerned with the long-term view of the organization. Business strategies focus on one line of business, building a strong competitive position. One useful framework is a seven-step approach (see Figure 1.2). By understanding strategy language and models, the HR professional can work with other executives to implement HR practices that enable strategy.

Key Terms

acquisition p. 10	merger p. 10
bankruptcy p. 10	mission statement p. 14
business strategy p. 12	procedures p. 21
capabilities p. 18	program p. 21
competitive advantage p. 17	realized strategy p. 6
core competencies p. 18	strategic implementation p. 21
corporate strategies p. 8	strategy p. 5
divestiture p. 9	turnaround strategy p. 9
dynamic capabilities p. 19	value proposition p. 20
emergent strategy p. 6	values p. 14
intended strategy p. 6	vision statement p. 14
liquidation p. 9	

Web Links

Excellent links for references on strategic planning:
www.strategyclub.com

Provides useful lists of the benefits and pitfalls of strategic planning:
www.entarga.com/stratplan/index.htm

A publication that provides articles, interviews, and case studies focused on strategic management and general business issues:
www.strategy-business.com

Collects examples of the application of balanced scorecards in businesses:
www.balancedscorecard.org

Required Professional Capabilities (RPCs)

The following RPCs are relevant to material covered in this chapter. The RPC number represents the CCHRA number assigned to the RPC as presented on the CCHRA website. All of the RPCs can be found in the Body of Knowledge at www.chrp.ca/rpc/body-of-knowledge.

RPC 1 Contributes to the development of the organization's vision, goals, and strategies with a focus on human capabilities

RPC 12 Develops business cases for HR initiatives and strategies

Discussion Questions

1. On the basis of the opening vignette and your own research, describe the current corporate strategy of Hudson's Bay Company, and compare the business strategies of The Bay and Zellers.
2. Identify companies currently operating under these corporate strategies: restructuring—turnaround, divestiture, liquidation, and bankruptcy; growth—incremental, international, and mergers and acquisitions.
3. Review these three mission statements and assess whether they meet the "person on a bus" test.

   • To provide book lovers and those they care about with the most inspiring retail and online environments in the world for books and life-enriching products and services.

   • X is dedicated to building a world-class national resource enabling Canadians to know their country and themselves through their published heritage, and to providing an effective gateway to national and international sources of information.

   • X is an independent campaigning organization that uses nonviolent, creative confrontation to expose global environmental problems and to force the solutions essential to a green and peaceful future.

4. The focus in this chapter (and in strategy literature) is on private companies. Check the websites of government departments and identify at least ten strategies (often called *plans* or *mission statements*). Can you identify any that correspond to some of the models of business strategies? Can you create a model or typology for public-sector organizations? To start, consult J. Tomkins, "Strategic Human Resources Management in Government: Unresolved Issues," *Public Personnel Management*, Vol. 31, No. 1 (2002): 95–110.

Exercises

1. Identify two companies working in the same sector (hotels, restaurants, and postsecondary institutions are good choices), one using a low-cost provider strategy and one using a differentiation strategy
2. Research these two companies' mission, vision, and value statements.
3. Discuss their differences in resources, capabilities, and core competencies.
4. Compare and contrast the practices of the two companies.
5. Write objectives for each of the following balanced scorecard categories for each company:

   i. Financial objectives.
   ii. Customer objectives
   iii. Learning and growth objectives
   iv. Internal business process objectives

Case LOBLAW COMPANIES LTD.

The Canadian food retailing sector had been growing at about 3 percent a year, and in 2010 it was a $83.9 billion business. There are a number of competitors in this sector, including Sobeys Inc., Metro Inc., Costco Canada Inc., Canada Safeway, and Walmart Canada Corp. Loblaw Companies Inc. is Canada's largest food distributor with sales of more than $30 billion, 1,000 stores, and 136,000 employees. The organizational objectives were to control costs through efficiencies and differentiate their products (through private-label brands such as President's Choice, No Name, Organics PC, and Joe Fresh) and its stores (through 22 different brand banners such as Loblaw, Fortinos, No Frills, Provigo, Zehrs, Wholesale Club, and Atlantic Superstore). In 2009, it acquired T&T, the largest Asian foods chain, to capitalize on the growing ethnic food market. Loblaw wants to see sales growth of 5 percent a year.

The largest threat to Loblaw's strategy is Walmart, the world's largest retailer. It has a growth strategy, opening hundreds of stores every year. Walmart arrived in Canada in 1994, by acquiring 122 Woolco stores. It quickly dominated, and in 2002 became the largest retailer in Canada, surpassing Eaton's (now bankrupt), Hudson's Bay, and Sears. Walmart not only used size and scale to compete (as did other retailers) but also mastered the use of technology to drive costs down. For example, its centralized information system tracked the operations of 5,000 stores worldwide, and linked them with about 30,000 suppliers, all in real time.

Sources: www.loblaws.com; "Loblaw Companies Limited: Company Profile," www.datamonitor.com; Z. Olyjnk, "Look Who's Eating Loblaw's Lunch," *Canadian Business*, vol. 80, no. 5 (February 26, 2007): 44.

Question

1. Conduct a SWOT analysis for Loblaw. As a group, assess the company against the strengths, weaknesses, threats, and opportunities contained in the SWOT matrix below.

SWOT Analysis

Potential Resource Strengths and Competitive Capabilities	
• A powerful strategy	• Superior intellectual capital relative to key rivals
• Core competencies in _____	• Cost advantages over rivals
• A distinctive competence in _____	• Strong advertising and promotion
• A product that is strongly differentiated from those of rivals	• Product innovation capabilities
• Competencies and capabilities that are well matched to industry key success factors	• Proven capabilities in improving production processes
• A strong financial condition; ample financial resources to grow the business	• Good supply-chain management capabilities

- Strong brand-name image/company reputation
- Good customer service capabilities

- An attractive customer base
- Better product quality relative to rivals

- Economy of scale and/or learning and experience curve advantages over rivals
- Wide geographic coverage and/or strong global distribution capacity

- Proprietary technology/superior technological skills/important patents
- Alliances/joint ventures with other firms that provide access to valuable technology, competencies, and/or attractive geographic markets

Potential Market Opportunities

- Openings to win market share from rivals
- Expanding the company's product line to meet a broader range of customer needs

- Sharply rising buyer demand for the industry's product
- Utilizing existing company skills or technological know-how to enter new product lines or new businesses

- Serving additional customer groups or market segments
- Online sales

- Expanding into new geographic markets
- Integrating forward or backward

- Falling trade barriers in attractive foreign markets
- Entering into alliances or joint ventures that can expand the firm's market coverage or boost its competitive capacity

- Acquiring rival firms or companies with attractive technological expertise or capabilities
- Openings to exploit emerging new technologies

Potential Resource Weaknesses and Competitive Deficiencies

- No clear strategic direction
- Behind on product quality, R&D, and/or technological know-how

- Resources that are not well matched to industry key success factors
- In the wrong strategic group

- No well-developed or proven core competencies
- Losing market share because _____

- A weak balance sheet; too much debt
- Lack of management depth

- Higher overall unit costs relative to key competitors
- Inferior intellectual capital relative to leading rivals

- Weak or unproven product innovation capabilities
- Subpar profitability because _____

- A product/service with ho-hum attributes or features inferior to those of rivals
- Plagued with internal operating problems or obsolete facilities

• Too narrow a product line relative to rivals	• Behind rivals in e-commerce capabilities
• Weak brand image or reputation	• Short on financial resources to grow the business and pursue promising initiatives
• Weaker dealer network than key rivals and/or lack of adequate global distribution capability	• Too much underutilized plant capacity

Potential External Threats to Company's Well-Being

• Increasing intensity of competition among industry rivals may squeeze profit margins	• Likely entry to potent new competitors
• Slowdowns in market growth	• Loss of sales to substitute products
• Growing bargaining power of customers or supplies	• Restrictive trade policies on the part of foreign governments
• A shift in buyer needs and tastes away from the industry's product	• Costly new regulatory requirements
• Vulnerability to industry driving forces	• Increased costs relating to utilities

Source: Thompson, Strickland, and Gamble, *Crafting and Executing Strategy 14/e* © 2005. Reprinted with the permission of the McGraw-Hill Companies, Inc.

Answers to HR Planning Today 1.4

1. Canada Post
2. Starbucks, and
3. Canadian Red Cross

ENDNOTES

1. Collis, D.J., and M.F. Rukstad. 2008. "Can You Say What Your Strategy Is?" *Harvard Business Review*, Vol. 86: 82–90.
2. Anthony, W.P., P.L. Perrewe, and K.M. Kacmar. 1993. *Strategic Human Resources Management.* Fort Worth, TX: Harcourt Brace Jovanovich.
3. Quinn, J.B. 1980. *Strategies for Change: Logical Incrementalism.* Homewood, IL: Richard D. Irwin.
4. Collins, J. 2001. *Good to Great.* New York: Harper Business.
5. Lengnick-Hall, C., and M. Lengnick-Hall. 1990. *Interactive Human Resource Management and Strategic Planning.* New York: Quorum Books.
6. Duane, M.J. 1996. *Customized Human Resource Planning.* Westport, CT: Quorum Books.
7. business.financialpost.com/2011/10/18/rim-unveils-next-generation-bbx-platform, retrieved on October 19, 2011.

8. Thompson, A.A., M.A. Peteraf, J.E. Gamble, and A.J. Strickland. 2010. *Crafting and Executing Strategy: The Quest for Competitive Advantage*, 18th ed. New York: McGraw-Hill Companies, Inc.

9. www.theglobeandmail.com/globe-investor/target-heads-north-in-zellers-deal/article1868308, retrieved on March 28, 2011.

10. www.bloomberg.com/news/2011-02-16/borders-book-chain-files-for-bankruptcy-protection-with-1-29-billion-debt.html, retrieved on March 28, 2011.

11. Thompson et al., 2010.

12. Thompson et al., 2010.

13. Woodcock, C.P., and P.W. Beamish. 2003. *Concepts in Strategic Management*, 6th ed. Toronto: McGraw-Hill Ryerson.

14. Certo, S.C., and J.P. Peter. 1993. *Strategic Management: A Focus on Process*, 2nd ed. Boston: Irwin.

15. Kaplan, R.S., and D.P. Norton. 2008. "Mastering the Management System." *Harvard Business Review*, January: 64–77.

16. Certo and Peter, 1993.

17. Kaplan and Norton, 2008.

18. Crossan, M.M., J.N. Fry, and J.P. Killing. 2002. *Strategic Analysis and Action*, 5th ed. Toronto: Prentice Hall.

19. Kaplan, R.S., and D.P. Norton. 2007. "Using the Balanced Scorecard as a Strategic Management System." *Harvard Business Review*, July/August: 150–161.

20. www.balancedscorecard.org, retrieved on July 28, 2011.

21. Peteraf, M.A., and J.B. Barney. 2003. "Unraveling the Resource-Based Tangle." *Managerial & Decision Economics*, Vol. 24: 309–323.

22. Hitt, M.A., R.D. Ireland, R.E. Hoskisson, W.G. Rowe, and J.P. Sheppard. 2002. *Strategic Management, Competitiveness and Globalization Concepts*. Toronto: Nelson Thomson Learning.

23. Ulrich, D., and N. Smallwood. 2004. "Capitalizing on Capabilities." *Harvard Business Review*, June: 119–127.

24. Barney, J.B. 1995. "Looking Inside for Competitive Advantage." *Academy of Management Executive*, Vol. 9: 49–61; Collis, J., and C.A. Montgomery. 1995. "Competing on Resources: Strategy in the 1990s," *Harvard Business Review*, Vol. 73, No. 4 (July/August 1995): 118–128.

25. Collis, D.J., and C.A. Montgomery. 2008. Competing on Resources. *Harvard Business Review*, Vol. 86: 140–150.

26. Hoskisson, R.E., M.A. Hitt, and R.D. Ireland. 2004. *Competing for Advantage*. Mason, OH: Thompson South-Western.

27. Thompson et al., 2010.

28. Collins, 2001.

29. Teece, D.J., G. Pisan, and A. Shuen. 1997. "Dynamic Capabilities and Strategic Management." *Strategic Management Journal*, Vol. 18: 509–533.

30. www.bloomberg.com/news/2011-02-16/borders-book-chain-files-for-bankruptcy-protection-with-1-29-billion-debt.html, retrieved March 28, 2011.

31. Thompson et al., 2010.

32. Thompson et al., 2010.

33. Dess, G.G., and G.T. Lumpkin. 2003. *Strategic Management: Creating Competitive Advantages.* Boston: McGraw-Hill.

34. Porter, M.E. 1985. *Competitive Advantage*. New York: Free Press.

Aligning HR with Strategy

CHAPTER LEARNING OUTCOMES

After reading this chapter, you should be able to:

- Understand the importance of strategic HR planning.
- Identify the risks associated with not planning.
- Discuss approaches to linking strategy and HR, including the barriers to becoming a strategic partner.
- List the characteristics of an effective HR strategy.

HR STRATEGY AT GOOGLE

Google has grown within a decade from a startup to a global company with a $180 billion market capitalization. Google's core business is its web search engine, which generates 99 percent of its revenue through advertising. Thanks to this cash cow, Google has been able to sponsor many innovative and competitive services, including its Gmail service, which was the first to have one-gigabyte storage, and Google Talk, which allowed free phone calls in North America. It has also entered the smartphone industry, in which its free Android operating system has quickly gained a 30 percent market share within two years.[1]

Google's success was in part due to its economies of scale in its financial, information, and technology resources. To keep growing, Google needs to continuously sense market opportunities and take action faster than others. Google knows that such dynamic capability cannot be generated from financial or physical resources alone, but also must come from the analytical, decision-making, and innovative capabilities of its human resources. Consequently, a software engineer at Google can receive up to $151,000 starting salary (excluding options, bonuses etc.), as against Apple ($149,000), Facebook ($138,000), and Microsoft ($128,000).[2] It is also famous for its extraordinary benefits for employees such as free food, varied recreational activities, and free services such as tax advice,

on-site child care, and doctors. Even at 2010 year-end, when the economy was still under recession, Google gave all employees a 10 percent raise plus a $1,000 bonus to retain valuable talents. It is not surprising that for five consecutive years, from 2007 to 2011, the company ranked among the top five on *Fortune* magazine's list of the best companies to work for.[3]

Google has strategically aligned its HR practices with the company's needs as well. To encourage innovation, it allows employees to spend 20 percent of their paid time doing anything they want. To help employees work better, the company has designed a course called "Managing Your Energy for Your Sustained Performance" for 2,000 first-year employees.[4] It has also established a talent analytics function consisting of 30 researchers, analysts, and consultants who have scientifically studied what types of human capital were strategic to the company's performance, what types of managers were effective or ineffective, and what types of HR practices enabled the recruitment and retention of the best talent.

As Google's vice-president of people operations has commented, "It's not the company-provided lunch that keeps people here. Googlers tell us that there are three reasons they stay: the mission, the quality of the people, and the chance to build the skill set of a better leader or entrepreneur. And all our analytics are built around these reasons."[5]

STRATEGIC HRM

Human resources management (HRM) can be viewed as an umbrella term that encompasses the following:

- Overarching HR *philosophies* that specify the values put on HR that inform an organization's policies and practices
- Formal HR *policies* that direct and partially constrain the development of specific practices, such as to increase workforce diversity
- Specific HR *practices*, such as recruitment, selection, and appraisal

Strategic HRM is the management of HR philosophies, policies, and practices to enable the achievement of the organizational strategy. Ideally, these philosophies, policies, and practices form a system that attracts, develops, motivates, and trains employees who ensure the survival and effective functioning of the organization and its members.[6] There is an emerging view that the discipline of HRM should be split into two areas, much like accounting and finance or sales and marketing.[7] One area would deal with transactional activities, such as payroll, which are routine but necessary, just like accounting. The second area would function like a decision science, concerned with the effective utilization of human capital, much like finance. In this model, strategic HRM would be concerned with decisions about HR practices, the composition and behaviours of employees, and the effectiveness of these decisions given various business strategies.[8] These strategic activities are comprehensive, are planned, and in their contribution to organizational success are considered high-long-term-value-added.[9]

While managers recognize implicitly that marketing strategy must support the business strategy, there is not the same sense among managers that HR programs can be designed to support the organizational strategy. And yet human capital issues are at the top of the CEO agenda, with more than half of the top priorities (attraction, retention, innovation) needing HR input.[10] According to recent surveys, three-quarters of Canadian organizations believed that HR was more influential now than five years ago; the reorganization of HR importance was especially higher among CEOs and senior managers (about three-quarters believed so) than other managers (about half).[11]

Strategic HRM
Interrelated philosophies, policies, and practices that facilitate the attainment of organizational strategy

THEORIES OF THE STRATEGIC MANAGEMENT OF HUMAN RESOURCES

HR practitioners themselves do not seem to value theory. HR is seen as atheoretical and problem-driven.[12] But the field is young, and perspectives are indeed emerging that can be seen as providing the theoretical underpinnings.

HRM Making Strategic Contributions

Human resources management, formerly called "personnel management," started as an administrative function and has traditionally been associated with costs in organizations. Its contributions were often measured by the number of disputes resolved, applicants recruited, total hours spent on training, etc. It is no wonder that many organizations attempted to minimize the size of the HR department by outsourcing administrative tasks to external vendors.

During the 1980s, strategic HR researchers and practitioners started to wonder whether HRM could make strategic contributions to organizations. Certain "high-performance" HR practices, such as selective hiring, extensive training, and competitive pay, came to be considered "best practices," because they were often found in the most successful organizations.[13] Cumulated research showed consistent evidence that the implementation of high-performance HR systems significantly predicted various organizational performance indicators, ranging from reduced employee turnover to improved quality and organizational performance.[14]

This perspective stimulated a broad implementation of high-performance HR systems in many businesses, as managers began to believe that investment in HR would eventually lead to higher financial performance. The term "human resources" was adopted, reflecting the recognition of personnel as valuable "resources" that create competitive advantage, an idea that can be traced back to the resource-based view.

Resource-Based View

The resource-based view was introduced in Chapter 1, in which the culture of Southwest Airlines was described as a resource that provided a sustained competitive advantage, because its culture is valuable, rare, and very difficult to imitate or substitute. The less a resource can be imitated, the more durable the source of competitive advantage. In addition to culture, a firm's human resources can create sustained competitive advantage if they meet all four criteria suggested by the resource-based view. First, employees who have superior performance because of their skills, commitment, or flexibility are *valuable*—they help the company beat out competitors by offering better service/unique products or reducing costs. The employee loyalty of Marks & Spencer, for example, helped reduce its labour costs to 8.7 percent, as against to an industry average of 10 to 20 percent. This dramatically added value to the company.[15]

Second, human resources can be *difficult for competitors to imitate*. If IBM introduces a new software package in January, Microsoft can probably imitate or duplicate this package by February of the same year. However, if IBM technical support people are trained and motivated to provide "knock-your-socks-off service," Microsoft will have a difficult time imitating this workforce within a month. Indeed, Porter estimates that it takes approximately seven years to duplicate a competitive edge in human resources. The competition can't just "buy" these employees, because their effectiveness is embedded in the HR systems of training, compensation, performance appraisal, and culture that allow them to work productively.[16]

Third, the best human resources are *rare*. "Talent war" describes the fierce competition among firms, especially in the high-technology industry, for the best talent. Almost 80 percent of Canadian organizations indicated that they had difficulty recruiting quality candidates with skills that were important to the organization or in high demand.[17] More reputable employers known for their advantage in attracting, developing, and keeping good talent are more likely to gain access to the best talent on the market. "Canada's Top 100 Employers" is an annual competition among Canadian businesses on their offerings to employees. Research in Motion was included for five consecutive years from 2007 to 2011, for their practices such as planning for retirement, providing a BlackBerry on the first day, offering tuition subsidies, and giving on-site care and services etc.[18] However, as its share price plummeted from $150 four years ago to below $10 today, its cumulative reputation as a best employer was ruined by its recent reshuffling of the boardroom and across-the-board layoffs of nearly a quarter of its workforce, which will damage its future ability to attract and retain top talent.

Finally, the value of human resources can be *hard to substitute*. As discussed in Chapter 1, dynamic capabilities are critical for today's businesses to continuously lead the competition. Dynamic capabilities allow businesses to be the first to discover new opportunities, to act faster than others to seize opportunities, and to quickly create the internal processes needed to realize these opportunities.[19] Other resources such as technology and physical resources do not have free will, and thus cannot substitute for decisions and changes made by human resources.[20] Take, for example, the competition between Apple and Nokia. Nokia was once known for its superior technology in producing the most reliable hardware. However, technology and resources do not regenerate by themselves. Yesterday's cutting-edge technology can become inadequate today. Apple bested Nokia in accurately sensing the potential market for smart phones, swiftly entering the business, and successfully regenerating its technology to become competitive in the market, largely due to the dynamic capabilities created by its human resources. HR department's role, then, is to develop a system that will facilitate and stimulate innovative thinking processes.

Therefore, a firm's human resources are more valuable for sustained competitive advantage than technological and physical resources, particularly in today's competitive and fast changing environment, because human resources are less visible, more complex, and can initiate change.[21] For these reasons, human resources are increasingly perceived as strategic resources. Given the unlimited potential of HR, how to exploit it is explained by the contingency perspective.

The Contingency Perspective

In Chapter 1 we learned that business strategies ranged from low-cost to high-differentiation. Although high-performance HR practices in general contribute to high performance, they may be more cost effective for businesses that pursue a differentiation strategy than for those implementing a low-cost strategy. This is called the *contingency perspective* of HRM. It is not difficult to imagine that employees working at Ritz Carlton would be very different from those working at Comfort Inn: they vary in their human capital (e.g. communication skills), as well as in the behaviours (e.g. customer orientation) that they display to customers. Such employee differences are largely shaped by the HR practices in place, and can be explained by the human capital and behavioural theories.

Human Capital Theory

Classical economists describe three types of resources or inputs used in the production of goods and services: land, capital, and labour. Labour, or **human capital**, refers to the collective sum of the attributes, experience, knowledge, and commitment that employees choose to invest in their work. This intangible asset comprises the knowledge, education, vocational qualifications, professional certifications, work-related experience, and competence of an organization's employees.[22] As researchers have noted, "In the new economic paradigm, as the demands for continuous change make innovation, adaptability, speed and efficiency essential features of the business landscape, the strategic importance of intellectual capital and intangible assets [has] increased substantially. While these assets are largely invisible . . . the sources are not. They are found in the human capital of the firm's employees."[23] From the perspective of human capital, employees are viewed as a capital resource that requires investment.[24]

Human capital
The sum of employees' knowledge, skills, experience, and commitment invested in the organization

Employees are of value to the organization to the extent that they work toward accomplishing organizational objectives. Costs incurred in training, motivating, compensating, and monitoring employees can be viewed as investments in human capital, just as maintenance of equipment is an investment in the capital of the firm.[25] Thus, human capital's value added can be estimated by:

$$\frac{\text{Total revenue} - (\text{operating expenses} - \text{total compensation costs})}{\text{Total compensation costs}}$$

Using this formula, it was estimated that the median human capital return on investment for Canadian organizations was $2.26, meaning that each dollar organizations invested on human capital generated $2.26 in return. Human capital return on investment also varied by industry, with finance, insurance, and real estate having the highest median return ($6.89), followed by manufacturing and construction ($2.19), and wholesale and retail trade ($2.02).[26] It is reasonable to expect that human capital return on investment would also vary by strategy, with differentiated organizations generating a higher return than low-cost organizations.

The advantages of an organization with effective HR practices may come, not only from having better resources, but also from making better use of these resources by achieving higher productivity per worker and matching the capabilities of employees with the strategy.[27] Organizations that compete on service excellence, for example, would invest on service-related human capital. Banks that invested in HR systems for service quality, such as selecting, training, and rewarding employees' service-related skills, had superior service-related human capital and subsequently higher customer evaluation of service quality.[28] To simplify, having a stock of human capital is similar to having a team of talented players. Knowing how to leverage their talents is like having skills in managing and coaching this team. So, too, without the right HR systems, the employees are less effective.

Behavioural Theory

The behavioural perspective suggests that different strategies require not only different human capital, but also different behaviours of employees. HR Planning Today 2.1 describes how employee behaviour can influence organizational outcomes.

An effective HR system first accurately identifies the behaviours needed to implement a strategy. For example, what kinds of employee behaviours are needed for Google to produce innovative ideas? This question may not sound difficult for HR managers. Providing expert opinion on human behaviour might be where the HR profession adds the most unique value. Most HR managers have a clear understanding of whether the company needs risk taking or rule following, competition or teamwork. HR's role is to tactfully challenge and refocus baseless ideas of human behaviour.[29] How to design the HR system to ensure that employees have the skills and opportunities to exhibit desired behaviours and are motivated to do so is more complex and requires deep thinking and systematic analysis.[30] In general, researchers considered performance

HR Planning Today (2.1

Sears: The Behavioural Link to Profits

Sears was one of the first organizations in the world to document the relationship between employee behaviour and the firm's performance. The company pioneered studies that defined and empirically verified the correlation between individual sales associates' behaviours, customer satisfaction, and financial performance. Sears executives have embraced a business strategy that relies on employees as the source of competitive advantage. After much research, Sears concluded that two employee attitudes (perceptions about their jobs and perceptions about the company) had a significant effect on employee retention and behaviour toward its company. The company made sure that employees received performance feedback from customers so that they could see the direct relationship between their behaviour and customer satisfaction. These changed employee behaviours then had a direct and dramatic effect on customer satisfaction and retention, which then impacted revenue growth, operating margins, and return on assets.

Source: M. Warech and J. B. Tracey, "Evaluating the Impact of Human Resources," *Cornell Hotel and Restaurant Administration Quarterly*, vol. 45, no. 4 (2004), pp. 376–387; B.E. Becker and M.A. Huselid, "Overview: Strategic Human Resources Management in Five Leading Firms," *Human Resource Management*, vol. 38, no. 4 (1999), pp. 287–301, copyright © 1999 John Wiley & Sons, Inc.; this material is used by permission of John Wiley and Sons, Inc.

appraisal, pay for performance, incentive plans, advancement opportunities, and benefits to enhance employee motivation to behave. Concomitantly, practices such as employee involvement, participation in decision making, voice and grievance, performance feedback, teamwork, and job enrichment operate to provide opportunities for employees to behave. Both practice bundles have shown significant impact on organizational outcomes.[31]

Behavioural perspective suggests that these HR practices should be further catered to a particular behavioural objective. For example, what kinds of HR practices will produce innovative behaviours? We learn from the opening vignette that Google encouraged innovative behaviours by selecting people with high creativity, providing them with time and freedom to innovate, and motivating them to innovate through various incentive programs. But this is only one of many ways of encouraging creativity; each method may be specific to each organization's culture and traditions. We will discuss the alignment of HR system with business strategy in more detail later in the chapter.

The behavioural perspective is particularly important as the HR department is asked to define and develop the behaviours necessary to achieve organizational capabilities of innovation, speed, and accountability.[32]

Strategic HR Planning

Despite the potential of HRM to make strategic contributions, HRM issues are often cited as a threat to an organization's ability to execute strategy. The free will, complex behaviours, and human capital make effectively planning and managing human resources extremely difficult.

A more traditional perspective of the HR planning concept implied that the organization was concerned only with possible problems of labour surpluses and shortages. The goal was to determine the knowledge, skills, and abilities (KSAs) required within broad organizational outcomes such as growth or decline. Much emphasis was put on the statistical techniques for analyzing resource supply and demand forecasting while ignoring managerial realities and support for the process.[33] This is now regarded as a narrow, linear approach to HR planning.

There is some concern that the narrow approach of HR planning has been preoccupied with resource supply and demand forecasting without considering the different HR practices required by fundamentally different strategies. For example, a company that decides to grow through the introduction of innovative products needs employees with different kinds of skills from a company that will grow through great customer service. Under traditional HR planning models, both strategies would require the acquisition and absorption of large numbers of employees, but the HR prescriptions for selection, training, and performance management, for example, would differ radically.

In this book, we are suggesting both an approach of forecasting supply and demand of human resources and an approach that calls for tailoring HR policies and practices to the organizational needs of the future. The proliferation of bankruptcies, mergers, and restructuring has affected our view of employees profoundly and highlighted the need for the input of HR professionals in formulating policy.

The Importance of Strategic HR Planning

Executives are demanding that the HR department move from articulating perceived value ("training builds employee skills") to demonstrating real value (the training results in fewer errors or more sales). As a member of the corporate team, the focus of HR must be on scoring points, not just coaching, training, or counting the number of players. The value of HR will be seen in its ability to deliver the behaviours needed to enable the organization's strategy. There are at least two reasons strategic HR planning is so important: (1) employees help an organization achieve success because they are strategic resources, and (2) the planning process itself results in improved goal attainment.

The value of employees as a resource must be placed within a strategic framework. In other words, a strategy itself can become obsolete, making current employee skills obsolete. Suppose, for example, that the current workforce may be valuable because of manual skills, but the market for the company's manufactured products is declining. Environmental analyses suggest that the corporation enter the high-tech field, with its demand for flexible, knowledgeable workers. By changing the strategy, the "value" of the current workforce is diminished. This requires HR planners to be forward-looking; when there is a vacancy, HR managers might not look for replacements for current skills, but rather consider what skills will enable the organization to implement its strategy a few years from now. A corollary is that employees can expect to face different HRM practices throughout their lifetimes, and even within a single organization. Employees might be asked to exhibit different behaviours, depending on strategic goals, and these behaviours will be motivated by different HRM practices.[34] HR planning ensures that human assets are managed and matched to the organizational strategy. Readers are invited to assess the HR planning efforts led by Billy Beane at the Oakland Athletics in the end-of-chapter exercises.

Improved Goal Attainment

Strategic HRM can improve an organization's performance. The goals of these HRM strategies are to shape employee behaviour so that it is consistent with the direction the organization identifies in its strategic plans. Organizations with clear strategies provide direction and meaning to employees and mitigate the need for control by substituting a consistency of purpose—in other words, a mission. This articulated vision for the future may result in a more effective organization through increased motivation and performance, lowered absenteeism and turnover, and heightened stability, satisfaction, and involvement.[35] HR Planning Today 2.2 illustrates how HSBC Canada used HR planning to facilitate a strategic change.

To summarize, strategy formulation is important to the attainment of organizational goals in order to align all HR functional strategies with overall strategy and to focus employees on important missions and goals of the organization. Research and observations have demonstrated that developing HR practices that support the strategy leads to improved strategy implementation.[36]

HR Planning Today (2.2

HSBC Canada: Upfront Planning

HSBC Canada is a subsidiary of the London-based HSBC Holdings plc with more than 60,000 employees. In 2009, the parent company decided to move all support functions including HR to shared services, in order to lower HR costs and help operational partners become more independent in HR services. In addition, HSBC launched a multiyear enterprise resource planning initiative to ensure that employees across the corporation use a consistent version of PeopleSoft HR application developed by Oracle. The subsidiaries were fully empowered to determine how to launch the change.

To lead this change, Pat Brosseau, vice-president of HR for HSBC Canada, emphasized the importance of HR planning. She had to reduce the number of HR generalists working with business-line colleagues. To this end, she and her team invested considerable effort into understanding what the new operating model would look like, defining the HR experience that all HSBC employees would have, and detailing each HR role. "We went into granular detail using process maps and policy reviews to understand, for example, exactly how the role of an employee relations specialist would differ from an HR generalist in the new operating model," she explained. Three factors helped the change progress:

- Within HR there is a change management unit consisting of three HR generalists with organizational design experience and skills, developed road maps, communication plans, and tactics for HR clients.
- HR professionals collaborate with the HSBC Canada project management team.
- HR professionals work with communications specialists in the corporate communications department to ensure the overall effectiveness of the communication plan.

Sources: Adapted from E. Krell. 2011. "Change within: Align your HR team's goals with corporate strategy." *HR Magazine*, August, 43–50. Reprinted with permission of the Society for Human Resource Management (www.shrm.org), Alexandria, VA, publisher of *HR Magazine*.

THE RISKS

Is there a downside to strategic HR planning? The strategic management of human resources seems beneficial, but some researchers point out that there are costs.[37] Research shows that these include the increased time and energy involved in making decisions, greater potential for information overload, impossible commitments to employees, and an overconcern with employee reactions that may be incompatible with industry conditions. As anyone who has gone through the strategy formulation and implementation process understands, the strategy formulation phase is relatively easy; motivating employees to commit to the strategy and implement it is far more difficult. A further problem is that any HR plan for the future may create employees' expectations that they have jobs for life and will be trained for those jobs, whereas the reality is that conditions change, and the plan may change, resulting in job losses.

Another problem, some would argue, is that organizations that commit to one strategy become blind to changes in the environment and lose their flexibility. However, incremental adjustments based on environmental scanning are part of strategy implementation. The risk of not having a strategy seems greater.

There are risks to not developing a strategy. Organizations that do not actively scan the environment face the danger of being out of touch with reality. Today's operating decisions may be based on yesterday's conditions. Comfortable with past success, the managers in these organizations focus on resolving internal problems, much like those who concentrated on making better horse carriages when automobiles were on the horizon.

One example of a company not in touch with reality was Consumers Distributing. It did not develop a strategy to match or surpass the changing distribution networks and customer-service levels of its competitors. The company, now bankrupt, continued to require customers to come to the stores and stand in line, often for out-of-stock items. Meanwhile, their competitors were offering electronic purchasing or were providing greeters at the door of the store who helped the customers find anything they wanted, all for a competitive price. MacMillan argues that firms that develop strategies gain an advantage and control their own destinies.[38] An apt cliché is "an organization that fails to plan, plans to fail."

LINKING HR PROCESSES TO STRATEGY

Strategic HRM has to facilitate the formulation and implementation of corporate and business-level strategies. Senior managers must focus on issues such as: What are the HR implications of adopting a strategy? What are the internal and external constraints and opportunities? Exactly what policies, practices, and philosophies contribute to the successful implementation of the strategy?

The basic premise is that every HR policy and practice must directly support the organization's strategy and objectives.[39] This does not happen as frequently as it should. Aligning HR strategy with business strategy can be done in one of these ways:

1. Start with organizational strategy and then create HR strategy.
2. Start with HR competencies and then craft corporate strategies based on these competencies.
3. Do a combination of both in a form of reciprocal relationship.

Let us examine each approach.

Corporate Strategy Leads to HR Strategy

A traditional perspective of HR planning views HRM programs as flowing from corporate strategy. In other words, personnel needs are based on corporate plans. If a firm decides to compete on the basis of offering low-cost products, HR policies and practices must align and be based on low labour costs. McDonald's is a good example. To illustrate the alignment of HR programs with business strategy, HR Planning Today 2.3 focuses on two strategies under Porter's model: the low-cost-provider strategy and the differentiation strategy. Although Porter recognized the importance of HRM, and even concedes that, in some firms, HRM holds the key to competitive advantage, he did not delineate any specific practices that can be aligned with business strategy. HR Planning Today 2.3 provides one of the few "recipes" for using HR strategies to support a business strategy.

HR Planning Today (2.3

HR Alignment with Two Strategies

Strategy 1: Low-Cost-Provider Strategy

A firm competing on cost leadership attempts to be the low-cost provider of a product or service within a marketplace. The product or service must be perceived by the consumer to be comparable to that offered by the competition and to have a price advantage. McDonald's uses this approach, as do Zellers and Timex.

Buyers are price sensitive, and businesses appeal to this price consciousness by providing products or services at prices lower than those of competitors. Survival is the ultimate goal, but organizations price low to gain market share (by underpricing competitors) or to earn a higher profit margin by selling at the going market rate. This strategy requires the company to balance the delivery of a product that still appeals to customers with not spending too much on gaining market share. McDonald's could deliver a cheaper hamburger, but would it have any taste? McDonald's could underprice its competitors, but it may risk its survival by going too low. The key is to manage costs every year.

The adoption of a low-cost-provider strategy by a firm has immediate implications for HR strategy. Costs are an important element of this strategy, so labour costs are carefully controlled. Efficiency and controlling costs are paramount. The implications of a low-cost-

provider strategy for six key components of HR are discussed below, but first we start with the job description of a typical employee working in a company that competes as a low-cost provider.

The Employee

To keep wages low, jobs have to be of limited scope so that the company can hire people with minimal skills at low wages. The job requires highly repetitive and predictable behaviours. There is little need for cooperative or interdependent behaviours among employees. The company directs its efforts at doing the same or more with less and capitalizing on economies of scale. Doing more with fewer employees is the goal of most organizations with a low-cost-provider strategy.

Risk taking on the part of the employee is not needed, but comfort with repetitive, unskilled work is necessary. Customers like those frequenting McDonald's are "trained" not to make idiosyncratic requests (such as a "medium-rare hamburger" or "hot mustard"), and so no unique response system is required. Employees are not expected to contribute ideas.

Another way to cut costs is to eliminate as many of the support or managerial layers as possible. The impact of cutting costs in this way is that employees may have to do more with less, make more decisions, and so on, which would require a more skilled employee. Alternatively, the

HR Planning Today 2.3 *(continued)*

jobs could be so tightly designed that little supervision is required, thus saving costs. Substituting technology for labour is another way to save costs.

We now look at six HR functions that will facilitate the personnel work at a lowcost-provider organization.

HR Planning

At the entry level, succession planning is minimal, ensuring only the feeder line to the next level. Outside labour markets are monitored to ensure that entry-level people are in adequate supply. The availability and use of fringe workers—those who are retired, temporarily unemployed, students, and so on—is part of the planning strategy, particularly if the employment market is offering better opportunities to the normal supply of low-skilled workers.

At the executive level, succession management assumes the same importance as in other organizations.

Selection

Recruitment is primarily at the entry, or lowest, level and is from the surrounding external labour market. Recruitment is by word of mouth, and application forms are available on-site, thus saving the costs of recruiting in newspapers. Most other positions are staffed internally through promotions. Thus, career paths are narrow.

Compensation

A low-cost-provider strategy includes lower wages and fringe benefits. Beyond the legal minimum pay requirements, firms with this strategy carefully monitor what their competitors are paying in the local labour market. These firms' strategy tends to be a lag strategy, where they attempt to pay wages slightly below industry norms.

One way of achieving these lower costs is to outsource production to sites with lower labour costs. In the United States, this means moving production from high-wage states, such as New York, to low-wage states, such as New Mexico. In Canada, wages are very similar across provinces, so firms analyze wage rates in countries such as India, which pay employees substantially less for similar productivity. Outsourcing has also meant moving the work from highly unionized plants, where

workers make $20 or more an hour, to non-unionized smaller sites, where workers are paid slightly more than the minimum wage.

Cost reduction in wages can also be achieved through the use of part-time workers, who receive no fringe benefits. Canadian organizations pay around 30 percent in fringe benefits, so the savings gained by using part-time workers is substantial among large employers. Food franchises employ part-time workers almost exclusively to reduce labour costs.

Pay for performance, such as incentive compensation that is linked to productivity, rewards individual effort. Group rewards are based on explicit, results-oriented criteria and the meeting of short-term performance goals.

Programs designed to reduce labour costs, such as outsourcing or using part-time workers, can easily be imitated by competitors, and so may produce no long-term competitive advantage. However, an innovative compensation scheme that cannot be duplicated by rivals may provide a competitive advantage. For example, in an arrangement between the Great Atlantic and Pacific Tea Company (A&P) and the United Food and Commercial Workers (UFCW), workers took a 25 percent pay cut in exchange for cash bonuses. If the store's employees could keep labour costs at 10 percent of sales by working more efficiently or generating more store traffic, they would receive a cash bonus of 1 percent of store sales. This arrangement resulted in an 81 percent increase in operating profits. However, unions were opposed to the spread of this practice, and so A&P's rivals in the low-margin food business were unable to reduce their labour costs in the same way. Any incentives for performance would reward cost savings, or improvements in efficiency, as this example shows.

Training

Training is minimal, as few skills are required. Any training is based on increasing efficiency in the current job, or specialization for the current position. Such training is fast and inexpensive. McDonald's can train a new hamburger flipper or cashier within a few hours. There is little to no investment in the long-term development of the employee, nor in the acquisition of skills for jobs other than the current one.

The training staff is lean, with the organization relying on outside suppliers for its limited training needs. However, most training takes place on the job in the form of direct instruction from or coaching by the supervisor. The jobs are so narrow in scope, so repetitive in nature, that little need for training exists.

Performance Evaluation

Short-term results, with explicit and standardized criteria, are used to evaluate an employee's performance. The feedback is immediate and specific. Individuals are held accountable only for their own behaviour or results, not for that of the team or the company. Only the supervisor provides input for the performance evaluation. Forms are kept to a minimum, and rating is done against check marks. Feedback, if based on a performance review, tends to be one-way, with little opportunity for the employee to debate the results or receive developmental feedback. Results are used for consideration for promotion.

Labour Relations

Low-cost providers try to prevent the formation of a union because they believe that unions drive up wages. Unions find low-cost providers, such as McDonald's, difficult to unionize. (Employees working part-time hours have little interest in unionization because they believe that this is a part-time job that they will leave in the near future, and they are unlikely to benefit from belonging to a union, to which they have to pay fees. It is also difficult to organize those working night shifts.) Furthermore, employees quit often, and many low-cost providers absorb turnover rates of 300 percent annually as a cost of doing business. High turnover has the primary advantage of keeping compensation levels low.

Now that we have an idea of how HR programs align with a low-cost provider strategy, let us examine what these programs would be like under a differentiation strategy.

Strategy 2: The Differentiation Strategy

In most markets, buyer preferences are too diverse to be satisfied by one undifferentiated product. Firms providing features that appeal to a particular market segment are said to compete on a differentiation strategy. A firm competing on the basis of a differentiation strategy will offer something unique and valuable to its customers. BMW, Polo Ralph Lauren, Rolex, and Hewlett-Packard's scientific instruments divisions are firms that compete successfully by charging a price premium for uniqueness. The primary focus is on the new and different. Observation, experience, and market research will establish what buyers consider important, what has value, and what buyers will pay for these features. Then the firm can offer a product or service that commands a premium price, increase unit sales within this niche, and gain buyer loyalty among those who value these features. The extra price outweighs the extra costs of providing these features.

A firm can differentiate itself from its competitors in many ways:

- Having quality products,
- Offering superior customer service,
- Having a more convenient location,
- Using proprietary technology,
- Offering valuable features,
- Demonstrating unique styling, and
- Having a brand-name reputation.

These different features can be anything. Common examples show some firms competing on service (Four Seasons Hotels), engineering design (BMW), image (Polo Ralph Lauren), reliability (Bell), a full range of products or services (Procter & Gamble), technological leadership (RIM), and quality (Honda).

Most of the time, these competitive advantages are combined, such as by linking quality products with proprietary technology and superior customer service, thus providing the buyer with more value for the money. The key in this strategy is to provide the differentiation that is perceived to be of value to customers while keeping costs down. For example, a slice of lemon in a glass of ice water delivered to the table is an obvious way to differentiate the restaurant, but at low cost. After-dinner mints are less expensive than valet parking, but may be equally appreciated by diners.

HR Planning Today 2.3 *(continued)*

A differentiation strategy calls for innovation and creativity among employees. HRM is affected in fundamentally different ways in organizations that want to use employees' brains rather than their limited (mainly manual) skills in the low-cost-provider strategy.

The starting point for aligning HR programming with a differentiation strategy is the employee.

The Employee

Organizations competing on a differentiation strategy require from their employees creative behaviour, a long-term focus, interdependent activity, and some risk taking, as well as an ability to work in an ambiguous and unpredictable environment. Their employees' skills need to be broad, and employees must be highly involved with the firm. Organizations encourage employees to make suggestions, through both informal and formal suggestion systems, for new and improved ways of doing their job. Employees at Corning Canada Inc., for example, submit their suggestions to their supervisors, who review them formally and give feedback directly to the employee. Contrast this with the traditional suggestion box, which many employees view as a recycling bin because of the lack of timely feedback.

HR Planning

In a company that has a differentiation strategy and that recognizes people are the key to competitive advantage, HR planning is taken very seriously. For example, at Sumitomo Metals in Japan, the business planning group reports to HR because the company understands that identifying what needs to be done is less difficult than planning how to do it.

Succession management is critical as employees have to possess many attributes to move ahead in the organization. Thus, a strong emphasis on developing skills for the future is part of the promotion policy. Investments in career moves, training, and developmental experiences are substantial. Long-term job security and reciprocal loyalty are the norm.

Selection

Companies with a differentiation strategy need employees who have a broad range of skills and the ability to learn from others. An innovative atmosphere requires employees who are self-motivated and do not require a great deal of supervision. Employees are selected for their abilities to think creatively, to be flexible in work attitudes, and to be able to work in teams. However, selection for these characteristics is more difficult and usually involves team interviews and behaviourally based evidence of innovative performance. Employees are normally recruited through reputation (word of mouth) or through graduate schools. Some testing for creative ability may be used.

Compensation

Compensation plans affect employee behaviour more directly than most HR practices. For example, Drucker describes a compensation scheme he implemented at General Electric (GE) in which pay for performance was based only on the previous year's results. As such, for ten years, GE lost its capacity for innovation because investing in innovation affects expenses and decreases profits, so everyone postponed spending on innovation.

However, compensation is carefully designed in firms that have a differentiation strategy. Pay rates may be slightly below average market rates but there are substantial opportunities to increase those base levels through incentive pay. Pay for performance is a large part of the compensation package and will be dependent on individual, group, and corporate results. These results are a combination of process and financial criteria and are set in advance, usually on a yearly basis.

There is a more varied mix of types of compensation; individuals may receive salary, bonus, or stock option incentives. Internal equity is of greater concern than equity with the external market. Egalitarian pay structures are associated with greater product quality. Nonmonetary rewards also play a larger role in HR strategy in these types of firms. At Honda, the team that designs a unique transportation vehicle is awarded a trip to Japan.

Training

Companies with a differentiation strategy have a strong training team. The focus of training is on both skills and attitudes. Process skills, such as decision making, the ability to work in teams, and creative thinking, are emphasized as much as skills needed for the current

HR Planning Today 2.3 *(continued)*

job. The training itself is seen as an opportunity to generate new ideas and procedures. Indeed, customers and cross-functional teams might be included in the training program. Developmental experiences are encouraged. The value of working in another division or another country is recognized and encouraged. Employees receive promotions or other job opportunities based, partially, on their willingness to undertake training and their track record in learning.

Performance Evaluation

In companies with a differentiation strategy, performance appraisal is based not on short-term results but instead on the long-term implications of behaviour. Processes that are deemed to lead to better results in the long term are rewarded. Thus, companies encourage and appraise attitudes such as empowerment, diversity sensitivity, and teamwork in an effort to build future bottom-line outcomes. Working beyond the job is encouraged, not punished. Failure is tolerated, although management tries to distinguish between bad luck and bad judgment or stupidity.

Evaluation tends to be based on a mixture of individual and group (and sometimes corporate) criteria. Thus, an individual might be evaluated on his or her ability to achieve results and to work as a member of the team, the group's performance might be measured against established quotas, and the company in terms of its overall financial performance.

Appraisals that include input from employees, functional experts, peers, and so on—360° evaluations—are the norm. Organizations in the service sector are more likely to include customers as sources of input for performance appraisal.

Labour Relations

Any structure or process that reduces the capacity to be innovative and flexible is difficult to tolerate. Traditional unions, with rigid collective agreements, are encouraged to work collectively toward a new union–management relationship. This relationship is characterized by shared information such as open books, shared decision making about best approaches, and shared responsibility for solving problems as they arise.

Sources: Adapted from R.S. Schuler and S.E. Jackson, "Linking Competitive Strategies with Human Resource Management Practices," *Academy of Management Executive*, vol. 1, no. 3 (1987), pp. 207–219; D. Ulrich, "Using Human Resources for Competitive Advantage," in R.H. Kilman and I. Kilman, eds., *Making Organizations Competitive*, San Francisco: JosseyBass, 1991; P.F. Drucker, "They're Not Employees, They're People," *The Harvard Business Review*, vol. 80, no. 2 (2002), pp. 70–77; M. Belcourt and S. Thornhill, "Growing from the Inside Out: Human Resources Practices for Growth Strategies," Proceedings of the Administrative Sciences Association of Canada, 1999.

But another perspective reverses this view, suggesting that employee competencies determine the business strategy.

HR Competencies Lead to Business Strategy

A competing view states that an organization cannot implement a strategy if it does not have the human resources necessary. Early into the 21st century, companies are scrambling to find qualified workers in many fields.

Small businesses seem to be better at this second approach. The owners of very small businesses are nimble and quickly recognize that if an employee has a certain capability, it can be exploited to develop new products or services. Diversity management efforts are currently building on this theme. For example, if the number of employees who speak Mandarin reaches a sufficient number within an organization, the observant executive will start to explore Asian markets.

This "skills determine strategy" outlook relies too heavily on employee capabilities and not enough on environmental analysis; nor is consideration given to changing HR practices in training or compensation to facilitate this change in strategy.

These perspectives represent two extremes on a continuum between organizational strategy and HR practices. The reality is closer to the concept of reciprocal interdependencies.[40]

Reciprocal Interdependency between HR Strategy and Business Strategy

An emerging perspective sees HR strategy as contributing to business-level strategy and vice versa. Increasingly, in large firms, senior HR vice-presidents are asked not only to review business plans to ensure consistency with HR strategy but also to provide input to this strategy based on HR strengths and weaknesses.

In this context, an organization chooses a business strategy, such as being a leader in innovative products, based on its in-house, highly educated, trained employees who have been socialized to value creativity. Simply phrased, an organization develops its employees and then capitalizes on their skills; the employees then learn new skills, and so it continues. In many ways, HR strategy generates the business strategy, and business strategy determines HR strategy. This concept of reciprocal interdependence is widely accepted in the HR strategy literature.[41]

An emerging view is that HR should build its strategies by starting with the issues facing the business. All HR programs should be created to solve real business problems and add value, thus becoming indistinguishable from the business.[42]

HR Becomes a Business Partner

The key point here is the concept of *concurrent strategy formulation.* Strategy development is conducted at the same time that HRM issues are considered. The HR senior management team moves from outsider status to insider status. The implications are not trivial; HR managers must understand the numbers language of business or the outcome expectations of non-profit organizations. They must be able to understand analyses presented by marketing, financial, and operational managers. Cost–benefit assessments of options within the HR domain will have to be prepared and defended. Entrepreneurial instincts will have to be sharpened, as HR managers will be expected to engage in scanning HR capabilities for business opportunities in this two-way approach to strategic HR planning. An example of this occurred when an organization was experiencing a rapid downward spiral in business. The traditional HR response would have been to prepare for downsizing the workforce. Instead the HR manager created a unit to lobby—successfully—the government to support two major contracts.[43]

Alternative solutions to problems have to be generated. For example, if the low-cost strategy depends on hiring personnel at minimum wage, HR managers have to develop strategies to deal with rapid training and high turnover rates. This option will have to be compared with outsourcing, use of robots, or even increasing wages to reduce the costs of turnover. The HR manager is no longer the auditor, but a partner and problem solver. Linkages between the HR manager and other managers, both formal and informal, ensure that this partnership role is enacted.

HR Planning Notebook 2.1

ARE YOU A STRATEGIC PARTNER?

Do you understand the business? What financial indicators are important to the company? Who are your customers, and what is your competitive advantage? What major technological changes will affect your work?

Do you know what the corporate plan is? Can you quickly list the major initiatives of your organization?

Do you align HR programs, policies, and practices with organizational strategies and goals? How can HR position the organization to succeed? Are the people management processes focused and measured on deliverables and not functions? Does HR report on effectiveness (the impact that the training program had on employee behaviour) or just efficiencies (such as the number of people being trained)?

Are major organizational decisions made with your input?

Count the number of times you answered yes. The higher the number, the greater the likelihood that you are a strategic partner or have the ability to be one.

STRATEGIC PARTNERING

Human resources professionals recognize the need to play a more strategic role within the organization. Although only 23 percent HR managers are playing that role now, executive teams expect most of them to be more strategic and to demonstrate added value over the next five years.[44] Why do executives ignore HR's contribution to strategy? Some argue that it is because management is not satisfied with HR services in general; that "people" issues belong only to HR, and HR can take care of any problems in executing the strategy.

These attitudes are changing, as organizations realize the impact that HRM strategy can have on organizational effectiveness and as HR managers develop the internal relationships to ensure that the strategy is effective. However, you cannot just ask to be on the executive team. It is like being in high school and asking to be on the basketball team. You have to prove yourself. HR Planning Notebook 2.1 poses the question, "Are you a strategic partner?"

BECOMING MORE STRATEGIC

HR departments are restructuring in order to be able to do the basics right (payroll, safety training, and so on) while enhancing the performance of business units and supporting strategic moves. Traditionally, HR has been organized into functional units (training, compensation, and so on). However, there are some more innovative practices, where the unit is organized according to the services provided, as outlined in HR Planning Notebook 2.2.

It seems feasible to design HR policies to match strategy, but what happens when an organization has more than one business strategy and more than one HR strategy? We attempt to answer that question in the next section.

HR Planning Notebook 2.2

A NEW VISION OF HR

Corporate HR

The key officer functions as a practice director, similar to what is found in consulting companies, and is on the executive team. Studies in the United Kingdom and Australia show that companies that included the HR director on the executive team experienced twice the growth in earnings per share compared to those who did not.[45]

Services Inc.

The part of HR that is administrative, estimated to be 60 percent to 70 percent of HR work, is located in a separate unit called Services Inc. The administrative burden is reduced through call centres and use of the Internet and intranet. The type of HR work done in Services Inc. includes compensation and benefits administration, training and education administration, staffing administration, and records management. There are three levels of service: Tier one is accessed by computer or telephone, and deals with minor things such as changes in addresses; everything is processed without human intervention. Tier two directs HR requests for information not listed on tier-one sites—such as questions about retirement eligibility or finding a course on innovation—to a call centre that can provide a quick response or explanation. Tier three comprises case workers—highly skilled professionals—who provide extensive and comprehensive assistance to complex issues such as employee relations or employee assistance.

Services Inc. is driven by cost reduction—it has to be the lowest cost and most efficient provider of service, whether outsourced or provided in-house. It may be located in Information Services or wherever appropriate as part of an organization-wide effort to provide services through the centralization of technology and call centres.

Solutions Inc.

This branch of corporate HR consists of HR subject-matter experts—all of whom possess professional credentials acquired through advanced study and extensive experience. Their role is to transform the organization through training and development, labour relations, compensation design, strategic staffing, and organizational development. They are responsible for creating solutions to organizational problems and for preparing the organization to achieve its strategic intents. These experts act like consultants to the organization and operate on a for-profit basis—that is, their efforts are measurable and must result in an increase in performance measures. The consultants are on the cutting edge of research and put innovative, state-of-the-art theories into practice.

Organization Capability Consultants

Operating as the third branch of corporate HR, the HR professionals in this unit are dispersed throughout the organization, providing guidance and assistance to operating units, with the goal of improving the effectiveness of the organization. If asked questions about changing benefits or dealing with a potential unionization threat, they hand out cards with the contact numbers for Services Inc. or Solutions Inc. They build organizational capabilities by aligning HR strategies, processes, and practices with the needs of the business. Their HR solutions should change existing processes to create "better-faster-cheaper" approaches.

Source: From MELLO. *Strategic Human Resource Management*, 1E. © 2002 South-Western, a part of Cengage Learning, Inc. Reproduced by permission. www.cengage.com/permissions

HR STRATEGY DIFFERENTIATION

Firms with more than one business strategy are likely to have more than one approach to HR strategy. As different divisions are responsible for realizing different aspects of the strategy, employees in different divisions may be encouraged to display different behaviours through appropriate HR practices. The challenge is to treat employees across divisions in an equitable fashion while motivating different behaviours that align with the divisions' strategies or functions. For example, 3M adopted HR practices that support innovation in the research and development branch while adopting policies that support low costs in the manufacturing branch. But to achieve equity, the company cultivated a culture of trust by implementing a series of HR practices such as educating employees on company's mission and objectives, ensuring compensation fairness, and facilitating communication to enhance employee engagement and perception of fairness.[46]

Recently researchers have suggested that HR strategy can be further differentiated based on jobs/positions within divisions. From a strategic perspective, different positions assume different roles in strategy implementation. Two considerations are: 1) when a position is directly responsible for creating the strategic capabilities of the business, and 2) when different job holders may vary substantially in their job performance, then the position is considered a strategic position.[47] For example, at Big Pharma, the strategic capability of the business is new product development, thus the R&D scientists would assume the most strategic role. Wal-Mart's strategic capability is its distribution and logistics systems that allow it to achieve high efficiency at low costs, thus the distribution and logistics specialists should be considered strategic positions. Organizations should have a special HR strategy for these strategic positions to make sure that they can attract, motivate, and retain top players in these positions.[48]

From a human capital perspective, even within the same positions, some individuals may deserve differential HR strategy than others for two reasons—because their human capital is 1) valuable to the business strategy and 2) unique (hard to replace).[49] For example, R&D scientists who have desirable skills in new product development in a particular domain, or founding members who have extensive experience within the company, may deserve differential HR management. Recent surveys showed that up to 67 and 58 percent of Canadian organizations had differential treatment (such as additional compensation, enhanced development opportunities, and career planning) for employees with rare skills and valuable skills, respectively.[50] Human capital was found to be significantly related to organizational performance, particularly when the human capital was unique to the organization.[51] The basic prescription is to design HR programs that support the business strategy.

Characteristics of an Effective HRM Strategy

The purpose of HR strategy is to capitalize on the distinctive competencies of the organization and add value through the effective use of human resources.[52] Effective HRM strategies include external and internal fit, and a focus on results.

Fit is an important consideration when designing HR programs. We look at two important types of fit: external fit and internal fit.

External Fit

HR programs must align with or fit the overall strategy of the organization. If the business strategy is to differentiate from competitors based on superior service, then selection and training programs should be developed to hire and train people in the skills and behaviours necessary to deliver superior service. Fit with other functional strategies is as important as fit with business strategies. HR senior management must be included in strategy discussions to be sure this happens. This is sometimes called the "best fit" approach to strategic HR, where HR strategies match organizational strategies.

Internal Fit

We look at two types of internal fit: a fit with other functional areas, such as marketing, and a fit among all HR programs. Fit with other functional areas is important. If the marketing department is developing an advertising plan that promises 24-hour access to customer service representatives but the HR plan does not include compensation differentials for shift work, the overall marketing strategy might fail.

HR programs must also be consistent with each other. That is, training, selection, and appraisal must work together to support a strategy. If the training department decides to teach employees to use the Internet to handle customer service, the staffing department must hire people who either are computer literate or who have the kinds of intelligence that enable them to learn computer skills rapidly. This working together is commonly referred to as "bundling" HR practices. The "best practices" approach, in which bundles of HR practices are internally consistent, suggests that there is a direct relationship between an internally consistent bundle of HR practices and firm performance.[53] If an organization adopts one best practice, such as structured interviewing, without adopting bundles of best practices that align with it, it will not increase the impact in a synergistic manner. However, there is disagreement as to what, exactly, these best practices are.[54]

Focus on Results

The hard work of deciding on strategy is not its formulation but its implementation and the tracking of results. Many HR managers do not have the resources or skills to measure results to see if the goals have been achieved. Unless the strategy contains performance measures—that is, is results oriented—it will be difficult to know how successfully the strategy was implemented. Chapter 14 presents various methods for evaluating programs.

Many HR programs are described as solutions looking for problems. Although HR managers insert the word "strategic" in front of HR programs, they fail to demonstrate the link to results. Before any HR program is introduced, the following chain needs to be developed.

HR program → employee human capital and behaviours
→ organizational strategy → organizational outcome

So, if the overall corporate outcome for a retailer is "growth in sales," and the strategy to do this is through customer service (a differentiation strategy), then what employee human capital and behaviours are required? If, for example, product knowledge and sales skills are needed, then HR programs could be designed to select and/or develop these skills.

SUMMARY

Strategic HRM is a set of distinct but interrelated philosophies, policies, and practices with the goal of enabling the organization to achieve its strategy. HR strategy is embedded in theories of the resource-based view of the firm, the behavioural perspective, and the human capital approach. By involving HR in discussions of strategic policies, an organization has a better chance of being effective in the implementation of these policies. There are various approaches to linking HRM strategies to organizational strategies. We can start with the corporate strategy that leads to the HR strategy, or start with the HR competencies that lead to the business strategy, or use a blend of the interrelationship of the HR strategy and the corporate strategy. Aligning HR strategy with the corporate strategy and with other functional strategies is important.

Key Terms

human capital p. 35
strategic HRM p. 33

Web Links

The *Canadian HR Reporter* website, with articles on strategic HRM:
www.hrreporter.com/hr_strategies

The HR strategy of the Department of Health and Social Services of the government of the Northwest Territories:
http://pubs.aina.ucalgary.ca/health/62245.pdf

Required Professional Capabilities (RPCs)

The following RPCs are relevant to material covered in this chapter. The RPC number represents the CCHRA number assigned to the RPC as presented on the CCHRA website. All of the RPCs can be found in the Body of Knowledge at http://www.chrp.ca/rpc/body-of-knowledge/

RPC 1 Contributes to the development of the organization's vision, goals, and strategies with a focus on human capabilities

RPC 2 Translates the organization's business plans into issues, priorities, and human resources strategies and objectives

RPC 6 Develops and implements a human resources plan that supports the organization's strategic objectives

RPC 7 Audits existing HR programs to ensure that they are aligned with business objectives

RPC 47 Develops an organization or unit design to fit a given set of business objectives and environmental factors

RPC 67 Develops people plans that support the organization's strategic objectives

Discussion Questions

1. "Employees are our biggest asset." "Yes, but unlike Mickey Mouse, they can walk out the door any time and all your investment in them will be lost." Explain why investments in human capital are important. Using the example of a great coach, explain why all is not lost if some of the team members quit.

2. Suppose that you are a senior HR manager at Research In Motion Inc. and you want to request $200,000 from senior executives to invest in diversity training. How would you make a business case to the executives? As a team, discuss the arguments that you will make. Be sure to talk about the contributions to organizational strategy and express the expected outcome in bottom-line figures.

3. Research the 10 most successful IT companies in the 1960s. Find out the top 10 IT companies today. How many companies did you find were on both lists? Why do you think many of the once most successful companies no longer exist? Discuss how the most successful companies today manage their human resources to be innovative.

Exercises

1. The HR function at Corning, Inc. uses a human capital approach to identify the implications of corporate strategy on HR services. Read about its approach in M.C. Brush and D.H. Ruse, "Driving Strategic Success through Human Capital Planning: How Corning Links Business and HR Strategy to Improve the Value and Impact of its HR function," Human Resource Planning, vol. 28, no. 1 (2005), pp. 49–61. In groups, discuss why Corning has chosen this approach and labelled it "HCP." Do you consider it effective? Does it share any features with the behavioural perspective, the resource-based view of the firm, or even the balanced scorecard?

2. Traditionally, Major League Baseball scouts chose players for their future potential, and selection decisions were made on gut instinct. Bill James studied baseball statistics for three decades and developed a method called Sabermetrics (based on rigorous statistical analysis) to determine a player's true value to the team. Sabermetrics is a process that analyzes past performance statistics (such as batting averages, earned run averages, bunting, stealing, getting on base, etc.) and links these to winning scores. These findings were not accepted until Billy Beane of the Oakland Athletics put Sabermetrics into practice. Watch the biographical sports movie "Moneyball" (2011) and learn about this approach. Identify the key competencies/capabilities of players that Billy Bean sought. Did they support the competing strategy of Oakland Athletics?

Case LINKING HR PRACTICES TO PERFORMANCE

Five Star, a luxury hotel in Auckland, New Zealand, was established in the early 1980s, renovated in the mid-1990s, and basically had not changed since. Competition was increasing as three more luxury hotels had opened in the area. The owners reacted by trying to upgrade the hotel and improve the customer service. In the hotel sector, customer service is the only differentiator from other hotels.

They created a vision statement that included a strategy for achieving their vision:

> Five Star is to be recognized as the **finest five-star property** in Auckland and a business leader in the hospitality industry. We will achieve this vision by recruiting and developing **customer-focused employees** who provide the highest level of guest service and by providing the **highest amenity level** of any hotel in Auckland (emphasis in original).

> By improving customer service, the owners hope to increase customer satisfaction and impact financial performance—the value chain, as demonstrated below:

Management Policies and Practices in a Quality-Focused Hospitality Industry Strategy

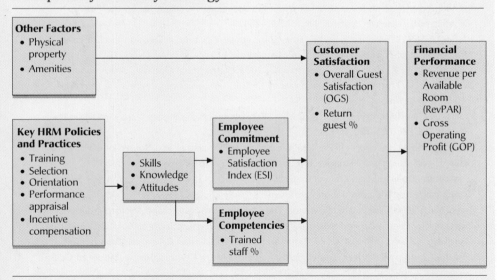

Source: Adapted from P. Haynes and G. Fryer 2000, "Human Resources, service quality and performance: a case study." *International Journal of Contemporary Hospitality Management*, Vol. 12, No. 4, pp. 240–248.

Questions

1. Develop a list of the competencies (skills, knowledge, and attitudes) that employees of this hotel need to demonstrate in order to become excellent at customer service.
2. Design the HRM selection, orientation, training, performance management, and incentive compensation program that will develop these competencies.

ENDNOTES

1. www.economist.com/node/17633138?story_id=17633138, retrieved on March 29, 2011.

2. www.economist.com/node/21528436, retrieved on September 9, 2011.

3. money.cnn.com/magazines/fortune/bestcompanies/2011/index.html, retrieved on March 29, 2011.

4. www.economist.com/node/21528436, retrieved on September 9, 2011.

5. Davenport, T. H., Harris, J., and Shapiro, J. 2010. "Competing on Talent Analytics." *Harvard Business Review*, Vol. 88: 52–58.

6. Jackson, S.E., and R.S. Schuler. 1995. "Understanding Human Resource Management in the Context of Organizations and Their Environments." *Annual Review of Psychology*, Vol. 46: 237–264.

7. Lawler, E.E., A.R. Levenson, and J.W. Boudreau. 2004. "HR Metrics and Analytics: Use and Impact." *Human Resource Planning*, Vol. 27, No. 4: 27–36.

8. Roos, G., L. Fernstrom, and S. Pike. 2004. "Human Resource Management and Business Performance Measurement." *Measuring Business Excellence*, Vol. 8, No. 1: 28–37.

9. Ruona, W.E.A., and S. K. Gibson. 2004. "The Making of Twenty-First Century HR: An Analysis of the Convergence of HRM, HRD and OD." *Human Resource Management*, Vol. 42, No. 1: 49–66.

10. "The New HR Executive." Corporate Leadership Council, September 2000.

11. Conference Board of Canada. June 2010. "Valuing Your Talent: Human Resources Trends and Metrics."

12. Ferris, G.R., A.T. Hall, M.T. Royle, and J.J. Martocchio. 2004. "Theoretical Development in the Field of Human Resources Management: Issues and Challenges for the Future." *Organizational Analysis*, Vol. 12, No. 3: 231–254.

13. Pfeffer, J. 1995. "Producing Sustainable Competitive Advantage Through the Effective Management of People." *Academy of Management Executive*, Vol. 9: 55–72.

14. Combs, J., Liu, Y., Hall, A., and Ketchen, D. 2006. "How Much Do High Performance Work Practices Matter? A Meta-analysis of Their Effects on Organizational Performance." *Personnel Psychology*, Vol. 59: 501–528.

15. Collis, D.J., and Montgomery, C.A. 2008. "Competing on Resources." *Harvard Business Review*, Vol. 86: 140–150.

16. Amit, R., and M. Belcourt. 1999. "Human Resources Processes as a Source of Competitive Advantage." *European Management Journal*, Vol. 17, No. 2 (April).

17. Conference Board of Canada, June 2010.

18. www.canadastop100.com/national, retrieved on July 28, 2011.

19. Teece, D.J. 2007. "Explicating Dynamic Capabilities: The Nature and Microfoundations of (Sustainable) Enterprise Performance." *Strategic Management Journal*, Vol. 28: 1319–1350.

20. Chadwick, C., and Dabu, A. 2009. "Human Resources, Human Resource Management, and the Competitive Advantage of Firms: Toward a More Comprehensive Model of Causal Linkages." *Organization Science*, Vol. 20: 253–272.

21. Paauwe, J., and P. Boselie. 2003. "Challenging Strategic HRM and the Relevance of the Institutional Setting." *Human Resource Management Journal*, Vol. 13, No. 3: 56–70.

22. Weatherly, L. 2003. "Human Capital: The Elusive Asset." *SHRM Research Quarterly* (Society for Human Resources Management).

23. Becker, B.E., and M.A. Huselid. 1999. "Overview: Strategic Human Resources Management in Five Leading Firms." *Human Resource Management*, Vol. 38, No. 4 (Winter): 287–301.

24. Hoskisson, R.E., M.A. Hitt, and R.D. Ireland. 2004. *Competing for Advantage*. Mason, OH: Thompson South-Western.

25. Schuller, R.S., and S.E. Jackson 2005. "A Quarter-Century Review of Human Resource Management in the U.S: The Growth in Importance of the International Perspective," *Management Review*, 16, 1, 11–35.

26. Conference Board of Canada, June 2010.

27. Wright, P.M., D.L. Smart, and G.C. McMahan. 1995. "Matches between Human Resources and Strategy Among NCAA Basketball Teams," *Academy of Management Journal*, Vol. 38, No. 4: 1052–1074.

28. Liao, H., Toya, K., Lepak, D. P., and Hong, Y. 2009. "Do they see eye to eye? Management and employee perspectives of high-performance work systems and influence processes on service quality." *Journal of Applied Psychology*, 94: 371-391.

29. Malley, M.O., and E. Lawler 2003. "What Is HR Good for Anyway?" *Across the Board*, 40, 4, 33–38.

30. Schuller and Jackson, 2005.

31. Subramony, M. 2009. "A Meta-analytic Investigation of the Relationship Between HRM Bundles and Firm Performance." *Human Resource Management*, Vol. 48: 745–768.

32. Ulrich, D., and N. Smallwood. 2004. "Capitalizing on Capabilities." *Harvard Business Review*, June: 119–127.

33. Zedeck, S., and W.F. Cascio. 1984. "Psychological Issues in Personnel Decisions." *Annual Review of Psychology*, Vol. 35: 461–518.

34. Schuler, R.S., and S.E. Jackson. 1989. "Determinants of Human Resources Management Priorities and Implications for Industrial Relations." *Journal of Management*, Vol. 15, No. 1: 89–99.

35. King, A.S. 1995. "Multi-Phase Progression of Organizational Ideology: Commitment." *Mid Atlantic Journal*, Vol. 31, No. 2: 143–160.

36. Lengnick-Hall, C., and M. Lengnick-Hall. 1990. *Interactive Human Resource Management and Strategic Planning*. New York: Quorum Books.

37. Lengnick-Hall, C., and M. Lengnick-Hall. 1988. "Strategic Human Resources Management: A Review of the Literature and a Proposed Typology," *Academy of Management Review*, Vol. 13, No. 3: 454–470.

38. MacMillan, I.C. 1983. "Seizing Competitive Advantage." *Journal of Business Strategy*: 43–57.

39. Anderson, W. 1997. "The Future of Human Resources: Forging Ahead or Falling Behind?" *Human Resources Management*, Vol. 36, No. 1 (Spring): 17–22.

40. Lengnick-Hall and Lengnick-Hall, 1988.

41. Bamberger, P., and A. Feigenbaum. 1996. "The Role of Strategic Reference Points in Explaining the Nature and Consequences of Human Resources Strategy." *Academy of Management Review*, Vol. 21, No. 4 (October): 926–958.

42. Wright, P.M., S.S. Snell, and P.H.H. Jacobsen. 2004. "Current Approaches to HR Strategies: Inside-Out Versus Outside-In." *Human Resource Planning*, Vol. 27, No. 4: 36–47.

43. Quinn, R.W., and W. Brockbank. 2006. "The Development of Strategic Human Resource Professionals." *Human Resource Management*, Vol. 45. No. 3: 477–494.

44. Brown, D. 2007. "C-Suite Understands Importance of HR." *Canadian HR Reporter*, Vol. 20, No. 2: 1, 20.

45. www.accenture.com, retrieved on April 5, 2006.

46. Schneider, B., and Paul, K.B. 2011. "In the Company We Trust." *HR Magazine*, Vol. 56: 40–43.

47. Becker, B.E., M.A. Huselid, and R.W. Beatty. 2009. *The Differentiated Workforce: Translating Talent into Strategic Action*. Boston: Harvard Business Press; Huselid, M.A., R.W. Beatty, and B.E. Becker. 2005."'A' Players or 'A' Positions? The Strategic Logic of Workforce Management." *Harvard Business Review*, December: 110–117.

48. Becker, Huselid, and Beatty, 2009; Huselid, Beatty, and Becker, 2005.

49. Lepak, D.P., and S.A. Snell. 1999. "The Human Resource Architecture: Toward a Theory of Human Capital Allocation and Development." *Academy of Management Review*, Vol. 24: 31–48.

50. Conference Board of Canada, June 2010.

51. Crook, T.R., J.G. Combs, S.Y. Todd, D.J. Woehr, and D.J. Ketchen Jr. 2011. "Does Human Capital Matter? A Meta-analysis of the Relationship Between Human Capital and Firm Performance." *Journal of Applied Psychology*, Vol. 96: 443–456.

52. Cooke, R., and M. Armstrong. 1990. "The Search for Strategic HR." *Personnel Management*, December: 30–33.

53. Buyens, D., and A.D. Vos. 2001. "Perception of the Value of HR." *Human Resource Management Journal*, Vol. 11, No. 3: 70–90.

54. Panayotopoulour, L., and N. Papalexandris. 2004. "Examining the Link Between Human Resource Management and Firm Performance." *Personnel Review*, Vol. 33, No. 5/6: 499–520.

CHAPTER 3

Environmental Influences on HRM

CHAPTER LEARNING OUTCOMES

After reading this chapter, you should be able to:

- Identify the sources that HR planners use to keep current with business and HR trends.
- Understand how environmental scanning is practised.
- Discuss the challenges in scanning the environment.
- Delineate the environmental factors, such as the economic climate, the political and regulatory context, and the social and cultural climate, that influence the practice of HRM.
- Describe the role of the stakeholder, and list several examples.

ENVIRONMENTAL SCANNING AT GM

General Motors (GM) was, for some business experts, associated with the birth of American capitalism. Back in 1955, the chairman of GM conceitedly stated that "What is good for General Motors is good for America." Now (at the beginning of the second decade of the 21st century) it has plunged into bankruptcy and then revitalized through $50 billion government bailout funds.[1] How is it possible that a corporation with money and expertise ended up with just 21 percent market share in 2008, from a position of 50 percent market share 50 years earlier?

Some experts feel that the failure was the myopic views held by management. GM's managers refused to adjust to a changing world for more than 30 years. GM managers thought that they understood that North American motorists loved big cars. They did not see or did not realize that the rising costs of fuel and increasing environmental awareness by consumers would demolish their core business of gas-guzzling SUVs. Ironically, GM was among the first to introduce the electric car, EV1, in 1996 but abandoned it in 2002 due to its high cost.

GM studied the competition, but in the wrong way. It appreciated the fact that the Japanese had cost and quality advantages, but did not seem to understand how to adapt these techniques to their own plants. To understand the cost advantages, GM purchased Japanese cars and disassembled them, looking for clues that explained their efficiencies. But while GM was studying these cars, the Japanese were already at the drawing board designing the next generation of cars. To rationalize the Japanese quality advantages, GM blamed the workforce and suppliers for quality and tried to "inspect quality" into the final product. They believed that the Japanese were able to produce superior products because their workers were docile and worked ten hours a day, singing the company song.

GM was myopic and did not seem to understand how factors can interact. Take, for instance, the interaction between the volume of cars sold and the price of fuel. In 1995, Jack Smith, CEO of GM, told investors to see the potential of the global market, because the North American market was saturated. He forecasted that GM would sell 10 million cars in China alone. When asked by an analyst, "Do you think that there will be an impact on fuel prices, if millions and millions of cars are purchased in developing countries?" the reply was, "We think that gas supplies will be adequate and gas prices will rise just at the rate of inflation."

In a reactive way, GM cut fixed operating costs by 22 percent and offloaded their extremely costly health benefits for retirees. (GM management did not foresee the huge costs of these agreements to care for aging retirees, who were more numerous than employees, which added about $1,400 to the cost of every vehicle.) But it was too late for GM. Toyota overtook GM as the world's largest car maker in 2008. When the demand for cars plummeted due to the economic crisis coupled with rising fuel prices, GM could not sustain its cash flow and filed for Chapter 11 reorganization in the United States in 2009. After receiving government bailout and rinsing off debts, GM was profitable again and had a successful initial public offering of US$33 a share.

The auto sector today is transforming rapidly. The world auto industry has suffered from four consecutive years of poor sales except in China, where sales doubled between 2007 and 2010.[2] The 2011 earthquake in Japan has impacted the market share of Japanese auto makers. GM, although also suffers from interruptions in parts supply in America and Europe, may outpace Toyota to be the biggest car maker later in 2011.[3] There are changes in how transportation is viewed in response to spiking fuel prices, energy risks, and climate change, and consumers are making adjustments through carpooling, biking, and public transportation. Out of GM's mess may emerge entrepreneurial ideas from those outside the auto industry, those who are scanning the environment, reading the trends, and responding innovatively.[4]

To understand strategic HR planning, we must understand how HRM is affected by the environment in which it operates. Just consider the past decade. Was your life touched by any of these events: the September 11, 2001 terrorist destruction of the World Trade Center in New York City; SARS (severe acute respiratory syndrome) in 2003, mainly in Toronto; the 2003 power failure that affected most of the power to Ontario and the northern United States; the 2008 economic meltdown; the H1N1 endemic in 2009; the 2011 nuclear plant crisis in Japan? HR planners want to track trends that influence the way in which employees can be managed. As a result of 9/11 and SARS, most large organizations now have emergency plans in place for the safety of their employees and buildings.

HR strategists need information about their environment in order to exploit the opportunities or cope with the threats. Environmental factors may influence different industries and businesses in a different way and to a different extent. The opening example shows that gas price and environmental concerns of customers influenced the strategic planning at GM; similarly, customers' attitudes towards nutrition and health may influence the business strategy of restaurants and food retailing chains. Being responsive to environmental changes is a prerequisite for building dynamic capabilities and gaining a first-mover advantage. It is important to note that following environmental changes is not only general managers' responsibility, but also HR managers'. Fear over pandemics, costs of fuels, technology development, and the demographics of the workforce all directly influence how work should be designed and how HR should be managed.[5] Being aware of knowledge workers' increasing preference for work–life balance and challenges, Google was among the first to create work–life balance programs as well as flexible job design to attract and motivate top talent. This created a competitive advantage in the company's human resources competency and engagement, which enabled the company to continuously grow and outperform others.

We will look first at the sources and methods HR planners use to track these trends.

ENVIRONMENTAL SCANNING SOURCES AND METHODS

Managers have to develop strategies and keep a keen eye on what is happening in the world outside the organization. **Environmental scanning** is the systematic monitoring of the major factors influencing the organization to identify trends that might affect the formulation and implementation of both organizational and HR strategies.

"Environment" is a fuzzy term; it covers factors as broad as national and multinational contexts that influence an organization. For example, managers are influenced by the culture in which they operate. A manager in Vancouver will treat her employees differently than a manager in New Delhi, and the employees in each city would have expectations about how managers should supervise. Environment also includes industrial environment, such as Porter's Five Competitive Forces.[6] HR practitioners who understand the competitive environment and its implications for their organizations can then develop practices that create competitive advantage.[7]

Environmental scanning
Systematic monitoring of trends affecting the organization

The analysis of the external environment consists of these stages:

- *Scanning:* An attempt to identify early signals of changes and trends in the environment. This information is ambiguous, incomplete, and unconnected.

- *Monitoring:* A systematic approach to following some key indicators that may affect the organization, such as legislative changes.

- *Forecasting:* After monitoring a trend, an attempt to project the possible impact on the organization.

- *Assessing:* An attempt to describe the impact of the monitored trend on the organization, and make a judgment of the probability of each of several possible outcomes.[8] For example, what would be the impact of a trend in the increase of social networking sites use? Some businesses may start using social network sites as a means to recruit and select talent.

In the past, HR managers monitored changes that might affect their programs and policies by reading newspapers or trade publications. They kept informed of issues regarding employment laws by subscribing to particular news services, and by being a member of the provincial HR association. The next section describes the sources that HR professionals might use to monitor trends in the environment.

Sources of Information

When developing strategies and determining their likely impact on an organization, HR professionals rely on many sources of information. These include publications, professional associations, conferences and seminars, and professional consultants.

Publications

HR professionals actively scan Canadian newspapers, business publications, and HR magazines, journals, and newsletters. We are fortunate enough to have access to not only a wide range of Canadian sources of information but also the extensive publication network originating in the United States. The authors' experience suggests that Canadian HR trends lag behind U.S. trends by a year or two. For example, workplace violence and employee retention were hot issues in the United States three years before they became important in Canada; the recession started in the U.S. in December 2007, but was not experienced in Canada until 2008. Thus, reading U.S. publications acts as an early warning signal for Canadian HR professionals. HR practitioners monitor many of the publications and websites listed in HR Planning Notebook 3.1.

Professional Associations

Canadian HR professionals and executives belong to a number of organizations that publish newsletters and updates on current events. Many of these, such as the Human Resources Professionals Association, have committees that actively scan the regulatory scene for upcoming changes. Some, like the Conference

Board of Canada, conduct research with their members to track trends. Relevant associations are listed in HR Planning Notebook 3.2.

Conferences and Seminars

Most professionals keep current with and even ahead of emerging trends by attending conferences, seminars, and workshops in Canada and the United States. The Human Resource Professionals Association, for example, attracts over 3,000 participants to its conference every February. Such events, including those sponsored by private organizations, are widely publicized in HR publications.

 HR Planning Notebook 3.1

PUBLICATIONS OF INTEREST TO HR PROFESSIONALS

Canadian

Canadian Business (www.canadianbusiness.com)

Canadian HR Reporter (www.hrreporter.com)

Canadian Journal of Learning and Technology (www.cjlt.ca)

The Financial Post Career & HR (www.financialpost.com/executive/careers-hr)

The Globe and Mail Report on Business (www.theglobeandmail.com/report-on-business)

HR Professional (www.hrpromag.com)

Ivey Business Journal (www.iveybusinessjournal.com)

Profit (www.profitguide.com)

Workplace Today (www.workplace.ca/magazine)

U.S. and International

Businessweek (www.businessweek.com)

Economist (www.economist.com)

Fortune (money.cnn.com/magazines/fortune)

HR Focus (www.hrfocusmagazine.com)

HR Magazine (www.shrm.org/publications/hrmagazine)

People Management (www.peoplemanagement.co.uk/pm)

Training (www.trainingmag.com)

Research Journals

Academy of Management Perspectives

Academy of Management Review

Benefits Canada

Business Horizons

Business Quarterly

California Management Review

Canadian Journal of Administrative Studies

Canadian Labour Law Reporter

Compensation

Compensation & Benefits Review

European Management Journal

Harvard Business Review

Human Resource Management

Journal of Applied Psychology

Journal of Business Ethics

Journal of Labor Research

Journal of Management

Journal of Staffing and Recruitment

Labor Studies Journal

Management Review

Occupational Outlook Quarterly

Organizational Behavior and Human Performance

Personnel

Personnel Journal

Personnel Psychology

Public Personnel Management

Training and Development Journal

HR Planning Notebook 3.2

ASSOCIATIONS OF INTEREST TO HR PROFESSIONALS

Administrative Sciences Association of Canada (HR division)

Canadian Association of Management Consultants

Canadian Council of Human Resource Associations (links to all provincial HR associations)

Canadian Human Resource Planners

Canadian Industrial Relations Association

Canadian Payroll Association

Canadian Public Personnel Managers Association

Canadian Society for Training and Development

Conference Board of Canada

Human Resource Planning Society

International Association for Human Resources Information Management Association

North American Human Resources Management Association

Society for Human Resources Management

Society for Industrial and Organizational Psychology

World at Work

Professional Consultants

Organizations that have an active interest in understanding the influence of potential trends often hire consultants to research or interpret these trends for them. The Hudson Institute is an example of a firm that specializes in this form of consulting. Most organizations have a person on staff, often the librarian, whose job is to bring information to the consultants' attention by actively scanning multiple sources.

HR Planning Today 3.1

The Experts Predict the Future of HRM

The Society for Human Resources Management attempted to forecast the workplace through the use of environmental scanning. They collected data from human resources professionals, and then used teams of individuals to filter the information in order to target which is truly critical. They also solicited opinions from HR expert panels and opinion leaders. They identified the following top ten trends that will have a strategic impact on the workplace:

- Continuing high cost of employee healthcare coverage in the United States
- Passage of federal healthcare legislation

- Increased global competition for jobs, markets, and talent
- Growing complexity of legal compliance for employers
- Changes in employee rights due to legislation and/or court rulings
- Large number of baby boomers (born 1945–1964) leaving the workforce at around the same time
- Economic growth of emerging markets such as India, China, and Brazil
- Greater need for cross-cultural understanding/ savvy in business settings

HR Planning Today 3.1 *(continued)*

- Growing national budget deficit
- Greater economic uncertainty and market volatility

Facing these environmental trends, the most common actions taken by organizations are:

- Linking employee performance and its impact on the organization's business goals
- Increasing expectations of employee productivity
- Taking steps to protect employees in the event of a major health epidemic
- Implementing policies and procedures aimed at protecting employee and customer data from identity threat

- Updating technology use policies for employees (use of social networking sites, email for non-business use, etc.)
- Changing company policy in response to federal regulations
- Investing in technology and services designed to protect company data in the event of disaster or cyber attack
- Increasing the use of technology to perform transactional HR functions
- Implementing wellness programs
- Increasing HR's role in promoting corporate ethics

Sources: Schramm, J. Coombs, J., and Victor, J. (2011, February). SHRM Workplace Forecast: The top workforce trends according to HR professionals. Reprinted with permission of the Society for Human Resource Management (www.shrm.org), Alexandria, VA, publisher of *HR Magazine*.

METHODS OF FORECASTING

HR professionals can use several methods to generate predictions about the future or extrapolate from current events to determine their impact on HR practices. These methods include trend analysis, the Delphi technique, nominal group technique, impact analysis, and scenario planning, which are discussed in detail in Chapter 6. An excellent evaluation of all these approaches can be found in Rothwell and Kazanas.[9] The steps of conducting a scenario-based HR planning are outlined in HR Planning Notebook 3.3. Readers are invited to experience a scenario-based technique as part of a group exercise at the end of this chapter.

Competitive Intelligence

Competitive Intelligence (or business intelligence) is a formal approach to obtain information about your competitors. Learning about competitors' moves early is critical for organizations to respond before the new offering materializes. However, surveys showed that only 23 percent of companies were able to do so.[10] The simplest method is to study their websites for information about their strategies and plans for product launches. Other companies train their employees to ask questions from vendors about the purchasing decisions of their competitors. Some organizations hire competitors' employees to obtain insider information about future plans. Other practices border on illegal or unethical. For example, Avon Products once allegedly hired private detectives to search through the dumpsters outside of the Mary Kay corporate offices. Information gathered through all these competitive intelligence methods must be subjected to two evaluation questions: Is the source reliable, and what is the likelihood of the information being correct?[11]

Competitive intelligence
A formal approach to obtain information about competitors

HR Planning Notebook 3.3

SCENARIO-BASED HR PLANNING

Step One: Identify three business scenarios that might be played out over the next five years (most desirable case, most likely case, and least desirable case).

Step Two: For each scenario, assess the firm's HR readiness. What are the challenges faced under each scenario (e.g., labour shortages, safety concerns). Then identify the HR department's strengths and weaknesses in relation to these challenges.

Step Three: Over the next five years, what are the likely trends with rivals, employees, and candidates? What are the threats posed by rivals? What are the predicted needs and motivations of key employees? What changes do we forecast in the quality and the quantity of our labour pool?

Step Four: For each scenario, identify HR initiatives and programs that must be undertaken to deal with the threats and opportunities. For example, to meet a labour shortage of skilled mechanics, a joint program with a community college might be established.

Source: Adapted from P. Boxall and J. Purcell, *Strategy and Human Resource Management*, 2nd ed. (New York: Palgrave Macmillan, 2008), Figure 11.1, p. 294.

CHALLENGES IN ENVIRONMENTAL SCANNING

There are problems in scanning the environment. These include our inability to accurately predict the future and to isolate what really is important to HR. Can we say what the world will look like in 2050? In 1900, could those working in HRM have predicted what it would look like in 2000? Not likely, because the field of HRM did not exist then. One hundred years ago, there were no payroll and benefits clerks. Even 20 years ago, it would have been difficult to forecast the flattening of organizations; downsizing; the impact of technology, outsourcing, and telecommuting; and a range of other changes we now experience. Most HR strategists limit themselves to a two- to three-year time frame and extrapolate from current trends.

Isolating the Critical from the Insignificant

So much change is happening in so many arenas that scanners have trouble picking out the truly important events. For example, which of these HR issues, taken from headlines in HR publications as this text is being written, are critical and which will prove insignificant: War for talent? Outsourcing all HR functions? Workplace privacy?

Four criteria have been suggested for identifying significant trends:[12]

1. Are there ripple effects (change in one aspect impacts another, such as social networking sites affecting both friendships and professional relationships)?
2. How profound are the impacts on people's priorities, roles, and expectations?
3. How large is the impact scope (number of people impacted)?
4. Will the changes endure over time?

One difficulty is that few trends exist in isolation—no issue is an island. Take the issue of the difficulty of finding employees where labour shortages exist. There is a growing concern that universities will be unable to find enough professors to replace all those expected to retire within the next ten years. If this problem is addressed in isolation, two solutions might be to (1) increase the number of spaces for doctoral students who then graduate to become professors and/or (2) recruit professors from other countries. But other trends may influence the ability to find enough professors. The policy of mandatory retirement is being challenged through the courts. The court challenges were successful in some provinces; therefore, some professors will not be forced to retire, and the shortages will not be as great as expected.

Just as there is a reaction for every action, for every trend there is a countertrend, and countertrends seem to develop in tandem with the trends. As globalization increases, so does "localization," and ethnic pride in customs and culture rises. This is not the same as the idea that the pendulum will always swing back. The current focus on work–life balance cannot be viewed just as a fad, with the resultant expectation that there will be another, replacement fad within a few years. The concepts underlying work–life balance will be embedded in our view of work, just as safety and labour laws are now permanently embedded in the culture of work.

We will now examine the major areas that these strategists typically scan.

ENVIRONMENTAL FACTORS

HR strategists monitor a number of factors more closely because they are more closely related to HRM. Following this tradition, we have included factors such as the economic climate, the political and regulatory context, and issues related to technology, demographics, and social values and norms. For each factor we have provided some current examples, keeping in mind that such examples quickly lose their relevance. In scanning each factor, we want to consider its potential impact on the organization and strategy in the near and the distant future, and how HRM can be adapted in response to the environmental changes.

Economic Climate

The economic indices we are so familiar with from the media are also important to HR strategists. Let us look at a few examples of how these indices influence HR managers who are:

- Concerned with the unemployment rate because it affects their ability to recruit
- Worried about the cost of fuel and the employees' willingness to commute
- Worried about the value of the Canadian dollar because it affects the company's ability to sell products internationally, and thus affects employment levels
- Troubled by the amount of public debt because it affects business taxes, and therefore a company's ability to survive and grow
- Anxious about interest rates because they affect how much a company is willing to borrow to grow its business and invest in employees

The recent economic recession, for example, has imposed many changes on HR management in businesses. Many employers try to reduce fixed costs by replacing permanent jobs with contingent jobs. Surprisingly, this trend applies not only to low-paid, low-skilled workers, but also to high-paid, high-skilled professionals and leaders. Business Talent Group, a company that provides leadership on demand service, reported that its client demands increased 50 percent in 2009.[13] An important role of HR managers will thus become outsourcing managers. Interestingly, a drop in demand for contingent, temporary, and contract employees (as reported by search and placement firms) can also predict an economic slowdown before these changes are reported by firms in their financial statements.

Other actions that were taken by HR managers to cope with the economic uncertainty include linking employee performance with organizational goals, increasing expectations of employee productivity, putting emphasis on succession planning and readiness, investing in leadership development, using non-cash rewards such as time off, time flexibility, and learning opportunities, and retraining employees for new jobs.[14]

Globalization

Another trend to watch is increasing globalization. Globalization is the growth in flows of trade and financial capital across borders. Globalization affects sovereignty, prosperity, jobs, wages, and social legislation. In North America, the North American Free Trade Agreement (NAFTA) was established in 1994 among Canada, the United States, and Mexico to gradually remove tariffs and other trade barriers in the region. It has almost tripled the trilateral merchandise trade since 1994 to nearly $1 trillion in 2008, which has significantly impacted businesses in these three countries. In particular, Canadian businesses exported C$381 billion and imported C$245 billion of merchandize through NAFTA in 2008. The labour market in Canada is also affected—it has been estimated that one in five jobs in Canada is related to international trade.[15] This has implications for recruiting and managing international human resources. Compared to the United States in particular, employees in lower-level jobs in Canada on average receive higher pay than their counterparts in the U.S., while those in higher-level positions and professionals earn less than those in the U.S. As NAFTA makes the workforce more mobile across the border, Canadian businesses need to work hard to retain the best knowledge workers.

The shift in the global economy has also been marked by the rapid growth of emerging economies such as India and China. These countries had workers who were willing to work longer hours for less money than workers in more developed countries. McDonald's has a great deal of experience in globalization, and when the company launches a restaurant in a new country, it works closely with all disciplines to "McDonaldize" a team so that they know the business inside out. Eighteen to 24 months before the restaurant is opened, the company starts with HR. Some of the HR challenges McDonald's has faced in other countries include the fact that part-time employment and multifunctional jobs simply did not exist.[16] HR managers will need to develop international competencies, as discussed in Chapter 11.

Political and Legislative Factors

Governments, both provincial and federal, can influence the business environment through political programs that result in changes to laws and regulations. For example, governments that wish to improve the climate for job creation emphasize tax cuts, provide tax incentives to develop jobs, increase job-training opportunities, and create balanced labour legislation. Governments can spur economic growth by reducing the public debt, balancing the budget, and cutting taxes. Such measures encourage businesses to invest in that province (or in Canada as a whole) and encourage consumers to spend, resulting in more jobs.

The employer–employee relationship is governed by a legal framework that includes common law (judicial precedents that do not derive from specific laws), constitutional law (e.g., the *Charter of Rights and Freedoms*, acts of federal and provincial parliaments), and contract law (e.g., collective agreements). You are probably familiar with some of these laws. For example, each province has employment standards that establish the maximum number of hours to be worked each day and human rights legislation that prohibits discrimination on the basis of sex, race, and so on. Additionally, governments often enact legislation that affects HR practices directly. For example, the government of Quebec mandates that every organization has to spend 2 percent of its payroll on employee training.

HR professionals need to continuously monitor legislative changes and ensure compliance with legal requirements. For example, Bill 168, an amendment to Ontario's *Occupational Health and Safety Act*, requires that effective June 15, 2010, businesses that employ more than five workers develop written policies to regulate workplace violence and harassment. Organizations need to develop and maintain procedures to allow workers to report incidents of threats, as well as to educate workers about the risk and communicate the policy and programs in place.[17]

The decisions not governed by law are usually governed by morals or an ethical code. The concept of ethics is not as clear as laws are. Ethical and moral decisions and practices go beyond the law, from "you must" to "you should." An employer can require an employee to work overtime and not pay him or her overtime rates (as required by the law). How? The employer gives the employee the title of "manager" (a category exempted from overtime regulations), even when the employee has no managerial responsibilities. Legal? Maybe, but not ethical.

Ethical issues are sometimes raised and resolved by employees, and sometimes organizations have official policies on ethics. For example, most organizations have explicit guidelines on the kinds of "gifts" (kickbacks) that employees may accept from suppliers. But most HRM ethical decisions are much more complicated. Should a company produce goods in a country that employs child labour? Should an organization eliminate one unit (laying off the staff in the process) only to subcontract the work to an outside supplier that employs workers at one-half the compensation rates? Since the 2007 recession, there has been increasing support for the role of government in regulating executive compensation (as advocated in the "Occupy Wall street" and "Occupy Bay street" demonstrations). Before government steps in with regulations, which may not happen any time soon, one important role of HR is to ensure pay equity and discourage risky behaviours of executives.[18]

Technological Factors

Technology is the process by which inputs from an organization's environment are transformed into outputs. Technology includes tools, machinery, equipment, and software. Technology has already had a large impact on HR and is predicted to continue to do so at an even faster pace—it took 75 years for telephones to reach an audience of 50 million people, 13 years for television to reach the same number, and only 4 years for the World Wide Web.[19] It is estimated that information technology (IT) allows companies to operate with 35 percent fewer HR employees.[20] HR Planning Today 3.2 identifies some of the trends in technology, and HR Planning Notebook 3.4 outlines the impact of technology.

Every HR function has the potential to become managed electronically. The trend started with payroll and benefits; now software is used to manage training data and succession management information. Online counselling for managers is available, and managers can complete performance appraisals interactively. E-learning is the single most used application on the web.[21] As the hardware becomes smaller and the software becomes smarter, we can expect most HR functions to be managed electronically. HR professionals will need to become technology savvy and/or learn skills of managing vendors of technology solutions.

Technology also transforms the organizational culture of how work is done. More than half of the Society for Human Resource Management companies reported that they used virtual work.[22] At Cisco, for example, the culture is "to work for the company, but not necessarily at a company location." Up to 56 percent of work is completed away from employees' desks; 63 percent of time is spent on teamwork, 35 percent of which is virtual; and 20 percent of employees use the Cisco virtual system to work remotely from home. These arrangements positively influence Cisco employees' job satisfaction and productivity, as is shown in a poll.[23] See Chapter 9 for a complete review of HR and IT.

However, there continue to be concerns about identity theft of employees' personal information and the vulnerability of technology to attack or disaster. According to a panel of technology experts, there will be heightened awareness of HR data privacy.[24] The line is blurring between personal and professional lives as employees answer email on vacation and use the phone to telecommute. Issues of the protection of intellectual property and the safeguarding of company secrets are made more difficult because of the ease of transferring information using technology.

HR Planning Today   3.2

Trends in Technology

- Virtual personal assistants that act like a secretary and take over routine tasks such as writing a letter, retrieving a file, or screening requests
- Smart mobile robots that will be able to run errands, do household chores, assist the disabled, and perform sophisticated factory work
- Electronic networking and portable information devices that will be used by the majority of the population to make calls, send email, and transmit data

Source: Adapted from T.L. Wheelen and J.D. Hunger, *Concepts in Strategic Management and Business Policy*, 11th ed. (Upper Saddle River, NJ: Pearson Prentice Hall, 2008).

HR Planning Notebook 3.4

IMPACT OF TECHNOLOGY ON ORGANIZATIONS

- *Requires changes in skills and work habits of employees:* Employees have to be provided with constant training, and skills are no longer viable for decades.
- *Elimination of some lower-level positions and layers of management:* Routine tasks, normally done by those lowest in the organization hierarchy, are automated, and the surviving employees need more advanced skills. Fewer managers and fewer layers of management are needed.
- *Less hierarchy, more collaboration:* The adoption of technology decreases the need for management as a supervisory control technique. Power has shifted from management to technical workers, who hold the knowledge about system processes.
- *Telecommuting options:* Telecommuting is estimated to be growing at 20 percent per year, allows employees to locate farther from their offices, and allows employers to choose office facilities farther from major cities.
- *Electronic monitoring and employee privacy:* One study estimated that 90 percent of employees have used their employer-provided computer for personal business on company time. Twenty-seven percent of employers monitor employee email. If an employee uses his break to access sites related to personal health-care issues, which the employer monitors, has this employee's right to privacy been violated?

Sources: Jeffrey A. Mello, *Strategic Human Resource Management*, 1st ed., © 2002, reprinted with permission of South-Western, a division of Thomson Learning, www.thomsonrights.com. SHRM, Workplace Forecast: A Strategic Outlook, 2004–2005, SHRM 2004.

Demographic Factors

Demographics, the study of population statistics, affect HR profoundly. The influence of women, the greying of the workforce, and the arrival of "Gen X's" and "Gen Y's" all influence HR policies.

Demographics
The study of population statistics

The Labour Market

The labour market is the most important demographic factor that should be monitored by HR professionals. A labour market is the area from which an organization recruits its employees. Such an area may be metropolitan, regional, provincial, national, or international. The number of people available for work depends on factors such as the unemployment rate, geographic migration, graduation rates from educational institutions, and so on. However, labour markets in the 21st century will become international. Ford, General Motors, and Nestlé already employ more people outside their countries than within. Because of India's huge population of English-speaking software engineers, companies such as Microsoft have employment centres in India. The labour market is changing, as is highlighted in HR Planning Notebook 3.5.

The labour market influences an organization's ability to implement strategy. An organization may decide to enter the high-tech field, only to discover itself unable to recruit enough electrical engineers to meet its personnel requirements, and so must abandon this particular strategy. Companies wishing to grow are facing problems in recruiting and retaining qualified scientists and technologists. There is a growing concern with the division of labour in Canada: the *shortage* of people with the right skills who can earn good money and expect benefits, and the *surplus* of people available to work in "McJobs." Human Resources and Skills Development Canada (HRSDC), the government department concerned with employment issues, is addressing this concern through its National Skills agenda, which will encourage companies to increase their training budgets by one-third (to be in line with other countries), and by requiring that 65 percent of adult immigrants have postsecondary education.[25]

Diversity

There is increasing diversity in the workforce. Terms such as "minority" and "majority" have lost their meaning. People may object to overly broad classifications such as "Asian," preferring, for example, "Japanese-Canadian" or

---

HR Planning Notebook 3.5

CANADIAN LABOUR MARKET FACTS

- From 2006 to 2010, the Canadian population increased for about 1.5 million, of which about 1 million increase were Canadian born, and about 0.5 million increase were landed immigrants. Of the total immigrants population in 2010 (over 6.2 million), 42 percent were from Asia and 35 percent from Europe.

- Visible-minority populations are growing fast and will rise from the current 16.2 percent of the population up to 23 percent of the Canadian population by 2017, meaning that about one of every five Canadians will be a member of a visible-minority group. In the United States, there will be no visible majority by 2050.

- Baby boomers, those born between 1945 and 1964, represent one-third of the population; those aged 55 to 64 are at a historic high of 3.7 million, and will represent 20 percent of the working population by 2016. The current average age of retirement is 61.6 years.

- Aboriginals have surpassed one million and make up 3.8 percent of the population, but have an unemployment rate of 13.2 percent.

- The participation rate of women grew by 13 percent since 1991, as against that of men at 6 percent. Women now represent 51 percent of the workforce. Women earned 61 percent of bachelor's degrees and over half of all master's degrees, but the majority of women, particularly those with children, have nonlinear or discontinuous careers.

- Sixty percent of adults aged between 25 and 64 had received postsecondary education. The number of jobs requiring a university education grew by one-third over the past ten years, those requiring a community college diploma grew by 3.3 percent, and those requiring a high school education decreased by 2 percent. Eighty percent of jobs require some postsecondary education and training. However, for every degreed professional there is a need for 15 to 20 technical support jobs.

Sources: Statistics Canada Conference, May 15, 2008, Toronto Canada; Statistics Canada, Census of Population 2006, Catalogue No. 97-558-XIE, 97-551-XWE, 97-560-XIE; estat.statcan.gc.ca; Industry Canada Small Business Research and Policy, Small Business Financing Profiles: Visible Minority Entrepreneurs; March 2005; Statistics Canada, Labour Force Survey, Catalogue no. 71-001-XIE, October 25, 2005; Salopek, J.J., "Straws in the Wind," *Training and Development*, 58, 1 (2004), 16.

"Korean-Canadian."[26] The increasingly diverse workforce demographics present challenges as well as opportunities for organizations to meet their talent needs. The ability of businesses to tap into underutilized pools of highly educated minority groups and effectively manage the diverse workforce will be an important source of competitive advantage in the future. A study of 800 members of the Human Resources Professionals Association found that 70 percent of companies had vision statements reflecting that they valued diversity. However, more than 74 percent of companies failed to allocate resources for diversity programs.[27] Organizations that tracked representation of diversity groups were more likely to do so for new hires (50 percent) than for a leadership succession pool (17 percent). As a result, although visible minorities represented 16.3 percent of the overall workforce, only 3.3 percent of senior executives were minorities.[28] Given the competition for critical skills, organizations that are able to exploit diverse talent will gain competitive advantage. Organizations may take advantage of inclusion programs, such as catering to communication styles and offering customizable benefits programs to engage different groups.[29]

Generational Differences

The supply of baby boomers (those born between 1946 and 1964) exceeds the demand for them in middle management and senior ranks. The combination of the surge of workers in their 50s and the flattening of organizations has created a cadre of plateaued workers who are approaching retirement. If a person starts working at 21, retires at 55, and dies at 89, this person will have spent 34 years at work and 34 years in retirement. Most boomers don't think their money will last that long. Surveys showed that 6 percent of the Canadian workforce that were eligible to retire in the next 12 months, only 1 percent expected to retire.[30] The *Income Tax Act* may have to be changed to allow phased-in retirement, and HR planners will have to make work adjustments to accommodate these requests.[31]

"Baby busters" (those born between 1965 and the mid-1970s) follow the boomers, who have created a bottleneck in the organization. There are far fewer baby busters, and most are very well educated and trained, so can command significant incomes.

Gen X employees (those born between 1965 and 1980) have lived with technology all their lives. They have fewer expectations of organizations and perceive themselves as independent agents. Members of Gen Y, born after 1981, are completely comfortable with technology and have a more global and tolerant outlook than people older than they. Gen Y employees are not very interested in climbing a career ladder; indeed, they assume that they will change jobs frequently. For HR managers, an important consideration is how to vary HR practices to engage and motivate these different generations of workers who also have different work values and preferences. HR managers also need to consider how to capitalize on Gen Y employees' knowledge and skills during the short period when they are hired by the company. Instead of continuing to employ people "from the shoulder down," HR managers need to unleash individuals' creativity "from the neck up."[32] Some considerations of intergenerational differences in HR management are outlined in HR Planning Today 3.3.

HR Planning Today 3.3

Workforce Strategies for Different Generations

	Baby Boomers	Generation X	Generation Y
Communication	Show respect Choose face-to-face	Get to the point Use email generally, but face-to-face to deal with issues	Orient them quickly Email and instant messaging are preferred
Development and job design	Acknowledge accomplishments Create an open work environment	Give them space to explore and find solutions Lighten up! Work can be fun	Provide feedback quickly Challenge them Outline the end game for each task
Recruitment	Use headhunters Advertise in newspapers	Go through social networks Create employee referral programs	Utilize technology (Facebook etc.) Allow space for parental input
Retention	Develop solutions to postpone retirement Highlight value and contributions to the company	Get over the notion of having to pay one's dues Provide flexible work solutions Set up clear steps for advancement	Find them a mentor Allow them to contribute to the community Introduce new opportunities frequently

Source: Adapted from Tapia, A., (2009). "The Emerging Diverse Workforce: Implications of a Global Demographic Tsunami for Organizations in Canada." Copyright Andrés T. Tapia 2009.

Social and Cultural Factors

Right to Privacy

Society can express its intent through laws and regulations, and in less formal ways within organizations through discipline and terminations. One issue getting more and more public attention is the right to privacy. Does the employer have a moral (and legal) right to monitor employee activities through video surveillance cameras or reading email? Dow Chemical Co. terminated 50 employees and disciplined another 200 because these employees downloaded, saved, or distributed offensive material using the company's email system. (Those who merely opened and deleted the material were not reprimanded.)[33]

Work–Life Balance

Another issue is the employee's attempt to balance a personal life with an ever-more-encompassing work life. Research on hours worked indicates that Canadians are spending more time at work. In 2001, the province of Ontario changed its employment standards to permit 60-hour workweeks, on a voluntary basis. Critics argue that the 60-hour workweek will become an implicit part of job expectations.[34] Many employees face the challenge of trying to spend quality time with their families while vigorously pursuing a career. People are generally most active in moving ahead in their careers between the ages of 25 and 45, exactly the stage at which most people raise their children. Both roles are demanding; both require long hours, during the same period (6 a.m. to 10 p.m.). The demographics of the aging workforce mean that working adults will be stressed by the extra demands of caring for their elderly relatives, estimated to consume about 23 hours each month.[35] Organizations have responded to this issue by increasing workplace flexibility. Some options include flex-time, part-time work, job sharing, telecommuting, elder care, and child care. The issue of employee well-being is also on the collective bargaining table, with unions asking for family support benefits such as subsidies for child and elder care, and access to wellness facilities. Although the unionized workforce is changing to include more women and older workers, many of the traditional union members, such as low-wage and hourly workers, factory and service workers, and outside workers, cannot take advantage of benefits such as flexible work hours, telecommuting, or on-site gyms.

Contingent Workers

Another significant trend in Canada is the continuing growth of contingency workers (part-time, temporary, seasonal, and contract workers). These workers may or may not voluntarily choose to pursue contingency employment and experience different work–life challenges than traditional workers.[36] For example, research shows that seasonal workers experience fewer developmental opportunities at work and are often treated as "costs" rather than "assets" in organizations. Not surprisingly, they report lower commitment to the organization and only focus on completing their assigned tasks.[37] As these contingent modes of employment continue to increase, HR needs to reconsider how to strategically manage these employees to gain competitive advantage. If the organization cannot promise long-term employment, benefits, or developmental opportunities, what other practices can be equally effective in engaging these employees?

Violence at Work

Violence in the workplace is also attracting attention. One study estimates that 5 percent of female employees in Canada and 4 percent of male employees reported being physically assaulted on the job.[38] Certain jobs, such as healthcare providers and those in enforcement or inspection, are at higher risk, along with those handling money and working alone at night. HR Planning Today 3.4 outlines some sociocultural trends worth monitoring.

Stakeholders

In addition to general environment, organizations also need to consider industrial and organizational environment, particularly the relevant groups in this context. Many groups have an influence on the organization's strategy. These groups, referred to as the *stakeholders*, hold expectations of the HR function that can influence HR strategy and practices.

Stakeholders are groups of people who have an interest in the projects, policies, or outcomes of an organization's decisions. Sometimes called constituent groups, they follow the actions of the organization and lobby to have their interests satisfied. These stakeholders affect strategy formulation.

Stakeholders
Groups of people who have vested interests in an organization's decisions

HR Planning Today 3.4

Sociocultural Trends

- Increasing environmental awareness.
- Low fertility rates; in Canada, the rate is now below replacement at 1.5.
- Changing household composition; for the first time in Canada, there are more households without children than with children.
- Expanding seniors market for goods and services, particularly healthcare-related.

Employees want more wages and job security, suppliers want longer-term relationships, customers want faster service, and shareholders want more dividends and higher stock prices. Organizations will often adapt their strategies to accommodate powerful stakeholders such as unions, regulatory agencies, or customers. Let us look at some of these organizational stakeholders and their interest in HR.

The Board of Directors and Senior Executives

This group develops the vision, mission, strategy, and objectives for the organization. As a group, the HR issues that interest them the most include the workforce implications of strategic options such as restructuring, outsourcing, mergers and acquisitions, and going international (all these HR implications are discussed in separate chapters in this text). They have a particular interest in succession management (Chapter 8) and leadership development.

Much of the research on HR planning recognizes the powerful influence of the CEO on the organization's ability to attain its goals. The concept of the rational manager is well embedded in our business psyche. We assume that the head of an organization carefully analyzes the environment—looking at competitors' actions and technological changes—and then decides the best strategy to exploit opportunities and corporate strengths. But hearts may be as influential as heads. Managers are more than rational actors; they have personal values, ethics, attitudes toward risk, and ambition.[39]

Research has shown that different types of strategies require different types of managers and executives. Studies of these managerial elites have found that managers with certain personalities—for example, those with a tolerance for ambiguity—managed firms with a growth strategy more successfully than those with a harvest strategy.[40]

Senior Management

Senior managers are typically responsible to the executives for the execution of the strategy and organizational performance. Therefore, they are most interested in the HR programs and practices that affect performance: workforce planning and utilization, incentive compensation, training and development, and performance management systems. They want metrics that spotlight performance indicators such as employee commitment scores, absenteeism, and turnover rate—all discussed in Chapter 14.

Supervisors

This group is responsible for the management of employees and their role in meeting organizational goals. As a group, they want HR to help them with recruitment, selection, compensation, training and development, coaching, and policy development. Their needs are often based on individual employee issues such as poor performance (and the need to terminate an employee) or difficulties in recruiting specialists.

Employees

Employees want the HR department to expedite their requests efficiently, confidentially, and fairly. They want HR policies that enable them to be satisfied at work, and to develop skills to be able to do their jobs, now and in the future. They are concerned with HR policies on compensation, training and development, health and safety, and overall working conditions.

As has been indicated earlier, sometimes an organization's strategy is influenced by the kinds of competencies it already possesses. Likewise, strengths can reside in the HR department itself. If the HR department has excelled in its ability to grow rapidly by attracting, hiring, and orienting highly qualified candidates, corporate venturing or a joint venture becomes an attainable goal. If culture management is the HR department's strength, mergers and acquisitions can be considered a strategic option.

Unions

The presence of unions in the environment will affect HRM strategy for firms entering new sectors with high unionization rates. The national unionization rate is stable at 32 percent, but another 21 percent of the workforce would join a union if given the choice.[41] (This unionization rate compares to 12.5 percent in the U.S.—and only 7.9 percent in the U.S. private sector—a rate that continues to decline.[42]) Employees who are currently unionized within an organization can influence strategy in two ways. One is a restrictive way, in which the collective agreement limits an organization's ability to make drastic changes in working methods or jobs to accommodate changes in strategic direction. A second way is that unions now play a larger role and are more cooperative than adversarial with regard to HR practices such as profit sharing, plant locations, selection procedures, and quality improvement. Savvy HR planners keep track of the policies of key unions such as the Canadian Auto Workers (CAW), because they set the benchmark for hourly workers in Canada. Any innovative benefit will filter through the economy and affect other organizations' negotiations. The key issues for unions are job security, income security, working hours, and inflation protection.[43] Unionized employees receive higher wages and have better working conditions than their non-unionized counterparts.[44] One potential trend worth watching is the rise in the unionization of managers. According to Statistics

TABLE 3.1

Issues Priority Matrix

		Probable Impact on Organization		
		High	Medium	Low
Probability of Occurrence	High	High priority	High priority	High priority
	Medium	High priority	Medium priority	Low priority
	Low	Medium priority	Low priority	Low priority

Source: Reprinted from *Long Range Planning*, vol. 17, no. 3, Campbell, J., "Foresight Activities in the USA: Time for a re-assessment," 1984, with permission from Elsevier.

Canada, 9 percent of managers are unionized, and the number has been slowly climbing.[45] Managers are interested in becoming part of unions in order to deal with their own compensation and workload issues.

Responding to External Factors

While it is interesting to attempt to assess all the changing factors that might affect your organization, the reality is that managers have limited time and resources to monitor everything. Most organizations use an issues priority matrix to determine which are the important trends that may affect them. Using the table below, managers can then rate, from high to low:

1. The probability of these trends actually occurring
2. The likely impact of each of these trends on the organization

A Proactive Approach

Some HR managers do not like passively observing the game through their windows; they want to participate and influence how the game is played. Thus, we find most professional associations have a group that lobbies for legislation that will favour the association membership. Most have public relations firms that try to shape the perception of the profession and its goals (thus influencing public opinion favourably toward regulations).

After the environmental scanning, companies can analyze the business environment to determine the impact on the organization and the actions that the organization needs to take. Organizations can use a SWOT analysis to determine the impact on the organization. HR Planning Today 3.5 describes in detail how one company scans the external environment to identify threats and opportunities.

Figure 3.1 summarizes the environmental and industrial factors that organizations need to scan and monitor to determine the impact on organizational strategy and HR management. On the basis of these analyses, organizations then further reposition the business competitive strategy and develop competitive advantage, as discussed in Chapter 1.

FIGURE 3.1

The Environmental Analysis Process

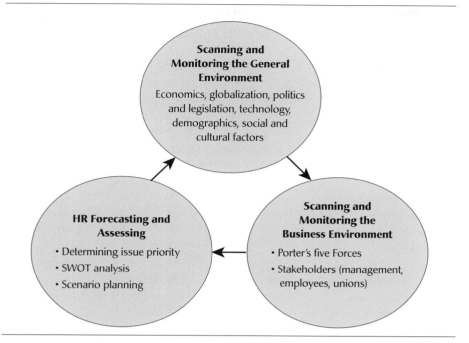

Scanning and Monitoring the General Environment
Economics, globalization, politics and legislation, technology, demographics, social and cultural factors

HR Forecasting and Assessing
• Determining issue priority
• SWOT analysis
• Scenario planning

Scanning and Monitoring the Business Environment
• Porter's five Forces
• Stakeholders (management, employees, unions)

HR Planning Today 3.5

The Global Wood Group

The Global Group of Companies (www.globaltotaloffice .com), with over 5,000 employees, is perhaps the largest manufacturing interest still operating in the Toronto area, as of 2008. Global Wood, which has developed over the past few years into the Global Wood Group, an autonomous division of the Global Group of Companies, designs and manufactures wood-laminate office furniture. On average, over 75 percent of its production is exported to and sold in the United States. Staff within the Global Wood Group continually scan the external environment through access to:

• *Professional associations:* Organizations such as the Wood Manufacturing Council and the Ontario Furniture Manufacturers Alliance lobby governments on behalf of manufacturers. Liaising with these groups provides the Global Wood Group with information that by 2004

the only restrictions that the United States would have on the importation of Chinese-manufactured wood furniture would apply to bedroom sets. As of 2002, Asian manufacturers controlled 48 percent of the American furniture market (American Home Furnishings Association) with annual sales of nearly US$2.8 billion, and it was estimated that their share of the market would increase by 30 percent over the following 2 years (U.S. International Trade Commission investigation 731-TA-1058).

• *Trade publications:* Publications such as *Offcuts*, *Wood Industry*, *Woodworking*, *Materials Management & Distribution*, and *Wood & Wood Products* revealed information about new products coming onto the market and the offerings of new manufacturers entering North America.

HR Planning Today 3.5 *(continued)*

- *Professional conferences and seminars:* At conferences hosted by organizations such as the Woodworking Council and the American Home Furnishings Alliance, Global Wood Group representatives were able to visit the displays of organizations selling machinery and equipment to furniture manufacturers and to ascertain which companies were purchasing machinery and what production techniques they were using.
- *External consultants and trainers:* ISO auditors visit Global Wood Group facilities for one week every year to review their processes. These auditors have international experience and provide recommendations regarding quality, safety, and environmental management, as well as production techniques, training, and logistics based on best practices from around the world. The Global Wood Group also utilizes outside training organizations to provide additional expert training for staff. This includes allowing employees to attend postsecondary courses.
- *Regular management meetings:* Senior management of the Global Wood Group meets on a weekly basis to review events and to discuss threats and opportunities and formulate strategies to address them.

Through these scanning activities, GW was able to assess threats and opportunities.

Threats

After extensive government reviews, including an investigation under the auspices of the International Trade Commission, the U.S. government decided to eliminate tariffs and restrictions on the importation of all wood furniture products with the exception of bedroom furniture. Manufacturers in China targeted first the residential market and by 2003 had control of the majority of this market in the United States. Using production and quality control techniques developed while manufacturing residential furniture, and the logistics and sales connections that went with it, these manufacturers then targeted the highly profitable commercial furniture market. The Global Wood Group increased their research, using government and industry documents to monitor lumber shipments,

equipment purchases, traffic through ports of entry, sales figures, and the marketing efforts of the Chinese manufacturers' representatives. At the same time, the Canadian dollar began its rise from just over 60 cents U.S. to par, which resulted in the loss of the price advantage that Canadian goods had held in the United States. In addition, the announced incremental increases in the minimum wage in Ontario, from $6.85 (as of 2003) to $10.25 (starting on March 31, 2010), created an inflationary impetus on wages. A number of furniture companies closed their manufacturing facilities in North America and in particular Ontario due to these complications.

Opportunities

But there were opportunities:

1. *Proximity to customers, which enabled a rapid response to order fulfillment:* The Global Wood Group decreased average turnaround time for orders from 30 days between receipt of the order and shipment to 5 days. Recent sharp increases in petroleum prices have increased the cost of shipping a 40-foot [about 12.2 metres] container from China to the United States by up to 30 percent. Rail prices in North America have remained relatively stable in comparison.

2. *The implementation of an internationally recognized quality management system (ISO 9001), which Global Wood combined with the introduction of environmental (ISO 14001) and occupational health and safety (OHSAS 18001) programs:* These require external auditing on a regular basis and conformance with internationally set standards. Adherence to these programs significantly improved quality, while reducing raw material use and lost time due to injuries and improving the work environment, thereby decreasing unwanted turnover. Every piece can be tracked to identify every worker who has handled it. Quality inspectors were eliminated and replaced with an internal responsibility system.

3. *A well-trained workforce:* Global Wood Group increased training phenomenally, both to improve production techniques and to implement and maintain the ISO programs. Beginning with the first day on the job, employees undergo intensive training

HR Planning Today 3.5 *(continued)*

following a prescribed checklist for each function and duty. The ISO/OHSAS programs require training on a quarterly basis, as well as the monitoring, documentation, and assessment of this training. Employees are empowered, and their roles have expanded beyond physical skills to mental skills such as inspection and quality control. This educated and trained workforce enabled the Global Wood Group to move from mass production to customized production. Rather than 1,000 identical units being manufactured, each unit can now be custom-ordered, with the workers responsible for matching the hardware, components, and colours with the size specified in the order.

4. *Access to raw material (wood laminate, which is manufactured in Northern Ontario and Quebec), allowing for delivery within one day:* This enabled Global Wood to expand the lines without increasing facility size, and storage areas to stockpile raw material were no longer required. Rather than pay for the removal of scrap wood, Global Wood workers were provided with bonuses for implementing ways and means to reduce the use of raw materials, waste, or scrap material. Eventually, a way was found to grind any remaining wood-based scrap and use it as a source of renewable energy, resulting in a reduction in material costs, waste costs, and energy costs.

5. *Access to latest trends in ergonomics and technology:* By changing the lines to be more ergonomic, Global Wood's lost-time claims were reduced to 0.02 percent of the industry average. By improving the work environment, the employee turnover rate was reduced from 24 percent to 6 percent. Implementing new techniques, such as the use of polyurethane glue and vacuum-assisted materials-handling devices, have improved production speed.

By successfully tracking changes in the operating and competitive environment and proactively making the necessary organization adjustment, Global Wood was able to track the following benefits over a three-year period:

- Increase in production (and orders) of 29 percent
- Increase in revenue of 30 percent, despite the rise of the Canadian dollar
- Reduction in scrap and waste materials of 26 percent
- Reduction in turnover of 18 percent
- Reduction in injuries of 81 percent
- Reduction in defects of 73 percent

As a result, the Global Wood Group has grown to become the most profitable part of the Global Group of Companies, and it now encompasses 12 separate corporations operating in Ontario and Alberta.

Source: Interview with Dan McGarry, Senior Divisional Manager HR (Consulting), Global Wood Group, July 10, 2008.

SUMMARY

HRM strategy is determined primarily by organizational strategy. However, there are environmental factors that shape HRM strategy, so HR managers and planners have to continually monitor the environment. Typically, they scan by reading publications, retaining memberships in professional associations, attending conferences, or using professional scanners. A number of methods, such as trend and impact analysis and the Delphi technique, are used to identify future trends. The environmental factors monitored include the economic climate, the political and regulatory climate, and social norms. Stakeholders such as shareholders, unions, customers, and executives contribute strongly to the formulation and implementation of strategy.

Key Terms

competitive intelligence p. 63
demographics p. 69

environmental scanning p. 59
stakeholders p. 73

Web Links

The website of Human Resources and Skills Development Canada is a good place to look for well-researched articles on trends in collective agreements, work–life balance, and other topics of interest to students and employers:
www.hrsdc.gc.ca

A Health Canada website that offers trends in workplace health and wellness:
www.hc-sc.gc.ca/ewh-semt/index_e.html

An excellent website of the Canadian Policy Research Networks, which tracks trends in work issues, such as rewards, job rotation, health and safety, and so on:
www.jobquality.ca

Required Professional Capabilities (RPCs)

The following RPCs are relevant to material covered in this chapter. The RPC number represents the CCHRA number assigned to the RPC as presented on the CCHRA website. All of the RPCs can be found in the Body of Knowledge at www .chrp.ca/rpc/body-of-knowledge.

RPC 3 Contributes to an environment that fosters effective working relationships

RPC 5 Keeps current with emerging HR trends.

RPC 8 Provides the information necessary for organization to effectively manage its people practices.

RPC 11 Gathers, analyzes, and reports relevant business and industry information (including global trends) to influence the development of strategic business HR plans

RPC 36 Stays current in terms of professional development

RPC 64 Researches, analyzes, and reports on potential HR issues affecting the organization

RPC 65 Forecasts HR supply and demand conditions

Discussion Questions

1. HR Planning Today 3.1 lists the top ten trends forecasted by experts in the United States. Discuss how these will impact Canadian trends.
2. Prepare an issues priority matrix, using some trends from each of the six environmental factors, on the trends that might impact the viability of Canada Post.
3. An economic trend to watch is the technology development. Discuss how this has impacted your life. Can you predict how it will impact the working patterns of employees? What policies should the HR department develop in anticipation of the continuing upgrade of technology?.

Exercises: Scenario Planning

The late Steve Jobs left behind a fast-growing Apple Inc. Practise the scenario planning technique for Apple using the steps below.

1. Form a group of four to six people. Discuss what Apple will experience following the decease of Steve Jobs, taking into consideration the changes that may occur in the general environment (economics, technology, globalization, legislation, demographics, sociocultural factors, etc.) and Apple's business environment (suppliers, competitors, customers, senior management, employees, etc.). Identify three business scenarios that might play out in the next five years (most desirable case, most likely case, and least desirable case).
2. For each scenario, assess the firm's readiness. What are the challenges faced under each scenario? Identify HR's strengths and weaknesses in relation to these challenges.
3. For each scenario, identify HR initiatives and programs that must be undertaken to deal with the changes.
4. Prepare a group report on the future of the job.
5. Present this report to the class.

After the presentations, discuss the challenges of predicting the future in this manner. Should HR planners not scan the environment because of these problems? Is there a better way?

Case WORK–LIFE FAMILY BALANCE

Magda Hyshka, manager of HR policies for TelPlus, the largest telecommunications company in Canada, had been asked by her director of HR to develop an innovative policy to address the work–family issues facing the company. As part of her research, Magda uncovered the following facts:

- Workers spend an average of 62 minutes a day (or ten days a year) commuting to and from work. The high cost of fuel is making this commuting increasingly expensive.

- Forty-six percent of workers reported moderate to high levels of stress in 1999, as against 64 percent in 1989; one in five workers reported high levels of stress in 1991—this changed to one in three in 1999; 10 percent of the workforce were depressed in 1999; two out of five disability claims were due to depression or anxiety.

- Three-quarters of female employees felt that commitment to families is a barrier to career advancement; 41 percent report postponing pregnancy or not having a child at all.

- Twenty-seven percent of employees report moderate to high levels of stress from balancing work and family responsibilities, an increase of 75 percent in a decade.

- Technology enabled employees to work seven days a week and at any time during the day or night, and many felt that they were expected to be available (online) all the time.

- Since the events of September 11, 2001, many Canadians are rethinking their commitment to work, with 81 percent intending to spend more time on personal matters and less on the job.

- While Canadians are insisting on more work–life balance, Asian workers with equivalent qualifications were willing to work long hours, for less than half the pay.

Magda also researched information from the United States, recognizing that Canada tends to lag behind the hot issues in the United States:

- The U.S. Bureau of Labor Statistics reported that work hours have been increased steadily until 2007. Twenty-five million Americans worked at least 49 hours per week, and 11 million Americans worked 59 hours a week. However, during the 2007–2009 recession, average weekly hours for employees decreased from 34.6 to 33.7 hours. Average work hours had bounced back to 34.3 hours by the end of 2010.

- Forty-six percent of employees feel overworked and overwhelmed and lack the time to step back and reflect on their work; 61 percent say they would give up pay to spend more time with their families; 36 percent state that they would be willing to take a pay cut to have a shorter commute.

- Caring responsibilities for children and elderly persons or both have been rising. Forty-four percent of Americans between the ages of 45 and 55 have aging parents as well as children under 21. Sixty-two percent of women with children under six are employed, and mothers with preschoolers make up the fastest-growing segment of the workforce. Sixty-six percent caregivers reported that they needed to shift work time or take time off to provide care, compared to 57 percent in 2004.

- Paradoxically, the number of Americans living alone has surpassed the number of married couples with children.

Sources: Y.A. Laroche, *Fine Balance,* Ottawa: Canadian Centre for Management Development, 2000; J. Schramm, J Coombs, and J. Victor, *Workplace Forecast,* Alexandria, Virginia: SHRM, February 2011.

Questions

Continue the research started by Magda. Prepare a report summarizing your findings and recommending policies that will help your employees cope with work–family balance issues.

ENDNOTES

1. www.economist.com/node/16846494. Retrieved on August 26, 2011.
2. www.economist.com/node/17493420. Retrieved on August 26, 2011.
3. www.economist.com/node/18712767. Retrieved on August 26, 2011.
4. Adapted from a July 13, 2008 broadcast of *The Michael Enright Show*, CBC Radio, available as a podcast; and Taylor, Alex, III. "Gentlemen, Start Your Engines." *Fortune*, January 21, 2008. Pp. 70.
5. Young, L. 2010. "The New Normal." *HR Professional*, February. Pp. 24–28.
6. Porter, M.E. 2008. "The Five Competitive Forces That Shape Strategy." *Harvard Business Review*, January 2008.
7. Schuler, R.S., and S.E. Jackson. 2005. "A Quarter-Century Review of Human Resource Management in the U.S.: The Growth in the International Perspective." *Management Review*, Vol. 16, No. 1: 11–35.
8. Certo, S.C., and J.P. Peter. 1993. *Strategic Management: A Focus on Process.* Boston: Irwin.
9. Rothwell, W.J., and H.C. Kazanas. 1988. *Strategic Human Resources Planning and Management.* Englewood Cliffs, NJ: Prentice Hall.
10. Coyne, K.P., and Horn, J. 2009. "Predicting Your Competitor's Reaction." *Harvard Business Review*, April. Pp. 90–97.
11. Wheelen, T.L., and Hunger, J.D. 2008. *Concepts in Strategic Management and Business Policy*, 11th ed. Saddle River, NJ: Pearson Prentice Hall.
12. Ofek, E., and Wathieu, L. 2010. "Are You Ignoring Trends That Could Shake Up Your Business?" *Harvard Business Review*, July/August. Pp. 124–131.
13. Conlin, M., Coy, P., and Herbst, M. 2010. "The Disposable Worker." *Business Week*, January 7, 2010: 32.
14. Schramm, J.J., Coombs, J., and Victor, J. 2011. "Workplace Forecast: The Top Workplace Trends According to HR Professions." SHRM.
15. www.international.gc.ca/trade-agreements-accords-commerciaux/agr-acc/nafta-alena/index.aspx?view=d. Retrieved on August 26, 2011.
16. Overman, S. 2002. "HR Is Partner in McDonaldizing Employees in New Countries." *HR News*, May. P. 7.
17. www.labour.gov.on.ca/english/hs/sawo/pubs/fs_workplaceviolence.php. Retrieved on March 31, 2011.

18. Young, 2010.
19. Patel, D. 2002–2003. *Workplace Forecast*. Alexandria, VA: SHRM; Schramm, J. 2005. "HR's Tech Challenges." *HR Magazine*, Vol. 50, No. 3: 152.
20. Chabrow, E. 2004. "World-Class Companies Use IT More Effectively for HR." *Information Week*, Vol. 10, No. 14: 18.
21. www.corporateleadershipcouncil.com, June 2002. Retrieved April 5, 2006.
22. Schramm, J. 2010. "At Work in a Virtual World." *HR Magazine*, Vol. 55: 152
23. Crush, P. (2009). Far-Sighted. *Human Resources*, December: 30–31.
24. Schramm, 2005.
25. Brown, D. 2002. "Ottawa Unveils National Training and Development Strategy." *Canadian HR Reporter*, Vol. 15, No. 5 (March 11): 3, 6.
26. Jamrog, J.J. 2002. "Current Practices: The Coming Decade of the Employee." *Human Resource Planning*, Vol. 25, No. 3: 5–12.
27. www.hrpa.ca/AboutHRPA/Documents/112007DiversityreleaseFINAL1.doc. Retrieved on March 31, 2011.
28. Conference Board of Canada. June 2010. "Valuing Your Talent: Human Resources Trends and Metrics."
29. www.hewittassociates.com/Lib/assets/NA/en-CA/pdf/DiversityTapia.pdf. Retrieved on March 31, 2011.
30. Conference Board of Canada, June 2010.
31. Langton, J. 2005. "Accountants Offer Two Cents on Aging Workforce." *Canadian HR Reporter*, Vol. 18, No. 4: 3.
32. Adams, A. 2010. "Changing Role of HR." *Human Resources*, June. Pp. 45–48.
33. Currie, M.B., and D. Black. 2001. "E-merging Issues in the Electronic Workplace." *Ivey Business Journal*, Vol. 65, No. 3 (January/February): 18–29.
34. www.jobquality.ca. Retrieved April 5, 2006; Anonymous. 2001. "Longer Work Weeks Unhealthy: Critics." *Canadian HR Reporter*, Vol. 14, No. 16 (September 24): 3.
35. Tomlinson, A. 2002. "Trickle Down Effects of Retiring Boomers." *Canadian HR Reporter*, Vol. 15, No. 11 (June 3): 1, 12.
36. Connelly, C.E., and Gallagher, D.G. 2004. "Emerging Trends in Contingent Work Research." *Journal of Management*, Vol. 30: 959–983.
37. Ainsworth, S., and Purss, A. 2009. "Same Time, Next Year? Human Resource Management and Seasonal Workers." *Personnel Review*, Vol. 38: 217–235.
38. Duncan, L. 2002. "An Ounce of Prevention: Ending Workplace Violence." *Canadian Employment Safety and Health Guide*, Vol. 256 (January): 3.
39. Guth, W.D., and R. Tagiuri. 1965. "Personal Values and Corporate Strategy." *Harvard Business Review*, Vol. 43, No. 5 (September/October): 123–132.
40. Gupta, A., and V. Govindarajan. 1984. "Business Unit Strategy Managerial Characteristics, and Business Unit Effectiveness at Strategy Implementation." *Academy of Management Journal*, Vol. 27: 25–41.
41. Brown, D. 2001. "Following Nortel's Lead? Really?" *Canadian HR Reporter*, Vol. 15, No. 20 (November 19): A1.
42. Sweeney, J. 2005. "Labor of Politics." *Wall Street Journal*, March 4, 2005: A14.
43. Brown, D. 2002. "CAW—Big Three Negotiations Set the Mark." *Canadian HR Reporter*, Vol. 15, No. 12 (June 17): 3, 12.
44. Lawler, E.E., and S.A. Mohram. 1987. "Unions and the New Management." *Academy of Management Executives*, Vol. 26, No. 1: 293–300.
45. Statistics Canada. *Labour Force Survey 2000: Perspectives on Labour and Income*. Catalogue No. 70-001-XIE. October 25, 2005.

PART 2

HR Planning

CHAPTER
4

Job Analysis

CHAPTER LEARNING OUTCOMES

After reading this chapter, you should be able to:

- Understand the central role played by job analysis in all HR activities, and especially in the effective conduct of HR planning.
- Comprehend the two essential elements of any job: methods and time standards.
- Explain common problems associated with the job analysis process.
- Identify the five steps of the job analysis process.
- Employ criteria to select job analysis methods that are best suited to the organizational jobs being examined.
- Develop analytical questions that will permit an in-depth examination of the knowledge, skills, abilities, and other attributes required for successful evaluation of jobs.
- Analyze the advantages and disadvantages of the most common methods of job analysis.
- Understand the benefits and disadvantages associated with using "competency modelling."

COMPETENCY-BASED ANALYSIS AND HR EDUCATIONAL TRAINING PROGRAMS

Over the past decade, the HR profession has both grown and changed dramatically in conjunction with changes in organizations and society at large. With increased globalization and complexity in organizational environments, it is critical that university- and college-based educational programs in human resources be reviewed and revised to align with the new demands and requests being made upon HR practitioners.

HR practitioners have expressed concern that the HR field needs to develop educational standards and processes similar to those in areas such as accounting and law, which tightly link learning outcomes to the world of work. However, to date, problems have arisen in effectively utilizing a competency approach to determine the number of elements that should be included in the HR educational curriculum, and their relative importance. For example, one competency-based model for HR education suggests that the educational process should prepare graduates to perform successfully in three work-related clusters: (1) HR practices, (2) business capabilities, and (3) managing change. Other frameworks propose (1) interpersonal and people management, (2) goals management, and (3) analytical reasoning, or a five-factor model of (1) HR technical proficiency, (2) goal and action management, (3) influence management, (4) business knowledge, and (5) functional and organizational leadership. The reader will notice considerable variations among these competing frameworks, and this is just at the top-level analysis of identifying major competency clusters. How, then, are educational professionals to utilize such disparate and vague articulations to guide their analysis of program and curriculum content?

One of the most telling indictments of the competencies approach in general is the lack of agreement over what constitutes a particular competency (e.g., what is "emotional intelligence"?) and its lack of specificity in guiding and differentiating workplace behaviours and performance. Also, it's far from apparent that these various competency factors are mutually exclusive. For example, typically one associates leadership ("functional and organizational leadership") with individuals who are able to articulate goals and ensure requisite action takes place to achieve their attainment, yet one of the aforementioned models separates "leadership" from "goal and action management." Furthermore, it often seems that these competency frameworks reflect a desired future state for HR in general terms, as expressed by those holding senior HR executive appointments, rather than providing effective specific guidance as to the knowledge, skills, abilities, and other attributes (KSAOs) required for entry-level HR graduates of university and college programs.

If competency-based approaches are to meaningfully inform work and job analyses for both HR practitioners and educational institutions, much more work needs to be done to fine-tune and demonstrate the real value of such an approach by avoiding buzzwords and vague generalities.[1]

INTRODUCTION

An organization's mission statement presents the guiding rationale for the activities of all subunits and employees. As we move down the organizational hierarchy from the executive suites to the production floor, corporate and divisional strategic goals are subdivided and allocated to various units as their operational goals. To attain the strategic and operational goals, it is necessary to develop short-run production and operational budgets, as well as to specify the division of labour, commonly referred to as partitioning the work process into manageable units called jobs. A **job** can be defined as a grouping of related duties, tasks, and behaviours performed by one or more individuals, namely jobholders. Each job will have one or more **positions**—in other words, the number of individuals who are performing the duties required by that specific job. The analysis of sub-divided work in the organization, both at the level of the individual job and for the entire flow of the production process, is referred to as **job analysis** and is the focus of this chapter. As HR planners, it is essential that we be knowledgeable about the nature of work and its overall contribution toward the attainment of the organization's mission.

It is important for us to see how each individual job, when aggregated with others in a process referred to as *departmentalization*, contributes to the performance of essential organizational tasks without unnecessary duplication or redundancy. Furthermore, as HR planners, we are responsible for determining the demand for and supply of personnel in the organization. In order to do this we must have detailed knowledge about the business strategies and the tasks that have to be carried out in the organization in order to achieve these goals. For these reasons, knowledge of the nature of the organization's work process, the job analysis process, and methods of evaluating jobs (based on factors that include working conditions, employee qualifications, and the educational training and skill requirements of each job) are essential components in the formulation of the successful HR planning system.[2]

Job analysis is not only a critical business practice to ensure legal compliance, but also the foundation of all effective talent management systems.

JOB ANALYSIS

Job analysis can be defined as an examination of the jobs in an organization with a view to documenting the tasks, duties, and responsibilities of a job and the knowledge, skills, abilities, and other attributes required for the successful performance of those jobs. The written outcomes of this process are referred to a **job description** and a **job specification** (see HR Planning Today 4.1). The difference between the two documents centres on whether the emphasis is on the tasks, duties, and responsibilities of the job (i.e., the job description) or on the competencies or KSAOs the jobholder must possess to be a successful performer in a specific job (i.e., the job specification). KSAOs are defined as follows:

- *Knowledge:* Knowledge is the body of information, usually of a factual or procedural nature, that allows an individual to perform a task successfully.

- *Skill:* Skill is the individual's level of proficiency or competency in performing a specific task. Level of competency is typically expressed in numerical terms.

- *Ability:* Ability is a more general, enduring trait or capability an individual possesses at the time when he or she first begins to perform a task.

- *Other attributes:* Other attributes include work experience.

HR practitioners refer to job analysis as the foundation for all HR activities, and there are extremely valid reasons for this assertion. Before we can meaningfully

Job

A grouping of related duties, tasks, and behaviours performed by one or more individuals, namely jobholders

Positions

The number of individuals who are performing the duties, tasks, and responsibilities of a specific job

Job analysis

The analysis of subdivided work in the organization, both at the level of the individual job and for the entire flow of the production process

Job description and job specification

The written outcomes (documents) produced by the job analysis process. The job description emphasizes the duties or tasks to be carried out on the job. Job specifications emphasize identifying the competencies the jobholder must possess to be a successful performer in the specified job.

HR Planning Today 4.1

Ensuring Job Descriptions Stay Relevant

Detailed written job descriptions can fail to maintain their relevance over time, as jobs change rapidly in today's dynamic global economy. Furthermore, if descriptions become outdated and do not reflect the changed realities of the contemporary job, they will be next to useless in facilitating the match between the individual's performance and career aspirations. Carla Joinson, a job analyst, recommends a minimalist approach to preparing job descriptions, reflecting a change in emphasis from detailed "skill-based" to shortened "role-based" documents. She suggests that shorter job descriptions, which are restricted to a few clearly written statements on the overall responsibilities and "roles" that will be performed by individuals holding specified jobs, are more much enduring and useful than the detailed and ponderous older descriptions. Detailed information on duties and tasks as contained in traditional job descriptions are not included in the new "minimalist job description." The advantage to this approach is that roles are more enduring than specific micro-level duties and tasks and will therefore provide better behavioural guidance over an extended period of time, and are flexible enough to maintain their relevancy to jobholders.

Source: Adapted from C. Joinson, "Refocusing Job Descriptions," *HR Magazine*, Vol. 46, No. 1 (January 2001): 66–72.

advertise jobs and recruit individuals to fill job vacancies identified by the HR planning process, to attract the desired applicants we must be able to specify the individual competencies that we seek. Once we have developed a pool of high-quality job applicants, the selection process will incorporate employment tests and interview questions based on the need to choose the individual who best meets the formal requirements for success identified by our job analysis process. The selection criteria that flow out of the job analysis process are also used in succession planning to appraise the organization's internal candidates for possible transfer or promotion to management or executive jobs. Once we have selected an individual to fill a job, he or she should be given a copy of the job description or specification for the job, which provides specific guidance on how to perform the job in accordance with the wishes of the organization. The performance appraisal process compares the individual's accomplishments over a predetermined period with the desired standards specified in the job description or specification. If the performance appraisal process reveals that the individual has deficiencies that can be rectified by training and development, specific programs or courses can be instigated to help the individual reach the desired standards. Furthermore, compensation systems in organizations typically use a classification process based on knowledge and skills, effort, responsibility, and working conditions, the four **compensable factors** of the job that are explicitly noted and formalized by the job analysis process.

Compensable factors
Skills, effort, responsibility, and working conditions

Finally, successful career-planning programs also draw heavily on the front-end requirement of a comprehensive job analysis. In planning future career moves, the individual and the organization note the employee's current KSAOs and level of performance and compare these to the KSAOs required in various target jobs for which the employee would like to apply. Once this information is collected through job analysis and documented in a job specification, the employee is informed of the explicit education and skills development that will be required prior to being considered for the target jobs. Job analysis, therefore, is not only a critical requirement for the proper implementation and operation of the HR planning process, as examined in this book, but also an essential pre-requisite for the success of virtually all other HR functions.[3]

Job analysis has a long history within the HR field. Efficiency expert Fred Taylor's **scientific management** studies were key contributions to the evolution of contemporary job analysis methods.[4] Taylor's industrial engineering approach focused on reducing costs and improving the efficiency of the manufacturing worker. In particular, his analysis process concentrated on finding the "one best way" to do any job. This approach, still a central feature of present-day job analyses, examines two main aspects of each job in the organization: (1) the methods *employed* and (2) the *time measurement* for task completion.

The first aspect is concerned with how the job incumbent performs the job—that is, with the minimum requirements for success in the job. These requirements include (a) the individual's knowledge of production techniques and processes (e.g., raw materials and other inputs, machinery, tools), cognitive (mental) abilities, mechanical abilities (e.g., principles and spatial relationships), and psychomotor abilities; and (b) the working conditions in which the job is performed (e.g., whether the work is done by the individual alone or in conjunction with other members of a team).

The second aspect common to all job analyses is time measurement, or the cycle/production time required to produce the good or service to the performance standards of the organization. This time standard is completely dependent on the first aspect, which is concerned with the methods employed (or how the job is performed). Obviously, changing the process from individual to team-based production and modifying the number of raw material inputs or steps in the production process will substantially change the output or number of items that can be produced on a time basis per hour, shift, or day.

Scientific management Examines two main aspects of each job in the organization: (1) the *methods employed* and (2) the *time measurement* for task completion

Job Analysis and HR Planning

The information derived from job analysis is absolutely vital in conducting effective HR planning. First, the analysis of jobs and work processes ensures that job descriptions and specifications accurate and reliable. By utilizing the most up-to-date information, we can help ensure that HR demand and supply can be effectively matched by means of recruitment activities, selection methods, and HR programs being properly aligned to attracting and retaining high-quality individuals to meet the needs of today and for the future. Second, changes in technological processes lead to certain jobs, programs, and processes becoming redundant over time, while new jobs and work activities develop and expand (e.g., information technology personnel). Job analysis allows HR programmers to suggest the most effective and efficient ways to (a) organize work, (b) differentiate "core" work activities from those that can be outsourced and/or curtailed, and (c) structure the organization, given key strategic business goals. Third, business is becoming increasingly global in its scope and operations, and work and job analysis procedures help organizational HR planners compare and contrast the degree of similarity or difference between geographically diverse operating units and personnel around the world, thereby facilitating more effective restructuring programs (mergers, acquisitions, divestitures, and so on). Furthermore, the need for high-performing organizational management has never been so apparent in organizations, and increasingly organizations are developing their own in-house management training centres, for example General Electric's John F. Welch Leadership Development Center in Crotonville, New York, Bank of Montreal's Institute for Learning in Toronto, and McDonald's Fred L. Turner Training Center in Oak Brook, Illinois. These programs can work effectively in helping to create continuity of effective management, by means of successful succession programs, only if they are based upon current, effective information derived from the validated personal requirements and behavioural performance standards that are outcomes of the job analysis process. All in all, job analysis is vital to ensuring the best fit between workers and work requirements, and the requisite complementarities of individual and organizational needs.

Problems Associated with Job Analysis

Having noted the importance of job analysis and its two constituent elements of methods and time, let's now turn to an examination of challenges associated with job analysis.

1. Job Analysis That Is Neither Updated nor Reviewed

Job analyses must be reviewed on a regular basis by incumbents, supervisors, HR staff, and so on to ensure that the written job requirements reflect the reality of contemporary job performance. Changes in organizational strategies, recent organizational changes (such as mergers, acquisitions, and divestitures; downsizing and restructuring) and any changes in technology, materials, and processes may affect how work should be efficiently organized into jobs. These changes must be incorporated to create job descriptions and specifications that accurately reflect how work is being organized into jobs and the corresponding set of KSAOs required of the job incumbents. Obsolete job descriptions not only fail to provide job incumbents with meaningful guidance as to their required duties and tasks, but also result in an HR planning process that is attempting to match individuals to jobs on the basis of information that is no longer valid.

2. Job Description or Specification That Is Too Vague

If job analysis is to provide important information to allow us to select the individual who best meets job requirements, we must be specific as to what those exact requirements are. For example, organizations often specify that applicants must have a certain number of years of experience in a certain functional area instead of specifying the exact skills or competencies the applicant should have learned over that period. Without this specific information, experience or time spent on the job has little relevance for selection. Similarly, organizations may mistakenly include elements such as "dependability" as one of their job requirements without giving specific examples of what constitutes dependable behaviour (e.g., the individual arrives on time for meetings with all preparatory work properly completed). To be an effective component of HR planning, the job analysis process must produce detailed and specific requirements for successful performance of each job in the work process.

3. Contamination and Deficiency

Although brevity and clarity are definite virtues with respect to job analysis (a short, clear job description is of great use to both job incumbents and supervisors), taken to an extreme these characteristics may cause problems during job analysis efforts. If our job description or specification fails to incorporate important aspects of the job that are required for success, this error of omission is referred to as **deficiency**. Conversely, if we include peripheral, unimportant aspects of a job in the formal job description, we run the risk of contaminating it by diverting attention from valid, important correlates of success. **Contamination** of the job analysis process may also lead to legal consequences if we use the information to select individuals on the basis of factors not related to the job that are considered discriminatory under provincial or Canadian human rights legislation. For job analysis, therefore, we should try to be as brief and clear as possible, but not at the expense of excluding any important behavioural or performance element of the job.

Deficiency
An error of omission that occurs when a job description or specification fails to incorporate important aspects of the job required for success

Contamination
An error that occurs when unimportant or invalid behaviours or attributes are incorporated into a job description or specification

4. Time and Costs of Job Analysis

Some organizations are deterred from conducting job analyses due to the significant time and costs perceived to be associated with the process. Typical costs include consulting fees for job analysts (if the organization does not have in-house HR staff with relevant qualifications); licensing fees associated with usage of copyrighted job analysis methods (e.g., the position analysis questionnaire); the costs of lost production (or overtime) involved with interviewing and surveying job incumbents, managers, and so on; and the administrative costs involved with codifying, analyzing, drafting, revising, and disseminating the information that results from the process. However, many organizations that bemoan the large time and cost expenditures associated with job analysis do so only because they have not conducted a proper cost–benefit analysis with respect to this decision. For example, organizations should also consider the time and cost savings (see HR Planning Notebook 4.1) that result from the following: (1) better matching of individual skills to organizational requirements (e.g., reduced costs, and often lower absenteeism and turnover, associated with training and development),[5] (2) incorporation of the benefits of organizational learning with respect to product and process improvements, (3) reduced job ambiguity and wastage, (4) clarification of operating procedures and job relationships, (5) explicit definition of performance expectations for individuals and teams, and (6) facilitation of other HR programs. If organizations consider the full costs and benefits associated with entering into the job analysis process, the decision whether to proceed is invariably very clear!

The Process of Job Analysis

The process of job analysis involves following five steps to maximize the potential for success. We now examine each of the five steps in turn, noting the actions required at each stage.

1. Determine the Job or Process to Be Analyzed

Although the desired outcome of a job analysis is to have a comprehensive record of all organizational jobs and their associated duties, skill requirements, working conditions, and so on, reality dictates that organizations normally select certain

HR Planning Notebook 4.1

SPEEDING UP JOB ANALYSIS

One of the oft-cited criticisms of job analysis is the time and cost associated with doing it properly. Darin Hartley's "Job Analysis at the Speed of Reality (JASR)" was designed to address these concerns by developing an abbreviated process that can create a validated task listing for most positions in approximately three hours. By utilizing approximately four to six job analysts, the group identifies six to twelve duty areas of each job, with each duty area typically containing from three to twelve "task statements" representing measurable activities.

The six steps of the JASR approach are:

1. Greet participants and conduct introductions.
2. Briefly explain the JASR process and participant roles.
3. Determine the scope of the job to be analyzed.
4. Identify the job's functional "duty areas."
5. Identify and list "task statements" for each "duty area."
6. Print the completed task list, and have it signed by the job analysts.

Source: Reprinted from *Job Analysis at the Speed of Reality*, by Darin Hartley, copyright © 2004. Reprinted by permission of the publisher: HRD Press, Inc., Amhurst, MA. (800) 822–2801. www.hrdpress.com.

well-defined jobs common throughout the industry that can be benchmarked externally—that is, the analysis commences with these well-known jobs first. Some of the factors that determine whether job analysis will be concurrent (all jobs analyzed at approximately the same time) or sequential (job analyses conducted in different stages over time) include (1) the degree to which the selected job is central or critical to the operations of the organization, (2) the availability of job analysts and other resources, and (3) the availability of external performance **benchmarks** for organizational jobs.

In the first instance, the more critical or central the job or process, the greater the tendency to analyze it and to defer examination of less central jobs or processes to a future time. The number and availability of job analysts, be they external consultants or internal HR specialists, are key factors influencing whether an organization is able to conduct concurrent job analysis or is forced to do it sequentially by stages.

Finally, the Canadian government's **National Occupational Classification (NOC)**, which contains standardized job descriptions on over 40,000 occupational titles, facilitates external benchmarking for the job analyst (see HR Planning Notebook 4.2).[6] The NOC and its U.S. counterpart, the **Occupational Information Network (O*NET)**, provide information on the main duties and employment requirements of each classified job, along with a listing of other job classifications that are similar to the one being analyzed.[7] This information is invaluable, as it facilitates comparison to similar jobs in other organizations with respect to required applicant specifications and performance standards for key duties and tasks.

Benchmarks
External comparators for organizational jobs and performance criteria

National Occupational Classification (NOC)
The Canadian federal government database that contains standardized job descriptions on thousands of jobs

Occupational Information Network (O*NET)
The U.S. government's most recent occupational database and equivalent to the NOC

HR Planning Notebook 4.2

CANADA'S NATIONAL OCCUPATIONAL CLASSIFICATION (NOC)

The National Occupational Classification (NOC) is the nationally accepted reference on occupations in Canada. It was established in 1992 in order to provide Canadians with definitive information on occupations and their associated requirements. It is an easy-to-understand framework that covers over 40,000 occupational titles, organized into 500 occupational group descriptions. The ten main occupational structure by skill type are:

0. Management Occupations

1. Business, Finance, and Administration Occupations

2. Natural and Applied Sciences, and Related Occupations

3. Health Occupations

4. Occupations in Education, Law, and Social, Community, and Government Services

5. Occupations in Art, Culture, Recreation, and Sport

6. Sales and Service Occupations

7. Trades, Transport, Equipment Operators, and Related Occupations

8. Natural Resources, Agriculture, and Related Production Occupations

9. Occupations in Manufacturing and Utilities

Each occupational title is denoted by a four-digit code. For example, the NOC code for Human Resources Manager is 0112. Human resources managers plan, organize, direct, control, and evaluate the operations of human resources and personnel departments, and develop and implement policies, programs, and procedures regarding human resources planning, recruitment, collective bargaining, training and development, occupation classification, and pay and benefit administration. They represent management and participate actively on various joint committees to maintain ongoing relations between management and employees. Human resources managers are employed throughout the private and public sectors.

Example Titles

manager, employee relations

manager, employment equity—human resources

manager, human resources

manager, industrial relations

manager, occupational health and safety

manager, pay and benefits

manager, training and development

manager, recruiting

Main Duties

Human resources managers perform some or all of the following duties:

- Plan, organize, direct, control, and evaluate the operations of human resources or personnel departments
- Plan human resources requirements in conjunction with other departmental managers
- Coordinate internal and external training and recruitment activities
- Develop and implement labour relations policies and procedures and negotiate collective agreements
- Administer employee development, language training, and health and safety programs
- Advise and assist other departmental managers on interpretation and administration of personnel policies and programs
- Oversee the classification and rating of occupations
- Organize and conduct employee information meetings on employment policy, benefits, and compensation and participate actively on various joint committees
- Direct the organization's quality management program
- Ensure compliance with legislation such as the *Pay Equity Act*

HR Planning Notebook 4.2 (continued)

CANADA'S NATIONAL OCCUPATIONAL CLASSIFICATION (NOC)

Employment Requirements

- A bachelor's degree in a field related to personnel management, such as business administration, industrial relations, commerce, or psychology

  or

- Completion of a professional development program in personnel administration is required.

- Several years of experience as a personnel officer or human resource specialist are required.

Additional Information

- Progression to senior management positions is possible with experience.
- Other joint committees led by human resources managers may focus on issues such as alcohol or drug addiction.

Source: National Occupational Classification 2011, 0112—Human Resources Manager, Human Resources and Skills Development Canada. Reproduced with the permission of the Minister of Public Works and Government Services Canada, 2012.

2. Determine Methods and Analyze the Job or Process

The second step in the job analysis process involves an appraisal of the most appropriate method(s) to use to study and record job-related behaviours. Selection criteria for job analysis methods include the following:

- *Cost:* Cost includes licence fees for such things as copyrighted questionnaires, training, and administration.

- *Time:* Time includes that spent on survey and interview training and assessment, data coding and analysis, and so on.

- *Flexibility of methods:* This criterion has to do with whether the method is appropriate for the particular circumstances (e.g., clerical service jobs as opposed to those in manufacturing).

- *Validity and reliability:* These criteria relate to whether the job analysis methods have been tested and found to be accurate measures of the job's essential elements and whether the results of these methods show a consistent pattern over repeated usage.

- *Acceptance:* Some job analysis methods, such as direct observation and videotaping of work performance, may be considered intrusive by the workforce and, therefore, may be met with resistance. Other methods, such as questionnaires and interviews, might be deemed more acceptable by the workers, who would then cooperate in providing information to the job analysts or persons collecting the job information. The aforementioned selection criteria are used to evaluate the following common methods of job analysis.

INTERVIEWS   To gather information about a job, a job analyst may interview job incumbents, as well as co-workers, supervisors, suppliers, clients, and subordinates. This type of all-round analysis of a job is referred to as **360° evaluation**, as the job analyst has input from individuals who are in the job under evaluation and in other jobs that relate to it. Not surprisingly, self-evaluations derived from this process tend to have a positive rating bias.

OBSERVATION   Observation of a job can be either direct or indirect. In *direct observation*, analysts observe the production line for worker behaviours and the skills required for job success. Recording of the number and duration of individual behaviours is normally captured on a standardized recording sheet.[8] *Indirect observation* can incorporate a variety of means, such as a videotaped recording of the job being performed, for subsequent analysis.

QUESTIONNAIRES   Numerous standardized questionnaires are used for job analysis. Some of the more frequently used instruments include (1) the Functional Job Analysis,[9] (2) the Job Diagnostic Survey,[10] and (3) the Position Analysis Questionnaire.[11]

These survey instruments are normally completed by jobholders, their supervisors, and people who work in other jobs that are related to the specific job being investigated.[12]

Typically, job analysis data derived from self-reports of incumbents, or current job holders, display the lowest levels of reliability, reinforcing the importance of gathering many sources of data to be used for job analysis.[13]

The questionnaires vary substantially, but common elements are questions concerning the following:

- Education, training, and skill requirements to be successful in the job

- Responsibility or accountability (e.g., with regard to budgets, specific duties and tasks performed, number and type of people supervised)

- Effort—the cognitive and physical demands placed on the individual

- Working conditions—whether the work is done by an individual or team, the equipment or materials used, the job context or the environmental conditions of work (e.g., telephone line repairperson), the work shifts or hours of work, the potential health hazards, and so on

JOURNALS AND DIARIES   This method of job analysis asks jobholders to maintain a written record of their job activities, and associated time expenditures, for a preset period that typically ranges from a complete work cycle or typical week to up to a month. Although the information can be useful in discovering actual time expenditures and activities—for example, it was a vital component of the Mintzberg (1973) research investigation into the nature of managerial work that asked managers to record their work activities and associated time expenditures—there can be the problem of selective reporting and bias as the respondent is fully aware that his or her time and activities are being monitored.

360° evaluation
Evaluation of attributes and performance dimensions of a job from "the full circle" around the job—that is, feedback from subordinates, superiors, co-workers, clients, and the jobholder him/herself

HR Planning Today (4.2

Rating Jobs Against New Values

Bayer Group AG, headquartered in Leverkusen, Germany, reorganized its three U.S. companies into one entity and in so doing revised its job analysis/evaluation processes. The new system was designed to meet the vision, culture, and goals of the unified company and to identify and measure competencies required for future organizational success. The existing Hay Guide Chart-Profile Method used previously was a starting point for the new system, although the language describing each work-value cluster was changed. Each of the following work-value clusters is matched to a numerical scale to enable Bayer to ensure internal equity through usage of point-based evaluation. Bayer's work-value dimensions are as follows:

1. *Improvement opportunity:* "Describes the requirement for and assesses the ability to improve performance within the context of assigned roles and rate of change in the work environment."

2. *Contribution:* "Describes the requirement for and ability to achieve results that improve performance and define success."

3. *Capability:* "Describes the total of proficiencies and competencies required to support effectiveness and progress."

Each of these three work-value clusters also incorporates various sub-elements, such as the following components of the capability cluster:

a. *Expertise and complexity:* "Measures the depth and breadth of specific technical and professional proficiencies and competencies required for expected individual and team performance."

b. *Leadership and integration:* "Measures the ability to manage, coordinate, integrate, and provide leadership for diverse people, processes, and organizational resources to achieve common goals and objectives."

c. *Relationship-building skills:* "Measures the requirements for meeting internal and external customers' needs through effective listening, understanding, sensitivity, and analytical abilities. This capability also measures the requirements for proactive persuasiveness, organizational awareness, and collaborative influencing skills necessary to effect desired change and build effective, enduring relationships."

Source: J. Laabs, "Rating Jobs Against New Values," *Workforce*, Vol. 76, No. 5 (May 1997): 38–49. Used with permission of ACC Communication/*Workforce*, Costa Mesa, CA. All rights reserved.

HR Planning Today 4.2 describes Bayer's revision of its job analysis and evaluation processes.

OUTPUT AND PRODUCTION ANALYSIS   Machine-generated output reports, as well as production reporting procedures, can obtain information about the job and its normal and peak levels of production. Although these techniques reveal little about the qualitative or process aspects of the job, they are useful in determining appropriate performance standards for output.

CURRENT JOB DESCRIPTIONS AND SPECIFICATIONS   In the quest for information about the job, a useful starting point, if a previous job analysis has been performed, is an examination of the existing job descriptions and specifications. Although the information contained in these documents is already dated, it is advantageous to see how the job in question has evolved and whether its component duties, tasks, and employee specifications, as well as the authority and status the job is accorded, have increased or diminished over time.

Despite Fred Taylor's best efforts, in fact there is no one best way to analyze a job, so most contemporary job analyses employ a combination of the aforementioned methods. This multi-method approach not only provides a more comprehensive examination of the job but also enables quantitative aspects (e.g., production reports, questionnaires, observation) and qualitative aspects (e.g., interviews, journals, observation) of each job to be analyzed.[14]

3. Examine the Recorded Data on the Job or Process

Having selected the most appropriate methods to analyze the job, job analysts record the knowledge, skills, and abilities; job-related behaviours, duties, tasks, and responsibilities; and working conditions of the job. The next step is to examine these data from a variety of perspectives to get a detailed profile of the current job. Some of the questions involved in the examination are as follows:

- What is the purpose of this job? Why does it exist?

- Where is the job physically performed? Are there compelling reasons why the job must be performed there?

- What is the sequence of behaviours required for successful job performance? Are there ways to modify the methods and process to improve the job both qualitatively (e.g., worker and client satisfaction, worker motivation) and quantitatively (e.g., output)?

- Who performs the job? What constitutes the employee specifications (e.g., education, training, skills, and so on) required for job success? Are these specifications optimal, or are they the minimum standards required for success on the job?

- What are the means of performing the job? Are the materials, machines, group processes (if applicable), and operating procedures congruent with effective performance of the job?

After addressing all these issues, the job analysts start to form a clearer picture of the present job profile. This information is used to draft the job description or specification, which should be reviewed not only by the job incumbents but also by their supervisors. Reference is also made to the NOC, which provides an external comparison for the validity of the emerging job documentation. Any inconsistencies or discrepancies in the findings are examined by all the job analysts and then taken back to the jobholders and supervisors for further feedback and elaboration.

4. Define and Formalize New Methods and Performance Standards for the Job or Process

So far in the process, the job analysts have (1) examined existing descriptions and specifications for the job (if previous analyses have been conducted), (2) analyzed data on the job as it is currently performed by the jobholder(s), and (3) compared the results of steps (1) and (2) to the job classification in the NOC and current practices in competitive firms. At this stage, the job analysts attempt to improve on current practices by recommending new methods and performance standards for the job. To do this, analysts must present the following questions to the incumbents and managers:

- Would you recommend any changes to materials, machinery, behavioural sequencing, training, or procedures to improve performance on the job?

- Are there any duties or tasks that should be added to or deleted from the job?

- Would you recommend any changes in the specifications (e.g., knowledge, skills, or abilities) for individuals selected to perform this job?

- What changes in working conditions would you recommend to improve performance on this job?

- What is your rationale for these recommended changes?

Having gleaned the collective wisdom of all relevant parties regarding the performance of the job under examination, the HR specialists or job analysts write the new description or specification. This will incorporate improvements in how the job is performed (i.e., methods) and revisions to performance and output standards (i.e., time). These changes are formalized into written documents—either a job description or a job specification.

A job description is job focused as it concentrates on the tasks, duties/responsibilities, and specific behaviours that are required to be a successful performer. These duties are listed in order of importance to the organization, with the most critical ones listed first. It is also common practice for job descriptions to indicate the amount or percentage of work time devoted to the performance of each job task. While this information is undoubtedly useful for the jobholder, it is important to remember that time-consuming tasks are not necessarily highly valuable or critical to the organization's success! Because of its emphasis on tasks, the job description is best employed for assessing individual performance.

Job specifications are person-focused as they detail the profile of the individuals who are required to perform the job. They concentrate on the knowledge, skills, abilities, experience, and physical capabilities required for job performance (e.g., the ability to clearly express ideas in oral communication) and are used by HR planners for recruitment and selection and by the organization in a number of talent management processes.

Both job descriptions and specifications contain the following information: (1) the job title, (2) the job code or classification number, (3) the compensation category, (4) the department or subunit, (5) the supervising job title (the title of the person to whom one reports), (6) the date of the approved description or specification, and (7) the name of the job analyst. This information facilitates quick access to the information by HR planners.

5. Maintain New Methods and Performance Standards for the Job or Process

It is one thing to have formal written documents specifying the duties, tasks, and KSAOs required for job success, but it is quite another to ensure that these new methods and standards for performance are put into practice. There are four main methods to help ensure use of the new techniques and to prevent relapses to the old, comfortable ways of performing on the job: (1) communication and training, (2) supervisory reinforcement, (3) employee feedback, and (4) reward systems.

As soon as the job description or specification with its new methods and standards has received final approval, the affected jobholders must be given a copy of the revised job description or specification. The process of formally communicating the job changes must also provide sufficient time for questions and answers to ensure that workers are clear on the new expectations for their job performance. Training and development programs may have to be instituted if there are significant changes in methods, materials, or the sequencing of behaviours required on the job.

After being formally notified of the changes, supervisors must spend considerable time ensuring that workers are, in fact, behaving in accordance with the new job procedures. (In a unionized environment, of course, the procedure for job reclassification will be specified under the terms of the collective agreement.) Coaching, modelling the desired behaviours, and reinforcing successful performance of the new methods are all effective techniques supervisors can employ to prevent relapses to the outdated, yet habitual, methods of performing the job.

Feedback is critical to the success of the job analysis process. We have already seen that all parties to the process must be consulted on an ongoing basis for their valuable input. Even after the written job analysis documents have been prepared, feedback is essential in ensuring the process has been successful. Employees must be given the freedom to express suggested improvements or concerns with respect to methods, performance standards, and so on if we expect them to become motivated and committed to their jobs. It is important to bear in mind that job analysis is a never-ending process of data gathering, coding, interpreting, and refining job methods and standards. Even if we "get it right" today, changes in technology, competitive practices, economic circumstances, and so on will ensure that we must change to reflect the realities of tomorrow. Besides, who is better able to provide valid feedback about the circumstances of the job than the actual jobholder?

A common downfall of job analysis efforts is that although the job methods and standards have changed, the organizational reward system has not been altered, and it reinforces the undesirable old job behaviours. Even if workers have been trained in the new methods of the job, and have been provided with a written copy of their revised job description and ample supervisory coaching, actual worker actions may be very different from formal requirements. For example, if the revised work process is team-based, but the compensation system conflicts with job descriptions by being disproportionately weighted toward evaluation of individual performance, we can expect to see unplanned, dysfunctional behaviours and conduct from members of the team. In this instance, worker demeanour may be dysfunctional from the perspective of the organization or the team, but extremely functional and rewarding from the individual's point of view! The oft-repeated dictum "What gets measured gets done" comes to mind, and if workers are still rewarded for their individual actions and not for their contributions to team success, conflicting organizational systems will ensure that we do not get the desired results from the job analysis process.

SPECIFIC JOB ANALYSIS TECHNIQUES

The final section of this chapter is devoted to an examination of specific job analysis techniques that are widespread in contemporary organizational usage. We will present five well-known and widely used techniques.

1. Critical Incidents Technique

Critical incidents technique
A qualitative process of job analysis that produces behavioural statements along a range from superior to ineffective performance for a specific job

The **critical incidents technique** is a qualitative process of job analysis that produces statements of behavioural examples along a range from superior to ineffective performance for a specific job.[15] Several experts, normally trained jobholders with considerable experience in the job that is being examined, are asked to identify the key dimensions of their job. Subsequently they describe for the analyst, in writing or verbally, specific critical incidents that relate to success, as well as those that lead to job failure. Once these critical incidents have been described, they are ranked with respect to their importance to success on the job. The behavioural statements are then used to provide specific guidance for HR planners in refining employee specifications for the job in question.

2. Position Analysis Questionnaire

Position Analysis Questionnaire (PAQ)
A common quantitative approach to job analysis consisting of 194 items to assess job characteristics in six different dimensions and relate them to human characteristics: (1) information input, (2) mental processes, (3) work output, (4) relationships with other workers, (5) job context and work satisfaction, and (6) other job characteristics.

The **Position Analysis Questionnaire (PAQ)**[16] was developed by Ernest McCormick as a structured job analysis checklist of 194 items or job elements used to rate a job. These job elements are incorporated into the following six dimensions:

1. *Information input:* How and where the worker obtains necessary information for job functioning
2. *Mental processes:* The types of planning, reasoning, and decision-making processes required by the job
3. *Work output:* The specific items produced by the worker and the tools he or she employs to produce them
4. *Relationships with other workers:* Important interpersonal contacts for the jobholder
5. *Job context and work satisfaction:* The physical and social working environments
6. *Other job characteristics:* Elements of the job that do not fall into the other five dimensions[17]

Although the job incumbent can complete the PAQ, typically a job analyst will interview the incumbent prior to directly observing his or her actions in fulfilling the performance requirements of the job. This enables the job analyst to score each of the 194 items on several five-point scales such as frequency of usage, importance to the specific job, and so on. The resultant quantitative score enables the comparison of jobs throughout the organization and for those jobs to be grouped according to similar scores on the six different dimensions.

3. Functional Job Analysis

Sidney Fine's **functional job analysis (FJA)** was used to establish the U.S. government's Dictionary of Occupational Titles (DOT) and had a strong formative influence on Canada's NOC.[18] The FJA employs a series of written task statements, each containing four essential elements: (1) a verb related to the task action being performed by the worker, (2) an object that refers to what is being acted on, (3) a description of equipment, tools, aids, and processes required for successful completion of the task, and (4) the outputs or results of task completion.[19] A compendium of various task statements covers all necessary tasks of the job and, although brevity and concise written statements are the norm, some analysts have devised as many as 100 statements for a job. The completed task statements are used to describe any job and contain three essential elements: (1) people (important interpersonal relationships on the job), (2) data (obtaining, using, and transforming data in aid of job performance), and (3) things (physical machinery, resources, and the environment). Each of these three dimensions is then rated on level of complexity and importance with respect to the job being analyzed. The result of the rating is a quantitative score that can be used to compare various jobs.

Functional job analysis (FJA)
Analyzes any job using three essential elements: (1) people (important interpersonal relationships on the job), (2) data (obtaining, using, and transforming data in aid of job performance), and (3) things (physical machinery, resources, and the environment); each of these three dimensions is then rated by level of complexity and importance

COMPETENCY-BASED APPROACHES

Over the past decade, concerns have been expressed that in today's business environment, characterized by increased globalization, extremely turbulent environments, and fierce competition, traditional job analysis may be unable to keep up with the rapid rate of change faced by most organizations.[20] Furthermore, a great many organizations, even those that are highly profitable entities, have reduced their complement of full-time workers by "downsizing," thereby producing flatter organizational structures with fewer workers and greater reliance on self-managed teams in achieving desired organizational outcomes.[21] In this context, the increased desire for flexibility and cross-training of employees has led to a trend of examining **competency** modelling in order to identify general worker requirements associated with a broad range or category of jobs.[22] Although traditional job analysis is still firmly entrenched in most organizations, it is also true that most organizations have started to examine competency-based practices and institute them into their work settings. Competency-based approaches have been used to develop successful professional performance for dentists, engineers, nurses, physicians, police officers, and so on.[23] Recent surveys have shown that approximately 75 to 80 percent of organizations have some sort of competency-driven applications currently in place.[24] HR Planning Today 4.3 describes the use of competency modelling.

Competency
Any knowledge, skill, trait, motive, attitude, value, or other personal characteristic that is essential to perform the job and that differentiates superior from solid performance

Competency advocates maintain that there are several differences in approach between more traditional job analysis methods and competency-based modelling. First, where traditional job analysis focuses on the KSAOs required

Core competencies
Characteristics that every member of an organization, regardless of position, function, or level of responsibility with the organization, is expected to possess

Role or specific competencies
Characteristics shared by different positions within an organization; only those members of an organization in these positions are expected to possess these competencies

to perform specific jobs and examines the linkages among those jobs, competency models focus on individual-level competencies that are common to a broader occupational group or an entire level of jobs (e.g., executives, production workers, supervisory management). There is a deliberate focus on a much broader set of classifying variables than is typical for traditional job analysis.[25] Competencies are typically categorized as **core competencies** (characteristics that every member of an organization, regardless of position, function, or level of responsibility with the organization, is expected to possess, e.g. "is a team player") or **role or specific competencies** (characteristics shared by different positions within an organization, e.g., obtains financial information from each project team leader and compiles a master budget for the entire organization).[27] Only those members of an organization in these positions are expected to possess these competencies.

HR Planning Today 4.3

Competency Models in Practice

The traditional job analysis focuses on jobs and involves the identification of necessary skills, knowledge, and abilities to carry out the tasks, duties, and responsibilities of the jobs. However, in today's knowledge economy, organizations are increasingly looking for flexibilities in maximizing the talents of their employees. A number of organizations have adopted a broader approach: shifting the focus from the job and the tasks to the person and what the person is capable of. Competencies include motives, traits, self-concept, attitudes or values, content knowledge, or cognitive or behavioural skills.

For example, 3M created a template of global leadership competencies. As a global technology company that started in 1902, 3M produces thousands of imaginative products, from those used in health care and highway safety to office products and abrasives and adhesives. The 12 competencies identified by the leadership team are organized into three categories:

• *Fundamental competencies:*
  o *Ethics and integrity:* Exhibits uncompromising integrity and commitment to 3M's corporate values, human resource principles, and business conduct policies. Builds trust and instills self-confidence through mutually respectful, ongoing communication.

  o *Intellectual capacity:* Assimilates and synthesizes information rapidly, recognizes the complexity in issues, challenges assumptions, and faces up to reality. Capable of handling multiple, complex, and paradoxical situations. Communicates clearly, concisely, and with appropriate simplicity.
  o *Maturity and judgment:* Demonstrates resiliency and sound judgment in dealing with business and corporate challenges. Recognizes when a decision must be made and acts in a considered and timely manner. Deals effectively with ambiguity and learns from success and failure.

• *Essential competencies:*
  o *Customer orientation:* Works constantly to provide superior value to the 3M customer, making each interaction a positive one.
  o *Developing people:* Selects and retains an excellent workforce within an environment that values diversity and respects individuality. Promotes continuous learning and the development of self and others to achieve maximum potential. Gives and seeks open and authentic feedback.

HR Planning Today 4.3 *(continued)*

- o *Inspiring others:* Positively affects the behaviour of others, motivating them to achieve personal satisfaction and high performance through a sense of purpose and spirit of cooperation. Leads by example.
- o *Business health and results:* Identifies and successfully generates product, market, and geographic growth opportunities, while consistently delivering positive short-term business results. Continually searches for ways to add value and position the organization for future success.

- *Visionary competencies:*
  - o *Global perspective:* Operates from an awareness of 3M's global markets, capabilities, and resources. Exerts global leadership and works respectfully in multicultural environments to 3M's advantage.

- o *Vision and strategy:* Creates and communicates a customer-focused vision, corporately aligned and engaging all employees in pursuit of a common goal.
- o *Nurturing innovation:* Creates and sustains an environment that supports experimentation, rewards risk taking, reinforces curiosity, and challenges the status quo through freedom and openness without judgment. Influences the future to 3M's advantage.
- o *Building alliances:* Builds and leverages mutually beneficial relationships and networks, both internal and external, which generate multiple opportunities for 3M.
- o *Organizational agility:* Knows, respects, and leverages 3M culture and assets. Leads integrated change within a business unit to achieve sustainable competitive advantage. Utilizes teams intentionally and appropriately.

Sources: J.I. Sanchez and E.L. Levine, "What Is (Should Be) the Difference Between Competency Modeling and Traditional Job Analysis?" *Human Resource Management Review*, Vol. 19 (2009): 53–63; M.E. Alldredge and K.J. Nilan, "3M's Leadership Competency Model: An Internally Developed Solution," *Human Resources Management*, Vol. 39, No. 2/3 (2000): 133–145; D. Dubois and W. Rothwell, "Competency-Based or a Traditional Approach to Training?" *T+D*, Vol. 58, No. 4 (2004): 46–57.

Second, some job analysts maintain that competency models are worker-focused, given their focus on identifying core competencies, whereas job analysis is much more focused on duties and tasks of work. In this regard, competency models include personality and value orientations (e.g. risk taking) into the mix of what is required to "fit in" and succeed in the culture of a particular organization.

Third, since much of the work in organizations is conducted by teams, it can be argued that team skills are much more relevant to today's organization than the classic approach of having each individual job finely delineated with well-defined boundaries. Management personnel recognize that workers know the limits of their jobs and could readily refuse to perform a task that fell beyond their written job description requirements. As a result, managers seek increased flexibility and control over workers' behaviours. On the other hand, unions are justifiably concerned about management abuses of authority in the new "competencies" approach, which lack the important safeguards of written documentation and well-defined limits to arbitrary displays of managerial power that are contained in traditional job descriptions and collective agreements.[28] Widespread problems with corruption, fraud, and executive misman-agement, as revealed in the corporate crashes of Nortel, Enron, and WorldCom, among others, show that unions, as the representatives of the organization's workforce, would be well advised to tread carefully with respect to innovations in this area.

On the downside, competency approaches have been subjected to widespread criticisms as to their utility, including that they are so broad and ill defined as to be of little practical use in guiding performance of job duties.[29] Second, competencies focus more on behaviours than results, and consequently focus on how individuals are expected to perform and not on their demonstrated achievements.[30] Third, there has been a great deal of confusion among workers, HR practitioners, and academics as to what exactly is incorporated into effective competency models. There are a very wide range of ideas as to what exactly

HR Planning Notebook 4.3

BEWARE THE "COMPETENCIES CULT"

Despite widespread usage by organizations in both the public and the private sector, recent research indicates that many "competency models" are of little utility in guiding individual behaviours to alignment with desired HR outcomes.

First, there is a problem associated with a lack of agreement as to what constitutes as "competency," whether it relates to specific behaviours, to outcomes of those behaviours, or to abilities, characteristics, or knowledge. As a result, there are significant differences between competencies which may be "task-" or "worker-" oriented.

Second, a major criticism of the competency approach is that because the models are derived from behaviour that has already occurred, they are at best "present-" oriented and more likely to be rigidly tied to past behaviours and processes. Accordingly, with many organizations facing increasingly fast and turbulent environments, competency models must be flexible and constantly reviewed/revised in order to stay relevant with the rapidly changing business environment.

Finally, inflexibly applied "deterministic" competency systems may give reassurance to managers that they have used "proper procedures" when in fact their overcomplicated detail, applied without

appropriate judgment and thought, can be a real hindrance to recruiting and selecting the most talented personnel.

How then to develop a relevant and future-oriented competency model? In order to avoid a competency model that exists on paper, but has little to no positive impact in reality, authors Robinson, Sparrow, Clegg, and Birdi (2007) recommend a three-phase competency methodology: (1) conduct interviews to develop scenarios of likely future business and behavioural requirements; (2) usage of questionnaires to identify and rank-order competencies as to their importance in the present and future; and (3) develop future competency profiles through usage of critical incident technique interviews to describe incidents in which future competencies were successful demonstrated.

Furthermore, competency models should not be seen as a straitjacket, but as only one of several HR tools, which should also include ability testing and biographically based interviews. Finally, managers must have the freedom and confidence to make justifiable decisions to recruit nonconformist and creative individuals who fall outside the confines of the competency taxonomy (Martin and Pope, 2008).

Sources: Adapted from P. Martin and J. Pope, "Competency-Based Interviewing—Has It Gone Too Far?" *Industrial and Commercial Training*, Vol. 40, No. 2 (2008): 81–86; M. Robinson, P. Sparrow, C. Clegg, and K. Birdi, "Forecasting Future Competency Requirements: A Three-Phase Methodology," *Personnel Review*, Vol. 36, No. 1 (2007): 65–90.

HR Planning Today 4.4

Assessing Competencies and Skills in the Workplace

Research shows that managers and workers have different perceptions about the competencies and skills associated with various jobs in organizations. The main discrepancies exist in the managers' and workers' different perceptions of "workplace autonomy" and "level of required skills." Workers report lower levels of autonomy in their jobs and higher levels of skill requirements for success than are reported by managers for the same jobs under analysis. Furthermore, it is suggested that workers do not see competency as a specific set of attributes, knowledge, skills, and abilities, but as the sum of their perceived experiences and meaning of work.

Sources: F. Green, "Assessing Skills and Autonomy: The Job Holder Versus the Line Manager," *Human Resource Management Journal*, Vol. 13, No. 1: 63–74; and J. Sandberg, "Understanding Human Competence at Work: An Interpretative Approach," *Academy of Management Journal*, Vol. 43, No. 1 (February 2000): 9–25.

constitutes a competency, and, as noted by Zemke, "the word 'competencies' today is a term that has no meaning apart from the particular definition agreed to by the person with whom one is speaking."[31] Fourth, it has been noted that competency modelling, far from being a novel or separate activity in relation to job analysis, is in fact merely an extension of job analysis that focuses on what is common across jobs and occupational groups and identifies the activities and worker characteristics that are core or critical on an organization-wide basis. Fifth, by focusing only on broad general competencies, it might easily be argued that a large portion of the activities required for an individual's successful performance in a job remains largely unexplained. Furthermore, it has been noted by a number of HR specialists that unlike job analysis, which is well understood by most HR practitioners and industrial/organizational psychologists, competency modelling is so ill defined that they see absolutely no value in its approach and expect it to die quickly![32]

See HR Planning Notebook 4.3 for more about the downside of competency modelling, HR Planning Today 4.4 for a discussion of assessment of workplace competencies and skills, and HR Planning Today 4.5 for a progressive Canadian example of competency modelling in action.

HR Planning Today 4.5

Cutting-Edge Canadian HRM: Competency Modelling at the YMCA of Greater Toronto

According to Melanie Laflamme, vice-president of HR for the YMCA of Greater Toronto, their recently developed competency model has been a huge factor in improving the effectiveness of their HR policies and programs. As a charitable organization with a mission of community involvement and providing leadership in building strong kids, families, and communities, the first step in formulating the competency model was the identification of specific role behaviours that augmented the key corporate values of (1) caring, (2) health, (3) honesty, (4) inclusiveness, (5) respect, and (6) responsibility.

HR Planning Today 4.5 *(continued)*

The usage of competency models is not new to the YMCA of Greater Toronto, as the organization was one of the first Canadian charities to develop and adopt competency-based human resources management in the early 1990s. Furthermore, in 1999 they adopted YMCA Canada's model of 29 competencies, which were important in performing various roles in the YMCA. However, in 2006 and 2007, it was recognized that specific elements of the YMCA of Greater Toronto's strategic plan, values, and core programs differed from those of other YMCA jurisdictions; hence the need to develop their own specific competency model. Focus groups were held with representatives from all key programming areas, and after considerable discussion and synthesis, agreement on the current competency model was reached.

Each competency consists of three progressively higher levels of mastery (A, B, and then C), and the level of mastery for any specific job is dependent upon the nature of the work and degree of complexity associated with that job. All employees of the YMCA of Greater Toronto are required to exhibit the appropriate mastery levels associated with their specific job on seven "Association-Wide Core Competencies," which apply to every job in the YMCA. These core competencies are:

1. Effective interpersonal communications
2. Ethics and self-management
3. Member focused
4. Relationship-building and partnering
5. Results focused
6. Teamwork and collaboration
7. Valuing diversity and social inclusion

In addition to meeting the requirements of these seven core competencies, YMCA leadership personnel must also exhibit the appropriate mastery of behaviours listed for their job under seven "Leadership Competencies" related to directing the strategies and people working under their direction. The leadership competencies are:

1. Association management and stewardship
2. Building community relationships and resources
3. Cross-functional integration
4. Leadership
5. People management
6. Planning and initiative
7. Strategic orientation and change management

The current competency model is the basis for all YMCA of Greater Toronto HR strategy, processes, and programs. Through identification of specific skills, behaviours, and knowledge required to perform a role, the competency model is the main HR tool used to guide job analyses and job design, recruitment selection and orientation, employee learning and development, rewards and recognition, and succession planning.

Following the completion of the competency model, requisite role behaviours were identified for each job and were written into the redefined job and its revised written description. These revised descriptions are then used to guide job performance for current job incumbents, and also form the basis of job posting information, as well as interview questions and testing associated with the recruitment and selection processes of new hires. If hired, the new employee is provided with an orientation process that reflects the aforementioned six key corporate values along with specific role requirements of the job for which they have been hired. Learning for the present job, and development processes for future jobs, are tied to performance criteria that reflect the degree to which the individual's job performance measures up to requirements on the current job, and desired role behaviours for future targeted jobs. By having detailed job specific behavioural requirements for all jobs, succession planning in the YMCA of Greater Toronto is facilitated, as talent gaps can be quickly identified, along with lists of potential successors, and their associated career planning and developmental needs to move from current to future job assignments.

According to Laflamme, the key benefits to the current competency model approach are (1) greater shared knowledge and understanding of what is being assessed and how the performance management

HR Planning Today 4.5 *(continued)*

system operates; (2) more effective behavioural-based structured interviews for recruitment, selection, and succession planning; (3) a much more comprehensive and complete picture of job requirements for recruit-

ment, selection, and succession purposes; and, perhaps most importantly, (4) an increased likelihood of hiring employees who will exhibit subsequent successful job performance.

Sources: Kenneth McBey interview of Melanie Laflamme, Vice-President of Human Resources Management, YMCA of Greater Toronto; the YMCA Leadership Competency Model.

SUMMARY

In this chapter, we have examined a number of important aspects of the job analysis process. We have noted how an organization's work process is divided into meaningful units of work called "jobs." The investigation of jobs focuses on two specific aspects, namely the methods employed to perform the job and the time standards for work completion. We have discussed a variety of traditional methods of job analysis (e.g., interviews, observation, questionnaires, journals and diaries, output and production analysis, and so on) including the recent trend of work analysis through competency-based approaches. Once job information has been collected and analyzed, it can be used in various talent management processes including HR planning—that is, to forecast and acquire the number of employees (quantity) and the KSAOs required in these individuals (quality), which is the topic we will turn to next.

Key Terms

benchmarks p. 94
compensable factors p. 90
competency p. 103
contamination p. 93
core competencies p. 104
critical incidents technique p. 102
deficiency p. 93
functional job analysis (FJA) p. 103
job p. 89
job analysis p. 89
job description p. 89

job specification p. 89
National Occupational Classification (NOC) p. 94
Occupational Information Network (O*NET) p. 94
positions p. 89
Position Analysis Questionnaire (PAQ) p. 102
role or specific competencies p. 104
scientific management p. 91
360° evaluation p. 97

Web Links

Government of Canada HRSDC's National Occupational Classification (NOC):
www5.hrsdc.gc.ca/noc/english/noc/2011/welcome.aspx

The U.S. Occupational Information Network (O*NET) is at:
www.doleta.gov/programs/ONET/

PAQ Services Inc. website is at:
www.paq.com

A useful guide to Internet resources on HR is available at:
www.hr-guide.com

Compliance tool for HR professionals in the United States:
http://hr.blr.com

Required Professional Capabilities (RPCs)

The following RPCs are relevant to material covered in this chapter. The RPC number represents the CCHRA number assigned to the RPC as presented on the CCHRA website. All of the RPCs can be found in the Body of Knowledge at www.chrp.ca/rpc/body-of-knowledge.

RPC 3 Contributes to development of an environment that fosters effective working relationships

RPC 8 Provides the information necessary for organization to effectively manage its people practices

RPC 21 Ensures the availability of information needed to support the management decision making processes

RPC 47 Develops an organization or unit design to align with business objectives and environmental factors

RPC 48 Contributes to improvements in the organization's structures and work processes

RPC 70 Develops systems and processes that link the career plans and skill sets of employees with the requirements of the organization

RPC 77 Analyzes position and competency requirements to establish selection criteria

Discussion Questions

1. One of the common reasons advanced for not conducting job analyses is the substantial cost that can be associated with such an undertaking. Present a more balanced perspective by identifying both the various benefits of conducting job analyses and the incremental costs that may occur if the process is not instigated.
2. This chapter describes the various methods that can be used to collect job information. What are the advantages and disadvantages of each of these methods? Are there certain jobs that are suited for each of these methods?
3. This chapter stressed that effective job analysis incorporates qualitative and quantitative aspects, as well as a multi-method approach. Why is this additional complexity an important component of an effective job analysis intervention?

4. Jobs and the nature of work itself are dramatically changing in our information-based, global economy. How will the emerging patterns of work affect the nature of organizational participation, the nature of our jobs, and the process we employ to conduct job analyses in the future?

5. Despite the widespread usage of "competency" models for job analysis/evaluation purposes, current research has shown that many of these models are next to useless. From your readings in the text, and from your readings of scholarly journals, develop a set of guidelines that might be used to develop effective competency models.

Exercises

1. Conduct a job analysis of your current job using one of the job analysis methods described in the chapter, as well as through identifying relevant competencies. Identify key stakeholders with whom you interact in order to perform your job duties, and interview them to derive valid information with respect to the tasks, information, accountabilities, roles, and KSAOs required to perform your job. Use this information to draft (1) a new/updated job description and (2) a set of competencies, related to your job. Compare these documents to the organization's current formal job description. Assess the similarities and differences between the documents produced by the two approaches, and attempt to identify why these differences occur.

2. How many jobs and positions are there in each of the following workplaces?

   a. A dental office where there are three practising dentists, four hygienists, three dental assistants, and two laboratory assistants.

   b. A consulting firm where there are two principals, three consultants, three associates, five analysts, and one office manager.

Case MADNESS AT MOOSEHEAD U

As a distinguished graduate of Moosehead University's HR program, you have been achieving considerable fortune and fame in your role as a consulting job analyst. Your success is reflected in your painfully fashionable clothes, your waterfront condo, your matching "his and hers" platinum Range Rovers, and of course your favourite possession, the isolated lakeside cottage in the Canadian Shield. Things are good! Well, things are good with *you* personally, but obviously there are problems that need to be addressed at your alma mater.

Just this morning you received a frantic phone call from Dr. Melinda Muckabout, the university's vice-president of administration, seeking to engage your professional services. It seems that she has been under considerable pressure from her boss, Dr. Hamish Haberdashery (VP academic), and the president, Dr. Carla Climber. They in turn have been receiving pointed directives for action from the funding arm of the provincial Ministry for Universities.

Specifically, the deputy minister has told them bluntly that if Moosehead doesn't take action within the next six months to implement "performance indicators" for university faculty members and professors, the university will be subjected to a severe funding cut. The politicians and civil servants are responding to ongoing pressure from students, parents, and other taxpayers for much greater emphasis on rewarding quality teaching, enhancing job performance, and obtaining accountability from all the provincial universities.

In your role as a job analyst, you will have your work cut out for you. Melinda lets you know that for every five faculty members on campus there are probably at least six different opinions on the core elements of a faculty member's job. To quote her exact words: "It's complete madness here!" The only internal policy guide is a Senate document that specifies in very general terms that a full-time faculty member has three areas of duties and responsibility: (1) teaching, (2) research and scholarly activities, and (3) service. There are many variations within each of these three categories. Teaching workloads vary enormously among professors with respect to the number of different courses and topics taught; whether the courses are introductory or advanced, undergraduate, or graduate level; whether they are "live" or delivered by Internet; the number of students in the classes themselves; and the degree of teaching and marking support made available by the university. The second category, "research and scholarly activities," is so incredibly broad as to almost defy description. It includes not only research and publications in journals, books, and practitioner magazines, but also theatre performances; media interviews; art gallery presentations; lectures to professional groups, the public, and other bodies; and lending professional expertise to groups within and outside the university itself. There are also huge variations among faculty members with respect to the funding support they receive for research, course releases from teaching, and general computer and facility support for these "scholarly" activities. The final category, service, typically incorporates serving on various university committees and task forces at the department-, faculty-, or university-wide levels; but it also incorporates service to community groups and outside agencies, activities that increase the prestige and visibility of the university.

Suddenly your decision to take the contract doesn't look so straightforward. Certainly this will be a much more difficult assignment than many you have taken on in the private sector.

However, over and above your fond attachment to Moosehead University, you realize that the university officials are relying on you to come through for them, as they will be hard pressed to sustain one more budget cut on top of the past decade of slashed budgets and decreased financial support. The finished documents you produce will be used not only to annually assess the performance of faculty members on key explicit job dimensions, but also to generate for each faculty member quantitative scores on these dimensions that can be used for compensation and "merit" pay. Furthermore, the finished documents will be of a quasi-legal nature, as they will guide and constrain decisions on faculty tenure and promotion, as well as the selection, training, developing, and career progression of Moosehead's faculty members. You certainly have your work cut out for you. It's time to get to it!

Source: K. McBey, "Madness at Moosehead U," 2002.

Question

As the consulting job analyst to Moosehead University, prepare an intake evaluation report that contains your recommended steps and sequencing of activities to conduct this work analysis. List the various stakeholders you will consult, and indicate specific methods and techniques you will employ in successfully completing this contractual assignment.

ENDNOTES

1. Graham, M., and L. Tarbell. 2006. "The Importance of the Employee Perspective in the Competency Development of Human Resource Professionals." *Human Resource Management*, Vol. 45, No. 3: 337–355; Hammonds, K. 2005. "Why We Hate HR." *Fastcompany.com*, Issue 97; McEvoy, G., et al. 2005. "A Competency-Based Model for Developing Human Resource Professionals." *Journal of Management Education*, Vol. 29, No. 3: 383–402:; Sincoff, M., and C. Owen. 2004. "Content Guidelines for an Undergraduate Human Resources Curriculum: Recommendations from Human Resources Professionals." *Journal of Education for Business*, Vol. 80, No. 2: 80–86.

2. Heneman, R. 2003. "Job and Work Evaluation: A Literature Review." *Public Personnel Management*, Vol. 32, No. 1: 47–73; Walker, J. 1994. "Integrating the Human Resource Function with the Business." *Human Resource Planning*, Vol. 17, No. 2: 59–77; Schuler, R.S., and J.W. Walker. 1990. "Human Resources Strategy: Focusing on Issues and Actions." *Organizational Dynamics*: 5–19.

3. Walker, J.W. 1980. *Human Resource Planning*. New York: McGraw-Hill.

4. McBey, K., and C. Hammah. 1990. "The Evolution of Managerial and Organizational Thought." In L. Allan, ed., *Introduction to Canadian Business*. Toronto: McGraw-Hill Ryerson.

5. McBey, K.J. 1996. "Exploring the Role of Individual Job Performance Within a Multivariate Investigation into Part-Time Turnover Processes." *Psychological Reports*, Vol. 78: 223–233.

6. Human Resources & Skills Development Canada, National Occupational Classification. 2006. www.hrsdc.gc.ca/eng/workplaceskills/noc/index.shtml.

7. Jeanneret, R., and Strong, M. 2003. "Linking O*NET Job Analysis Information to Job Requirement Predictors: An O*NET Application." *Personnel Psychology*, Vol. 56, No. 2: 465–480; United States Department of Labor. 1994.

8. Jenkins, G.D. 1975. "Standardized Observations: An Approach to Measuring the Nature of Jobs." *Journal of Applied Psychology*, April: 171–181.

9. Fine, S. 1974. "Functional Job Analysis: An Approach to a Technology for Manpower Planning." *Personnel Journal*, November: 813–818; Fine, S., and W.W. Wiley. 1971. *An Introduction to Functional Job Analysis*. Kalamazoo, MI: Upjohn Institute for Employment Research.

10. Hackman, R., and G. Oldham. 1974. *The Job Diagnostic Survey: An Instrument for the Diagnosis of Jobs and the Evaluation of Job Redesign Projects.* Springfield, IL: National Technical Information Service; Hackman, R., and G. Oldham. 1975. "Development of the Job Diagnostic Survey." *Journal of Applied Psychology*, Vol. 60: 159–170.

11. McCormick, E.J., P.R. Jeanneret, and R.C. Meecham. 1972. "A Study of Job Characteristics and Job Dimensions as Based on the PAQ." *Journal of Applied Psychology*, Vol. 56, No. 4 (August): 347–368.

12. Jones, R., J. Sanchez et al. 2001. "Selection or Training? A Two-Fold Test of the Validity of Job Analytic Ratings of Trainability." *Journal of Business and Psychology*, Vol. 15, No. 3: 363–389; Mueller, M., and G. Belcher. 2000. "Observed Divergence in the Attitudes of Incumbents and Supervisors as Subject Matter Experts in Job Analysis: A Study of the Fire Captain Rank." *Public Personnel Management*, Vol. 29, No. 4: 529–558.

13. Dierdorff, E., and M. Wilson. 2003. "A Meta-Analysis of Job Analysis Reliability." *Journal of Applied Psychology*, Vol. 88, No. 4: 635–646.

14. Chang, I., and B. Kleiner. 2002. "How to Conduct Job Analysis Effectively." *Management Research News*, Vol. 25, No. 3: 73–82; Reynolds, R., and M. Brannick. 2001. "Is Job Analysis Doing the Job? Extending Job Analysis with Cognitive Task Analysis." *Society for Industrial and Organizational Psychology*, July; Schuler and Walker, 1990; Godet, M. 1983. "Reducing the Blunders in Forecasting." *Futures*, Vol. 15, No. 3 (June): 181–192; Mahmoud, E. 1984. "Accuracy in Forecasting: A Survey," *Journal of Forecasting*, Vol. 3, No. 2 (April): 139–159.

15. Leeds, P., and R. Griffith. 2001. "Critical Incident Inter-rater Agreement Among Security Subject-Matter Experts." *Journal of Security Administration*, Vol. 24, No. 1: 31–46; Flanagan, J.C. 1954. The Critical Incidents Technique." *Psychological Bulletin*, Vol. 51: 327–358; Ghorpade, J.V. 1988. *Job Analysis: A Handbook for the Human Resource Director.* Englewood Cliffs, NJ: Prentice Hall.

16. Fine, S. 1974. "Functional Job Analysis: An Approach to a Technology for Manpower Planning." *Personnel Journal*, November: 813–818; Fine, S., and W.W. Wiley. 1971. *An Introduction to Functional Job Analysis.* Kalamazoo, MI: Upjohn Institute for Employment Research.

17. McCormick, E.J. 1976. "Job and Task Analysis." In M.C. Dunnette, ed., *Handbook of Industrial and Organizational Psychology.* New York: Rand McNally.

18. Harvey, R. 2002. "Functional Job Analysis." *Personnel Psychology*, Vol. 55, No. 1: 202–206; Fine, S. 1974. "Functional Job Analysis: An Approach to a Technology for Manpower Planning." *Personnel Journal*, November: 813–818; Levine, E.L. 1983. *Everything You Always Wanted to Know about Job Analysis.* Tampa, FL: Mariner Publishing.

19. Harvey, 2002; Henderson, R. 1993. *Compensation Management*, 6th ed. Reston, VA: Reston Publishing.

20. Buhler, P. 2002. "Tips to Improved Staffing Decisions." *Supervision*, Vol. 63, No. 10: 20–23; Ashkenas, R., D. Ulrich, T. Jick, and S. Kerr. 1995. *The Boundaryless Organization.* San Francisco: Jossey-Bass.

21. Hayden, S. 1999. "Competency Based Management." *IHRIM Journal*, Vol. 3, No. 1: 16–18.

22. Prien, E., K. Prien, and L. Gamble 2004. "Perspectives on Nonconventional Job Analysis Methodologies." *Journal of Business and Psychology*, Vol. 18, No. 3: 337–348; Catano, V., S. Cronshaw, W. Wiesner, R. Hackett, and L. Methot. 2001. *Recruitment and Selection in Canada*, 2nd ed. Toronto: Nelson Thomson Learning.

23. Schippmann, J., R. Ash, M. Battista et al. 2000. "The Practice of Competency Modeling." *Personnel Psychology*, Vol. 53, No. 3 (Autumn): 703–737.

24. Schippmann et al., 2000.

25. Sanchez, 1994.

26. Catano et al., 2001, p. 176.

27. Intagliata, J., D. Ulrich, and N. Smallwood. 2000. "Leveraging Leadership Competencies to Produce Leadership Brand: Creating Distinctiveness by Focusing on Strategy and Results." *Human Resources Planning*, Vol. 23, No. 3: 12–23.

28. Harvey, R., and M. Wilson. 2000. "Yes Virginia, There Is an Objective Reality in Job Analysis." *Journal of Organizational Behavior*, Vol. 21, No. 7: 829–848; Schippmann, J., R. Ash, M. Battista et al. 2000. "The Practice of Competency Modeling." *Personnel Psychology*, Vol. 53, No. 3 (Autumn): 703–737.

29. Lievens, F., J. Sanchez, and W. De Corte. 2004. "Easing the Inferential Leap in Competency Modeling: The Effects of Task-Related Information and Subject Matter Expertise." *Personnel Psychology*, Vol. 57, No. 4: 881–1003; Schippmann, J., R. Ash, M. Battista et al. 2000. "The Practice of Competency Modeling." *Personnel Psychology*, Vol. 53, No. 3 (Autumn): 703–737.

30. Fine, S. 1974. "Functional Job Analysis: An Approach to a Technology for Manpower Planning." *Personnel Journal*, November: 813–818; Fine, S., and W.W. Wiley. 1971. *An Introduction to Functional Job Analysis.* Kalamazoo, MI: Upjohn Institute for Employment Research.

31. Fine, 1974.

32. Hemphill, J.K. 1960. *Dimensions of Executive Positions.* Columbus: Ohio State University.

The HR Forecasting Process

CHAPTER LEARNING OUTCOMES

After reading this chapter, you should be able to:

- Identify the three different categories of HR forecasting activity and their relationship to the HR planning process.
- Understand the considerable advantages that accrue to organizations from instituting effective HR forecasting procedures.
- Discuss the rationale for giving special attention to specialist, technical, and executive personnel groups in the HR forecasting process.
- Comprehend the impact of environmental and organizational variables on the accuracy and relevant time periods for future estimates of HR demand and supply.
- Identify the various stages in the process of determining net HR requirements.
- Understand the policy and program implications of an HR shortage or an HR surplus.

THE IMPENDING TALENT SHORTAGE—REALLY?

It may be a little challenging to comprehend the concept of a shortage of workers when our national unemployment rate has been hovering at over 7 percent since early 2009, after the economic meltdown in 2008. However, with Canada's fertility rate at below 2 percent in the past decades and our increasing aging workforce, projections by many institutions have shown that it is going to be a "sellers' market" in not-too-distant future. Other countries around the world are also not immune to the talent shortage challenge. According to a survey conducted by Manpower that involves almost 40,000 interviews in 39 countries around the world, one in three employers faced challenges in acquiring the necessary talent. The Conference Board of Canada forecasted that by 2020, there will be a labour shortfall of 950,000 workers.[1] Estimates by Andrew Ramlo and Ryan Berlin of the Urban Futures Institute show that the projected shortfall might get as high as 14 million workers by 2055.[2] Organizations who want to grow and remain competitive in their industry sector will have to focus their efforts on strategic workforce planning in order to ensure they will have the right number of people with the right KSAOs to perform the work and achieve their organizational strategies. For example, Google announced in January 2011 its biggest hiring spree ever of 6,000 workers globally[3] and Target, the second-largest retailer in the United States, has already started recruitment efforts as it plans to open up to 135 stores across Canada by March 2013.[4]

HR forecasting
The heart of the HR planning process; can be defined as ascertaining the net requirement for personnel by determining the demand for and supply of human resources now and in the future

Transaction-based forecasting
Forecasting that focuses on tracking internal change instituted by the organization's managers

Event-based forecasting
Forecasting concerned with changes in the external environment

Process-based forecasting
Forecasting not focused on a specific internal organizational event but on the flow or sequencing of several work activities

HR forecasting, which constitutes the heart of the HR planning process, can be defined as ascertaining the net requirement for personnel by determining the demand for and supply of human resources now and in the future. Environmental scanning, as discussed in Chapter 3, is an important step before forecasting can take place. Once the senior management team has decided on the organizational strategy, the demand for and supply of workers can be determined and specific programs can be developed to reconcile the differences between the requirement for labour in various employment categories and its availability, both internally and in the organization's environment. Programs in such areas as training and development, career planning, recruitment and selection, and managerial appraisal are all stimulated by means of the HR forecasting process.

FORECASTING ACTIVITY CATEGORIES

Forecasting activity can be subdivided into three categories: (1) transaction-based forecasting, (2) event-based forecasting, and (3) process-based forecasting.[5]

- **Transaction-based forecasting** focuses on tracking internal change instituted by the organization's managers.

- **Event-based forecasting** is concerned with change in the external environment.

- **Process-based forecasting** is not focused on a specific internal organizational event but on the flow or sequencing of several work activities (e.g., the warehousing shipping process).

HR Planning Today 5.1

HR Forecasting in a Global Economy

Organizations that operate globally face additional challenges to their effective and efficient use of human resources. For instance, differences in time zones and the vast geographic dispersion of operational units and workforces can present a problem. Technology can help companies through use of the Internet and organizational intranets, as well as email and videoconferencing systems. Global HR planning managers should encourage employee collaboration through:

- Maximizing use of technology such as email
- Explicitly scheduling work to take advantage of time zone differences that can be used to the company's advantage (e.g., preparation of a contract by employees in an advanced time zone, which can then be sent to a client firm that is in a time zone several hours behind that of the preparing unit)
- Elimination of redundant costs through centralizing data in the HRMS

Source: Adapted from C. Solomon, "Sharing Information Across Borders and Time Zones," *Workforce*, Vol. 3, No. 2 (March 1998), pp. 12–18.

All three categories are important in order to have a comprehensive method for ascertaining HR requirements.

Forecasting is only an approximation of possible future states and is an activity that strongly favours quantitative and easily codified techniques. As a result, it is important to make an explicit effort to obtain and incorporate qualitative data into our analyses.[6] Furthermore, more successful HR forecasting processes use both qualitative and quantitative data, and a number of studies have clearly shown that accuracy of prediction improves significantly when we use a variety of forecasting techniques[7] (see HR Planning Today 5.1 and 5.2). Effective forecasting also hinges on obtaining a fine balance between global and local control of the process. A study of multinational corporations operating in Ireland showed that most of the firms that were analyzed adopted a local approach to forecasting, with the (global) headquarters maintaining a vigilant yet loose monitoring of financial costs and other performance criteria.[8]

The Strategic Importance of HR Forecasting

A great number of important benefits accrue to organizations that take the time to institute effective HR forecasting processes, and the forecasting techniques employed do not have to be sophisticated to be of value to the firm.[9] A few of the more important advantages of HR forecasting are discussed below.

1. Reduces HR Costs

Effective HR forecasting focuses on a comparison between the organization's current stock of workforce KSAOs (e.g., experience) and the numbers, skill competencies, and so on desired in the workforce of the future. This inherent comparison facilitates a proactive, sequential approach to developing internal

HR Planning Today 5.2

Successful Workforce Planning

Given the plethora of organizational CEOs who state that "people are our greatest asset," it might be assumed that HR and workforce planning activities would be among the best-developed functions in organizations and regularly receive top priority with respect to funding and other resource allocations. In reality, many organizations devote insufficient time and resources to HR planning activities, which have three main factors associated with their success. Specifically, HR planning should be:

- Strategic and forward looking
- Comprehensive and encompass all employee groups and management functions

- Tailored to the specific culture and attributes of the organization to which it is being applied

Furthermore, by being proactive and avoiding the "feast or famine" swings in personnel numbers associated with reactive workforce staffing, HR planning can dramatically cut labour costs, increase productivity, reduce the number of "surprises," and rectify problems before they grow more complex and costly. In order to achieve these ends, workforce planning should give priority to forecasting and assessment, recruitment and selection, leadership development, and succession planning programs.

Sources: Adapted from J. Sullivan, "Workforce Planning: Why to Start Now," *Workforce*, Vol. 81, No. 12 (November 2002), 46–50; and J. Woodard, "Three Factors of Successful Work Force Planning," *The Journal of Government Financial Management*, Vol. 50, No. 3 (Fall 2001), 36–38.

workers and is concurrent with activities focused on obtaining the best external recruits from competitors, universities, and training programs.[10] In this manner, organizations can reduce their HR costs as they take a long-run planning approach to HR issues. This means that organizations will be less likely to have to react in a costly last-minute crisis mode to unexpected developments in the internal or external labour markets. Proper planning will ensure that any inefficiencies can be avoided as much as possible: consider a situation in which an organization does not have enough work for all its employees but still has to continue to pay wages and benefits, or, alternatively, in which an organization faces an increase in work demands and will have to pay overtime for its current workers.

2. Increases Organizational Flexibility

An oft-cited advantage of HR forecasting is that its proactive process increases the number of viable policy options available to the organization, thereby enhancing flexibility.[11] With regard to labour supply considerations, forecasting processes develop program options that can determine whether it is more advantageous and cost-effective to retrain or develop current members of the workforce to fill anticipated job openings or fill these openings with external recruits who already possess the required competencies and skills. Given that HR forecasting is predicated on trends, assumptions, scenarios, and various planning time horizons, the process itself encourages the development of a wide range of possible policy options and programs from which the HR staff can select. Furthermore, each of the various HR programming options are ranked, subjected to cost–benefit analyses, and allocated organizational resources after being carefully examined as part of the HR forecasting process.

3. Ensures a Close Linkage to the Macro Business Forecasting Process

A serious problem develops in some organizations when the HR planning process is not aligned to the overall business goals of the organization.[12] The implementation of an HR forecasting process helps to eliminate the possibility that personnel policies will veer away from the overall operating and production policies of the organization. First, HR forecasting, although an ongoing process, takes its lead from specific production, market share, profitability, and operational objectives set by the organization's top management. These objectives have been established through proactive internal and environmental scans of market and competitor strengths, weaknesses, opportunities, threats, resources, and policy actions.[13]

Once these have been established, specific HR forecasting analyses are set in motion to determine the feasibility of the proposed operational objectives with respect to time, cost, resource allocation, and other criteria of program success. The HR analyses are subsequently sent back to top management, and they either confirm the viability of the original business objectives or indicate that changes (e.g., the allocation of additional resources) need to be made to enable the objectives to be met.

The business forecasting process, therefore, establishes overall organizational objectives, which are input into the HR forecasting process.[14] Management can then determine whether the explicit objectives, with their associated specific performance parameters, can be met with the organization's current HR policies and programs or whether specific changes have to be instituted, with their associated costs, to achieve the objectives. These analyses and the subsequent feedback of the HR forecast summaries to senior management help to ensure that the top decision makers in the organization (1) are aware of key HR issues and constraints that might affect organizational plans for success and (2) ensure that the HR objectives are closely aligned with the organization's operational business objectives.[15]

4. Ensures That Organizational Requirements Take Precedence over Issues of Resource Constraint and Scarcity

As we present each step of the HR forecasting process in sequence throughout this book, it will quickly become evident that the first step in the process is the calculation of organizational requirements, or **demand** for human resources. Determining the source of personnel—that is, the availability or **supply** of workers—is done only once the process of evaluating personnel requirements for current and future time horizons has been finalized. This sequence is not accidental, and it reinforces the fact that attainment of desired organizational goals and objectives must take priority over all issues concerning resource scarcity and other implementation issues.

Human resources demand
The organization's projected requirement for human resources

Human resources supply
The source of workers to meet demand requirements, obtained either internally (current members of the organization's workforce) or from external agencies

Key Personnel Analyses Conducted by HR Forecasters

Although the forecasting process for personnel in an organization is conducted to determine the number of employees and the skill competencies required by sub-units, as well as the entire organization, a number of personnel categories typically are given greater-than-average attention in the forecasting process. These categories are discussed below.[16]

1. Specialist/Technical/Professional Personnel

Workers holding trade qualifications that are in high demand or that require lengthy preparatory training for attainment of skill competency constitute a key area of focus for HR forecasting. In our increasingly global economy, these workers will be in high demand by competitive firms both in Canada and abroad, which means we will have to give special attention to programs to induce these workers to join our organization. Furthermore, we must give attention to benchmarking compensation schemes to meet or lead industry standards so as to attract and retain people who perform well in these categories. With respect to supply issues, a longer lead time is often required to recruit technicians and professionals because of the need for a more comprehensive and larger geographic search for this specialist talent pool.

2. Employment Equity–Designated Group Membership

Designated groups
Groups deemed to require special attention due to the persistent disadvantages they face in the labour market; the four designated groups include people of Aboriginal descent, women, persons with disabilities, and members of visible minorities

Federal and provincial governments in Canada have enacted employment-equity legislation and guidelines that require organizations to ensure employment practices are fair and equitable and that the composition of their workforce reflects the rapidly changing face of Canadian society. Four **designated groups** require special attention with respect to their degree of use or equitable employment in organizations:

1. People of Aboriginal descent
2. Women
3. Persons with disabilities
4. Members of visible minorities

Particular attention must be paid to monitoring members of these designated groups with respect to the opportunities they receive for employment, promotion, training, and so on as compared to those received by the dominant population of the organization.[17] Furthermore, the composition of the organizational workforce should reflect the underlying characteristics of the society in which it is embedded, so the supply issue, as it relates to proportional representation of designated groups in the organization, is a key area for HR forecasting.

3. Managerial and Executive Personnel

To be successful, any organization must ensure that its executives and managers possess the skills required for success in their specific environmental niche, especially those who possess the hot and critical skills. Executives (CEO, president, vice-presidents, and so on) interact with key environmental stakeholder groups on behalf of the organization and are responsible for setting the goals for the organization's future direction. Managers, acting as the supervisory layer of authority between executives and the operating shop-floor level, are responsible for coaching, directing, training and developing, and controlling worker behaviours to achieve the goals established by the executive group. Although there is no shortage of managers and executives who can function effectively in relatively benign, predictable, environmental situations, researchers believe that organizational leaders who are able to transform organizational culture and anticipate external change, and who possess the dynamic personal attributes necessary to unify the organization, are very rare in most public- and private-sector organizational settings.[18] For this reason, not only must greater attention be paid to identifying leadership talent within the organization, but also assessments or appraisals must be conducted to match the "right person to the right job at the right time."[19] The organization's survival and future success depend directly on succession and replacement planning!

4. Recruits

As was the case with succession and replacement planning, recruiting trainees is extremely important to the success of the organization's overall HR policies. When determining whether to obtain trainees from the internal workforce or externally, a wide variety of factors must be considered. For example, selecting current employees to attend training courses leading to promotion rewards loyalty and past performance and simultaneously diminishes the need for the organizational socialization of newcomers from outside. However, current employees might be very comfortable with the status quo and existing methods of organizational operation, and therefore might not be well suited for employment on novel, creative work processes that differ substantially from established practices. Furthermore, new entrants can bring insights into how competitors structure and operate their businesses and may, as well, bring with them the latest trends and practices taught in universities and specialist training agencies. The relative balance of internal to external personnel to be selected for training courses is a key factor in the HR forecasting and programming operations of many organizations.

The important relationship between effective HR planning processes and the organizational bottom line has been revealed by researchers at the University of Sheffield and is described in HR Planning Today 5.3.

The goal of HR forecasting is to obtain sufficient numbers of trained personnel who will be able to perform successfully in jobs when those jobs need to be filled. To do this, the forecasting process has five stages:[20]

1. Identify organizational goals, objectives, and plans.
2. Determine overall demand requirements for personnel.
3. Assess in-house skills and other internal supply characteristics.
4. Determine the net demand requirements that must be met from external, environmental supply sources.
5. Develop HR plans and programs to ensure that the right people are in the right place.*

*Source: Adapted from Randall S. Chuler, and James W. Walker, 1990. "Human Resources Strategy: Focusing on Issues and Actions," *Organizational Dynamics* (Summer): 4–19.

Before turning to aspects concerned with determining personnel demand, we will examine the effects of environmental uncertainty and of planning time horizons on HR forecasting.

HR Planning Today 5.3

Profitable Personnel

Critics have applied the sarcastic label "big hat, no cattle" to HR managers whom they believe have little effect on the performance of the organization. The United Kingdom's University of Sheffield Effectiveness Program disputes this assertion, because its research discovered that not only was "people management" critical to business performance, but it far outstripped the emphasis on quality, technology, competitive strategy, or research and development in its influence on the organization's bottom-line performance. Although research findings with respect to the relationship between individual satisfaction and job performance have been mixed, the Sheffield research found that at the macro level, satisfaction of the work group across a wide range of areas—for example, developing skills, creativity, and recognition processes—was critical to organizational productivity.

Source: Adapted from M. West and M. Patterson, "Profitable Personnel," *People Management*, Vol. 4, No. 1 (January 1998), pp. 28–31.

ENVIRONMENTAL AND ORGANIZATIONAL FACTORS AFFECTING HR FORECASTING

The HR forecasting process is extremely complex. The forecasting process requiring specific numerical and skill competency targets for personnel to be met despite operating in circumstances of high uncertainty.[21] This uncertainty arises both from external environmental factors and from inside the organization itself. Given this uncertainty and the natural rate of change resulting from operating in a turbulent, global economy, the key factor for HR forecasters is to incorporate flexibility into the program responses associated with demand and supply forecasts (see Chapter 3).

HR FORECASTING TIME HORIZONS

As environmental and organizational factors increase the level of uncertainty for HR forecasters, flexibility in the programs they devise to balance personnel demand and supply is necessary. The key point to consider from an analysis of environmental and organizational factors is that uncertainty decreases our confidence in our ability to predict the future accurately and hence reduces the HR forecasting time horizon.[22] Large organizations with substantial resources and sizable numbers of well-trained personnel who also perform well may be better able to weather the storms of future change in environmental, economic, technological, and competitive market factors. If this is the case, they will be able to extend their HR forecasting process further into the future with greater confidence in the accuracy of their predictions. Irrespective of their situation with regard to environmental and internal factors, organizational forecasters use several different time horizons for forecasting. Although there are variations among organizations with respect to how they define their specific time parameters, the typical HR forecasting time horizons are as follows:[23]

1. *Current forecast:* The current forecast is the one being used to meet the immediate operational needs of the organization. The associated time frame is up to the end of the current operating cycle, or a maximum of one year into the future.

2. *Short-run forecast:* The short-run forecast extends forward from the current forecast and states the HR requirements for the next one- to two-year period beyond the current operational requirements.

3. *Medium-run forecast:* Most organizations define the medium-run forecast as the one that identifies requirements for two to five years into the future.

4. *Long-run forecast:* Due to uncertainty and the significant number and types of changes that can affect the organization's operations, the long-run forecast is by necessity extremely flexible and is a statement of probable requirements given a set of current assumptions. The typical long-run forecast extends five or more years ahead of the current operational period.*

*Source: Adapted from Bechet, T.P., and J.W. Walker. 1993. "Aligning Staffing with Business Strategy," *Human Resource Planning*, Vol. 16, No. 2: 1–16; Walker, J.W. 1980. Human Resource Planning. New York: McGraw-Hill.

The outcome of forecasts derived from these four time horizons leads to predictions and projections. A **prediction** is a single numerical estimate of HR requirements associated with a specific time horizon and set of assumptions, whereas a **projection** incorporates several HR estimates based on a variety of assumptions.[24] The forecasting term **envelope** is synonymous with projection, as one can easily visualize the four corners of an envelope, each corner containing a specific prediction; for example, corner 1 contains an optimistic sales assumption (time 1), corner 2 a pessimistic sales assumption (time 1), corner 3 an optimistic sales assumption (time 2), and corner 4 a pessimistic sales assumption (time 2). The four corner predictions serve to anchor the envelope, which may also contain a number of other specific predictions (e.g., the most likely assumption, which may be to maintain the current sales level). The use of a combination of predictions and projections provides the necessary forecasting flexibility required to cope with the uncertainty and change associated with the environmental and organizational factors described previously.

HR forecasters therefore devise a set of alternative **scenarios**, each with its own set of assumptions and program details associated with HR functions such as training and development, staffing (advertisement, recruiting, and selection), and succession or replacement planning.[25] Naturally, organizations must also conduct **contingency planning** to have HR policy responses ready if substantive unanticipated changes occur. Contingency plans are brought into action when such severe changes to organizational or environmental factors completely negate the usefulness of the existing HR forecasting predictions or projections (e.g., a substantial drop in consumer demand occurs due to adverse public relations, as was seen in the Classic Coke and Tylenol cases).

DETERMINING NET HR REQUIREMENTS

Thus far we have discussed the importance of HR forecasting, key personnel groups targeted for special attention, and forecasting time horizons. The final part of this chapter addresses the process of determining net HR requirements. The next two chapters will be devoted to an examination of specific methods used to determine HR demand (Chapter 6) and HR supply (Chapter 7), but for now we will lay the foundation for these chapters by examining the overall process.

Prediction

A single numerical estimate of HR requirements associated with a specific time horizon and set of assumptions

Projection

Several HR estimates based on a variety of assumptions

Envelope

An analogy in which one can easily visualize the corners of an envelope containing the upper and lower limits or "bounds" of the various HR projections extending into the future

Scenarios

A proposed sequence of events with its own set of assumptions and associated program details

Contingency plans

Plans to be implemented when severe, unanticipated changes to organizational or environmental factors completely negate the usefulness of the existing HR forecasting predictions or projections

1. Determine HR Demand

As we mentioned briefly, it is essential that we calculate our requirement or demand for personnel in terms of numbers and obligatory skill competencies before we consider how we will meet those requirements (i.e., what supply or source of personnel to use). In determining demand, a variety of factors must be considered. First, each organizational subunit has to submit its net personnel requirement to the corporate forecasting unit, based on future needs for labour required to meet the agreed-on corporate and subunit objectives (e.g., market share, production levels, size or expansion, and so on). It is critical to note that this HR demand figure must incorporate the individuals needed to maintain or replace the current personnel who quit, retire, die, are fired or otherwise terminated, or take long-term leave (e.g., for reasons such as disability, training courses, and so on), as well as the replacements for individuals who are promoted or transferred out of the department. All these elements must be included in the calculation of departmental or subunit HR demand. These subunit labour demands are then aggregated and used as the starting point for the HR demand forecasts.

Next, planned future changes in organizational design or in restructuring (e.g., expansion of certain departments, downsizing of mid-level management, planned redundancy, elimination of specific jobs), with their associated increases or decreases in staffing levels, must be incorporated into the equation to revise the aggregated net departmental demand requirements. Furthermore, forecasters have to consider how to replace non-productive paid time (e.g., vacation and sick days) either by increasing demand for full- or part-time personnel (i.e., slack resources[26]) or perhaps by using overtime with the existing set of current employees to prevent loss of productive capacity and required level of service to organizational clients. Finally, consideration of all these issues leads us to the *net HR demand*, broken down into the forecasting time horizons mentioned previously and containing (1) the number of employees required by each subunit and by the organization in total and (2) the employee skill sets, competencies, or specifications required for each of the positions. Finally, we conduct a cost estimate (HR budget) for the net HR demand figure to determine whether our forecasts are realistic, given financial resource considerations. Often, at this stage, subunits are asked to rank their HR demand, identifying jobs that are most critical to the achievement of their departmental objectives.[27]

2. Ascertain HR Supply

Step one produced an estimate of personnel requirements or demand. Step two examines exactly how we plan to fill the anticipated future requirements for personnel. In essence, there are two supply options:

1. **Internal supply**, which refers to current members of the organizational workforce who can be retrained, promoted, transferred, and so on to fill anticipated future HR requirements
2. **External supply**, which refers to potential employees who are currently undergoing training (e.g., university students), working for competitors, members of unions or professional associations, or in a transitional stage, between jobs, or unemployed

Internal supply
Current members of the organizational workforce who can be retrained, promoted, transferred, and so on to fill anticipated future HR requirements

External supply
Potential employees who are currently undergoing training (e.g., university students), working for competitors, members of unions or professional associations, or are in a transitional stage, between jobs, or unemployed

Typically, most organizations use a mix of both internal and external supply, rewarding loyal employees who perform well with promotion and advancement possibilities and recruiting outside individuals who possess competencies not held by the present workforce.

With respect to internal supply, the ability to meet HR demand hinges on the size of the current workforce and especially its abilities. The number and the KSAOs of the workforce are analyzed using the HRMS, which contains a personal record or skills inventory of each member of the workforce. Included in the inventory are items such as employee name, seniority, classification, part- or full-time work status, work history and record of jobs held in the organization, education, training, skill competencies, history of performance appraisals, and future jobs desired by or recommended for the individual, as well as hobbies and interests that may be useful for organizational planning.[28] For example, a computer search of the HRMS database might enable us to quickly determine the numbers, names, and employment status of, and performance records for, all employees who have successfully completed a graduate degree in statistics. If the search procedure fails to find a sufficient number of employees with the necessary KSAOs to meet HR demand, the policy options would be either to identify and retrain employees with related KSAOs who perform well or to turn to external sources for personnel.

Although some organizations hire recruits externally only when their internal searches and job posting or bidding process fail to identify sufficient numbers of high-quality internal candidates,[29] there are several other reasons many organizations use external labour to meet their HR demand. First, and most obviously, if it is necessary to expand our operations without increasing labour efficiency or implementing labour-saving technology, we might have to increase the size of the workforce by hiring externally. Second, internal employees are socialized and might be comfortable in their modus operandi, whereas external applicants can introduce to the organization competitive insights and highly creative novel operational techniques recently learned in external institutions. Third, an internal candidate might be considerably more expensive (due to collective agreement provisions relating compensation to seniority) than an individual who is recruited from outside the organization. Fourth, the use of *headhunters*, specialist personnel placement firms that have detailed knowledge and an extensive network of industry contacts, might enable the organization to lure away from competitive firms proven high performers with distinctive profiles of competencies and experience not possessed by the organization's current executives/professionals. Finally, if organizational objectives require a shift in operating techniques, culture, and past practices, hiring external candidates is often desirable for shaking up the organization.

Irrespective of the reasons why organizations seek external recruits, the key factor in determining whether the organization will be effective in meeting HR requirements from external supply sources is an analysis of how HR policies are perceived by individuals who are potential employees. By benchmarking competitor practices with respect to compensation, it is possible to examine staffing and compensation policies to make them more attractive to high-quality applicants. An organization's ability to attract the "cream of the crop" will be substantially enhanced if the organization is perceived as being the industry leader with

HR Planning Notebook 5.1

CATEGORIZING FORECASTING MODELS

Forecasting models can be categorized in three ways: (1) time-series models, (2) cause-and-effect models, and (3) judgmental models. Time-series models use past data in order to extrapolate and extend trends into the future. These models are simple to use and are typically confined to short-term forecasting. An example of a time-series model is trend forecasting. Cause-and-effect models assume that an ongoing relationship exists between one or more causal or "independent" variables that produce change in the target or "dependent" variable. An example is the sig-

nificant negative relationship existing between market rate of interest (cost of capital) and the demand for construction workers. Cause-and-effect models are used for short-, medium-, and long-term HR forecasting; the best-known example is regression, discussed in Chapter 6. Finally, judgmental models are used for new ventures, situations in which past data do not exist or are unreliable, or when the forecasting period extends into the distant future. They rely on the subjective judgments of experts to derive the forecasts; one widely used example is the Delphi technique.

Source: Adapted from Jain, C. 2002. "Benchmarking Forecasting Models," *The Journal of Business Forecasting Methods and Systems*, Vol. 21, No. 3 (Fall), pp. 18–20.

respect to compensation, rather than just meeting or lagging behind its competitors. As well, recruiting policies must be fine-tuned to ensure communication is established with the appropriate labour markets. For example, it might be possible to fill many production jobs from local labour market sources, but specialized technicians and professionals may require external recruiting, which is national, if not international, in scope. In this case, additional resources, time, and effort may be required if we are expected to fully meet the numerical and KSAO requirements specified by our HR demand process. Finally, obtaining external applicants requires not only identifying where these individuals live and work, but also ascertaining the most appropriate media to use to contact and attract them. These media may include job fairs, open houses, and career days, as well as advertising in industry and professional association journals, publications, newspapers, and websites read by potential external applicants who are trained in the skills needed.

HR Planning Notebook 5.1 refers to different ways of categorizing HR forecasting models.

3. Determine Net HR Requirements

The third step in the process involves the determination of net HR requirements. Personnel who can fill organizational HR demand requirements must be found from either internal or external supplies:

external supply requirements = replacement + change supply components

replacement = hiring to replace all normal losses

change supply = increase (or decrease) in the overall staffing level

(Normal losses are those that result from retirements, terminations, voluntary turnover, promotions, transfers, and leaves must be replaced to keep the workforce size at the current level.)

Recall from our earlier discussion of HR demand that future personnel requirements must not only replace the current workforce employees (in terms of numbers and skill competencies) but also reflect desired future changes to staffing levels. Therefore, the first element in deriving our external supply calculation is to meet our *replacement needs*—that is, to maintain operations at the current level by hiring new employees to replace workers who have left due to firing, transfers, retirements, promotions, leaves, and so on. Next, if we are to increase or decrease our staffing levels, based on organizational and subunit objectives, we have to consider the *change component* that moves the overall size of the workforce to its new future level. This process can be represented by the following equation:

$$\text{external supply} = \text{current workforce size} \times (\text{replacement \% per year} + \text{change \% per year})$$

Using the example of an organization with a current workforce size of 1,000 workers, an annual historical replacement/loss rate of 11 percent, and a desired future growth rate of 7 percent, the net external supply requirement is that 180 individuals be hired per year:

$$\text{external supply} = 1{,}000 \, (0.11 + 0.07) = 110 + 70 = 180$$

Of the new hires, 110 people are allocated strictly to replacement of departing workers, and the other 70 individuals constitute the change requirement for new growth.

Another organization with a workforce of 450, which has a historical annual replacement/loss rate of 8 percent and a corporate downsizing policy that will reduce overall staffing levels by 9.5 percent, has the following supply requirement:

$$\text{external supply} = 450 \, (0.08 + [-0.095]) = 36 - 43 = -7$$

(In the equation above, note that the figure 43 has been rounded up from 42.75.) In this case, the annual replacement/loss rate is insufficient on its own to reduce the size of the organization's workforce to the desired lower staffing level. The result is a net HR surplus, and the organization must not only institute a freeze on external hiring but also further reduce the current internal workforce complement by seven positions to meet the mandated downsizing policy!

In many cases, the existence of a collective agreement between management and the union representing the employees may, due to seniority and layoff articles in the agreement, result in the organization not being able to specify which workers are to be terminated.

HR Planning Notebook 5.2 discusses ways in which an organization may fine-tune its HR forecasting models.

4. Institute HR Programs: HR Shortage and HR Surplus

When a forecast of HR demand is reconciled with the current workforce supply of personnel (i.e., HR internal supply), the result is the net HR requirement,

HR Planning Notebook 5.2

TIPS ON TUNING UP YOUR HR FORECASTING MODELS

HR forecasting models attempt to align an organization's human capital with strategic business direction by projecting future demand and supply requirements. By implementing a systematic process of analyzing our current workforce and identifying talent gaps between desired present and future states, we devise programs to attain these desired future states. However logical and straightforward this appears conceptually, there are a variety of compounding issues that can thwart the actual usage and comprehension of HR forecasting models in everyday life.

First, a key problem for HR forecasting is the dilemma between desiring simplistic, easy-to-use HR processes that are readily understood by a variety of organizational decision makers and the reality that a multitude of individual, organizational, and environmental factors significantly impact human resources supply and demand. These variables compete for consideration and incorporation into your modelling process. Remember the principle of parsimony, which dictates that additional causal factors should only be incorporated into a forecasting model if it makes a significant marginal increase to prediction power.

Second, the issue of data collection time intervals should be considered when evaluating your HR forecasting model. Time lags in data collection lead to discrepancies between HR forecasts and actual requirements for personnel. These discrepancies are less likely to occur if the collection frequency in a time-series analysis is increased. Australian researchers found that the utility of a model forecasting demand for emergency room personnel increased when data collection was changed from monthly to daily or hourly observations.

Third, Korean researchers investigating HR forecasting for the information security industry found that frequent feedback of relevant forecasting information helped reduce the problems caused by time lags between separate forecasting of HR demand and HR supply models. Causal factors for HR demand were most strongly related to size and growth of the business sector and its operational capability, while key causal factors related to HR supply were demand for specific occupational training resulting from the perceived attractiveness of certain types of employment.

Finally, the whole concept of HR forecasting may seem daunting to many small enterprises, but successful HR forecasting models don't have to be comprehensive or expensive, just systematic and sustained. Try segmenting your jobs into three categories—strategic, core, and non-core—as a starting point for your HR strategic planning. Ensure that your analyses are both qualitative and quantitative in nature, and combine data from interviews from business leaders with data on worker performance and potential.

Sources: Adapted from R. Champion, L. Kinsman, et al., "Forecasting Emergency Department Presentations," *Australian Health Review*, 31, 1 (February 2007); S. Park, S. Lee, et al., "A Dynamic Manpower Forecasting Model for the Information Security Industry," *Industrial Management & Data Systems*, 108, 3 (2008), 368–384; C. Hirschman, "Putting Forecasting in Focus," *HR Magazine*, 52, 3 (March 2007), 44–50.

which will be either a shortage or a surplus (unless we are exceedingly lucky and achieve parity with an exact balance of the two!).

$$\text{HR shortage} = \text{HR demand} > \text{HR internal supply}$$

HR shortage

That which occurs when demand for HR exceeds the current personnel resources available in the organization's workforce (HR internal supply)

Simply stated, an **HR shortage** means that forecasted HR demand requirements cannot be satisfied solely by use of the current internal workforce supply of employees, even with them working overtime. Therefore, policy options focus on external supply considerations of recruitment, selection, and compensation schemes to attract new employees. It might be possible to hire part-time employees, full-time employees, contract or freelance workers to address the deficit. Similarly, it might be possible to recall any workers (depending on their KSAOs and training) who were laid off because of past lower levels of HR demand. Also, retired employees might be enticed back to work on at least a part-time basis by means of attractive, flexible work schedules. The use of temporary workers also can help the organization meet a short-run HR shortage, although in the long run further attention to providing promotion and transfer opportunities for internal workers by means of training and development programs usually proves more advantageous.

$$\text{HR surplus} = \text{HR demand} < \text{HR internal supply}$$

An **HR surplus** occurs when the internal workforce supply exceeds the organization's requirement or demand for personnel. In this instance, a number of policy options can be considered. Employees might be laid off to reduce the excess labour supply to a level equal to the demand requirements. Alternatively, employers might terminate employees if certain jobs are considered redundant and the skill sets associated with these jobs will not be required in the future. **Job sharing** occurs when two or more employees perform the duties of one full-time position, each sharing the work activities on a part-time basis. This policy option is gaining strength in Canadian industry as it allows the company to retain valued employees, albeit with reduced hours and lower income levels, with the intention of reinstating them to full-time status once HR demand levels increase at some time in the future, usually when the economy rebounds. **Worksharing** is a federal government program that aims to avoid temporary layoffs through a redistribution of work, earnings, and leisure time. The program provides income support to employees through the Employment Insurance benefits for the amount of work reduction of between 20 to 60 percent. This arrangement has to be agreed upon by both the employer and the employees, and with the unions in unionized environments.

Other programs for addressing an HR surplus include reducing the number of hours, shifts, or days worked by each worker so that all workers can be retained, while reducing overall work hours to the level required by operational demand imperatives. Secondments or leaves occur when the organization lends some of its excess workforce to community groups or permits those surplus workers to take educational leave or training away from the operational workplace. **Attrition** is the process of reducing an HR surplus by allowing the size of the workforce to decline naturally due to the normal pattern of losses associated with retirements, deaths, voluntary turnover, and so on. This decrease of internal supply over time can be accentuated by a **hiring freeze**, which is a prohibition on all external recruiting activities. Early-retirement packages attempt to induce surplus workers to leave the organization when granted severance benefits and outplacement assistance. Finally, if internal supply exceeds HR demand for specific positions, organizational retraining and development, assistance with the expenses associated with moving to a better labour market (geographic mobility), and transfer and demotion can also be considered possible policy options for the organization's affected personnel.[30]

HR Planning Today 5.4 outlines the experiences of one key Canadian corporation in aligning its corporate values with its HR processes.

HR surplus
That which occurs when the internal workforce supply exceeds the organization's requirement or demand for personnel

Job sharing
That which occurs when two or more employees perform the duties of one full-time position, each sharing the work activities on a part-time basis

Worksharing
A federal government program that aims to help organizations mitigate temporary layoffs through a redistribution of work, earnings, and leisure time

Attrition
The process of reducing an HR surplus by allowing the size of the workforce to decline naturally because of the normal pattern of losses associated with retirements, deaths, voluntary turnover, and so on

Hiring freeze
A prohibition on all external recruiting activities

HR Planning Today 5.4

Cutting-Edge Canadian HRM: Sapient Canada—Aligning Culture and Core Values with Key HR Processes

Sapient Corporation, headquartered in Cambridge, Massachusetts, provides IT strategy and marketing design consulting services for clients worldwide based out of 22 offices in Canada, the United States, Europe, and India. Sapient Canada has 185 staff (and 47 temporary international "travellers"), and its synergistic HR processes and operations have helped ensure its consistent placement in "The Top 100 Employers in Canada."

The company's corporate core values of "openness, people growth, leadership, client focus, creativity and growth" are explicitly incorporated into the selection and succession processes, with the goal of finding qualified employees who best fit these values. Furthermore, Sapient Canada's people-oriented culture is inclusive and minimizes hierarchical distinctions as exemplified by the "open table" office design, with only two offices (no cubicles) in the whole building, ensuring that all employees, including the managing director and top staff, sit at tables with the rest of the workforce.

Leadership development programs rely extensively upon formal mentoring for the top 20 potential employees, and informal mentoring and buddy systems for new and other ongoing employees. Feedback is both encouraged and expected, and all Sapient Canada employees receive mandatory semiannual performance assessments, over and above the regular coaching and counselling activities demonstrated on a day-to-day basis. These 360° PPG (people, performance, and growth) performance appraisals include a self-appraisal component, along with qualitative and quantitative assessments of performance provided by a variety of employee and manager-nominated external assessors. Managers are themselves evaluated on their effectiveness in developing their personnel, and there are very real financial and career

consequences if they do not perform the employee PPG review and other HR processes in a highly competent and timely fashion.

Leaving aside a compensation scheme that pays a premium over prevailing market rates for top-quality personnel, other factors that enable successful retention of key performers include ample opportunities for further education and learning, organizational support for corporate social responsibility community improvement initiatives, and a comprehensive and integrated awards and recognition program. Approximately every six to eight weeks, Sapient Canada has a mandatory professional development day and social activity, during which time employees are instructed on topics such as work–life balance, developing business and career plans, and so on. Employees are seconded or given time away from billable projects in order to join in community improvement initiatives. A broad range of awards, from "Rookie of the Year" (for new hires) to the "Founders Awards," promote recognition of exemplary performance and demonstration of core values.

HR forecasting processes are based upon ongoing, real-time bottom-up and top-down forecasting processes. Bottom-up HR forecasting at Sapient Canada is derived from aggregating the labour demand forecasts of various business consulting projects and their requirements for various type of employee skills, knowledge, expertise, and qualifications. These business plan–driven forecasts are augmented by top-down HR forecasts predicated on strategic analysis of business and HR trends, leading to anticipatory hiring today of personnel with competencies and attributes that will be required by Sapient's operations in future. This multi-tier HR forecasting process operates in real time with comprehensive evaluations conducted at least monthly by the HR staff.

Source: Kenneth McBey Interview of Lou-Ann Paton, Amanda Peticca-Harris, and Brad Simms of Sapient Canada.

SUMMARY

This chapter has examined a wide variety of aspects associated with HR forecasting. The advantages of instituting effective forecasting procedures include reducing the costs of HR, increasing the flexibility of the organization, ensuring a close link to the process of business forecasting, and ensuring that the requirements of the organization take precedence over other specific issues. Some groups—executives or specialist/technical personnel, especially those with hot and critical skills, for example—attract special attention in the HR demand and supply reconciliation process. Both environmental and organizational factors have a tremendous impact on various forecasting procedures, and many of these factors have to be addressed explicitly in HR forecasting procedures. The various stages associated with the HR forecasting process are determining the demand, ascertaining the supply, determining net HR requirements (formulae were supplied), and instituting the program. Finally, we discussed the policy implications of reconciling HR demand and supply, ending up with either an HR shortage or an HR surplus, and the various programs that may have to be instituted by organizations to address these varying situations; these programs include job sharing, attrition, and a hiring freeze.

The next two chapters are devoted to an examination of specific techniques used by organizations to calculate HR demand and supply. Chapter 6 presents specific techniques employed by organizations to derive HR demand forecasts while Chapter 7 focuses on HR supply forecasts.

Key Terms

attrition p. 131

contingency plans p. 125

designated groups p. 122

envelope p. 125

event-based forecasting p. 118

external supply p. 126

hiring freeze p. 131

HR forecasting p. 118

HR shortage p. 130

HR surplus p. 131

human resources demand p. 121

human resources supply p. 121

internal supply p. 126

job sharing p. 131

prediction p. 125

process-based forecasting p. 118

projection p. 125

scenarios p. 125

transaction-based forecasting p. 118

worksharing p. 131

Web Links

The Canadian government's Human Resources and Skills Development website is at:
www.hrsdc.gc.ca/en/home.shtml

The Canadian government's advisory website on HR management for employers is located at:
http://hrmanagement.gc.ca/gol/hrmanagement/site.nsf/en/hr10777.html

For information on human resources planning at the Canadian federal government, go to Treasury Board of Canada Secretariat:
www.tbs-sct.gc.ca/hrh/ip-eng.asp

Guidelines from the government of Saskatchewan on HR planning are located at:
www.psc.gov.sk.ca/workforceplanning

Statistics Canada website is at:
www.statcan.gc.ca

The U.S. Bureau of Labor Statistics website is at:
www.bls.gov

Information on workplace trends and forecasting is available from the U.S. Society for Human Resource Management at:
www.shrm.org/Research/Pages/default.aspx

Information on the federal government's worksharing program can be found at:
www.servicecanada.gc.ca/eng/work_sharing/index.shtml

Required Professional Capabilities (RPCs)

The following RPCs are relevant to material covered in this chapter. The RPC number represents the CCHRA number assigned to the RPC as presented on the CCHRA website. All of the RPCs can be found in the Body of Knowledge at www.chrp.ca/rpc/body-of-knowledge.

RPC 6 Develops and implements a human resources plan that supports the organization's strategic objectives

RPC 7 Audits existing HR programs to ensure they are aligned with business objectives

RPC 9 Audits existing HR programs to ensure they are aligned with business objectives

RPC 11 Gathers, analyzes, and reports relevant business and industry information (including global trends) to influence the development of strategic business HR plans

RPC 65 Forecasts HR supply and demand conditions

RPC 66 Identifies the data required to support HR planning

RPC 67 Develops people plans that support the organization's strategic directions

RPC 73 Identifies the potential source of internal and external qualified candidates

Discussion Questions

1. Over the past decade, there have been dramatic employment shifts in many industries because of product life cycles and technological change, as well as general changes in demand for workers with specific KSAOs—for example, in computer and systems engineering. Select a particular industry and conduct a literature review and Internet search for business and labour employment statistics related to its operations (access the websites for industry associations and Statistics Canada). On the basis of this historical review and your knowledge of current business trends, forecast possible employment shifts for the specific industry you selected. How would you use this information as an HR planner?

2. A wide range of HR programming options is available to address either an HR shortage or an HR surplus. However, these programs have widely divergent consequences for the workforce, service to clients, and the local labour market, as well as for the organization's financial bottom line. Identify specific criteria to evaluate and differentiate the effectiveness of the various HR program options.

3. Discuss the strategic importance of HR planning. What are the direct and indirect costs that organizations incur when they experience sustained periods of labour shortages and labour surpluses?

Exercise

Why is strategic HR planning important to organizations? Describe the potential negative outcomes if (1) a hospital does not have enough nurses, (2) a university does not have enough professors, (3) Best Buy does not have enough salespersons in stores.

Case SUN MICROSYSTEMS

Sun Microsystems has experienced extremely rapid growth as the company has evolved from an entrepreneurial operation to a major player in the computer systems industry. As a result, there is a strong need to forecast and identify managerial and executive talent both within and outside the corporation. Ken Alvares, vice-president of human resources, is well aware of the need to "grow" high-potential employees into these key managerial appointments.

Sun has 600 directors, which is the entry-level executive job, and these individuals report to 110 vice-presidents, who in turn report to the president and the 11 executives who sit on Sun's senior management team. Alvares pays close attention to the profile and performance of each of these individuals: "We watch the directors closely, but give more attention to the VPs. We look at each person's particular profile and tailor individual coaching to their needs." Because of this policy, the forecasting and developing of senior managerial and executive talent at Sun takes on a very personalized approach, one that seems to be working, at least to date.

Alvares says he has a good idea who would fill a job if something happened to a specific person, but he is still unsatisfied with Sun's system. "When you look at our bench strength, I don't get the feeling that we've got ourselves covered. I worry about developing people to step up to the next level. In some cases, I have one guy who can fill 10 jobs. If I have to use him, then I'll have to do some scrambling."

Source: Society for Human Resource Management, "Heirs Unapparent: Sun Microsystems," *HR Magazine*, 1999. Reprinted with the permission of HR Magazine, published by the Society for Human Resource Management (www.shrm.org), Alexandria, VA.

Question

Prepare a report analyzing Sun Microsystems' forecasting program for managerial and executive talent. What additions, modifications, or changes would you make to this program?

ENDNOTES

1. Conference Board of Canada. 2000. "Wanted: Skilled Workers to Fill the Upcoming Labour Shortage." *Performance and Potential 2000–2001*. Chapter 3.

2. Ramlo, Andrew, and Ryan Berlin. 2006. *A Perfect Storm: Sustaining Canada's Economy During Our Next Demographic Transformation*. Urban Futures Institute. ISBN 1-894486-54-4.

3. Liedtke, Michael. 25 January 2011. "Google to Hire 6,000 More Workers." Associated Press. www.thestar.com/Business/Companies/Google/article/927913.

4. Dana Flavelle. 23 Sept. 2011. Target Plans Up to 135 Canadian Stores by 2013. www.thestar.com/business/article/1058457—target-finalizes-its-canadian-stores-inks-deal-with-sobeys.

5. Atwater, D.M. 1995. "Workforce Forecasting." *Human Resource Planning*, Vol. 18, No. 4: 50–53.

6. Godet, M. 1983. "Reducing the Blunders in Forecasting." *Futures*, Vol. 15, No. 3 (June): 181–192.

7. Patterson, B. 2003. "Weighing Resources." *HR Magazine*, Vol. 48, No. 10: 103–108; Hogan, A. 1987. "Combining Forecasts: Some Managerial Experiences with Extrapolation." *Socio-Economic Planning Sciences*, Vol. 2, No. 3: 205–211; Mahmoud, E. 1984. "Accuracy in Forecasting: A Survey." *Journal of Forecasting*, Vol. 3, No. 2 (April): 139–159.

8. Bechet, T. 2000. "Developing Staffing Strategies That Work: Implementing Pragmatic, Nontraditional Approaches." *Public Personnel Management*, Vol. 29, No. 4: 465–478; Wagner, R., S. Hlavacka, and L. Bacharova. 2000. "Slovakia's Health System: Hospital Human Resource Planning in Slovakia." *Journal of Management in Medicine*, Vol. 14, No. 5/6: 383–407; Monks, K. 1996. "Global or Local? HRM in the Multinational Company: The Irish Experience." *International Journal of Human Resource Management*, Vol. 7, No. 3 (September): 721–735.

9. Pynes, J. 2004. "The Implementation of Workforce and Succession Planning in the Public Sector." *Public Personnel Management*, Vol. 33, No. 4: 389–404; Stone, T., and J. Fiorito. 1986. "A Perceived Uncertainty Model of Human Resource Forecasting Technique Use," *Academy of Management Review*, Vol. 11, No. 3: 635–642; Meehan, R., and B.S. Ahmed. 1990. "Forecasting Human Resources Requirements: A Demand Model." *Human Resource Planning*, Vol. 13, No. 4: 297–307.

10. Schramm, J. 2005. "Planning Ahead." *HR Magazine*, Vol. 50, No. 10: 152–153; Bechet, T. 2000. "Developing Staffing Strategies That Work: Implementing Pragmatic, Nontraditional Approaches." *Public Personnel Management*, Vol. 29, No. 4: 465–478; Walker, J.W. 1980. *Human Resource Planning*. New York: McGraw-Hill.

11. Wagner, R., S. Hlavacka, and L. Bacharova. 2000. "Slovakia's Health System: Hospital Human Resource Planning in Slovakia." *Journal of Management in Medicine*, Vol. 14, No. 5: 6, 383–407; Beck, B.M. 1991. "Forecasting Environmental Change." *Journal of Forecasting*, Vol. 10, No. 1: 3–19; Schuler, R.S. 1989. "Scanning the Environment: Planning for Human Resource Management and Organizational Change." *Human Resource Planning*, Vol. 12, No. 4.

12. Bechet, T. 2000. "Developing Staffing Strategies That Work: Implementing Pragmatic, Nontraditional Approaches." *Public Personnel Management*, Vol. 29, No. 4: 465–478; Fulmer, W. 1990. "Human Resource Management: The Right Hand of Strategy Implementation," *Human Resource Planning*, Vol. 12, No. 4: 1–11.

13. Helton, K., and J. Soubik. 2004. "Case Study: Pennsylvania's Changing Workforce: Planning Today with Tomorrow's Vision." *Public Personnel Management*, Vol. 33, No. 4: 459–474; McEnery, J., and M. Lifter. 1987. "Demands for Change: Interfacing Environmental Pressures and the Personnel Process." *Public Personnel Management*, Vol. 16, No. 1 (Spring): 61–87.

14. Fulmer, W. 1990. "Human Resource Management: The Right Hand of Strategy Implementation." *Human Resource Planning*, Vol. 12, No. 4: 1–11.

15. Schuler, R.S., and J.W. Walker. 1990. "Human Resources Strategy: Focusing on Issues and Actions." *Organizational Dynamics*, Summer: 4–19.

16. Adapted from Burack, E.J., and N.J. Mathys. 1996. *Human Resource Planning: A Pragmatic Approach to Manpower Staffing and Development*, 3rd ed. Northbrook, IL: Brace Park.

17. Grabosky, P., and D. Rosenbloom. 1975. "Racial and Ethnic Integration in the Federal Service." *Social Science Quarterly*, Vol. 56, No. 1 (June): 71–84.

18. Zaleznik, A. 1977. "Managers and Leaders: Are They Different?" *Harvard Business Review*, Vol. 55, No. 3 (May): 67–78.

19. Bucalo, J. 1974. "The Assessment Center: A More Specified Approach." *Human Resource Management*, Fall: 2–12.

20. Adapted from Schuler, R.S., and J.W. Walker. 1990. "Human Resources Strategy: Focusing on Issues and Actions." *Organizational Dynamics*, Summer: 4–19.

21. Helton, K., and J. Soubik. 2004. "Case Study: Pennsylvania's Changing Workforce: Planning Today with Tomorrow's Vision." *Public Personnel Management*, Vol. 33, No. 4: 459–474; Beck, B.M. 1991. "Forecasting Environmental Change." *Journal of Forecasting*, Vol. 10, No. 1: 3–19.

22. Beck, B.M. 1991. "Forecasting Environmental Change." *Journal of Forecasting*, Vol. 10, No. 1: 3–19; Butinsky, C.F., and O. Harari. 1983. "Models vs. Reality: An Analysis of 12 Human Resource Planning Systems." *Human Resource Planning*, Vol. 6, No. 1: 11–20.

23. Adapted from Bechet, T.P., and J.W. Walker. 1993. "Aligning Staffing with Business Strategy." *Human Resource Planning*, Vol. 16, No. 2: 1–16; Walker, J.W. 1980. *Human Resource Planning*. New York: McGraw-Hill.

24. Burack, E.J., and N.J. Mathys. 1996. *Human Resource Planning: A Pragmatic Approach to Manpower Staffing and Development*, 3rd ed. Northbrook, IL: Brace Park.

25. Fink, A., B. Marr, A. Siebe, and J. Kuhle. 2005. "The Future Scorecard: Combining External and Internal Scenarios to Create Strategic Foresight." *Management Decision*, Vol. 43, No. 3: 360–381; Millett, S., and Zelman, S. 2005. "Scenario Analysis and a Logic Model of Public Education in Ohio." *Strategy & Leadership*, Vol. 33, No. 2: 33–41; Van Der Heihden, K. 2000. "Scenarios and Forecasting: Two Perspectives." *Technological Forecasting and Social Change*, Vol. 65, No. 31: 36; Mason, D.H. 1994. "Scenario-Based Planning: Decision Model for the Learning Organization." *Planning Review*: March/April 1994: 6–11.

26. Thompson, J. 1967. *Organizations in Action*. New York: McGraw-Hill.

27. Burack, E. 1995. *Creative Human Resource Planning and Applications: A Strategic Approach*. Englewood Cliffs, NJ: Prentice Hall.

28. Greengard, S. 2001. "Make Smarter Business Decisions: Know What Employees Can Do." *Workforce*, Vol. 80, No. 11: 42–46; Martin, R. 1967. "Skills Inventories." *Personnel Journal*, January: 28–83; Kaumeyer, R.H. 1982. *Planning and Using a Total Personnel System*. New York: Van Nostrand Reinhold; Seamans, L. 1978. "What's Lacking in Most Skills Inventories." *Personnel Journal*, March: 101–106.

29. Connolly, S. 1975. "Job Posting." *Personnel Journal*, May: 295–299.

30. McLaughlin, G. 1975. "A Professional Supply and Demand Analysis." *Educational Record*, Vol. 56, No. 3 (Summer): 196–200.

Determining HR Demand

CHAPTER LEARNING OUTCOMES

After reading this chapter, you should be able to:

- Understand the importance of demand forecasting in the HR planning process.
- Recognize the linkages between the HR plan, labour demand forecasting techniques, and the subsequent supply stage.
- Compare and contrast the advantages and disadvantages of various demand forecasting techniques: index/trend analysis, expert forecasts, the Delphi technique, the nominal group technique, HR budgets (or staffing tables), envelope/scenario forecasting, and regression analysis.

PROJECTING LABOUR DEMAND IN CANADA

The Canadian economy is expected to create about 1.9 million new jobs over the next ten years.

Due to globalization and the shift to a knowledge economy, demand for labour in both the primary and manufacturing sectors has declined in the past ten years. Over the past three years, the manufacturing sector has lost nearly 250,000 workers as a result of intensified competition from emerging economies, rising costs of raw materials (including energy), and the appreciation of the Canadian dollar. The increase in demand for labour has been driven mainly by the growth in the service sector, which includes construction and all service industries. This sector accounts for 78 percent of economic activity and 84 percent of total employment in Canada.

The number of retirements in the Canadian economy is expected to rise markedly over the next decade. This means that the vast majority of job openings over the period 2006–2015 will be due to the need to replace retired workers in existing jobs. It is expected that close to 3.8 million positions will be freed up by retirements over the next ten years.

Management occupations are expected to be most affected by retirement pressures over the decade. The management occupations where retirement pressures will be the most intense include managers in health, education, social and community services, and legislators and senior management.

The highest rate of expansion demand is expected to be in occupations that require a university degree, spurred by the continued shift to a knowledge-based economy and by increased public spending in the healthcare sector (e.g., engineers and engineering technicians, computer and information systems professionals, university professors, physicians, and registered nurses).

About two-thirds of all job openings (those due to new job creation plus those due to retirements) over the next ten years will be in occupations usually requiring postsecondary education (university, college, or apprenticeship training) or in management occupations.

Source: Human Resources and Skills Development Canada (2007). Looking Ahead: 10-Year Outlook for the Canadian Labour Market (2006–2015). Policy Research Directorate, Strategic Policy and Research Branch.

METHODS OF FORECASTING

HR professionals can use several methods to generate predictions about the future or extrapolate from current events to determine their impact on HR practices. These methods can be both quantitative and qualitative. Quantitative methods include ratio analyses, trend analysis, and regression analysis. Qualitative methods include envelope/scenario planning, impact analysis, the Delphi technique, and the nominal group technique.

Successful organizations combine statistically driven quantitative forecasts with more qualitative expert processes to achieve the most comprehensive demand forecasts possible.[1] As well, organizations must consider demand for personnel not only for the current operational period but also well into the future to ensure that the right numbers of workers with the requisite skills and competencies are ready and available to work when the organization requires them.

Trend/Ratio Analysis

Trend analysis is a quantitative approach that attempts to forecast future personnel needs by extrapolating from historical changes in one or more organizational indices. A single index, such as sales, or ratio, such as sales per employee, might be used. However, more complex modelling or multiple predictive techniques, used by professional planners, rely on a combination of several factors.

Trend analysis
A forecasting method that extrapolates from historical organizational indices

  Ratio analysis involves examining the relationship between an operational index and the demand for labour (as reflected by the number of employees in the workforce) and is a relatively straightforward quantitative demand forecasting technique commonly used by many organizations.[2] For example, an organization my choose to look at the ratio of amount of sales per employee. Although sales level is probably the most common index used by organizations, other operational indices are (1) the number of units produced, (2) the number of clients serviced, and (3) the production (i.e., direct labour) hours. Similarly, although the relationship between the operational index and workforce size (number of employees) can be calculated for the entire organization, as well as for the department or operational subunit, some organizations use trend analysis to ascertain demand requirements for (1) direct labour and (2) indirect labour (e.g., HR staff). HR Planning Notebook 6.1 shows an example of trend/ratio analysis.

Ratio analysis
A quantitative method of projecting HR demand by analyzing the relationship between an operational index and the number of employees required

 HR Planning Notebook 6.1
TREND/RATIO ANALYSIS

Puslinch Pottery

Year	Sales ($ Thousands)	Number of Employees	Ratio (Sales [$ Thousands] per Employee)
2009	$2,800	155	18.06
2010	3,050	171	17.83
2011	3,195	166	19.25
2012	**3,300**	**177**	**18.64**
2013	3,500[a]	188[b]	18.64[c]
2014	3,600[a]	193[b]	18.64[c]
2015	3,850[a]	207[b]	18.64[c]

[a]Time now is the year 2012. We are forecasting labour demand for 2013, 2014, and 2015, and therefore sales figures for those years are future estimates.
[b]Employee numbers are historical, except for the figures for 2013, 2014, and 2015, which are our future HR demand forecasts.
[c]The index used to calculate future demand (number of employees) can be the most recent figure, or an average of the up-to-date period (e.g., the past four years, for which the average is 18.44). In this trend analysis, the most recent ratio (18.64) for the year 2012 was used for forecasting.

There are five steps to conducting an effective trend analysis.

1. Select the Appropriate Business/Operational Index

The HR forecaster must select a readily available business index, such as sales level, that is (1) known to have a direct influence on the organizational demand for labour and (2) subjected to future forecasting as a result of the normal business planning process.

2. Track the Business Index over Time

Once the index has been selected, it is necessary to go back in time for at least the four or five most recent years, but preferably for a decade or more, to record the quantitative or numerical levels of the index over time.

3. Track the Workforce Size over Time

Record the historical figures of the total number of employees, or, alternatively, the amount of direct and indirect labour (see above) for exactly the same period used for the business index in step 2.

4. Calculate the Average Ratio of the Business Index to the Workforce Size

Obtain a ratio by dividing the level of sales for each year of historical data by the number of employees required to produce that year's level of sales. This ratio is calculated for each year over the period of analysis so that an average ratio describing the relationship between the two variables over time can be determined.

5. Calculate the Forecasted Demand for Labour

Divide the annual forecast for the business index by the average employee requirement ratio for each future year to arrive at forecasted annual demand for labour. For example, obtain future sales forecast figures for the next five years. For each of the years, divide the level of sales by the average employee requirement ratio to obtain the forecasted numerical demand for labour for each future year.

Although trend/ratio analysis is widespread due to its ease of use, remember that the analysis incorporates only the relationship between a single business variable and demand for labour (workforce size). By design, any single-variable relationship provides a simplistic forecast for demand. For more comprehensive analyses that reflect a variety of factors affecting business operations, such as interest rates, level of unemployment, consumer disposable income, and so on, the quantitative techniques normally employed are multivariate regression or other similar modelling/programming models.[3] Although these sophisticated, multiple-predictor techniques require detailed knowledge of statistics and systems programming, we will present an example of simple regression later in the chapter.

Regression Analysis

Another quantitative demand forecasting technique to be discussed in this chapter is regression analysis.[4] Regression analysis is a very effective quantitative forecasting technique for short-, medium- and long-range time horizons and can be easily updated and changed.[5] This section presupposes that readers possess a basic knowledge of statistical techniques, as instruction in statistics is not the focus of this book. The section will enable HR practitioners to understand the essence of what regression can do for them[6] but will not explain the mathematical derivation of the regression equation from first principles. Readers who would like more information about such statistical methods should refer to any one of a number of high-quality statistical textbooks. Regression is such a powerful technique for forecasting demand, however, that we will present a brief and simple explanation of the underlying rationale and basic principles behind its use in HR planning.

Simply put, **regression analysis** presupposes that a *linear relationship* exists between one or more *independent (causal) variables*, which are predicted to affect the *dependent (target) variable*—in our instance, future HR demand for personnel (i.e., the number of personnel required). Using reasoning similar to that used in trend analysis, regression projects into the future on the basis of the past historical relationship between the independent and dependent variables. *Linearity* refers to the observed relationship between the independent and dependent variables. For example, if a per-unit increase or decrease in the level of sales and the market rate of interest result in a concurrent associated change in HR demand (the dependent variable), then the assumption of linearity might be met and regression analysis could be used for our demand forecasting. If, however, the relationship between the independent and dependent variables was random or nonlinear (e.g., curvilinear "U-shaped" relationships, which exist between individual performance and turnover, or stress and motivation), the use of normal regression procedures would not be valid, and/or specialized regression adjustment would have to be used. If there are several causal or independent variables, such as the market interest rate (i.e., the cost of capital), the unemployment rate, the organization's sales level, and so on, then the analysis is referred to as a *multivariate regression analysis*. Because of the complexity of the calculations, such multiple regressions are inevitably carried out by statistical software programs such as SPSS (Statistical Program for the Social Sciences) or the SAS Programming Language. For our purposes, we will present an example of what is referred to as *simple regression*: a prediction model based on the impact on HR demand (the dependent variable) of a single causal independent variable.

Regression analysis
Presupposes that a linear relationship exists between one or more independent (causal) variables, which are predicted to affect the dependent (target) variable—in our instance, future HR demand for personnel (i.e., the number of personnel)

Simple Regression Prediction Model

The simple regression prediction model is as follows:

$$Y = A + BX$$

Y = the *dependent variable* (HR demand, i.e., number of personnel required)
A = constant (intercept)
B = the slope of the linear relationship between X and Y
X = the *independent/causal variable* (e.g., level of sales, production output)

where:

$$B = \frac{\sum XY - N(\bar{X})(\bar{Y})}{\sum(X^2) - N(\bar{X})^2}$$

$$A = -Y - B\bar{X}$$

In other words, the predicted value for HR demand (Y) will be a function of a constant starting point (A) (i.e., the value of Y when $X = 0$) plus the interaction between the value of the causal/independent variable (X) multiplied by a slope factor (B). Let's turn to a specific example to make sense of it all.

Regression Exercise

As HR planning manager for Keele Kontainers Ltd., a dynamic, fast-growing company located in Wawanesa, Manitoba, you have an important task to fulfill. To continue the company's history of successful growth, you need to forecast the number of marketing personnel required for $8 million and $10 million of sales activity. You have the following historical information available to guide your regression analysis and HR demand forecast:

X: Sales Level ($ Millions)	Y: Number of Marketing Personnel
2.0	20
3.5	32
4.5	42
6.0	55
7.0	66

Note that the above information represents five sets of observations for both the independent (X) and the dependent (Y) variables: set 1 (2.0; 20), set 2 (3.5; 32), set 3 (4.5; 42), and so on. Record that $N =$ the number of sets of observations, in this instance, five.

There are five steps to conducting the regression analysis:

1. *Calculate XY, X², average X(X̄), and average Y(Ȳ):* We can do this by extending the two columns shown above to a four-column set. *XY* is simply the result of multiplying each observation set's *X* level by the associated *Y* level, and X^2 is determined by multiplying the *X* value by itself:

X: Sales Level ($ millions)	Y: Number of Marketing Personnel	XY	X^2
2.0	20	40	4.00
3.5	32	112	12.25
4.5	42	189	20.25
6.0	55	330	36.00
7.0	66	462	49.00
23.0	215	1,133	121.50

Average X or $\bar{X} = 23/5 = 4.6$

Average Y or $\bar{Y} = 215/5 = 43.0$

Recall that:

$$N = 5 \text{ and } Y = A + BX$$

2. *Calculate the value of B (slope of the linear relationship between X and Y):*

$$B = \frac{\Sigma XY - N(\overline{X})(\overline{Y})}{\Sigma(\overline{X}^2) - N(\overline{X})^2}$$

Plug in the values calculated in step 1; therefore:

$$B = \frac{1133 - (5)(4.6)(43)}{121.5 - (5)(4.6)^2}$$

$$B = \frac{1133 - 989}{121.5 - 105.8^2} = 9.17$$

3. *Calculate A (constant or intercept):* Recall that:

$$Y = A + BX$$

Then:

$$A = \overline{Y} - B\overline{X}$$

Plug in the values calculated in step 1; therefore:

$$A = 43 - (9.17)(4.6) = 0.82$$

4. *Determine the regression prediction equation:* We know that the general prediction model for regression is:

$$Y = A + BX$$

For our specific problem, we have calculated A and B, so we insert these values into the equation, which will be used to calculate our HR demand (Y) as follows:

$$Y = 0.82 + (9.17)(X)$$

What does this mean? For our comparison between the level of sales (the independent/causal variable represented by X) and the predicted HR demand for marketing personnel (the dependent variable represented by Y), even when level of sales is at a zero level (i.e., less than $1 million of sales), the A value (the constant/intercept) shows that we have one marketing person (0.82 of a person rounds to 1.0). Furthermore, the prediction model shows that for every one unit ($1 million) increase in the level of sales (the independent variable X), there is a predicted increase of 9.17 marketing staff (Y) associated with that change.

5. *Calculate predicted HR demand (Y) by inserting values for X:* To predict our HR demand for marketing personnel at $8 million and $10 million of sales,

as has been asked of us, we simply plug these levels into the values of X as follows:

For $8 million of sales ($X = 8$)

$$Y = A + BX = 0.82 + (9.17)(8) = 74.18$$

or 74 marketing staff are required.

For $10 million of sales ($X = 10$)

$$Y = A + BX = 0.82 + (9.17)(10) = 92.52$$

or 93 marketing staff are required.

As we can see, regression models can be extremely valuable tools for the HR planner. In our calculation of the simple regression problem above, we used five years or sets of observed historical data for our organization with respect to matching levels of sales and their relationship to levels of marketing personnel (HR demand). Most recent sales levels of $7 million of sales were associated with a marketing staff size of 66 personnel. We wish to predict into the future what our personnel requirements for $8 million and $10 million of sales will be. Our calculations of the regression equation noted that for every $1 million increase in sales, our marketing staff increased by approximately 9 (9.17) personnel, indicating the linear relationship between the two variables. Furthermore, we now know that for $8 million and $10 million of sales, we require 74 and 93 marketing staff respectively. This valuable forecasting technique enables us to plan and execute recruitment, selection, training, and development programs in a planned, proactive fashion to ensure the trained marketing staff are on hand exactly when required by the organization.

HR Planning Notebook 6.2 introduces another model for estimated HR demand.

HR Planning Notebook 6.2

ESTIMATING HR DEMAND USING COHORT ANALYSIS AND LONGITUDINAL INDIVIDUAL DATA

Among several approaches to gathering data for the purposes of forecasting HR demand, cohort analysis and individual longitudinal data are two of the most common. Cohort analysis focuses on demand estimates based upon changes at the *cohort*, or *group*, level, whereas the longitudinal approach monitors movement flows at the level of the *individual*. In a recent HR forecasting study conducted in Ireland, use of the cohort or group approach for forecasting was found to substantially underestimate actual HR demand requirements. The cohort method failed to capture many of the dynamic flows and factors that impact HR movement in many occupations. The authors strongly recommend the use of individual-level longitudinal data for ascertaining HR replacement demand.

Source: Adapted from R. Fox and B. Comerford, "Estimating Replacement Demand: Lessons from Ireland," *International Journal of Manpower*, 29/4 (2008), 348–361.

QUALITATIVE FORECASTING TECHNIQUES

Direct managerial input is the most commonly used method for determining workforce requirements.[7] Using experts to arrive at a numerical estimate of future labour demand is considered to be a qualitative process for determining future labour requirements, because it is a detailed process of stating assumptions, considering potential organizational and environmental changes, and deriving a rationale to support the numerical estimate.

A wide variety of individuals may be considered experts for their knowledge of organizational operations, competitive HR practices, international trends in the labour markets, and so on.[8] First and foremost, the organization's own line managers, who each have detailed knowledge of workload, responsibilities, and overall task responsibilities for a department, possess important insights into how future demand for labour should or might change in the manager's own areas of responsibility. Second, the organization's HR and business planning staffs certainly have critical information to provide wise guidance in forecasting future levels of labour demand. For example, the planning staff may use econometric and strategic models to predict the future level of sales of, or demand for, the organization's goods and services, as well as provide important insights into future economic indicators affecting labour demand such as interest rates, change in gross national product, level of consumer disposable income, savings, and so on. The HR staff, whether they are HR generalists or a team of HR planning specialists, are able to draw up a detailed set of assumptions with respect to industry, local, and international labour market trends that affect how the organization organizes and employs its own workforce. Third, business consultants, financial analysts, university researchers, union staff members, industry spokespersons, and others possess detailed knowledge of specific industries or types of organizational activity and are able to give rich, detailed, and largely impartial judgments on future labour demand because of their external perspective relative to the organization. Finally, but not exclusively, federal, provincial, and local governmental staff and officials are important individuals to consult, because they possess knowledge of future environmental changes in labour and business legislation that can dramatically change labour demand not only for a specific organization but also for the industry in general. For example, pending legislation to ban the use of certain materials in product manufacturing might cause a substantial drop in demand for these products and hence an associated reduction in demand for employees who are involved in their manufacture.

Governmental ministries and departments, most specifically those devoted to labour, HR, and economic development, and of course, the highly regarded Statistics Canada, can all provide expert information for our labour demand forecasting process. Irrespective of which experts we select, a number of options are available for obtaining labour demand estimates and assumptions from those concerned. Interviews, questionnaires (conducted in person or by mail or email), and telephone conference calls are some of these options, but other techniques can be employed to maximize the benefit of each expert's contributions in specific circumstances. We now turn our attention to some of these methods of facilitating high-quality labour demand forecasts.

Envelope/Scenario Forecasting

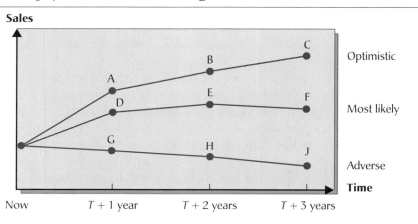

Note that A = Staffing table A; B = Staffing table B, etc.

Envelope/Scenario Planning

Envelope/scenario
forecasts

Projections, or multiple-
predictor estimates, of
future HR demand based
on a variety of differing
assumptions about how
future organizational
events will unfold

Envelope/scenario forecasts are based on the premise that because we have no certain knowledge of the future course of events, we would be well served by developing several plausible sets of outcomes. Based on certain assumptions, experts search for causality by linking cause-and-effect events together. Scenarios are developed by having brainstorming sessions with line managers and HR managers, who formulate the group's combined expert view of the workforce five years or more in the future, and then work back in time to identify key change points.[9] The group members then try to make sense of the various future states by further developing and discussing the linkages and courses of action that will lead from the present to the proposed future scenarios.[10] Figure 6.1 illustrates envelope/scenario forecasting.

This flexible demand forecasting process is much more useful for incorporating the effects of uncertainty and change into our strategic HR planning process than is consideration of the single assumption of an HR budget. Each of the scenarios or predicted future states contains its own set of assumptions, resulting in an entirely different estimate presented in *a single staffing table for each specific course of action.* In this way, an organization's HR staff are able to develop, with the associated staffing tables, future scenarios that are optimistic (e.g., sales levels will increase by 10 to 15 percent), realistic or most likely (e.g., sales levels will increase by 5 to 10 percent), or pessimistic (e.g., sales levels will remain constant or increase by less than 5 percent). Furthermore, as we consider the optimistic, realistic or most likely, and pessimistic scenarios extended into the future, the impact of the time horizon (e.g., year 1, year 2, year 3, year 4, and year 5) forms the shape of a letter envelope. The optimistic and pessimistic

HR Planning Notebook 6.3
SCENARIO-BASED HR PLANNING

Step 1: Identify three business scenarios that might be played out over the next five years (most desirable case, most likely case, and least desirable case).

Step 2: For each scenario, assess the firm's HR readiness. What are the challenges faced under each scenario (e.g., labour shortages, safety concerns, and so on)? Then identify the HR department's strengths and weaknesses in relation to these challenges.

Step 3: Over the next five years, what are the likely trends with rivals, employees, and candidates?

What are the threats posed by rivals? What are the predicted needs and motivations of key employees? What changes do we forecast in the quality and the quantity of our labour pool?

Step 4: For each scenario, identify HR initiatives and programs that have to be undertaken to deal with the threats and opportunities. For example, to meet a labour shortage of skilled mechanics, a joint program with a community college might be established.

Source: Adapted from Figure 11.1 (page 294) in Boxall, P. & Purcell, J., *Strategy and Human Resource Management*, 2nd edition (2008), (New York: Palgrave MacMillan).

scenarios, and their associated staffing tables, constitute the four corners of the envelope from the initial time period to the final time period being forecasted. Other scenarios are plotted as midpoints on the envelope. By means of this comprehensive, explicit set of staffing tables, which reflect a wide variety of future organizational circumstances, the scenario/envelope technique allows us to have ready access to flexible, preplanned demand estimates when circumstances rapidly change.

HR Planning Notebook 6.3 outlines how HR planning can be integrated with scenario planning.

Impact Analysis

Impact analysis a forecasting method in which past trends are analyzed by a panel of experts who then predict the probability of future events. Past trends are analyzed by a panel of experts who then attempt to identify future demand and study their effects on the extrapolated trend.[11] Unlike trend analysis, which is an objective statistical technique, impact analysis relies on subjective, but expert, judgments.

Impact analysis
Forecasting method in which past trends are analyzed by a panel of experts to predict future HR demand

Delphi Technique

The **Delphi technique**, named after the Greek oracle at Delphi and developed by N.C. Dalkey and his associates at the Rand Corporation in 1950, is an especially useful qualitative method for deriving detailed assumptions of long-run HR demand.[12] This forecasting technique is "a carefully designed program of sequential, individual interrogations (usually conducted through questionnaires) interspersed with feedback on the opinions expressed by the other

Delphi technique
A process in which the forecasts and judgments of a selected group of experts are solicited and summarized in an attempt to determine the future HR demand

participants in previous rounds."[13] Its key feature is that once a group of experts is selected, the experts do not meet face to face.[14] Instead, a project coordinator canvasses them individually for their input and forecasts by means of a progressively more focused series of questionnaires.

The advantage of the Delphi technique is that it avoids many of the problems associated with face-to-face groups, namely reluctance on the part of individual experts to participate due to (1) shyness, (2) perceived lower status or authority, (3) perceived communication deficiencies, (4) issues of individual dominance and groupthink (i.e., group conformity pressures), and so on.[15] Because the Delphi technique does not employ face-to-face meetings, it can serve as a great equalizer and can elicit valid feedback from all expert members. It is also advantageous that the Delphi technique can effectively use experts who are drawn from widely dispersed geographical areas.[16] See HR Planning Today 6.1 for more details on the Delphi technique.

HR Planning Today 6.1

The Delphi Technique in Action

The Delphi technique is used in a wide variety of applications for HR forecasting. For example, an agricultural research organization started by deriving nine organizational core competencies from interviews and internal organizational documentation. The experts were identified by the organization, which asked them to respond to set of questionnaires based on the Delphi technique. The questionnaires investigated:

1. The importance of human competencies in the future

2. The capacity of the organization's current human resources

3. Ranking the nine organizational core competencies in order of priority

HR policy interventions were developed from the resulting information.

A three-round Delphi procedure was used to identify the basic competencies of research chefs, who develop new products, create new recipes, and conduct food testing. Thirty-three expert chefs were involved in the Delphi undertaking, and they were asked questions concerning:

1. Factors differentiating successful from less successful research chefs

2. Knowledge and skills required by successful research chefs

3. How tasks for a research chef differ from those of an ordinary chef

The experts identified 19 basic competencies that a successful research chef should possess.

Finally, subsequent to the September 11, 2001 terrorist attacks on the United States, the Delphi technique was used by the government and insurance and risk managers to estimate the possibility of future losses due to terrorism, and the likely types of terrorist acts various organizations might experience. Experts used the Delphi technique to analyze databases on landmarks, tourist attractions, "vital points," and property assessment data to come up with their forecasts.

Sources: Adapted from T. Guimaraes et al., "Forecasting Core Competencies in an R&D Environment," *R&D Management*, Vol. 31, No. 3 (July 2001), 249–255; K. Birdir and T. Pearson, "Research Chefs' Competencies: A Delphi Approach," *International Journal of Contemporary Hospitality Management*, Vol. 12, No. 3 (2000), 205–209; and B. Coffin, "Forecasting Terrorism Losses," *Risk Management*, Vol. 49, No. 11 (November 2000), 8–9.

There are disadvantages associated with the Delphi technique, as indeed there are with all forecasting techniques. In particular, because of the series of questionnaires administered to derive a forecast, the time and costs incurred when using the Delphi technique can be higher than those incurred when using alternative forecasting methods. Another deficiency is that since the results cannot be validated statistically, the process is greatly dependent on the individual knowledge and commitment of each of the contributing experts.[17] Furthermore, if the experts are drawn from one specific field, their common professional training might guide them along a single line of inquiry rather than pursuing more innovative and creative courses of action. Finally, if insufficient attention has been paid to developing criteria for the identification and selection of experts, the personnel selected to derive the demand forecasts may lack sufficient expertise or information to contribute meaningfully to the process.[18] There are six steps associated with using the Delphi technique for HR demand forecasting.

1. Define and Refine the Issue or Question

During this stage, a project coordinator is assigned, and he or she works with the HR staff to determine the specific personnel category or activity that will be the focus of the Delphi technique. It is essential that the group targeted for HR forecasting be well defined so that relevant, focused, and detailed feedback based on a minimum of assumptions (redundant assumptions are associated with loss of the experts' time) can be derived.

2. Identify the Experts, Terms, and Time Horizon

The project coordinator, normally in conjunction with the HR staff, identifies and selects a team of individuals deemed to be experts with respect to the specific personnel grouping that requires a forecast. Next, given that in many cases the group of experts will include individuals who are not members of the organization, it is important for both parties to reach agreement on the terms and conditions for participation in the forecasting process, as well as setting the context and explicitly defining the nature of the work. For example, the team of experts must be absolutely clear on which jobs constitute "production workers" if those experts are being asked to derive a demand forecast for this category. Similarly, the exact time horizon(s) must be specified for the personnel category being analyzed.

3. Orient the Experts

In addition to identifying the relevant time horizon(s) and clarifying which personnel groups are of interest, the orientation process for experts includes an overview of the demand forecasting decision process (which is very similar to the structural framework in which you are now engaged!). The experts are told either that there will be a predetermined number of questionnaire iterations or that the sequence will continue until a majority opinion exists among the experts.

4. Issue the First-Round Questionnaire

The project coordinator sends each expert the questionnaire by courier, fax, mail, or email and includes a time frame for completing and returning it. Typically, this first questionnaire focuses on defining both the explicit assumptions made by each of the experts and the background rationale supporting his or her particular demand estimate.

5. Issue the First-Round Questionnaire Summary and the Second Round of Questionnaires

Following the completion of the first questionnaire, the project coordinator sends the second and subsequent rounds of questionnaires to the experts with a written summary of the findings from the previous round. The aim of the subsequent questionnaires is to focus the experts' initial assumptions and estimates by providing summarized feedback from all members of the group. Points of commonality and conflict are identified in the summary, as is the need to clarify specific assumptions identified by the responses to the previous round.

6. Continue Issuing Questionnaires

The project coordinator continues to issue questionnaires until either all the predetermined questionnaire stages have been completed and summarized or the group reaches a clear majority decision. In either case, the majority or *n*th-round summary summarizes the experts' future demand estimate for the HR category under analysis.

Nominal Group Technique

Nominal group technique (NGT)

Long-run forecasting technique utilizing expert assessments

Although the **nominal group technique (NGT)** is also a long-run, qualitative demand forecasting method, it differs from the Delphi technique in several important respects. First, unlike in the Delphi technique, the group does, in fact, meet face to face and interact, but only after individual written, preparatory work has been done and all the demand estimates (idea generation) have been publicly tabled, or written on a flip chart, without discussion.[19] Second, each demand estimate is considered to be the property of the entire group and to be impersonal in nature, which minimizes the potential for dominance, personal attacks, and defensive behaviour in support of estimates presented in the group forum.[20] Finally, the expert forecast is determined by a secret vote of all group members on their choice of the tabled demand forecasts. The estimate receiving the highest ranking or rating during the voting process is deemed to be the group's forecast.[21] See HR Planning Today 6.2 for more information on the NGT.

There are seven steps associated with implementing the NGT.

1. Define and Refine the Issue or Question and the Relevant Time Horizon

This step is similar to the first step of the Delphi technique. The HR forecasting staff or coordinator is responsible for identifying the specific personnel category or activity that will be the focus for the NGT. The more refined the problem definition, the more likely it is that relevant, focused, detailed feedback will be derived with a minimum of redundant assumptions. Second, it is essential that the time horizon(s) of interest for the demand estimate be clearly specified. Overall, the issue is often phrased as a question: "What will ABC Corporation's demand for

HR Planning Today (6.2

Assessing the Utility of the Nominal Group Technique

Studies have shown that nominal group technique (NGT) is especially effective for brainstorming sessions to ensure all participants have an equal voice in the sessions, and when a problem or issue stems from several widely diverse causes. Furthermore, studies have shown that NGT provides highly reliable and valid qualitative data that is ranked by importance, and is superior to that derived from focus group sessions. Nominal group sessions investigating teaching performance competencies on 13 dimensions (technical knowledge, planning and organizing, managing interaction, commitment to teaching objectives, proactive orientation, student development orientation, class presentation ability, impact on the class, adaptability and flexibility, personal motivation, listening skills, oral communication skills, and presentation skills) were dramatically superior to information obtained from focus groups. The study predicted that nominal group technique will replace focus groups as the qualitative research method of choice and will reduce the need for the administration of surveys.

Sources: Adapted from B. Andersen and T. Fagerhaug, "The Nominal Group Technique," *Quality Progress*, Vol. 22, No. 2 (February 2000), 144–145; and B. Langford et al., "Nominal Grouping Sessions vs. Focus Groups," *Qualitative Market Research*, Vol. 5, No. 1 (2002), 58–70.

production workers be in the year 2017 (or five years from the present)? Please provide your demand estimate and the explicit assumptions and rationale supporting your forecast."

2. Select the Experts

In the second step, the coordinator or HR forecasting staff selects the individuals who have expert knowledge of the specific personnel group being analyzed. Experts are then contacted to confirm their participation in the process and to schedule the time for the face-to-face meeting.

3. Issue the HR Demand Statement to the Experts

Next, the coordinator sends each of the experts a concise statement of the HR demand he or she is being asked to address. As discussed in the first step, the issue is normally framed as a question that the experts are being asked to answer, and an accompanying sheet of terms, definitions, and assumptions may accompany the question or issue statement.

4. Apply Expert Knowledge, State Assumptions, and Prepare an Estimate

Having received the issue or question posed by the coordinator on behalf of the organization, each expert now considers his or her specific knowledge of the particular personnel group that is the subject of the demand estimate. In particular, experts will undoubtedly have personal insights or insider information not available to other members of the group and should explicitly state the various assumptions that arise from this information, as well as their numerical estimate of demand. In this way, once the nominal group meets face to face, the supporting rationale for what may be widely divergent demand estimates quickly becomes apparent to the group as a whole.

5. Meet Face to Face

Having prepared their individual assumptions and a numerical estimate of demand, the experts then meet face to face. The first item of business will be a brief presentation of each expert's demand estimate with the associated supporting assumptions. Individual interaction and discussion are strictly forbidden so as not to stifle creativity. The coordinator will arrange for individual introductions and ice-breakers to facilitate group interaction only after all estimates have been tabled either prior to or at the beginning of the meeting. He or she will also specify the process for the nominal group's subsequent actions.

6. Discuss the Demand Estimates and Assumptions

After each expert has presented his or her demand estimate, the process shifts to detailed analyses and group discussion of the estimates and their assumptions. To minimize individual defensiveness and personal ownership of estimates, group members are asked to focus on ascertaining supportive information for estimate assumptions and to avoid attacks on the soundness of any specific estimate. The question, answer, and discussion session continues until all pertinent information affecting the HR demand estimates has been presented to the satisfaction of the experts in attendance, or at least to the point where all positions and assumptions are clear to group members.

7. Vote Secretly to Determine the Expert Demand Assessment

A secret vote is taken, and the estimate drawing the highest ranking or number of votes from the experts is selected to be the group's HR demand estimate solution to the question posed in the first step.

Readers are invited to experience a nominal group technique as part of a group exercise at the end of this chapter.

HR BUDGETS: STAFFING TABLE

HR budgets are quantitative, operational, or short-run, demand estimates that contain the number and types of personnel (i.e., personnel classes, such as bank clerks, loans officers, and branch managers) required by the organization as a whole and for each subunit, division, or department (see Table 6.1 for a hypothetical example for the firm "Ennotville Eateries").[22] These HR budgets, prepared by the HR staff in conjunction with line managers, take into consideration information from historical company staffing trends, competitor staffing practices, industry and professional associations, and Statistics Canada.

The HR budget process produces a **staffing table**, which contains information related to a specific set of operational assumptions or levels of activity (e.g., maintain the current organization structure, increase the sales level by 5 percent over last year's level). The staffing table presents the total HR demand requirement, as well as the number of personnel required, by level (e.g., vice-presidents) and function (e.g., marketing personnel).

HR budgets

Quantitative, operational, or short-run demand estimates that contain the number and types of personnel (i.e., personnel classes, such as bank clerks, loans officers, and branch managers) required by the organization as a whole and for each subunit, division, or department

Staffing table

Total HR demand requirement for operational or short-run time periods

TABLE 6.1

Staffing Table and HR Budget, Ennotville Eateries

Staff Demand Requirements	Sales ($ millions)			
	$1–10	>$10–25	>$25–50	>$50–75
Administrative Positions				
President	1	1	1	1
Vice-presidents	1	1	2	3
Marketing managers	1	1	2	2
Sales staff	4	7	10	18
HR staff	2	4	5	7
Treasurer	1	1	1	2
Financial staff	3	5	7	9
Clerical and general staff	5	8	12	14
Production Positions				
Executive chef	1	1	1	1
Chef	2	4	5	6
Cook	8	15	25	35
Haggis helper	10	20	30	40
Saucier	1	3	5	6

In this way, HR planners can determine short-run future demand requirements for subunits and the organization as a whole. This enables budgeting processes to incorporate changes in compensation costs linked to the level of future personnel demand.

HR Planning Today 6.3 provides information on e-recruiting and how it can be used to help meet HR demand.

HR Planning Today 6.3

Meeting HR Demand Requirements Through E-Recruiting

Utilizing information systems technology to meet HR demand requirements is not only cost- and time-efficient compared to placing ads in journals or hiring recruiting firms but also allows applicants to submit résumés from the comfort of their own homes. Organizations such as Hewlett-Packard, Dell Computer, and Cisco Systems conduct e-recruiting by placing job postings online (company or third-party Internet career websites), and use tracking systems that sort résumés and candidates by conducting content-based analyses of the applicants' résumés. However, e-recruiting should not be regarded as a stand-alone tool; it should be incorporated into an integrated HR system that also uses behavioural and skills assessments, job analysis,

HR Planning Today 6.3 *(continued)*

performance management, and training tools to enhance individual and team productivity and satisfaction. These integrated systems increase the demand for effective decision-making and communication skills, and highlight the fact that fast and efficient data collection is insufficient without fast and efficient decisions resulting from the process.

With online recruiting sites often being the first point of contact between the potential applicant and the organization, it is critical that the technological processes associated with e-recruiting do not frustrate and deter applicants, especially the "best and brightest" who are well versed in leading-edge technology. Cumbersome application forms with poor instructions, accompanied by lengthy and marginally relevant online test and assessment instruments, can discourage applicants, as can the fact that having completed the online process, many people do not even receive a thank-you message acknowledging the receipt of their application. This can leave applicants feeling that the company is cold, impersonal, untrustworthy, and perhaps even manipulative in its relations with employees, perceptions that can prove extremely detrimental to any firm.

Sources: Adapted from E. Goodridge, "Online Recruiters Feel the Pinch," *Information Week*, No. 837 (May 14, 2001), 83–84; B. Cullen, "E-Recruiting Is Driving HR Systems Integration," *Strategic Finance*, Vol. 83, No. 1 (July 2001), 22–26; and I. Kotlyar and L. Karakowsky, "If Recruitment Means Building Trust, Where Does Technology Fit In?" *Canadian HR Reporter* (October 7, 2002), 21.

HR Planning Today (6.4

Cutting-Edge Canadian HRM: ARXX: HR Processes of a Global Leader in Green Building Solutions

Hank and Henry Mesen, founders of Canada's ARXX Corporation, developed a revolutionary new "building block" approach to the construction of houses and buildings that uses a combination of recycled Styrofoam and concrete. The insulated blocks utilize approximately 2,400 pounds (about 1,089 kilograms) of Styrofoam taken out of landfills (based on an average house), the foam shape being connected by wire or plastic web inserts reinforced with steel bars. The foam blocks fit together like LEGO. Cement is then poured between the foam blocks to complete the lightweight, environmentally friendly structure. The web design enables screws, drywall, and siding to be applied directly to the wall without strapping.

Among the many benefits of this revolutionary approach to building include lightweight materials (each form weighs about 10 pounds), and the fact that it uses no trees and creates no waste in the building process. The homes are fire-retardant; are warmer in winter and cooler in the summer, which saves on energy costs; and have been tested to withstand a bomb blast and gunshots. Furthermore, these innovative foam building blocks are ideal for building in remote locations without trees, in cold or hot weather, and in areas lacking in skilled construction labour.

Not surprisingly, due to the success resulting from extremely high demand for these products, ARXX Corporation is aggressively expanding, and has acquired four other construction companies in the past year alone. Christine Thrussell, corporate HR manager, based in Cobourg and Markham, Ontario, is extremely busy developing HR policies and processes to support widely dispersed operations in Canada, the United States, Mexico, Australia, and the Middle East. ARXX currently has 85 full-time employees, and "Rapid Acquisition Teams" made up of Canadian and U.S. project managers who are sent to hire local workers and oversee local construction projects all over the world. In view of the wide geographic dispersal of its building operations, ARXX trains its project managers in interviewing skills, enabling them to conduct extended behaviourally based, structured interviews

HR Planning Today 6.4 *(continued)*

in the field by utilizing these skills, in combination with written job descriptions, to ascertain whether job candidates possess two key elements: (1) the requisite knowledge, skills, and abilities to perform the job (job descriptions focus); and (2) whether they fit into the ARXX corporate culture of green sustainable practices of "people and the environment" and the key corporate values of "creativity, integrity, honesty, and quality." HR forecasting and personnel demand estimates are derived from business activity information relayed at weekly department head/director meetings (e.g., finance, HR, IT, accounting, sales, technical services), often conducted via videoconference.

Although leadership training programs have not yet been formalized, ARXX requires that all personnel in leadership appointments name a designated successor for their position. The company supports develop-

mental education and training programs, professional conferences, and the establishment of mentoring relationships in the workplace. Due to rapidly expanding demand for these innovative building products, combined with a compensation practice of paying between 5 and 15 percent above prevailing market rates, and a corporate culture that reinforces the primacy of people and the environment, the key HR issue is not retention of personnel, but ensuring the ongoing supply of trained personnel to meet future project requirements. By delegating responsibility for interviewing and meeting local HR demand to the local project manager level, while retaining overall HR evaluation at the corporate level, ARXX has developed fast-paced and organic human resource processes that are well suited to the dynamic nature of the market for its innovative, environmentally friendly building products.

Source: Kenneth McBey. Interview of Christine Thrussell, Corporate HR Manager, ARXX Corporation.

SUMMARY

In this chapter, we examined various techniques that organizations use to forecast future requirements for HR demand. We noted that index/trend analysis examines the historical relationship between workforce size and a measure of operational efficiency, such as sales, to determine the ratio between the two measures for forecasting purposes. Expert forecasts revealed that there are a number of individuals, not necessarily just those who are HR staff, who have valid information on organizational policies, procedures, and planned future changes. This information can have a dramatic impact on deriving accurate forecasts of numbers and types of employees required for the organization's workforce of the future.

With respect to experts, we saw that the Delphi technique and the nominal group technique can be used effectively to obtain demand estimates from individuals while minimizing the time wastage and interpersonal dominance that often occurs in group settings. The HR budget process produces staffing tables that are concerned with short-run operational time horizons in planning HR demand. Specifically, the staffing table presents a prediction of the number of personnel required, listed by authority or functional level, given a specific set of assumptions regarding the future organizational activity. Plotting a wide variety of possible future scenarios produces what is referred to as envelope forecasting of HR demand, in which each corner of the envelope has its own specific staffing table.

Finally, we demonstrated the tremendous usefulness of the regression analysis technique in determining future workforce requirements. Our example of simple regression revealed how this statistical technique can enable us to be proactive with respect to determining future HR requirements and planning and programming to fulfill those requirements.

We have examined specific techniques associated with the first element of HR forecasting—that is, the calculation of demand or requirement for personnel. In Chapter 7, we look at specific methods used to ascertain personnel supply. The sources of labour supply derive from either the current organization (internal workforce) or the external environment.

Key Terms

Delphi technique p. 149
envelope/scenario forecasts p. 148
HR budgets p. 154
impact analysis p. 149
nominal group technique (NGT) p. 152

ratio analysis p. 141
regression analysis p. 143
staffing table p. 154
trend analysis p. 141

Web Links

For a background briefing on the current and future labour market shortage in Canada, go to:
www.hrsdc.gc.ca/eng/publications_resources/research/categories/labour_market_e/sp_615_10_06/shortages.shtml

For information about what government is going with respect to education to better equip the workforce in Ontario, go to:
www.tcu.gov.on.ca/eng/about/newsletter/nl0611.html

For Statistics Canada standard industry classification, go to:
www.statcan.gc.ca/concepts/industry-industrie-eng.htm

HRM Guide to labour participation and demand (for the United Kingdom) can be found at:
www.hrmguide.co.uk/hrm/chap3/ch3-links4.htm

The government of Canada's HR resources for business are listed at:
www.hrmanagement.gc.ca

Information on the government of Saskatchewan's human resource planning is at:
www.psc.gov.sk.ca/workforceplanning

Required Professional Capabilities (RPCs)

The following RPCs are relevant to material covered in this chapter. The RPC number represents the CCHRA number assigned to the RPC as presented on the CCHRA website. All of the RPCs can be found in the Body of Knowledge at www.chrp.ca/rpc/body-of-knowledge.

RPC 34 Develops and administers a departmental or project budget

RPC 65 Forecasts HR supply and demand conditions

RPC 72 Identifies the organization's staffing needs

Discussion Questions

1. The Delphi technique and the nominal group technique are often used to facilitate creative and innovative solutions to HR demand issues. What are the similarities and differences between the two methods? List the conditions associated with successful employment of each of these two demand forecasting techniques.
2. Ratio or trend analysis can be a very effective method for determining HR demand. Identify a wide variety of relevant indices that can be used for this demand forecasting technique in different organizational contexts, including public not-for-profit organizations, as well as in diverse industrial settings in the private sector.
3. One of the sources to ensure Canada can keep up with labour demand is through immigration. The Citizenship and Immigration Canada (CIC) periodically publishes a list of occupations that are qualified under the skilled immigrant category. To be considered a skilled worker under the federal skilled worker category, one has to have one year of continuous full-time or equivalent part-time paid work experience in at least one of the following eligible occupations within the last ten years:

- 0631 Restaurant and Food Service Managers
- 0811 Primary Production Managers (Except Agriculture)
- 1122 Professional Occupations in Business Services to Management
- 1233 Insurance Adjusters and Claims Examiners
- 2121 Biologists and Related Scientists
- 2151 Architects
- 3111 Specialist Physicians
- 3112 General Practitioners and Family Physicians
- 3113 Dentists
- 3131 Pharmacists
- 3142 Physiotherapists
- 3152 Registered Nurses
- 3215 Medical Radiation Technologists
- 3222 Dental Hygienists & Dental Therapists
- 3233 Licensed Practical Nurses

- 4151 Psychologists
- 4152 Social Workers
- 6241 Chefs
- 6242 Cooks
- 7215 Contractors and Supervisors, Carpentry Trades
- 7216 Contractors and Supervisors, Mechanic Trades
- 7241 Electricians (Except Industrial & Power System)
- 7242 Industrial Electricians
- 7251 Plumbers
- 7265 Welders & Related Machine Operators
- 7312 Heavy-Duty Equipment Mechanics
- 7371 Crane Operators
- 7372 Drillers & Blasters—Surface Mining, Quarrying & Construction
- 8222 Supervisors, Oil and Gas Drilling and Service

Do any of these occupations surprise you? Do you think there are ways we can train and retrain Canadians who are already living in this country to work in some of these occupations?

Exercises: The Nominal Group Technique

1. Using the Nominal Group Technique.
   A. Form a group of four to six people. If you are working with a group of students, you will be discussing the future of the student role, or "job." If you are working with a group of people in the same occupation or job, your group will be discussing the future of that occupation or job. Appoint a group leader.
   B. Ask everyone to individually list the trends that may change, at some likely future time, the work methods or work outcomes for the "job" under consideration. Try a time span of three, five, or ten years. (Allow 15 minutes for this step.)
   C. Have each person then state the first item on his or her list and record this item on a flip chart or greenboard so that others can see it.
   D. Have each person, in turn, continue to state items until all are listed. If an item is mentioned more than once, the group leader should ask for the number of people who listed this item. Record that number beside the item to give a rating of frequency.
   E. Ask each person to discuss the relevance of his or her items to the job.
   F. When all items are listed, ask each person to assign a rating from 1 to 10 to each item on the flip chart, 1 being the most important influence on the job and 10 being the least important. This is a rating of importance.

G. Analyze the results.

H. Use these results to prepare a group report on the future of the job.

I. Present this report to the class.

(Note that many of these steps can be done with group software, such as Lotus Notes.)

After the presentations, discuss the potential challenges of predicting the future in this manner. Should other methods be used to supplement this method? What are some of your suggestions?

2. As HR forecasting manager for the Downsview University Dating Service, you have been faced with a tremendous increase in customer demand over the company's five years of operations. As a result, you are using regression analysis to ascertain future requirements for staff to handle customer inquiries. In particular, you need to forecast the number of customer service representatives required for 5,000 and 7,000 dating contracts. The following information will help guide your regression analysis:

X: Dating Contracts (Thousands)	Y: Customer Service Representatives	XY	X^2
1.5	9		
2.0	14		
3.0	21		
3.8	25		
4.2	27		

Case TALENT POACHING: HOW TO LURE A STAR EMPLOYEE TO WORK FOR YOU

Hiring an employee from a rival firm can mean bringing on someone who already knows your industry and business, and can bring valuable new knowledge and even clients to you. Small wonder that recruiters are often asked to bring home that particular prize.

Still, enticing as it is, hiring from the competition requires caution and a certain degree of finesse, especially for a small business owner. The process is loaded with pitfalls: you don't want to get a reputation as a poacher, start a tit-for-tat talent war with a competitor, or, worst of all, get sued for breaching a non-compete agreement.

So, before wading into such treacherous waters, here are a few things to consider.

Take the Subtle Approach

If you can afford it, hiring a search firm to find candidates can help keep you at an arm's length from the potentially distasteful business of poaching. A good search firm uses a polished, subtle approach. They'll talk with potential candidates about "an opportunity" in vague terms, until they can gauge interest.

Look Before You Leap

Perhaps the most important thing to think through is whether the candidate you're eyeing is really worth the trouble. You don't want to get stuck with someone else's headache, says Martin Kartin, principal of boutique search firm Martin Kartin and Company in New York. "You want to make sure you're recruiting talent, as opposed to recruiting a résumé," he says. "The biggest mistake small companies make is to look at the résumé in terms of what the person says he has done, and what company the person has been with, and they automatically say 'Oh, that's great.' Even if they have the right job with the company, it doesn't mean that they are a qualified candidate," he warns.

Watch for Legal Troubles

If it turns out that the candidate you've been eyeing at a competitor is as good as you hoped, and you want to begin talking with him or her more seriously about joining your firm, a critical step is to find out whether he or she has a non-compete agreement with their current employer.

Sell Your Story

And don't forget that you need to sell such prospects on what you and your company have to offer. After all, why should they leave their job and join you? You need to make your opportunity sound more attractive than what they've already got. And remember, it's not just about money. Most people are motivated by things they weren't offered at their previous job: the leadership, recognition, opportunity, and more innovation and excitement.

Questions

1. Do you think poaching is ethical? Would you do it?
2. What can you do to ensure you are recruiting talent, not recruiting a résumé?
3. What can you do to prevent other companies from poaching your star employees?

Source: Adapted from Hillary Johnson, "How to Poach an Employee from a Competitor," Inc.com, Jan 31, 2011 found at http://www.inc.com/guides/201101/how-to-poach-an-employee-from-a competitor.html

ENDNOTES

1. Schuler, R.S., and J.W. Walker. 1990. "Human Resources Strategy: Focusing on Issues and Actions," *Organizational Dynamics*, Summer: 5–19.
2. Elbo, R. November 15, 2000. "In the Workplace: Competing with Poaching Employers." *BusinessWorld*, 1–3; Cascio, W.F. 1991. *Applied Psychology in Personnel Management*, 4th ed. Englewood Cliffs, NJ: Prentice Hall; Ward, D. 1996. "Workforce Demand Forecasting Techniques." *Human Resource Planning*, Vol. 19, No. 1: 54–55.

3. Al-Harbi, K. 2000. "Optimization of Staff Numbers in the Process Industries: An Application of DEA." *International Journal of Manpower*, Vol. 21, No. 1: 47–55; Meehan, R., and B.S. Ahmed. 1990. "Forecasting Human Resources Requirements: A Demand Model." *Human Resource Planning*, Vol. 13, No. 4: 297–307.

4. Drui, A.B. 1963. "The Use of Regression Equations to Predict Manpower Requirements." *Management Science*, Vol. 9, No. 4 (July): 669–677.

5. McDermott, R. 2001. "Using Simple Multiple Regression to Establish Labour Rates." *Healthcare Financial Management*, Vol. 55, No. 9: 50–57; Georgoff, D.M., and R.G. Murdick. 1986. "Manager's Guide to Forecasting." *Harvard Business Review*, Vol. 64, No. 1; Meehan and Ahmed, 1990.

6. McDermott, 2001; Tullar, W. 1991. "Theory Development in Human Resource Management." *Human Resource Management Review*, Vol. 1, No. 4 (Winter): 317–323.

7. Ward, 1996.

8. Anonymous. 2005. "Tool Forecasts Labour Needs." *On-Site*, Vol. 49, No. 6: 10–11; Gatewood, R.D., and E.J. Gatewood. 1983. "The Use of Expert Data in Human Resource Planning: Guidelines from Strategic Forecasting." *Human Resource Planning*, Vol. 6, No. 2 (June): 83–94.

9. Van der Heijden, K. 2000. "Scenarios and Forecasting: Two Perspectives," *Technological Forecasting and Social Change*, Vol. 65: 31–36; Mason, D.H. 1994. "Scenario-Based Planning: Decision Model for the Learning Organization." *Planning Review*, Vol. 22, No. 2 (1994): 6–11. Bechet, T.P., and J. W. Walker. 1993. "Aligning Staffing with Business Strategy." *Human Resource Planning*, Vol. 16, No. 2: 1–16. Burack, E.H., and N.J. Mathys. 1996. *Human Resource Planning: A Pragmatic Approach to Manpower Staffing and Development*, 3rd ed. Northbrook, IL: Brace Park.

10. Van der Heijden, 2000; Ward, 1996.

11. Burack, E.H., and N.J. Mathys. 1987. *Human Resource Planning: A Pragmatic Approach to Manpower Staffing and Development*, 2nd ed. Lake Forest, IL: Brace-Park Press.

12. Passmore, D., E. Cebeci, and R. Baker. 2005. "Market-Based Information for Decision Support in Human Resource Development." *Human Resource Development Review*, Vol. 4, No. 1: 33–49; Luthans, F. 1992. *Organizational Behavior*, 6th ed. New York: McGraw-Hill.

13. Helmer, O., cited in Bramwell, L., and E. Hykawy. 1999. "The Delphi Technique: A Possible Tool for Predicting Future Events in Nursing Education." *Canadian Journal of Nursing Research*, Vol. 30, No. 4: 47–58.

14. Passmore et al., 2005; Fusfeld, A.R., and R.N. Foster. June 1971. "The Delphi Technique: Survey and Comment." *Business Horizons*, Vol. 14, No. 3 (June 1971): 63–74.

15. Loo, R., and K. Thorpe. 2003. "A Delphi Study Forecasting Management Training and Development for First-Line Nurse Managers." *The Journal of Management Development*, Vol. 22, No. 9: 10, 824–825; Hampton, D.R., C.E. Summer, and R.A. Webber. 1987. *Organizational Behavior and the Practice of Management*, 5th ed. Glenview, IL: Scott Foresman; Milkovich, G., A. Annoni, and T. Mahoney. 1972. "The Use of Delphi Procedures in Manpower Forecasting." *Management Science*, Vol. 19, No. 4 (December): 381–388; Milkovich, G.T., and T.A. Mahoney. 1978. "Human Resource Planning Models: A Perspective." *Human Resource Planning*, Vol. 1, No. 1 (1978): 19–30.

16. Bramwell, L., and E. Hykawy. 1999. "The Delphi Technique: A Possible Tool for Predicting Future Events in Nursing Education." *Canadian Journal of Nursing Research*, Vol. 30, No. 4: 47–58.

17. Loo, R., and K. Thorpe. 2004. "Making Female First-Line Nurse Managers More Effective: A Delphi Study of Occupational Stress." *Women in Management Review*, Bradford, Vol. 19, No. 1/2; and Chan, C., and K. McBey, et al. 2004. "Nursing Crisis: Retention Strategies for Hospital Administrators." *Research and Practice in Human Resource Management*, Vol. 12, No. 2: 31–56; Meehan and Ahmed, 1990.

18. Bramwell and Hykawym, 1999.

19. Fraser, C., and A. Fraser. 2000. "Measuring the Performance of Retail Managers in Australia and Singapore." *International Journal of Retail & Distribution Management*, Vol. 28, No. 6: 228–243; Van de Ven, A.H. 1974. *Group Decision-Making Effectiveness.* Kent, OH: Kent State University Center for Business and Economic Research Press.

20. Rohrbaugh, J. 1981. "Improving the Quality of Group Judgement: Social Judgement Analysis and the Nominal Group Technique." *Organizational Behavior and Human Performance*, October: 272–288.

21. Fraser, C. 2000. "The Influence of Personal Characteristics on Effectiveness of Construction Site Managers." *Construction Management & Economics*, Vol. 18, No. 1: 29–36; Delbecq, A.L., A.H. Van de Ven, and D.H. Gustafson. 1975. *Group Techniques for Program Planning.* Glenview, IL: Scott Foresman; Green, T.B. 1975. "An Empirical Analysis of Nominal and Interacting Groups." *Academy of Management Journal*, March: 63–73.

22. McBeath, G. 1992. *The Handbook of Human Resource Planning: Practical Manpower Analysis Techniques for HR Professionals.* Oxford: Blackwell.

CHAPTER

7

Ascertaining HR Supply

CHAPTER LEARNING OUTCOMES

After reading this chapter, you should be able to:

- Understand the relationship between demand and supply forecasting techniques in the HR planning process.

- Recognize the importance of the human resources management system (HRMS) in implementing effective supply forecasting procedures.

- Comprehend the critical relationship between supply forecasting and succession planning.

- Discuss and evaluate the advantages and disadvantages of the following specific methods of determining external and internal supply of an organization's personnel:

  a. Skills and management inventories

  b. Succession/replacement analysis

  c. Markov models

  d. Linear programming

  e. Movement analysis

  f. Vacancy/renewal models

TRENDS IN THE CANADIAN LABOUR FORCE

The composition of the Canadian labour force has changed quite significantly in the past few decades and will continue to become more diverse in the next few decades. Women's participation in the labour force has increased. And whereas in 1981 there were about six working-age Canadians for every person aged 65 and over, that number has decreased to less than five in 2010, and is projected to be less than three by 2031.

The Aboriginal population is projected to grow much faster than the non-Aboriginal population. And since the Aboriginal population is much younger than the average Canadian, with a median age in 2006 of only 26.5 years, compared to 39.5 years for all Canadians, they can be a source of labour supply. The change in the source countries of immigrants arriving from non-European countries since the 1980s has also contributed to the increasing diversity of the Canadian labour force. In 1981, only about 14 percent of all immigrants were from Asia, but that has increased to 41 percent in 2006 and is projected to account for 55 percent of all immigrants to Canada by 2031. The proportion of immigrants from Africa has also been increasing and is also projected to rise in the next two decades.

Visible minorities, who accounted for only 5 percent of the Canadian labour force in 1981, are projected to reach 33 percent of the labour force by 2031. In certain provinces, such as Ontario and British Columbia, this number may reach 40 percent.

According to the latest projections by Statistics Canada, by 2031, the Chinese and South Asians will remain the largest groups, the Black and Filipino groups will double in size, and the Arab and West Asian populations will grow the fastest, most likely tripling in size.

Canada's increasingly diverse workforce will play an integral role in filling the impending talent shortage as discussed in the opening vignette in Chapter 5. In order to ensure Canada's prosperity and competitiveness on the global stage, Canadian organizations in both the private and public sectors will need to attract and fully utilize the human capital of all Canadians, irrespective of their age, gender, race/ethnicity, and immigration status.

Rob Norris, the provincial Minister for Advanced Education, Employment and Labour, agrees that there is already a "talent challenge" in Saskatchewan—a struggle to find talent to sustain and enhance Saskatchewan's growth. Norris suggested that attracting additional Saskatchewan Métis and First Nations people and immigrants into the workforce would also help to decrease the number of job vacancies in the province. The Province has done extensive recruitment of workers in the Philippines to fill vacancies in the hospitality sector. Other sectors such as mechanical repair facilities, early learning schools, and retirement facilities are seeing the value in hiring visible minorities.[1]

In the preceding chapter, we examined a variety of methods used to forecast HR demand. Many of these procedures (e.g., trend analysis, the Delphi technique, the nominal group technique) can also be used to determine personnel supply.

When considering the issue of supplying personnel to meet organizational demand, one aspect of the analysis is quite simple. Our personnel must be obtained from a source that is either *internal* (current employees) or *external* (individuals currently not employed by the organization), or more commonly, some combination of these. Many organizations give preference to internal supply, because selecting these individuals for training and development, and subsequent promotion, enables the organization to reinforce employee loyalty and performance. Other reasons for giving preferential consideration to your own workforce to fill job openings include the following:

1. Your employees are already socialized to the norms, rules, and procedures of your organization.
2. You possess detailed knowledge (as listed on their HRMS skill inventories) of their performance and KSAs over time (e.g., work history and experience).

We now turn our attention to this latter point concerning organizational databases on current workforce members—namely skills and management inventories.

SKILLS AND MANAGEMENT INVENTORIES

The first step in supply analysis is an examination of the number and capabilities of current employees. Skill inventories and management inventories contain information on the capabilities of your employees.[2] A **skills inventory** is an individualized personnel record held on each employee except those currently in management or professional positions. Typically, a skills inventory contains information for each individual on the following areas:

1. Personal information (e.g., name, employee number, job classification and compensation band, emergency notification, and telephone number)
2. Education, training, and skill competencies (e.g., certificates, licences, and diplomas or degrees completed, including the area of specialization, dates of attendance, and names of the institutions attended)
3. Work history (e.g., date of hire, seniority, current job and supervisor, and previous jobs held in the organization and the dates associated with them)
4. Performance ratings (i.e., a numerical score of the employee's history of performance in jobs in the organization)
5. Career information (e.g., future jobs desired by employee and those recommended by supervisors)
6. Hobbies and interests (including community and volunteer associations), and willingness to relocate.[3]

> Skills inventory
> An individualized personnel record held on each employee except those currently in management or professional positions

This skills inventory record is entered into an organization's HRMS database and can be searched when looking for people with the skills and competencies required by a specific job. For this reason, skills inventories must be kept current, and employees should be given frequent opportunities to update or correct their personal entries; otherwise, an employee may not be considered for a job that he or she could fill successfully.

Management inventories can be considered to be enhanced skills inventories, because they contain all the above information and the following:

> Management inventory
> An individualized personnel record for managerial, professional, or technical personnel that includes all elements in the skills inventory with the addition of information on specialized duties, responsibilities, and accountabilities

1. A history of management or professional jobs held
2. A record of management or professional training courses and their dates of completion

3. Key accountabilities for the current job (i.e., organizational resources, including the size of the budget controlled, the number of subordinates, important organizational outcomes for which the incumbent is primarily responsible)
4. Assessment centre and appraisal data
5. Professional and industry association memberships.

Only when an organization has a properly maintained HRMS, complete with the skills and management inventories described above, is it really able to assess correctly the numbers and competency levels of its current workforce. In this way, HR planners can determine the organization's workforce strengths and weaknesses and plan training and development courses accordingly, while noting which job openings must be filled from external sources because current employees lack the skill competencies required.

Succession/Replacement Analysis

Succession planning is critical to effective organizational functioning.[4] With demographic trends predicting even greater shortages in the market supply of skilled labour, organizational succession planning is now assuming much greater importance. It is absolutely essential that organizations create systems that meaningfully reward managers for developing and retaining their employees, or it is very likely that these critical tasks will not be performed.[5] Furthermore, the highly dynamic and changing global business environment is forcing HR managers to expand their succession planning beyond the traditional identification of a shortlist of replacements for specific jobs. Increasingly, the focus is on identifying and developing the broad skills and behaviours (i.e., competencies) that will be required by the organization to accomplish its competitive strategy.[6]

There are two aspects to succession planning: (1) *long-term succession*, a process of providing training and work experience to enable individuals to assume higher-level job appointments in the future, and (2) *short-term emergency replacement* of individuals who have quit, been terminated because of performance problems, have died, and so on.[7] Succession planning can help the organization be more effective in filling vacant positions.

There are several reasons succession planning is critical for effective HR planning:[8]

1. Succession planning enables an organization to respond appropriately and stay on track when inevitable and unpredictable changes occur. It provides for continuity and future direction even in the turmoil of change.
2. It helps develop people as they prepare for new experiences and jobs, and this development can also help improve their performance in current positions.
3. When succession planning takes into account employees' performance and promotes them for it, employees are positively motivated.
4. It supports new organizational structures and flexibility by explicitly providing backups to various positions, thereby reducing organizational dependency on any one employee.
5. It saves time and money by having plans already in place to enable smooth internal employee movement and continuity; therefore, external hiring is an exception to the process.

For more discussion on the topic of succession planning/management, please see Chapter 8.

It should come as no great surprise that the skills and management inventories described in the previous section are extremely useful information for succession and replacement planning. Furthermore, they are important for matching an individual's qualifications to the requirements of a specific job in the organization (e.g., it is easy to derive shortlists of potential successors, such as employees with a degree in marketing, with performance ratings of "above average" or better over the past three years, and fluently bilingual in English and French) and for identifying possible successors for specific positions. The key requirement for succession and replacement planning to function effectively is that supervisors, in conjunction with the HR staff, must develop *succession/replacement charts and tables* for key executive, managerial, and professional jobs in the organization (see Figure 7.1 and Table 7.1 for examples). The information that fuels this process is derived not only from current managerial assessments of subordinates but also from information contained in the inventories concerning education, training, and skills, as well as historical records of each potential successor's performance appraisals. Obviously, given the large amount of personal information used and the sensitive nature of the information,

FIGURE 7.1

Example of Succession/Replacement Chart

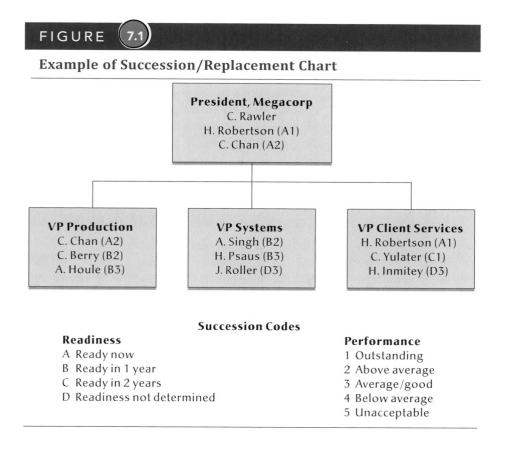

Succession Codes

Readiness	Performance
A Ready now	1 Outstanding
B Ready in 1 year	2 Above average
C Ready in 2 years	3 Average/good
D Readiness not determined	4 Below average
	5 Unacceptable

TABLE (7.1)

Example of Succession/Replacement Table

Keith Kiltmakers Chief Executive Officer (Position A01)

Incumbent	Employee Number	Current Appointment and Tenure[a]	Expected Date of Movement
Robert James	060422	CEO	06 April 2010
Potential Successors		**Succession**	**Codes**
June Catharine	070121	VP Operations (A21)/61	H, F
Roderick Alexander	010753	VP Legal (B24)/52	S, D
Kenneth James	010956	VP HR (D19)/48	B, F, D
Donald Martin	290959	VP Systems (C24)/16	Y, D

[a]The tenure of the current appointment is listed in number of months' duration.

succession planning documents are highly confidential. Access to the succession/replacement charts and tables, and to their supporting documentation, must be strictly controlled and limited on a "need to know" basis to such people as the CEO, the vice-president of HR, HR planning staff, and divisional executives. Access by divisional executives should be restricted solely to their own area of responsibility.[9] Although a manager should naturally consider his or her current subordinates in the process of developing succession plans, the skills and management inventories are important to ensure that other employees who have been transferred or seconded to other divisions, or are working in areas different from those for which they received functional training will not be overlooked. In fact, such employees will be identified by the search capabilities of the HRMS.

HR supply and succession aren't important for just corporations. HR Planning Today 7.1 discusses the importance of planning for succession in family businesses.

The first type of document used in succession planning is referred to as a *succession/replacement chart*. As you will notice from Figure 7.1, it closely resembles a typical organizational chart in that it represents the organizational hierarchy and the key jobs with their inherent reporting relationships. However, on closer inspection, the succession/replacement chart provides more detailed information on each job, specifically, the name of the current job incumbent and a shortlist (determined by managers in conjunction with the HR staff) of the top internal candidates who might replace the incumbent if and when he or she leaves the job.

An important aspect of the succession/replacement chart is the **succession readiness code**, which is listed next to the names of all employees. This code contains two elements of information essential for succession planning:

1. The employee's level of *performance* in the current job (e.g., represented by a value between 1 and 5, where 1 = outstanding and 5 = 5 unacceptable)
2. The employee's *readiness for movement or promotion* (e.g., A = ready now, B = probably ready within one year, C = needs development [i.e., probably ready in two years], D = not suitable for this job)

Succession readiness code Code listed next to the names of all potential successors; contains two elements of information essential for succession planning: (1) the employee's level of performance in the current job and (2) the employee's readiness for movement or promotion

HR Planning Today (7.1)

Take Steps to Keep Business All in the Family

A study by Deloitte & Touche states that the majority of Canada's family businesses are facing a leadership crisis due to a lack of succession planning. John Bowey, a Deloitte & Touche partner, says that family businesses in Canada account for 4.7 million full-time jobs, 1.3 million part-time jobs, and $1.3 trillion in annual sales. Furthermore, customers often prefer these businesses because of the personal contact and perceived high standards of credibility and quality. However, a full 75 percent of family business owners believe that the future success of their business depends wholly on them, reflecting a failure to develop future leaders and a neglect of the succession and replacement planning process. Almost half (44 percent) of these same business owners doubt their businesses will survive once they bow out of the operations. To cast a further dire light on the situation, 27 percent of the family business owners plan to retire within five years, a further 29 percent in six to ten years, and 22 percent in eleven to fifteen years.

Source: Adapted from Ian Harvey, "Be Careful to Keep Biz All in the Family," *Toronto Sun*, Jan 19, 1999. Reprinted with permission.

By including the two elements of the succession coding next to the name of each employee on the succession chart, we are able to get an accurate, although admittedly incomplete, picture of the state of succession readiness for each department and for the entire organization. Because no chart can capture all the information required for succession decisions, tables are used for supplementation.

Although we will have to refer back to specific inventories, performance appraisal records, and assessment centre reports (which summarize the potential of employees after they complete a series of tests) to get further information on potential successors, one of the key benefits of a succession/replacement chart is that it allows us to identify what are referred to as **ripple** or **chain effects**: one promotion in the organization can cause several movements in the organization as a series of subordinates are promoted to fill the sequential openings.[10] The succession/replacement chart, with its graphic illustration of ripple or chain effects, allows us to determine HR blockages or problem areas.[11] For example, the organization might not be able to immediately promote a top-performing potential successor to a particular position because no subordinates to the potential successor are trained and ready to replace him or her. The successor who was rated second, but who has ensured that his or her departmental subordinates have been properly trained by being exposed to increasingly more challenging job assignments and are therefore ready to be promoted themselves, might be chosen by the organization to replace the jobholder leaving.

The second document produced for succession/replacement planning is referred to as a *succession/replacement table* (see Table 7.1). We have seen how the succession/replacement chart gives an important yet incomplete pictorial representation of the state of succession readiness throughout a department or the entire organization. The succession/replacement table complements the succession/replacement chart in that it provides additional information on each specific job, the incumbent jobholder, and all potential internal successors.

Ripple **or** chain effects
The effect caused when one promotion or transfer in the organization causes several other personnel movements in the organization as a series of subordinates are promoted to fill the sequential openings

Being consumed by day-to-day sales operations can spell disaster for organizations that don't consider their HR supply in the long-term context. HR Planning Today 7.2 presents information on the looming succession crisis among Canada's car dealerships.

A succession/replacement table is prepared for each key job in the organization. In considering a replacement for the HR planning manager, for example, although the succession/replacement chart provides us with the top two or three candidates and their succession codes, all it may indicate is that promoting any of these individuals might be problematic for a variety of reasons (e.g., because of their performance or lack of training). By turning to the succession/replacement table, we get a list of *all* potential internal successors, not just the shortlist or top three individuals, as well as a very detailed information code for each candidate. Typically, a series of alphanumerical code combinations will provide us with important information not presented on the succession/replacement chart because of space limitations (e.g., using the coding from Table 7.1, in "(A21)/61" the "A" might signify a manufacturing operations position [#21], with 61 being the number of months in the current position). Succession/replacement table codes summarize information on personal career and training preferences, long-run historical data on performance appraisal, family, geographical posting preferences, and so on, all of which may affect movement or promotion and are not included on the succession/replacement chart.

The succession/replacement tables and charts are very useful tools for HR planners who are analyzing the state of the current workforce. Once we have used these two instruments of succession/replacement analysis, other details concerning specific job blockages or problems with our current internal

HR Planning Today   7.2

The Future of Retirement Around the World

A comprehensive study on global attitudes to aging and retirement published in 2004 shows that for many people traditional retirement is a thing of the past: 80 percent want to scrap mandatory retirement and 75 percent want to keep working in their maturity. The study interviewed over 11,000 adults in ten nations and territories: Brazil, Canada, China, France, India, Japan, Hong Kong, Mexico, the United States, and the United Kingdom. In six of the ten societies surveyed, alternating work and leisure was seen by the majority as the ideal lifestyle.

Highlights from the study include:

- Canadians view their later years as a time of reinvention, ambition, and close relationships with friends and family.
- Americans view their later years as a time for opportunity, new careers, and spiritual fulfillment, but are less focused on family or health than are other countries.
- The French view these years as a time of dreams and aspirations, but also as a time of worry, and they are concerned about being a burden to their families.
- The British view later life as a time of self-sufficiency, independence, and personal responsibility, counting on neither government nor family to care for them.
- Brazilians view later life as a time for slowing down, relaxing, and spending time with their families, relatives, and friends, and they expect significant support from their children.
- Mexicans see it as a time for continued work and hard-earned financial stability.

HR Planning Today 7.2 *(continued)*

- In China, younger generations view retirement as an opportunity for a new life but continued careers, while older generations want to stop working and relax. All Chinese people view family as an important source of happiness and support.
- Respondents from Hong Kong view it as a time for rest, relaxation, and the enjoyment of accumulated wealth, which is seen as the cornerstone of well-being.

- Respondents from India view later life as a time to live with and be cared for by their families.
- The Japanese look forward to their later years as a time of good health, family considerations, and continued fulfillment from work.

In Canada, mandatory retirement is now a thing of the past. Canadians can choose when and how they want to bow out of the labour force—see below.

Regional Breakdown of Retirement Rules by Province/Territory

Alberta	No mandatory retirement age
British Columbia	Law to eliminate mandatory retirement took effect January 2008
Manitoba	No mandatory retirement age
New Brunswick	No mandatory retirement age, but companies allowed to enforce it under "the terms or conditions of any retirement or pension plan."
Newfoundland & Labrador	Law to eliminate mandatory retirement took effect May 2007
Northwest Territories	No mandatory retirement age
Nova Scotia	Law to eliminate mandatory retirement took effect July 2009
Nunavut	No mandatory retirement age
Ontario	Law to eliminate mandatory retirement took effect January 2008
Prince Edward Island	No mandatory retirement age
Quebec	No mandatory retirement age
Saskatchewan	Law to eliminate mandatory retirement took effect November 2007
Yukon	No mandatory retirement age

Sources: HSBC, "The Future of Retirement in a World of Rising Life Expectancies," 2005. The study was conducted by market research company Harris Interactive under the guidance of HSBC and Age Wave; CBC News "Mandatory Retirement Fades in Canada," October 18, 2010.

workforce and the resultant requirement to process new hires from external sources become much clearer.[12] Chapter 8 contains further detailed information on succession planning/management.

Markov Models

Markov models are the most popular technique used for contemporary supply-side HR planning applications.[13] These models are widely used in both educational and personnel planning processes.[14] Furthermore, they have been found to be most useful in stable work environments where career paths are better

Markov model

A model that produces a series of matrices that detail the various patterns of movement to and from the various jobs in the organization

defined. A **Markov model**, also referred to as a *probabilistic* (using probabilities of various movement options) or *stochastic model*,[15] determines the pattern of employee movement throughout an organization's system of jobs.[16] Markov analysis produces a series of matrices that detail the various patterns of movement to and from the wide variety of jobs in the organization. When considering *employee movement patterns* in the organization, an employee has five possible options:

1. Remaining in the current job
2. Promotion to a higher classified job
3. A lateral transfer to a job with a similar classification level
4. Exit from the job (e.g., termination, layoff, voluntary leaving by the employee)
5. Demotion (which is relatively rare)[17]

Probabilistic or Markov models do not examine individual employees but instead examine overall rates of movement between various job levels, and this movement between jobs is based on historical movement patterns.[18] It is normally assumed, for calculation purposes, that the pattern of employee movement is relatively stable over time. If this is not the case, then adjustments have to be made to the historical data to allow them to be used for HR planning in the present day. Markov model data should be based upon movement during "typical" business operations. However, if environmental conditions change dramatically, the information should be adjusted, using the HR planners' best judgment. It is important to note that Markov techniques depend on stable transition probabilities, so dynamic and unstable environmental scenarios may preclude the effective usage of Markov models.[19] See HR Planning Today 7.3 for an example of a Markov model.

There are three main steps to using a Markov model for HR planning purposes.[20] First, we collect historical data on mobility rates between jobs in the organization. Second, based on this data we develop matrices to forecast future personnel movement between jobs. Third, we use the forecasts of the model to analyze our HR policies and programs, and instigate the necessary adaptive measures.[21]

By using employee movement data from the past five years or so, we are able to calculate *transitional probabilities*, or the likelihood that an individual in a specific job will exhibit one of the five aforementioned movement behaviours, normally one year into the future. By multiplying the total number of employees or positions in a particular job (e.g., 18 managers) by the associated probabilities for each of the five possible movement scenarios, the HR planner derives numerical data on employee flow patterns throughout the organization, and between various job levels (see Table 7.2).

The sequences of movements between various job states are referred to as *Markov chains.*[22] (Markov chains are derived from the model and can be considered a subset of the model as they refer to movement sequences between specified job states, not the overall matrix.) Detailed examination of the Markov model enables us to determine the number of external recruits required at various levels of the organizational hierarchy to fill openings caused by turnover, termination, promotion, and so on. Furthermore, we earlier referred to blockages or problems in succession planning, and these problems become readily apparent when we use

TABLE 7.2

Markov Model

Ottermere Outbound Adventures

		Year 2013			
		Chief Outfitter	**Outfitter**	**Guide**	**Exit**
Year 2012	Chief Outfitter ($n = 4$)	3(.75)	—	—	1(.25)
	Outfitter ($n = 12$)	1(.08)	9(.75)	—	2(.17)
	Guide ($n = 16$)	—	3(.19)	9(.56)	4(.25)
	Supply ($n = 32$)	4	12	9	7

Note: The probabilities (percentages) of various movement options are expressed horizontally and sum to 1 (100 percent).

this supply model using historical trends of movement probability. The Markov model enables us to determine the specific number of replacements or successors required for any job family annually, as well as for specified future planning periods (based on normal attrition assumptions), which can help us to be more proactive in our external recruitment programs. Additionally, we can calculate the chain of movement from an entry-level job all the way to the CEO appointment, along with forecast times of arrival, stay, and departure, in conjunction with breaks in career progression along the way. In fact, White refers to the length of a vacancy chain (the number of personnel who will move as a result of having to replace one individual) as its *multiplier effect*, and his study of U.S. churches showed that for any one retiring minister, a chain of movement for five subsequent ministers was created.[23] The length of an average chain is approximately three.[24] Apart from its obvious appeal for the career planning of individuals who have upward aspirations in the organization,[25] HR planners can use the derived information to plan when training and development courses, job rotations, and so on should be conducted for a specific group of employees, on the basis of predicted time to move from their current jobs to target jobs several levels higher in the organization's hierarchy.[26] Therefore, a Markov model has great value for determining:

1. The number of personnel who move annually, and over specified time periods, between various job levels
2. The number of external hires that are required by the organization, and where the specific jobs are needed
3. The movement patterns and expected duration in specified jobs associated with patterns of career progression for employees in the organization (i.e., career paths)[27]
4. The number and percentage of all starters at a particular job level who will successfully attain a future target job level by a specified time period[28]

All this information provides us with important insights in calculating the most appropriate balance between training and promoting internal employees on the one hand, and external recruiting on the other. All in all, the Markov model is a very useful tool for analyzing HR supply.

HR Planning Today (7.3

Using Markov Models to Forecast Ocean Deck Officers

An interesting application of Markov models concerns its usage by the Taiwanese Ministry of Communications to develop a five-year moving average of the "transitional probabilities" to ascertain that the supply of ocean deck officers would be able to meet forecast demand. The key forecasting issue was that the demand for deck officers was rising annually and exceeded supply, due to expansion in the local economy that resulted in an increased number of ships operating from Taiwan. The forecasting issue was of critical importance for several reasons. First, Taiwan is a significant maritime power as two local carriers—the Evergreen and Yang Ming shipping companies—rank among the 20 biggest shipping companies in the world. Second, because Taiwan is a maritime nation, the shipping industry is a key contributor to the success of the local economy.

The Markov model was derived from historical information about the current number of shipping officers in the four hierarchical levels (masters, chief officers, ship officers, and deck officers), the seniority time at each level, and the supply of new shipping officers who have obtained their certificates of proficiency. Demand information was obtained from the five-year plot of the grand total of ships that operated

domestically and ships that used Taiwan as their flag of convenience.

The resulting findings, which reconciled demand with supply, came up with a number of important conclusions. Not only did the study confirm that demand exceeded supply for shipping officers, but the forecasts also predicted that this situation would worsen in the future, leading to a 64 percent shortage in positions just three years into the future. Second, the worst imbalance in supply was for the lower-ranking positions, specifically deck officers and shipping officers. Concurrent research determined that graduates from the marine university in Taiwan perceived military service in the navy as offering the most prestigious and desirable jobs following graduation and that they would prefer not to work on a commercial vessel. Policy recommendations that derived from the study included (1) having the government establish ocean internships to support the shipping industry, (2) encouraging increased support for maritime colleges and universities to expand training programs for their ships' officers, (3) aggressively encouraging crew members to seek opportunities to train for their officer certificates, and (4) helping alleviate supply shortages by conducting overseas recruiting.

Source: Adapted from Lin, C., S. Wang, and C. Chiang. 2001. "Manpower Supply and Demand of Ocean Deck Officers in Taiwan," *Maritime Policy & Management*, Vol. 28, No. 1, pp. 91–102. Reprinted with permission of Taylor and Francis, Ltd. http://www.tandf.co.uk.

Linear Programming

Linear programming
A complex mathematical procedure commonly used for project analysis in engineering and business applications; it can determine an optimum or best-supply mix solution to minimize costs or other constraints

Linear programming is a mathematical procedure commonly used for project analysis in engineering and business applications. It has utility for HR planners because it allows us to determine the future supply of personnel based on achieving the best staffing outcome while taking into account certain constraints such as labour costs.[29] Furthermore, conditions such as desired staffing ratios (e.g., the internal/external mix of employees) can be programmed into the equation for determining HR supply. The optimum or best supply-mix solution is provided by the model, and the best conditions obviously vary across organizations.[30] Some companies may seek to minimize turnover or total labour costs, while others may seek to achieve an optimum level of staffing with respect to designated groups (e.g., visible minorities, women, Aboriginal people, people with disabilities) in all job levels throughout the organization.[31] By providing the level of personnel supply that is best with respect to explicitly defined constraints or criteria, linear programming enables us to calculate "what if" scenarios by changing or relaxing various model assumptions in order to determine the impact these changes will have on final numerical requirements for supply, both internal and external. To use linear programming, our assumptions have to be similar to those used in regression analysis (discussed in Chapter 6), namely that the mathematical model has to contain variables that have *linear relationships* among the various constituent elements. If this situation does not hold, we have to employ nonlinear or quadratic programming techniques to determine supply requirements. As linear programming is a relatively complex mathematical procedure normally performed on a computer, a detailed presentation on this technique is beyond the scope of this book.

Movement Analysis

Movement analysis is a technique used to analyze personnel supply, specifically the chain or ripple effect that promotions or job losses have on the movements of other personnel in an organization.[32] Specifically, we are able to identify the total number of vacant or open positions in the organization or department, as well as the total number of personnel movements that are caused by replacing and filling these vacant positions. The total number of personnel movements is always greater than or equal to the number of vacant positions to be filled. If we rely solely on external personnel, the number of vacant positions to be filled is exactly equal to the number of new hires obtained by the organization, as there are no internal promotions of current employees to replace the losses. Conversely, if we rely heavily on current employees (i.e., internal supply) to fill position openings, the total number of personnel movements will be greatly in excess of the number of open positions, because any one opening (e.g., due to a promotion or termination) will result in a whole chain of subordinates sequentially moving up one authority level to fill the gaps.[33] Movement analysis enables the HR planner to select the desired mix or percentage of internal and external supply for those positions requiring replacements, ranging from a promote-from-within policy to the other extreme of replacing losses entirely through hiring personnel from outside the organization.

Movement analysis can be performed for the organization as a whole, although analysts normally find it more useful to conduct separate analyses for each department, division, or functional area.[34] The normal planning time horizon is one year, and we start by identifying the number of personnel in each authority or compensation-band level at the start of the forecasting period. Next, we consider changes in the level of staffing for the department—that is, whether we are going to increase the number of jobs in some or all authority levels or downsize to reduce the total number of employees in the department. Having increased or decreased the personnel requirement from that which was forecast at the start of the period, we now turn to calculating the losses requiring replacement for each authority level of the department. We are interested only in losses (e.g., because of promotions, transfers out of the department, voluntary turnover, termination) that need to be *replaced*; therefore, it is important that we not "double-count" positions that have already been incorporated into the staffing changes column! We add changes in staffing level to personnel losses requiring replacement to

Movement analysis
A technique used to analyze personnel supply, specifically the chain or ripple effect that promotions or job losses have on the movements of other personnel in an organization

HR Planning Notebook 7.1

MANAGING THE FIRM'S INTERNAL LABOUR MARKET: LESSONS FROM THE FIELD

Professors at Simon Fraser University's Faculty of Business Administration have uncovered four lessons in properly using internal labour markets to supply the organization's staffing requirements based on their study of a large manufacturing firm:

1. Managers should recognize that there are often *multiple internal labour markets* typically operating in one firm.

2. Managers should conceptualize their staffing task as managing a system of human resource *flows*.

3. Managers need to develop an appreciation for the *temporal* and *situational contexts* within which staffing decisions are made.

4. Staffing decisions themselves can be appropriately viewed as garbage-can models (a classic model of decision making) in which *multiple issues* and *multiple criteria* are typically invoked in matching individuals and jobs.

Source: Adapted from L. Pinfield and V. Bushe, "Managing the Firm's Internal Labour Market: Lessons from the Field," Burnaby, BC: Faculty of Business Administration, Simon Fraser University. Paper presented at the Western Academy of Management Annual Meeting, Spokane (April 1992).

give us the total number of positions requiring replacement. At this stage, having determined the total number of positions to be filled, the actual number of personnel movements, as briefly described previously, can vary widely, depending on our organization or department's desired policy concerning the supply mix of internal and external replacements. To demonstrate, we now turn to a practical example of a movement analysis.

Movement Analysis Exercise

As HR forecasting manager of Keele Kontainers Ltd., your focus of interest is the organization's finance department. You wish to determine (1) the total number of positions requiring replacements over the next one-year period, and equally important, (2) the impact these openings will have on the current employees' movements throughout the department. Keele Kontainers has a policy of "promote from within" for all authority levels above the basic entry level (level 9), which obviously must be filled externally with new recruits. The finance department does not have any personnel in authority levels 1 to 3 inclusive (i.e., president, senior vice-president, vice-president); the senior appointment is a level 4 (senior manager) position. On the basis of historical trends and information provided by the strategic planning cell, you know the following:

1. A 5 percent staffing (position) increase for each of authority levels 6 to 9 inclusive will be required to meet additional financial processing activity in the department; one additional senior manager (level 4) will be required, as management wants one senior manager to handle financial forecasting while one senior manager is responsible for financial claims (i.e., current operations); six additional managers (level 5) will be required to supervise the financial analysts and clerks (i.e., the increases in levels 6 to 9 mentioned above) added over the course of the year.

2. Historical annual loss rates include the following:

    a. Retirements (requiring replacements): two positions for level 5, 15 percent of current positions for levels 6 to 9 inclusive

    b. Turnover = resignations (voluntary) + terminations (involuntary):

        Levels 5 and 6 = 10% of positions at start of period
        Level 7 = 15% of positions at start of period
        Level 8 = 20% of positions at start of period
        Level 9 = 25% of positions at start of period
        Note: The loss rates can be grouped into one column or broken into individual components (e.g., terminations, retirements).

3. The numbers of personnel/positions at the start of the year are as follows:

    Level 4 (senior manager) = 1
    Level 5 (manager) = 6
    Level 6 (senior analyst) = 20
    Level 7 (analyst) = 32
    Level 8 (clerk) = 40
    Level 9 (clerical assistant) = 50

In calculating our movement analysis, we construct two separate tables: the first determines the total number of positions to be filled, while the second identifies the internal and external personnel movements required to fill the open positions identified. When conducting a movement analysis, there are two rules to follow:

1. Work from the top down. Start at the highest authority or hierarchy level in the organization, because normal personnel movement in organizations is upward as people are promoted to replace higher-level losses.
2. Calculate the movement figures for one authority or compensation level at a time.

Let's construct a movement analysis table, shown in Table 7.3, and use historical information to calculate position replacement requirements or positions to be filled.

By using historical information, we are able to determine that the finance department, with 149 positions at the start of the year, requires 68 positions to be filled over the year. These positions are needed because of a planned staffing increase of 15 positions and because 53 individuals are required to replace personnel losses (i.e., losses due to retirements, resignations, and terminations). The calculations to arrive at these numbers are straightforward. For example, the increased staffing requirement for level 7 is determined by multiplying the original number of positions at that level by the percentage increase (i.e., $32 \times 0.05 = 1.6$ positions), and because we don't normally hire fractions of people, the requirement is for two new positions! Similarly, total personnel losses for level 8 consist of 14 positions, which is the sum of six retirements (i.e., 40 starting positions $\times$ 15%) plus eight turnover losses (i.e., 40 starting positions $\times$ 20%).

TABLE 7.3

Number of Positions to Be Filled

Authority Level	Number of Positions at Start of Period	Staffing Changes	Personnel Losses	Positions to Be Filled
4	1	1	0	1
5	6	6	3	9
6	20	1	5	6
7	32	2	10	12
8	40	2	14	16
9	50	3	21	24
	149	15	53	68

Sources: Adapted from E.H. Burack and N.J. Mathys, *Human Resource Planning: A Pragmatic Approach to Manpower Staffing and Development*, 3rd ed. (Northbrook, IL.: Brace Park, 1996); D. Bartholomew, *Stochastic Models for the Social Sciences* (New York: Wiley, 1982); E. Burack and J. Walker, *Manpower Planning and Programming* (Boston: Allyn & Bacon, 1972); R. Grinold and K. Marshall, *Manpower Planning Models* (New York: Elsevier North-Holland, 1977); R. Niehaus, "Models for Human Resource Decisions," *Human Resources Planning*, Vol. 11, No. 2 (1988): 95–107; J. Walker, *Human Resources Planning* (New York: McGraw-Hill, 1980); and H. White, *Chains of Opportunity: System Models of Mobility in Organizations* (Cambridge, MA: Harvard University Press, 1970).

Starting with the "Positions to Be Filled" column from Table 7.3, we construct a second table, Table 7.4, that reveals the employee movement at all levels of the finance department caused by promotions to fill the identified vacancies.

What does this all mean? Overall, to fill the 68 positions that require replacements over the next year, a total of 167 movements will occur in the finance department due to the ripple or chain effect on promotions. In Table 7.3, note

TABLE 7.4

Personnel Movement

Positions to Be Filled			Total Ripple or Chain Movement						Personnel Movement
1		—		—		—		—	1
9	+	1		—		—		—	= 10
6	+	1	+	9		—		—	= 16
12	+	1	+	9	+	6		—	= 28
16	+	1	+	9	+	6	+	12	= 44
24	+	1	+	9	+	6	+	12	+ 16 = 68
68		5		36		18		24	16 = 167

Sources: Adapted from E.H. Burack and N.J. Mathys, *Human Resource Planning: A Pragmatic Approach to Manpower Staffing and Development*, 3rd ed. (Northbrook, IL.: Brace Park, 1996); D. Bartholomew, *Stochastic Models for the Social Sciences* (New York: Wiley, 1982); E. Burack and J. Walker, *Manpower Planning and Programming* (Boston: Allyn & Bacon, 1972); R. Grinold and K. Marshall, *Manpower Planning Models* (New York: Elsevier North-Holland, 1977); R. Niehaus, "Models for Human Resource Decisions," *Human Resources Planning*, Vol. 11, No. 2 (1988): 95–107; J. Walker, *Human Resources Planning* (New York: McGraw-Hill, 1980); and H. White, *Chains of Opportunity: System Models of Mobility in Organizations* (Cambridge, MA: Harvard University Press, 1970).

that for level 5, although we start off with having to find replacements for nine open positions, we also have to promote one individual from level 5 to fill the requirement for an additional senior manager at level 4. Therefore, the total number of individual movements at level 5 is ten, although only nine open positions had to be filled at that level. Similarly, at level 6, in addition to having to fill six open positions, we also have to promote nine individuals to fill the openings one level higher at level 5, and one individual must be promoted to replace the level 5 individual who was promoted to level 4. Although there were only six open positions at level 6, the ripple or chain effect of sequential movement means that 16 individuals had to move to fill the organizational job openings. Furthermore, our assumption that we promote from within means that all 68 new hires originate from outside (i.e., from an external supply) at the entry level of clerical assistant (level 9). All other vacancies are filled by upward movement of current employees. Additionally, 99 promotions occur for current employees (i.e., internal supply) as is reflected in the ripple or chain effect matrix (i.e., 99 promotions = 5 + 36 + 18 + 24 + 16). In other words, movement analysis has allowed us to identify that for this year's need to fill 68 position vacancies, a total of 167 individual moves will be required because of extensive promotion from within. If we were to balance external and internal supply, the only adjustment would be that fewer individuals would be promoted from within the organization. This would lead to a decrease in the individual moves to a number closer to the number of open positions to be filled.

Using movement analysis, not only can an organization estimate the number of internal promotions and external hires, but it can also use the information for planning purposes and ensure it is able to devote enough resources in the training and development of its current employees (i.e., the 99 employees who would have taken up positions at higher levels) and in the recruitment of the 68 new hires.

Vacancy Model

The **vacancy model**, sometimes referred to as a **renewal** or **sequencing model**, analyzes flows of personnel throughout the organization by examining inputs and outputs at each hierarchical or compensation level.[35] Vacancy models have been found to have more predictive capacity than Markov models over short- and long-term periods (of three, five, and ten years),[36] although the common time frame for this model is one year into the future. It is important that we always calculate our personnel supply requirements one level at a time in a "top-down" fashion, beginning at the highest relevant authority level, because the normal direction of personnel movement in an organization is from the bottom to the top. The rationale behind the vacancy model is simple: the supply needs of each salary level are determined by staffing changes—the number of personnel promoted away from the level and any personnel losses (e.g., retirements, departures, terminations).

Organizational policy will determine the extent to which these openings will be filled by internal and external supply. Personnel losses are normally based on historical trends with respect to the percentage of personnel at each level who normally exit from that level annually, while growth estimates are based on the normal business forecasting process. Overall, vacancies in the organization lead

Vacancy, renewal, or sequencing model
Analyzes flows of personnel throughout the organization by examining inputs and outputs at each hierarchical or compensation level

to a sequence of internal promotions from lower levels as the open positions are filled by the replacement personnel. The vacancy model identifies the specific number of external and internal personnel required at each level and for the organization as a whole.

We now present an illustrative example of the vacancy model.

Vacancy Model Exercise

Hamish's Hamburgers and Eats offers high-quality, low-cost snacks and meals to budget-conscious students at Moosehead University. From the following information, calculate the company's vacancy model for next year's HR supply forecast.

1. Staffing changes: None (i.e., stable size)

2. Personnel losses during the year:

   Level 1 (president)   = 100% (compulsory retirement)
   Level 2 (vice-presidents) = 15%
   Level 3 (managers)   = 17%
   Level 4 (team leaders)   = 20%
   Level 5 (associates)   = 25%
   Level 6 (trainees)   = 50%

3. Personnel replacement policy (% external supply : % internal supply)

	% External Hiring	% Internal Promotion
Level 1	0	100
Level 2	10	90
Level 3	20	80
Level 4	30	70
Level 5	55	45
Level 6	100	0

Remember that the key to successful completion of the model is to start your calculations at the top of the organization and work down one level at a time. So let's start our analysis at level 1, the position of the president:

Level	No. of Personnel at Start of Year	Annual Losses	Promotions to Level	Level Outflows	External Hiring
1	1	1	1	1	0

The president of Hamish's will be retiring this year, so there will be an annual loss of one person. The company's personnel replacement policy states that for the president's job (level 1), all (100 percent of) loss replacements will come from internal promotions, in this case, from level 2 below. Therefore, there is one promotion to level 1 (from level 2) with no external hires, and annual losses are exactly equal to outflow at that level. Now consider the situation for level 2:

Level	No. of Personnel at Start of Year	Annual Losses	Promotions to Level	Level Outflows	External Hiring
1	1	1	1	1	0
2	6	1	2	2	0

Having completed level 1, we now calculate the personnel flows one level lower in the organization's authority or compensation system. For level 2, the annual losses are one, consisting of the number of personnel at that level at the start of the year multiplied by the historical loss rate (i.e., 6 × 0.15 = 0.9, rounded to one person). Next, it is crucial to note that the outflows from level 2 are not the same as losses, because we must take losses due to termination, retirement, and so on of one person and add to that the one individual who was promoted to level 1 to replace the retiring president. Therefore, our total personnel outflows from level 2 are two people. Total outflows from any organizational level are equal to losses at that level plus promotions to higher levels.

Now we refer to the company's personnel replacement policy, which dictates that we are required to replace the two personnel who left level 2 by 10 percent external hires and 90 percent internal promotions. Naturally, we do not deal in fractions of people, so 2 × 0.9 = 1.8, which is rounded to two persons. Both replacements are promoted from level 3, and we do not hire any individuals externally for the level 2 losses. The analysis continues in like manner until all organizational levels have been completed. The finished vacancy model is as follows:

Level	No. of Personnel at Start of Year	Annual Losses	Promotions to Level	Level Outflows	External Hiring
1	1	1	1	1	0
2	6	1	2	2	0
3	18	3	4	5	1
4	45	9	9	13	4
5	88	22	14	31	17
6	156	78	0	92	92
	314	114	30	144	114

In this instance, our vacancy model meets the specified requirement of a stable workforce size (i.e., no growth) as annual personnel losses of 114 are exactly replaced by 114 new hires from outside the organization. Furthermore, we know that in addition to the 114 annual losses (from a stable organizational workforce of 314), there are 144 total personnel movements, consisting of 114 new hires from external supply sources and 30 internal promotions across all levels. If instead of a no-growth scenario we predict a staffing increase or decrease, the above table is merely revised with the growth percentages (e.g., 5 percent at level 3, 8 percent at level 5) multiplied by the original number of personnel in each level to arrive at a column containing the revised (increased or decreased) number of personnel. This adjusted number of personnel is then used as the base point for calculating losses, promotions, and other flows from and to each authority level in the organization. Given the vacancy model information, it is possible to calculate the promotion rate (sometimes called the *upward mobility rate)* for each authority level in the organization. For example, the promotion rate for level 4 is 8.8 percent, which is obtained by dividing 4 (the four people who were promoted to level 3) by 45 (the total number of personnel who are in level 4). As we can see, the vacancy model is a very useful tool for ascertaining specific personnel supply requirements for internal promotions of current employees, as well as for specifying the exact number of external new hires required at each level of the organization.

HR Planning Today 7.4

Developing Effective Employee Retention Policies

Although most organizations tend to devote considerable time and resources to the process of *attracting* new workers, a great many fall short by not putting enough emphasis on *retaining* the high-quality personnel they currently employ. In order to rectify this situation, studies note the importance of making retention policies a top corporate priority. Several studies have clearly shown that managers at all levels should be held responsible for the retention of their personnel, and managerial performance evaluation should incorporate specific measurable goals in this matter. Greater importance should be given to identifying high-performing and high-potential employees, and their associated values, interests, needs, and so on, before they leave to work for competitors. Organizations should conduct a demographic analysis and compensation reviews by using their HRMS. These analyses will enable HR planners to identify potential gaps in the personnel ranks and develop policies to ensure sufficient well-trained, high-quality employees are on hand over the medium and long term. Other retention policy recommendations include (1) forming a "retention task force" to include HR personnel, line unit managers, and senior executives; (2) reinforcing employee loyalty and performance by "promoting from within" wherever possible; (3) measuring turnover on an ongoing basis at corporate, division, and local levels, utilizing multiple measures; (4) holding line managers responsible for retention; and (5) reviewing and addressing compensation and working condition issues before they become issues for dissatisfaction that prompt employees to leave the organization.

Sources: Adapted from M. Young, "The Case of the Missing CEO," *Canadian HR Reporter*, February 14, 2000: 117–120; and M. Abrams, "Employee Retention and Turnover: Holding Managers Accountable," *Trustee*, Vol. 55, No. 3 (March 2002), T1–T4.

HR supply isn't just a matter of finding new workers; as HR Planning Today 7.4 points out, retention planning is a vital component of effective HR supply.

HR Planning Today 7.5 discusses how labour shortages lead to flexible HR processes.

HR Planning Today 7.5

Shortages in Labour Supply Lead to Flexible HR Processes

As labour markets become increasingly global, and demand for highly skilled personnel intensifies from potential employers all over the world, organizations that were initially resistant to adopting innovative HR practices have been forced to change. With employers being unable to fill key HR demand from domestic Canadian and U.S. sources, managers that once ignored the need for diversity in workplace policies, and flexible practices such as telecommuting, flexible working hours, and so on, have been forced to adopt these practices to stay competitive in attracting and retaining skilled personnel.

- The city of Calgary has targeted the United Kingdom in an attempt to attract city planners, bus drivers, and firefighting personnel. There are already a significant number of British personnel holding down permanent positions in Calgary's police force, and the cultural similarities between the United Kingdom and

HR Planning Today 7.5 *(continued)*

Canada have helped ease their adjustment to working in a new country.

- Organizations such as hospitals, which were once quite restrictive about their access policies, are now holding recruiting "open houses" and job-shadowing days to encourage workers to think about employment with their

institution. With approximately 20 percent of Windsor Regional Hospital's workforce of 3,000 expected to retire in between three to five years, the hospital has introduced the "Take a Walk in My Shoes" program, which has drawn 150 people to spend a few hours with a staff person shadowing their daily activities and work.

Sources: Adapted from K. Cryderman, "City Hall Blitzes U.K. for Workers: Calgary Looks Overseas to Fill 250 Jobs," *Calgary Herald*, March 20, 2008, A1; G. Macaluso, "Health Jobs Taken for Test Drives; Forecasting Future Vacancies, Hospital Welcomes Public to Shadow Employees," *The Windsor Star*, September 20, 2008, A3; J. Schramm, "Coping with Tight Labour," *HRMagazine*, 52/6 (June 2007), 192.

HR SUPPLY AND RETENTION PROGRAMS

Any presentation on HR supply would be incomplete without a discussion of the need for organizations to monitor and control levels of absenteeism and employee turnover ("labour wastage," in British parlance). It may be helpful to think metaphorically of the organization's supply of employees as the level of water in a bathtub. Even with the water taps fully open and water pouring into the tub, if the drain plug is not in place, inevitably we will soon be looking at an empty tub! Organizationally, even if we are highly successful in *recruiting* a large number of high-quality applicants (a situation that is increasingly rare for most organizations, given demographic and competitive factors), if we are unable to *retain* experienced, high-performing employees, we face dire consequences, not only in the short run in failing to achieve desired organizational goals but also, perhaps even more critically, in an inadequate HR supply and lost opportunities for future succession.[37] Apart from normal levels of retirement and voluntary turnover, high levels of involuntary turnover normally signify a mismatch between the individual and the organization. Attention should be paid to selection procedures to ensure that proper skills and competencies are possessed by the individual, as well as to orientation and training and development in ensuring that personnel are provided with clear guidance with regard to their employment and desired performance levels. HR Planning Notebook 7.2 addresses the issue of leadership talent for the future.

With labour shortages projected for the next decade, retention programs are no longer an option for most North American companies; they are fast turning into a key requirement for organizational survival.[38] The costs of replacing current workers and acquiring new ones can be staggering. Apart from "hard" costs (e.g., advertisements, headhunter and recruiting fees, interview training and travel costs, administration expenses, cost of lost production, bonuses or increased salaries to act as inducements to join, and so on), there are also the "softer" elements (such as lost business and customer contacts, decreased quantity or quality of work due to training and "learning curve" gaps, orientation and training time, decline in team morale and productivity, and increased turnover due to the "follow me" effect) to consider. It is estimated that the cost of replacing a trained worker ranges from 70 to 200 percent of the departing person's annual salary![39] Successful retention

HR Planning Notebook 7.2

ENSURING THE SUPPLY OF LEADERSHIP TALENT FOR THE FUTURE

The IBM Global Human Capital Study, which surveyed 400 organizations in 40 different countries worldwide, found that "lack of leadership capability" and the challenge of "building leadership talent" were the primary challenges facing contemporary organizations.

Providing for continuity of leadership supply into the future needs to be an *ongoing, dynamic process*, not just a once-a-year review and formal written report on the performance and potential ratings of a select group of "high potentials."

First, there can be problems associated with *rigid and early categorizations* of whether employees are seen as "high potential," given that many future successful leaders take time to blossom and show their leadership abilities in the best light. Conversely, it is all too common that early designated "superstars" fail to deliver the expected performance, being later exposed as blatant self-promoting political game players who are highly adept at looking good, rather than doing good by helping others and sharing in the work as well as the credit and recognition.

Second, any effective leadership program must augment its *formal* developmental systems with ongoing *informal* "ear to the ground" identification of leaders who may be overlooked by managers and HR staff in their compilation of the leadership talent pool list.

There are several steps that can be taken to help ensure successful development of future leadership supply:

1. Ascertain the competency and numerical demands for leaders according to future strategic imperatives, not just based on current operational situations.

2. Analyze your current leadership talent pools and identify talent gaps that need to be addressed.

3. Resist the temptation to contract out leadership assessment and talent review processes to external third parties. Knowledge of your leadership talent pools, and development of personnel, must be top corporate strategic imperatives.

4. "Grow and flow." Wherever possible, use internal personnel rather than external hires to fill open leadership appointments. Not only does this increase the potential for reward by offering lateral transfers across and upwards in the organization, it also increases organizational flexibility and discourages "talent hoarding" by any one department or manager.

5. Develop your leadership personnel by a combination of methods including "stretch" assignment, formal education, and work on projects of strategic importance. Remember the importance of providing effective and timely feedback in the development of your leadership supply.

6. Your top leadership talent always has alternatives to working in your organization. Lack of consideration for their total life involvements, including family, friends, and outside interests, may see you ending up the loser, as key employees depart to work in better balanced and/or more rewarding organizational contexts.

Sources: Adapted from J. Dauby, "Planning for Tomorrow's Leaders," Rural Telecommunications, 25/1 (Jan/Feb 2006); C. Watkin, "How to Manage Leadership Talent Strategically," www.peoplemanagement.co.uk, November 01, 2007; The IBM Global Human Capital Study 2008: Unlocking the DNA of the Adaptable Workforce, IBM Global Business Services, Belinda Tang (source).

programs not only consider the organization's desire to "fill the job slots" but also explicitly attempt to address the needs of its workforce. Organizations that demonstrate flexibility and a genuine effort to assist their employees are perceived to be more attractive places to work (see HR Planning Today 7.6). Retention can be greatly facilitated by offering effective communication programs, maintaining an enjoyable and collegial work atmosphere, designing *meaningful jobs*, formulating and administering performance and compensation systems that identify and differentially reward better performers—based on clearly communicated criteria—and offering more flexible and attractive work arrangements (e.g., flextime, telecommuting, cafeteria-style benefit plans). Mentoring programs have also been found to be highly effective for retention through positively influencing individual commitment and potential for career success, and thereby reducing turnover intentions.[40] The need is clear, as is the fact that our employees—or "human capital"—are our key competitive advantage, self-renewing resources that clearly make the difference between organizational success or failure.[41] After years of short-sighted "downsizing" and "restructuring" initiatives, a great many of which have severely crippled organizations' development of intellectual capital and customer service delivery, many organizational managers still don't seem to get it. Until they take action to become "preferred employers" to their employees, by working hard to rebuild trust and mutual commitment, organizations will continue to have HR supply and retention problems, which will prove increasingly costly given looming demographic shortages in the labour force.[42] (See HR Planning Notebook 7.3.) The onus is on organizational and HR managers to deliver! HR Planning Today 7.7 illustrates one successful company that does just that.

HR Planning Today (7.6

Worksharing

Worksharing is a program designed to help companies facing a temporary downturn in business avoid layoffs by offering Employment Insurance income support to employees who work a reduced workweek while the company undergoes recovery. Employers retain employees and avoid expensive rehiring and retraining costs, and employees continue working and keep their skills up to date.

Worksharing was first used in Germany in 1927 and was introduced in Canada in 1977. It is also currently available in the United States, including Arizona, Arkansas, California, Connecticut, Florida, Iowa, Kansas, Maryland, Massachusetts, Minnesota, Missouri, New Hampshire, New York, Oklahoma, Oregon, Rhode Island, Texas, Vermont, and Washington.

To be eligible to participate in the program in Canada, the employer must have been in business in Canada for at least two years and be able to show that the need for reduced hours is temporary and unavoidable. The employer has to produce a recovery plan detailing how the company will recover from the temporary downturn in business and return to normal hours by the end of the agreement. Worksharing ranges in duration from 6 to 26 weeks, with a possible extension of up to 12 weeks. Companies have to obtain consent from their employees, and in unionized environments from the unions as well.

The program has benefited many companies and individuals. As of March 2010, there were about 5,500 active worksharing agreements nationally, benefiting close to 135,000 participants.

Source: Media Release: Government of Canada Protects Jobs Through Work-Sharing: Canada's Ecomonic Action Plan Extends and Enhances Program to Minimize Impact of Recession on Workers. URL: http://news.gc.ca/web/article-eng.do?nid=523909. Human Resources and Skills Development Canada, 2010. Reproduced with permission of the Minister of Public Works and Government Services Canada, 2012.

HR Planning Notebook 7.3
WINNING THE WAR FOR TALENT

Organizations cannot afford to lose experienced, talented employees. Given that highly qualified, high-performing staff will always have alternative employment options, what are some of the steps organizations can take to help attract and retain talented employees? The following recommendations are drawn from the research literature:

1. Train managers in strategies for the retention of employees, and hold them accountable for retention.

2. Pay is not the main reason for losing talent. Pay attention to "toxic" bosses and co-workers, bad management practices, and a lack of autonomy and respect at work.

3. Implement flexible working arrangements to facilitate work–life balance (e.g., flexible work hours, compressed workweek, telecommuting, job sharing, daycare centres, and so on).

4. Reward fairly, consistently, and differentially on the basis of performance and results. Give recognition to employee preferences for different types of work benefits (time off, non-monetary rewards such as travel or goods, tuition assistance, pension plans, life insurance, and so on).

5. Hold regular feedback and career development discussions with your employees.

6. Recognize that talented, highly motivated employees do not view training as a discretionary item that should get cut during the first round of annual budget reviews!

7. Deal with "slackers" and underperformers! Talented employees resent being burdened with additional stress and workload.

8. Reward organizational seniority in addition to rewarding performance.

9. Identify "high (turnover) risk" occupations, classifications, and personnel, and develop appropriate talent retention strategies.

10. Develop a managerial academy to teach talented employees the technical and interpersonal skills necessary to assume higher managerial positions in the future.

11. Review and pare to a minimum the following potential "dissatisfiers": rules, regulations, micromanagement, policy manuals, meetings, and so on.

12. Take action on talent management; don't just meet, discuss, or prepare a report.

Employee retention will soon become the number one priority for HR professionals (Frank & Taylor).

Sources: Adapted from F. Frank and C. Taylor, "Talent Management: Trends That Will Shape the Future," Human Resource Planning, Vol. 27, No. 1 (2004): 33–42; J. Greenwald, "Benefits Programs Aim to Keep More Moms in the (Work) Family," Business Insurance, Vol. 38, No. 5 (2004); "The Return of Work/Life Plans, HR Focus, Vol. 81, No. 4 (2004); K. Hilton and J. Soubik, "Case Study: Pennsylvania's Changing Workforce: Planning Today with Tomorrow's Vision," Public Personnel Management, Vol. 33, No. 4 (2004): 459–474; C. Trank, S. Rynes, and R. Bretz, "Attracting Applicants in the War for Talent: Differences in Work Preferences Among High Achievers," Journal of Business and Psychology, Vol. 16, No. 3 (2002): 331–345; M. Hay, "Strategies for Survival in the War of Talent," Career Development International, Vol. 7, No. 1 (2002): 52–56; S. Langan, "Finding the Needle in the Haystack: The Challenge of Recruiting and Retaining Sharp Employees," Public Personnel Management, Vol. 49, No. 4 (2000): 461–478.

HR Planning Today 7.7

Cutting-Edge Canadian HRM: Leadership Development and Retention at Ceridian Canada

With over 40 years of experience, Ceridian Canada provides its 40,000 Canadian customers with a wide range of best practice–based HR and information solutions, allowing them to focus upon their core business activities. Approximately 1,450 payroll and HR staff operate out of 11 different office locations across Canada, providing HR solutions in HRIS/HRMS, payroll, recruiting, work–life wellness, learning and development, employee assistance programs (EAP), and HR consulting.

The Canadian arm of Minneapolis-based Ceridian Corporation can also draw upon the resources of the large multinational company, which operates worldwide in 40 different countries. Ceridian Canada has a continuing record of workplace innovation and has been recognized as being one of "The Top 100 Employers in Canada" for the past five years.

This ongoing record of success has drawn heavily upon Ceridian Canada's focus upon ensuring *employee engagement*, a key metric that is measured annually by an external third party. By ensuring that leadership appointments are fully cognizant of the various drivers of employee engagement, Ceridian helps to ensure long-run continuity of supply of their own HR staff, and thereafter, being able to provide quality HR solutions offered to their organizational clients.

Ceridian Canada's Core Leadership Development program focuses on imparting to their managerial appointments the fundamental drivers of employee engagement in three learning modules: *organizational* drivers, *manager* drivers, and *employee* drivers. Organizational drivers of employee engagement focus on the importance of communications, organizational standards, and a culture for innovation and risk taking as cornerstones of securing an engaged and committed employee. Building upon the macro organizational factors, every manager is responsible to provide his/her employees with effective feedback, rewards, and recognition, which explicitly link each employee's performance to key organizational goals. Finally, employee drivers of engagement are focused on personal and career devel-

opment of employees, with managers learning coaching and facilitating skills to help enable long-run engagement and "embeddedness" of employees to Ceridian Canada.

The fourth and final module of Ceridian Canada's Core Leadership Development program is focused on *change management and communication*. In this module, managers are taught action plans and strategic approaches to guiding effective change processes, and the critical need for ongoing effective communication throughout the process.

Specialized leadership development is not a single, defined program but instead comprises a series of possible developmental initiatives focused on succession planning and the need to have ready successors for leadership appointments throughout the organization. The succession planning model used for specialized leadership development is drawn from the Corporate Leadership Council and consists of three key attributes of effective leaders: (1) aspiration, (2) ability, and (3) engagement. Possible elements of this developmental phase often include advanced educational and learning opportunities and "stretch" assignments/projects that are strategic in nature.

We have already discussed how Ceridian Canada's focus upon employee engagement in its leadership development program helps to ensure a long-run supply of highly motivated and performing employees. This approach also has considerable downstream beneficial effects in that highly engaged employees are less likely to leave the organization, leading to Ceridian Canada having a lower-than-average rate of employee disengagement and turnover. With managers being trained to pay attention to employee engagement, and the differing degrees to which employees feel valued and challenged in their current roles, this enables the organization to be more proactive in addressing situations that otherwise may cause absenteeism and turnover. Furthermore, by having exit interviews contracted to an external third party, Ceridian Canada's retention program receives unbiased feedback from recent leavers, providing valid information that serves as the basis for workplace policy and program improvements.

Source: Interview documentation provided to Kenneth McBey by Heather Turnbull-Smith, Director of National Learning & Development, and Vittoria Sgambelluri, Team Administrator, Ceridian Canada Ltd.

SUMMARY

This chapter presented six models or techniques used by organizations to determine future HR supply requirements. Skills and management inventories contain information that allows a detailed analysis of the current workforce to determine whether we can meet the demand for personnel replacement from current employees in the organization. Succession/replacement analysis expands on the inventories approach by using succession/replacement charts and tables to identify specific replacements for key organizational jobs and to examine whether problem areas or blockages would occur if specified individuals were to be promoted or transferred. The Markov model uses historical patterns of individual movement between jobs in the organization and attaches transitional probabilities for promotion, transfer, and remaining in the particular job for an annual or specified future period. In this way, we are able to derive exact numbers of open positions throughout the organization and can track career progression and the time required for individuals to reach specified target jobs. Linear programming uses mathematical equations to determine the optimal or best mix of personnel supply given specified constraints, such as minimizing labour cost or achieving a desired mix of diverse employee group memberships. Movement analysis enables the identification of not only the location and number of open positions that must be filled by the organization but also the total number of individuals who will be moved to fill these openings. The vacancy model provides specific information on total personnel flows into and out of each authority or compensation level, as well as for the organization as a whole. Accordingly, we are able to calculate the exact numbers of internal promotions and external recruits that will be required by the organization.

Finally, we concluded our discussion of HR supply by pointing out the need for organizations to develop retention programs to control absenteeism and turnover.

Key Terms

linear programming p. 176
management inventory p. 167
Markov model p. 174
movement analysis p. 177
ripple or chain effects p. 171

skills inventory p. 167
succession readiness code p. 170
vacancy, renewal, or sequencing
    model p. 181

Web Links

The government of British Columbia's Labour Force Statistics on HR supply and other indices can be found at:
www.aved.gov.bc.ca/labourmarketinfo

Canadian HR Reporter is at:
www.hrreporter.com

To search for jobs available at the U.S. federal government, go to the official site USAJOBS at:
www.usajobs.gov

The United Kingdom's HR professional association, the Chartered Institute of Personnel and Development, has a website at:
www.cipd.co.uk

Information on the supply and demand of the British labour force can be found at HRM Guide UK's website at:
www.hrmguide.co.uk/hrm/chap3/ch3-links4.htm

Required Professional Capabilities (RPCs)

The following RPCs are relevant to material covered in this chapter. The RPC number represents the CCHRA number assigned to the RPC as presented on the CCHRA website. All of the RPCs can be found in the Body of Knowledge at www .chrp.ca/rpc/body-of-knowledge.

RPC 65 Forecasts HR supply and demand conditions

RPC 68 Assesses the effectiveness of people and talent management plans

RPC 69 Maintains an inventory of people talent for the use of the organization

RPC 73 Identifies the potential source of internal and external qualified candidates

RPC 74 Evaluates the relevance of alternatives to recruitment (developing, outsourcing, contingent workers, agencies, etc.).

Discussion Questions

1. This chapter discusses some of the reasons for giving preferential consideration to your own workforce to fill job openings. Are there any disadvantages? What can management do to mitigate these potentially negative effects?
2. A Markov model provides important information to the HR supply analyst with respect to movement or flows of personnel through various jobs in the organization. Discuss how this supply-forecasting technique might also provide useful information to rank-and-file members (i.e., non-HR staff) of the organization's workforce.
3. Movement analysis is concerned with the ripple effects or workforce movements resulting from various supply policy options selected by the organization. Discuss the various implications of using internal sources of labour (i.e., the current workforce) rather than external sources of labour (i.e., recruits) for the supply needs of an organization. What advantages, disadvantages, costs, and benefits are associated with the different options?

4. The Canadian Nurses Association's latest projection shows that the shortage of nurses will grow by almost five times over the next decade and that Canada will be short almost 60,000 registered nurses by 2022. Discuss the factors that have led to the shortage. What do you think can be done to alleviate this shortage?

Exercise

1. Dave's Dumpsters offers a low-cost disposal system for the high-quality campus food served at Moosehead University, as well as for many other institutions of higher learning. The company has retained your services on a lucrative contract to calculate the vacancy model for next year's HR forecast, based on the following assumptions:

   a. Workforce complement at beginning of period (i.e., before staffing changes):

   Salary level 1 = 1
   Salary level 2 = 4
   Salary level 3 = 18
   Salary level 4 = 40
   Salary level 5 = 75
   Salary level 6 = 136

   b. Organizational growth: 5 percent increase in each salary level with the exception of salary level 1 (CEO), which remains at one position.

   c. HR losses during year:

   Salary level 1 = 100%
   Salary level 2 = 20%
   Salary level 3 = 22%
   Salary level 4 = 25%
   Salary level 5 = 30%
   Salary level 6 = 50%

   d. HR supply policy:

	Outside %	Inside %
Salary level 1	0	100
Salary level 2	10	90
Salary level 3	20	80
Salary level 4	30	70
Salary level 5	50	50
Salary level 6	100	0

   Source: Exercise created by K. McBey, 2002.

Case   HR PLANNING AT M&K

1. Workforce complement at M&K as of the end of this year is as follows:

CEO	Level 1	1
Executive Vice-President	Level 2	5
Senior Vice-President	Level 3	10
Vice-President	Level 4	20
Director	Level 5	100
Senior Manager	Level 6	200
Manager	Level 7	400
Associate	Level 8	500
Assistant	Level 9	1,200

2. The staffing levels for CEO and EVPs are to remain unchanged next year. The number of SVPs and VPs required are dependent on annual revenues. Staffing levels for SVPs and VPs are considered to be optimal in this year. Revenues generated for the year 2011 was $2 billion with 10 SVPs and 20 VPs. The revenue level for next year is expected to reach $3 billion.

3. The company is planning to open three additional offices across the country next year. Each office requires 5 directors, 15 senior managers, 30 managers, 50 associates, and 80 assistants.

4. The company will also be outsourcing its payroll and benefits administration to DES next year. The company is also getting rid of its donut business because they are not "good for you." Currently, 15 directors, 20 senior managers, 30 managers, 50 associates, and 150 assistants are involved in these activities.

5. Introduction of a new computer system will increase the productivity of the assistants by 50 percent but will require hiring a team of technical staff which will include 5 senior managers, 10 managers, and 50 associates.

6. Forecasted losses for next year are as follows:

	Quits	Dismissals	Retirements
Level 1	0%	0%	0%
Level 2	20%	0%	20%
Level 3	10%	0%	10%
Level 4	10%	0%	0%
Level 5	40%	5%	0%
Level 6	15%	10%	0%
Level 7	50%	5%	0%
Level 8	30%	10%	0%
Level 9	40%	5%	0%

7. M&K has two HR supply policies, as follows:
   (a) Exclusively "promote from within"
   (b) A combination of internal promotion and external hires, as follows:

	Inside	Outside
Level 1	100%	0%
Level 2	80%	20%

(Continued)

	Inside	Outside
Level 3	70%	30%
Level 4	60%	40%
Level 5	50%	50%
Level 6	40%	60%
Level 7	30%	70%
Level 8	20%	80%
Level 9	0%	100%

8. According to information stored on M&K's comprehensive HRIS system, annual employee movements between levels 5 to 9 in last year are as follows:

	Level 4	Level 5	Level 6	Level 7	Level 8	Level 9	Exit	Total
Level 5	10	80	5				5	100
Level 6		10	160				30	200
Level 7			20	360			20	400
Level 8				70	455		175	700
Level 9					300	500	200	1,000

9. M&K has also been tracking their revenues against the number of managers they have on staff. Below is the information obtained from M&K's ERP:

Year	No. of Managers	Revenues ($B)
This year (year X)	400	2
Year X – 1	320	1.8
Year X – 2	250	1.5
Year X – 3	200	1.3
Year X – 4	150	1.0

Questions

1. Estimate the total HR demand for M&K for next year, by job level.
2. Estimate changes in HR supply for M&K for next year, by job level.
3. Calculate the number of employee movements if M&K uses:
   (a) Exclusively a "promote from within" policy, or
   (b) A mix of internal and external supply as detailed in item 7(b)
   As HR Director, what do you see as some of the talent strategies and plans that have to be in place to facilitate each of the above options?
4. Calculate the transitional probabilities of movements for levels 5 to 9 on the basis of information provided in item 8.
   Using the calculated transitional probabilities, what employee movements (at levels 5 to 9) might take place next year?
5. Using information provided in item 9, estimate the number of managers that M&K would need using regression analysis if revenue levels:
   (a) Increases to $2.5B
   (b) Increases to $3.5B
   How many managers would M&K have to let go if revenues drop to $1.5B?

ENDNOTES

1. Martel, L., E.C. Malenfant, J.D. Morency, A. Lebel, A. Belanger, and N. Bastien. 2011. "Projected Trends to 2031 for the Canadian Labour Force." *Canadian Economic Observer*, Vol. 24, No. 8: 3.1–3.21; Sharpe, A., J.F. Arsenault, S. Lapointe, and F. Cowan. 2009. "The Effect of Increasing Aboriginal Educational Attainment on the Labour Force." *Output and the Fiscal Balance*. Research Report 2009-3. Ottawa: Centre for the Study of Living Standards; Statistics Canada. 2005. *Population Projections of Visible Minority Groups, Canada, Provinces and Regions*. Catalogue No. 91-541-XIE. Ottawa: Statistics Canada. Statistics Canada. 2010. *Projections of the Diversity of the Canadian Population*. Catalogue No. 91-551-X. Ottawa: Statistics Canada.

2. Buhler, P. 2004. "Managing in the New Millennium." *SuperVision*, Vol. 65, No. 2: 20–23; Martin, R. 1967. "Skills Inventories." *Personnel Journal*, January: 28–83; Kaumeyer, R.H. 1979. *Planning and Using Skills Inventory Systems*. New York: Van Nostrand Reinhold.

3. Schwarzkopf, A., R. Mejias et al. 2004. "Effective Practices for IT Skills Staffing." *Communications of the ACM*, Vol. 47, No. 1; 83–88; Martin, R. 1967. "Skills Inventories." *Personnel Journal*, January: 28–83; Seamans, L. 1978. "What's Lacking in Most Skills Inventories." *Personnel Journal*, March: 101–106.

4. Pynes, J. 2004. "The Implementation of Workforce and Succession Planning in the Public Sector." *Public Personnel Management*, Vol. 33, No. 4: 389–405; Cooke, R. 1995. "Succession Planning." *Credit Union Management*, October: 27–28.

5. Rothwell, W. 2002. "Putting Success into Your Succession Planning." *Journal of Business Strategy*, Vol. 23, No. 3: 32–37.

6. Guinn, S. 2000. "Succession Planning Without Job Titles." *Career Development International*, Vol. 5, No. 7: 390–394.

7. Rothwell, W. 2011. "Replacement Planning: A Starting Point for Succession Planning and Talent Management." *International Journal of Training and Development*, Vol. 15, No. 1: 87–99.

8. Pynes, J. 2004. "The Implementation of Workforce and Succession Planning in the Public Sector." *Public Personnel Management*, Vol. 33, No. 4: 389–405; Cooke, R. 1995. "Succession Planning." *Credit Union Management*, October: 27–28.

9. Cooke, 1995.

10. White, H. 1970. "Matching Vacancies and Mobility." *Journal of Political Economy*, Vol. 78, No. 1 (January): 97–105.

11. Foot, D., and R. Venne. 1990. "Population, Pyramids, and Promotional Prospects." *Canadian Public Policy*, Vol. 16, No. 4 (December): 387–398.

12. Foot and Venne, 1990: 387–398.

13. Bechet, T.P., and W.R. Maki. 1987. "Modeling and Forecasting: Focusing on People as a Strategic Resource." *Human Resource Planning*, Vol. 10, No. 4: 209–217; Konda, S., and S. Stewman. 1980. "An Opportunity Labor Demand Model and Markovian Labor Supply Models: Comparative Tests in an Organization." *American Sociological Review*, Vol. 45, No. 2 (April): 276–301; Weigel, H., and S. Wilcox. 1993. "The Army's Personnel Decision Support System." *Decision Support Systems*, Vol. 9, No. 3 (April): 281–306.

14. Bartholomew, D.J. 1973. *Stochastic Models for the Social Sciences*. London: Wiley; Law, H. 1977. "A Projection Model and a Rational Policy for the Supply and Demand of Human Resources from an Educational Institution." *Applied Mathematical Modeling*, Vol. 1, No. 5 (June): 269–275.

15. Meehan, R., and B.S. Ahmed. 1990. "Forecasting Human Resources Requirements: A Demand Model." *Human Resource Planning*, Vol. 13, No. 4: 297–307.

16. Heneman, H.G., and M.G. Sandiver. 1977. "Markov Analysis in Human Resource Administration: Applications and Limitations." *Academy of Management Review* (October): 535–542; Vassiliou, P.C. 1976. "A Markov Chain Model for Wastage in Manpower Systems." *Operational Research Quarterly*, Vol. 27, No. 1: 57–70.

17. Gans, N., and Y. Zhou. 2002. "Managing Learning and Turnover in Employee Staffing." *Operations Research*, Vol. 50, No. 6: 991–1007; Bechet, T.P., and W.R. Maki. 1987. "Modeling and Forecasting: Focusing on People as a Strategic Resource." *Human Resource Planning*, Vol. 10, No. 4: 209–217.

18. Blakely, R. 1970. "Markov Models and Manpower Planning." *Industrial Management Review*, Winter: 39–46.

19. Stone, T., and J. Fiorito. 1986. "A Perceived Uncertainty Model of Human Resource Forecasting Technique Use." *Academy of Management Review*, Vol. 11, No. 3: 635–642.

20. Zeffane, R., and G. Mayo. 1995. "Human Resource Planning for Rightsizing: A Suggested Operational Model." *American Business Review*, Vol. 13, No. 2 (June): 6–17.

21. Zeffane and Mayo, 1995: 6–17.

22. Gans, N., and Y. Zhou. 2002. "Managing Learning and Turnover in Employee Staffing." *Operations Research*, Vol. 50, No. 6: 991–1007; Nielsen, G.L., and A.R. Young. 1973. "Manpower Planning: A Markov Chain Application." *Public Personnel Management*, March: 133–143.

23. White, H. 1970. *Chains of Opportunity: System Models of Mobility in Organizations*. Cambridge, MA: Harvard University Press.

24. Stone, T., and J. Fiorito. 1986. "A Perceived Uncertainty Model of Human Resource Forecasting Technique Use." *Academy of Management Review*, Vol. 11, No. 3: 635–642.

25. Gridley, J. 1986. "Who Will Be Where When? Forecast the Easy Way." *Personnel Journal*, Vol. 65, No. 5 (May): 50–58.

26. Sandefur, G. 1981. "Organizational Boundaries and Upward Job Shifts." *Social Science Research*, Vol. 10, No. 1 (March): 67–82; Bartholomew, D. 1996. *Mobility Measurement Revisited in the Statistical Approach to Social Measurement*. San Diego: Academic Press.

27. Tuma, N. 1976. "Rewards, Resources, and the Rate of Mobility: A Nonstationary Multivariate Stochastic Model." *American Sociological Review*, Vol. 41, No. 2 (April): 338–360.

28. Rowland, K., and M. Sovereign. 1969. "Markov Chain Analysis of Internal Manpower Supply." *Industrial Relations*, October: 88–99; Glen, J.J. 1977. "Length of Service Distributions in Markov Manpower Models." *Operational Research Quarterly*, Vol. 28, No. 4: 975–982.

29. Al-Harbi, K. 2000. "Optimization of Staff Numbers in the Process Industries: An Application of DEA." *International Journal of Manpower*, Vol. 21, No. 1: 47–55; Gans, N., and Y. Zhou. 2002. "Managing Learning and Turnover in Employee Staffing." *Operations Research*, Vol. 50, No. 6: 991–1007; Weigel, H., and S. Wilcox. 1993. "The Army's Personnel Decision Support System." *Decision Support Systems*, Vol. 9, No. 3 (April): 281–306.

30. Patz, A.L. 1970. "Linear Programming Applied to Manpower Management." *Industrial Management Review*, Vol. 11, No. 2 (Winter): 131–138.

31. Gans, N., and Y. Zhou. 2002. "Managing Learning and Turnover in Employee Staffing." *Operations Research*, Vol. 50, No. 6: 991–1007; Walker, J.W. 1980. *Human Resource Planning*. New York: McGraw-Hill.

32. Bartholomew, D. 1982. *Stochastic Models for the Social Sciences*, 3rd ed. New York: John Wiley; Bartholomew, D. 1996. *Mobility Measurement Revisited in the Statistical Approach to Social Measurement*. San Diego: Academic Press; Burack, E.H., and N.J. Mathys. 1996. *Human Resource Planning: A Pragmatic Approach to Manpower Staffing and Development*. 3rd ed. Northbrook, IL: Brace Park; White, H. 1970a. *Chains of Opportunity: System Models of Mobility in Organizations*. Cambridge, MA: Harvard University Press;

White, H. 1970. "Matching Vacancies and Mobility." *Journal of Political Economy*, Vol. 78, No. 1 (January): 97–105.

33. Geerlings, W. and Van Veen, K. 2001. "Simulating Patterns of Organizational Careers." *Computational and Mathematical Organization Theory*, Vol. 7, No. 4: 287–310; White, H. 1970. *Chains of Opportunity: System Models of Mobility in Organizations*. Cambridge, MA: Harvard University Press; White, H. 1970b. "Matching Vacancies and Mobility." *Journal of Political Economy*, Vol. 78, No. 1 (January): 97–105.

34. Monks, K. 1996. "Global or Local? HRM in the Multinational Company: The Irish Experience." *International Journal of Human Resource Management*, Vol. 7, No. 3 (September): 721–735.

35. Geerlings, W., and K. Van Veen. 2001. "Simulating Patterns of Organizational Careers." *Computational and Mathematical Organization Theory*, Vol. 7, No. 4, 287–310; White, H. 1970. *Chains of Opportunity: System Models of Mobility in Organizations*. Cambridge, MA: Harvard University Press; White, H. 1970. "Matching Vacancies and Mobility." *Journal of Political Economy*, Vol. 78, No. 1 (January): 97–105; Bartholomew, D. 1982. *Stochastic Models for the Social Sciences*. 3rd ed. New York: John Wiley; Bartholomew, D. 1996. *Mobility Measurement Revisited in the Statistical Approach to Social Measurement*. San Diego: Academic Press.

36. Konda, S., and S. Stewman. 1980. "An Opportunity Labor Demand Model and Markovian Labor Supply Models: Comparative Tests in an Organization." *American Sociological Review*, Vol. 45, No. 2 (April): 276–301.

37. McBey, K., and L. Karakowsky. 2000. "Examining Sources of Influence on Employee Turnover in the Part-Time Work Context." *Leadership and Organization Development Journal*, Vol. 21, No. 3: 136–144.

38. Kohl, N. 2000. "HR Managers Losing the Retention Game." *Pro2Net*, November 7: 2.

39. North, N., E. Rasmussen et al. 2005. "Turnover Amongst Nurses in New Zealand's District Health Boards: A National Survey of Nursing Turnover and Turnover Costs." *New Zealand Journal of Employment Relations*, Vol. 30, No. 1: 49–63; Kohl, N. 2000. "HR Managers Losing the Retention Game." *Pro2Net*, November 7: 2.

40. Gram, J. 2004. "New Approaches to Human Resource Forecasting in the Public Sector." *Public Manager*, Vol. 32, No. 4; Joiner, T., T. Bartram, and T. Garreffa. 2004. "The Effects of Mentoring on Perceived Career Success, Commitment and Turnover Intentions." *Journal of American Academy of Business*, Vol. 5, No. 1–2: 164–171.

41. Lofgren, E., S. Nyce et al. 2002. "Will You Be Stranded by a Worker Shortage?" *Electric Perspectives*, Vol. 27, No. 3: 22–29.

42. Walker, J. 2003. "Perspectives: Where Are We Going?" *Human Resource Planning*, Vol. 26, No. 1: 14–16.

Succession Management

CHAPTER LEARNING OUTCOMES

After reading this chapter, you should be able to:

- Understand why succession management is important.
- Trace the evolution of succession management from its roots in replacement planning, comparing the two models with respect to focus, time, and talent pools.
- List the steps in the succession management process.
- Compare and contrast the job-based and competency-based approaches to aligning future needs with strategic objectives.
- Discuss the four approaches to the identification of managerial talent.
- Describe several ways to identify high-potential employees.
- Evaluate the advantages and disadvantages of the five management development methods: promotions, job rotations, special assignments, formal training, and mentoring and coaching.
- Recognize the difficulties in measuring the success of a management succession plan.
- Outline the employee's role in the succession management process.
- Describe the role of HR in succession management

SUCCESSION MANAGEMENT AT EDWARDS LIFESCIENCES

Edwards Lifesciences is a manufacturer of medical products with more than $1 billion in sales and 5,700 employees. Its CEO dedicates 20 percent of his time to talent management issues. This highly profitable company attributes its succession management success to its identification of 75 critical positions (which it refuses to reveal for competitive reasons). Each of these 75 positions has at least two employees identified as replacement candidates. The company spends millions of dollars annually to develop qualified candidates for these positions, including e-learning initiatives and weeklong leadership programs for upper management and promising talent. Almost 70 percent of jobs are filled by internal candidates. Every board meeting and every management meeting includes an item on succession management. For their program to track and retain candidates for critical positions, Edwards Lifesciences was awarded the 2007 Optimas Award for Competitive Advantage.[1]

Sources: Ruiz, G. "Edwards Lifesciences: Optimas Award winner for Competitive Advantage" www.workforce.com, retrieved October 13, 2008.

IMPORTANCE OF SUCCESSION MANAGEMENT

Succession management
The process of ensuring that pools of skilled employees are trained and available to meet the strategic objectives of the organization

Executives of any organization must develop the next generation of leaders, just as sports teams need to develop the next generation of players. **Succession management** refers to the process of ensuring that pools of skilled employees are trained and available to meet the strategic objectives of the organization. (Succession management might be viewed as part of the talent management process of an organization that focuses on the flow of employees, starting from selection to career management to exit, through the organization.)

Succession management used to focus mainly on the CEO. However, there must be a pipeline of talent for the most critical roles:

1. The CEO
2. The senior management team (executives)
3. Critical roles based on long-term value to the organization (such as scientists or customer relationship specialists)[2]

Succession management consists of a process of identifying employees who have the potential to assume key positions in the organization and preparing them for these positions. The identification of talent is always paired with ongoing programs to develop that talent. Succession management ensures continuity in leadership and, like any rookie program, develops the next generation of players. The goals of succession management programs are to identify and prepare future leaders and to ensure business continuity.[3] Other drivers are outlined in Figure 8.1. The first priority of any succession management program is to have a plan to replace its leaders. Organizations with positive reputations for leadership brands tend to outperform their peers.[4]

As Peter Drucker says, the ultimate test of good management is succession management, ensuring that there is a replacement for the CEO.[5] Organizations must prepare for expected and unexpected turnover, for key players do die, retire, or quit. Unfortunately, only about half of organizations answered "yes" when asked the question "If your president or CEO resigned today, do you know who would take charge of the company?"[6] At McDonald's, the excellent succession

FIGURE 8.1

Drivers of Succession Management Programs

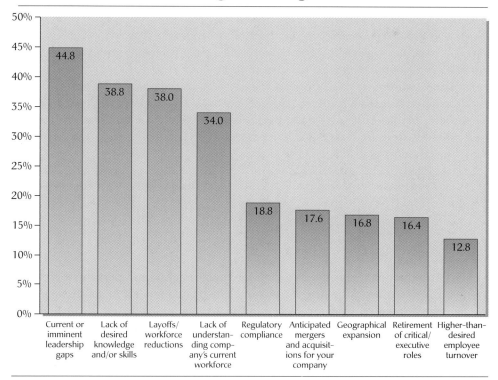

Source: Frauenheim, E. 2009, "Talent Planning for the Times" *Workforce Management*, 88, 11, pp.37-39, (October), 41-43. Retrieved May 27, 2011, from ABI/INFORM Global.

management program enabled them to designate a replacement within six hours of their CEO's sudden death, compared to a more typical delay of six months. The research shows that delays in naming a successor result in decreasing operating performance, and that these negative effects can last up to two years.[7] Fiery young entrepreneurs who build hugely successful businesses often see them fail in the hands of their untrained children. Many Canadian dynasties (e.g., Eaton's, Simpsons) have failed because their heirs were incapable of managing the business. See HR Planning Today 8.1 for a discussion of the problems facing family firms.

Succession management is needed even when retirements and company sell-outs are predictable. The baby boomers who currently hold most of the leadership positions are retiring. Twenty percent of top management positions and 25 percent of middle management positions will become vacant in in the near future, and retirements of baby boomers (the first of whom turned 65 in 2011) will accelerate this trend.[8] And 75 percent of executives are worried about their ability to develop leaders.[9] Yet this worrying does not result in action plans, as only 26 percent of companies report having a formal succession plan in place.[10] About one-half of the HR managers surveyed in 2011 don't consider grooming potential leaders a high priority.[11]

HR Planning Today 8.1

Family Firms Fail

Family-owned businesses represent a significant part of the economy in Canada, generating $1.2 *trillion* in revenues and employing 4.7 million full-time employees and 1.3 million part-time employees. Four out of five owners will retire in the next 15 years; and 65 percent indicate that they have no process for succession management. Nearly half of these owners believe that the business will not survive without them, which could result in an economic disaster for Canada. They are right. Research has established that hereditary owners have a poor track record; businesses handed to sons and daughters fail 50 percent of the time. There is no such thing as the "lucky sperm club"—the factors that drive entrepreneurs to succeed cannot be passed down. As A. Mac Cuddy, the bitter founder of Cuddy International, a multimillion-dollar poultry producer whose company was torn apart in a family feud among his five sons, said, "You can hire better than you can sire."

Sources: "Successful Successors," *Canadian Business*, Vol. 80, No. 7 (March 26, 2007): 7–9; "Leadership Crisis," *CMA Management*, Vol. 73, No. 5 (June 1999): 25–27; M. McClearn, "A New Era," *Canadian Business*, Vol. 75, No. 5 (March 18, 2002): 24; T. Watson, "The Rich 100—Succession: Family Circus," *Canadian Business*, Vol. 74, No. 24 (December 31, 2000): 104–110.

At minimum, firms need to plan for replacements, and personnel planning was the first step in the march toward sophisticated models of succession management. Some reasons for succession management are listed in HR Planning Notebook 8.1. The next section traces this evolution.

Evolution of Succession Management

Replacement planning

The process of finding replacement employees for key managerial positions

Replacement planning can be defined as the process of finding replacement employees for key managerial positions: If the CEO dies, who will be prepared to take over that position? Is there a replacement for the vice-president of marketing if she suddenly quits to take another job? The events of September 11, 2001 tragically presented a worst-case scenario. Bond trading firm Cantor Fitzgerald lost 700 of its 1,000 World Trade Center staff, including most of its executives.

Formal and methodical replacement planning has existed for over 30 years. This section examines how replacement planning has evolved into succession management by:

- Broadening the focus
- Expanding the time horizon
- Creating a talent pool of replacements
- Improving the evaluation system

Broader Focus

The focus of replacement planning was the job, and having a replacement ready to fill that job if the incumbent died or quit. This concept referred mainly to the succession and replacement charts for the high-level or key positions in the organization. Each key position was represented by a box on the chart, with the name

HR Planning Notebook 8.1

WHY ORGANIZATIONS HAVE SUCCESSION MANAGEMENT PROGRAMS

1. Improve internal candidate pools.

2. Assure business continuity.

3. Reduce skill gaps.

4. Retain employees.

5. Help individuals realize their career plans within the organization.

6. Develop leaders more quickly.

7. Encourage the advancement of diverse groups.

8. Improve employees' ability to respond to changing environmental demands.

Sources: K. Lamoureux, "Developing Leaders," *Leadership Excellence*, Vol. 25, No. 7 (July 2008): 11, 12.; A. Paradise, "Many Barriers Inhibit Success of Succession Planning," *T+D*, Vol. 64, No. 6 (2010): 60.

and possible retirement or departure date of the incumbent in the box. Below the box were the names of two or three potential successors, with codes next to their names. These would be, for example, codes such as "PN" for "promotable now" or "RD" for "ready with development."

In short, replacement planning consisted of a periodically updated table of employees who might be nominated if a need arose. This type of planning focused on the high-potential candidates (replacement track stars), all ready to step into vacant positions, and in doing so set off a chain effect throughout the organization. This model assumed that people have single careers within one organization. Thus, replacements were replicas of the current jobholders.

This planning depended on a stable future, in which the knowledge, skills, attitudes, and other attributes (KSAOs) of future managers looked pretty much like those of the current managers. Jobs of the next five to ten years were assumed to be identical to the existing jobs. Organizational structures (i.e., how the organization was set up along divisional lines, product lines, or functional lines) were unchanging, and few new competitors were seen on the horizon. Obviously, this type of scenario just doesn't exist for most companies.

In replacement planning, the starting point was the job, whereas in succession management, the starting point is the strategy of the organization. Employees are selected on the basis of long-term goals, and the developmental plans for employees are aligned with strategic plans, not position replacements.

A case might best illustrate how succession management aligns with strategy. Traditionally, the goal of a large utility like Ontario Hydro was to provide safe, reliable energy. Its core competencies were reliability of distribution, measurement of consumption, and the maintenance of its power plants. However, deregulation and a more competitive environment forced Ontario Hydro to compete on price and services. Sales and marketing were the new competencies needed. The strategy changed from providing energy to marketing energy. Thus, in the long run, Ontario Hydro must identify or develop managers who have not only sales and marketing abilities but also the ability to change a production culture to one of marketing.[12]

Time Horizon

The traditional planning approach was concerned with immediate and short-term replacements. Who is our backup for the vice-president we are planning to promote in six to twelve months? A strategic focus of under one year is a "business as usual" perception, which, if repeated, will not be true over a ten-year period. This short time perspective does not allow for the intake or career management of those with different skills in growth areas.

Succession management looks at a longer term (after ensuring that immediate replacements are in place) and focuses on a future of two years or more. Obviously, this is harder to do, and so, rather than identify one replacement, succession managers identify talent pools.

Talent Pools

Traditional models of HR planning looked at succession as the passing of the baton to the next capable runner. Managers would identify their top performers and groom them for success. Sometimes two or three successors would be identified, and they would be in a race to the finish line of executive promotion. This practice may have worked when organizations consisted of dozens of levels, each manager having many assistant managers. Currently, organizations have found that their designated backup personnel fill only 30 percent of the open positions for which they were slotted.[13] Flatter organizations with fewer "apprentices" can no longer rely on this approach. The key is not to develop a specific successor to fill any position (done by about one-third of organizations) but to develop several multiple successors (about two-thirds of organizations do this) for every position.[14] The place to start is with positions that are difficult to fill because of talent shortages.

As employees cannot trust organizations to provide lifetime job security, so too organizations cannot rely on single individuals or a small group of employees for their succession plans. Organizations are trying to identify and develop as many employees as possible to ensure employee departures and changing needs will not leave them harmed.

At MDS, many of the high-potential employees are not aware of being tracked, because "we do not want to create a culture in which some people feel they are special and others feel their potential is not being recognized."[15]

By not telling employees this, companies risk having employees leave the organization for one that offers better opportunities, and they also risk having to groom someone who may not want the job. (However, most employees realize their special status through the frequency of their promotions, assignments, and training.) Employers must avoid promises such as "You will become CEO in five years"; such promises are an implicit contract that may be judged to be binding.

Does identifying many successors solve these problems? Surely competition among successors will ensure that the best candidate wins by trying harder and demanding better training. Furthermore, if one successor does not develop to the potential that was anticipated or quits the organization, then others are willing and ready. But this approach has problems too. One is that candidates might sabotage each other by not sharing important information or by raiding key employees to improve their own track records. As well, many might engage in managing impressions and performing for short-term results in order to be evaluated more highly. This strategy does not encourage team playing, which is a force in organizational culture.

There is no easy solution to these problems. At NCR, the management development plan is labelled Project 64K, because it is meant for all 64,000 employees, not an elite group. At Johnson & Johnson, the focus is on the top 700 managers.[16]

The key is to communicate to these star employees that they are valued and that they have leadership potential, without ever promising anything. Another approach is to tell high potential employees about their status, and then explain that they will be given a series of developmental challenges, and their potential will be continually assessed.

Any organization needs a pool of talent and must develop many employees with flexible job skills and competencies. A "pool" is a good description of the next generation of talented leadership because the term implies fluidity and responsiveness to the impact of forces. The talent pool is considered a corporate resource and is not the property of individual organizational units. This evolution from personnel planning to succession management has led to a model of generating pools of leadership talent within an organizational context of global competition, environmental turbulence, de-layered organizations, and new technologies.

Talent segmentation, the identification of employees who are critical to the success of the organization, is expected to become as important as customer segmentation.[17]

Furthermore, a succession management approach should not depend only on internal candidates, but should also track external candidates. Rather than rely on inbred internal managers, the new generation of succession managers tracks high performers in the external market, thus ensuring that new skills and ideas flow into the organization. Large companies such as IBM and AT&T have recruited over half their executives from outside the organization to obtain the skills that these mega-companies were unable to predict they would need or to develop internally. HR Planning Notebook 8.2 compares the advantages and disadvantages of internal and external candidates. The list of advantages of internal candidates is more robust than for those of external candidates, and the reality is that about two-thirds of internal candidates do succeed.[18] Moreover, it appears that when a company is doing well, internal candidates are favoured to sustain high performance, because they possess valuable firm-specific knowledge.[19] But overall, it appears that companies that are performing well do better by hiring from within, and those companies that are struggling show better returns by hiring outsiders.[20]

Rating System

Traditional planning relied on the identification of the replacement people by a single rater. Previously, only the boss of the high-potential employee supplied information about that employee, and the information on which succession plans were based could be both out of date and unreliable. The gathering and recording of these judgments may have been seen as a personnel function, which incorporated little understanding of the real needs of the organization. Thus, managers may not have bought into the process.

HR Planning Notebook 8.2

INTERNAL VERSUS EXTERNAL

Advantages of Internal Candidates

- Organizations have more and better information about internal candidates.
- Organizations that offer career development and opportunities to internal candidates increase commitment and retention among their employees.
- Internally developed leaders preserve corporate culture.
- Internal candidates can hit the road running, because they know the organization, its people, and its processes. Other employees know the internal candidate, and there is less internal disruption waiting to see who the new executive is and what changes he or she will make. Internally chosen executives do not replace those who report to them as often as external candidates do; externally chosen candidates often get rid of the "old guard."

- Recruitment and selection costs are lower. For example, the replacement cost of a CEO is estimated to be $750,000, including the use of a search firm and lost opportunities getting the external candidate up to speed. Additionally, internal candidates do not have to be compensated at the higher levels demanded by external candidates (who face the risk of starting in a new organization).

Advantages of External Candidates

- The external candidate may have better skills to lead the organization through a major transformation or change in strategy.
- The external candidate brings new knowledge and skills to the organization and prevents the organization from becoming inbred and stale.

HR Planning Notebook 8.3

COMPARISON OF REPLACEMENT PLANNING WITH SUCCESSION MANAGEMENT

Factors	Planning	Management
Environment	Stable	Dynamic
Focus	Jobs	Strategy
Time frame	6–12 months	2+ years
Selection criteria	Job experience	Competencies
Appraiser	Immediate manager	360° feedback
Selection pool	Internal	Internal and external
Successors	Slated individuals	Talent pools
Development	Limited	Flexible, multiple

In a succession management approach, several raters give current evaluations on an employee's performance. The increasing use of 360° feedback mechanisms sheds light on various aspects of any candidate's style and performance. HR Planning Notebook 8.3 compares replacement planning and succession management.

Succession Management Process

The succession management process links replacement planning and management development. Until recently, in some organizations, succession planners worked with one database, management trainers with another. Now, both databases are integrated, with succession managers working in strategic planning committees, performance management groups, and organizational learning and training functions.

The succession management process is simple to understand but difficult to implement. The process involves five steps, each of which we will now consider in some detail.

1. Align Succession Management Plans with Strategy

Management development must be linked to business plans and strategies. If the business plan focuses on global markets, then managers have to be trained to manage global businesses. How does this translate into everyday skills? To build global talent, an organization could start by asking these questions: What are the specialized skills and perspectives necessary to compete globally? How many managers possess these skills? What percentage of employees could represent the firm to the world? How many could have an extended dinner with key international customers?[21]

The strategic connection is important, so organizations must start with the business plan. Using this, coupled with environmental scanning, managers try to predict where the organization will be in three, five, or ten years.

2. Identify the Skills and Competencies Needed to Meet Strategic Objectives

From the strategic plan, managers can then develop a list of the employee skills and competencies needed. There are at least two approaches to identifying the characteristics of successful managers: the job-based approach and the competency-based approach.

JOB-BASED APPROACH   The first impulse is to start with the job. We know that employees have jobs with duties and responsibilities (discussed in Chapter 4). The job-based approach suggests that employees who have significant experience as managers, and who have acquired job skills such as motivating, delegating, marketing, or managing finances, will make successful managers. Additionally, organizations such as Procter & Gamble insist that their leaders understand the marketing of brand names.

Others suggest that this job-based approach to successors is inadequate because jobs change rapidly. Furthermore, the increase in knowledge work has led many organizations to search for a different approach to employee development, particularly for those employees at the managerial level. Therefore, many organizations are turning to a competency-based approach, in which the capabilities of individuals are the primary focus.[22]

COMPETENCY-BASED APPROACH   Competencies are groups of related behaviours that are needed for successful performance.[23] They are measurable attributes that differentiate successful employees from those who are not. These competencies are a collection of observable behaviours and can be "hard" or "soft." Hard competencies might be the ability to build new technologies. Soft competencies might be the ability to retain top talent. Given an uncertain future in which skill needs change rapidly, succession management should focus on the development of competencies.

Consulting firms are the perfect example of companies in which the skills and capabilities of individuals drive the business, and business opportunities drive the development of new capabilities. Thus a list of skills (rather than jobs or positions) forms the basis for succession management. Rather than moving *up* a career ladder, individuals move *through* a certification process, developing increasingly complex capabilities along the way. There may be several skill acquisition paths, rather than one sure path to the top.

A good place to start preparing a list of competencies is to look at what experts have said about the competencies of successful managers. Many lists are available that outline the kinds of generic skills and competencies managers should possess. HR Planning Notebook 8.4 presents a list of these characteristics.

The skills that managers need to possess are endless, and each "expert" develops a preferred list. These lists could be used as a starting point and then be customized to identify and develop managers in any organization. By emphasizing competencies rather than job skills, individuals will be more flexible in adapting to changing organizational needs. ("Skills" and "competencies" are

---

HR Planning Notebook 8.4

MANAGERIAL COMPETENCIES

- *General mobility skills and knowledge:* These competencies facilitate reemployment and include effectiveness in group process, communication skills, and flexibility and adaptation.
- *General managerial core competencies:* These competencies were identified by studying successful managers and include "being able to build a cohesive team" and "being able to persuade employees to accept much needed organizational changes."

- *Detailed, job-specific competencies:* Job-specific competencies vary by function, but in HR would include "the ability to implement a change program" and to "identify the best selection tool to identify high-potential candidates." These abilities would vary by level, with a junior manager mastering the ability to identify performance gaps in a subordinate and a senior manager being able to initiate change programs to improve performance.

Source: Adapted from E.H. Burach, W. Hochwarter, and N.J. Mathys, "The New Management Development Paradigm," *Human Resource Planning*, vol. 20, no. 1 (2000), pp. 14–21.

terms that are often used interchangeably. However, skills are narrower and refer more specifically to skills for one job; competencies are broader and can be applied to many jobs at many levels. For example, proficiency in PowerPoint and installing Windows are skills; the ability to think creatively and work in teams are competencies.) Catano and his colleagues provide a full discussion of competencies; they distinguish between several types:

- *Core competencies:* Characteristics, such as thinking skills, that every member of the organization is expected to possess
- *Role or specific competencies:* Characteristics, such as business knowledge, shared by different positions within an organization
- *Unique or distinctive competencies:* Characteristics, such as expertise in media relations, that apply only to specific positions within an organization[24]

3. Identify High-Potential Employees

After we know what competencies are needed, we can turn to the identification of employees who might ultimately acquire these sets. Regularly scheduled discussions about succession force the leaders of the organization to think about the future of the business and the kinds of employee skills needed to facilitate the chosen strategy. By concerning themselves with the future directions of the organization, executives focus on the managers who will guide that future. The performance appraisal process becomes meaningful and not just another personnel form to complete. Executives come to "own" the succession and development plans, because they are integral to the success of the organization.

In HR, we often state that the best predictor of future performance is past performance. Executives must be able to move beyond descriptions of high-potential employees that use descriptions such as "She is very bright and very strategic" and "He has the support of his team" to listing specific achievements.[25]

Organizations use several approaches to identify managerial talent, including the following:[26]

1. *Temporary replacements:* At the most primitive level, most individual managers will have identified a designated backup and potential successor. This is done in case the manager is away from the office for extended periods (e.g., vacations, training). A manager who fails to pick a successor may never be promoted, as no replacements would be ready to succeed him or her.
2. *Replacement charts:* At the next level, some organizations prepare replacement charts with predicted departure dates of the incumbents, along with a shortlist of possible successors. This is usually done around performance appraisal time, using the performance evaluation data. Typically, a handful of senior executives targets a diverse list of employees for growth and creates annual development plans. These executives stay in touch with each individual assigned to them and become responsible for the development of the leadership competencies of those individuals. The list identifies those candidates who are ready now, those who will be ready in three to five years, and the long shots. These approaches tend to replicate current strengths (and weaknesses) and are not necessarily future oriented, nor are they strategically aligned with the needs of the business. This

stair-step approach is too rigid during times when organizational structures are changing rapidly and employee loyalty is weak.

3. *Strategic replacement:* A more advanced succession management program exists in an organization that is less inclined simply to replicate existing incumbents, but instead identifies the leadership competencies it needs, on the basis of organizational plans. The organization then tries to support and train these managers from within. The identification of high-potential people moves beyond the evaluations conducted by one or two managers. The Public Service Commission of Canada, for example, uses a formal assessment centre to identify those public servants who will become the future executives in the federal public service. Wary of evaluations done by only one individual with one perspective on employee performance, many organizations are moving to a 360° evaluation. For many employees, such an evaluation is the first time they have received feedback on how others perceive them. Some employees have likened the experience to holding up a mirror, others to a breath of fresh air.[27] Employees who had undergone 360° feedback reported that they felt their peers often knew better than their managers how to improve their performance.*

The above three systems favour the selection of internal candidates. As a result, these systems have a motivating impact on employee performance. However, they are limited in their ability to introduce new ways of thinking and working, and may not suit the strategic direction of the organization. In the next approach, the managers more actively scan the environment to identify and retain top talent.

4. *Talent management culture:* Many organizations, whose CEOs lie awake at night worrying about their ability to find and keep top talent, have adopted a talent management culture.[28] The winners in the war for talent have developed a talent mindset—that is, they believe that talent matters and it must be developed not only at the top level but also at all levels. Managers are committed to define and model an employee value proposition that answers the question, "Why would a talented person want to work here?" The employee "brand" is managed as much as the company brand. See HR Planning Today 8.2 for a discussion of brand positioning to attract and retain employees. Organizations with employer brands outperformed others in three critical areas: revenue, net income and share price.[29] Managers actively scan the environment (e.g., for the actions of their competitors or the actions of the world's best industry leaders in other areas with overlapping functions, such as finance or logistics) looking for external talent. They have developed both internal and external lists of high-potential candidates.*

Recruitment is opportunistic—that is, when a top candidate is found, that person is hired regardless of whether there is a vacancy. For example, MDS, a medical supply company, is so interested in securing talent that it will hire even when no position is open, and make that person an "executive-in-residence" and give him or her a special project to manage until a vacancy arises.[30] As David Guptil, vice-president of HR for Lafarge Canada, a large supplier of construction materials, states:

*Source: Joinson, C. 1998. "Developing a Strong Bench," *HRM Magazine* (January): 92–96.

HR Planning Today 8.2

Building the Brand: An Employee Value Proposition

Some companies develop an employee value proposition (EVP) that will help attract and retain employees. They base this EVP on concepts that they have learned in customer attraction and retention. An EVP is a brand positioning aimed at employees so that the company will be seen as an employer worth working for, and all company messages sent to the labour market are compelling and consistent. Key candidates seem to be attracted to companies that pose one of four brand positions:

- A "winning" company, which is characterized by growth and development
- A "big risk, big reward" company, which offers great potential for advancement and compensation
- A "save the world" organization, which is attractive to those wanting a mission
- A "lifestyle" company, in which employees want flexibility and a good relationship with the boss

Sources: S. Cliffe, "Winning the War for Talent," *Harvard Business Review*, Vol. 76, No. 5 (September/October, 1998): 18–19; S. Hood, "The PR of HR," *HR Professional* (February/March 2001): 17–21.

What keeps me awake at night is my very thin bench strength. … We are resisting that temptation to scale back on strategic recruiting. And when I say strategic recruiting, what I mean is that you don't wait for a vacancy and the predicted retirees. I and our senior managers are always on the lookout for talent that may be available. If I find a very talented person … my freedom is to go out and hire that person whether we have a vacancy or not.[31]

The process of continually searching for talent is correlated with success. A McKinsey study found that nearly one-third of HR directors at top-performing companies constantly search for talented executives, as against less than 10 percent at average-performing companies.[32] These talent management companies analyze turnover statistics and always include in their reports the reasons for the voluntary turnover. Managers, not HR, have the responsibility for identifying and cultivating talent.

Finally, some companies operate with all four approaches, using replacement planning for highly predictable jobs such as accounting, and talent management to deal with rapid changes in strategic needs.

Assessing employees to identify high-potential candidates must be done both fairly and accurately: fairly so that employees buy into the process and feel that the search for talent is an equitable procedure, and accurately so that the selection process is both reliable and valid. Organizations typically use the direct supervisor's informal judgments and formal evaluations such as performance appraisals and assessment centres. (More information can be found in the performance evaluation chapter of any introductory HRM text.) Caterpillar's annual talent assessment includes the employee's manager, the business unit manager, and the executive office. The discussion centres on the employee's next three moves and the kinds of career experiences needed for these moves.[33] HR Planning Notebook 9.5 contains a brief description of common assessment methods. Usually about 10 percent of employees are identified as high-potential. Syncrude Canada Ltd., an oil producer, with headquarters in Fort McMurray, Alberta, has identified about 8 percent of its 3,600 employees as high-potential.[34]

However, the use of annual reviews of talent can result in a mechanical approach leading to the goal of completing the forms provided by HR, rather than quality dialogues about leaders. Some managers simply update forms to meet a deadline. A better process would be to commit to quarterly reviews and the allocation of one full day to choose the top candidates by ranking them against all other candidates. Even these discussions can become politicized when:

- Executives rate their own candidates too positively;
- People are hesitant to criticize the choices of others;
- Members distrust the motivation of others' recommendations ("passing the trash");
- Running conflicts between executives result in cheap shots about candidates; or
- Information about the best players is withheld as executives want to own this talent.

HR Planning Notebook 8.5

TECHNIQUES FOR ASSESSING EMPLOYEE POTENTIAL

- *Performance appraisals:* Managers identify high-potential employees through performance appraisal systems. Raters, who may include the supervisor, colleagues, customers, and subordinates of an employee, evaluate the employee against some pre-developed standards. The goal is to identify and communicate the employee's performance strengths and weaknesses. The information is then used for developmental purposes so that gaps in performance can be closed. High-potential employees are tracked in this way using a standardized organizational assessment tool. Managers are forced to identify high-potential employees through performance appraisal systems and may be rewarded for developing employees.

- *Assessment centres:* Assessment centres involve a process by which candidates are evaluated as they participate in a series of exercises that closely resemble the situations faced on the job. Simulations include negotiating a merger, handling the press, managing interdepartmental conflicts, or making a decision without all the facts.

Trained and experienced managers observe the candidates' behaviour during this process and provide an evaluation of their competence and potential. The newest form of assessment centres is the acceleration centre, in which the first stop is a website where candidates can learn everything about the fictitious company they will manage for a day. All testing, correspondence, and decisions are completed online, enabling the assessors to compare candidates more objectively.

- *Human Resources Management Systems (HRMS):* Large amounts of information about employees' KSAOs can be stored in databanks and used to identify employees with needed skills. Employee files can document their experiences, skills, abilities, and performance evaluations. Employees' interests and career objectives may also be recorded. Basic matching to identify high-potential candidates is simplified with an effective HRMS. A useful feature of an HRMS is its ability to construct scenarios. Planners can create "what if?" models to determine the effect of employee movements.

To minimize the politics involved in identifying talent, management should develop a set of principles such as "Talent is managed in the larger interests of the company. Managers are simply stewards of this talent, and companywide interests prevail."[35]

4. Provide Developmental Opportunities and Experiences

Before we discuss the methods used to develop managers, we should first consider two issues:

- Are leaders born or made?
- Should organizations produce their own managerial talent or buy it on the open market?

Born or made? Many great leaders have had no formal management training. Shouldn't we just select leaders with the inherent qualities of leaders and not try to teach leadership skills?

Peter Drucker, considered by many to be the founder of management as a discipline, is credited with saying, "Most managers are made, not born. There has to be systematic work on the supply, the development, and the skills of tomorrow's management. It cannot be left to chance."[36]

Buy or make? Organizations invest many dollars and other resources to develop managers, but perhaps experienced, trained managers could simply be hired from other organizations.

Some organizations do prefer to pick up their needed executive talent by buying it on the open market. For example, Elliot Whale, president and CEO of Dylex Ltd., had been president of Toys "R" Us (Canada) Ltd. and director of player personnel for the Toronto Blue Jays baseball club before he moved to Dylex. Selecting outsiders allows companies to bring in fresh perspectives, people who can lead the organization through a transformation. By bringing in an outsider, the board of directors sends a strong message to employees and shareholders that the old way of doing things is going to change.[37] Other organizations feel strongly that they want to indoctrinate and train their own leaders, who then have a deep commitment to the organizational vision.

There are no easy answers to these questions. Organizations may find outstanding leaders by chance, or they may commit to the development process. Some may choose to hire from the outside to obtain fresh approaches; others will commit significant time and money to train their own managers. However, most large organizations have a policy of promotion from within. There are many advantages to this: the organization has accurate records of employees' past performance, and employees understand and are committed to organizational objectives, know the ropes, and know how to get things done. Another reason to recruit internally is that CEOs recruited from the outside delivered annual returns 3.7 percent lower than insiders.[38] Most large organizations have formal management development programs to ensure a ready supply of "promotables." Let us look at some of the methods such organizations use.

MANAGEMENT DEVELOPMENT METHODS In the succession management process, the focus in management development is on the development of competencies, not just on job preparation. Because the goal is to develop many skills that may be needed in an uncertain future (in contrast to simply replicating the skills of the present incumbents), management is much more open to various approaches to develop the talent pool. More traditional approaches might have relied on a senior leadership course and one developmental assignment, perhaps mimicking exactly what the current CEO did. The key point is that the approach has changed from one of providing training to fill jobs to one of providing experiences to realize leadership potential. The most common development methods are promotions, job rotations, special assignments and action learning, formal training and development, and mentoring and coaching.

Promotion

An employee's upward advancement in the hierarchy of an organization

Promotions   A **promotion** refers to an employee's upward advancement in the hierarchy of an organization and usually involves increased responsibilities and compensation. Traditional models of management development saw managers moving up a pyramid, managing larger and larger units until they reached their appointments at the top. Each organization had its favourite route to the top, some through sales, others through operations. These paths became worn over time, and few succeeded by using other paths, such as an HR track. One organization used a system of temporary rotations, resulting in a win–win combination. Senior executives nearing retirement were given the option of a week's vacation in every month, which they welcomed, and were replaced by high-potential employees who could try new leadership skills in a safe setting. In flat organizations, where promotions are rare, a preferred developmental method is job rotations—developing managers horizontally rather than vertically.

Job rotations

A process whereby an employee's upward advancement in the hierarchy of an organization is achieved by lateral as well as vertical moves

Job Rotations   **Job rotations** are lateral transfers of employees between jobs in an organization. Rotations involve a change in job assignments but not necessarily more responsibility or money. For example, one way of orienting a new employee quickly is to place him or her in a new department every few weeks, providing an overview of the organization. The CEO of Maritime Life Insurance believes that rotation is the best indicator of whether an employee is ready for a top position. To avoid costly placement decisions, staff with potential are placed in a variety of roles across the organization. Succeeding at rotation is a prerequisite for a top-level position.[39]

Rotations have several motivational benefits for employees, including the reduction of boredom and fatigue. Trying out new jobs also benefits employees who have reached a career plateau. The development of additional skills may increase an employee's job and career prospects. Almost all the research suggests that job rotation makes employees more satisfied, motivated, involved, and committed.[40]

From the organization's standpoint, rotations are useful for orientation and career development. Rotations allow an employee to increase his or her experience. A common use of job rotation is to take a functional specialist, such as an accountant, and rotate this specialist through both HR and operations in preparation for management positions. An information technology specialist, before a rotation in sales, might try to sell his idea to management by saying, "We have to invest in a multiprotocol router," and might be met with complete incomprehension. After a rotation through the sales department, the same specialist might sell the same program by explaining, "We're building an infrastructure so that salespeople can get access to product or inventory information from anywhere." The technician has learned a business skill.[41] Jet Form, an Ottawa-based business with about 650 employees, uses cross-functional mobility as a key part of its strategic planning.[42] The results are encouraging, and employees are regularly rotated between functions to increase their knowledge and skills.

Besides the additional knowledge of the functional areas, such as sales, and management areas, such as business knowledge, the rotated employee is making contacts and establishing a network that might prove useful in the future. Learning new ways of doing things, with different co-workers and bosses, also might make employees more adaptable in their managerial jobs. The research shows that rotation improves an employee's knowledge of the organization (e.g., of business, strategy, and contacts) and improves his or her ability to cope with uncertainty. Furthermore, employees who have tried out several jobs gain a better insight into their own strengths and weaknesses. However, job rotation produces generalists and should be supplemented by training for any specific skills needed.

Of course, the downside of employee rotations includes the increased time needed to learn the new jobs, the cost of errors while learning, and the loss of efficiency that otherwise is gained through repetition and specialization.[43] In other words, workload may increase for the employee while productivity decreases, and other employees absorb additional work and stress in efforts to socialize, orient, and train the newcomer.

At the managerial level, employers should be concerned about producing a short-term orientation in the organization's leadership ranks. Employees in six-month jobs may put their efforts into creating fast results, which might hurt the unit in the long term. For example, employees with a short-run focus may neglect plant safety in a rush to exceed production quotas. Furthermore, the rotation of managers places new expectations on performance, creates new goals, and results in reassignment of work, producing stress on the unit managed by rotation.[44]

One approach is to give an employee a number of assignments within the company or a related sector. Ultimately, managers may be better formed by developing skills horizontally, throughout an organization, rather than by developing specialized skills vertically, up a career ladder.

Special Assignments and Action Learning   On-the-job learning is still a favoured path to the development of managerial skills. Most organizations test high-potential employees by giving them an assignment in addition to their regular duties. For example, the manager of corporate banking might be placed on a task force that is considering the acquisition of another bank. A manager who needs international experience might be sent to work in China with a vendor to the company. In another case, a team of managers might be given a special assignment, such as developing an equity plan for the organization or developing an e-commerce plan for the company. These types of special projects enable candidates for future executive positions to network and test their skills in new environments. Mistakes must be tolerated, as candidates may quickly assume that these special assignments are synonymous with failure, fostering a culture of fear in which no employee dare be innovative or take bold measures, and finally, derailment from the fast track. Remember the story about the executive called into his boss's office expecting to be fired because of a business decision that cost the company a million dollars. The CEO instead gives him another special assignment, reasoning, "Why should we fire you? We just invested $1 million in your development." Interviewers for executive positions routinely ask candidates about a difficult challenge or unsuccessful project. If the candidates indicate no failures, the executive search firm concludes that the candidate is not open about these experiences, or he or she may not have the skills to handle an unsuccessful project in the next assignment. The best assignments are those that entail a high degree of risk and accountability, such as launching a new business or turning around a struggling project. If these are coupled with decision-making authority and the opportunity to manage a large group of people, this is the recipe for producing effective executives.

Formal Training and Development   Management training and education is big business. Hundreds of thousands of dollars may be spent preparing one executive to become the CEO of the organization. This cost appears relatively minor when it is estimated that the total career investment in an individual employee is 160 times the initial starting salary.[45] In this book, we use the term "management development," but others label a similar process "executive education" or "leadership training" or a combination of any of these words.

According to a study of U.S. organizations, 87 percent offer management development programs that were designed, developed, and delivered in-house.[46] Only a small number use external vendors. The majority of companies use traditional and passive instructional techniques and rate them least effective, but they are fast and easy to use. Most use lectures, seminars, and discussion groups more often than behaviour modelling and experiential learning.[47] Senior managers need the soft skills of delegation and motivation, rather than hard technical skills such as website development or benefits management. Thus we would recommend that role-playing, case studies, behaviour modelling, and action learning, which are effective techniques, be used as training methods for management development. In most cases, the effectiveness of the training method is evaluated by the "smile sheets"—course evaluation sheets in which participants rate the course and instructors—at the end of the program rather than the application of the learned skills on the job. Techniques for increasing the extent to which training is then applied to and endures in the performance of the job have been described by Belcourt and Saks.[48] Critics believe that these training programs teach very specific skills that might not be robust enough to stand the test of time and successfully prepare managers for rapidly changing environments.

Many companies prefer an educational approach that broadens intellectual skills such as the ability to analyze. These companies turn to universities to teach their executives conceptual skills, which would be useful in many situations. Others create their own training centres, which they label corporate universities.

U.S. organizations, more than 1,000 of them, have begun opening corporate universities—available only to the employees—because these organizations view training as a lifelong process, rather than as discrete courses taken occasionally. Most of these universities focus on building competencies and skills that are aligned strategically to meet both employee and corporate needs. Individual corporate universities offer a wide range of courses, which together constitute something resembling a mini-MBA. Through case studies and action learning, the courses offer managers a chance to practise and receive feedback. Unlike professional athletes or musicians, managers seldom get a chance to practise their skills and try out new ideas and methods. Sometimes these corporate universities have mentors on staff, often with more than 20 years in the business, who coach and assist in the transfer of knowledge.

Mentoring and Coaching   Many very successful managers explain that their successes resulted directly from having been mentored: A senior executive took an interest in them and their careers at a critical time in their lives. **Mentors** are executives who coach, advise, and encourage junior employees. The mentor takes an active interest in the career advancement and the psychosocial development of the protégé. Career development aspects include examining approaches to assignments and learning how tasks should be handled, which conferences or networks have high career value, and which senior managers to emulate. Psychosocial considerations include building the self-confidence of the protégé, as well as offering counselling and friendship to make him or her aware of the political open doors and open pits of the organization. Studies show that protégés do indeed derive these psychosocial benefits (increased confidence, self-esteem, reduced feelings of isolation etc.) as well as career benefits (increased compensation, promotions, career development opportunities, etc.).[49] One company offers coaching to help high-potential candidates understand the executive derailers—those personality traits that might cause an otherwise effective executive to fail (such as arrogance, micromanagement, risk aversion, volatility, and low tolerance for ambiguity).[50]

Mentoring used to happen informally, but organizations have recognized the value of having a senior manager take a career interest in a junior employee and so have started formal mentoring programs. One survey showed that 70 percent of highly productive organizations have mentoring programs, and employees in these programs report greater career satisfaction and experience faster career growth.[51] These programs link executives who have the motivation and time to nurture managerial talent with employees who are motivated to advance quickly. Two-thirds of the topper-forming companies provide high-potential employees with frequent access to the CEO, and opportunities to interact on projects with senior managers.[52] Mentors are almost always more senior people who volunteer within an organization, while coaches tend to be paid counsellors from outside the organization. Internal mentors are best for strengthening and assuring continuity of organizational culture.[53] The advantages of external coaches are described in HR Planning Notebook 8.6.

While it is necessary for discussion purposes to separate management development methods, all companies will use a combination of methods. Some focus on formal programs, such as a three-week leadership course followed by an assignment in a foreign country. Other companies, such as 3M, allow their employees to choose assignments and to work on ad hoc committees to manage new projects, as well as giving them free time to tinker and play with ideas. Cisco, a leader in hardware and software technology, uses the 3E Model: 70 percent of development occurs through **E**xperience (assignments, rotations, special projects), 20 percent through **E**xposure (feedback, mentoring, and shadowing), and 10 percent through **E**ducation (readings, e-learning, and courses).[54] The choice of

Mentors
Executives who coach, advise, and encourage junior employees

HR Planning Notebook 8.6

BENEFITS OF EXTERNAL COACHES

For the Organization	For the Individual
Retain high performers with incentives other than financial rewards.	Reconnect the individual with personal values or missions.
Develop key employees for succession planning.	Provide clarity and focus to accelerate the achievement of goals.
Guide individuals and organizations through transition.	Compress learning time to optimize skills by building competencies faster through one-on-one coaching.
Change skills and attitudes for long-term sustainable results.	Translate leadership theories and concepts into "useful insights" to affect communication, decision making, and overall strategies.
Give new perspectives on business experience and practices.	

Sources: Adapted from L. Hyatt, "Best Practices for Developing Great Leaders," *Workplace Today*, January 2003: 14–17; G. Voisin, "When to Use an Internal or External Coach," *HR Professional*, June/July 2001: 30–33.

a method depends on the employee's learning style and the goals to be achieved. Learning about foreign cultures is best done by spending time in a foreign office or with representatives from overseas, not from a book; nor is shadowing an IT employee the best way to learn about IT.

Table 8.1 outlines the most common leader development activities, and how HR managers rate their effectiveness.

Some companies follow these processes but press the fast-forward button for candidates to intentionally accelerate their development. These candidates are part of an acceleration pool and

- obtain assignments that offer the most intense learning and high visibility,
- spend less time in assignments,
- are given stretch assignments,
- receive more training,
- are given developmental activities designed especially for them, and
- are assigned a mentor, but
- are not guaranteed promotion.[55]

Companies that do this well are called "academy companies"—a kind of executive finishing school—known for breeding the best leaders. In Canada, these incubators are PepsiCo, IBM, General Electric, Procter & Gamble, Petro-Canada, and Manulife Financial.[56] Headhunters go to these companies to poach new leadership blood. These top companies for leaders offer many benefits, as outlined in HR Planning Notebook 8.7. Does this mean that companies risk losing leaders if they invest in them? Not necessarily, according to research by Canadian professors Jack Ito and Celeste Brotheridge, who concluded that supervisory support for career development strengthens employee's intentions to stay.[57] Generally, providing opportunities to grow and develop new skills is seen as a good retention tool.

HR Planning Notebook 8.7

ACADEMY COMPANIES

Academy companies offer these experiences to become top companies for leaders:

- Working abroad/international experiences
- 360° feedback to assess and critique leadership attributes, skills, and traits
- Assessment centre solely for leadership development of high potentials
- Mentor with admired senior leader
- Rotational job assignments

- Spending 10 percent to 24 percent of top leadership's time on talent management issues
- Organization has special/different career development process to retain high potentials
- Organization prepares specific development plans for high potentials
- Organization makes lateral moves attractive to high potentials

Source: Donlon, J.P. 2007. "Best companies for Leaders" *Chief Executive*, December 2007, 230, 58–62.

TABLE 8.1

Use and Effectiveness of Leader Development Activities

Use	% Very Effective	% Moderate or Extensive Use
Special projects within one's own job responsibilities	77	69
Special projects outside of one's own job responsibilities	46	55
Expatriate assignments	26	54
Coaching with internal coaches or mentors	48	45
Formal workshops	85	42
Coaching with external coaches or mentors	28	42
Articles/books	65	27
Tests, assessments, or other measures of skills	52	26
Computer-based learning	38	16

Notes: Leaders rated effectiveness; HR professionals rated usage; table made from bar graph.

Source: Bernthal, P. & Wellins, R. 2006. "Trends in Leader Development and Succession," *Human Resource Planning*, vol. 20, Issue 2, p. 35.

Another reason for using different methods is that the development of a senior executive may take 25 years. It is unusual to see a vice-president of a large company who is younger than 40 years old. So some companies, such as Walmart, start early, grooming the store managers under a mentoring system to take on more and more responsibility.

5. Monitor Succession Management

Some succession plans are placed on an executive's top shelf, ready to be dusted off to prepare for the annual discussion. They do not form part of a strategic plan, nor are they used to guide employee development. To measure the effectiveness of succession management, succession planners used to count the number of predicted "high-potential replacements" with the actual number of those placed in the position. However, if the needs of the business change dramatically, this may be a poor way of measuring. Others suggest measures such as:

- Increased engagement scores
- Increased positive perceptions of development opportunities
- High potentials' perceptions of the succession management process
- Higher participation in developmental activities
- Greater numbers involved in the mentoring process[58]

Nevertheless, there are internal ways to judge whether a succession management program is successful, including HR metrics, which may be viewed as lag measures such as:

- Increased average number of candidates for key positions
- Reduced average number of positions having no identified successors
- Increased percentage of managers with replacement plans
- Increased percentage of key positions filled according to plans
- Increased ratio of internal hires to external hires in key positions
- Increased retention rates of key talent
- Increased percentage of positive job evaluations after promotion
- More positive assessment of the quality of preparedness for new roles
- Increased number of bosses as talent developers[59]

The above measures need benchmarks, perhaps simply improvements over the previous year for the organization. Benchmarks will emerge for these measures. For example, one benchmarking organization suggests that effective organizations have 1.6 candidates for each key role.[60] However, one study found that the single most important driver of an effective plan was that the executive team modelled the behaviour, believed in it, and held managers accountable (in performance reviews and bonuses) for developing employees. Top-performing companies allocate 20 percent of executive bonuses to leadership development and assess them on the ability to retain this talent.[61]

One expert asked, "If this process worked perfectly and everything happened the way it was supposed to happen, what would the results look like?"[62] The answer? Employees would receive regular feedback based on the assessment process and would participate in development plans. The best result would be an organization with skilled employees prepared to contribute to the goals of the organization under changing conditions. Organizations measure their success not only by the percentage of positions filled by designated high-potential employees but also by attitude surveys of these employees, as well as exit interviews if these high potentials leave the organization. The word "success" in succession is illuminating in that studies are starting to show that corporations with strong succession management programs are higher performers measured by revenue growth, profitability, and market share.[63]

Another international study surveyed thousands of leaders, employees, and HR staff from 117 organizations in 14 countries and identified the following characteristics as critical to perceptions of succession management effectiveness:

- A timeframe for achieving planned action

- Flexible adjustments to changes in strategic plans

- The sharing of information about the nomination process performance and rankings with identified candidates

- Visible support from top management

- The involvement of line management in the identification and development of candidates.[64]

So far, we have examined succession management from the organizational perspective. We will now consider the employee's perspective.

EMPLOYEE ROLE IN SUCCESSION MANAGEMENT   A top-down, organization-directed approach to succession management assumes that employees are ready and willing to be prepared for the next generation of leadership. A top-down approach treats employees as pieces in a chess game. But employees are not pawns; their voices need to be heard.

The first consideration is that an employee's relationship with any organization is not permanent. The employee can quit, or the employer can terminate him or her. Today's new employment contract does not guarantee jobs to anyone, even to those performing competently. The former contract was built on an implied promise of a long-term, mutually satisfying relationship. However, market forces create turbulence that sometimes causes companies to restructure or fail. These changes have resulted in a change in the psychological contract that an employee has with the employer. The traditional employment contract with the organization was built on an implicit understanding that the employee would work hard, would develop additional skills provided mainly by the employer, and, in return, would be promoted on a regular basis. At a minimum, the employer would reward the loyalty and efforts of employees with job security. This contract is dead. Today's career model may be perceived as a transactional one in which benefits and contributions are exchanged for a short period.[65] The new contract, transactional in nature, lists the responsibilities and rights of each party in the employer–employee relationship, and employees want this contract stated

HR Planning Notebook 8.8

COMPARING TRADITIONAL AND EMERGING CAREER MANAGEMENT CONCEPTS

Characteristics	Traditional	Emerging
Employment contract	Implicit	Explicit
Duration	Long term	Useful term
Career responsibility	Employer	Self-directed
Career identity	Organization	Profession/occupation
Benefits	Focus on security	Focus on experience
Loyalty	To the organization	Profession, friends, family
Mindset	Inward, political	Outward, entrepreneurial
Development	Formal training	Work experiences
Career progression	Vertical	Horizontal
Employment stability	Job security	Employability
Role of manager	Control/coordination	Coach
Career goal	Corporate success	Meaningful contributions

Source: Adapted from D. Hall and J.E. Moss, "The New Protean Career Contract: Helping Organizations and Employees Adapt," *Organization Dynamics*, Winter 1988, pp. 22–37; E.F. Craig and D.T. Hall, "The New Organizational Career: Too Important to Be Left to HR?" *Reinventing HRM: Challenges and New Directions*, R.J. Burke and C.L. Cooper, eds. (New York: Routledge, 2005).

explicitly in writing. If loyalty to any organization still exists, it is to the professional organization, to a network of peers, and to certifiable credibility that confers collegiality and respect. HR Planning Notebook 9.8 contains a comparison of the two concepts of career management.

This transactional view of employer–employee relationships suggests that as organizations develop employees, they must take into consideration employee aspirations and goals. Employees will participate in management development programs more eagerly if their goals match the succession plans of the company. Employees will enthusiastically engage in self-development if they are aware of the strategic goals of a company, thus enhancing their own job security or marketability. If, for example, employees of *The Globe and Mail* knew that the company was changing from a newspaper publishing business to an international information marketing business, employees would likely undertake, on their own time and at their own expense, to study languages or marketing. Managerial preferences cannot be the sole determinant in employee development. Career counselling and discussions at performance appraisal time will help ensure that the employee's voice is heard. While organizations cannot promise lifetime employment, competition for leadership talent is so intense that high-potential employees must be given a reason to stay with an organization.

An added benefit of listening to employees is the opportunity to customize the development plan. Employees are very aware of their strengths and weaknesses and their preferred learning styles. One employee might suggest that she could learn decision making by being given a leadership role; another might prefer a seminar on decision making. Some organizations, such as Ford Financial, which has 20,000 employees around the world, provide information to employees that enables them to make their own career plans. Ford Financial has a sophisticated skill and competency-based learning program with direct links to the company's three core businesses and job requirements. Employees can determine the skills and competencies needed for any job within the organization, then undertake a self-development plan to master any of the 15 knowledge domains, 80 functional areas, and 800 separate skills.[66]

By creating a process that invites employee participation, succession managers are more likely to gain employee commitment to and ownership of the plans. We turn now to a discussion of the role of HR in this process.

MANAGING TALENT: THE HR ROLE   Most researchers and consultants will argue that the CEO should own the succession management function, and that HR should simply provide some tools for doing so. But HR are professionals and know more about succession management best practices (and pitfalls) than CEOs do. HR should own the talent management process in order to mitigate three types of risk to an organization:

1. *Vacancy risk:* Organizations that are unable to fill key vacant positions quickly with effective leaders may suffer business losses and/or an inability to move forward on strategic goals.
2. *Readiness risk:* HR must develop employees so that when opportunities arise, there are qualified and motivated personnel in place.
3. *Transition risk:* In addition to preparing employees for key roles, HR must develop programs to retain key employees, and to monitor competitors and others to be able to quickly identify external candidates.[67]

In order to manage these risks, HR promotes a culture of talent management, develops successors for all key positions, identifies gaps between current competencies and those needed in the future, and encourages development at all levels.

SUMMARY

In this chapter, we defined succession management and contrasted it with personnel planning. The five-step model of effective succession management includes these steps: (1) align succession management plans with strategy; (2) identify the skills and competencies needed to meet strategic objectives; (3) identify high-potential employees; (4) provide developmental opportunities and experiences through promotions, job rotations, special assignments and action learning, formal training and development, and mentoring and coaching; and (5) monitor succession management. The employee's role in the process must be considered. The HR function has to assume responsibility for the succession management process.

Key Terms

job rotations p. 214
mentors p. 217
promotion p. 214

replacement planning p. 202
succession management p. 200

Web Links

The Canada Public Service Agency publishes a step-by-step protocol on succession planning:
www.psagency-agencefp.gc.ca/gui/speng.asp

A succession management process guide by the province of Nova Scotia:
www.gov.ns.ca/psc/pdf/InnovationGrowth/SuccessionManagement.pdf

Required Professional Capabilities (RPCs)

The following RPCs are relevant to material covered in this chapter. The RPC number represents the CCHRA number assigned to the RPC as presented on the CCHRA website. All of the RPCs can be found in the Body of Knowledge at www.chrp.ca/rpc/body-of-knowledge.

RPC 6 Develops and implements a human resources plan that supports the organization's strategic objectives

RPC 64 Researches, analyzes, and reports on potential people issues affecting the organization

RPC 67 Develops people plans that support the organization's strategic objectives

RPC 68 Assesses the effectiveness of people and talent management plans

RPC 69 Maintains an inventory of people talent for the use of the organization

RPC 70 Develops systems and processes that link the career plans and skill sets of employees with the requirements of the organization

RPC 73 Identifies the potential source of internal and external qualified candidates

RPC 145 Determines the most effective learning and development initiatives required for organizational success

RPC 146 Develops and implements training and development activities to address current capabilities and future training needs

RPC 148 Designs career development programs that align with business needs

RPC 151 Uses a variety of methods to deliver development programs

RPC 152 Develops and implements measurement tools and processes to evaluate program effectiveness

RPC 153 Helps supervisors and managers to identify career options for employees that align with business needs

RPC 154 Provides assessment tools for career development

RPC 156 Assists employees in identifying career paths, and establishing learning plans and activities required for achieving personal and organizational success.

RPC 157 Facilitates the implementation of development work assignments

RPC 158 Monitors, documents, and reports on career development activities

Discussion Questions

1. Ganong Bros. Ltd., a manufacturer of candy and chocolates, is based in St. Stephen, New Brunswick. In 2008, for the first time in its 135-year history, an outsider succeeded a member of the Ganong family as president of the company. (Two children who work in the business were deemed "not ready.") This decision is a result of two years of succession planning by the Ganong board, which is dominated by outsiders. What are the advantages and limitations of choosing an outsider to head the company?
2. About half of all Canadian companies offer paid leave to volunteer, ranging from one day to two weeks annually. According to Mario Paron, KPMG's chief HR officer, "Employees return with a fresh perspective . . . new skills learned in a nontraditional environment . . . learning and sensitivity in dealing with people from different backgrounds, that is invaluable when they return to work."[68] Do you think that volunteering is a good management developmental tool? Why or why not?
3. This chapter has focused mainly on managers, implying that they are the key talent that needs to be managed. However, there are people who believe that the organization's most critical employees are not those who make the highest salary, but those who have the most impact on the customer: for example, the couriers at FedEx and the street sweepers at Walt Disney World. Describe why these people should be considered key talent, and what succession management plans could be used for them.
4. PepsiCo's leadership development program is well described on its website (see www.pepsico.com/Purpose/Sustainability/Talent-Sustainability.aspx). Assess the program against the steps outlined in this chapter. List the measures that you would use to evaluate the effectiveness of PepsiCo's program.

Exercise

Consider the following three scenarios:

1. Lee Ki Chung managed all the operating systems for 8 Star Manufacturing Company. Always reliable and never absent, Lee was indispensable. One day, Lee phoned to say that he had been diagnosed with cancer, had to enter treatment immediately, and did not know when he would return to the office.

2. The president of Overseas Banking Corporation, the second-largest bank in the country, had chosen as his successor the vice-president of finance. However, as the president's retirement date approached, he began to worry that this star employee could no longer handle the stress and long hours of banking. The VP was absent for extended periods as he tried to deal with his son, who was a drug addict, which in turn caused problems in his marriage.

3. Hi Tech Corp is a company created by the next generation of Bill Gates clones. They had succeeded in attracting the best and brightest to help them build a billion-dollar company to develop the ultimate software applications. On Tuesday, October 10, the entire design team announced they were quitting to start a rival company and recapture that entrepreneurial culture of the early years.

Could succession management have mitigated the impact on the organization of any of these situations? How could succession management mitigate the seriousness of the consequences?

Case 1   THE PEOPLE DEVELOPMENT FRAMEWORK AT FORD OF CANADA

The North American automotive industry has been facing significant challenges in recent years as the "Big Three" restructure their operations to respond to increased foreign competition, difficult economic conditions, and shifting demand as consumers migrate toward more fuel-efficient vehicles. In light of these dynamic business conditions, Ford of Canada relies heavily on organization and personnel planning processes and tools to ensure that the organization structure, internal selection practices, and succession management systems are aligned to support the future needs of the firm and the needs of its employees. With a strategic focus on maintaining a "People Development Framework," succession planning is a key element of the organization and personnel planning function.

The HR team reviews four major areas of focus in order to make better decisions about the organization's future direction for personnel requirements. In addition to assessing the impact of external factors such as world events, the changing marketplace, and workforce demographics, team members regularly review the operational plans in place so that functional HR objectives and action plans are properly developed and aligned to meet the long-term goals of the business. Ongoing reviews of the organization structures are conducted to ensure that the delivery of the organization's business priorities is achieved in an efficient, flexible, and affordable manner by assessing factors such as the size of the organization, the percentage of resources deployed at each level and function, and the attraction and retention potential of the leadership level and salary grade system. Lastly and most importantly, the "people equation" is evaluated on an ongoing basis to ensure that the organization has the right people in the right positions at the right time to help the organization achieve success.

Personnel development committees (PDCs) play a central role within Ford of Canada to identify and match employee capabilities to key positions to ensure appropriate bench strength is in place. Committees exist for three broad levels of the organization including senior executive, business unit management, and line management, and PDC composition includes managers from all functional business areas to ensure cross-functional opportunities can be efficiently explored and utilized for employee development. In conjunction with department managers, PDC members are charged with the responsibility of identifying employees who demonstrate outstanding leadership abilities, strong and continual learning, and superior job performance, and then matching employees to key positions.

PDCs assess candidate bench strength for particular key positions or job families using a visual aid called a "T" chart. Employees immediately qualified are plotted on the horizontal section of the "T" while employees with future potential who require further development are identified in rank order in the vertical region of the tool. Using a graphic aid such as a "T" chart allows review committees and managers to see and compare bench depth across key positions; it further assists in the communication process as succession planning information moves vertically to other PDCs as vacancies are being filled or when bench strength is being assessed.

An integral component of the People Development Framework is the engagement and participation of the individual employee in his or her own professional development and career management. With consultation from their immediate supervisors, employees are engaged in the process through the completion of a Leadership Development Employee Profile (LDEP) and an Individual Development Plan (IDP) on an annual basis. The LDEP acts as an internal résumé to capture individual employee information for PDC or hiring manager review that includes current position details, previous Ford position history, the employee's viewpoint on Ford, and non-Ford key accomplishments, as well as preferred developmental assignments.

The IDP reinforces the need for each employee to invest in his or her own professional development and provides an opportunity for career planning activities to further develop strengths and areas of improvement in alignment with career goals and business needs. Plans are developed between an employee and supervisor that identify developmental actions that improve current assignment performance and also position the individual for their desired future assignments. While partnership with the supervisor is necessary for establishing the content and implementation timing of an IDP, it is inherently critical that employees take personal ownership of the formation and maintenance of their own career plans for this tool to be successful.

As Ford of Canada business units strive to "do more with less" in a manner that delivers an efficient, profitable, and competitive position, an assessment of key position requirements and employee leadership and technical competencies is critical to ensure that employee developmental needs and placements support the delivery of the desired business outcomes. The process tools and governance structure under the People Development Framework serves to reinforce the inherent linkage and shared responsibility between employee, manager, and PDCs in the success of the organization and of individual employees.

Source: Case prepared by Ron Derhodge, Human Resources Manager, Parts Distribution Centre, Ford Motor Company of Canada, Limited.

Question

Analyze the effectiveness of Ford's succession management program. Include in your report the strengths and weaknesses of the model and suggestions for increasing its effectiveness.

Case 2 EXECUTIVE SUCCESSION MANAGEMENT PROGRAM AT EMEND MANAGEMENT CONSULTING INC.

When company executives and boards need advisory services on succession, they sometimes seek external support, from consulting firms such as EMEND. Ellie Maggio, CEO and Managing Director of EMEND, describes the *necessary* transformed interest of Boards and executives in succession planning:

> *Over the past decade, succession plans have really become important due to CEO departures leaving organizations scrambling. Moreover, heightened board governance and regulatory compliance have raised the bar on this important function. If succession plans are not implemented, shareholders may view their investment at risk.*

At EMEND, when working with boards, a six-step process is used in developing executive succession management programs:

1. Plan

- Determine or clarify CEO and board expectations of the succession management process
- Ensure top-level responsibility/accountability
- Ensure plan is business oriented, pragmatic, and endorsed at the highest levels

2. Assess

- Review executive contracts for content related to succession plans and how they may relate to development plans, performance plans, compensation plans, termination, retirement, organization departure, and transition
- Review existing replacement plans, performance reviews, talent/high potential/development plans

3. Strategize

- Engage executives in the development of the new/refined program
- Ensure clear linkages to other programs related to risk management, talent management, performance management, and compensation programs
- Ensure the succession management method and process is reflective of stakeholder requirements

4. Develop

- Create talent review criteria/competency models for executive and critical jobs
- Develop talent review tool(s) linked to the leadership development program, performance management process, and executive compensation
- Develop talent review process steps and timeline for implementation

5. Implement

- Conduct talent reviews (e.g., 180°/360° assessments)
- Analyze talent reviews and link findings to criteria/competency models
- Facilitate the process by using an electronic "talent skills inventory"
- Communicate succession plans and ensure internal and external transparency
- Educate/train decision makers

6. Track and Measure

- Develop metrics to measure success of the new program. Metrics may include but are not limited to:
    i. Quality/readiness of potential leaders
    ii. Number of vacancies
    iii. Success rate of new executives
    iv. Executive assessment of new plan
    v. Identification of potential leaders
    vi. Response and completion rate of plans
    vii. Ratings from employee satisfaction surveys
- Track success and make enhancements as required

Source: Correspondence with Ellie Maggio, CEO and Managing Director, EMEND Management, June 2011.

Questions

1. What steps might you include or remove from this process?
2. What additional techniques might be used to assess talent?
3. How would this process apply to non-executive succession planning?

ENDNOTES

1. Ruiz, G. "Edwards Lifesciences: Optimas Award Winner for Competitive Advantage," www.workforce.com, retrieved on October 13, 2008.

2. Conlon, R. Smith, R.V. 2010. "The Role of the Board and the CEO in Ensuring Business Continuity." *Financial Executive*, Vol. 26, No. 9: 52–55.

3. Paradise, A. 2010 "Many Barriers Inhibit Success of Succession Planning." *T+D*, Vol. 64, No. 6: 60–61.

4. McLaughlin, V. Mott. C. 2010 "Leadership Brand Equity: HR's Role in Driving Economic Value." *Strategic HR Review*, Vol. 9, No. 4: 13–19.

5. Drucker, P. 1998. "Management's New Paradigms." *Forbes*, October 5: 152–177.

6. "Succession Management in C-Suite Is Lagging: A Korn Ferry Study Finds That the Majority of Companies Do Not Have a C Suite Succession Plan in Place." *T+D*, Vol. 64, No. 1 (2010): 23.

7. Behn, B.K., Dawley, D.D., Riley, R., and Yang, Y. 2006. "Deaths of CEOs: Are Delays in Naming Successors and Insider/Outsider Succession Associated with Subsequent Firm Performance?" *Journal of Managerial Issues*, Vol. 18, No. 1: 32–45.

8. St. Onge, S. 2007. "Planning Ahead." *CA Magazine*, Vol. 140, No. 1 (January/February): 51–52.

9. Anonymous. 2008. "Top Trends for 2008: Leadership Talent and Metrics Will Be Key." *HR Focus*, Vol. 85, No. 1: 8.

10. Anonymous. 2008. SHRM Workplace Forecast. www.shrm.org, retrieved on October 5, 2008.

11. Immen, W. 2011. "Getting a Jump on the Fast Track." *The Globe and Mail*, June 25, 2011, p. B18.

12. Leibman, M., R. Bruer, and B.R. Maki. 1996. "Succession Management: The Next Generation of Succession Planning." *Human Resources Planning*, Vol. 19, No. 3: 16–29.

13. Byham, W.C. 2002. "A New Look at Succession Management." *Ivey Business Journal*, Vol. 66, No. 5 (May/June): 10–12.

14. Corporate Leadership Council, 2003. *Hallmarks of Leadership Success: Strategies for Improving Leadership Quality and Executive Readiness*. New York: Corporate Executive Board.

15. Immen, W. 2005. "Rising Stars Get a Chance to Shine." *The Globe and Mail*, November 16, pp. C1, C3.

16. Fulmer, R.M. 1997. "The Evolving Paradigm of Leadership Development." *Organizational Dynamics*, Spring: 59–72.

17. Boudreau, J.W., and P.M. Ramstead 2005. "Talentship, Talent Segmentation, and Sustainability: A New HR Decision-Science Paradigm for a New Strategy Definition." *Human Resource Management*, Vol. 44, No. 2 (Summer): 129–136.

18. Bernthal, P., and R. Wellins. 2006. "Trends in Leader Development and Succession." *Human Resource Planning*, Vol. 29, No. 2 (2006): 31–40.

19. Hoskisson, R.E., M.A. Hitt, and R.D. Ireland. 2004. *Competing for Advantage*. Mason, OH: Thomson South-Western.

20. Conlon, R. Smith, R.V. 2010. "The Role of the Board and the CEO in Ensuring Business Continuity." *Financial Executive*, Vol. 26, No. 9: 52–54.

21. Eichlinger, B., and D. Ulrich. 1996. "Are You Future Agile?" *Human Resource Planning*, Vol. 11, No. 2: 30–41.

22. Lawler, E.E. III. 1994. "From Job-Based to Competency-Based Organizations." *Journal of Organizational Behaviour*, Vol. 15: 3–15.

23. Catano, V.M., S.F. Cronshaw, W.H. Wiesner, R.D. Hackett, and L.L. Methot. 2010. *Recruitment and Selection in Canada*. 4th ed. Toronto: ITP Nelson.

24. Catano et al., 2010.

25. Kessler, G.C. 2002. "Why the Leadership Bench Never Gets Deeper: Ten Insights About Executive Talent Development." *Human Resources Planning*, Vol. 25, No. 1: 32–45.

26. Joinson, C. 1998. "Developing a Strong Bench." *HRM Magazine*, January: 92–96.

27. Lenz, S.S., and S. Wacker. 1997. "Career Development in an Uncertain World." Paper presented at the Human Resource Planning Society Symposium, Ithaca, New York.

28. Gore, N. 2000. "Managing Talent Replaces Static Charts in a New Era of Succession Planning." *Canadian HR Reporter*, Vol. 13, No. 15 (September 11): 12.

29. McLaughlin, B., and Mott, C. 2010. "Leadership Brand Equity: HR Leaders' Role in Driving Economic Value." *Strategic HR Review*, Vol. 9, No. 4, pp. 13–19.

30. Immen, 2005.

31. Guptil, D. 2003. "HR Leaders Talk." *Canadian HR Reporter*, February 10: 16.

32. Yancey, G.B. 2001. "Succession Planning Creates Quality Leadership." *Credit Union Executive Journal*, Vol. 41, No. 6 (November/December): 24–27.

33. Fulmer, R., S. Stumpf, and J. Bleak. 2009. "The Strategic Development of High Potential Leaders." *Strategy and Leadership*, Vol. 37, No. 3 (2009): 17–22.

34. Newell, E. 2001. "CEOs Talk." *Canadian HR Reporter*, Vol. 14, No. 17 (October 8).

35. Kessler, 2002: 34.

36. Walter, G. 1996. "Corporate Practices in Management Development." *Conference Board*, Report No. 1158-96-RR. New York: Conference Board Inc., 89.

37. Church, E. 1998. "New-Style CEOs Follow Zig-Zag Path." *The Globe and Mail*, February 20, p. B23.

38. Gagne, C. 2004. "Get Good Help." *Canadian Business*, Vol. 77, No. 14/15: 71–72.

39. Black, B. 2002. "CEOs Talk." *Canadian HR Reporter*, October 7: 17.

40. Campion, M.A., L. Cheraskin, and M.J. Stevens. 1994. "Career-Related Antecedents and Outcomes of Job Rotation." *Academy of Management Journal*, Vol. 37, No. 6 (December): 1518–1525.

41. Horwitt, L. 1997. "It's Your Career: Manage It." *Network World*. March 17: 39–43.

42. Francis, K. 2001. "CEO's Talk." *Canadian HR Reporter*, Vol. 14, No. 11 (June 4): 17.

43. Horwitt, 1997.

44. Chereskin, L., and M.A. Campion. 1996. "Study Clarifies Job Rotation Benefits." *Personnel Journal*, November: 31–38.

45. Dahl, H.L. 1997. "Human Resource Cost and Benefit Analysis: New Power for Human Resource Approaches." *Human Resource Planning*, Vol. 11, No. 2: 69–78.

46. Walter, 1996.

47. For a fuller discussion of these methods, see Saks, Alan M., and Robert R. Haccoun. 2010. *Performance Management Through Training and Development*, 5th ed. Toronto: Nelson.

48. Belcourt, M., and A.M. Saks. 1998. "Benchmarking Best Training Practices." *Human Resource Professional*, December 1997/January 1998: 33–41.

49. Haynes, R.K., and R. Ghosh. 2008. "Mentoring and Succession Management: An Evaluative Approach to the Strategic Collaboration Model." *Review of Business*, Vol. 28, No. 2 (Winter 2008): 3–7.

50. Byham, 2002.

51. Butyn, S. 2003. "Mentoring Your Way to Improved Retention." *Canadian HR Reporter*, January 27: 13.

52. Hewitt Associates Inc. 2005. "How the Top 20 Companies Grow Great Leaders." *Research Highlights*. Toronto: Hewitt Associates.

53. Haynes and Ghosh, 2008: 3.

54. Chatman, J. O'Reilly, C., and V. Chang. 2005. "Cisco Systems: Developing a Human Capital Strategy." *California Management Review*, Vol. 47, No. 2 (Winter 2005): 137–167.

55. Busine, M., and B. Watt. 2005. "Succession Management: Trends and Practices." *Asia Pacific Journal of Human Resources*, Vol. 43, No. 2: 225–237.

56. Pitts, G. 2005. "Need a Leader: Just Look for a GE Graduate." *The Globe and Mail*, July 11, p. B11.

57. Ito, J., and C.M. Brotheridge. 2005. "Does Supporting Employees' Career Adaptability Lead to Commitment, Turnover or Both?" *Human Resource Management*, Vol. 44, No. 1 (Spring): 5–19.

58. Bernthal and Wellins, 2006.

59. Corporate Leadership Council, 2003; Fulmer, R.M. 2005. "Keys to Best Practice Succession Management." *Human Resources*, October 14, 2005: 17–18.

60. Anonymous. 2010. "2010 Benchmarks: Key Measures to Monitor." *HR Focus*, Vol. 87, No. 1: 1, 13–15.

61. Hewitt Associates Inc., 2005.

62. Borwick, C. 1993. "Eight Ways to Assess Succession Plans." *HRM Magazine*, Vol. 38, No. 4: 109–114.

63. Willins, R., and W. Byham. 2001. "The Leadership Gap." *Training*, Vol. 38, No. 5 (March): 98–106.

64. Bernthal, A., and R.S. Wellins. 2003. *The Leadership Forecast: A Benchmarking Study*. Pittsburgh, PA: Developmental Dimensions International.

65. Hall, D., and J.E. Moss. 1988. "The New Protean Career Contract: Helping Organizations and Employees Adapt." *Organization Dynamics*, Winter: 22–37.

66. Greengard, S. 2001. "Make Smarter Business Decisions: Know What Employees Can Do." *Workforce*, Vol. 80, No. 11 (November): 42–46.

67. Lockwood, N. "Talent Management: Driver for Organization Success." *HR Magazine*, Vol. 51, No. 6 (June 2006): 1–12.

68. Lane, P. "Time Off to Save the World." *National Post*, July 26, 2008.

CHAPTER 9

Information Technology for HR Planning

This chapter was adapted from a chapter written by Victor Y. Haines III.

CHAPTER LEARNING OUTCOMES

After reading this chapter, you should be able to:

- Describe the benefits of information technology (IT) solutions for human resource planning (HRP).
- Explain how different IT solutions can be leveraged to improve HR planning.
- Identify specific IT applications for HR planning.
- Apply the process of IT acquisition and implementation.
- Project into the future a number of new IT applications for HR planning.
- Ensure system and data security.

SOFTWARE FOR HR PLANNING

Some observers are skeptical that software products by themselves will aid a company's human resources planning efforts. But as organizations seek to expand their talent management programs to include mid-level leaders and not just top executives, computerized systems with databases are crucial, says Jim Holincheck, an analyst at the research firm Gartner.

Succession-planning software typically allows companies to do such things as assess the risk that various leaders may leave the company, list possible replacements for managers, and document the strengths and credentials of up-and-coming employees. Besides managing succession and career development plans for more employees, software products in this field have other benefits, advocates say. These include more-up-to-date information than paper-based plans done once a year and an improved ability to search for candidates from within a company.

Auto parts and services chain Pep Boys is convinced it made a sound investment when it began using software from SuccessFactors about a year ago, says Liviu Dedes, the firm's director for training and organizational development. The software was part of a broader succession-management overhaul, which included a set of 84 round-table discussions throughout the country on employees' potential. According to Dedes, SuccessFactors' software helped the company overcome problems it discovered when it reorganized its business in 2004. The chain, with some 20,000 employees and nearly 600 stores throughout the United States and in Puerto Rico, wanted to double the number of area directors to 84 in a period of two months. It was a "very painful" event, thanks to internal and external talent pools that were "shallow," Dedes recalls. For one thing, he says, Pep Boys' paper-based system made it hard to notice quality candidates even in the neighbouring areas. The company also had inconsistent measures of people's potential. SuccessFactors' software, which Pep Boys accesses over the web, has helped the company standardize its employee reviews around a set of competencies and also made it much easier to see the aspirations and abilities of some 2,000 managers throughout the company, Dedes says. Far from being a bust, human resources planning software served as a catalyst for the company to reflect on and improve its approach to succession management, Dedes says: "It was a great opportunity to rethink ourselves and revise the process we were using."[1]

Source: Adapted from Frauenheim, E. 2006. "Software Products Aim to Streamline Succession Planning." *Workforce Management Online*, www.workforce.com, January.

IT AND HRM

Information technology (IT)
All of the hardware and software, including networking and communication technologies

In this age of electronic human resources management (eHR), there is a pressing need to better leverage technology for planning purposes. **Information technology (IT)** can help project correct demand and supply levels on the basis of realistic scenarios. Because of its powerful storage and retrieval capabilities, IT can support HR planning and career development plans. However, before we get into such planning capabilities, let's have a look at the bigger picture and explore how IT is reshaping HRM.

The HR department has always been the custodian of employee information. All those forms that are completed by employees giving information about their education, training, job experience are stored as data. This data can be used to locate employees for promotions or transfers, and help managers plan for labour shortages or surpluses. Obviously, using technology to mine this data is faster, cheaper and more effective than any paper-based system. According to industry analysts, "HR without technology is becoming an unthinkable proposition."[2] The use of IT for HRM has increased at a fast pace over the last couple of decades. As a result, HR professionals have been able to handle a greater workload and achieve operational and strategic efficiency. Compared to paper-based systems, IT provides better data storage, information retrieval, and tools for analysis— capabilities that help alleviate the burden of transactional activities. This allows more time and resources to be dedicated to the more strategic roles of business partner and change agent.[3] Workforce analysis capabilities and related dashboards and scorecards, for instance, help human resources managers collect and interpret data to measure the success of their efforts (a topic more thoroughly covered in Chapter 14).[4]

A recent study found that IT makes a difference to HR.[5] First, the study found that the five applications that received the highest levels of IT support were (1) storing important data such as wages, vacation, and sick time; (2) transferring employee data between HR and outside payroll systems; (3) generating organizational charts; (4) posting jobs openings within the organization; and (5) tracking labour costs. The five HR applications that received the lowest levels of IT support were (1) providing employees with self-assessment and career development guidance; (2) providing employees with ergonomics assessment assistance; (3) measuring the needs and results of diversity initiatives; (4) letting employees make changes to their own benefits records; and (5) online service delivery of employee assistance programs. More to the point, the results show that IT usage is significantly associated with HR's greater involvement in supporting the successful implementation of business strategy and delivering tangible results. IT usage is also associated with greater HR involvement in the strategic roles of business partner and change agent, and with more positive assessments of the technical and strategic effectiveness of the HR function. Taken together, these findings suggest that IT can indeed help HR professionals reduce the burden of administrative transactional tasks, including the processing of hundreds of forms. Smart use of technology allows HR professionals to dedicate themselves to being strategists and achieving results instead of being bogged down with "administrivia." As a result of the shift to more strategic roles, prompted in part by technology, HR professionals, more now than ever before, need to be experts in their area of specialization (i.e., functional HR delivery) and possess knowledge of the business.[6]

Within HR, some basic requirements are now being met with IT. Employee benefits and payroll management are typically automated in one way or another. These are basic transactional activities that have a long history of IT use. Such transactional activities can also be outsourced to an outside company. More strategic and analytic operations, however, are only just starting to benefit fully from the capabilities of automation. In the area of employee recruitment, for instance, the use of web-based job sites, portals, and kiosks to attract job applicants is ever increasing. In the area of performance management, several software solutions are now available to streamline the multisource (or 360°) feedback process. These more strategic and analytic operations are rarely outsourced. This would explain why, as HR outsourcing continues to grow, most organizations resort to selective outsourcing.

HR Planning Notebook 9.1

PROPERTIES OF ADVANCED INFORMATION TECHNOLOGIES

- Basic characteristics:
  - o Better data storage capacity
  - o Improved transmission capacity
  - o Higher levels of processing capacity
- Communication properties:
  - o To communicate more easily and less expensively across time and geographic location
  - o To communicate more rapidly and with greater precision to targeted groups
  - o To record and index more reliably and inexpensively the content and nature of communication events
  - o To more selectively control access and participation in a communication event or network

- Decision-aiding ability:
  - o To store and retrieve large amounts of information more quickly and inexpensively
  - o To more rapidly and selectively access information created outside the organization
  - o To more rapidly and accurately combine and reconfigure information as to create new information
  - o To more compactly store and quickly use the judgment and decision models developed in the minds of experts, or in the mind of the decision maker, and store as expert systems or decision models
  - o To more reliably and inexpensively record and retrieve information about content and nature of organizational transactions

Advanced information technologies share a number of properties, which are summarized in HR Planning Notebook 9.1.[7] For human resources planning, the decision-aiding properties are clearly the most valuable. Human resources planning involves juggling large amounts of information. Relevant data needs to be accessed in a timely manner to inform decision making. This is where IT can be of greatest value for HR planning.

NEW SERVICE DELIVERY MODELS

Gaining access to data in a timely manner is a constant challenge. The good news is that computer capacity is increasing at a steady pace; computers have doubled in capacity every 24 months since 1970, and there is no reason to expect a slowdown in the near future. HR is leveraging this computer capacity to improve service delivery and, by doing so, is transforming itself.[8]

HR Planning Today   9.1

Apps for HR

Increasing usage of mobile technology has created an "apps" culture for some organizations. In some instances HR departments are offering apps for HR, which include obtaining and sharing legal information and benefits. Mobile applications are also being adopted for other HR functions such as recruiting, scheduling work and e-learning.

Source: Anonymous, "Growing Use of Apps Expanding Operations of HR Professionals," *HR Focus*, Vol. 87, No. 11 (November 2010): 4–5; B. Roberts, "Mobile Workforce Management?" *HR Magazine*, Vol. 56, No. 3: 67–30.

Web-Based HR

Web-based HR allows service delivery that pushes employees and managers into making transactions. Self-service is an important web-based service delivery model. Another is web-based HR service centres that allow employees easy access to their data (e.g., job postings, personal data, access to learning solutions) through online access to information, resulting in quicker responses from experts. Hence, rather than outsource, HR may consolidate its services into an internal HR service centre and operate the centre with its own HR practitioners.

Web-based HR processes and practices are also gaining momentum. E-recruiting and **e-learning** are highly visible applications; in addition, some organizations are now conducting pre-employment testing on the Internet. For an example of such web-based capabilities involving applicant tracking and hiring management, you might want to try the demo available at www.hr-soft.com.

E-learning
The process of learning contents distributed in digital format via computers over the Internet or other network

Enterprise Portals

Enterprise portals are but one of many IT tools that allow efficient access to relevant content and applications. HR portals are sophisticated websites that are designed to communicate a range of human resources information and a variety of organizational resources. They provide a single site for employees to access HR services. They are, in a sense, "HR's front door"[9] as they offer a web-based access point to all information sources, tools, and systems needed to consume HR services effectively. Employees can access the portal to share information and collaborate more effectively with customers, partners, and suppliers using a secure infrastructure. The portal might also allow employees to sign up for direct deposit or view their time cards. Employees may also gain access to a knowledge repository and e-HR functions.

Enterprise portals
Knowledge communities that allow employees from a single or multiple companies to access and benefit from specialized knowledge associated with tasks

Self-Service

Self-service is based on the principle that data is most effectively captured at source. Under this principle, self-service allows employees and managers to communicate with and affect databases. For example, employees might input and edit personal information such as their address, emergency contact, and so on. Employees and managers might also be authorized to apply for travel reimbursement and enroll for benefits or training classes. In some organizations, employees can use self-service to view job openings within the company, create application materials, apply for a position, and check the status of pending applications. Employees might also use self-service applications to model retirement options or enroll in benefits programs. Managers may use self-service to access authorized information about the employees they supervise. They may also use self-service to complete a requisition to fill an open position. Managers might further use the system to compile employee absenteeism and turnover data, to forecast HR demand, or to manage employees from recruitment to the annual employee review and compensation planning. This is how employee self-service (ESS) and manager self-service (MSS) applications are changing service delivery models as HR service consumers no longer need to interact directly with HR service providers.

Self-Service
A technology platform that enables employees and managers to access and modify their data via a web browser from a desktop or centralized kiosk

IT FOR HR PLANNING

IT can be leveraged to better manage several activities involved in HR planning. For instance, available information on employees' participation in training, their competencies, and their performance levels may help determine the most competent employee for a position. Easy access to data may also help management identify areas where available talent is lacking for adequate succession. Moreover, technology can be leveraged to gauge client satisfaction with the service levels provided by the HRM department, and electronic surveys are increasingly used to conduct climate or engagement surveys. As a result, IT can support the different steps of the strategic HR planning process.

Besides providing better information processing and decision-making models, some technology applications are highly responsive to the particular requirements of HR planning. Here we review workforce analytics, workforce management and scheduling, forensic reporting, skills inventories, replacement charts, and succession management applications.

Workforce Analytics

Business intelligence

The applications and technologies for gathering, storing, analyzing, and providing access to data to help users make better business decisions

Workforce analytics applications address the challenge of getting **business intelligence** for strategic decision making. The best applications provide on-demand access to workforce performance, dashboards that place information at the manager's fingertips, enabling root-cause analysis, comparisons, and trending. Such workforce analytics applications organize information and present key data in ways that are simple to understand.

Having human resources data is valuable, but having the ability to sift quickly through data is even more so. Workforce analytics applications help do some of the analysis that is needed for strategic HR planning. Depending on the organization's needs, workforce analytics solutions might provide a breakdown of employees by age or turnover rates across multiple areas of the business. The key to effective workforce analytics applications is their ability to provide the right information, in the right form, at the right time. The types of data required for HR planning are outlined in HR Planning Today 9.2.

Within the realm of analytics, dashboards contain the key metrics of strategy all in one place. They are used to visualize metrics, charts, and data. HR dashboards contain the employee information required to make critical business decisions. They allow companies to view, drill down, and analyze workforce performance data across geographies, business units, and other organizational

HR Planning Today 9.2

Information Needs for HR Planning

In order to determine whether an organization will have suitably trained and prepared employees in place for future job openings, the employer needs to collect the following types of information: employee name, contact numbers, current position and compensation, education, training, languages spoken, experience by years, position levels, performance appraisals, and career interests.

entities. Examples of metrics include the cost of the HR function per employee; or the cost/benefit of an employee training program. Some dashboards monitor enterprise goal alignment and help identify performance deficiencies that require more attention. Scorecards illustrate performance on key metrics over time. A scorecard application, for instance, might track revenue per employee, cost of hire, or voluntary separation by length of service.

Workforce Management and Scheduling

The logistics of workforce management and scheduling are often quite complex. Workforce scheduling and optimization software provides applications for deploying employees most effectively. In a contact centre, for example, the planning process might involve accurately forecasting call volumes, handle times, and overhead to determine staffing and scheduling requirements. Once these forecasts are available, the software application could quickly create schedules that take into account work rules, call volumes, agent preferences, and training/meeting times. Then managers could make scheduling adjustments as call volumes and other variables change. As is reported in HR Planning Today 9.3, such workforce management software solutions have indeed come a long way.

Forensic Reporting

Canadians report experiencing high levels of stress, and the first signs of burnout may be higher levels of absenteeism or turnover or accidents. Grouped together, along with accidents and reduced vacation requests, these factors might offer an early signal of decreases in productivity. If the stress continues, the organization may face higher workers' compensation rates, higher recruitment and selection costs, and increases in the demand for overtime. The need to schedule the remaining workforce will become increasingly important.[10]

HR Planning Today 9.3

Workforce Management Has Come a Long Way

The field of workforce management technology has come a long way. Years ago, applications focused on the administrative task of tracking workers' hours to prevent underpayment or overpayment. The products now include sophisticated planning and scheduling tools. The idea is to create optimal master schedules that match the peaks and valleys of staffing needs, taking into account employee performance, employee preferences, and labour rules, such as limits to minors' working hours.

A key to the progress on workforce management software is recent computing advances, according to the Bernstein report. "As a result, it is possible to generate optimal schedules using both constraints and preferences in an efficient time frame," the report says. "For example, a 10-employee schedule might be generated in 1 to 3 seconds, a 20-employee schedule in 1 to 5 minutes and a 500-employee schedule in 15 to 60 minutes."

Source: E. Frauenheim, "Scheduling Software Sees Surge in Demand," *Workforce Management*, Vol. 85, No. 19 (2006): 36.

Skills Inventories

Skills inventories represent a valuable source of information for assessing the internal supply of talent (see Chapter 7). IT applications that support the development of skills inventories typically contain a personal record or skills profile of each member of the workforce. Included in the inventory are items such as employee name, seniority, classification, part- or full-time work status, work history and record of jobs held in the organization, education, training, skill competencies, areas of expertise, talents, history of performance appraisals, and future jobs desired by or recommended for the individual, as well as hobbies and interests that may be useful for organizational planning. This information can (and should) be stored in a database that allows easy search and retrieval, enabling managers to identify and fill knowledge voids.

An automated skills inventory provides a quick and easy way to collect skills information. Web-based skills inventories are designed to help develop a listing of specific skill sets as employees complete their online individual assessment. Such automated skills inventories allow managers to quickly identify employees with critical competencies and ensure that training is connected to strategic business needs. They help match up the right set of workers for a project. They help track skills with the aim of getting the right talent at the right time, a critical capability in today's knowledge economy. When used in such a way, automated skills inventories become an integral part of IT enhanced competence management.

Replacement Charts

Replacement planning designates the process of finding replacement employees for key managerial positions. Replacement charts are often used to support this process. These include predicted departure dates of the incumbents, along with a shortlist of possible successors. Replacement charts include employee performance appraisal data and information about how ready possible successors are to fill those key managerial positions. Some IT applications ease the process of replacement planning by providing timely and user-friendly access to replacement charts.

Replacement planning software solutions generally allow decision makers to determine which positions have sufficient "bench strength" and which positions need further planning. In the area of talent management, Authoria offers online navigation of divisional and corporate-wide organizational charts, allowing the manager to track incumbents and candidates and obtain specific information from the résumé, or historical pay or performance details (www.authoria.com). Such products are most useful for large organizations where the volume of data is sufficient to require software support for the process.

Succession Management

The process of succession management is information-intensive requiring information on competencies, talent pools, developmental plans, performance assessments from different sources, and developmental opportunities. IT solutions can help structure and manage this information, making succession planning more effective and widespread to include mid-level leaders and not just top executives.

HR Planning Today 9.4

Cisco's Pathfinder Solution

In September 2001, Cisco took a first step to implement its "build" strategy: it created the Pathfinder software application that allowed managers to post openings for jobs within high-growth areas. Pathfinder's corresponding online database, I-Profiler, allowed employees to voluntarily enter their résumés for consideration. The profiles captured employees' work and educational experience, skills, and technical qualifications, and detailed their career aspirations for development discussions with their managers. Line managers had access to each of their employees' profiles to better assess existing skills on their teams. Pathfinder was the first tool designed specifically to advertise job openings internally.

Source: J. Chatman, C. O'Reilly, and V. Chang, "Cisco Systems: Developing a Human Capital Strategy," *California Management Review*, 47, 2 (2005), p. 153.

There are, for example, several tools available to conduct multiple-source or 360° feedback performance assessments. Other succession management IT solutions, such as Nardoni Strategic Solutions, include more functionalities. The company's Succession Pulse™ allows users to analyze comprehensive data on employees, positions, and developmental activities (www.nardoni.com). It will locate and compare successors based on competency search and comparison.

One meaningful activity involved in succession management involves helping individuals realize their career plans within the organization. This may be done by advertising internal opportunities for continuous learning and growth. The Pathfinder software application implemented at Cisco Systems, for example, was an important component of its new "build" talent strategy (see HR Planning Today 9.4).

Another approach to helping individuals realize their career plans is to allow employees to assess their own skills as a basis for career planning and training. The reporting functions of some software solutions allow employees to record and track their competencies and to perform comparative analysis against their job position as well as other positions in the organization. They may also include a skills dictionary containing skills data for all positions.

DIFFERENT SOLUTIONS FOR DIFFERENT NEEDS

There is an amazing diversity of software solutions for HRM and HR planning. Organizations may favour a comprehensive human resource information system (HRIS) or a specialty product focused on a single area, such as applicant tracking. Within these two broad categories, the marketplace offers a range from low-cost, to mid-market, to costly high-end systems. In this section, we review these options, and also enterprise solutions such as those offered by SAP or PeopleSoft.

HRIS

The **human resources information system (HRIS)** offers an integral solution for the HR department. It includes the software, hardware, support functions, and system policies and procedures used to gather, store, and report human resources data. The system collects, stores, maintains data, and retrieves information about employees and their jobs.

Human resources information system (HRIS)

A comprehensive across-the-board software system for HRM that includes subsystems or modules

The HRIS provides access to a large database through a variety of modules that automate diverse functions. As such, the HRIS is an integrated solution that includes several subsystems or modules such as recruitment and selection, time and attendance management, payroll, training and development, pension administration, and so on. The HRIS thereby covers most if not all of the important subsystems of HRM. It is the primary transaction processor, editor, record-keeper, and functional application system that lies at the heart of all computerized HR management work.

Specialty Products

Specialty products

Software solutions for specific/specialized applications that may or may not interface with the main database

Numerous **specialty products** are available that enable the automation of discrete tasks and responsibilities. They have the ability to address specific needs as they are focused on a single area of HRM. They thereby offer the advantage of going in-depth into a particular business activity.

Meade estimates that such specialty products or functional applications number between 1,500 to 2,000.[11] They include compensation planning solutions that allow managers to compare various salary recommendations or scenarios relative to budget. The time and attendance software offered by Kronos can track days, hours, overtime, and vacation balances (www.kronos.com). Other applications assist in managing training schedules and budgets. A company named SIPC, for example, developed a software system that is specialized in tracking training expenses (www.sipc.qc.ca). Given the legislation in Quebec regarding training and development, the SIPC software solution was designed to help managers prepare the reports relative to employer investments in employee training and development.

Such specialty products may be easily acquired off-the-shelf by smaller companies as less costly solutions for addressing specific challenges. They are also likely to interface with a company's more comprehensive HRIS or ERP base system.

Enterprise Solutions

Enterprise resource planning (ERP)

Commercial software systems that automate and integrate many or most of a firm's business processes

Enterprise resource planning (ERP) solutions are based on software that integrates data from diverse applications into a common database. They cover the fullest range of organizational activities and processes, including finance, logistics, production, accounting, and HRM. ERP computer systems are used by large corporations around the world, adopted with the aim of achieving substantial cost savings and improved access to "tried and tested" solutions, new releases, and an opportunity to update procedures and align them with the so-called "best practices."

SAP, the world's third-largest independent software provider with more than 76,000 customers in more than 120 countries around the world, offers an ERP that includes four functional areas: financials, human capital management, operations, and corporate services (www.sap.com). Human capital management, the HR part of SAP's ERP solution, is described in HR Planning Today 9.5.

Relational database

A database that can share information across multiple tables or files, which allows the same information to exist in multiple files simultaneously

The ERP approach promotes the use of a single, shared **relational database** for critical information across the organization. This fosters the enforcement of consistent processes and procedures throughout the organization and ensures that administrative units can easily share information and communicate with one another. For HR, the enterprise-wide solution provides a platform for a better integration of HR and finance in the management of payroll.[12] When HR finds it difficult to obtain budget approval for investments in an HRIS solution, the

HR Planning Today 9.5

SAP's Human Capital Management

The SAP ERP Human Capital Management (SAP ERP HCM) solution is a complete and integrated human capital management solution that delivers unmatched global capability. SAP ERP HCM gives organizations in all industries worldwide the tools needed to manage their most important asset: people. The solution equips executives, HR professionals, and line managers to hire the best talent, and train and cultivate the skills of their workforce.

Using one unified software suite for all talent management processes, an organization can more readily understand where the workforce's talents lie—and align the goals of employees with organization's overarching business strategy. With real-time insight into the workforce, an organization can benefit fully from human-capital strategies and programs, and measure the workforce's contributions to the bottom line.

Automation of all core human resources processes, such as employee administration, payroll, and legal reporting, increases efficiency and supports compliance with changing global and local regulations.

Source: "SAP ERP Human Capital Management: Operational Excellence and Innovation in HCM," SAP website, accessed at www.sap.com/solutions/business-suite/erp/hcm/index.epx. This publication contains references to the products of SAP AG. SAP, R/3, xApps, xApp, SAP NetWeaver, Duet, PartnerEdge, ByDesign, SAP Business ByDesign, and other SAP products and services mentioned herein are trademarks or registered trademarks of SAP AG in Germany and in several other countries. Business Objects and the Business Objects logo, BusinessObjects, Crystal Reports, Crystal Decisions, Web Intelligence, Xcelsius and other Business Objects products and services mentioned herein are trademarks or registered trademarks of Business Objects in the United States and/or other countries. SAP AG is neither the author nor the publisher of this publication and is not responsible for its content, and SAP Group shall not be liable for errors or omissions with respect to the materials.

enterprise-wide solution offers an opportunity for automation along with other administrative functions. HR professionals may also gain credibility as a result of their effective involvement in an ERP implementation. The ERP approach, however, is often quite costly with a lengthy implementation, as it involves significant organizational and contextual change.[13] HR may get sidelined in the process of integrating a whole range of functions across the organization. Also, because ERP systems are built with "generic users" in mind, they may not be well adapted to the specific practices and requirements of the HR user group in any given company. This may create tensions regarding the organization's unique identity.[14]

SELECTING TECHNOLOGY SOLUTIONS FOR HRM

Organizations rarely develop their own systems; most acquire software from a vendor. But with so many vendors and technology solutions out there, the HR professional needs guidelines. This section presents an overview of the selection process. For a more comprehensive treatment of this topic, consult specialized books.[15]

Conduct a Needs Analysis

Needs regarding HR technology are constantly evolving. Nevertheless, writes James G. Meade, "You are best off if you define those needs, at least in outline form, and plan for software that will meet the needs as they evolve."[16] A systematic needs analysis will involve collecting information about the organization (e.g., size, industry demands), its technical environment (e.g., hardware, operating systems, network environment, database, installed software, telecommunications, possible application service providers), and the needs of its HR department. With

HR Planning Notebook 9.2

NEEDS ANALYSIS QUESTIONS

- Is the human resources department spending too much time on manual processing?
- Are there too many data security risks involved with manual processing?
- Is the current human resources management system obsolete?
- Are we able to ensure an adequate follow-up of health and safety incidents?
- Are we being responsive to current business priorities?

- Will we be able to keep up with company growth?
- Are we managing our human capital as a strategic asset?
- Are we maintaining too much redundant information?
- Which requests for information is the human resources department unable to respond to?
- Would it be more efficient to integrate our different legacy systems into a single database?

regard to such needs, Meade suggests exploring areas in which the HR department is not accessing critical information in an accurate or timely manner. For instance, if benefits enrollment takes almost two months, this wait time might be considered a problem. Some of the questions that may help identify such gaps are presented in HR Planning Notebook 9.2.

It is also helpful to consider what information requests the HR department responds to, what reports and documents it uses, what information passes through the HR unit, and what manual records are maintained—in short, the information processing needs of the HR function.

Explore the Marketplace

The marketplace offers a wide variety of software solutions and matching the right solution to one's needs can be a difficult task. Therefore, it is important to get to know the vendors and what they have to offer by contacting software providers to ask for some literature and demo disks. Industry periodicals offer reviews of HR software, and HR professionals can participate in vendor exhibitions, meet the vendors, attend conferences, and gather documentation. By exploring the market, HR professionals can further specify their needs on the basis of a more complete understanding of available software solutions, and ultimately come up with a shortlist of a handful of prospective vendors.

Issue a Request for Proposal

The next step in the selection process is to issue a requests for proposal (RFP) to a short list of vendors. This basically involves communicating what is sought from vendors. A well-structured RFP contains two parts. The first describes your company and your system requirements; the second specifies the information you need from the vendor, such as product information, customer references, and so on.

Interested vendors then set up sales calls in which they show demos of their product. See HR Planning Notebook 9.3 for recommendations from the Society for Human Resource Management about what to require from vendors in an RFP.

HR Planning Notebook 9.3

RECOMMENDED RFP CONTENTS

- An overview that describes your company
- A description of your software need and the employee population it will support
- Desired systems functionality
- Required technical environment/specifications

- A request for pricing
- A request for customer references
- Details on customer service/support available from the vendor
- A request for sample contract terms

Evaluate Vendors and Products

Careful vendor selection is critical to the success of any software acquisition process. Meade suggests that **scripted demos**[17] be used at this stage. A scripted demo is an in-person demonstration of the product that follows a clear agenda that you have prepared for the vendors. This ensures that the demo focuses on your organization's needs.

At this stage of the acquisition process it is also useful to obtain references from users of the product you are considering, both technical and functional staff. They can provide timely information about the product, its ease of use, levels of support offered by the vendor, and address other concerns as well (e.g., ease of implementation).

> **Scripted demo**
> An in-person demonstration of the product that follows a clear agenda (in fact, a written script) that you have prepared for the vendors

IMPLEMENTING AND EVALUATING TECHNOLOGY

Implementing HR technology should be considered a major organizational change. Investing in technology does not necessarily ensure its effective implementation. Timely adoption and transformation can turn the HRMS into a competitive advantage. Much can go wrong at this stage, and most implementation failures can be traced back to one or several of the reasons listed in HR Planning Notebook 9.4.

As you might have noticed, some of the difficulties involved are technical in nature, while others relate to human behaviour and resistance to change. Knowing this, it then becomes clear that the success of information technology implementation efforts is as much a function of human interaction as it is of appropriate technology.

This section reviews some of the key issues relating to technology implementation. We also include some criteria for evaluating HR technology.

Typical Implementation Process

Organizations adopt either a process- or a technology-driven approach to HR technology implementation.[18] A process-driven approach adapts technology to existing HR processes. Organizations that adopt such an approach would try very hard to tailor the IT application to their unique processes. A technology-driven approach, conversely, adapts HR processes to technology. With such an approach, organizations review their processes so as to align them with existing time-tested technology solutions.

HR Planning Notebook 9.4

IT IMPLEMENTATION PITFALLS

- Lack of user involvement
- Incomplete definition of needs
- Change of needs
- Lack of support through management
- Lack of planning
- Lack of resources
- New technology

- Size and complexity of the project
- Lack of technical knowledge
- Lack of knowledge on new technologies
- Project no longer needed
- Unrealistic expectations
- Unclear goals
- Unrealistic time frames

Whatever the approach, implementing HR technology, especially large-scale HRIS of ERP projects requires an effective change or organizational development strategy. This strategy would typically include selecting a project manager and putting together a project team. The implementation phases, from implementation planning to parallel testing, are listed in HR Planning Notebook 9.5. HR professionals involved in an HR technology project would be well advised to consult a specialized textbook for a more in-depth treatment of these implementation phases.[19]

As for other significant changes in projects, the successful implementation of HR technology rests upon a number of key success factors, including top management support for the project. It has been found, for instance, that face-to-face communication in a user training session is more effective than written communication during system implementation.[20] We might add that the implementation plan should involve users early in the project, ideally during the design process or in the planning stage of system implementation.

HR Planning Notebook 9.5

HR TECHNOLOGY IMPLEMENTATION

- Implementation planning
- Input of the steering committee
- Ongoing communications to all interested parties
- Policy and procedure development
- Project team training
- Installation

- Fit analysis
- Modification
- Interfaces
- Conversion
- User (and technical support) training
- Unit and integrated testing
- Parallel

Source: G.M. Rampton, I.J. Turnbull, and J.A. Doran, 1999, *Human Resources Management Systems: A Practical Approach,* 3rd ed. Scarborough, ON: Carswell.

Business Process Re-engineering

Automation and business process re-engineering go hand in hand; it would not make sense to automate before reviewing processes. Likewise, process review needs to consider opportunities for automation. HR systems can provide unique opportunities to consolidate work and eliminate steps in otherwise complex processes. Employee involvement in the early stages of planning results in a more successful implementation and a general upskilling of employees. IT often plays an important enabling role in business process re-engineering projects.

The principles of **business process re-engineering**[21] are quite straightforward. They involve rethinking organizational processes in light of enabling technologies. In some cases, business process re-engineering involves going back to the drawing board and recharting processes altogether. The implications for HR technology implementation are that HR professionals need to fully understand their processes and determine how new IT can be leveraged to streamline them. This can involve changing anything that gets in the way of business performance.

Ensuring Data Security

Employers have an obligation to protect employees' personal records, medical records, and employment tests. Because of the sensitive nature of HR data, it is important that the system provide robust security to protect such data, especially with more and more employees transporting data on their personal flash drives and MP3 players.

Legislation in Canada requires that personal information used for an administrative purpose be as accurate, up to date, and complete as possible. With regard to the collection of personal information, only that information which relates directly to a business should be collected and maintained in the HRIS. There must be a proper balance between what an individual is expected to divulge and what information employment and management decisions require. This legislation also sets boundaries for the use of personal information. Such information should only be used for the purpose for which it was obtained or compiled, or for a use consistent with that purpose.

Another golden rule is that only authorized persons should have access to employee data. Some security features that restrict access include login security, row-level security (record security), and field-level security (data field).[22] Procedures to further protect data include the usage of PINs and passwords; the usage of encryption devices or software when sending sensitive email; smart cards or tokens; provision of regular, ongoing education and reinforcement of clearly defined organizational policies; and turning off systems when they are not in use.

System security further protects sensitive data. Secure operating systems and dependable computer programs are, of course, important. Another key to security is limiting access to computer resources. Company policies, for instance, can physically limit access to computers to only those who will not compromise security. This might involve restricting entrance to a property, a building, or a room.

Business process re-engineering
The fundamental rethinking and radical redesign of business processes to achieve dramatic improvements in critical, contemporary measures of performance, such as cost, quality, service, and speed

EVALUATING HR TECHNOLOGY

Technology acceptance
Extent to which users intend or actually use technology as a regular part of their job

User satisfaction and system usage are important indicators of HRIS success.[23] Drawing from the **technology acceptance** and user satisfaction streams of research, a study found that attitudes toward IT are influenced by behavioural beliefs about technology usefulness and ease of use.[24] These beliefs, in turn, are influenced by information satisfaction and system satisfaction, which result from information quality and system quality (see HR Planning Notebook 9.6). An audit that includes these different measures may provide useful insights into HR technology effectiveness.

A more sophisticated evaluation might include an analysis of the costs and benefits of the IT solution.[25] Similarly, a return on investment (ROI) approach would involve putting a dollar sign on the dollars saved through the HR system.[26] A company might find, for instance, that its HR system has led to lower costs of hiring, better succession planning, or reduced printing and distribution costs.

Competitive Advantage

Beyond simply evaluating how well the system is performing, it might also be useful to assess the contribution of HR technology to competitive advantage. This contribution would occur when HR systems facilitate the development of firm-specific competencies, produce complex social relationships, and generate tacit organizational knowledge.[27]

Looking at system performance from this angle, the question becomes "How then can IT be leveraged to cultivate these capabilities?" Many available technology applications exist that can help firms develop internal labour

---

HR Planning Notebook 9.6

SAMPLE TECHNOLOGY EFFECTIVENESS ITEMS

- Attitude:
  - Using this HR technology is very enjoyable.
- Usefulness:
  - Using this HR technology enhances my effectiveness on the job.
- Information satisfaction:
  - I am very satisfied with the information I receive from this HR technology.
- System satisfaction:
  - Overall, my interaction with this HR technology is very satisfying.
- Information quality:
  - This HR technology produces comprehensive information (completeness).
  - The information provided by this HR technology is well laid out (format).
  - There are few errors in the information I obtain from this HR technology (accuracy).
  - The information provided by this HR technology is always up to date (currency).
- System quality:
  - This HR technology operates reliably (reliability).
  - This HR technology makes information very accessible (accessibility).
  - This HR technology can be adapted to meet a variety of needs (flexibility).
  - This HR technology effectively integrates data from different areas of the company (integration).
  - This HR technology provides information in a timely fashion (timeliness).

markets through job posting and career-pathing. E-learning further allows the just-in-time acquisition of firm-specific knowledge. These technology solutions may also facilitate the development of firm-specific competencies. E-recruiting can increase the probability of hiring individuals whose values and beliefs are congruent with the organization's culture, which may contribute to the development of richer social relationships within the firm. Also, implementation of ESS applications may reinforce a culture of employee participation and engagement.

If distinctive competencies are a major source of competitive advantage, providing employees with easy access to a pool of expertise through knowledge repositories, they might further contribute to organizational performance. Such **knowledge management** practices or enablers allow successful knowledge sharing, improved learning, and new knowledge creation.

Whatever the perspective on competitive advantage, HR professionals and planners need to consider how IT may develop organizational resources and capabilities. This should lead to wiser technology investments based upon a clearer understanding of firm-specific opportunities for improvement.

LOOKING AHEAD

The world of eHR is renewing itself at a rapid pace. That is why it is important for HR professionals to keep looking for new opportunities for improved planning capabilities through technology. One way of staying abreast is to network and participate in the activities and workshops of professional associations specialized in HR systems. The Canadian Association of Human Resource Management Systems Professionals (HRMSP) is one such association (www.hrmsp.org). Another way to stay current is to engage in conversations with vendors and industry specialists, such as Richard Rousseau (see HR Planning Today 9.6).

Knowledge management
A systematic and organizationally specified process for acquiring, organizing, and communicating both tacit and explicit knowledge so that employees may make use of it to be more effective and productive in their work[28]

HR Planning Today 9.6

A View from Inside: Interview with Richard Rousseau

What is your role in the world of HR technology?

For over 20 years, I have been promoting and selling V.I.P. for D.L.G.L., a Canadian HRMS software provider, author of V.I.P., a bilingual, totally integrated North American product for HR, payroll, time capture and scheduling, and pension system for large corporations. I represented the technology community for eight years on the Canadian Council of Human Resources Associations, five of which as treasurer for the new CHRP standards project. As president and co-founder of the HRMS Professionals Association, a not-for-profit organization founded in 2005, it is my role to promote

the objective of HRMSP, which is to provide to the HR community the knowledge on how they can become more efficient by using technology, either through seminars or user testimonials; raise the level of awareness of existing tools; and share ideas that would help them move from the day-to-day "administrivia" to decision-making management.

What are some of the significant trends in HR technology that you are noticing?

The major trends revolve around self-service portals, business intelligence metrics, and outsourcing.

HR Planning Today 9.6 *(continued)*

ESS portal is mostly utilized by major industries. Corporate priorities and objectives will determine the usage of ESS. One can just give access to its employees to consult and print their pay stub, view their absenteeism profile, or even enter their time sheet, areas that show direct financial ROI. Another may give the rights to update personal information, contact information, and consult benefits and/or pension plans. MSS portal is the most revolutionary management approach. It transfers some "administrivia" HR/payroll responsibilities to line managers, allowing HR and payroll professionals to focus on strategic issues. It offers a direct communication opportunity between managers and employees. Although many MSS solutions are offered by vendors, this concept has a slow implementation pace as, in many cases, it often challenges the culture of the organization; managers are reluctant to take on extra duties. Business intelligence (BI) metrics is a win-win solution for all HR professionals. BI allows HR professionals to better strategize on HR issues by reporting and measuring HR data. A picture is worth a thousand words. Examples are BI graphs on headcount male/female, retirement projections, and average salary by gender. Outsourcing is a never-ending debate between what are the core business, value-added activities, organizational efficiency, and costs. Organizations need to determine their priorities and focus on the business needs.

What do companies that are successful with HR technology understand that others don't?

They are more efficient and proactive. HR technology has changed their way of working and analyzing HR data. It has created value for the organization. A company that offers ESS or MSS gives a direct message to its employees—you are competent and trustworthy. Information is input at source, avoiding duplicate entries and possible human errors. An HRMS offers automated workflow processes; a rules-based system eliminates human interpretation of corporate policies. Cost savings often come from simple improvements in their business processes—online pay stub, online absenteeism profile, and efficient scheduling system—not by eliminating jobs.

Source: Richard Rousseau is Vice President Sales & Industry Relations at D.L.G.L., President of HRMS Professionals Association and Chairman, 2008–2009, of the Canadian Payroll Association.

SUMMARY

This chapter presented an overview of HR technology and described some specific applications. The big challenge that lies ahead is to add strategic functionality to core HR processes. Much strategic functionality can be found in strategic HR planning applications. IT can support workforce analytics, management and scheduling, forensic reporting, skills inventories, replacement planning, and succession management. Such applications may be made available on an HRIS, specialty product, or ERP.

Depending on the organizational context, HR professionals may call upon different IT solutions. In the process, a thorough understanding of business and HR needs is a good starting point. A keen awareness of the HR technology market will prove invaluable when acquiring new software solutions. HR professionals will then need to deploy their change management skills when implementing new IT solutions. Communication and training are keys to successful HR technology implementation. HR may also find some opportunities for realigning processes and service delivery with IT. Finally, evaluating the IT solutions with various methodologies may reveal opportunities for improvement.

Key Terms

business intelligence p. 238
business process re-engineering p. 247
e-learning p. 237
enterprise portals p. 237
enterprise resource planning (ERP) p. 242
human resources information system
   (HRIS) p. 241

information technology (IT) p. 234
knowledge management p. 249
relational database p. 242
scripted demo p. 245
self-service p. 237
specialty products p. 242
technology acceptance p. 248

Web Links

Canadian Association of Human Resource Management Systems Professionals
(HRMSP):
www.hrmsp.org

International Association for Human Resource Information Management
(IHRIM):
www.ihrim.org

Required Professional Capabilities (RPCs)

The following RPCs are relevant to material covered in this chapter. The RPC number represents the CCHRA number assigned to the RPC as presented on the CCHRA website. All of the RPCs can be found in the Body of Knowledge at www .chrp.ca/rpc/body-of-knowledge.

RPC 15 Ensures the HR information management function is fully capable of support the organizations' strategic and operational needs.

RPC 16 Provides the organization with timely and accurate HR information.

RPC 18 Contributes to development of specifications for the acquisition and/or development of HR information management systems and for their implementation.

RPC 19 Evaluates alternatives for meeting current and future information management needs.

RPC 20 Contributes to the development of information management systems.

RPC 21 Ensures the availability of information needed to support the management decision making process.

Discussion Questions

1. In Canada, air traffic control is managed by NAV Canada, which has an international reputation for the management of air traffic controllers. If you were a manager, what data would you find useful to schedule the shifts for air traffic controllers?

2. Replacement charts are necessary to plan for promotions and transfers. What information should the EVP HR of a large corporation be requesting in order to fill a Director of HR planning position?
3. Databases used for HR management and planning contain a wide variety of personal and sensitive data that require the organization to set security, privacy, and usage policies. What legislative and ethical requirements of data security need to be considered?

Exercises

1. Using the Internet, find providers that offer performance appraisal software. Analyze the marketing material, and prepare a recommendation for adoption of a particular company, comparing the strengths, weaknesses and benefits of the providers.
2. Identify one activity involved in strategic HR planning (scheduling, succession planning, management development, and so on). Explore the Internet to find a software solution for that activity. Provide information on the vendor and describe the software solution in terms of its data requirements, technical and reporting capabilities, data security features, and price. Print out a couple of sample reports if available.
3. In the search for talent, employers often try to identify external candidates. What are the advantages and disadvantages of virtual job fairs for employers? For candidates?

Case 1 BUILDING TALENT AT CISCO SYSTEMS

In an article, Chatman, O'Reilly, and Chang describe the human capital strategy at Cisco Systems, a leader in the data networking equipment market (www.cisco.com). This strategy could be described as "build" talent strategy geared at developing the next generation of leaders. It was developed in response to changes in market conditions. The company now needs people who can help their customers solve business problems rather than just technical problems. Managers need to be able to cross-functionally coordinate and mobilize the pieces of Cisco needed to solve complex customer problems.

Cisco's "build" strategy involved developing leaders who have a different skill set and who embrace a different organizational culture than the previous generation. The new Cisco would therefore focus more on motivating and developing internal talent, particularly leaders. This involved providing rich development opportunities within an environment of continuous learning and challenge. Cisco also needed to get better at moving resources and retraining.

Several new initiatives demonstrated the company's commitment to the new human capital strategy. Cisco developed a system that allowed managers to post openings for jobs within high-growth areas. Cisco University was the focal point for all career management and a cornerstone of Cisco's effort to conceptualize the development of human capital within Cisco. It was defined as more than a corporate university or a centralized training centre; rather, it was described as an initiative that involved career management and development, with linkages to feedback, job opportunities, coaching, training, and mentoring. The company also revised its performance management and development process to improve performance and support talent development. In addition, Cisco implemented a succession management process that allowed the company to identify the top 20 percent of its leaders, assess their progress, and evaluate future opportunities. The company also launched customized 360° feedback to provide managers with a feedback report from the people they worked with.

The significant transition from a "buy" to "build" human capital strategy was a daunting challenge. Cisco wanted nothing less than a new generation of leaders focused on the customer and working across functions effectively. While focusing on customers and customer success, elements of the old culture needed to remain strong. All this in a large company that has been through some troubling times. There is also the challenge of maintaining this emphasis on leadership development when the market picks up and people are stretched and don't have much time for development.

Source: Adapted from Jennifer Chatman, Charles O'Reilly, and Victoria Chang, "Cisco Systems: Developing a Human Capital Strategy," *California Management Review,* Vol. 47, No. 2 (2005): 137–167.

Question

How might IT be leveraged to support Cisco's human capital strategy and enhance decisions about its talent resources? Identify and explain three specific software applications that might help this company better manage some elements of its HR strategy.

Case 2 SUSTAINING TALENT WITH STRATEGIC WORKFORCE PLANNING SOFTWARE AT ENERGY RESOURCES CONSERVATION BOARD

At the Energy Resources Conservation Board (ERCB), an independent and quasi-judicial agency of the Government of Alberta, a key challenge for this not-for-profit organization includes recruiting and retaining talent.

The ERCB regulates approximately 1,500 oil and gas companies and manages a budget of approximately $175 million. Given the demographic profile of the ERCB's approximately 1,000 employees, the ERCB expects the departure of 300 employees due to retirements alone in the next five years. In addition, the ERCB has an estimated average loss of 80 people per year for other reasons. To address the looming labour shortage, the ERCB undertook a strategic workforce planning (SWP) initiative. According to Susan Cassidy, Manager of Human Resources at ERCB, "SWP is about determining actions we need to take today to provide the workforce we need for tomorrow. It is taking the steps today to ensure we have the right people, in the right job, with the right skills, at the right time."

Part of ensuring the ERCB can meet workforce requirements of the future includes going through a process of SWP and analyzing how technology can assist in that process in a strategic way, a challenge often faced by HR departments.[29] As Ms. Cassidy indicates, "Data collection is an essential component of workforce planning. Collecting data and turning it into management information that can be acted upon is the essence of SWP." Acquiring the appropriate software was a necessary step to achieve this level of data collection. The ERCB solicited request for proposals from potential outside providers and settled on Aruspex, a niche provider of SWP. Costing about $85,000 annually, Aruspex software works to collect relevant data, creating scenarios and generating reports to help address development plans and sustainability strategies. Essentially, Aruspex "provides more than anecdotal evidence—it provides good information that is creditable."

The adoption of strategic workforce planning suggests a shift from "manpower planning," which includes headcounts and forecasting used for budgetary purposes, to strategic planning which looks at replacement and succession from a holistic perspective—using technology as a leveraging tool. As Ms. Cassidy indicates, "technology has gone beyond Excel spreadsheets which were associated with 'manpower planning' and we realized more was needed."

Source: Correspondence with Susan Cassidy, Manager, Resources, at Energy Resource Conservation Board and Former Chair of the Board of the Human Resources Calgary, June 2011

Question

Strategic workforce planning is one example of how the HR function might be improved by information technology. In this case we see that software assists with the ERCB being able to meet the needs of the future. How might IT be leveraged in other areas of HR for the ERCB and perhaps other organizations?

ENDNOTES

1. Adapted from Frauenheim, E. 2006. "Software Products Aim to Streamline Succession Planning." Workforce Management Online, www.workforce.com, January.

2. HRfocus. 2007. "HRIT 'Report Card': Trends for 2008 Plans." *HRfocus*, December, Vol. 84, No. 12: 1, 11–15.

3. Ulrich, D., and W. Brockbank. 2005. *The HR Value Proposition*. Boston, MA: Harvard Business School Press.

4. Frauenheim, E. 2007. "Keeping Score with Analytics Software." *Workforce Management*, Vol. 86, No. 10: 6–7.

5. Haines, V.Y., III, and G. Lafleur. 2008. "Information Technology Usage and Human Resource Roles and Effectiveness." *Human Resource Management*, Vol. 47, No. 3: 525–540.

6. Bell, B.S., S.-W. Lee, and S.K. Yeung. 2006. "The Impact of E-HR on Professional Competence in HRM: Implications for the Development of HR Professionals." *Human Resource Management*, Vol. 45, No. 3: 295–308.

7. Huber, G.P. 1990. "A Theory of the Effects of Advanced Information Technologies on Organizational Design, Intelligence, and Decision Making." *Academy of Management Review*, Vol. 15, No. 1: 47–71.

8. Gueutal, H.G., and C.M. Falbe. 2005. "eHR: Trends in Delivery Methods." In H.G. Gueutal and D.L. Stone, eds., *The Brave New World of eHR: Human Resources Management in the Digital Age*, pp. 190–225. San Francisco: Jossey-Bass.

9. Gueutal and Falbe, 2005, pp. 190–225.

10. Matwichuk, D. 2011. "HRIS an Early Warning System for Employee Burnout." *Canadian HR Reporter*, Vol. 24, No. 8 (April 25): 23.

11. Meade, J.G. 2003. *The Human Resources Software Handbook: Evaluating Technology Solutions for Your Organization*. San Francisco, CA: Wiley. P. 293.

12. Newman, M., and C. Westrup. 2005. "Making ERPs Work: Accountants and the Introduction of ERP Systems." *European Journal of Information Systems*, Vol. 14: 258–272.

13. Mabert, V.A., A. Soni, and M.A. Venkataraman. 2001. "Enterprise Resource Planning: Common Myths versus Evolving Reality." *Business Horizons*, May/June: 71–78.

14. Pollock, N., and J. Cornford. 2004. "ERP Systems and the University as a 'Unique' Organization." *Information Technology & People*, Vol. 17, No. 1: 31–52.

15. Meade, 2003; Rampton, G.M., I.J. Turnbull, and J.A. Doran. 1999. *Human Resources Management Systems: A Practical Approach*, 2nd ed. Scarborough, ON: Carswell.

16. Meade, 2003, p. 84.

17. Meade, 2003, p. 117.

18. Pollock and Cornford, 2004, pp. 31–52.

19. Rampton et al., 1999.

20. Kossek, E.E., W. Young, D.C. Gash, and V. Nicol. 1994. "Waiting for Innovation in the Human Resources Department: Godot Implements a Human Resource Information System." *Human Resource Management*, Vol. 33, No. 1: 135–159.

21. Felstead, A., D. Gallie, F. Green, and Y. Zhou. 2010. "Employee Involvement, the Quality of Training and the Learning Environment: An Individual Level Analysis." *The International Journal of Human Resource Management*, Vol. 21, No. 10: 1667.

22. Ashbaugh, S., and R. Miranda. 2002. "Technology for Human Resources Management: Seven Questions and Answers." *Public Personnel Management*, Vol. 31, No. 1: 7–20.

23. Haines, V.Y., III, and A. Petit. 1997. "Conditions for Successful Human Resource Information Systems." *Human Resource Management Journal*, Vol. 36, No. 2: 261–275.

24. Wixom, B.H., and P.A. Todd. 2005. "A Theoretical Integration of User Satisfaction and Technology Acceptance." *Information Systems Research*, Vol. 16, No. 1: 85–102.

25. Rampton et al., 1999.

26. Meade, 2003.

27. Lado, A.A., and M.C. Wilson. 1994. "Human Resource Systems and Sustained Competitive Advantage: A Competency-Based Perspective." *Academy of Management Review*, Vol. 19, No. 4: 699–727.

28. Alavi, M., and D.E. Leidner. 1999. "Knowledge Management Systems: Issues, Challenges and Benefits." *Communications of AIS*, Vol. 1: 1–37.

29. E. Lawler and J. Boudreau,. "What Makes HR a Strategic Partner?" *People and Strategy*, Vol. 32, No. 1 (2009): 14–22.

3

Strategic Options and HR Decisions

CHAPTER 10 DOWNSIZING AND RESTRUCTURING

CHAPTER 11 STRATEGIC INTERNATIONAL HRM

CHAPTER 12 MERGERS AND ACQUISITIONS

CHAPTER 13 OUTSOURCING

CHAPTER 14 EVALUATION OF HR PROGRAMS AND POLICIES

NEL

257

Downsizing and Restructuring

This chapter was written by Professor Terry H. Wagar, Department of Management, Sobey School of Business, Saint Mary's University, Halifax, Nova Scotia.

CHAPTER LEARNING OUTCOMES

After reading this chapter, you should be able to:

- Appreciate the importance of defining "downsizing."
- Be familiar with the complexity of the downsizing decision.
- Recognize the need to address concerns of both the victims and survivors of downsizing.
- Be aware of the ethical issues and consequences of downsizing.
- Understand what downsizing strategies are effective in enhancing organizational performance.
- Comprehend the concept of the "psychological contract."
- Develop an awareness of the importance of HRM in managing the downsizing process.

DOWNSIZING: A THING OF THE PAST?

"Canada Shed 54,000 Jobs in October 2011." "RIM Woes Worry 500 Workers in Bedford." "Tories Cite Deficit in Eliminating Auditing Jobs."[1] No, these are not old headlines from the downsizing era of the 1990s. They are a small sample of employee cutbacks announced in 2011.

Around the globe, we are seeing massive job cuts, and the global financial crisis is having a major impact on employers and employees. Consider the case of Hewlett-Packard (HP). During the five-year tenure of CEO Mark Hurd, which ended in August 2010, HP's profits increased about 18 percent a year and its stock price more than doubled.

According to traditional measures of performance, HP was a huge success. However, in 2009, HP cut more than 24,500 jobs. Not surprisingly, morale dropped, and about two-thirds of employees indicated that they would leave HP if they got another job offer. There were also cuts in research and development—former HP engineer Charles House stated, "That's why HP had no response to the iPad." According to Professor Wayne Cascio, an expert on downsizing, cutting jobs in knowledge-based firms is particularly harmful, because "each departure disrupts the social networks where ideas are generated and work gets done."[2]

Sources: P. Galagan. 2010. "The Biggest Losers: The Perils of Extreme Downsizing," T+D, November: 27–29; *The Globe and Mail*, June 21, A4; *The Chronicle Herald*, June 18, 2011, C1. Republished with permission The Halifax Herald Ltd.

THE DOWNSIZING PHENOMENON

In the 1990s, organizations became obsessed with reducing the workforce and operating in a "lean and mean" fashion. While most of the past decade saw an increased focus on employee retention and winning the war for talent, downsizing has returned with a flourish beginning around 2008. The global financial crisis and the huge debt burdens facing governments around the world suggest that cost cutting and downsizing are unlikely to disappear in the near future.

However, there is growing evidence that firms can become too "lean," and downsizing may cut into the muscle of the organization. Furthermore, a number of the reductions have been characterized as "mean"—destroying the lives of victims of cutbacks and leaving a demoralized and frightened group of **survivors** of downsizing. In today's environment, downsizing and restructuring are critical components of HR planning.

Historically, the focus of many organizations was on growth or the "bigger is better" syndrome. As a result, managers responsible for developing a **downsizing strategy** often had little experience in effectively managing the HR planning process and very little guidance from the management literature. Although the past 20 years have seen a considerable volume of articles on downsizing and restructuring, the suggestions they contain often are based on a single experience, are not supported by research, and frequently are in conflict. For instance, should cuts be targeted or across the board? Will the firm's stock price increase or decrease when the firm announces a major layoff or restructuring? Should an employer carry out all of the cuts at once or stage them over a period of time? Does downsizing improve organizational performance?

Downsizing is not just a Canadian phenomenon. Organizations around the world are striving to improve their competitive position and respond to the challenges of a global economy. For example, Nokia Siemens Networks (the world's second-largest mobile infrastructure maker) recently announced that it will

Survivors
Employees remaining with an organization after a downsizing

Downsizing strategy
Strategy to improve an organization's efficiency by reducing the workforce, redesigning the work, or changing the systems of the organization

eliminate more than 17,000 jobs worldwide by 2013 (about 23 percent of its workforce) in an effort to cut costs by $1.35 billion a year. According to Strategy Analytics analyst Phil Kendall "the Chinese have shaken up the operational environment by originally selling cheap hardware and won business that way, but have now built up a credible reputation and become quite competent technology providers. All of the big traditional Western infrastructure vendors have really had to work hard to fight off the threat."[3]

In some instances, employers are planning massive cutbacks. The U.S. Postal Service, which does not receive any taxpayer funding, is hoping to cut 220,000 jobs (out of a workforce of about 650,000 employees) and close about 300 processing facilities. Proposals by the Postal Service to cancel Saturday mail and increase rates above inflation have not been supported by Congress, and the Postal Regulatory Commission and mail volumes are falling as more people communicate electronically and pay bills online.[4]

Furthermore, downsizing is not restricted to the private sector; governments intent on managing costs reduced public service employment in dramatic ways, and cutbacks in traditionally secure industries such as education, health care, and government have become common.

Defining Downsizing and Restructuring

It is important to clarify what is meant by "downsizing." Managers and academics use the word to mean a number of different activities; for a summary of words used to describe downsizing, see HR Planning Notebook 10.1. Obviously, it is difficult to understand the effect of downsizing if we do not understand clearly what it means.

Kim Cameron, a leading scholar in the area of organizational change, has defined **downsizing** as follows:

> *Downsizing is a set of activities undertaken on the part of management and designed to improve organizational efficiency, productivity, and/or competitiveness. It represents a strategy implemented by managers that affects the size of the firm's workforce, the costs, and the work processes.*[5]

Note that the Cameron definition is not the only one. Some definitions are much narrower or broader. For example, Datta, Guthrie, Basuil, and Pandey defined employee downsizing as "a planned set of organizational policies and practices aimed at workforce reduction with the goal of improving firm performance," while Sheaffer, Carmeli, Steiner-Revivo, and Zionit referred to downsizing as "a selective reduction in organizational resources, including different combinations of reductions in physical, financial, organizational and human resources."[6]

Cameron identifies three types of downsizing strategies:

- **Workforce reduction:** Typically a short-term strategy aimed at cutting the number of employees through such programs as attrition, early retirement or voluntary severance packages, and layoffs or terminations. While a number of these approaches allow for a relatively quick reduction of the workforce, the problem is that their impact is often short-term, and in many instances the organization loses valuable human resources.

Downsizing
Activities undertaken to improve organizational efficiency, productivity, and/or competitiveness that affect the size of the firm's workforce, its costs, and its work processes

Workforce reduction
A short-term strategy to cut the number of employees through attrition, early retirement or voluntary severance packages, and layoffs or terminations

HR Planning Notebook 10.1

EXAMPLES OF WORDS USED TO DESCRIBE DOWNSIZING

axed	rationalized
building-down	reallocated
chopped	rebalanced
compressed	redeployed
consolidated	redesigned
declining	reduction-in-force
degrown	redundancy elimination
dehired	re-engineered
demassed	reorganized
derecruitment	reshaped
destaffed	resized
disemployed	resource allocation
dismantled	restructured
displaced	retrenched
downshifted	RIF'd
downsized	rightsized
fired	slimmed
involuntarily separated	slivered
personnel surplus reduction	streamlined
ratcheted down	workforce imbalance correction

Sources: Various, including K. Cameron, "Strategies for Successful Organizational Downsizing," *Human Resource Management*, Vol. 33 (1994): 189–211; M. Moore, *Downsize This* (New York: Harper Perennial, 1996); L. Ryan and K. Macky, "Downsizing Organizations: Uses, Outcomes and Strategies," *Asia Pacific Journal of Human Resources*, Vol. 36 (1998): 29–45; C. Tsai and Y. Yen, "A Model to Explore the Mystery Between Organizations' Downsizing Strategy and Firm Performance," *Journal of Organizational Change Management*, Vol. 21 (2008): 367–384.

Work redesign

A medium-term strategy in which organizations focus on work processes and assess whether specific functions, products, and/or services should be eliminated

- **Work redesign:** Often a medium-term strategy in which organizations focus on work processes and assess whether specific functions, products, and/or services should be changed or eliminated. This strategy, which is frequently combined with workforce reduction, includes such things as the elimination of functions, groups, or divisions; the reduction of bureaucracy; and the redesign of the tasks that employees perform. Because some planning is required, this strategy takes somewhat longer to implement and gets away from the problem of the organization simply doing what it always has done but with fewer people.

- **Systematic change:** A long-term strategy characterized by changing the organization's culture and the attitudes and values of employees with the ongoing goal of reducing costs and enhancing quality. By its very nature, this strategy takes considerable time to implement. The thrust of the strategy is to consider downsizing as an evolutionary part of an organization's life with the goal of continuous improvement: Employees assume responsibility for cutting costs and searching for improved methods and practices. Because of the human and financial commitment required for strategy, the impact on the organization's bottom line is rarely immediate, and consequently the approach is less than appealing to firms that focus on short-term profits or budget goals.*

*Source: Cameron, K. 1994. "Strategies for Successful Organizational Downsizing," *Human Resource Management* 33: 189–211.

Although some downsizing efforts were limited to reducing the size of the workforce, many employers discovered that merely cutting back the number of people in the organization was insufficient to achieve organizational goals. Consequently, some firms began giving more attention to "restructuring" the workplace.

There are three types of "restructuring": (1) portfolio restructuring, which involves changes to the organization's business portfolio (changes in the mix and/or percentage makeup of the organization's businesses, including divestures and acquisitions); (2) financial restructuring, which may include such financial changes as reducing cash flow or increasing levels of debt; and (3) organizational restructuring, which is "any major reconfiguration of internal administrative structure that is associated with an intentional management change program."[7] While portfolio and financial restructuring are important, the emphasis in this chapter will be on organizational restructuring. It is necessary, when considering downsizing, to distinguish an approach involving a reduction in the number of employees with one based on a strategically oriented organizational redesign or restructuring.[8]

In order to provide more information on the extent to which employers are restructuring the workplace and introducing organizational change, the results of two surveys conducted in 2007 were merged; the findings are shown in Figure 10.1. Overall, about 32 percent of Canadian organizations are involved in an extensive restructuring program. The most common activities include redesigning jobs, eliminating unnecessary tasks, and contracting out. However, there is considerable variation across organizations with respect to restructuring and change efforts.

Why Do Organizations Downsize?

There are several reasons organizations decide to downsize the workforce. Some of the factors most commonly mentioned are:

- Declining profit
- Business downturn or increased pressure from competitors
- Merging with another organization, resulting in duplication of efforts
- Introduction of new technology
- The need to reduce operating costs
- The desire to decrease levels of management
- Getting rid of employee "deadwood"

Systematic change
A long-term strategy that changes the organization's culture and attitudes, and employees' values, with the goals of reducing costs and enhancing quality

FIGURE 10.1

Restructuring and Organizational Change

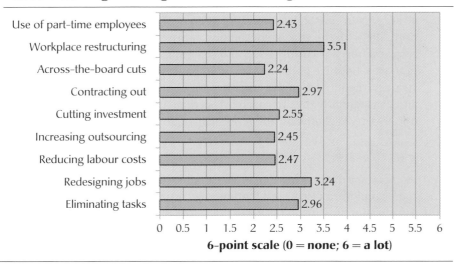

6-point scale (0 = none; 6 = a lot)

Use of part-time employees	2.43
Workplace restructuring	3.51
Across-the-board cuts	2.24
Contracting out	2.97
Cutting investment	2.55
Increasing outsourcing	2.45
Reducing labour costs	2.47
Redesigning jobs	3.24
Eliminating tasks	2.96

Simply put, many organizations engage in downsizing because managers perceive that cutting people will result in reduced costs (costs being more predictable than future revenues) and improved financial performance. In addition, labour costs are often seen as easier to adjust relative to other expenditures (such as capital investment). Still, there is considerable evidence that workforce reduction programs often fail to meet their objectives, as has been observed by Pfeffer:

> Layoffs don't even reliably cut costs. When a layoff is announced, several things happen. First people head for the door—and it is often the best people (who haven't been laid off) who are the most capable of finding alternative work. Second, companies often lose people they don't want to lose. Managers also underestimate the extent to which layoffs reduce morale and increase fear in the workplace. A survey by the American Management Association found that 88% of the companies that downsized said that morale had declined.[9]

There are some organizations that drastically reduce the workforce and employ a severe reduction strategy despite stable or increasing demand and a favourable competitive environment.[10] This development, which has been mentioned by HR managers in personal interviews, may be due to a variety of reasons including a decision to follow the lead of other firms engaging in cutback management and an increasing desire to operate in a "lean and mean" fashion. At other times, the decision to lay people off may be unavoidable:

> The Citadel Halifax Hotel announced that it was closing the hotel in January 2012. The hotel will be demolished and a new hotel is planned to be ready in about 16 months. As a result of the closure, 80 unionized hotel

staff are being laid off which has lead [sic] to the filing of a grievance by the union. According to company CEO Steve Gilbin, "our people have done a magnificent job running this hotel and we do want them back when we reopen. We have issues to resolve there but we feel we can come to a good conclusion."[11]

The Downsizing Decision

Going through a downsizing can be a very painful and difficult experience. However, some senior executives believe that reducing the workforce is just part of the job. One executive, when discussing his role in a cost-cutting plan at a previous company, stated, "I don't get frustrated any more. I just fire people."[12]

Too often, organizations embark on a downsizing program without careful consideration of whether there are feasible alternatives to downsizing. Study after study reveals that many downsizings are not well planned, frequently ignore the linkage between downsizing and the strategic direction of the organization, and underestimate the impact of downsizing on the organization and its human resources. Proactive organizations plan for downsizing by careful planning.

Alternatives to Downsizing

Downsizing can be a costly strategy for organizations to pursue, and, as a result, it is desirable to investigate whether alternatives to downsizing exist. In a number of instances, organizations discover that pursuing different alternatives to downsizing may eliminate the need to reduce the workforce or allow for a less severe downsizing strategy. Different approaches are summarized in HR Planning Notebook 10.2.

 HR Planning Notebook 10.2

ALTERNATIVES TO EMPLOYEE CUTBACKS: SOME HR STRATEGIES

Several alternatives are available to organizations faced with the challenge of cutting costs. These include:

Medium-Term Cost Adjustments

- Extending reductions in salary
- Voluntary sabbaticals
- Lending employees
- Exit incentives

Short-Term Cost Adjustments

- Hiring freeze
- Mandatory vacation
- Reducing the workweek
- Reducing overtime
- Reducing salaries
- Short-term facility shutdowns
- Obtaining cost-reduction ideas from employees

Source: Adapted from F. Gandolfi, "HR Strategies That Can Take the Sting Out of Downsizing-related Layoffs," *Ivey Business Journal Online*, July/August, 2008.

INPLACEMENT AND OUTPLACEMENT ISSUES

Inplacement
Reabsorbing excess or inappropriately placed workers into a restructured organization

Outplacement
Providing a program of counselling and job-search assistance for workers who have been terminated

In examining the downsizing decision, it is necessary to consider both inplacement and outplacement issues.[13] **Inplacement** refers to a career management approach aimed at reabsorbing excess or inappropriately placed workers into a restructured organization, while **outplacement** focuses on the provision of a program of counselling and job search assistance for workers who have been terminated.

In a survey of Canadian manufacturing firms, I asked organizations that had gone through downsizing to report on the benefits they provided to displaced workers. These results are provided in Figure 10.2. The most common benefits were severance pay, continuation of employee benefits, outplacement counselling, and an extended notice period. A minority of firms provided retraining assistance or family counselling.

Some Ethical Considerations

Consider the experience of one female manager who was downsized.

> *I actually did the rounds and said goodbye to a few key people. And the thing that was really upsetting was that I went in to see senior people such as the chief executive officer; I went into his office and he just came out and saw me talking to his secretary and said, "What is wrong?" Because he saw*

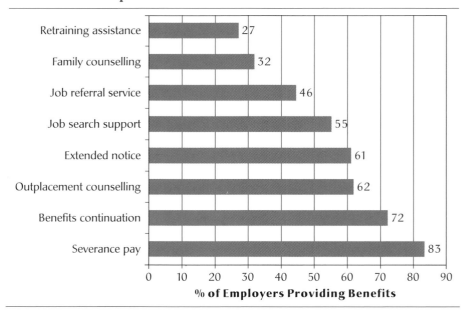

FIGURE 10.2

Benefits to Displaced Workers

Benefit	%
Retraining assistance	27
Family counselling	32
Job referral service	46
Job search support	55
Extended notice	61
Outplacement counselling	62
Benefits continuation	72
Severance pay	83

% of Employers Providing Benefits

my face. And I said "I've just been retrenched." And he was shocked because he didn't know, because it was his second in command who handled operational issues. So he basically said "I'm really sorry" . . . but you know, "See you later. There's nothing I can do."[14]

Is it unethical to downsize? Downsizing is, in most circumstances, perfectly legal. Of course, there may be contractual provisions (such as terms of a collective agreement) and legal restrictions (such as human rights legislation, labour or employment standards, or the common law of wrongful dismissal) that restrict how an employer may engage in downsizing. For example, labour standards codes often require that an employer provide a specified period of notice before engaging in a mass layoff.

Assuming that a downsizing is legal, can it still be unethical? There is evidence that downsizing may have negative impacts on laid-off employees, survivor employees, and the downsizers. When confronted with the need to make decisions about downsizing, managers may use economic, accounting and ethically based rationales.[15]

A number of downsizings may infringe on principles of distributive, procedural, and interactional justice (see "Perceptions of Justice" later in this chapter). Moreover, communication during a downsizing may be mismanaged, and managers may use and abuse information as a source of power. For instance, organizations may choose to conceal information from employees (such as failing to inform employees about impending job loss) or distort information concerning the financial status of the business.[16]

Downsizing may be considered a breach of the psychological contract that exists between an employer and employee (i.e., an individual worker's perception of the agreement he or she has with the employer). In addition, downsizing may also involve the violation of social contracts; an organization is a member of different local communities, and a failure to adhere to certain values and mores (an ethical floor or basic standards of ethics) would result in the organization being considered a "poor" corporate citizen.

One employee, after being informed by his boss that his employment with the company had been terminated, stated the following:

As I say, the relationship between my boss and myself was pretty intense, and I think (the meeting) ends up with something like him saying, "Well Ben, this is very unfortunate. I do wish you all the very best in your future and hope everything will work out," something to that effect. And I responded with, "Look Chris, let's not mess around. You hate my guts, and I can assure you that I hate yours."[17]

Planning for Downsizing

Assuming the organization has decided to embark on a downsizing strategy, planning is essential. Some key issues include the following:

- Determining how many people will lose their jobs.

- Determining who will be let go. For example, will the decision be made on the basis of seniority, performance, or potential?

- Determining how the reduction will be carried out. For example, to what extent will the organization use attrition, early retirement or voluntary severance programs, and layoffs or termination? The approaches to workforce reduction vary in terms of the degree of protection to employees and the time it takes to implement them.

- Determining the legal consequences. For example, organizations often ignore or are unaware of legal requirements when downsizing the workforce. Some areas of law to consider include the law of wrongful dismissal, employment standards legislation, trade union law, existing collective agreement provisions, and human rights legislation.

- Designing current and future work plans. This issue represents a key challenge for the organization and is frequently neglected.

- Implementing the decision. Implementation includes such elements as the communication of the termination decision, the timing of the decision, security issues, severance payments, outplacement counselling, and communications with remaining employees.

- Performing follow-up evaluation and assessment of the downsizing efforts. Although this step is critical, it is often ignored in many organizations.*[18]

*Source: Amundson, N., W. Borgen, S. Jordan, and A. Erlebach. 2004. "Survivors of Downsizing: Helpful and Hindering Experiences," The Career Development Quarterly 52: 256–271, 260.

Adjusting to Job Loss

Workers who have lost their job frequently experience tremendous pain. As well, job loss can be very difficult for family members. Furthermore, many downsized employees are very bitter and angry with their former employer. A U.S. study of downsized workers revealed that 67 percent would never work for their former company again, 54 percent would not recommend that others purchase the organization's products or services, and 11 percent considered going to the media and talking about their layoff experiences.[19] As indicated in HR Planning Today 10.1, losing a job may have benefits for some employees.

Still, for most employees, job loss is a traumatic experience. Consider the responses from two victims of downsizing:[20]

Victim 1: *Money was limited. I felt very un— . . . I didn't like to go out in the day. I remember my wife said to me, "Why don't you go and mow the lawn?" And I didn't want to go out there because, it's interesting, you just felt that people are watching you. And you have this feeling of, "He can't even support his family." Look at him. He is failing.*

Victim 2: *I was out of work for seven months. I was trying very hard to get a job. That did have a dramatic effect on me and my family. My kids were going to private school. I'd paid a whole year up front. But it affected them. My kids said at one point, and this really cut me up, they said "Daddy, if we haven't got any money, we don't have to have Christmas this year." And that really upset me.*

HR Planning Today (10.1

Can Losing a Job Be a Good Thing?

While job loss is not typically considered a favourable experience, a study of 30 men and women who lost their job and were using an outplacement firm revealed that losing a job may have some positive aspects. Some of the benefits resulting from job loss identified by participants were:

- The opportunity to reflect on their careers and a chance to think about what they really want to do.
- A chance to get out of a job they didn't like. A number of the participants, upon reflection,

concluded that they weren't satisfied with what they had been doing.
- More time for family and a better work–life balance.

Although some participants felt considerable stress and anxiety associated with job loss, others felt relief. More positive views tended to occur as time passed. Still, individuals with young families still felt considerable pressure to get back into the workforce.

Source: Adapted from S. Klie, "The Upside of Job Loss," *Canadian HR Reporter*, October 22, 2007, 1–2.

In Mackenzie, British Columbia, workers were devastated after the town's largest employer, AbitibiBowater, shut down its two sawmills and its paper mill and the remaining sawmill in town was closed four months later.

> *According to one worker, "I wanted to stay here forever. But all the mills are going down. There's nothing more. The town is dying." People are trying to sell their homes and work elsewhere. As another employee stated: "I was out the door right away, suitcase in hand, off to my next job." However, others worry about the community: "Who will be the scout leaders, the hockey coaches? The whole social fabric of the community starts to fall apart."*[21]

If a single organization acting alone decides to engage in workforce cutbacks, the employees have the option of seeking alternative employment; however, in an economy in which several firms are downsizing, frustrated employees have few alternative employment opportunities.[22] Still, firms that have not treated employees well may encounter difficulties in attracting and keeping quality employees when the demand for workers is high. A poll of almost 7,000 employees indicated that 84 percent would search for a new job if they heard that their company was planning layoffs.[23]

A number of organizational interventions and practices have been identified as helping previously employed workers adjust to job loss and secure new employment.[24] They include the following:

- Advance notification of layoffs, which gives employees time to deal with the reality of job loss and seek future employment

- Severance pay and extended benefits, which provide an economic safety net

- Education and retraining programs, which give individuals time to acquire marketable skills

- Outplacement assistance to inform employees of new job opportunities and to improve their ability to "market" themselves

- Clear, direct, and empathetic announcement of layoff decisions

- Consideration of HR planning practices that represent alternatives to large-scale layoffs

Still, organizations don't always manage the process properly. As one employee observed:

You know, they [former employees] were told that their positions were being eliminated, they were given counselling—financial and counselling about their package . . . but then they were actually ushered right out the door and I think that is despicable. People that had been with the company for 20 years that had been very good employees are made to think that they've done something wrong . . . very, very demeaning.[25]

White-collar and upper-management jobs are also no longer immune to downsizing. In 2011, more than 200,000 jobs have been lost in the global financial services industry (as against 174,000 in 2009) and more downsizing is anticipated as the debt crisis in Europe worsens. Victims of downsizing are observing that it is harder and harder to find work in the industry as firms continue to cut back on staff. One employee called his wife when he lost his job—she was at home watching *The Company Men,* which is a movie about downsizing.[26] It has been observed that "downsizing has turned into one of the inevitable outcomes of living in a global economy where continual adjustments to products, services, and the price of labour are needed to remain competitive."[27] HR Planning Today 10.2 summarizes recent evidence concerning employment status and suicide risk.

HR Planning Today (10.2

Examining Employment Status and Suicide Risk

Is losing a job associated with a greater risk of suicide? What about being unemployed for a long period of time? In a forthcoming article, Tim Classen and Richard Dunn examine these questions using U.S. panel data over a 10 year period. Their major findings include the following:

- Recent job loss (unemployed less than five weeks) was not associated with a difference in suicide risk in men versus women.

- A narrower measure of recent job loss (based on mass-layoff events) was positively associated with the suicide rate for both men and women. The authors estimate one additional suicide for every 4,200 men who became unemployed as part of a mass layoff and one additional suicide for every 7,100 women who were part of a mass layoff.

- Suicide risk increases for both men and women who experience long periods of unemployment.

Source: Adapted from T. Classen and R. Dunn, "The Effect of Job Loss and Unemployment Duration on Suicide Risk in the United States: A New Look Using Mass-Layoffs and Unemployment Duration," *Health Economics,* Vol. 21 (March 2012): 338–350.

One article describes the situation as follows:

What's going on here? Didn't companies hack away layers of management during downsizings of the late 1980s and the rightsizings following the dot-com crash of the early 2000s? They did, but "business runs in cycles. When the economy is buoyant, as it has been in recent years, there is less cost discipline and companies add head count. But when a downturn hits, the high salaries of managers are an obvious expense to trim because you get more savings per body.[28]

THE "SURVIVORS" OF DOWNSIZING

While we see media accounts of people rebounding from downsizing and starting a new life for themselves, the reality is that for many individuals, the pain of being downsized is very severe. The impact on family life, career plans, and personal esteem are devastating and the social costs can be enormous.

What about the survivors of a downsizing? How do employees who remain with an organization react? Here is a description of a typical response, also known as survivor syndrome:[29]

The initial anger and pain are often followed by fear and cynicism. Stress, bred of uncertainty and the necessity of doing more with less, skyrockets. Trust in the company and its management plummets. Employees who remain spend their days juggling more work and avoiding anything that approaches risk taking or innovation.

Surviving a downsizing can be traumatic and there is growing evidence that perceptions of job insecurity (even in the absence of a downsizing) may be associated with negative consequences for employees and employers. Job insecurity has been defined as "an individual's expectations about continuity in a job situation" or "overall concern about the future existence of a job."[30] In other words, even employees in organizations that have not downsized the workforce may have perceptions of job insecurity, which has been related to impaired well-being, increased stress, mental distress, and lower job satisfaction.[31]

Perceptions of Justice

Perceptions of fairness and equity play a key role in understanding how survivors of a downsizing react to the experience. In examining the survivors of downsizing, three types of justice warrant consideration:[32]

- **Procedural justice:** The procedures (or "decision rules") used to determine which employees will leave or remain with the organization.

- **Interactional justice:** The type of interpersonal treatment employees receive during the implementation of the downsizing decision.

- **Distributive justice:** The fairness of the downsizing decision. For example, responses from employees may include feelings of guilt after seeing co-workers lose their jobs, support for the downsizing decision as necessary for the firm, or feelings of unfairness and concern that further layoffs may put their own job in jeopardy.*

*Source: Armstrong-Stassen, M. 1993. "Survivors' Reactions to a Workforce Reduction: A Comparison of Blue-Collar Workers and Their Supervisors," *Canadian Journal of Administrative Sciences* 10: 334–343.

Procedural justice
Procedures or rules used to determine which employees will be downsized

Interactional justice
The interpersonal treatment employees receive during the implementation of the downsizing decision

Distributive justice
The fairness of the downsizing decision

Consider the response of one disgruntled employee who was laid off from a chemical company and sabotaged the computer system, resulting in more than $20 million in damages. In a letter to the company president, he wrote:

> I have been loyal to the company in good and bad times for 30 years. I was expecting a member of top management to come down from his ivory tower to face us with the layoff announcement, rather than sending the kitchen supervisor with guards to escort us off the premises like criminals. You will pay for your senseless behaviour.[33]

Examining Justice and the Threat of Plant Closure

HR Planning Today 10.3 addresses the issue of fairness and commitment to the organization after downsizing. The following example provides an opportunity to think about employee perceptions of justice in light of a threatened plant closure. Both employees who survive the layoff and those who lose their jobs might well feel that distributive, procedural, and interactional justice were severely lacking.

In early November of 2011, senior management threatened to close the Bowater Mersey Paper Company in Brooklyn, N.S. unless energy and cost-saving measures were found. Brooklyn is a small town of just over 1,000 people and the paper company first opened the mill in 1929. Local government officials and members of the public made it clear that the company was critical to the success and survival of the region.

The company wanted to reduce labour costs from $97 a tonne to $80, and in mid-November informed the union that it wanted to cut about 110 of 250 bargaining-unit employees. The current collective agreement, negotiated in 2009, was scheduled to expire in 2014; but since signing the agreement, the union had agreed to a 10 percent wage reduction, an 8 percent benefits reduction, and 4 percent in labour reductions. On November 16, 2011, 51.7 percent of workers voted in favour of cutting 110 jobs in an effort to save the plant.

In addition to labour-cost reductions, the local government gave Bowater Mersey a 15 percent tax break and also granted a reduction on power rates.

HR Planning Today (10.3

Fairness and Commitment After Downsizing

What is the relationship between downsizing and affective organizational commitment (the level of emotional attachment to, identification with, and involvement in the organization)? Do the perceptions of survivors and victims differ? The results of a recent study indicate that:

- Fairness was correlated with higher organizational commitment when considering the responses of both survivors and victims of downsizing.

- Procedural fairness was more important than distributive fairness for downsizing survivors.
- The impact of fairness is greater in countries with a more individualistic culture (rather than a collectivistic culture).
- Fairness is more important if the downsizing was undertaken in order to maximize profits rather than out of economic necessity.

Source: D. van Dierendonck and G. Jacobs, "Survivors and Victims, a Meta-analytical Review of Fairness and Organizational Commitment After Downsizing," *British Journal of Management*, 2010.

As employees grappled with whether to accept severance packages, and people debated the success of the "Occupy" movement, which had spread to cities around the globe, it was revealed that two senior executives who directed the company's restructuring efforts had received attractive severance packages. Former CEO David Paterson got a severance of $1.338 million, a restructuring award of $765,000, a $430,000 bonus, and $150,000 monthly to act as a consultant for six months; former Chief Financial Officer William Harvey got a severance of $1,346,181 and a consultancy fee of $40,000 a month. Bowater Mersey employees are being given severance of 1.5 weeks' pay for each year of service.[34]

Survivor Reactions

There is considerable evidence that downsizing may produce a number of dysfunctional behaviours among the employees who remain with the organization. Some of these impacts are discussed below:[35]

- *Negative attitudes and behaviours:* In a number of downsizings, employees who retain their jobs report increased job insecurity, fear, stress, and burnout. They may also experience lower self-confidence and self-esteem, reduced job satisfaction, and lower commitment to the organization. Not surprisingly, these factors may lead to increased turnover, absenteeism, and lateness.

- *Reduced performance capabilities:* There is growing evidence that it is not necessarily the poor performers who leave the downsized organization. Of particular concern is the fear that the best employees will leave, because quality workers are more attractive to other firms. This result undermines the HR activities of the organization.

- *Lower organizational productivity:* Negative employee attitudes and behaviour, in conjunction with lower performance capabilities, may destroy or markedly harm team activities and result in lower productivity (see HR Planning Today 10.3).*

  *Source: Mone, M. 1994. "Relationships between Self-Concepts, Aspirations, Emotional Responses, and Intent to Leave a Downsizing Organization," *Human Resource Management* 33: 281–298.

A recent study examined various forms of downsizing and the perceptions of almost 14,000 employees. Employees who had not experienced downsizing were compared to individuals who had been subject to layoffs, outsourcing (moving work to outside entities such as contractors or consultants, resulting in job loss), and offshoring (moving work to foreign entities outside the company). The major findings included the following:

- Survivors of layoffs had reported lower perceived organizational performance, lower job security, reduced attachment to the organization, and a higher intention to quit their job compared with employees who had not experienced downsizing.

- Survivors of offshoring perceived that their employer's organizational performance was lower, manager fairness was lower, and commitment to the organization was not as high compared to respondents who had not been downsized. However, outsourcing survivors did not differ significantly in their attitudes relative to employees who had not been downsized.*[36]

*Source: Maertz, C., J. Wiley, C. LeRouge, and M. Campion. 2010. "Downsizing Effects on Survivors: Layoffs, Offshoring and Outsourcing," *Industrial Relations*, 49: 275-285.

Impact on the "Downsizers"

Although there has been a fair bit of research on the survivors of downsizing, what about the individuals who carry out the downsizing and actually terminate members of the workforce? In one study, detailed interviews were conducted with ten managers responsible for implementing the downsizing. The results showed that participating in the downsizing process was very difficult for a number of the managers. Of particular note was the experience of social and organizational isolation, a decline in personal health and well-being, and an increase in family-related problems.[37] Another study revealed that having to carry out the downsizing (being the "executioner") is emotionally taxing and the downsizers develop mechanisms to distance themselves emotionally, physically, and cognitively from the task. Experienced downsizers were more able to develop coping mechanisms and an emotional numbness to the task.[38] Downsizers may begin speaking in less personal terms to describe their job—for instance, a workforce reduction may be described as a realignment or "revectoring."

While the involvement of some downsizers may be restricted to behind-the-scenes administrative tasks (such as blocking employee access to computers), others have a more direct role including identifying the people to be laid off, carrying out the actual layoffs, and dealing with employees immediately after the layoff decision:

> *People stare at you funny, they won't even say "Hello" to you. You know, they think you made the personal decision yourself. . . . What was my name for it? A grim reaper.*[39]

There is often extreme emotion on the part of the downsizer:

> *A manager I dealt with here, broke down and cried. Cried during the training sessions. Got too emotional herself. Cried during the delivery of the message. I felt that the person did not display the managerial or directorial responsibilities that they have to the company. Got too emotional and too personal.*[40]

FINANCIAL PERFORMANCE AND DOWNSIZING

Do organizations that have reduced their workforces perform better than other firms? This is an important question. One would expect organizations engaging in downsizing anticipate that their financial performance will thereby improve.

How does the stock market react to downsizing announcements? While some analysts suggest that downsizing will improve the value of a firm's stock, investors generally respond negatively to the announcement of a layoff, particularly if the reduction is due to financial factors or involves a large-scale, permanent cutback of employees.

One study indicated that downsizing had a negative impact on stock market returns, and this was even more pronounced for larger downsizings. However, the negative effects associated with downsizing were reduced or eliminated when the firm adopted a relocation strategy in which specific units and functions were targeted for layoffs; targeted cuts allow the firm to retain the most valuable human resources, whereas across-the-board cutbacks result in the loss of quality employees. If engaging in a large downsizing is inevitable, firms with disengagement incentives/strategies (incentives to leave) are viewed more favourably by the stock market relative to firms without such incentives/strategies.[41]

When we look at financial performance outcomes, academic research does not paint a very clear picture; some studies suggest downsizing is linked to increased profitability while others indicate it is linked to poorer financial performance. Why the conflicting results? In examining the various studies, it is difficult to make comparisons, because authors don't use similar measures of performance, and each defines downsizing somewhat differently. In addition, the research tends to look at workforce reduction behaviour without considering the overall downsizing strategy.

However, there is some U.S. evidence supporting the position that improved return on assets and common stock might be related, at least in part, to the downsizing strategy employed by the organization.[42] Firms following a "pure employment" downsizing (a workforce cutback of at least 5 percent but little change in plant and equipment expenditure) did not outperform other firms in their industry. However, "asset downsizers" (firms that cut at least 5 percent of the workforce accompanied by a decline of at least 5 percent in expenditures on plant and equipment) generated higher returns relative to industry competitors.

In addition, a study of Fortune 500 companies revealed that firms that had downsized their workforce had substantially poorer financial results up to two years later. However, these results began to dissipate by the third year. The findings were particularly negative for employers reducing 10 percent or more of the workforce. In addition, there was modest evidence that the use of more frequent (ongoing) layoffs was associated with poorer performance.[43]

It appears that the link between organizational performance and downsizing is complex, and that the likelihood of a successful downsizing might be associated with a number of factors surrounding the downsizing. A study of large firms over an 18-year period indicated that downsizing is more likely to be successful (as measured by better financial performance) when firms have higher levels of slack (excess resources, which can include inventory, working capital, and people), the downsizing is broadly based (i.e., the focus not only is on reducing the number of people but also involves organizational redesign), and the approach to downsizing is proactive (planned out rather than in response to declining performance).[44] These findings support a number of the suggestions provided earlier in the chapter.[45]

Consequences of Downsizing

Many downsizing efforts fall well short of meeting organizational objectives, and are carried out with little strategic planning or consideration of the costs to the individuals and the employer.[46] More often, job cuts represent a short-term reaction to a much more complex problem. While senior executives often focus on financial issues during a reorganization, the benefits of restructuring frequently fail to transpire if HR issues are not carefully thought out and resolved appropriately.

HR Planning Today (10.4

Are Employees in a Downsized Organization More Likely to Quit?

What are the implications for employee quit behaviour if an organization downsizes? Does investment in human resources management practices moderate the quit rate? These questions were addressed in a study by Trevor and Nyberg. Among their major findings were the following:

- Downsizing was associated with a higher quit rate. This finding has implications for an organization that may lose more people than desired, because the downsizing in turn impacts on the quit rate. As well, higher performers may be among those who decide to voluntarily leave the organization.

- Higher quits are frequently associated with negative consequences, compounding the negative effect of the downsizing. The authors found that if just 1 percent of the workforce is downsized, post-downsizing voluntary turnover rates increase by about 31 percent.
- If downsizing is unavoidable, adopting practices such as job embeddedness (e.g., flextime, on-site child care, and defined-benefit plans) and procedural justice prior to the downsizing may reduce the consequences of downsizing resulting from higher voluntary turnover, induce the least valuable employees to leave, and encourage the most valuable employees to stay.

Source: Adapted from C. Trevor and A. Nyberg, "Keeping Your Headcount When All About You Are Losing Theirs: Downsizing, Voluntary Turnover Rates, and the Moderating Role of HR Practices," *Academy of Management Journal*, (2008), Vol. 51, 259–276.

Despite the guilt associated with permanently reducing the workforce, a growing number of firms are willing to downsize and are discovering that workforce reduction can lead to many unwanted consequences.[47] Some of these consequences include the high human costs, psychological trauma experienced by both those let go and the survivors, reduced employee commitment, lower performance among employees due to job insecurity, greater attention by management to the downsizing process while ignoring customer and client needs, a shift from innovation to protection of one's turf, lower morale, potential litigation by employees who believe that they are victims of discrimination, and a loss of valuable employees (see HR Planning Today 10.4).

A study of almost 2,000 Canadian workplaces indicated that establishments reporting employee cutbacks also had lower overall employee satisfaction and less favourable employer–employee relations.[48] A second study examined "serial downsizers" (i.e., firms that had downsized the workforce both when the study began and five years later). The serial downsizers had the poorest scores when considering changes in employee satisfaction (e.g., poorer morale, quality of work life, commitment to the organization). While the "late downsizers" (those organizations that had downsized only recently) also had negative scores on the employee satisfaction measures, the "early downsizers" did not significantly differ from those employers that did not downsize throughout the period of the study. In other words, it appears that the negative people consequences associated with the early downsizing had dissipated over the five-year period.[49]

One issue that has received little attention is the effect of downsizing on the organization's *reputation for corporate social performance (RCSP)*. Reputation for corporate social performance can be defined as "the firm's reputation for principles, processes and outcomes related to the social impact of the firm's operations."[50] An organization's RCSP is one of the most important intangible assets of a business and an important source of competitive advantage. In addition, it may be critical to attracting and retaining quality employees. Although considered an acceptable business practice, there is evidence that downsizing has a negative impact on an organization's RCSP and is even more pronounced for organizations that had high financial performance prior to the downsizing.[51]

Another issue beginning to attract attention is the relationship between downsizing and employee safety. The research evidence suggests that downsizing creates job insecurity, which is strongly associated with low levels of job satisfaction. Low job satisfaction, in turn, is related to safety motivation (the incentive to work safely) and safety knowledge (an understanding of safe operating procedures). When safety motivation is low, employees are less likely to engage in "safety compliance," that is, comply with safety procedures and carry out their work in a safe manner. Finally, lower levels of safety compliance are associated with more workplace accidents. It is suggested that during a downsizing, employees concerned with keeping their jobs view productivity as more important than safety. However, in downsizings in which employees perceived the safety climate as positive and the organization viewed safety as very important, the negative outcomes associated with job insecurity were not seen.[52]

Effective Downsizing Strategies

If an organization is not "lean and mean" enough, downsizing might be an appropriate strategic response. However, cutting the number of people in an organization is not a quick fix; prior to embarking on any workforce reduction effort, firms should carefully consider the consequences. Considerable care and planning must go into the decision, and the reasons for the reduction must be effectively communicated to employees. In addition, managers frequently have little experience or training with regard to downsizing and restructuring.

From a strategic perspective, an important decision involves answering such questions as: Should we downsize? When should we do it? How should we do it? The focus should be on *rightsizing*, which involves establishing a shared vision of the organization and a clearly stated strategy supported by management, understood by employees, and involving a sense of "ownership" by members of the firm.[53]

It is critical that the HR department play a very active role in the early stages of formulating a downsizing strategy. There is evidence that negative outcomes associated with downsizing might be mitigated by increased communication and employee participation and systematic analysis (in advance) of tasks and personnel requirements.[54] In addition, senior management has to take an aggressive, visible, and interactive role in formulating the downsizing strategy. However, the identification, development, and implementation procedures should involve the employees. In many instances, the identification of inefficiencies and areas where improvements are possible is best left to employees, who typically are in a better position to make such judgments.

Strategic Downsizing

Why do so many workforce reduction programs fail to meet expectations? Many organizations engaging in downsizing had no policies or programs to address problems associated with cutting human resources, and several organizations failed to anticipate the dramatic impacts workforce reduction has on the work environment, employees, customers, and clients. Furthermore, a number of downsizing efforts were not integrated as part of the organization's overall strategic plan.[55]

An effective downsizing depends on comprehensive planning for change; proper communication of the plan; credibility of the organization with employees, customers, suppliers, and other stakeholders; and consideration and compassion both for employees who are terminated and those remaining.[56] Moreover, firms engaging in downsizing typically focus only on workforce reduction aspects of the strategy and ignore the more time-consuming but critical strategies of redesigning the organization and developing a systematic strategy predicated on massive cultural change within the firm. Research in both Canada and the United States indicates that while almost all organizations engaging in downsizing focus on the first component (workforce reduction), only about one-half make some attempt at work redesign and less than one-third implement a systematic change strategy.

One study compared the effect of the three downsizing strategies (workforce reduction, organizational redesign, and systematic change) on two performance outcome measures (cost reduction and quality improvement).[57] It found that the workforce reduction strategy was negatively related to organizational performance, while the organizational redesign and systematic change strategies were associated with improved performance. In other words, firms that simply focus on reducing the number of employees typically will find that the results fail to meet organizational objectives. Moreover, mutual trust between employees and senior management plays an important role in the success of organizational redesign and systematic change strategies. The creation of a culture of trust is essential prior to embarking on a downsizing strategy.

Effective and Ineffective Downsizing Strategies

A number of studies have pointed out downsizing strategies and practices that do not work. For instance, Cameron, Freeman, and Mishra developed a list of six best practices in downsizing firms:

1. Downsizing should be initiated from the top but requires hands-on involvement from all employees.
2. Workforce reduction must be selective in application and long-term in emphasis.
3. Special attention should be paid both to those who lose their jobs and to the survivors who remain with the organization.
4. Decision makers should identify precisely where redundancies, excess costs, and inefficiencies exist and attack those specific areas.
5. Downsizing should result in the formation of small, semi-autonomous organizations within the broader organization.
6. Downsizing must be a proactive strategy focused on increasing performance.*[58]

*Source: Cameron, K., S. Freeman, and A. Mishra. 1991. "Best Practices in White Collar Downsizing: Managing Contradictions," *Academy of Management Executives* 5: 57–7.

Although the importance of communication is widely acknowledged, it appears that communication during downsizing is particularly difficult because of the negative effect on the informal communication networks in an organization. It is important to (1) attend to rumours, (2) provide survivors with available information on the downsizing, (3) ensure that survivors are aware of the new organizational goals, (4) make expectations clear, (5) tell survivors that they are valued, and (6) allow time for grieving.[59]

THE "NEW DEAL" IN EMPLOYMENT AND THE PSYCHOLOGICAL CONTRACT

You're expendable. We don't want to fire you but we will if we have to. Competition is brutal, so we must redesign the way we work to do more with less. Sorry, that's just the way it is. And one more thing—you're invaluable . . . We're depending on you to be innovative, risk-taking, and committed to our goals.[60]

What does this mean for employees? In many organizations, we have moved away from the expectation of lifetime employment.[61] Rather, workers should prepare for a "multiorganizational career" and recognize that it is highly unlikely that they will remain with the same organization throughout their working lives.

An important part of the employment relationship is the **psychological contract** (those unwritten commitments between employers and employees). Over the past two-and-a-half decades, the psychological contract between employers and employees has changed dramatically. Historical notions of job security and rewards for loyal and long service to the organization have, in many instances, been replaced by ongoing change, uncertainty, and considerable shedding of employees. Associated with such developments are the considerable pain, stress, and hardship inflicted on employees, including both workers who have lost jobs and survivors who remain with an organization (see HR Planning Today 10.5).

A number of organizations try, as part of their HR planning and development activities, to hire from within the firm (where possible). Such organizations develop internal labour markets in which new employees are hired at specific "ports of entry," and other positions are filled through internal transfers and promotions. Historically, employers and employees often had an implicit contract

Psychological contract

An unwritten commitment between employers and their employees that historically guaranteed job security and rewards for loyal service

HR Planning Today 10.5

Losing a Job and Social Withdrawal

What is the impact of losing your job on your social life? Using data from high school graduates tracked over a 45-year period, a just-released study revealed that being laid off once made people approximately 30 to 35 percent less likely to join a social organization. Study author Jennie Brand indicated, "We found that workers who were displaced were less likely to participate in arranged activities, whether church groups and church attendance, charitable organizations—a big one was youth groups and community groups—and even social gatherings with friends or country club organizations."

It should also be noted that individuals who were downsized only once were less likely to engage in social activities than those who had been laid off more frequently. It was speculated that individuals working in jobs with low job security become more accustomed to downsizing and are not as negatively affected by the experience as those who are downsized for the first time.

Source: Adapted from "Layoffs Lead to Social Withdrawal," *Vancouver Sun*, September 2, 2008, C7. Material reprinted with the express permission of CanWest News Service, a CanWest Partnership.

based on the notion that there was a mutual commitment by both employers and workers to long-term employment, and job hirings were viewed as "implicit contracts" in which employees are given certain assurances regarding security of wages and employment. However, such contracts have been radically altered or have ceased to exist in many organizations.

Does it really matter if the psychological contract is breached (i.e., the perception is that that one party has failed to live up to its obligations)? In one study, employees who perceived that their employer breached the psychological contract were more likely to report lower levels of trust in the employer, reduced performance, increased use of sick leave, and a greater intention of leaving the organization. When asked to assess the perceived breach of a psychological contract associated with downsizing, individuals with a strong belief in the ideologies of market competition or shareholder interest were significantly less likely to indicate a breach of the psychological contract than ones who believed in the ideology of employee worth (i.e., an obligation on the part of organizations to focus on employee interests).[62]

Downsizing and "High Involvement" HRM

High-involvement human resources management

A commitment to human resources management practices that treat people as assets

Over the past two decades, some employers have been giving more and more attention to what has become known as **high-involvement human resources management**. A number of organizations are introducing programs such as self-managed work teams, selective hiring, extensive training, labour–management committees, and incentive compensation. However, a number of these same firms have also undertaken (or are planning to undertake) large-scale restructuring. From the perspective of the employee, these strategies appear to be in competition: If human resources are so valuable and worthy of development, why is the organization getting rid of its assets? Management credibility is destroyed, because employees view the notion of high-involvement HRM as diametrically opposed to the shedding of workers: employee involvement and empowerment programs require employee attachment and commitment, while downsizing programs focus on organizational detachment.

Can high-performance work practices exist in an environment of layoffs and restructuring? It has been argued that downsizing may be incompatible with the introduction of high-performance work practices, because team-based work requires relatively stable membership of team members, and high-performance work practices are based on the notion of substantial employee commitment to the organization.

There is some evidence that organizations with more high-performance work practices may also be more likely to engage in workforce reduction. However, such firms are also more likely to use less harsh approaches (such as attrition and voluntary severance packages) and less likely to rely on compulsory layoffs.[63] A new study of Canadian firms that had engaged in downsizing revealed that organizations with a more extensive use of high-performance work practices had lower levels of labour productivity following downsizing, unless such employers also had high levels of consideration for employee welfare and morale—in other words, it is important that organizations with high-performance work practices also maintain trust and commitment following downsizing by focusing on fair treatment, involvement, and communication.[64] The relationship between layoffs and human resources management is discussed further in HR Planning Today 10.6.

HR Planning Today ⟨ 10.6 ⟩

HRM, Competitive Advantage, and Layoffs

What is the impact if a high-involvement workplace resorts to layoffs? Can investment in human resources management reduce the negative consequences often associated with layoffs?

In a large study of Canadian workplaces, Zatzick and Iverson found that workplaces with a greater number of high-involvement work practices suffer more from layoffs than those with fewer practices. In other words, the competitive advantage of a high-involvement workplace may be threatened if there are layoffs.

A number of firms, when engaging in layoffs, also cut back on their investment in human resources management. However, Zatzick and Iverson's research revealed that the negative effect on productivity associated with layoffs may be mitigated by continued investment in high-involvement practices. The authors conclude that layoffs are more likely to be successful when they are part of a planned strategic change rather than part of a cost-cutting exercise.

Source: Adapted from C. Zatzick and R. Iverson, "High-Involvement Management and Workforce Reduction: Competitive Advantage or Disadvantage," *Academy of Management Journal*, Vol. 49, No. 5 (2006), 999–1015.

A recent book, *The Enemy of Engagement* (by Tom Agnew and Mark Royal), discusses the importance of addressing employee needs in difficult economic times and the focus on doing more with less. According to Tom Agnew, "We're downsizing, we're cutting costs, we're cutting expenditure . . . and I can't, as a manager, focus on my people because I'm so focused on making sure that I spend less money and we get the stuff done with the same amount of people. From an employee perspective, when they hear we have to do more with less—what does that mean? You want me to work harder, you want me to work longer, and in all likelihood, you're going to give me less resources to do it—and you're not going to pay me any more."[65]

Human resources experts have a considerable role to play in downsizing and restructuring. Some considerations are as follows:

- Advising on restructuring the organization (work groups, teams, departments, and so on) to maximize productivity and retain quality performers.

- Developing skill inventories and planning charts to evaluate the impact of a downsizing on HR needs and projected capabilities.

- Communicating the downsizing decision effectively.

- Evaluating the downsizing program after completion. This includes an assessment of who left the organization and who remains. Some key issues include job design and redesign, worker adjustment to change, the need for employee counselling, organizational communication, and a review of the appropriateness of HRM policies and programs (training, compensation and benefits, orientation of employees into the "new" organization, etc.).*[66]

*Source: Mone, M. 1994. "Relationships between Self-Concepts, Aspirations, Emotional Responses, and Intent to Leave a Downsizing Organization," *Human Resource Management* 33: 281–298.

Labour Relations Issues

Consider the decision by Navistar to close its Chatham, Ontario truck manufacturing plant. Employees at the plant, who are represented by the Canadian Auto Workers, have been on layoff status for two years because the union and employer have been unable to reach a collective agreement. According to CAW President Ken Lewenza, "Closing the Chatham plant is a devastating blow to the workers, the families and the communities. Despite our relentless efforts since 2009 to reopen the idled facility and get our members back to work, Navistar has remained rigid and is moving ahead with plans to shutter the plant."[67]

Practitioners in unionized organizations often face additional challenges when participating in the restructuring process. In any downsizing involving a union, it is critical that management representatives *read* the collective agreement—while this should go without saying, in many instances practitioners do not follow this advice. The collective agreement often outlines the procedures to be followed in the event of a reduction of bargaining unit employees. Of particular relevance are clauses addressing notice-period requirements in the event of a layoff and provisions dealing with seniority.

There has been a movement in labour relations toward greater cooperation between labour and management and the emergence of new employment relationships. However, changes in managerial attitudes and behaviours are necessary if cooperation between labour and management will succeed; unfortunately, many downsizing programs have destroyed positive labour relations programs. One study of workforce reduction in the unionized environment revealed that labour–management climate was lower (the quality of the labour–management relationship was more adversarial) for those bargaining units that experienced a reduction of the workforce. Of note was that this result was consistent when considering *both* employer respondents and union officials.[68]

A second study explored the adoption of high-performance work practices in unionized environments and the role of employment security. The results indicated that the use of high-performance work practices declined as union representation increased. However, this finding was affected by the employer's commitment to job security. Among companies with a low commitment to job security, the use of high-performance work practices declined markedly as the percentage of the workforce represented by a union increased. However, where commitment to job security was high, the use of high-performance work practices rose modestly as unionization increased. In other words, providing employment security appears to temper the effect of unionization on the adoption of high-performance work practices.[69]

Should unions participate in management-initiated restructuring efforts? One case study documented the experiences of three union locals involved in the process of restructuring. Each union local negotiated with the employer over the issue of workplace restructuring, but the substance of the bargaining as well as the level of involvement by the union and its members varied noticeably. However, it is possible to identify two distinct union responses. The *interventionist* response was characterized by early involvement in the restructuring process and the involvement of a broad cross-section of the union membership in the development and implementation of the new form of work organization.

HR Planning Today 10.7

Unionized Employees' Perceptions of Role Stress and Fairness During Downsizing

Do union members who survive a downsizing have lower job satisfaction and less favourable attitudes toward the union? Very little research has examined the effects of downsizing on union members' attitudes and perceptions. A study of unionized workers in a Swedish hospital sheds some light on the consequences of downsizing in a unionized environment.

Downsizing was associated with reduced levels of job satisfaction and perceptions of poorer health but was not related to union members' satisfaction with their union. However, union members who perceived that their union treated employees fairly during the downsizing reported higher levels of job satisfaction and well-being.

Source: Adapted from J. Hellgren and M. Sverke, "Unionized Employees' Perceptions of Role Stress and Fairness During Organizational Downsizing: Consequences for Job Satisfaction, Union Satisfaction and Well-Being," *Economic and Industrial Democracy*, Vol. 22 (2001), 543–568.

On the other hand, the *pragmatic* response was one in which the union relied on the employer to make workplace changes and then negotiated with management over the impact of such changes. While this response is not surprising, the study results indicate that it may not be the optimal response—in redesigning the work, management has limited information about the work itself and workplace norms, the change does not proceed through a series of steps in which union input is sought, and the lack of involvement in the process leads to lower commitment to change on the part of the union and its members.[70]

It remains to be seen how true cooperation can exist when the job security of employees is threatened. By way of example, union leaders frequently report that joint committees and employee involvement programs are designed to get workers to make suggestions that increase productivity at the cost of job security. Although a positive labour climate is often associated with favourable organizational outcomes, achieving such a climate is very difficult, and several good relationships have been destroyed when firms embarked on a program of cutting jobs. Furthermore, there is evidence that downsizing may be harmful to the health of employees (see HR Planning Today 10.7).

SUMMARY

HR planning plays an important role in the development and implementation of an effective downsizing strategy. The "job for life" approach has been radically changed in the past decade, resulting in a number of new challenges for both employees and employers. It does not appear that the downsizing phenomenon is over, and consequently HR professionals must have a solid understanding of how to manage the downsizing process.

There is considerable evidence that many downsizings fell far short of achieving the goals that senior management expected. In a number of organizations, downsizing was followed by lower morale, greater conflict, reduced employee commitment, and poorer financial performance. Moreover, many downsizings were carried out without considering the strategic objectives of the organization, and many employers failed to assess how downsizing would affect its victims, surviving employees, the organization, customers, or society. Managing human resources in a time of cutback management presents several unique challenges to the HRM professional.

Key Terms

distributive justice p. 271
downsizing p. 261
downsizing strategy p. 260
high-involvement human resources
   management p. 280
inplacement p. 266
interactional justice p. 271

outplacement p. 266
procedural justice p. 271
psychological contract p. 279
survivors (of downsizing) p. 260
systematic change p. 263
workforce reduction p. 261
work redesign p. 262

Web Links

A site that tracks layoff announcements:
www.layoffwatch.com

A site with an extensive collection of articles about downsizing:
http://topics.nytimes.com/top/reference/timestopics/subjects/layoffs_and_job_reductions/index.html

Required Professional Capabilities (RPCs)

The following RPCs are relevant to material covered in this chapter. The RPC number represents the CCHRA number assigned to the RPC as presented on the CCHRA website. All of the RPCs can be found in the Body of Knowledge at www.chrp.ca/rpc/body-of-knowledge.

RPC 1 Contributes to the development of the organization's visions, goals, and strategies with a focus on human capabilities

RPC 4 Guides and advises the organization in the development and application of ethical practices

RPC 6 Develops and implements a human resources plan that supports the organization's strategic objectives

RPC 8 Provides the information necessary for organization to effectively manage its people practices

RPC 14 Uses communication strategies to advance organizational objectives

RPC 16 Provides the organization with timely and accurate HR information

RPC 43 Serves as a change agent to support organizational development initiatives

RPC 50 Plans for and manages the HR aspects of organizational change

RPC 64 Researches, analyzes, and reports on potential people issues affecting the organization

RPC 65 Forecasts HR supply and demand conditions

RPC 67 Develops people plans that support the organization's strategic objectives

RPC 88 Develops and implements procedures for employee departures

RPC 90 Advises on alternatives to terminations

Discussion Questions

1. What can managers embarking on an organizational downsizing do to minimize the impact of the process on the "survivors" of downsizing?
2. In light of the negative consequences often associated with downsizing, why do organizations downsize? Why do so many downsizings fail to meet organizational objectives?
3. "It is a lot harder downsizing unionized employees." Do you agree with this statement? Discuss some of the challenges associated with downsizing in a union environment.
4. What is the "psychological contract"? Why has it changed over the past 25 years? When considering the next ten years, what changes to the psychological contract do you envision?
5. Can a high-involvement human resource management strategy succeed in an organization that is also going through a downsizing?

Exercises

1. Discuss the following statement: "Restructuring is unavoidable. Firms that want to survive and prosper in the global economy need to engage in restructuring strategies."
2. Interview three employees who are survivors of a downsizing. Ask them to discuss how the downsizing was conducted and its effects on them personally and on the organization.
3. Meet with an HRM professional or a senior management official whose organization has gone through a downsizing. Ask the individual to describe the downsizing strategy employed by his or her organization. Consider Cameron's three downsizing strategies of workforce reduction, work redesign, and systematic change. To what extent did the organization use any or all of these strategies?

Case   A DOWNSIZING DECISION AT THE DEPARTMENT OF PUBLIC WORKS

Kathleen Pool is a human resources officer with a municipal government in a town of just over 25,000 people. A well-known consulting firm, in cooperation with senior government officials, recently completed a detailed audit of government operations. As a result of the audit, selected government departments (including the Department of Public Works) were targeted for restructuring. The consultants made it clear in their report that they believed that the budget allocation for the Department of Public Works was "adequate" and recommended that the department receive a 2 percent annual increase in funding for the next two years. Note that operating costs for the department are projected to increase at a rate of about 4.0 percent annually.

Kathleen has been given the responsibility of managing the restructuring at the Department of Public Works. Rather than directing the department to cut a specific number of jobs, Kathleen has been asked to develop a restructuring strategy that will meet the town's mission of "providing quality service to its residents in a cost-effective manner." She is currently reviewing the operating policies at the Department of Public Works.

The Department of Public Works is responsible for such tasks as garbage collection, basic sidewalk and road maintenance, city parks and arenas, installation of street signs and parking meters, and snow removal. At the present time, employees work in one of three subunits: garbage collection, parks and recreation, or city maintenance. Each of the subunits is housed in a separate building, and has its own equipment and supplies, and its own operating budget. As well, while employees can formally apply to transfer to a different subunit, the managers of the subunits involved and the Director of Public Works (who is responsible for the overall operation of the Department) must all agree. Unless a vacancy at one of the subunits arises, it is rare that any employee transfer will be approved.

In 2006, the Department of Public Works underwent a considerable downsizing and 4 percent of its permanent positions were cut. In addition, the department stopped its practice of hiring summer students from local high schools and universities in an effort to cut costs. Prior to this, students were employed over the summer to help with special projects and to cover vacation periods for full-time employees. In 2009, a smaller cutback of 2 percent of the workforce took place.

In 2010, the municipality brought back the practice of hiring summer students. This decision was welcomed by the full-time employees at the Department of Public Works, in particular because it allows the employees much more flexibility in selecting their vacation time. From 2006 to 2009, management put considerable restrictions on when employees could go on vacation; employees with ten or more years of service could have a maximum of one week's vacation in July or August while employees with less than ten years of service were not permitted to go on vacation during these two months. Under the collective agreement, management has the right to determine the vacation schedule of unionized employees.

In reviewing turnover data for the Department of Public Works, Kathleen found that very few full-time employees quit their jobs to pursue other employment opportunities. In addition, dismissals for cause were rare; over the past ten years, only two employees were terminated for cause. In both cases, the union lost the discharge grievance at an arbitration hearing.

Since the late 1990s, the municipality has had a local consulting firm conduct surveys of both municipal employees and the users of government services. A summary of the findings from the employee survey (for Department of Public Works employees only) is contained in Table 10.1. Note that each of the items (such as employee morale) is measured on a five-point scale (1 = very low; 5 = very high). Similarly, Table 10.2 contains summary information

TABLE 10.1

Summary Results from a Survey of Public Works Employees

Year	Employee Morale	Employee Commitment to Department	Overall Employee Job Satisfaction	Intention to Stay with the Municipality
2005	3.89	3.72	4.02	4.77
2006	2.21	1.99	2.34	4.11
2007	2.36	2.22	2.87	3.77
2008	2.65	2.62	3.22	3.99
2009	2.38	2.33	2.66	4.44
2010	2.88	3.01	2.99	4.5
2011	3.54	3.52	3.88	4.72

TABLE 10.2

Summary Results from a Survey of Municipal Residents

Year	Level of Satisfaction with the Board of Public Works	Quality of Service Provided by the Board of Public Works
2005	3.95	3.88
2006	3.22	3.01
2007	3.34	3.24
2008	3.65	3.66
2009	3.56	3.49
2010	3.78	3.72
2011	4.01	3.98

from the survey of municipal residents concerning the performance of the Department of Public Works. Again, respondents were asked to reply using a five-point scale (1 = very low and 5 = very high). Note that on both the employee survey and the users of government services survey, there were only minor differences in the results when the data were broken down by subunit (garbage collection, parks and recreation, or city maintenance).

Questions

1. Outline the issues that Kathleen should consider prior to designing a restructuring strategy.
2. Design a strategy to restructure the Department of Public Works. Be sure to provide support for the decisions/recommendations you propose.
3. A recent newspaper editorial suggested that the town contract out the collection of garbage. What are the advantages/disadvantages of contracting out services that had been provided by government?

ENDNOTES

1. The sources of these headlines are "Canada Shed 54,000 Jobs in October." *The Chronicle Herald*, November 5, 2011, p. B1; "RIM Woes Worry 500 Workers in Bedford." *The Chronicle Herald*, June 18, 2011, p. C1; "Ottawa Eliminating Auditing Jobs." *The Globe and Mail*, June 21, 2011, p. A4.
2. This example comes from an article by Galagan, P. 2010. "The Biggest Losers: The Perils of Extreme Downsizing." *T+D*, November: 27–29.
3. "Nokia Siemens Networks to Slash 17,000 Jobs Worldwide by 2013." *Winnipeg Free Press*, November 23, 2011.
4. Stephenson, E. 2011. "U.S. Postal Service Looks to Cut 220,000 Jobs." *Canadian HR Reporter*, August 15.
5. Cameron, K. 1994. "Strategies for Successful Organizational Downsizing." *Human Resource Management*, Vol. 33: 189–211.
6. Datta, D., J. Guthrie, D. Basuil, and A. Pandey. 2010. "Causes and Effects of Employee Downsizing: A Review and Synthesis. *Journal of Management*, Vol. 36: 282; Sheaffer, Z., A. Carmeli, M. Steiner-Revivo, and S. Zionit. 2009. "Downsizing Strategies and Organizational Performance." *Management Decision*, Vol. 47: 951.
7. McKinley, W., and A. Scherer. 2000. "Some Unanticipated Consequences of Organizational Restructuring." *Academy of Management Review*, Vol. 25: 735–752.
8. Kane, B. 2000. "Downsizing, TQM, Re-engineering, Learning Organizations and HRM Strategy." *Asia Pacific Journal of Human Resources*, Vol. 38: 26–49.
9. J. Pfeffer, "Lay off the Layoffs." *Newsweek*, February 15, 2010.
10. Love, E., and N. Nohria. 2006. "Reducing Slack: The Performance Consequences of Large Industrial Firms, 1977–93." *Strategic Management Journal*, Vol. 26: 1087–1108.
11. B. Erskine, "Hotel to be Razed, Rise Again." *The Chronicle Herald*, September 9, 2011, p. C1.
12. *Financial Post*, June 30, 2001, p. C2.
13. Latack, J. 1990. "Organizational Restructuring and Career Management: From Outplacement and Survival to Inplacement." In G. Ferris and K. Rowland, eds., *Research in Personnel and Human Resources Management*. Greenwich, CT: JAI Press.

14. Vickers, M. 2009. "Journeys into Grief: Exploring Redundancy for a New Understanding of Workplace Grief." *Journal of Loss and Trauma*, Vol. 14: 412.

15. See Arce, D., and S. Xin Lee. 2011. "Profits, Layoffs and Priorities." *Journal of Business Ethics*, Vol. 101: 49–60.

16. See Rosenblatt, Z., and Z. Schaeffer. 2000. "Ethical Problems in Downsizing." In R. Burke and C. Cooper, eds., *The Organization in Crisis: Downsizing, Restructuring and Privatization*. Malden, MA: Blackwell.

17. Vickers, 2009: 410.

18. Amundson, N., W. Borgen, S. Jordan, and A. Erlebach. 2004. "Survivors of Downsizing: Helpful and Hindering Experiences." *The Career Development Quarterly*, Vol. 52: 260.

19. "If You Must Lay Off." *Canadian HR Reporter*, April 22, 2002, p. 4.

20. These quotes are taken from Parris, M., and M. Vickers. 2010. "'Look at Him . . . He's Failing': Male Executives' Experiences of Redundancy", Vol. 22: 350.

21. Mickleburgh, R. "There's Nothing More: The Town is Dying." *The Globe and Mail*, May 17, 2008, p. S3.

22. Cappelli, P. 1995. "Rethinking Employment." *British Journal of Industrial Relations*, Vol. 33: 563–602.

23. Immen, W. 2008. "When Flames of Fear Lick at Your Feet." *The Globe and Mail*, May 7, 2008, p. C1.

24. Feldman, D., and C. Leana. 1994. "Better Practices in Managing Layoff." *Human Resource Management*, Vol. 33: 239–260.

25. Amundson, N., W. Borgen, S. Jordan, and A. Erlebach. 2004. "Survivors of Downsizing: Helpful and Hindering Experiences." *The Career Development Quarterly Review*, Vol. 52: 256–271, 260.

26. See Abelson, M., and A. Choudhury. 2011. "Wall Street Faces 'Darkest Days' as Jobs Vanish." *Financial Post*, November 22; Ho, K. 2009. "Disciplining Investment Bankers, Disciplining the Economy: Wall Street's Institutional Crisis and the Downsizing of 'Corporate America.'" *American Anthropologist*, 111: 177–189.

27. Kets de Vries, M., and K. Balazs, 1997. "The Downside of Downsizing." *Human Relations*, Vol. 50: 11–40.

28. Immen, W. 2008. "Managers in the Crosshairs." *The Globe and Mail*, August 6, 2008, p. C1.

29. Lee, C. 1992. "After the Cuts." *Training*, Vol. 29: 17–23.

30. See Davy, J., A. Kinicki, and C. Scheck. 1997. "A Test of Job Security's Direct and Mediated Effects on Withdrawal Cognitions." *Journal of Organizational Behavior*, Vol. 18: 323–349; Rosenblatt, Z., and A. Ruvio. 1996. "A Test of a Multidimensional Model of Job Insecurity: The Case of Israeli Teachers." *Journal of Organizational Behavior*, Vol. 17: 587–605.

31. Sverke, M., and J. Hellgren. 2002. "The Nature of Job Insecurity: Understanding Employment Uncertainty on the Brink of a New Millennium." *Applied Psychology: An International Review*, Vol. 51: 23–42.

32. Armstrong-Stassen, M. 1993. "Survivors' Reactions to a Workforce Reduction: A Comparison of Blue-Collar Workers and Their Supervisors." *Canadian Journal of Administrative Sciences*, Vol. 10: 334–343.

33. See A. Molinsky and J. Margolis. 2006. "The Emotional Tightrope of Downsizing: Hidden Challenges for Leaders and their Organizations." *Organizational Dynamics*, Vol. 35: 145–159, 146.

34. A series of articles relating to the Bowater Mersey case appeared in *The Chronicle Herald*. See, for example, "Bowater Boss Plays Hardball on Cost Cuts." November 11, 2011, p. C2; "Bowater Mersey Workforce Could Get Chopped in Half." November 15, 2011, p. A1; "Bowater Mersey: Concessions or Closure?" November 16, 2011, p. A1; "Bowater Workers Accept Cuts." November 17, 2011, p. A1; "Bowater Gets 15% Tax Break." November 18, 2011; "Papermaker Brass Split $4-Million Payout." November 19, 2011, p. A1; "Bowater Workers Weigh Options." November 24, 2011, p. C1.

35. Mone, M. 1994. "Relationships Between Self-Concepts, Aspirations, Emotional Responses, and Intent to Leave a Downsizing Organization." *Human Resource Management*, Vol. 33: 281–298.

36. Maertz, C., J. Wiley, C. LeRouge, and M. Campion. 2010. "Downsizing Effects on Survivors: Layoffs, Offshoring and Outsourcing." *Industrial Relations*, Vol. 49: 275–285.

37. Wright, B., and J. Barling. 1998. "The Executioner's Song: Listening to Downsizers Reflect on their Experiences." *Canadian Journal of Administrative Sciences*, Vol. 15: 339–355.

38. Gandolfi, F. 2009. "Executing Downsizing: The Experience of Executioners." *Contemporary Management Research*, Vol. 5: 185–200.

39. Clair, J., and R. Dufresne. 2004. "Playing the Grim Reaper: How Employees Experience Carrying Out a Downsizing." *Human Relations*, Vol. 57, No. 12: 1608.

40. Molinsky and Margolis, p. 152.

41. Nixon, R., M. Hitt, H. Lee, and E. Jeong. 2004. "Market Reactions to Announcements of Corporate Downsizing Actions and Implementation Strategies." *Strategic Management Journal*, Vol. 25: 1121–1129.

42. Cascio, W., C. Young, and J. Morris. 1997. "Financial Consequences of Employment-Change Decisions in Major U.S. Corporations." *Academy of Management Journal*, Vol. 40: 1175–1189.

43. DeMeuse, K., T. Bergmann, P. Vanderheiden, and C. Roraff. 2004. "New Evidence Regarding Organizational Downsizing and a Firm's Financial Analysis." *Journal of Management Inquiry*, Vol. 16: 155–177.

44. Love and Nohria, 2006.

45. An excellent review of the relationship between downsizing and both employer and employee outcome measures is provided in Datta, D., J. Guthrie, D. Basuil, and A. Pandey. 2010. "Causes and Effects of Employee Downsizing: A Review and Synthesis." *Journal of Management*, Vol. 36: 281–348.

46. Cascio, W. 2002. *Responsible Restructuring: Creative and Responsible Alternatives to Layoffs*. San Francisco: Berrett-Koehler.

47. Tomasko, R. 1990. *Downsizing: Reshaping the Corporation of the Future*, 2nd ed. New York: AMACON.

48. Wagar, T. 1998. "Exploring the Consequences of Workforce Reduction." *Canadian Journal of Administrative Sciences*, Vol. 15: 300–309.

49. Wagar, T., and K. Rondeau. 2002. "Repeated Downsizing, Organizational Restructuring and Performance: Evidence from a Longitudinal Study." *Proceedings of the Administrative Sciences Association of Canada (HRM Division)*. Winnipeg. For a study with similar results based on data from New Zealand see Gilson, C., F. Hurd, and T. Wagar. 2004. "Creating a Concession Climate: The Case of the Serial Downsizers." *International Journal of Human Resource Management*, Vol. 15: 1056–1068.

50. Zyglidopoulos, S. 2004. "The Impact of Downsizing on the Corporate Reputation for Social Performance." *Journal of Public Affairs*, Vol. 4: 13.

51. Zyglidopoulos, 2004: 11–25. Also see Bergstrom, O., and A. Diedrich. 2011. "Exercising Social Responsibility in Downsizing: Enrolling and Mobilizing Actors in a Swedish High-Tech Company." *Organization Studies*, Vol. 32: 897–919.

52. For an interesting review of the safety–job insecurity issue, see Probst, T. 2004. "Job Insecurity: Exploring a New Threat to Employee Safety." In J. Barling and M. Frone, eds., *The Psychology of Workplace Safety*. Washington: APA, 2004. pp. 63–80.

53. Hitt, M., B. Keats, H. Harback, and R. Nixon. 1994. "Rightsizing: Building and Maintaining Strategic Leadership and Long-Term Competitiveness." *Organizational Dynamics*, Vol. 23: 18–32; Lamarsh, J. 2009. "How Companies Reduce the Downside of Downsizing." *Global Business and Organizational Excellence*, November/December: 7–16.

54. Cameron, K. 1994. "Strategies for Successful Organizational Downsizing." *Human Resource Management*, Vol. 33: 189–211. Also see Chadwick, C., L. Hunter, and S. Walston. 2004. "Effects of Downsizing Practices on the Performance of Hospitals." *Strategic Management Journal*, Vol. 25: 405–427.

55. Galagan, 2010.

56. Kammeyer-Mueller, J., H. Liao, and R. Arvey. 2001. "Downsizing and Organizational Performance: A Review of the Literature from a Stakeholder Perspective." In G. Ferris, ed., *Research in Personnel and Human Resource Management*. Amsterdam: JAI Press. Pp. 269–329.

57. Mishra, A., and K. Mishra. 1994. "The Role of Mutual Trust in Effective Downsizing Strategies." *Human Resource Management*, Vol. 33: 261–279.

58. Cameron, K., S. Freeman, and A. Mishra. 1991. "Best Practices in White Collar Downsizing: Managing Contradictions." *Academy of Management Executive*, Vol. 5: 57–73.

59. Dunlap, J. 1994. "Surviving Layoffs: A Qualitative Study of Factors Affecting Retained Employees After Downsizing." *Performance Improvement Quarterly*, Vol. 7: 89–113.

60. O'Reilly, B. 1994. "The New Deal: What Companies and Employees Owe One Another." *Fortune*, June 13, pp. 44–52.

61. Cappelli, P. 1995. "Rethinking Employment." *British Journal of Industrial Relations*, Vol. 33: 563–602.

62. Rust, K., W. McKinley, G. Moon-Kyungpook, and J. Edwards. 2005. "Ideological Foundations of Perceived Contract Breach Associated with Downsizing: An Empirical Investigation." *Journal of Leadership and Organizational Studies*, Vol. 12: 37–52.

63. Iverson , R., and C. Zatzick, "High Commitment Work Practices and Downsizing Harshness in Australian Workplaces." *Industrial Relations*, Vol. 46: 456–480.

64. Iverson, R. and C. Zatzick. 2011. "The Effects of Downsizing on Labor Productivity, the Value of Showing Consideration for Employees' Morale and Welfare in High Performance Work Systems." *Human Resource Management*, Vol. 50: 29–44.

65. See Lauren LaRose, "Employee Frustration Cited as Workplace's Silent Killer." *The Chronicle Herald*, November 27, 2011, p. A9. Also see Roth, W. 2009. "Downsizing: The Cure That Can Kill." *Global Business and Organizational Excellence*, September/October: 46–52.

66. Mone, M. 1994. "Relationships Between Self-Concepts, Aspirations, Emotional Responses, and Intent to Leave a Downsizing Organization." *Human Resource Management*, Vol. 33: 281–298.

67. A. Ananthalakshmi and L. Adler, "Navistar to Shutter Ontario Plant." *The Globe and Mail*, August 2, 2011.

68. Wagar, T. 2001. "Consequences of Work Force Reduction: Some Employer and Union Evidence." *Journal of Labor Research*, Vol. 22: 851–862.

69. Liu, W., J. Guthrie, P. Flood, and S. MacCurtain. 2009. "Unions and the Adoption of High Performance Work Systems: Does Employment Security Play a Role?" *Industrial and Labor Relations Review*, Vol. 63: 109–127.

70. Frost, A. 2001. "Reconceptualizing Local Union Responses to Workplace Restructuring in North America." *British Journal of Industrial Relations*, Vol. 39: 539–564.

CHAPTER
11

Strategic International HRM

This chapter was written by Dr. Stefan Gröschl, ESSEC Business School, France, and is based on a previous edition's chapter by Dr. Xiaoyun Wang, I.H. Asper School of Business, University of Manitoba, Winnipeg, Manitoba; and Dr. Sharon Leiba-O'Sullivan, Department of Management, Faculty of Commerce and Administration, University of Ottawa, Ottawa, Ontario.

CHAPTER LEARNING OUTCOMES

After reading this chapter, you should be able to:

- Identify key challenges influencing human resources (HR) practices and processes within an international context.
- Identify key characteristics of strategic international HRM (SIHRM).
- Understand the relationship between different approaches of SIHRM and corporate business strategy options.
- Understand the impact of globalization and internationalization on key HR practices and processes.

THE WOULD-BE PIONEER

When Linda Myers accepted a human resources position at SK Telecom in South Korea, she thought it was the opportunity she'd long been working toward. . . . For someone who'd spent years consulting on expatriate transitions, this seemed like a dream job. . . . Myers had never heard of SK when a recruiter emailed her, in July 2007. "Dear Mr. Myers," the email began. "They assumed I was a man," she recalls. It was an innocent mistake, but it foreshadowed the misunderstandings to come. . . . The recruiter's initial email marked the start of a six-month interview process, including trips to New York and Santa Clara, California. . . . "I was working with a young man who spoke enough English to be the liaison for his boss, who spoke a little bit less English," Myers recalls. That was to be expected in negotiations with a Korean company for a job in Korea, but the two-language game of telephone sometimes led to confusion. Still, she pressed ahead. In October, SK Telecom formally offered her a job. . . .

On the ground in Seoul, . . . one early shock was the homogeneity of not only her office but also the city: Government estimates indicate that foreigners account for 2.4 percent of the population. . . . Another surprise was her inability to communicate effectively. . . . She recalls having to ask for an interpreter at her first meetings at SK. And even with an assistant and colleagues who spoke English, she found it difficult to get the information she needed. As she saw it, even diplomatic inquiries could be construed as confrontational and critical. She was also unprepared for the company's rigid hierarchy. . . . Moreover, she was constantly aware of being female. Aside from secretaries, she was almost always the only woman in the room.

In spite of these challenges, Myers advanced at SK. Four months after her arrival, she moved on to be head of Global Talent at SK Holdings. But leadership shakeups changed the tenor of this role. Myers felt increasingly left out of key meetings and conversations, in part because language was still a problem, even though, according to SK, she by then had a mostly bilingual team, including three non-Koreans. Although Myers saw her role as that of a change agent, she struggled to implement new practices and policies. "At the lower and middle levels, I think that people were very excited, very eager for change," she explains. "But at the top, most of the leadership was nervous." . . . By early 2009, Myers could tell she was on her way out. "My team leaders would barely speak to me," she says. Finally, her boss called her into his office and explained that although they had extended her contract once, they would not do so again.[1]

Source: Reprinted by permission of *Harvard Business Review*. From "The Would-be Pioneer" by S. Green, April 2011. Copyright ©2012 by Harvard Business School Publishing Corporation. All rights reserved.

Struggling to fit in is a key challenge for managers in their overseas assignments, and one of many critical HR aspects in the internationalization of Canadian companies and their employees. Fast-growing economies such as Brazil, Russia, India, China, and South Africa represent significant business opportunities and require Canadian companies to expand beyond their national boundaries. Despite the weakened global economy, Canada has remained one of the top ten home economies with the highest outflow of foreign direct investments. According to the 2010 World Investment Report, in 2009, Canadian companies invested 38.1 billion Canadian dollars abroad.[2] The same report listed Canadian financial institutions such as the Bank of Nova Scotia, the Royal Bank of Canada, Manulife Financial Corporation, Canadian Imperial Bank of Commerce, and the Toronto Dominion Bank among the top 50 financial transnational companies worldwide[3]

HR Planning Today (11.1

Investing Abroad

It will be interesting to observe how non-financial Canadian companies respond to the current global economic instability and uncertainties. With fast-changing environmental factors such as oil prices and foreign market developments, how will Canadian companies successfully position themselves internationally? How will Canadian businesses respond to the ongoing economic crisis in the United States? While the latter remains the leading foreign market for Canadian companies Canadian direct investments in the U.S. decreased from $289 billion in 2008 to $250 billion in 2010.[4] By benefiting from a weaker U.S. dollar, the United States might continue to import less from and export more to Canada. Canadian companies might have to diversify their foreign investments across a wider range of countries and regions. In 2010, for example, the European Union as a whole accounted for only 25.5 percent of Canada's total foreign direct investment, followed by South and Central America with 5.4 percent, Africa with 0.5 percent and Asia/Oceania with 9 percent.[5] Greater diversification into European countries and other growing markets such as China and South Africa requires Canadian organizations to operate in increasingly complex business environments, and to consider the appropriateness and effectiveness of organizational processes and managerial practices in a wide range of very different cultural and legal settings. Comparative international and cross-cultural management researchers[6] and multinational teams[7] concluded that, in particular, the planning and managing of human resources play a key role in the successful expansion of organizations across national borders.

(see also HR Planning Today 11.1). Yet entering growing economies and new markets means not only greater business opportunities for Canadian firms, but also a wide range of strategic and operational HR challenges.

KEY CHALLENGES INFLUENCING HR PRACTICES AND PROCESSES WITHIN AN INTERNATIONAL CONTEXT

When entering new markets, organizations are confronted with a wide range of challenges mostly related to socioeconomic, political, and technological aspects. Following is a brief discussion of some of the key issues HR managers face when their organizations expand across national borders.

Workforce Diversity

Many articles in academic journals and the popular press have documented Canada's growing workforce diversity. While the different dimensions of diversity provide Canadian organizations with many opportunities, Canada's workforce diversity also produces a wide range of HR-related challenges, including the integration and accommodation of an increased number of older workers and employees with disabilities, diverse gender identities, and aspects related to ethnic and cultural differences among employees. The complexity of the current workforce diversity will grow with each foreign market Canadian organizations decide to enter, multiplying the workforce diversity–related challenges HR managers currently face. Strategic international human resources management (SIHRM) systems must consider and accommodate the needs of an increasingly diverse labour force and tailor international HR policies and practices accordingly.

Employment Legislation

HR managers of organizations operating across Canada are faced with a complex provincial and federal employment legislation framework. When crossing national borders, Canadian HR managers encounter additional host-country employment legislation—and in the case of a European Union (EU) member state being the host country, employment laws and regulations of the host country and the EU. This wide range of home and host-country employment legislations represent a key challenge to HR managers and the development and implementation of employment policies, processes, and practices in Canadian organizations operating internationally.

The Role of the HR Function

HR departments are often understaffed, underfunded, and limited to a supporting role with little key decision-making power. Yet employment legislation, socioeconomic, and technological differences in local markets demand sophisticated SIHRM systems. The creation of such systems requires sufficient financial and human resources and support. It is crucial that HR managers responsible for the development and implementation of such systems be equipped with the necessary staff and are integrated in the organizational strategic decision-making process and the development of organizational goals and objectives. Previous chapters have shown the importance and the challenge of matching HRM practices with organizational goals. Within an international context, this matching process becomes even more challenging and, at the same time, even more imperative for the successful expansion beyond national borders.

Flexibility

Flexibility

The ability to respond to various demands from a dynamic competitive environment

In an international context, the changes are dramatic and fast, though they differ from country to country. In such a dynamic global competitive environment, SIHRM systems need to be flexible to quickly adjust their policies and practices to respond to the changes. **Flexibility** is defined as a firm's ability to respond to various demands from a dynamic competitive environment.[8] Yet, no matter how capable the HR manager is, it is impossible to expect him or her to be aware of all the changes in the international competitive environment. Advanced SIHRM systems, however, can obtain a high level of fit and flexibility by developing a strategic approach toward the management of international workforces.

Security

While Afghanistan and Iraq have been known for many years for their unsafe business environments, recent terrorist attacks in Pakistan and India, violent societal upheavals in Egypt, Bahrain, Tunisia, Algeria, Libya, and Syria, and organized crime and increased kidnappings in Venezuela, Mexico, Honduras, Nigeria, Somalia, and Sudan[9] have raised serious concerns among internationally operating businesses for their expatriate employees' security. Sophisticated

HR support structures in areas of employee security and safety including risk assessment processes, precautionary actions and procedures, and contingency planning are critical aspects in ensuring that employees and their families deployed in dangerous or troublesome parts of the world always return home safely. Establishing close relationships with Canadian governmental overseas representatives (Canadian embassies, chambers of commerce, consulates, high commissions) in countries in which employee security is a concern to foreign businesses is only one of many proactive and precautious security measurements.[10]

STRATEGIC INTERNATIONAL HUMAN RESOURCES MANAGEMENT

The UPS example in HR Planning Today 11.2 illustrates the size, geographical distribution, and level of internationalization of many multinational enterprises, highlighting the need for the methodical and careful planning of a strategic international HR approach.

Strategic international HR planning typically involves projecting global competence supply, forecasting global competence needs, and developing a blueprint to establish global competence pools within companies so that the supply of global managers worldwide will be sufficient to coincide with the multinational company's (MNC) global strategies. Attracting and retaining managers who are competent to represent the company in a global arena have been rated as the most critical goals of international HRM by multinational corporations (MNCs).[11]

Moreover, international HR planning needs to fit with both the internal factors, such as a firm's strategies, competencies, and existing HR system, and the external factors including local economic, political, social, cultural, legal, and

> Strategic international HR planning
>
> Projecting global competence supply, forecasting global competence needs, and developing a blueprint to establish global competence pools within companies

---

HR Planning Today 11.2

UPS Around the World

In 2001, the $30 billion multinational company UPS employed more than 360,000 people in 200 countries and territories. For the core business, 13 regional directors had a total of 72 district managers reporting to them. And each of those 72 district managers ran an operation the size of a Fortune 1000 company. Besides its core business, UPS managed several other business units with revenues in excess of $1 billion.[12] The size and geographical distribution of UPS creates a wide range of HR implications and challenges: respecting and adjusting to 200 or more different employment and human rights legislations, and industrial relations; selecting the right level or mix of centralizing and decentralizing UPS' HR function across countries, companies, and business units; creating HR structures and reporting systems supporting UPS' HR strategic role and operational responsibilities in a proactive and flexible way; and responding to the wide range of different cultural value systems in UPS' decision-making process about the level of standardization or adaptation of HR policies, processes, and practices. Failing to address these challenges can lead to a wide range of costly implications for UPS—from employment lawsuits due to, for example, lacking awareness of local employment practices, to labour relations disputes and strikes, and in the worst-case scenario, to surrendering and retreating from a foreign market.[13]

Source: J. Kirby, "Reinvention with Respect," *Harvard Business Review*, November 2001, p. 117.

HR Planning Today 11.3

Global Compensation Packages

According to Expatica, an online resource for internationals living abroad, findings from a Mercer HR Consulting survey indicate a trend toward global compensation packages among North American and Europe-based MNCs, including pay in relation to the market, short- and long-term incentive policies, and consistent processes of job grading and levelling. Expatica quotes Mark Edelstein from Mercer in London, who argues that compensation strategies are becoming more and more important for the success of MNCs, and that pay is being increasingly managed from a global perspective—to support global expansion efforts, manage labour costs more effectively, develop internal equity, or ensure effective governance.[14] Yet the development of such global compensation packages creates a wide range of challenges for HR compensation experts. There is, for example, the question of how standardized such global compensation packages can or should be—especially considering the differences in costs of living, taxation policies, and other host-country-specific regulations influencing employees' compensations. When it comes to internal equity, justifying and explaining compensation gaps between a home-country manager working side by side with a host-country manager can be a rather sensitive and complex task. Thus, HRM has to carefully weigh the advantages and disadvantages of such a compensation strategy before developing global compensation policies.

Strategic international HRM
Human resources management issues, functions, policies, and practices that result from the strategic activities of multinational enterprises and that affect the international concerns and goals of those enterprises

Fit
The degree to which the needs, demands, goals, objectives, and/or structure of one component are consistent with the need, demands, goals, objectives, and/or structure of another component

HR systems. A fit and, as mentioned earlier, flexible SIHRM system is critical for firms to successfully implement their international strategies and to gain competitive advantage. Studies found that MNCs globalize HR practices issues such as pay systems, management development, or employee communications (see HR Planning Today 11.3). With other issues, such as wage determination, hours of work, forms of job contract, and redundancy procedures that are subject to local laws and convention, MNCs tend to follow the local practices, although the extent to which SIHRM practices fit with the local environment or with home headquarters varies from company to company and from country to country.[15]

Strategic thinking is needed for SIHRM to project HR supply and to forecast HR needs for the foreign subsidiaries. Therefore, **strategic international HRM** is defined as "human resource management issues, functions, and policies and practices that result from the strategic activities of multinational enterprises and that impact the international concerns and goals of those enterprises."[16]

Strategic IHRM Fits with Corporate International Business Strategies

As mentioned in previous chapters, HR planning should fit with the overall business strategies of the firm. This principle should apply to SIHRM as well. **Fit** is defined as "the degree to which the needs, demands, goals, objectives and/or structure of one component are consistent with the need, demands, goals, objectives, and/or structure of another component."[17] Based on this principle, SIHRM approaches and policies will be influenced by the overall corporate international strategies, the type of product or service, and the organizational structure and culture (*internal fit*). At the same time, it is important to consider the local legal, political, economic, and cultural factors (*external fit*). The internal and external fits of SIHRM are vital to the effective implementation of a corporate strategy.

The Domestic Stage

Organizations applying a **domestic strategy** become international by exporting goods abroad as a means of seeking new markets, focusing on domestic markets, and exporting their products without altering the products for foreign markets. Because this is an initial step of going international and there is no subsidiary in foreign countries, there is very little demand on the HR department to conduct its practices any differently than domestic HR practices. Usually, an export manager is appointed by headquarters to take charge of the exporting business.

Domestic strategy
Internationalizing by exporting goods abroad as a means of seeking new markets

The Multidomestic Stage

As the firm develops expertise in the international market and as the foreign market grows in importance for the success of the organization, a subsidiary is typically set up, reflecting a **multidomestic strategy**.[18] Management at this stage realizes that there are "many good ways" to do business and that cultural sensitivity is important to be successful in the local market. A polycentric perspective is a trademark of this stage, and firms use the multidomestic strategy to develop culturally appropriate products for local markets.

Multidomestic strategy
A strategy that concentrates on the development of foreign markets by selling to foreign nationals

In line with this polycentric business strategy, the company's SIHRM system will apply an **adaptive IHRM approach**, adopting local HR practices in their host country's subsidiaries. French lodging giant ACCOR is taking this approach, and has adopted many local HRM practices in its U.S. subsidiaries in order to attract and retain local employees. Following an adaptive IHRM approach, a local executive is usually hired to take charge of the subsidiaries' HR management. The advantage of this method is that the local HR manager for the subsidiaries is familiar with local issues, and there is no language barrier between the HR manager, local partners, and employees. Hiring a local HR manager can also guarantee the consistency of the HR practices with the local legal system and environment. One disadvantage is if the local HR manager does not know the corporate culture well enough to reflect the overall corporate strategies and the corporate principles in the subsidiary HR system. Nevertheless, because HRM is very sensitive to local legal and economic systems, compared to other business functions, such as finance and manufacturing, HRM has mostly adhered to local practices in many multinational corporations.[19]

Adaptive IHRM approach
HRM systems for foreign subsidiaries that will be consistent with the local economic, political, and legal environment

The Multinational Stage

When more and more MNCs enter the same market, the competition from other multinationals forces management to shift its strategy, resulting in the standardization of its products and services around the world to gain efficiency. Such a **multinational strategy** promotes a price-sensitive perspective with limited emphasis on cultural differences.[20]

Multinational strategy
Standardizing the products and services around the world to gain efficiency

Following the company's multinational business strategy, HR systems will be standardized across its subsidiaries all over the world. Numerous MNCs, such as Ernst & Young, have adopted such an **exportive IHRM approach** to reduce transaction costs, ensure the consistency of their corporate policies all over the world, and gain control over their subsidiaries.[21] The advantage of this approach is that the HR managers at headquarters have a "tried and true" HR system and can readily implement it efficiently in subsidiaries in other countries.

Exportive IHRM approach
Transferring home HRM systems to foreign subsidiaries without modifying or adapting to the local environment

The disadvantage is that the local environment will not have been considered in the HR system, and the fit with the local system will be missing, which might cause problems for the subsidiaries' management.

The Global Stage

Global strategy

Introducing culturally sensitive products in chosen countries with the least amount of cost

Integrative IHRM approach

Combining home HR practices with local practices and selecting the most qualified people for the appropriate positions no matter where these candidates come from

Companies adopting a **global strategy** are striving to introduce culturally sensitive products, with the least amount of cost. To accomplish this, resources and materials within regional branches are reallocated globally to make quality products at the lowest cost. A geocentric perspective is taken by the company management at this stage.

Fitting this global business strategy is an **integrative IHRM approach** combining home HR practices with local practices. The best HR policies and practices will be chosen for the foreign subsidiaries. For example, some Japanese companies have transferred some of their HR practices, such as job flexibility, intensive on-the-job training, teamwork, and cooperative relations between management and employees, to North America, but abandoned other practices, such as the use of uniforms.[22] With this approach, not only can the best context-free HR practices be transferred to subsidiaries but also sound foreign practices can be learned and transferred to headquarters. The decision making regarding HR policies and practices will be jointly in the hands of headquarters and foreign subsidiaries. Therefore, this approach usually goes along with the global strategy and is recommended for the purpose of mutual learning between headquarters and subsidiaries. The challenge of using this approach is that the HR managers at headquarters need to have a geocentric or global perspective, be culturally sensitive, and be able to strategically move HR resources around the subsidiaries and headquarters, as illustrated by Four Seasons' Golden Rule policy outlined in HR Planning Today 11.4.

HR Planning Today 11.4

Four Seasons' Golden Rule

While Four Seasons recognizes and responds to local differences at the same time, the Canadian hotels and resorts company thrives for global integration through globally uniform standards. Within the HR context, for example, Four Seasons' key standard has been the "Golden Rule":

Human resource management at Four Seasons started and ended with "The Golden Rule," which stipulated that one should treat others as one would wish to be treated. "The Golden Rule is the key to the success of the firm," founder and CEO [Isadore] Sharp emphasized, "and it's appreciated in every village, town, and city around the world."[23]

While Sharp promotes the Golden Rule as a successful global HR tool in Four Seasons, BP's manager of HR global operations for Europe considers the Golden Rule inappropriate for his human resources management philosophy. He argues that managers and employees should not treat each other the way they themselves wish to be treated, but the way the other wishes to be treated.[24] These two rather contrasting views show how companies can use different employee relations philosophies in recognizing and responding successfully to global standardization and to local differences.

Companies may not practise one of the above corporate strategies exclusively at any one time; rather, they might simultaneously implement the four strategies for different products at the same time. Of the different IHRM approaches, it is not difficult to see that the adaptive approach has the highest external fit, the exportive approach has the highest internal fit, and the integrative approach has the maximum fit both internally and externally. The integrative approach is highly recommended, because, as mentioned above, both internal factors and external factors are important to successfully implement corporate international strategies.

KEY HR PRACTICES AND PROCESSES WITHIN AN INTERNATIONAL CONTEXT

The global expansion of organizations particularly influences the management of their human resources. While during the economic crisis some Canadian companies announced cuttings of their expatriate assignments, in the 2011 Employee Relocation Policy Survey by the Canadian Employee Relocation Council the majority of Canadian companies expected the number of foreign assignments and relocations to remain steady or to continue to increase.[25] Similarly, according to the Brookfield GRS's 2011 Global Relocation Trends Survey, 61 percent of respondents expected the number of relocations to increase, with China, India, and Brazil as the primary emerging destinations.[26] A number of key HR areas demonstrate how HR processes and practices are influenced by the internationalization of organizations and the expatriation of managers.

Recruitment

In the domestic context, one of the key strategic decisions in recruitment is the internal recruitment versus external recruitment. This two-option decision has a three-option parallel in the international domain and includes recruitment opportunities such as **home-country nationals (HCNs)**, **parent-country nationals (PCNs)**, and **third-country nationals (TCNs)**. HCNs are individuals from the subsidiary country who know the foreign cultural environment well. PCNs are individuals from headquarters who are highly familiar with the firm's products and services, as well as with its corporate culture. TCNs are individuals from a third country who have intensive international experience and know the corporate culture from previous working experience with the corporate branches in the third country.

While each recruitment option has its strategic advantages and disadvantages (see HR Planning Notebook 11.1), it is crucial that any staffing decisions be based on the MNC's short and long-term strategies and follow best recruitment practices. The latter include the development of a job analysis identifying job specifications and providing the basis for job descriptions.

Each specific assignment might have different job descriptions and require different knowledge, skills, and abilities (KSAOs), which is similar to domestic assignments. However, general KSAOs are also required to carry out these assignments in a foreign context. Caligiuri and Di Santo's[27] empirical study identified a list of abilities, knowledge, and personality characteristics essential for global managers with different positions in diverse cultures.

Home-country nationals (HCNs)

Individuals from the subsidiary country who know the foreign cultural environment well

Parent-country nationals (PCNs)

Individuals from headquarters who are highly familiar with the firm's products and services, as well as with its corporate culture

Third-country nationals (TCNs)

Individuals from a third country who have intensive international experience and know the corporate culture from previous working experience with corporate branches in a third country

▶ HR Planning Notebook 11.1

STRATEGIC ADVANTAGES AND DISADVANTAGES OF KEY RECRUITMENT OPTIONS

	Advantages	Disadvantages	SIHRM
PCNs	• Well versed in company's needs and norms	• Potential unfamiliarity with the cultural norms of the host country (including norms of supervision) • Possible blocking of HCNs' career progression within the firm • Considerable costs of relocating abroad	Strong exportive SHRM approach
HCNs	• Familiarity with the host-country culture	• Limited familiarity with firm's own operations • PCNs at headquarters may lack sufficient understanding of the subsidiary's needs, and corporate strategy for the subsidiary may suffer as a result	Strong adaptive SHRM approach
TCNs	• Greater familiarity with the host-country culture than PCNs (if, that is, the TCNs come from a proximal nation) but loyalty will be to the firm (rather than to the host country per se) • Relocation costs lower than for PCNs • Enhanced career development opportunities by allowing employees from the various subsidiaries to move to other subsidiaries • Improved understanding of the subsidiaries' needs by the corporation and vice versa through greater interaction between TCNs positioned in regional or corporate headquarters and PCNs	• Some cross-cultural preparation may still be required • Potentially suffering from a lack of knowledge of the corporate culture • Use of TCNs is often part of a strategy that entails the use of employees from many nationalities (including HCNs and PCNs), increasing the overhead for expatriate relocation across the entire firm considerably • Using TCNs to the exclusion of HCNs may create the same problem of blocked career advancement that occurs when PCNs are used in this manner	Mixture of exportive and adoptive SIHRM approach

Once the international assignment needs have been identified and the appropriate recruitment pool has been chosen, the right candidates must be selected.

Selection

Selecting the right candidates for global assignments is crucial for the long-term success of both the MNC and the individual managers. While companies in the 2003/2004 Global Relocation Trends Survey[28] planned to invest in better selection and preparation of their of their expatriates to improve their return on investment (ROI), the latest surveys show a different picture (see HR Planning Today 11.5).

HR Planning Today 11.5

International Selection and Preparation

Many companies responding to the 2003/2004 Global Relocation Trends Survey planned to invest in better selecting and preparing their managers for their foreign assignments and beyond. Yet, due to the global economic crisis in the past few years, companies revised and adjusted their programs and investments to the economic challenges. In the 2011 Global Relocation Trends Survey, 75 percent of companies reduced assignment expenses. In particular preparation processes such as cross-cultural training initiatives were hit by the cost cuttings. According to the report, just 74 percent of companies provided cross-cultural preparation—the lowest percentage in the history of this report.

Only 18 percent of respondents had a formal candidate pool for international assignments. Among the international assignees, only 9 percent were 20 to 29 years old (tied for the lowest percentage in the report's history), 18 percent were women (compared

to a historical average of 16 percent), 68 percent of international assignees were married, and less than half (47 percent) had children accompanying them, an all-time low. According to the report, companies continue to struggle to arrange spouse/partner employment during international assignments. While 60 percent of spouses/partners were employed before assignments only 12 percent found employment during their partners' assignments.

While 86 percent of respondents prepared cost estimates before an assignment and 67 percent tracked costs during an assignment, only 25 percent of respondents compared estimated with actual costs, the lowest percentage in the history of this report. And despite the economic pressures, only 8 percent of companies formally measured return on investment (ROI). Half of all companies argued that the principal reason for not measuring ROI was that they did not know how to achieve it.

Source: Brookfield GRS, "The 2011 Global Relocation Trends Survey," http://knowledge.brookfieldgrs.com/content/insights_ideas-grts, retrieved on June 25, 2011.

Personality as a Selection Criterion

The five-factor personality model (FFM)[29] has been demonstrated as being crucial to expatriate adjustment.[30] These five factors are emotional stability, extraversion, openness, agreeableness, and conscientiousness (see HR Planning Notebook 11.2 for a detailed explanation). Expatriates who scored high on these five dimensions were found to be better adjusted in overseas assignments.[31] This personality model should be used for selecting the potential global managers. The instrument for measuring these dimensions of personality can be found at www3.parinc.com.

Trainability as a Selection Criterion

Research so far appears to have presumed that cross-cultural training (CCT) is the panacea for most expatriate ills.[32] Yet it is quite possible that some individuals are simply more cross-culturally adaptable than others, and that, accordingly, CCT will have a more positive effect on them. Other researchers have also observed that there is a synergistic relationship between selection and training.[33] If you select someone who is "ready to hit the ground running," you are less likely to need to invest costly training dollars in that person. Therefore, the question of selecting for trainability is an important one. **Trainability** refers to an

Trainability
An individual's ability to acquire certain skills to a desired level of performance

HR Planning Notebook 11.2
FIVE-FACTOR MODEL OF PERSONALITY

Emotional stability: Individuals who score high on emotional stability are usually calm, even-tempered, and relaxed, and they are able to face stressful situations without becoming upset or rattled.

Extraversion: Individuals who score high on extraversion are sociable, like people, and prefer large groups and gatherings; they are also assertive, active, and talkative. They like excitement and stimulation and tend to be cheerful in disposition. They are upbeat, energetic, and optimistic.

Openness to experience: Individuals who score high on openness are curious about

both inner and outer worlds, and their lives are experientially rich. They are willing to entertain novel ideas and unconventional values, and they experience both positive and negative emotions more keenly than do closed individuals.

Agreeableness: Individuals who score high on agreeableness are fundamentally altruistic. They are sympathetic to others and eager to help them and believe that others will be equally helpful in return.

Conscientiousness: Individuals who score high on conscientiousness are purposeful, strong-willed, and determined.

Source: P.T. Costa, Jr., and R.R. McCrae, *Revised Neo Personality Inventory.* Lutz, Florida: Psychological Assessment Resources, Inc., 1992. Reprinted with permission.

individual's ability to acquire certain skills to a desired level of performance.[34] Preliminary conceptual research on expatriate trainability has observed that the various cross-cultural KSAOs may be classified according to their stable properties (e.g., personality) versus their dynamic properties (e.g., knowledge, skills).[35] Put simply, we may be able to gain incremental success in our selection efforts if we select expatriates who possess a minimum level of the stable characteristics (e.g., extraversion), because such individuals may be better able to acquire the interpersonal skills (e.g., developing and maintaining relationships with culturally different others) that contribute to that success.

Other Personal Characteristics

Many other different antecedent factors of cross-cultural adjustment have been identified in the literature. These include cultural knowledge, stress-management skills, conflict resolution skills, communication skills, and cognitive flexibility.[36] Several authors have simplified the above lengthy list into the following three dimensions of cross-cultural competencies:[37]

- Self-maintenance competencies, which refer to the capability to substitute sources of reinforcement when necessary and deal with alienation and isolation

- Relationship competencies, which refer to the capability to develop and maintain relationships with home-country nationals (HCNs)

- Perceptual competencies, which refer to the capacity to understand why foreigners behave the way they do, to make correct attributions about the reasons or causes of HCNs' behaviour, and to correct those attributions when they prove incorrect

Selecting candidates on the basis of their true potential, using the above criteria, means choosing global managers for their personality, trainability, interpersonal skills, and attitudes, regardless of whether they are PCNs, HCNs, or TCNs. A capable global manager should be able to work in different countries to successfully implement his or her headquarters' strategies. This is usually the integrative approach, which seeks, for the most part, to place the best-qualified person in the position, regardless of the nationality of that person. In order to select the best person at the right time for the right place, managers should start by identifying the best potential global managers, then put them through training and help them develop their global careers.

PRE-ASSIGNMENT TRAINING

The well-being of these expatriates and their families in the local country depends largely on how well they were prepared for the global assignment. Cross-cultural training for global managers and their accompanying relatives plays a crucial role in this pre-assignment process. Studies have consistently found that cross-cultural training positively influences expatriate self-development, interpersonal skills, and cross-cultural perception. Training was also found to have a major impact on the adjustment and effectiveness of expatriate managers.[38] Researchers have been calling for firms to conduct more formalized CCT for years.[39] However, in reality, many firms still fail to heed this call[40] (see HR Planning Today 11.5).

Aside from the economic pressures and challenges, reasons for the limited investment in CCT could be a lack of coordination with HR planning activities. Many firms select their expatriates too quickly, which precludes a lengthy training process. According to the Canadian Employee Relocation Council (CERC)'s 2011 employee relocation policy survey, only one-third of the survey's responding companies give more than two months' notice of an impending assignment.[41] Because of the improper usage of expatriate training, many companies have not benefited from the training.[42]

Strategic HR planning is needed for training in order to meet the goals of career development for global managers and to focus on the development of global competencies as defined previously. Ptak et al. interviewed professionals who were experienced in expatriate training.[43] These professionals were asked to suggest some useful guidelines for overseas training. The researchers found that effective training should emphasize five points: (1) assess and evaluate the needs of training for expatriates; (2) clarify the purpose and goals of training that are relevant and applicable to participants' daily activities; (3) plan and design the training programs to meet training goals; (4) implement the training plan; and (5) use several techniques to increase the effectiveness of training programs. Based on the work of Ptak and colleagues, HR Planning Notebook 11.3 outlines four steps for guiding the effective training.

HR Planning Notebook 11.3

GUIDELINES FOR EFFECTIVE TRAINING

Training planning: Assess and evaluate the needs of training for every selected potential global manager. Clarify the purpose and goals of training that are relevant and applicable to global managers' daily activities. Plan and design the training programs to meet training goals.

Training contents: Training can cover many areas depending on the needs of individual managers, ranging from technical training and managerial training to interpersonal skills training and cultural training. Typically, cultural training involves the following aspects: (1) area studies programs that include environmental briefings and cultural orientations; (2) culture assimilators—essentially multiple-choice questions about cultural characteristics; (3) language training; (4) sensitivity training (which could include role-playing exercises and behavioural modelling videos designed to raise awareness of cultural differences in behaviour); and (5) field experiences, such as visits to the restaurants of the target nationality or actual visits to the host country itself. These cultural training activities are not only useful for the global managers but also helpful for their spouses and children.

Training approaches: Several training approaches have been used in reality, ranging from (1) an information-giving approach (such as lecture-based area briefings), to (2) behavioural modelling videos or case studies that offer vicarious learning, to (3) the most experiential forms (e.g., training based on role-playing and immersion in the form of field experiences). These three methods should be encompassed in the

training plan according to the training needs. An information-giving approach will increase the knowledge competency of the global managers; the other two approaches will increase the trainees' other skills, such as interpersonal and analytical skills. All methods will be effective if they are planned properly to meet the training needs of the global managers, but the experiential methods are usually considered more "rigorous" (i.e., as having a greater degree of trainee involvement).

Treating the international assignment as on-the-job training: Global experience has been found to be the best way to help employees gain global competence. For example, Warner-Lambert has its Global Leadership Associates Program (GLAP), which is designed to rotate potential global managers through various foreign Warner-Lambert businesses. By gaining experience in different cultures and functions, these managers will acquire the skills, ability, and knowledge to lead anywhere in the world. This requires, however, mentoring at the host-country site by, for example, other expatriates at the host-country site or by HCNs. Moreover, to fully regard the international assignment as part of a long-term career development process, a plan must be in place for the expatriate's return to the home country (presuming, that is, that the PCN is to remain a PCN or to become a TCN). This, unfortunately, is where a lot of organizations fall short, and it has led to what has become known as the "repatriation issue."

Sources: R.L. Tung, "Selecting and Training of Personnel for Overseas Assignments," *Columbia Journal of World Business*, Vol. 16 (1981): 68–78; S. Black and M.E. Mendenhall, "Cross-Cultural Training Effectiveness: A Review and a Theoretical Framework for Future Research," *Academy of Management Review*, Vol. 15, No. 1 (1990): 113–136; R.L. Tung, "Selection and Training Procedures of U.S., European, and Japanese Multinationals," *California Management Review*, Vol. 25, No. 1 (1982): 57–71; P. Caligiuri and V. Di Santo, "Global Competence: What Is It, and Can It Be Developed Through Global Assignments?" *Human Resource Planning*, Vol. 24, No. 3 (2001): 27–35; and J.P. Katz and D.M. Seifer, "It's a Different World out There: Planning for Expatriate Success Through Selection, Pre-departure Training, and On-site Socialization," *Human Resources Planning*, Vol. 19, No. 2 (1996): 32–47.

POST-ASSIGNMENT ACTIVITIES
Repatriation

Repatriation usually means that the PCNs, TCNs, or even HCNs (working in headquarters as part of a career development plan) finish their overseas assignment and come back to their home headquarters or home subsidiaries. It is somehow expected that one will encounter "culture shock" when moving to another country. That one might experience culture shock upon return from abroad is usually not a concern. Yet research[44] indicates that the "big picture" of the cross-cultural adjustment process is that it is not just a U-curve process (i.e., the high of the post-arrival honeymoon, the low of the cultural shock experience, and the eventual regained high of adjustment and mastery), but rather a W-curve process, with the last "V" of the "W" happening in the form of "reverse culture shock" on return to the home country.[45] (See also HR Planning Today 11.6.)

It has been argued that reverse culture shock upon repatriation leads to several serious consequences for the employee and the organization, for example:

- Prior to the return home, the employee may become anxious at the thought of having no appropriate position to return to; this anxiety can affect productivity abroad and work adjustment shortly after repatriation.[46]

- The employee may become dissatisfied with his or her standard of living upon return, having become accustomed to the special status that accompanied the expatriate position.[47]

- Co-workers may not be interested in hearing about the repatriate's experiences; lots of things have gone on in their own lives over the last few years, and they've had their own preoccupations and focus.[48]

- The repatriate's job may not make as much use of internationally acquired KSAOs as it could.[49] In this case, "out of sight, out of mind" is the operative phrase.[50] (HR Planning Today 11.6 illustrates how this attitude can create "perpetual expatriates" and deprive a firm's headquarters of badly needed international competencies).

Despite the negative consequences of not having well-developed repatriation processes for their international assignees, companies continue to pay little attention to the return of their expatriate employees. In the 2011 Global Relocation Trends Survey, 95 percent of respondents held repatriation discussions, 74 percent of companies had written repatriation policies, yet only 14 percent of companies had a formal repatriation strategy linked to career management and retention.[51] And in the CERC Relocation Trends Survey 2011, participating companies that had formal repatriation policies were at 33 percent—down from 44 percent in 2009.[52]

Clearly, a career development plan for global managers will minimize these negative consequences; the MNC can also make the most of the repatriate's internationally developed KSAOs by treating them as candidates for global managers. The career planning for repatriates will also let the soon-to-be-repatriated individual have a clearer idea of what's in store, which will go a long way toward minimizing these negative consequences.

Repatriation
The process of PCNs, TCNs, or even HCNs returning to their home headquarters or home subsidiaries

HR Planning Today 11.6

Once Abroad, Always Abroad?

According to the 2006 GMAC Global Relocation Services Survey, 23 percent of repatriates left the company within the first year. The 2004 survey reported 13 percent of repatriates left with the first year, and 10 percent within two years. In the 2002 survey firms, admitted a 44 percent expatriate turnover rate, half of whom left their firms within the first year of re-entry. According to the different GMAC surveys, explanations for repatriate turnover included:

- "Employees with international experience are more likely to leave the company" (2002 survey)
- "Most expatriates leave to pursue other expatriate assignments that they view as beneficial to their careers" (2004 survey)
- "Expatriates anticipate a lack of attractive positions to return to in the home country and seek out better opportunities outside their company" (2006 survey)

These findings have been confirmed by a study by CIGNA International Expatriate Benefits, the National Foreign Trade Council (NFTC), and WorldatWork suggesting that a major problem of repatriation was the employees' status upon return and the lack of commitment to have a job for the employee upon their return. The same study reported that 77 percent of those surveyed are more likely to accept an international position with another employer than a domestic position with their current employer. Eighty-seven percent would accept another overseas assignment with their current employer.

It is important to note that while 39 percent of the multinationals in the 2002 GMAC survey did not know their expatriate attrition rate, this figure almost doubled in the 2004 survey, with 69 percent of responding firms indicating that they did not know when expatriates had left.

Considering the financial and non-financial resources (e.g., training and development) companies invest in their international assignees, it comes as a big surprise that companies do not keep track of expatriate attrition rates and, indirectly, their return of investment. Losing international assignees because of a lack of employment or career opportunities in home-country operations is not only a great monetary loss but also most of all a non-monetary loss (knowledge and skills transfer, management development, relationship and network building, and so on), and might also have a negative impact on other candidates for overseas assignments. It is important for HR professionals to have arranged with the expatriate prior to his departure clear career objectives, and to communicate with the expatriate on a regular basis while he/she is on assignment to discuss any potential career path changes, and to better prepare him/her and the family for a potential reverse culture shock upon their return home. As mentioned earlier, it seems that for many companies the support and preparation for an international assignee stops with his/her departure to the host country. Yet, as we can see from the study results above, company and HR responsibilities for an expatriate need to be more comprehensive, including all stages of an international assignment—in particular, the repatriation of the employee and his/her family.

Sources: GMAC-Global Relocation Services, U.S. National Foreign Trade Council and SHRM Global Forum, *Global Relocation Trends 2002 Survey Report* (2002); *2004 Survey Report*; and *2006 Survey Report*. These reports are available from the GMAC Global Relocation Services website, www.gmacglobalrelocation.com/survey.html, and J. Handel, "Out of Sight, Out of Mind," *Workspan*, June 2001, pp. 54–58.

Career Development

Two issues are of great importance for the long-term career development of global managers. The first is to regard the international assignment as merely one step in an overall career development plan. The second is to ensure that the next step (i.e., the candidate's subsequent assignment) makes good use of the

HR Planning Today 11.7

An Effective Repatriation Policy

Colgate-Palmolive Co. recognized the wealth of information it already had on expatriate skills—in a system not originally designed for that purpose. Coleen Smith, New York–based vice president for global people development, says that the company began putting together a global succession-planning database almost 10 years ago. "It has taken a variety of forms over the years," she says. While Colgate-Palmolive's database is primarily for succession planning, it also contains data on each manager's experience with or awareness of particular cultures. The information is made available throughout the company's worldwide network. "Senior leaders," Smith says, "have come to expect a certain level of information, which we really manage through our global succession-planning database."

The example of Colgate-Palmolive shows how a comprehensive global HR information system (HRIS) can support multinational enterprises and their expatriates in making international assignments more successful. Including manager's experience with or awareness of particular cultures in the HRIS can help companies to make more informative decisions in the selection of the right candidate for the overseas appointment. A global HRIS could also help companies to develop and communicate effectively clear and long-term career objectives and paths for its global managers, and better plan and prepare an expatriate's repatriation in terms of creating and providing appropriate employment opportunities that are in line with the returning manager's career objectives. While initially costly in their development, the long-term benefits of such HRIS should not be underestimated—in particular when considering the many failed expatriate assignments and heavy financial and non-financial losses associated with such failures.

Source: R. O'Connor, "Plug the Expat Knowledge Drain," *HR Magazine* (October 2002), 101–107. SHRM

KSAOs developed internationally, as these will serve as a source of competitive advantage to the firm. There are a number of ways to incorporate KSAOs acquired internationally into the repatriates' subsequent career development. The repatriate could serve as a mentor or formal trainer to future expatriates or provide input into the CCT process by recounting critical incidents experienced abroad. Alternatively (or as well), the repatriate can apply his or her understanding of the subordinate's needs by eventually serving as a long-distance supervisor to other expatriates. HR Planning Today 11.7 provides anecdotal evidence of how consideration of the repatriation issue proved to be effective for Colgate-Palmolive.

Another option is for the expatriate not to be repatriated but instead to join the pool of global managers and remain an international employee for the duration of his or her career, rotating from subsidiary to subsidiary, as outlined in HR Planning Today 11.8.

Performance Appraisal

Two broad categories of global assignments exist: technical/staff specialist and managerial.[53] The managerial expatriate may perform technical/staff specialist roles as well (usually at a low- or mid-level managerial position) or may hold a higher-level managerial position, such as being the general manager of the entire subsidiary itself. Performance criteria should be developed ahead of time, and the criteria will vary according to the particular international assignment under consideration.

HR Planning Today (11.8

International Relocation Activities and Policies of Companies Operating in Canada

On a biannual basis, the Canadian Employee Relocation Council (CERC) conducts surveys of employee relocation policies and practices of organizations with operations in Canada. The 2011 survey confirmed that Canadian businesses remain very active in the global marketplace, with almost 50 percent relocating employees internationally. Forty-two percent of companies expect short-term international relocations to increase over the next 12 months, and 32 percent of respondent companies anticipate that long-term international transfers will increase over the same period.

The key organizational challenges for successfully relocating international assignees include family concerns, tax implications, and housing. The average cost of a permanent relocation for a homeowner is reported at $97,500. The average costs for a short-term assignment for a homeowner is $69,000 and for long-term assignments for homeowners is $108,000. The vast majority of companies, 81 percent, continue to manage their international relocation through a written policy, with 51 percent reporting they manage international mobility with policies specific to international moves, and 33 percent through one centralized global policy. Seventy-one percent of companies provide a cost of living allowance for their expatriates on long-term assignments, and 58 percent provide a cost-of-living allowance for their employees on short-term assignments.

The number of companies that provide international medical coverage programs for their expatriates has increased from 31 percent in 2009 to 51 percent in 2011. Ninety-seven percent of companies pay the tuition fees for school children of their international assignees, and 75 percent provide educational assistance at private schools.

Most of the 46 percent of companies with tax reimbursement policies prefer the tax equalization method when managing reimbursements. Ninety percent of companies report to counsel their international assignees on tax related aspects, and to provide tax preparation assistance during their assignments. The home country remains the preferred option for payroll purposes, for determining base salaries for short- and long-term assignments, and for maintaining employee pension plans.

Source: CERC, "2011 Employee Relocation Policy Survey—Executive Summary" (Toronto: Canadian Employee Relocation Council, 2011).

This might sound straightforward—after all, the job has objectives, and the objectives become criteria for evaluation. But, in the international realm, several additional environmental factors combine to make the choice of criteria significantly more complex than they would first appear:

- One such factor is the extent of interaction that the position requires.[54] A technical position in one context may demand greater interaction with HCNs than would a similar position in another context. For example, a computer specialist charged with the task of resolving a database problem might have relatively greater isolation when performing the task than, say, a marketing manager charged with establishing a local distribution network. The greater the amount of interaction demanded, the greater the extent to which performance is contingent on the expatriate's cross-cultural skills. Expatriates hired in operational element positions may face a different kind of challenge.

Such individuals, particularly those with managerial responsibilities, will often be faced with tasks that may both be novel and require considerable interaction with the environment. Such cross-cultural contextual factors will need to be incorporated into the performance targets set (either as criteria or as a moderator of the level at which other targets are set). Otherwise, the set of criteria used may not be truly valid in content.

- Expatriates sent abroad to serve as upper-level managers, such as the general manager of a subsidiary, are often evaluated on the basis of the subsidiary's bottom-line results. But how comparable are these results internationally? Differences in accounting systems and financial reporting across countries can often lead to misinterpretation of results.[55] For example, Peruvian accounting rules count sales on consignment as firm sales.[56] Can this measure of sales performance be reliably and fairly used as an indicator of successful performance if none of the firm's other subsidiaries count their sales figures this way?

- Another complicating factor is the volatility of the foreign labour market. If labour costs are high in a particular host country (e.g., Hong Kong) but not in any of the other countries in which the firm's subsidiaries operate, is it fair to penalize the general manager operating in the country with high labour costs for lower returns because of costs that are beyond his or her control? Or, if the skill level of HCNs is fairly low, but the host-country government requires the firm to employ a minimum percentage of locals in their operations, can the resultant lacklustre productivity levels (as compared to other subsidiaries of the firm) be justly blamed on the general manager?

- In addition, telecommunication and transportation infrastructures are severely lacking in many host countries, which adds to the time inefficiencies (and hence, costs) of doing business in these places.[57] Sometimes the infrastructure may exist, but it may operate in a way that is thoroughly foreign to the expatriate. Performance may be fairly slow until the expatriate has reached a more advanced level in his or her learning curve regarding "the way things are done around here" (i.e., in the host country). All of the above must be taken into consideration when setting target levels for performance.

Therefore, the international performance appraisal should be conducted within the contextual considerations mentioned above. Everything we know about performance appraisals says that measuring observable behaviour (e.g., using behaviourally anchored rating scales, or BARS) is the most valid and reliable means of assessing performance. When using this standardized instrument (BARS) for an international assignment, it is recommended to have both host-country supervisors and subordinates and home-country supervisors and subordinates perform the appraisal.[58] When taking the bottom-line financial results as appraisal criterion, the targets should be set in accordance with the environmental considerations mentioned above.

Compensation

Expatriates and their families will usually incur the following categories of cash outlays:[59] (1) goods and services (food, personal care, clothing, household furnishings, recreation, transportation, and medical care); (2) housing (major costs associated with the employees' principal residence); (3) income taxes (payments to federal and local governments for personal income taxes); (4) reserve (contribution to savings, benefits, investments, education expenses, social security taxes, etc.); and (5) shipment and storage (major costs associated with shipping and storing personal and household effects). Employees working in any particular subsidiary may come from a multitude of countries; consequently, the first three of these outlay categories are where the greatest discrepancies can arise if the firm does not take careful action.

The multinational firm has several choices to make regarding how to cover these expenses. For example, salary can be paid at the home rate rather than the local rate or in the home currency rather than local currency. Ceilings can be established for payment of certain expenses (or certain expenses can be completely prohibited if excessive). The expatriate candidate should be informed of these ceilings in advance. The firm can also alter the combination of the package according to its direct and indirect compensation components to alleviate the effects of tax discrepancies across borders.[60] Finally, benefits such as home leave allowances (trips home) are commonly offered.[61]

By having a policy for the firm's strategic approach to international compensation, the firm will increase the likelihood that the above choices will be made in a fairly consistent manner and that there exists some incentive to be posted abroad. Three common policy options typically are considered: (1) a home-based policy, (2) a host-based policy, and (3) a region-based policy:[62]

- The home-based policy approach links the expatriate's and TCN's base salary to the salary structure of the relevant home country. For example, a Canadian executive transferred to Mexico would have his or her compensation package based on the Canadian base salary level rather than that of the host country, Mexico. The advantage is that this policy (1) creates equity with home-country colleagues and (2) can be cheaper when some home countries have lower wages than the host country (e.g., if a Mexican employee was stationed in a Canadian subsidiary for a while). The key disadvantage is that international staff performing the same function in a given subsidiary may be paid at different base salaries merely due to an accident of birth location. This option can become a problem when the expatriate has been bouncing around from subsidiary to subsidiary over many years and no longer identifies himself or herself as a birth-country national.

- The host-based policy approach links the base salary to the salary structure in the host country but retains the home-country salary structure for other international supplements (e.g., cost-of-living adjustment, housing, schooling, and other premiums). The one advantage of this approach is that it attracts PCNs or TCNs to a higher-paying location. Disadvantages are that it does not eliminate inequities between PCNs and TCNs unless the home-country supplements are phased out (something that would apply primarily to expatriates who are unlikely to be repatriated to their country of origin).

- Finally, the region-based policy compensates expatriates working in their home regions (e.g., Canadians working in North America) at somewhat lower levels than those who are working in regions far from home. This approach has the advantages of (1) providing incentives for distant foreign relocation and (2) allowing significant cost savings, since those stationed in neighbouring countries will not receive the same premiums as those travelling farther away, and so it remains a promising option.[63]

LABOUR RELATIONS

Knowledge of the types of unions that exist in a country (i.e., the union structure) and the rate of unionization in that country can be critical to international HR managers. This is because union activities can influence the HR practices that may be implemented and how implementation may proceed.

At least four types of unions can be identified:[64] industrial, craft, conglomerate, and general. Industrial unions represent all grades of employees in an industry; craft unions are based on skilled occupations across industries; conglomerate unions represent members in more than one industry; and general unions are open to all employees in the country. This diversity of types of unions can be found to varying extents in different countries.[65] For example, Canada's union structure is industrial, craft, and conglomerate. In the United States, all four types of union structures exist, although the U.S. has white-collar unions as well. Germany's union structure is primarily industrial and white-collar, and Norway's is both industrial and craft. Japan's union structure consists of enterprise unions, which operate within the enterprise and have the employees of this enterprise as its members.

In addition to the diversity in types of unions, nations vary in their rates of unionization. In 2010, the United States' unionization rates was at 11.4 percent; Japan's rate was slightly higher, at 18.4 percent, followed by Germany's at 18.6 percent and Canada's at 27.5 percent. Some of the highest rates of unionization exists in Scandinavian countries such as Sweden (68.4 percent) and Finland (70 percent).[66] There is a global trend of union density decrease, and the reasons are manifold and often region-bound. For North America as a whole, the declining union density throughout the past decades has been caused by "institutional weakness (absence of sectoral employers' associations and comprehensive wage bargaining structures), decentralization and fragmentation of union organizations and industrial relations."[67] The reasons for Canada's higher union density in comparison to the United States have been "the larger size of the public sector in Canada . . . and the more positive public sentiment towards unionisation."[68]

Awareness of practical differences in labour relations, while laudable, is by itself insufficient. International HR managers need to translate this awareness into practice. Labour relations activities can constrain MNCs' abilities to influence wage levels (perhaps even to the extent that labour costs become noncompetitive).[69] Such activities may also limit the ability of MNCs to vary employment levels at will, and may hinder or prevent global integration of the operations of the MNC.[70]

Accordingly, international HR managers have to devise strategies to improve the fit between their labour relations activities and the external environment. Strategic compensation might be limited in countries with strong governmental or union wage interference. Firms operating in such countries may need to find other ways of maintaining low costs. Staffing may be affected in countries that limit the firm's ability to implement redundancy programs.[71] In such countries, worker retraining may be important because of the economic necessity to cross-train and retain workers to adapt to environmental and technological changes affecting the firm rather than lay off workers.[72] In short, the presence of unions need not be disastrous for the international firm; rather, the wise international HR manager will simply learn the constraints posed by the local union conditions and devise an effective strategy to plan accordingly.

SUMMARY

This chapter has addressed many of the strategic issues and decisions that have to be taken into consideration in the context of managing employees internationally. Organizations seeking to expand their businesses globally would do well to do the following: first, recognize the strategic decision issues inherent in managing the HR function in an international context; second, strive to make these decisions in ways that take into account their firm's strategic objectives and recognize the added complexity that the international context brings; and third, the continuous career development of global managers should be arranged starting from the point of expatriate selection, followed by ongoing training and career arrangement after repatriation. Overall, all SIHRM practices and issues should be implemented strategically and a global competence pool should also be developed strategically.

Key Terms

adaptive IHRM approach p. 299
domestic strategy p. 299
exportive IHRM approach p. 299
fit p. 298
flexibility p. 296
global strategy p. 300
home-country nationals (HCNs) p. 301
integrative IHRM approach p. 300
multidomestic strategy p. 299

multinational strategy p. 299
parent-country nationals (PCNs) p. 301
repatriation p. 307
strategic international HRM p. 298
strategic international HR planning
   p. 297
third-country nationals (TCNs) p. 301
trainability p. 303

Web Links

A well-designed site that caters to the Canadian expatriate; it provides information and resources—including a forum—that are equally useful to Americans and other expatriates or those wishing to become so:
www.canuckabroad.com

The Canadian Employee Relocation Council provides information about workforce mobility and employee relocation at its site:
www.cerc.ca

To view a listing of global expatriate sites; regional and country expatriate websites; and expatriate forums, discussion groups, and blogs, visit:
www.transitionsabroad.com/listings/living/resources/expatriatewebsites.shtml

For embassy contacts and information about consulates around the world, visit:
http://w01.international.gc.ca/cra-rce/index.aspx

For listings for and links to online newspapers from around the world, go to:
www.onlinenewspapers.com

Required Professional Capabilities (RPCs)

The following RPCs are relevant to material covered in this chapter. The RPC number represents the CCHRA number assigned to the RPC as presented on the CCHRA website. All of the RPCs can be found in the Body of Knowledge at www .chrp.ca/rpc/body-of-knowledge.

RPC 11 Gathers, analyzes, and reports relevant business and industry information including global trends

RPC 69 Maintains an inventory of HR talent for the use of the organization

RPC 73 Identifies potential source of qualified candidates

RPC 86 Develops deployment procedures (e.g., transfers, secondments and reassignments).

Discussion Questions

1. In this chapter we have highlighted strategic advantages and disadvantages of key recruitment options. Identify and discuss key host environmental and organizational aspects that influence your choice of recruitment.
2. Much of the discussion and many of the company examples given in this chapter have been about MNCs. Yet many small and medium-sized enterprises (SMEs) have also started to have operations overseas. Considering their rather limited HR infrastructures and resources in comparison to large MNCs, discuss how HR managers of these SMEs can deal just as successfully with the HR challenges that emerge when operating beyond national borders.
3. In this chapter we have discussed different forms of industrial relations. Discuss in which way HR managers can respond to the potential constrains on their companies' international HR policies and practices as a result of operating within a different trade union context.

Exercises

1. The global business environment has been hit by a number of regional events that have had profound implications for the global and local strategies of MNEs. Select a recent world event, identify the specific HR implications that may arise from this, and devise policies as to how these may be handled.

2. Despite its widely illustrated importance for preparing expatriates and their families for international assignments, CCT is often not included in the preparation process. In pairs, discuss which cross-cultural aspects you would include in your company CCT training program; why you consider them as important; and how these aspects can be operationalized by what kind of training methods.

3. Ask an employer for an interview with one of the company's expatriates who has recently returned back home or arrange for a phone interview with an expatriate currently on an international assignment. Discuss his/her experiences, and how he/she was prepared and supported by the company during the different stages of an international assignment. How do the interviewee's views differ from the studies and findings discussed in this chapter? Why?

Case DANGEROUS ASSIGNMENTS

On June 24, 1998, Edward Leonard, of Creston, B.C. and a diamond driller working for Terramundo Drilling Inc. were kidnapped by members of the Revolutionary Armed Forces of Colombia (FARC) in the northeast of Colombia. Leonard's capturers wanted to negotiate a deal for gold mining shares with Greystar Resources Ltd., a gold mining company from Vancouver and the owner of claims in Colombia's Santander province for which Terramundo and Leonard were contracted to drill core samples.

Leonard's boss, Terramundo's Norbert Reinhart, wanted to purchase his employee's freedom by paying $100,000 to the FARC guerrillas. On October 6, 1998, in a meeting with the guerrillas, Reinhart and the ransom money were exchanged with Leonard. While Reinhart was hoping to walk away with Leonard after the money exchange, the FARC realized that Reinhart was the president of Terramundo and thought that in him they had an even better hostage. After 94 days of captivity, and some complicated and complex negotiations between the FARC, local contact persons, and Canadian governmental and company officials, Norbert Reinhart was released on January 8, 1999.

The case shows the dangers of frontier mining (which has had a strong tradition in Canada) and illustrates some of the potential challenges for employees on international assignments. At the same time, the case has started a strong debate about the responsibilities of companies operating in industries and geographic regions dangerous to their employees, and the necessity for precautious actions and support structures protecting international assignees. (In the same year in which Reinhart was taken hostage, more than 2,100 people were kidnapped in Colombia, including at least 43 foreigners.)

Source: "Homecoming for a hero," by T. Fennell and S. Timmins. *Maclean's,* January 25, 1999.

Questions

1. Was it the right decision in the first place for Terramundo to operate in a region well known for being controlled by FARC guerrillas, and in which kidnapping was a very common way to fund FARC activities?
2. Did Reinhart do the right thing to get involved in the way described and help his employee? What were Reinhart's alternatives and options?
3. What can companies operating in industries such as the mining or oil business do to protect their international assignees? What should be the role of the HRM function?
4. When sending your employees into remote and dangerous geographic regions, should all employees (i.e., both home and host-country employees) get the same employment support and workplace safety and security support? Is the reality reflecting or in line with your response?

ENDNOTES

1. Green, S. 2011. "The Would-Be Pioneer." *Harvard Business Review*, April: 124–126.
2. United Nations Conference on Trade and Development. 2010. *World Investment Report 2010*, www.unctad.org/en/docs/wir2010_en.pdf, retrieved on May 26, 2011.
3. United Nations Conference on Trade and Development. 2010. *World Investment Report 2010*.
4. Foreign Affairs and International Trade Canada. 2011. *Foreign Direct Investment Statistics*, www.international.gc.ca/economist-economiste/statistics-statistiques/investments-investissements.aspx?lang=eng, retrieved on May 27, 2011.
5. Foreign Affairs and International Trade Canada, 2011.
6. For example, Schneider, S., and J.L. Barsoux. 2003. *Managing Across Cultures*. London: Prentice Hall.
7. For example, Brodbeck, F., M. Frese, S. Akerblom, G. Audia, G. Bakacsi, et al. 2000. "Cultural Variation of Leadership Prototypes Across 22 European Countries." *Journal of Occupational and Organizational Psychology*, Vol. 73, No. 1: 1–30.
8. Sanchez, R. 1995. "Strategic Flexibility in Product Competition." *Strategic Management Journal*, Vol. 16, Special Issue: 135–159.
9. Beckett, D. 2011. "Why Kidnap and Ransom Insurance?" February 21, http://thecanadianexpat.com/index.php/2011/02/21/why-kidnap-ransom-insurance, retrieved on June 20, 2011.
10. For a list of Canadian governmetal representatives in different countries, go to www.voyage.gc.ca/contact/offices-list_liste-bureaux-eng.asp.

11. Cuthill, S. 2000. "Managing HR Across International Borders." *Compensation and Benefits Management*, Vol. 16, No. 3: 43–45.
12. Kirby, J. 2001. "Reinvention with Respect." *Harvard Business Review*, November: 117.
13. Ferner, A. 1997. "Country of Origin Effects and HRM in Multinational Companies." *Human Resource Management Journal*, Vol. 7, No. 1: 19–37; Rosenzweig and Nohria, 1994.
14. Expatica, "Multinationals Go for Global Compensation Programmes." March 24, 2005. www.expatica.com/actual/article.asp?channel_id=7&story_id=18404, retrieved on September 13, 2007.
15. Ferner, A. 1997. "Country of Origin Effects and HRM in Multinational Companies." *Human Resource Management Journal*, Vol. 7, No. 1: 19–37; Rosenzweig, P.M., and N. Nohria. 1994. "Influences on Human Resource Management Practices in Multinational Corporations." *Journal of International Business Studies*, Vol. 25: 229–251.
16. Taylor, S., S. Beechler, and N. Napier. 1996. "Toward an Integrative Model of Strategic International Human Resource Management." *Academy of Management Journals*, Vol. 21, No. 4: 959–985.
17. Nadler, D., and M. Tushman. 1980. "A Model for Diagnosing Organizational Behavior." *Organizational Dynamics*, Vol. 9, No. 2: 35–51.
18. Dowling, P., M. Festing, and A. Engle. 2008. *International Human Resources Management: Managing People in a Multi-national Context*. London, UK: Thomson Learning.
19. Rosenzweig and Nohria, 1994.
20. Harvey, M., C. Speier, and M.M. Novicevic. 2001. "Strategic Human Resource Staffing of Foreign Subsidiaries." *Research and Practice in Human Resource Management*, Vol. 9, No. 2: 27–56.
21. Bonache, J. 2000. "The International Transfer of an Idea Suggestion System." *International Studies of Management and Organization*, Vol. 29, No. 4: 24–44.
22. Beechler, S., and J. Yang. 1994. "The Transfer of Japanese-Style Management to American Subsidiaries: Contingencies, Constraints, and Competencies." *Journal of International Business Studies*, Vol. 25: 467–491; Bonache, 2000.
23. Hallowell, R., D. Bowen, and C.I. Knoop. 2003. "Four Seasons Goes to Paris: '53 Properties, 24 Countries, 1 Philosophy.'" *Harvard Business School*, January 8.
24. Presentation by Michael Schmidt, Manager of HR Global Operations Europe, keynote speaker at the Bertelsmann Stiftung Conference. 2008. *Synergie durch Vielfalt*, Berlin, Germany.
25. Canadian Employee Relocation Council. 2011. "2011 Employee Relocation Policy Survey." www.cerc.ca/LinkClick.aspx?fileticket=Y7rfVwX9bUg%3d&tabid=135, retrieved on June 20, 2011.
26. Brookfield GRS. 2011. "Global Relocation Trends Survey." knowledge.brookfieldgrs.com/content/insights_ideas-grts, retrieved on June 26, 2011.
27. Caligiuri, P., and V. Di Santo. 2001. "Global Competence: What Is It, and Can It Be Developed Through Global Assignments?" *Human Resource Planning*, Vol. 24, No. 3: 27–35.
28. GMAC Global Relocation Services, National Foreign Trade Council, and the SHRM. 2004. "Global Forum Global Relocation Trends 2003/2004 Survey Report." www.nftc.org/default/hr/GRTS%202003-4.pdf, retrieved on June 23, 2011.
29. Costa, P.T., and R.M. McCrae. 1992. *Revised NEO Personality Inventory* (NEO-PI-R) *and NEO Five-Factor Inventory* (NEO-FFI) *Professional Manual*. Odessa, FL: Psychological Assessment Resources, Inc.
30. Deller, J. 1997. "Expatriate Selection: Possibilities and Limitations of Using Personality Scales." In Z. Aycan, ed., *Expatriate Management: Theory and Research*. Greenwich, CT: Jai Press: 93–116; Ones, D.S., and C. Viswesvaran. 1997. "Personality Determinants in the Prediction of Aspects of Expatriate Job Success." In Z. Aycan, ed., *Expatriate Management: Theory and Research*. Greenwich, CT: Jai Press, pp. 63–92.
31. Ones and Viswesvaran, 1997.

32. Gröschl, S., P. Dowling, M. Festing, and A. Engle. 2008. *International Human Resources Management: A Canadian Perspective*. Toronto: Nelson Publishers.

33. Wexley, K.N., and G.P. Latham. 1991. *Developing and Training Human Resources in Organizations*, 2nd ed. New York: Harper-Collins.

34. Tannenbaum, S.I., and G. Yukl. 1992. "Training and Development in Work Organizations." *Annual Review of Psychology*, Vol. 43: 399–441.

35. For example, Leiba-O'Sullivan, S. 1999. "The Distinction Between Stable and Dynamic Cross-Cultural Competencies: Implications for Expatriate Trainability." *Journal of International Business Studies*, Vol. 30, No. 4: 709–725.

36. Mendenhall, M., and G. Oddou. 1985. "The Dimensions of Expatriate Acculturation." *Academy of Management Review*, Vol. 10: 39–47; Walton, S.J. 1990. "Stress Management Training for Overseas Effectiveness." *International Journal of Intercultural Relations*, Vol. 14: 507–527; Black, J.S., and M. Mendenhall. 1990. "Cross-Cultural Training Effectiveness: A Review and a Theoretical Framework for Future Research." *Academy of Management Review*, Vol. 15, No. 1: 113–136; Abe, H., and R.L. Wiseman. 1983. "A Cross-Cultural Confirmation of the Dimensions of Intercultural Effectiveness." *International Journal of Intercultural Relations*, Vol. 7: 53–67; Parker, B., and G.M. McEvoy. 1993. "Initial Examination of a Model of Intercultural Adjustment." *International Journal of Intercultural Relations*, Vol. 17: 355–379.

37. For example, Black, J.S., and M. Mendenhall. 1991. "The U-Curve Adjustment Hypothesis Revisited: A Review and Theoretical Framework." *Journal of International Business Studies*, 2nd Quarter: 225–247; Mendenhall and Oddou, 1985.

38. For example, GMAC Global Relocation Services, National Foreign Trade Council, and the SHRM. 2004. "Global Forum Global Relocation Trends 2003/2004 Survey Report," www.nftc.org/default/hr/GRTS%202003-4.pdf, retrieved on September 4, 2008; and Gröschl et al., 2008.

39. Belcourt, M., and P.C. Wright. 1996. *Managing Performance Through Training and Development*. Toronto: Nelson Canada; Feldman, D. 1989. "Relocation Practices." *Personnel*, Vol. 66, No. 11: 22–25; McEnery, J., and G. Des Harnais. 1990. "Culture Shock." *Training and Development Journal*, Vol. 44, No. 4: 43–47.

40. Brookfield GRS. 2011. "The 2011 Global Relocation Trends Survey." http://knowledge.brookfieldgrs.com/content/insights_ideas-grts, retrieved on June 25, 2011.

41. Canadian Employee Relocation Council. 2011. "CERC Relocation Trends Survey 2011." www.cerc.ca/LinkClick.aspx?fileticket=Y7rfVwX9bUg%3d&tabid=135, retrieved on July 11, 2011.

42. Black, S., and H.B. Gregersen. 1991. "When Yankee Comes Home: Factors Related to Expatriate and Spouse Repatriation Adjustment." *Journal of International Business Studies*, Vol. 22, No. 4: 671–694; Thomas, D.C. 1998. "The Expatriate Experience: A Critical Review and Synthesis." *Advances in International Comparative Management*, Vol. 12: 237–273; Tung, R.L. 1981. "Selecting and Training of Personnel for Overseas Assignments." *Columbia Journal of World Business*, Vol. 16: 68–78.

43. Ptak, C.L., J. Cooper, and R. Brislin. 1995. "Cross Cultural Training Programs: Advice and Insights from Experienced Trainers." *International Journal of Intercultural Relations*, Vol. 19, No. 3: 425–453.

44. For example, see Lazarova, M., and P. Caligiuri. 2001. "Retaining Repatriates: The Role of Organizational Support Practices." *Journal of World Business*, Vol. 36, No. 4, 389–401; Suutari, V., and C. Brewster. 2003. "Repatriation: Empirical Evidence from a Longitudinal Study of Careers and Expectations Among Finnish Expatriates." *International Journal of Human Resource Management*, Vol. 14, No. 7: 1132–1151.

45. Black and Mendenhall, 1991; see also Gröschl et al., 2008.

46. Black and Gregersen, 1991.

47. Black and Gregersen, 1991.

48. Harvey, M.G. 1982. "The Other Side of Foreign Assignments: Dealing with the Repatriation Dilemma." *Columbia Journal of World Business*, Vol. 17, No. 1: 52–59.
49. Beck, J.E. 1988. "Expatriate Management Development: Realizing the Learning Potential of the Overseas Assignment." In F. Hoy, ed., *Best Papers Proceedings, Academy of Management 48th Annual Meeting*, August 1988. Anaheim, CA: 112–116; Tung, 1988.
50. Handel, J. 2001. "Out of Sight, Out of Mind." *Workspan*, June: 54–58.
51. Brookfield GRS. 2011. "The 2011 Global Relocation Trends Survey." http://knowledge.brookfieldgrs.com/content/insights_ideas-grts, retrieved on June 25, 2011.
52. Canadian Employee Relocation Council. 2011. "CERC Relocation Trends Survey 2011." www.cerc.ca/LinkClick.aspx?fileticket=Y7rfVwX9bUg%3d&tabid=135, retrieved on July 11, 2011.
53. Dowling, P.J., Schuler, R.S., and Welch, D.E. 1994. *International Dimensions of Human Resource Management*, 2nd ed. Belmont, CA: Wadsworth Publishing Company.
54. Dowling, Schuler, and Welch, 1994.
55. Dowling, Schuler, and Welch, 1994.
56. Garland, J., R.N. Farmer, and M. Taylor. 1990. *International Dimensions of Business Policy and Strategy*, 2nd ed. Boston: PWS-Kent.
57. Gröschl et al., 2008.
58. Dowling, Schuler, and Welch, 1994.
59. Gröschl et al., 2008; Dowling, Schuler, and Welch, 1994.
60. Bishko, M.J. 1990. "Compensating Your Overseas Executives, Part I: Strategies for the 1990s." *Compensation and Benefits Review*, May/June: 33–34.
61. "Trends in Expatriate Compensation." *Bulletin to Management*, October 18, 1990: 336.
62. Anderson, J.B. 1990. "Compensating Your Overseas Executives, Part 2: Europe in 1992." *Compensation and Benefits Review* , July/August.
63. Dowling, Schuler, and Welch, 1994.
64. Gröschl et al., 2008.
65. Katz, J.P., and S.W. Elsea. 1997. "A Framework for Assessing International Labor Relations: What Every HR Manager Needs to Know." *Human Resource Planning*, Vol. 20, No. 4: 16–25.
66. OECD. "Trade Union Density." http://stats.oecd.org/Index.aspx?DataSetCode=UN_DEN, retrieved on July 12, 2011.
67. Visser, J. 2006. "Union Membership Statistics in 24 Countries." *Monthly Labor Review Online*, Vol. 129, No. 1. www.bls.gov/opub/mlr/2006/01/art3full.pdf, retrieved on September 23, 2008.
68. Visser, 2006.
69. Gröschl et al., 2008.
70. Gröschl et al., 2008.
71. Katz and Elsea, 1997.
72. Katz and Elsea, 1997.

CHAPTER 12

Mergers and Acquisitions

CHAPTER LEARNING OUTCOMES

After reading this chapter, you should be able to:

- Understand the various types of mergers and acquisitions.
- Explain why organizations merge and the methods used to achieve a merger.
- Identify the financial and human impacts of mergers.
- Describe the issues involved in blending cultures.
- Discuss how a merger affects HR planning, selection, compensation, performance appraisal, training and development, and labour relations.

BIG IS BEAUTIFUL

In 2006, Rogers Communications Inc., a Canadian communications and media company, bought 93 retail stores in order to integrate them with their existing Rogers Video and Fido stores, with the goal of providing a one-stop retail experience. Combined under one brand, Rogers Retail, the new operation would be among the ten largest retail chains in Canada.

Francois Chevallier, vice-president of retail systems for Rogers Retail, had four months to assure the successful integration of these stores into Rogers' culture and operations. The first step was to put together the transition team, and the two most important functional experts were the IT expert and the HR expert. The immediate task was to hire nine managers and 500 employers. They had to devise strategies to retain key employees, particularly the retail supervisors who tend to leave soon in the New Year, after receiving their year-end bonuses. As Francois noted, "The amount of communication involved in a transition like this is staggering." To cope with the deluge of email, Rogers set up an intranet site, which sent email advisories alerting employees to updates. After employees were hired, the training could not begin until the new operating systems were chosen and the new business rules for small stores were developed. Francois is very satisfied with the acquisition: "Just three months after the transition, the new stores are our best performers."[1]

Mergers and acquisitions (M&As) play a critical part in a corporation's survival, growth, and profit strategies. Many great companies were built on a track record of mergers and acquisitions; they include GE, Thomson, Alcan, and Power Financial. After the economic slowdown of the past few years, merger activity in Canada is returning to its previous high levels in Canada; therefore, HR professionals should add the ability to manage a merger as part of their skill set.[2]

The number and value of mergers and acquisitions hit a peak in 2007, before the economic crisis. Buyers are increasingly focused on M&A as a growth strategy, but sellers are reluctant, as valuations are rising and economic conditions improving.[3] About one-half are typically domestic deals—Canadian companies buying Canadian companies.[4] But in the world of mergers and acquisitions, Canadian companies are more often the prey, not the hunters. Foreign companies have acquired Canadian companies, such as HBC, Canada's oldest organization, and our natural resource companies, such as Inco, the mining giant based in Sudbury. A New York–based private equity firm acquired Intrawest, the owner of Whistler Blackcomb and other ski resorts, for US$2.8 billion. Henry Mintzberg, Canada's management guru, suggests that Canadians are less aggressive, being seen more as northern mice, rather than northern tigers. The result of this takeover activity is that we end up with shells, which means less work for head office specialists in advertising, law, financial services, and human resources.[5]

There are concerns about foreign takeovers that go beyond the loss of head office jobs, and this issue is discussed in HR Planning Today 12.1.

Before we embark on a discussion of the motives for mergers, readers are encouraged to become familiar with the terms used to describe them.

HR Planning Today (12.1)

Issues: Foreign Ownership of Canadian Companies

One in five Canadian companies has a foreign owner. Critics of foreign ownership posit a number of reasons against foreigners controlling Canadian based companies. They argue that CEOs based in Canada will make decisions that help the Canadian economy, such as keeping R&D in Canada, as well as other specialists in HR, marketing, law, etc. Profits will remain in Canada. Canadian companies will use Canadian suppliers, while foreign-owned ones will trust the relationships they have with suppliers in their home country.

However, the facts do not support all these allegations. Foreign firms that took over Canadian companies created as many jobs as they eliminated. They also created more head office jobs than Canadian firms during the same period. However, there is strong public opinion that foreign ownership should be restricted in certain sectors such as banking, telecommunications, and culture. Recently, the government blocked a deal by a foreign company to acquire Potash Inc., one of the first times the regulators have protected a natural resource.

Source: Adapted from Prasad, S. 2006 "The urge to merge", *Toronto Star*, August 6, 2009, page 12.

DEFINITIONS

A merger is a consolidation of two organizations into a single organization.[6] Within mergers, there are three categories:

- A **horizontal merger** is the merging of two competitors, who combine to increase market power. These mergers typically are subject to review by regulators who fear monopoly power in the marketplace. The merging of Coles Books and SmithBooks to form Chapters (which was then acquired by Indigo) is an example of competitors uniting to achieve economies of scale and to withstand the attack from American mega-bookstores. HR Planning Today 12.2 describes a merger of two big competitors.

Horizontal merger
The merging of two competitors

- A **vertical merger** occurs when a buyer and a seller (or supplier) merge to achieve the synergies of controlling all factors affecting a company's success, from the production of raw goods to manufacturing to distribution and retail sales. A real estate agency might merge with a real estate developer, for example.

Vertical merger
The merger of a buyer and seller or supplier

- A **conglomerate merger** occurs when one company merges with another but the two companies have no competitive or buyer–seller relationship. In other words, they are in different businesses competing in different markets. Although Tata, the largest, most successful conglomerate (primarily a motor company) in India, achieved most growth organically, the company did buy VSNL (an international telecommunications company) to enter the telecommunications business.

Conglomerate merger
The merger of two organizations competing in different markets

An acquisition is the purchase of an entire company or a controlling interest in it. The purchase of Federated Department Stores by Robert Campeau is a public example. By acquiring Federated Department Stores for $6.6 billion, Campeau, a Canadian, became the fourth-largest retailer in the United States.

HR Planning Today 12.2

A Rough Ride

One of the mergers that attracted a great deal of attention was the multibillion-dollar merger of Chrysler and Daimler-Benz. There are always problems merging two cultures, but this merger posed additional problems because the rivals were also from two different countries. Behaviours based in national differences are very difficult to identify and describe. For example, the Daimler-Benz German culture is strong on formality, which the Americans judged as brutal and harsh, whereas to the Germans it meant respect. Likewise, the Germans saw the American informal or casual way of doing business as "goofy" and "acting like a game show host." Added to this mix were the two fiercely competitive organization cultures with each "rival" trying to establish who was best at what. In the end, the merger did not work. After a decade of problems and billions of dollars lost, Daimler-Benz sold the ailing Chrysler division for a fraction of what they had paid for it. Observers think that Daimler-Benz was so preoccupied with the Chrysler problems that their lack of attention to the Mercedes division caused it to lose its status as the number one luxury car in the world.

Sources: L. Jack, "Oh Lord, Won't You Buy Me," *Marketing Week*, May 22, 2008, p. 2; D. Brown, "Everything's Fine, and Then. . . . ," *Canadian HR Reporter*, October 22, 2001, p. 1.

Consolidation
The joining of two or more organizations to form a new organization

A **consolidation** occurs when two or more companies join together and form an entirely new company. In this case, the assets and liabilities of both companies are taken on by the third company, usually after the original ones are dissolved. Burroughs and Sperry, two computer manufacturers, consolidated to form UNISYS. Three hospitals in Toronto—York Finch, Humber Memorial, and Northwestern General—merged in response to budget cutbacks.

Takeover
One company acquiring another company

A **takeover** occurs when one company seeks to acquire another company. Usually, this term denotes a hostile transaction, but it can mean a friendly merger as well. A hostile takeover involves acquisition of a company against the wishes of its management. ClubLink, known for operating 18-hole golf courses, was the target of a hostile takeover bid from Tri-White Corp. The ClubLink management team campaigned successfully to win the support and votes of more than 50 percent of the outstanding shareholders, and the bid was unsuccessful.

For the purposes of this chapter, M&As will be treated as one category, that of two or more companies joining together. The next section examines three motives for merging.

THE URGE TO MERGE

Companies merge for three reasons: strategic benefits, financial benefits, and/or the needs of the CEO or managing team.

Strategic Benefits

Companies that have growth as a strategic objective can expand in many ways: leveraging current customers, opening new markets internationally, corporate venturing, and M&As. The first three are slower methods. Acquisitions of companies in different regions or serving different markets are much quicker than internal expansion. Compaq and HP both sell computers but target two different markets: home offices and home entertainment customers. Their merger created more sales than two single brands.

Another strategic rationale that can be achieved through mergers and acquisitions is the strengthening of competitive position. Pfizer, a pharmaceutical company, took over its competitor, Warner-Lambert, in order to obtain the powerful cholesterol drug Lipitor. Companies may want to acquire competencies that make their core competency less imitable.[7]

Companies may acquire or merge with others to achieve complementarities. Different types of synergies can be achieved through M&As. (*Synergy*, a term taken from the physical sciences, refers to the type of reactions that occur when two substances or factors combine to produce a greater effect together than would result from the sum of the two operating independently. More simply stated, synergy can be described as a state in which two plus two equals five.) **Operating synergy**, which usually is referred to as *economies of scale* (decreases in per-unit costs), is the cost reduction produced by a corporate combination. Compaq and HP can renegotiate contracts with suppliers for memory chips and hard drives to save a total of $3 billion annually.[8] The merger of Inco and Falconbridge resulted in savings of $350 million achieved through synergies.[9] These gains are achieved by the spreading of overhead, the increased specialization of labour and management, and the more efficient use of capital equipment. Closely related to the economies-of-scale benefit is the *economy-of-scope advantage*: the ability of a firm to use one set of inputs to produce a wider range of products and services.[10] Banks, for example, like to use their bank tellers (now called "financial consultants") to do not only banking but also mortgage financing, car loans, and so on. Another type of synergy may occur when the acquiring firm believes that it can manage the target firm better and could increase its value. For example, a small firm may benefit significantly by using the larger firm's distribution networks and experienced management. It is important that the majority of anticipated synergies be identified and captured in the first year of the deal to ensure success.[11]

Companies may merge to gain access to new markets. For example, Canada's two satellite radio businesses, XM and SIRUS Canada, merged in 2011, a deal that quadrupled XM's revenue and customer base.[12]

Diversification may be another strategic motive. A company may wish to reduce its dependency on a market that is cyclical in nature to capitalize on excess plant or employee capacity. For example, a ski resort might acquire a golf course in order to fill its hotel rooms and restaurants during the stagnant summer months. General Electric pursued this diversification strategy; not wanting to depend entirely on electronics, the company became a diversified conglomerate by acquiring insurance businesses, television stations, plastics manufacturing businesses, credit card businesses, and so on over a ten-year period.

Companies may even wish to redefine their businesses through acquisitions. Nortel Networks made a series of acquisitions in the 1990s to move from being a supplier of switches for traditional voice networks to a supplier of technology for the Internet. Of course, this strategy is not always successful.

Companies may also wish to achieve the benefits associated with vertical integration and horizontal integration. **Vertical integration** refers to the mergers or acquisitions of companies that have a buyer–seller relationship. Such

Operating synergy
The cost reductions achieved by economies of scales produced by a merger or acquisition

Vertical integration
The merger or acquisition of two organizations that have a buyer–seller relationship

a move may ensure either a dependable source of supply or control over quality of the service or product. PepsiCo acquired KFC, Taco Bell, and Pizza Hut and thus ensured the distribution of its products in these restaurant outlets. (However, Coke then convinced Wendy's and other fast-food chains that selling Pepsi in their outlets would indirectly benefit their competitors.[13])

Horizontal integration refers to the increase in market share and market power that results from M&As of rivals. Western Canada's BC Telecom and TELUS merged to become a stronger regional telephone company that was better able to compete against Bell Canada's launch of a new national company. When acquisitions are impractical for organizations (perhaps because target companies are not for sale or too expensive) firms might turn to strategic alliances. For example, Cisco Systems is an active acquirer of small firms, but also engages in R&D alliances with Intel and other technology giants.[14]

Horizontal integration
The merger or acquisition of rivals

Financial Benefits

Organizations look to M&As to achieve some financial advantages. The main reason is to reduce expenses by reducing headcount, factories, and/or branches. Other financial goals include the following:

- Organizations expect to reduce the variability of the cash flow of their own business. An organization lowers its risk by putting its "eggs in different baskets." However, a counterargument suggests that executives cannot manage unrelated businesses and must focus on and protect the core business from competitive and environmental pressures. The suggested wisdom is to put eggs in similar baskets.[15]

- Organizations expect to use funds generated by their own mature (or cash cow) businesses to fund growing businesses. However, some experts argue that the advantages of using one division to fund another division might be risky in the long run. Labelling one business in the portfolio a "cash cow" and another a "star" has negative effects. Employees in the "mature" business might feel neglected, as resources are poured into the star, and may reduce their commitment to production and innovation. Management might misjudge which businesses have potential for market share increases and which do not. For example, most industry observers viewed the piano market as having slow or no growth. However, Yamaha saw the industry quite differently: it looked worldwide for market share, saying, "Anyway, we are not in the piano business, we are in the keyboard business."[16] Sometimes slow-growth, highly competitive industries offer stable (not risky) returns.

- There may be tax advantages to the takeover, which vary by country. Considerable tax losses in the acquired firm may offset the income of a parent company.

- It is expensive to enter new markets and to develop new products. Acquisitions result in more rapid market entries than internal innovation and product development do. They provide speedy access to new markets and to new capabilities, as exemplified by pharmaceutical companies that purchase biotechnology companies for their scientists and patents.[17]

- Astute corporations may analyze the financial statements of a company and decide that the company is undervalued. By acquiring the company, and sometimes by merging it with the administration already in place, a company can achieve financial gains. However, the success of the valuation driven acquisition depend on timing economic cycles.

The overriding goal is to increase the shareholders' wealth.

Management Needs

Some argue that corporate life is a game, and managers love to play it. The theory here is that managers seek to acquire firms for their own personal motives, and economic gains are not the primary consideration.[18] This hypothesis might help explain why some firms pay questionably high premiums for their takeover targets.

One theory examines the "incentives" or payoffs to the CEOs if they engage in acquisition behaviour. Managers may pursue their personal interests at the expense of stockholders. For example, there is a positive correlation between the size of the firm and management compensation, and so CEOs can expect higher salaries for managing larger firms.[19] Other, more indirect incentives might include the prestige or status of owning larger firms or companies in fashionable sectors, such as entertainment or sports.

Another perspective examines the unconscious motives of CEOs. Robert Campeau's takeover of Allied Stores and Federated Department Stores has been subject to "armchair" analysis because he overpaid for his acquisitions and ultimately went bankrupt servicing the debt. Speculation on his motives ranges from the simple need to prove himself to complex theories espoused by psychoanalysts. But does the research support the theory that managers make decisions based on Freudian or unconscious motivators?

Most of the work in this area analyzes the role that a manager's unconscious desires or neuroses play in formulating corporate strategy or decision making.[20] Some research is based on the intensive analyses used by therapists to explore motives. A few studies attempt to link personality characteristics, such as the need for power, with growth strategies.[21] One study found that the greater the ego of the acquiring company's CEO—as reflected in the CEO's relative compensation and the amount of media attention given to that CEO—the higher the premium the company is likely to pay.[22] However, few studies arrived at helpful conclusions that would explain the behaviour of executives.

Merger Methods

How do companies merge? The process, in a friendly environment, is relatively simple. The management of one company contacts the management of the target company. Sometimes an intermediary is used, such as an investment banker or, in smaller firms, a colleague who makes an introduction. During the first tentative talks, the boards of directors are kept informed of the procedures, and ultimately, they approve the merger. Friendly deals can be completed quickly. Hostile takeovers become dramatic, with management pushing for *poison pills* and seeking *white knights* to protect themselves. The term "poison pills" refers to the right of key players to purchase shares in the company at a discount—around 50 percent—that makes the takeover extremely expensive. "White knights" are buyers who will be more acceptable to the targeted company. There is even a "Pac-Man" defensive manoeuvre, by which the targeted company makes a counteroffer for the bidding firm.

The Success Rate of Mergers

How do we define merger success? In publicly owned companies, the goal would be to increase shareholder value ($2 + 2 = 5$). In private companies, the goal would be to increase ROI (return on invested capital). Many studies have established that only about 15 percent achieve the financial goals that were envisioned.[23] Acquisitions of related businesses fare better than acquisitions of businesses unrelated to the parent business.[24] The novice M&A management team does as poorly as the experienced team. Why? Perhaps because every merger is different, with different synergies and cultures.

Not only is the merged firm at risk, but the subsidiaries are also. There is some indication that a merger occupies so much management time, attention, and other resources that the original businesses are neglected. Executives of HP and Compaq spent more than one million person-hours planning for the integration.[25] There are enormous challenges in joining two companies. The problems include integrating computer systems, eliminating duplication, re-evaluating supplier relationships, reassuring clients, advising employees, and reconfiguring work routines.

The success rate may also vary by sector and by size. The manufacturing sector, for example, differs from the service sector. In the manufacturing sector, much more is fixed, with capital investments already made, with technology controlling process, and with lower job skills. The service sector, in contrast, relies on social-control mechanisms, which are highly subject to culture management. As such, the risk is greater with acquisitions in the service sector.

Size appears to influence success rates. A large firm can absorb a small firm in a relatively inconsequential fashion. The merger of two large firms generates more problems.

Financial Impact

For many reasons, the financial returns are rarely those that were envisioned. Acquisitions, on average, resulted in increases of 25 percent for the target firms, and zero economic profits for the bidding firms.[26] Sometimes, a premium price was paid, and the company is unable to service the debt or recover the investment. At other times, the forecasted economies of scale or complementarities are not achieved. The market may have changed, resulting in revised forecasts.

During the merger of two healthcare facilities in the United States, chaos was created in the resulting company by the collapsing of 525 branches into 350, the attempt to standardize the two facilities' computer systems, the termination of a tenth of the workforce, an attempt at a second acquisition, and the need to defend the company against a barrage of lawsuits.[27] The result was that outstanding bills jumped 30 percent in one year, payment times increased from 109 days to 131 days, earnings were down substantially, revenues were less than those of previous years, and the stock price dropped.

Overall, studies by consulting company McKinsey & Co. report that only 23 percent of mergers end up recovering the costs incurred in the deal, and about half of those analyzed by the American Management Association resulted in

HR Planning Notebook 12.1

REASONS FOR FAILURES OF M&As

- Integration difficulties
- Inadequate evaluation of target
- Large or extraordinary debt
- Inability to achieve synergy
- Too much diversification

- Managers overly focused on acquisitions
- Too large an acquisition
- Difficult to integrate different organization cultures
- Reduced employee morale due to layoffs and relocations

Source: F.R. David, *Strategic Management: Concepts and Cases*, 12th ed. (Toronto: Pearson Prentice Hall 2009), p. 169.

profit reductions.[28] Four out of five fail to produce any shareholder value.[29] Most devastating of all for merger maniacs was the analysis that demonstrated that non-acquiring companies (i.e., those that made no acquisitions) outperformed acquiring companies on Standard & Poor's industry indices.

Many mergers fail because the buyer overextends itself financially.[30] The buyer borrows heavily and then must engage in cost-cutting to service the debt. Assets are spun off, employee numbers are reduced, and the new company is left in financial shambles.

Even if the overall financial picture of the merged company appears rosy, there are indications that different functional areas suffer. For example, a firm that has to use cash to pay for the debt incurred in acquiring another business now has less to spend on certain projects that can be postponed, such as research and development.

An overall summary of the reasons for failures is provided in HR Planning Notebook 12.1.

The specialists in post-integration mergers at PricewaterhouseCoopers have conducted research that compares the goals of mergers to their success rates (see HR Planning Notebook 12.2). As you will note, most of the studies of mergers have examined U.S. mergers. One of the few studies to examine the mergers of Canadian companies shows a different trend. From an analysis of all mergers between 1994 and 2000, two Canadian academics concluded that there are positive and significant returns to shareholders, in contrast to American studies, which show negative or insignificant returns. Why? One explanation is that Canadian capital markets, industries, and companies are much smaller.[31] However, there are some winners, namely the merger advisers. The Campeau–Federated Department Stores deal alone generated approximately US$500 million in fees for M&A advisory firms.[32]

Impact on Human Resources

The real costs of a merger may be hidden—that is, not evident when analyzing financial records. Takeovers result in human displacement, and the cost of losing the best sales rep, who either is anxious about her job or does not wish to work for the acquired company, cannot be measured in accounting terms. The time involved in replacing this employee with a new one represents a cost to the employer. Research has shown that that M&As cause increases in insecurity

HR Planning Notebook 12.2

GOALS OF MERGERS AND ACHIEVEMENT RATES

Goals	Rationale for Deal (%)	Rate of Achievement (%)
Access to new markets	76	74
Growth in market share	74	60
Access to new products	54	72
Access to management/tech talent	47	51
Enhanced reputation	46	48
Reduction in operating expenses	46	39
Access to distribution channels	38	60
Access to new technologies	26	63
Reduction in number of competitors	26	80
Access to new brands	25	92

Source: K. Frers and A. Chadha. 2000. "Why You Can't Create a Purple-Footed Booby." *Canadian HR Reporter* (November 20), p. 16. Adapted by permission of Carswell, a division of Thomson Canada Ltd.

among employees, lower levels of satisfaction at work, less affective commitment, and a loss of trust in the firm and its top managers. This is particularly true in hostile acquisitions.[33]

Another study showed that nearly half of the senior executives in large acquisitions leave within a year of the takeover, and 75 percent leave within three years.[34] Add to this the thousands of jobs that are lost in the restructuring or downsizing of the merged companies. That is a national effect. The organizational effects are that it takes from 6 to 18 months for an organization to assimilate the results of an M&A, and the productivity loss is estimated to be 15 percent.[35] The loss of employee productivity stems from many sources:

- Employees go underground, afraid to make themselves visible or do anything that may put their jobs at risk.

- Overt sabotage occurs when employees deeply resent the turmoil the merger is causing in their lives.

- Self-interested survival tactics emerge, including hiding information from team members to accumulate a degree of power (the employee feels that he or she is "the only one who really knows how things work around here").

- A resigned attitude appears, stemming from the belief that no amount of work will prevent one from being fired.[36]

- Employees spend at least one hour a day dealing with rumours and misinformation, and/or engaging in job-search activities.[37]

But the real cost is to the thousands of employees who lose their jobs. Those who survive are affected in different ways. Most experience stress and anxiety, with a resultant loss of productivity.

To summarize, the feeling among those experienced in M&As is that, while mergers are forged for strategic and financial reasons, they succeed or fail for human reasons. Experts estimate that employee issues are responsible for the failure of one-third to one-half of mergers.[38] These issues include the difficulty in blending cultures, reduction in service levels, poor motivation, loss of key people and clients, and the loss of focus on longer-term objectives.[39]

The next section examines what many consider to be the greatest challenge of M&As—the blending of corporate cultures.

CULTURAL ISSUES IN MERGERS

In an effort to increase the probability that the merger will work, many managers are turning to the principal reason they fail: the meshing of cultures. The friendly merger of TransCanada Pipelines Ltd. and Nova Corp. has been described as "GI Joe meets the Care Bears."[40] The nearly US$10-billion merger of Nortel and Bay Networks met with skepticism about its possible success, principally because of a predicted clash between the cultures of a traditional telephone equipment manufacturer with a brash upstart newcomer.[41]

Culture is the set of important beliefs that members of an organization share. These beliefs are often unspoken and are shaped by a group's shared history and experience. Culture can be thought of as the "social glue" that binds individuals together and creates organizational cohesiveness.[42] Cultures, growing slowly over time, are not easy to describe, and employees are often aware of their corporate culture only when they try to integrate with people from another organization with a different one.

Culture
The set of important beliefs that members of an organization share

It is estimated that mismanagement of the culture is responsible for as high as 85 percent of all merger failures.[43] The longevity of an organization's culture cannot be underestimated. Canadian Airlines International was formed by merging about half a dozen different airlines. A decade after the merger, employees still referred to themselves as veterans of Wardair or Canadian Pacific Airlines—that is, they retained their original cultures. Integrating two cultures is a difficult process. Early on, the merger executives have to decide if one culture will be grafted onto that of the other, or if the two will merge to create a third culture.

In some cases, firms that are aware of the difficulties of merging cultures attempt to negotiate, in the form of a contract, many aspects in advance. The assignment of positions or the acceptance of a culture, such as one of empowerment, seems like good advance planning. But those who have been through this process liken it to a marriage. The couple might agree, in writing, on who will do the dishes and how many children they want, but the day-to-day living may be quite different, and the assumptions change over time. Recognizing this, some employees might choose to leave the corporation rather than endure the pain of culture mergers.

Anthropologists have something to say about the blending of cultures. According to researchers, four options are open to those involved in M&As:[44]

- *Assimilation:* Assimilation occurs when one organization willingly gives up its culture and is absorbed by the culture of the acquirer or the dominant partner.

- *Integration:* Integration refers to the fusion of two cultures, resulting in the evolvement of a new culture representing (one hopes) the best of both cultures. This form rarely occurs, because the marriage is rarely one of two equals, and one partner usually dominates.

- *Deculturation:* Sometimes the acquired organization does not value the culture of the dominant partner and is left in a confused, alienated, marginalized state known as deculturation. This is a temporary state, existing until some integration or separation occurs.

- *Separation:* In some instances, the two cultures resist merging, and either the merged company operates as two separate companies or a divorce occurs.*

*Berry, J.W. 1990. "Social and Cultural Change," In H.C. Triandis and R.W. Brislin, eds., *Handbook of Cross-cultural Psychology*, 5th ed. Boston: Allyn & Bacon.

Merging two cultures is difficult. How can a rule-bound, bureaucratic organization such as the Bank of Montreal merge with the "cowboys" of the brokerage firm Nesbitt Burns? To complicate this issue, the acquiring company typically wants to retain the entrepreneurial spirit of the target company and to infuse this spirit into its own troops. Instead, the entrepreneur is squashed by the rules and rigid decision making of the parent company. For example, Novell purchased WordPerfect (then owned by Corel) and managed to stifle the innovative talent it had bought.

The level of difficulty in merging two cultures is increased when the merger is one between companies from two different countries, that is, an international M&A. For example, Canadians tend to look to employee task forces and committees to provide input on decisions; people from other countries expect their managers to provide direction. Mexicans want more structure and definition of roles and responsibilities than do Canadians. In one case, a merger was stalled because Mexicans needed this information but would not ask for it as it was seen as questioning management's authority.[45]

The blending of cultures can take years. As in all organizational change programs, a process must be undertaken. The first step is to identify the differences, to ensure that employees are aware of the differences and can verbalize or label them. There are many cultural assessment tools—such as the Merging Cultures Evaluation Index—that enable companies to identify the cultural fit between merged companies.[46] Is one company entrepreneurial and the other risk averse? Does one have programs of team building while the other rewards individual achievements? Our recommendation is to appoint a sprinter to deal with urgent matters. Likewise, we suggest that a team of "long-distance runners" be appointed to address broad issues of mission statements, the creation of culture to achieve the strategic goals, and similar matters. Part of their mandate would be to measure current attitudes, solicit opinions, and give the employees a voice in the process.

Here is an example of how this is done. Two hospitals that merged had very different cultures, which did not blend. One had a culture of controlling employees; the other a culture of encouraging employees.[47] The hospitals began the culture-blending process by conducting a comprehensive audit, using a paper-and-pencil diagnostic tool. The results were terrible, and the only positive finding was that *everyone* wanted a change. Two teams were appointed, one to change the culture of both hospitals to a culture of employee development and the other to help form this new culture.

Sometimes, cultural characteristics common to both merging companies can be identified. For example, two very different firms found out that they both put top priority on customer service, and this common focal point became the link for their merger. Sometimes a superordinate goal can be created.

The formation of task forces or one-off projects has integration as a subgoal. As is the case when warring nations are forced to fight together against an alien force, the ways in which two corporate cultures are more similar than different are apparent when a superimposed goal becomes the catalyst. American Express uses this technique regularly. Managers from merging firms work together on projects to develop new products or services, for which the merged firms can claim ownership. Besides integration, such projects have other benefits: They develop in-house talent, provide an opportunity to solicit broad perspectives, and facilitate transfers as the project ends.[48] General Mills used an integration team as part of a successful strategy in its acquisition of Pillsbury (see HR Planning Today 12.3). While all of this seems time consuming, it may, in fact, save time in the longer term. Organizational change experts realize that time spent ensuring employee buy-in will speed implementation. If time is not spent ensuring that employees are committed to the changes, employees will resist the changes.

HR Planning Today 12.3

HR Systems Effective in Acquisition

In 2001, General Mills acquired Pillsbury. The goal of General Mills was to double revenues, be a market leader in 14 food categories, and be in a position for international growth in every country in the world, through the dough business. Both companies were the best in their class, not only having brand icons like the Pillsbury Doughboy but also having won many awards for being best employers. Conscious of the research that demonstrated that most acquisitions fail, the vice-president of HR set out to manage the process of integrating 10,500 General Mills employees with 16,000 Pillsbury employees.

The integration strategy started with a transition team who anticipated the fundamental concerns of employees: (1) Will I have a job in the new organization? (2) How do I win? (i.e., how can I do my best and reap rewards?) and (3) Do I have a future here?

The transition team paid attention to three areas:

1. Develop the systems that mattered most to employees: rewards, performance management, and individual development.

2. Sequence the implementation of these systems at a pace that employees could absorb.

3. Use the climate survey to monitor employee feedback and concerns.

The acquisition was a success. During the first 12 months of the integration, turnover dropped to 5.4 percent from 9.9 percent (General Mills) and 17.8 percent (Pillsbury). They were able to retain 98 percent of the top value creators. Although business results were disappointing in the first fiscal year, the following year sales increased by 32 percent, and net earnings doubled. These results are attributed directly to the integration strategy, and prove that HR systems can be key drivers of success in a merger or acquisition.

Source: F.R. David, *Strategic Management: Concepts and Cases*, 12th ed. (Toronto: Pearson Prentice Hall 2009), p. 169.

Another approach is to "seed" the company with experienced managers who "walk the talk" and can facilitate the adoption of the new culture. However, just transferring personnel from one company to another may only increase the differences between them and promote subcultures or cliques. "Living together" before the marriage may also help ease merger shock. Japanese companies usually have worked on a joint venture or a collaborative project, designed to assess cultural fit, before they acquire another company. Turf battles are a problem unless companies establish the new structure, including the reporting relationships, early in the merger process.

Consultants specializing in post-merger integration practices at PricewaterhouseCoopers believe that two cultures cannot be merged by just waving the common-vision banner above the employees. They suggest these specific steps be undertaken:

- *Deploy role models:* Those in highly visible positions of authority should exemplify the new and desired behaviours.

- *Provide meaningful incentives:* Shower the role models and employees who replicate the desired behaviours with quick and visible rewards.[49]

More radical measures may be necessary. Some companies force employees who are opposed to the merger or cannot adapt to the new culture into early retirement or some other exit option. However, this will result in knowledge loss for the organization. Researchers are recognizing that employees' knowledge and abilities—the organizations set of capabilities—might not appear on the balance sheet but are crucial to the success of an organization. The difficult part of the merger is to merge these intangible assets of two organizations.[50]

Often, the acquiring firm managers see themselves as conquering heroes, feeling that they have won and the acquired managers are losers. In one merger, this attitude caused 96 percent of valuable store managers of the acquired company to leave within six months of the acquisition.[51] North American firms are the most likely to adopt a centralized, micromanagerial attitude to an acquisition, rather than an adoption of the best practices of both companies.[52] An acquisition could be seen as a stimulus to review all HR practices, and to learn about both organizations. The cultural integration issues are described in HR Planning Today 12.4. The steps necessary to do a cultural audit or due diligence are outlined in HR Planning Notebook 12.3.

HR ISSUES IN M&As

Experts in HRM have much to say about increasing the success rate of mergers. Indeed, when HR is involved early in the process, the merger is more likely to be successful.[53] The impact of a merger on HRM is discussed below, using the familiar functional areas of HR.

HR Planning

In a merger, planning moves beyond the traditional concepts of HR planning for several reasons. HR planning in an M&A situation has several dimensions that are not part of the normal planning process.

HR Planning Today (12.4

The Blending of Cultures: Integration of Pet Valu and Bosley's

Pet Valu opened its first store in 1976 when the owners invested in a small space to start a business distributing pet supplies. Over 35 years later, Pet Valu has become one of the largest players in the pet food and supply industry, with over 400 stores across Canada and the United States servicing thousands of customers. Its staff has grown to over 1,300 employees.

Although the Toronto-based pet-supply retailer achieved some of its growth organically, the purchase of the company by private equity allowed it to significantly increase its ability to expand. In 2009, Roark Capital Group, a franchise-focused, private-equity firm, bought Pet Valu from its previous owners for a reported $144 million. Since the sale to Roark, Pet Valu has had more funds to dedicate to the renewal of the chain and growth.

A new goal of Pet Valu became non-organic growth via acquisitions. Pet Valu being a new acquisition, it was important to achieve the anticipated sales targets forecasted in order to rationalize the purchase by showing early returns to stakeholders. A more long-term goal of Pet Valu was to move into new markets and grow the business across Canada and the United States. In 2010, Pet Valu acquired Bosley's Pet Food Plus Inc., a smaller specialty retailer chain of pet food and supplies with 23 stores across British Columbia. Bosley's story was similar to Pet Valu's: it had been in business for over 30 years with mainly corporate stores. The unique feature of Bosley's was its focus on holistic and specialty brands in a market known as a leading-edge innovator of natural and holistic pet products. An attractive feature of Bosley's was that "its stores typically had higher sales than comparable stores," as Christine Martin Bevilacqua, Vice-President of Human Resources, points out. However, post-acquisition, there were several integration challenges. For example, although Bosley's had payroll employees, they did not have a fully developed HR function. Christine describes the overall challenge:

Figuring out the balance between integration and letting them [Bosley's] stand alone. Some
places we wanted to integrate and some places we didn't want to add bureaucracy. . . . [Bosley's] had a good brand, so we still wanted to foster that entrepreneurial spirit and allow them to be successful in their market.

Ms. Martin Bevilacqua recalls the approach to integration of the two businesses:

We treated them [Bosley's] like a client; it wasn't like they were acquired and now they are subservient. . . . They were often doing better in their individual store sales and we didn't want to tamper with that. So, [after the sale] we allowed them to operate separately . . . while trying to figure out where we could add real value. After a HR audit, we knew what they had and what they needed. We met with the General Manager and key operational management, and gave them an overview of all the things we had that might be helpful and let them pick and choose.

Some early wins were achieved in terms of standardizing processes. First, Bosley's participated in the development and implementation of Pet Valu's online learning sales module for store employees, which teaches effective ways to utilize product knowledge in the sale of products to customers. Second, they decided to use Pet Valu's materials for effective and standardized recruitment and employee appraisals. Ms. Martin Bevilacqua describes what happened:

It was a sort of sharing backwards of what would be value to them [Bosley's] rather than telling them to follow a whole bunch of procedures. . . . They choose what ones they want to start with. . . . If you take over a company you often just enforce the larger organization's standards. . . . But we let them pick and choose what they would like to invite in, knowing that we had as much to learn from them as what we could provide in terms of resources.

HR Planning Today 12.4 *(continued)*

Early on, it was not as straightforward as giving tools and practices away to the newly acquired retailer chain. Ms. Martin Bevilacqua indicates that "at first we drowned Bosley's in involvement." However, later she indicates that this eventually worked in their favour, as Bosley's felt comfortable approaching HR on their own because they began to value the new resources available to them. Christine recalls the integration approach:

> An easy and immediate way of building bridges on things that maybe they [Bosley's] didn't have the time or resources to address . . . where you can create synergies that make sense and then balancing these synergies with what good for

the business. . . . *Slowly but surely we were essentially making them part of the larger organization.*

Pet Valu's approach to acquisition integration positioned the company for double-digit growth in sales for stores. It also gave Pet Valu a model for future purchases, something core to their strategic plan. In the end, the acquisition allowed Pet Valu to achieve its strategic goals of entering a new market and establishing operations. Ms. Martin Bevilacqua summarizes, "While the first two steps were straightforward, the ultimate goal was sharing resources through integration, and this is where HR was able to add value."

Source: The Canadian Press. 2009. "Pet Valu sold to U.S. private equity firm." *The Toronto Star*, Online, (July 6), Available: http://www.thestar.com/business/article/661481. (Accessed June 2, 2011). Correspondence with Christine Martin Bevilacqua, Vice President, Human Resources Management, Pet Valu Inc., June 2011.

 HR Planning Notebook 12.3

THE CULTURAL DUE DILIGENCE CHECKLIST

Research tells us that those companies that actively manage their cultures attain higher revenues and profits than those that do not. This is particularly important during a merger, but indeed less than 10 percent of companies actively spend time on cultural fit issues during integration. Here are the steps:

1. Conduct a cultural audit of each organization, through qualitative research (e.g., interviews, focus groups) or through quantitative surveys.

2. Identify similarities and differences, and discuss these. Create a new employee value proposition from the strengths of each culture.

3. Use acculturation strategies such as cross-functional seminars and graduation ceremonies (to let go of the "old"), and provide cultural mentors to strengthen integration.

4. To overcome cultural challenges, celebrate small wins, acknowledge value in past practices, and measure progress at regular intervals.

Sources: "HR Issues Are Bottom of M&A Checklists," *Personnel Today*, January 6, 2004, p. 3; S.H. Applebaum and J. Gandlel, "A Cross Method Analysis of the Impact of Culture and Communications upon a Health Care Merger: Prescriptions for Human Resources Management," *Journal of Management Development*, Vol. 78, No. 6 (2003): 108–116; M. Johne, "The Human Factor: Integrating People and Culture after a Merger," *CMA Management*, Vol. 74, No. 3 (2000): 30–37; R. Miller, "How Culture Affects Mergers and Acquisitions," *Industrial Management*, Vol. 42, No. 5 (2000): 22–27; K. Walker, "Meshing Cultures in a Consolidation," *Training and Development*, Vol. 52, No. 5 (1998): 83–88.

1. The Contingency Plan

Strategic planners must be aware of the board of directors' interest in M&As. Based on this expressed interest, a contingency plan that can be implemented when a deal is in play should be prepared. The plan should identify the contact person and the merger coordinator, who should have received training in effective merger management. The contact person should develop a plan, one similar to emergency plans developed for fires or gas leaks; it should outline the chain of command, methods for communicating, procedures to follow during a takeover, and negotiation skills training and media response training for the senior team. It should also identify a transition team.[54] Some companies even keep lists of compatible white knights (in cases of being targeted for acquisition) and prepare lists of consultants who are experts in negotiation techniques or productivity enhancement methods. Some organizations that grow through acquisitions have a dedicated M&A specialist on their HR team.[55]

2. HR Due Diligence

The second element of HR planning in an M&A situation is the need to conduct a due diligence review.[56] *Due diligence* is a process through which a potential acquirer evaluates a target firm for acquisition.[57] Hundreds of questions are asked about areas from tax implications to differences in culture, in order to ensure that the right price is paid and that the chances of success are measured. The first question to be asked is how the transaction is structured, as this affects the treatment of employees, as is described in HR Planning Notebook 12.4. Researchers have found that there is a tendency for hard criteria to drive out soft criteria: in other words, if the numbers look good (reduced head count, more customers, etc.), any issues about culture differences tend to be dismissed.[58]

From an HR perspective, the due diligence would include a review of the following:

- Collective agreements
- Employment contracts

HR Planning Notebook 12.4
SHARE OR ASSET PURCHASE

Share purchase: The purchaser acquires the shares of a company. The corporate entity continues to exist, and employees are retained.

Asset purchase: The purchaser acquires all or some of the company's shares, but there is a different corporate entity that continues the management of the business. Employees of the company are transferred to the purchaser (i.e., no longer work for the seller), and a new employment relationship must be worked out with the purchaser. In general, the purchaser has no legal obligation to hire all or some of the employees or provide them with the same working conditions and terms. But in practice, most purchasers do so in order to carry on with business and to limit liability for terminations.

Source: D. Corbett, "HR Issues in M&A," *HR Professional* (August/September 2002), pp. 18–21.

- Executive compensation contracts (particularly "golden parachutes": lump-sum payments made to executives who lose their jobs as a result of an M&A)
- Benefit plans and policies
- Incentive, commission, and bonus plans
- Pension plans and retirement policies
- Workers' Safety and Insurance Board (WSIB) statements, claims, assessments, and experience rating data
- Employment policies
- Complaints about employment equity, health and safety, wrongful dismissal, unfair labour practices, and applications for certification and grievances

Sometimes these liabilities (e.g., an enriched retirement plan) or obligations (e.g., an incentive plan) may kill the deal. Pension plans are often the deal killers. Pension plan liabilities (defined benefits, for example) can impact profit estimates. Changes to the pension plan may affect employee morale and productivity.[59] Once the legal obligations have been thoroughly assessed, the level of employees' knowledge, skills, abilities, and other attributes (KSAOs) must be evaluated. The HR planning team then addresses the suitability of current management talent and cultural fit. A deal may be aborted if talent shortfalls are extreme or if the cultures are seriously incompatible. There are several ways to assess employee capabilities, including:

- Reviewing all employee documentation (CVs, performance appraisal reports, etc.) and then conducting interviews with the managers at a minimum of four levels[60]
- Determining contractual obligations with regard to early retirements, terminations, promised new jobs and pre-merger levels of turnover[61]

Despite the obvious benefits of involving the HR team in due diligence, only four out of ten companies do so.[62]

3. Transition Team

A third element of HR planning is the need to appoint a transition team. This is necessary because of the urgency of the M&A situation and the information gaps and employee stress that characterize it:

- *Urgency:* Staffing decisions, such as terminating, hiring, evaluating, and training, become urgent. Planners don't have the luxury of planning in three-year periods, during which orderly succession proceeds as predicted. Job analyses must be conducted immediately to identify duplicate positions and new work processes. Soon after the merger is announced, decisions about the retention of employees and the reassignment of others have to be made and executed humanely. At the same time, marketable employees are finding jobs elsewhere and customers are re-examining their business relationships. The uncertainty impedes productivity and new business development.

- *Information gaps:* While both companies might have excellent plans for employees and reams of documentation, these plans have to be adjusted to the merged needs. For example, the targeted company may have prepared succession plans for its finance department, but now most of these positions (and people) are redundant because the bidder may have its own finance department. Furthermore, the merged company may use its combined resources to seek businesses in new countries (with different financial reporting or tax laws), and neither of the merged companies may have that expertise. Thus, the information accumulated to date may have to be updated rapidly and revised in light of the new needs. The loss of capable employees, those who are marketable and can easily find other jobs, also results in the need to update plans continuously during a merger. Upon the announcement of its merger, AOL Time Warner immediately created an online tutorial that explained the reasons for the merger, how it affected employees, and career opportunities under the new regime.[63]

- *Stress:* The moment that the companies go "into play," employees are stressed because they are aware of the traditional fate of employees in merged companies. Most employees realize that most positions are duplicated. A transition team, whose sole concern is HR issues in the merger, must be appointed. The transition team may be the most important determinant of merger success. The role and responsibilities of the transition team are outlined in HR Planning Notebook 12.5.

The goals of the transition team are to retain talent, maintain the productivity (both quantity and quality) of employee performance, select individuals for the new organization, integrate HR programs (e.g., benefits, incentive plans), and take the first steps toward the integration of cultures. Some have adopted a 100-day strategy. The anxiety felt by employees and other stakeholders is lessened when the merger team announces that within 100 days of closing, all job decisions will have been made. The impact that this team can have on the retention of key employees is so great that some companies, like Dow Chemical, have a permanent "integration" team that manages all acquisitions, and is able to build on previous successes.[64]

As the transition team is handling the urgent matters, the HR planners can undertake the revisions necessary to prepare HR plans. Employee skills inventories must be updated and succession plans revised. If the business enters new sectors and they require new labour pools, these labour pools have to be identified and the need for them assessed. Employment equity data have to be revised and, perhaps, resubmitted to the relevant agencies. On the basis of the revised strategic plans, the HR department must revise and align its plans and produce a new forecast for HR requirements.

A review of the HR policies will likely reveal three types of situations:

- *Complementary:* One company might focus on career development, while the other focuses on benefits.

- *Duplicated:* Both companies have identical human resources information systems (HRIS).

HR Planning Notebook 12.5

THE TRANSITION TEAM

Senior vice-presidents of HR who have had a lot of experience in mergers recommend that a transition team be appointed to deal with the concerns of employees in mergers. These persons cite the need to deal with employee stress before the stress renders employees incapable of working. In addition, it is known that employees who have access to information about their future are less likely to begin a job search and leave the organization. Communication is critical, and employees should be the central focus of communication efforts.

Here are some elements of a good merger management process:

- *A formal announcement:* When a merger or acquisition is announced, the CEO should issue a statement containing the following items of information:
  o The rationale for the merger—that is, its intended benefits
  o General information about both companies
  o Information about changes in the corporate name and structure, particularly changes in key management positions
  o Plans for employee reductions
  o Plans for recognizing and working with the union

  o Plans for changes in products or services
  o Detailed information about changes in benefits, or the date for decisions about such changes
- *A merger hotline:* When Inland Gas purchased Mainland Gas, creating BC Gas, the company immediately set up a hotline so that employees could call the vice-president of HR and ask direct questions. Another company created a video in which the CEO talked about the changes.
- *A managerial toolkit:* This toolkit included identifiable support resources who could address employee concerns and fears.[65] The board of directors should be provided with a list of possible questions and answers.
- *A newsletter or web page:* Experts agree that the formation of communication channels must be swift and consistent, and all communication must be honest. One company created a fictional employee ("Frank") who, on behalf of the workforce, asked questions about the merger and reported back to the employees, from their perspective.

Source: Adapted from T.J. Galpin and M. Herndon, *The Complete Guide to Mergers and Acquisitions*, San Francisco, CA: Jossey-Bass, 2000.

- *Contradictory:* One organization uses the performance management system for career development while the other uses its system to support incentive pay programs, by measuring employee productivity to determine bonuses or merit pay.[66]

Selection

Retention and reduction, paradoxically, are two critical areas that must be addressed immediately. The typical scenario is that over two-thirds of executives are replaced within three years.[67] Duplicate positions and redundant employees must be terminated, and highly qualified employees in critical positions must be motivated to stay. The first critical question is "How many employees does the merged company need?" The answer is not to eliminate the most jobs possible in an attempt to operate a lean and mean corporation; the result would be work overload and stress. The answer may lie in benchmarking statistics. Increasingly, HR professionals are developing benchmark data by sector. For example, one merged hospital, which employed six full-time workers per occupied bed, reduced the number of employees to match the benchmark of four full-time workers per occupied bed.[68]

Of course, it is not just the numbers of employees that are subject to analysis but the types of employees. One company classified workers in these ways:

- Critical to ongoing operations

- Critical to retain through to the close of the deal

- Highly marketable

- Potentially redundant[69]

Key workers must be identified and offered retention bonuses and employment agreements. Employees are offered incentives to stay at least until the deal closes—often, for periods after the closure. The superstar financial brokers at Merrill Lynch were offered a one-time retention bonus of 110 percent of their take-home pay (more than $1 million a year) by CIBC in order to retain them. The retention bonus was structured as a five-year loan so that each year 20 percent of the loan was forgiven.[70]

Reductions might be necessary. The dismissal process can be heartbreaking, as is described in one merger case.[71] In the rush to terminate quickly, some employees were notified by voice mail or email or in hurried and short meetings with strangers. A supervisor was forced to fire three of his employees before being fired himself. His termination was particularly difficult to understand, as his performance reviews had been excellent. As wave after wave of salespeople were laid off, customers became confused about their contacts. Departing employees took advantage of this and went to the competition, taking the business relationships with them.

Chapter 10 covered this aspect of restructuring in detail. A number of decisions must be made immediately. Employees will want to know if they will be offered employment in the merged company; if not, they will want to know what the severance packages contain. If jobs are offered, can employees choose not to accept them? For those wary of the new owner or who fear being dumped once the sale closes, will there be a safety net? For those who are terminated, will assistance such as financial planning, job relocation, and career planning be offered? Will benefits continue for a short adjustment period? One organization, which could not promise job security to its employees, did promise to position them for work in the new organization or outside it.[72] This pledge was kept; employees were trained, at organizational expense, for other positions. Part of the training included seminars in which employees were taught to be responsible for their own development and were given assistance to develop a survival kit called Making Me Marketable. Jobs were reanalyzed to focus on basic skills. For example, the job specifications for a patient-care technician stated that a high school diploma was required, but a review showed that certain skills, and not a high school diploma, were needed to do the job. Managers used their contacts and networks to assist departing employees. Employees were encouraged to work on cross-functional teams to expand their horizons and skills. The result was that productivity did not diminish dramatically, as occurs in most mergers. Furthermore, the downsizing and exodus were orderly, lessening the stress on remaining employees. The culture was changed, and employees were rewarded.

Those who stay with the newly acquired or merged company face several fates:

- *Demotion:* Under the new organizational structure, some employees are given less responsibility, less territory, or fewer lines due to amalgamation.

- *Competition for the same job:* Some companies force employees to compete for their old jobs by having to apply as new candidates for a position.

- *Termination:* If not successful in the competition, employees are then let go. Sometimes, the acquiring firm waits until it can obtain its own appraisal of employee capabilities and has a chance to determine fit.

The survivors have adjustments to make, and these were detailed in Chapter 10. Like employees involved in a restructuring, the survivors of a merger are dealing with their loss of identity as the company changes, a lack of information and the resultant anxiety, a lack of protection from adverse effects over which they have no control, the loss of colleagues, and a change in their jobs.[73] Those remaining with the corporation will need to know about compensation plans.

Compensation

Two companies with two different compensation systems have to merge their systems, adopt one, or create a new one. AOL Time Warner replaced the straight salary system of Time Warner with the AOL system of salary plus stock options.[74] Incentive plans have to be aligned to support the merger strategy. But consideration can be given to incentives to make the merger work. BC Gas gave each employee 50 free shares and introduced an attractive stock purchase plan to promote commitment to the new company.[75]

In a merger, a major issue for the HR department is the integration of benefit plans. Which company's plan should be adopted? Employees obviously wish for the most favourable benefits, but organizations are concerned with cost. If the buyer's benefit packages are significantly lower than the seller's programs, any attempt to match this would result in staggering additional costs.[76] However, when benefits are removed or reduced in the integration of companies, employees may experience loss of morale. More seriously, if employees are subjected to materially different compensation packages, they could sue for constructive dismissal. Thus, for employees in the process of considering their futures with the organization, the resolution of the benefits package may affect their decision.

The best resolution of this problem would be to conduct a cost–benefit analysis of the benefits, package by package. For example, childcare centres or health and wellness centres may seem to be costly benefits. But if the number of sick days and mental health days taken is reduced or employee turnover is diminished, then the benefits may outweigh the costs. Pension concerns will be high. Although there are regulations governing certain pension credits, different approaches to pension plan transfers must be analyzed, as variances can run into the millions of dollars.

For employees who are being terminated, retaining certain benefits during the months or years after the merger may be a humane way to soften the adverse effects of the merger. Companies may wish to offer extended medical and dental coverage, modified retirement plans, and some counselling to deal with unemployment and with career plans.

Performance Appraisal

During a merger, employees undergo stress, and productivity can be expected to drop. Focusing on long-term goals may be difficult and so short-term goals should be substituted. Business is not as usual. The role of the manager may change from one of supervisor to one of coach. Employees may play it safe and may require constant positive reinforcement for the work they do accomplish under the new house rules.

One model describes employee behaviour during a merger as falling into one of three categories: not knowing (remedied by more communication), not able (the solution is training), or not willing (a strong case for performance management through feedback and incentives).[77]

Performance appraisals for development purposes may have to be redone. The merged company may be larger or engaged in different businesses, allowing for more or different promotion paths and developmental experiences. Employee intentions and aspirations under the new regime will have to be redocumented.

Stress levels may necessitate a relaxation of the rules and more counselling and coaching. Personal problems (such as financial or marital difficulties), rather than performance problems, may surface as the stress begins to affect employees.

Training and Development

After the strategic plan has been developed, an inventory of the KSAOs needed to align with the strategy should be undertaken. Information based on previous needs analyses might have to be revised in light of the new strategy, which may create new jobs.

Managers and peers may need some additional training in the role of coach and counsellor. Every employee might benefit from stress reduction or relaxation programs. Developmental programs, such as overseas assignments or executive exchanges, or long-term educational opportunities, may be put on hold while the new organization establishes long-term plans.

Labour Relations

Unionized employees are covered by a collective agreement, which is a legally binding document. Typically, these agreements set out the conditions under which job changes must occur. Various issues will need to be considered.

HR Planning Today (12.5

HR Making a Difference in Mergers

- Encana was created in 2002 out of the acquisition of Alberta Energy Co. by PanCanadian Energy. The transaction has been called a stunning success, and the share price has risen 14 percent since its initial listing. Officials attribute this success to speed, saying "The quicker you remove uncertainty the better off you are. We all know mergers that have dragged on for a year or two, and that would be extremely counterproductive." One week after shareholders gave their approval, layoffs were announced internally. Within four weeks, employees were given the names of their new supervisors, their compensation packages, and a high-performance contract, which outlined career objectives and goals for the year.

- TD Bank acquired Canada Trust in 1999, and had to integrate 1,500 branches, 44,000 employees, 10 million customers, and $265 billion in assets. Senior executives immediately notified employees about how their jobs would be affected. Realizing that if a glitch occurred in its bank machine network, which handles 700 transactions per second, customers, as well as employees and shareholders, would resist the merger, branches were converted in waves, starting on the East Coast.

Source: J. Kirby, "The Trouble with Mergers," *Canadian Business*, vol. 77, issue 4 (February 16, 2004), pp. 65–75.

For example, will unionized employees continue with the same working conditions and benefits, as negotiated, or will the contracts be renegotiated? At a minimum, the collective agreements must be read to determine what provisions exist for job security and what the notification periods are for layoffs and terminations. Merger experts say that unions should be informed and involved from the outset of the merger so that they can make valuable contributions. Unions are perceived as independent from management and can help to obtain the trust and confidence of the workforce to participate in a change program. Those companies that involved unions had reduced labour disruptions and grievances.[78]

As you can see, HR plays a pivotal role in the success of M&As. Today, fully two-thirds of all deals now involve HR professionals in due diligence.[79] Read about HR practices in two very successful deals in HR Planning Today 12.5.

SUMMARY

The focus of this chapter was the HRM implications of M&As. Mergers are undertaken to provide a strategic benefit or a financial benefit, or to fulfill the psychological needs of the managers. The financial and other results of mergers are not always as positive as expected, and the effect on staff can be devastating, whether or not employees stay with the merged company. The culture of the previously separate companies and the new merged company is the area that experts say is the most important predictor of merger success. The merger has an impact on each of the functional areas—HR planning, selection, compensation, performance appraisal, training and development, and labour relations.

Key Terms

conglomerate merger p. 323
consolidation p. 324
culture p. 331
horizontal integration p. 326
horizontal merger p. 323

operating synergy p. 325
takeover p. 324
vertical integration p. 325
vertical merger p. 323

Web Links

Provides policies and reports about business in Canada:
www.canadaonline.about.com

Required Professional Capabilities (RPCs)

The following RPCs are relevant to material covered in this chapter. The RPC number represents the CCHRA number assigned to the RPC as presented on the CCHRA website. All of the RPCs can be found in the Body of Knowledge at www.chrp.ca/rpc/body-of-knowledge.

RPC 41 Contributes to the development of the organization's vision, goals, and strategies with a focus on human capital

RPC 42 Guides and facilitates change in organizational culture and/or values consistent with business strategies

RPC 43 Serves as a change agent to support OD interventions

RPC 45 Monitors and reports on the progress of major change initiatives

RPC 47 Develops and organization or unit design to align with business objectives and environmental factors

RPC 50 Plans for and manages the HR aspects of organizational change

RPC 97 Provides advice and counselling for employees

Discussion Questions

1. What are the reasons that a company would acquire another company? Search the business press for a recent acquisition, and rank the reasons for the acquisition as explained by the analysts and/or executives.
2. Describe the effects that a merger may have on employees. What can management do to lessen the more negative effects of a merger? What can employees do to protect themselves when they start to hear rumours of a merger?

3. One of the urgent issues facing executives immediately after the merger is announced is the retention of key employees. How would you define or describe a key employee? What methods would you use to identify key employees? Describe some programs you might use to retain your key employees during and after the merger.

Exercise

The term "merger" implies a merging of two organizations' systems and culture. The term "acquisition" implies that that acquired company will be forced to adopt the systems and culture of the parent company. But in reality, there are five options: (1) dual companies: run the two side by side (Best Buy and Future Shop are owned by the same company); (2) the parent company dominates (Scotiabank purchases many Caribbean banks); (3) the acquired company dominates (Saatchi and Saatchii was acquired by Publicis, the world's fourth-largest advertising and communication company, which adopted S&S's operating systems and culture—a kind of reverse takeover); (4) blend the best of both (this was done in the acquisition of Gillette by Procter & Gamble); and (5) build a new company (Burroughs and Sperry united to build a new company, UNISYS).

In groups, discuss the advantages and limitations of each of these options.

Case MOLSON COORS AND ACQUISITIONS

The history of Molson started over 220 years ago when John Molson invested in a little log brewery. Over the past two centuries, Molson had acquired a steamship line, a luxury hotel, and a theatre. In 2005, Molson and Coors merged to become the third-largest beer maker in the world, with a market cap of US$8 billion. After two centuries of M&A experience, one would expect Molson to be experts on the management and integration of acquisitions. This case will describe two acquisitions, both breweries—one successful and the other a failure.

In 2002, Molson acquired Brazil's second-largest beer maker, Kaiser, for US$765 million. Four years later, the company was worth US$68 million, thus experiencing one of the worst corporate losses in Canadian business history. The acquisition was costing $100 million dollars a year just to survive, and Molson lost 50 percent of the market share. Analysts suggest that one of the reasons for the failure was the use of North American management techniques in the very different South American business climate. The company should have delegated decision making to local operators and had at least one independent director on the board from Brazil. The bureaucracy in Brazil is overwhelming, and it is vital to have local partners who understand this. The second error was the attempt to bring the Brazilian beer, Bavaria, to Canada in an attempt to penetrate the premium beer category. This too was a disaster, one not helped by the soft-porn marketing campaign, and Bavaria is no longer being sold in Canada.

In 2005, Molson Coors Brewing bought a craft brewer, Creemore Springs Brewery, for $17 million. The brewery had $10 million dollars in sales. Interestingly, Molson spent $20 million on the transaction costs associated with the merger. Creemore was a highly successful small-time brewery, which the foremost authority on beer called one of the two best lagers in North America. The image of a small-time brewer that did not advertise and cared deeply about the product was at risk when Creemore was acquired by Molson, which specialized in mainstream beers. Creemore produces about 40,000 hectolitres of beer (about 12 million bottles), as against the 48 million bottles produced by Molson Coors. It is very tempting to view the acquisition of Creemore as creating opportunities for economies of scale, entering new markets, and all the other reasons why companies acquire other companies. Indeed, some of the advantages have occurred: Creemore uses the larger company's distribution systems and gets better discounts on purchases. But Creemore decided not to use Molson's canning operations, which can produce 1,000 cans a minute, and instead retained a production facility in Creemore, producing 21 cans a minute. Creemore has the same brewmaster and almost all the same employees, and management has almost complete decision-making authority.

Sources: A. Holloway, "The Molson Way," *Canadian Business,* April 9, 2007; vol 80, Issue 8, page 36 and A. Holloway "Tale of two brews," *Canadian Business,* June 5, 2006, vol. 79, Issue 12, page 63.

Questions

1. Using HR Planning Notebook 12.2, what do you think were the reasons for the acquisitions in both cases?
2. Develop the HR plans under these two scenarios: (a) a full integration of Kaiser and (b) the hands-off acquisition of Creemore Springs.

ENDNOTES

1. Chevallier, F. 2007. "Leading a Rapid Retail Transformation—Acquisition of 93 Stores Required Quick Integration and Standardization Across Canada." *Optimize*, Vol. 6, No. 6: 35.
2. Wells, S.J. 2004. "Merging Compensation Strategies." *HR Magazine*, Vol. 49, No. 5: 66–74; Bryson, J. 2003. "Managing HRM Risk in a Merger." *Employee Relations* 25, Vol. 2: No. 14–31.
3. SDC Thompson Reuters, retrieved on May 30, 2011.
4. Anonymous, "Merger and Acquisition Outlook." *CA Magazine*, Vol. 141, No. 4: 10.
5. Pitts, G. 2005. "Timid Canada Falls Prey to a Global M&A Boom." *The Globe and Mail*, October 12, p. B9.
6. Schraeder, M., and D.R. Self. 2003. "Enhancing the Success of Mergers and Acquisitions: An Organizational Cultural Perspective." *Management Decision*, Vol. 41, No. 5: 511–523.
7. McIntyre, T.L. 2004. "A Model of Levels of Involvement and Strategic Roles of Human Resource Development (HRD) Professionals as Facilitators of Due Diligence and the Integration Process." *Human Resource Development Review*. Vol. 3, No. 2 (June 2004): 173–183.

8. Edwards, C., and A. Park. 2002. "HP and Compaq: It's Showtime." *BusinessWeek*, June 17, 2002: 76–77.

9. Gilbert, C., K. Louiseeize, and A. Larmour. 2005. "Exploring the Inco Merger." *Northern Ontario Business*, Vol. 26, No. 1: 1–2.

10. Master, L.J. 1987. "Efficient Product of Financial Services: Scale and Scope Economies." *Federal Reserve Bank of Philadelphia*, January/February: 15–25.

11. Ficery, K. Herd. T., and Pursche, B. 2007. "Where Has All the Synergy Gone? The M&A Puzzle." *The Journal of Business Strategy*, Vol. 28, No. 5: 29–35.

12. "XM, Sirius Moves Closer to Merger in Canada." 2011. *The Globe and Mail*, February 17, 2011, p. B1.

13. Anand, J. 2000. "A Match Made in Heaven." *Ivey Business Journal*, Vol. 64, No. 6 (July/August): 68–73.

14. Graebner, M., K. Eisenhardt, and P. Roundy. 2010. "Success and Failure in Technology Acquisitions: Lessons for Buyers and Sellers." *The Academy of Management Perspectives*, Vol. 24, No. 3: 73.

15. Lubatkin, M.H., and P.J. Lane. 1996. "Post—The Merger Mavens Still Have It Wrong." *Academy of Management Executive*, Vol. 10, No. 1 (February): 21–39.

16. Hamel, G., and C. Prahalad. 1989. "Strategic Intent." *Harvard Business Review*, Vol. 3: 73.

17. Hosskisson, R.E., M.A. Hitt, and R.D. Ireland. 2004. *Competing for Advantage*, Mason, OH: Thompson South-Western.

18. Roll, R. 1986. "The Hubris Hypothesis of Corporate Takeover." *Journal of Business*, Vol. 59, No. 2 (April): 197–216.

19. Kroll, M., P. Wright, L. Toombs, and H. Leavell. 1997. "Form of Control: Determinant of Acquisition Performance and CEO Rewards." *Strategic Management Journal*, Vol. 18, No. 2 (February): 85–96.

20. Kets de Vries, M.F.R. 1991. "Introduction: Exploding the Myth That Organizations and Executives Are Rational." In M.F.R. Kets de Vries and Associates, eds., *Organizations on the Couch: Clinical Perspectives on Organizational Behavior and Change.* San Francisco: Jossey-Bass.

21. Rovenpor, J.L. 1993. "The Relationship Between Four Personal Characteristics of Chief Executive Officers and Company Merger and Acquisition Activity." *Journal of Business and Psychology*, Vol. 8, No. 1 (Fall): 27–55.

22. Zwieg, P.L. 1995. "The Case Against Mergers." *BusinessWeek*, October 30: 122–130.

23. Guerrero, S. 2008. "Changes in Employee Attitudes at Work Following an Acquisition: A Comparative Analysis." *Human Resource Management Journal*, Vol. 18, No. 3: 216–236.

24. Gaughan, P.A. 1996. *Mergers, Acquisitions, and Corporate Restructuring.* New York: John Wiley & Sons.

25. Edwards and Park, 2002.

26. Barney, J.B., and W.S. Hesterly. 2008. *Strategic Management and Competitive Advantage*, 21st ed. Upper Saddle River, NJ: Pearson Prentice-Hall. P. 317.

27. Schonfeld, E. 1997. "Have the Urge to Merge? You'd Better Think Twice." *Fortune*, March 31: 114–116.

28. Fisher, A. 1994. "How to Make a Merger Work." *Fortune*, Vol. 129, No. 2 (June 24): 64–66.

29. Laroche, L., G. Gitelson, and J. Bing. 2001. "Culture Shock." *CMA Management*, Vol. 75, No. 1: 40–44.

30. Kadlec, R.E. 1990. "Managing a Successful Merger." *Business Quarterly*, Autumn.

31. Yuce, A., and A. Ng. 2005. "Effects of Private and Public Canadian Mergers." *Canadian Journal of Administrative Sciences*, Vol. 22, No. 2: 111–125.

32. Harshbarger, D. 1990. "Mergers, Acquisitions, and the Reformatting of American Businesses." In D.B. Fishman and C. Cherniss, eds., *The Human Side of Corporate Competitiveness.* Newbury Park, CA: Sage Publications.

33. Guerrero, 2008.

34. Galpin, T.J., and M. Herndon. 2000. *The Complete Guide to Mergers and Acquisitions.* San Francisco, CA: Joss-Bassey.

35. Laroche et al., 2001.

36. Hollister, M. 1996. "Competing Corporate Cultures Can Doom Acquisition." *Human Resource Professional*, January/February: 7–10.

37. Laroche et al., 2001.

38. Dackert, I., P.R. Jackson, S. Brenner, and C.R. Johansson. 2003. "Eliciting and Analyzing Employees' Expectations of a Merger." *Human Relations*, Vol. 56, No. 6: 26–32.

39. Bryson, 2003.

40. Howes, C. 2001. "There Is More to a Merger Than Making a Buck: Making Cultures Fit." *Financial Post*, February 2: C5.

41. Bernhut, S. 2000. "Bridging Cultures Adding Value in a Merger." *Ivey Business Journal*, Vol. 64, No. 3: 53–58.

42. Cartwright, S., and C.L. Cooper. 1993. "The Role of Culture Compatibility in Successful Organizational Marriage." *Academy of Management Journal*, Vol. 7, No. 2: 57–70.

43. Pekala, N. 2001. "Merger They Wrote: Avoiding a Corporate Culture Collision." *Journal of Property Management*, Vol. 66, No. 3: 32–37; Miller, R. 2000. "How Culture Affects Mergers and Acquisitions." *Industrial Management*, Vol. 42, No. 5: 22–27.

44. Berry, J.W. 1990. "Social and Cultural Change." In H.C. Triandis and R.W. Brislin, eds., *Handbook of Cross-cultural Psychology*, 5th ed. Boston: Allyn & Bacon.

45. Laroche et al., 2001.

46. Corporate Leadership Council. 2001. "Cultural Assessment Tools for Mergers and Acquisitions." July.

47. Riddel, A., and F. Lipson. 1996. "Bankrupt Hospital Lands on Its Feet." *Personnel Journal*, August: 83–86.

48. Koeth, B. 1985. "Expressly American: Management's Task Is Internal Development." *Management Review*, February: 24–29.

49. Frers, K., and A. Chada. 2000. "Why You Can't Create a Purple-Footed Booby." *Canadian HR Reporter*, Vol. 13, No. 20: 16.

50. Klie, S. 2009. "HR Perspective Makes Acquisitions a Success." *Canadian HR Reporter*, Vol. 22, No. 14 (August 10): 10–11; Konpichayanond, P. 2009. "Knowledge Management for Sustained Competitive Advantage in Mergers and Acquisitions." *Advances in Developing Human Resources*, Vol. 11, No. 3: 375.

51. Anonymous. 2009. "M&As Fail Far Too Often and It's Avoidable." *Canadian HR Reporter*, Vol. 22, No. 14: 11.

52. Rees, C., and Edwards, T. 2008. "Management Strategy and HR in International Mergers: Choice, Constraint And Pragmatism." *Human Resource Management Journal*, Vol. 19, No. 1: 24–39.

53. Anonymous. 2005. "HR's Growing Role in M&A Due Diligence." *HR Focus*, Vol. 82, No. 8 (August): 1–5.

54. Stuart, P. 1993. "HR Actions Offer Protection During Takeovers." *Personnel Journal*, June: 84–95.

55. Anonymous. 2008. "Cognizant Post Recognizes HR's Role in Mergers." *Workforce Management*, Vol. 87, No. 10: 12.

56. Walker, J. 1992. *Human Resource Management.* New York: McGraw-Hill.

57. Hoskisson, R.E., M.A. Hitt, and R. D. Ireland. 2004. *Competing for Advantage.* Mason OH: Thompson South-Western.

58. Marks, M., and Mirvis, P. 2011. "Merge Ahead: A Research Agenda to Increase Merger and Acquisition Success." *Journal of Business and Psychology*, Vol. 26, No. 2: 161–168.

59. Leisy, B. 2009. "5 Questions: Addressing HR Risk." *Workforce Management*, Vol. 88, No. 1: 8; Sorhaitz, K., and McCullagh, D. 2011. "Merge Ahead." *Benefits Canada*, Vol. 35, No. 4: 38–40.

60. Kummer, C. 2008. "Motivation and Retention of Key People in Mergers and Acquisitions." *Strategic HR Review*, Vol. 7, No. 6: 5–10.

61. Tanuer, B., and Gonzalez-Duarte, R. 2007. "Managing People in Radical Changes (M&As): The Adoption of Intrinsically Consistent HRM Strategies in Brazilian Companies." *International Journal of Manpower*, Vol. 28, No. 5: 369–383.

62. Galpin and Herndon, 2000.

63. Adams, M. 2002. "Making a Merger Work." *HR Magazine*, Vol. 47, No. 3: 52–57.

64. Klie, S. 2009. "HR Perspective Makes Acquisitions a Success." *Canadian HR Reporter*, Vol. 22, No. 14 (August 10): 10–11.

65. Parks, N. 2004. "Managing the HR Challenges of a Major Global Merger." *Strategic HR Review*, Vol. 4, No. 1: 24–27.

66. Kemp, A., and P. Lytwyn. 2002. "Merging HR Departments: How to Make It Work." *HR Professional*, August/September: 29–30.

67. Tannous, G.F., and B. Chang. 2007. "Canadian Takeover Announcements and the Job Security of Top Managers." *Canadian Journal of Administrative Sciences*, Vol. 24: 250–267.

68. Riddel and Lipson, 1996.

69. Wade, M., and B. Zimmerman, 2003. "Please Don't Go: Retaining Key People During the Ups and Downs of M & A's." *Workspan*, Vol. 46, No. 11: 50–56.

70. Alphonso, C. 2002. "Top Staff Gain Clout in Mergers." *The Globe and Mail*, May 29, p. C1.

71. Schonfield, E. 1997. "Have the Urge to Merge? You'd Better Think Twice." *Fortune*, March 31, pp. 114–116.

72. Riddel and Lipson, 1996.

73. Walker, 1992.

74. Buchanan, R., and M. Daniell. 2002. "The Leadership Testing Ground." *Journal of Business Strategy*, Vol. 23, No. 2: 12–17.

75. Kadlec, 1990.

76. O'Rourke, R.W., and B.R. Berg, 2005. "Avoiding Costly Benefits Bloopers in Mergers and Acquisitions." *Employee Benefit Plan Review*, Vol. 60, No. 1: 11–14.

77. Galpin and Herndon, 2000.

78. Bryson, 2003.

79. Brown, D. 2005. "More HR Input Leads to More Merger Success: Study." *Canadian HR Reporter*, Vol. 18, No. 1: 1–2.

CHAPTER
13

Outsourcing

CHAPTER LEARNING OUTCOMES

After reading this chapter, you should be able to:

- Define outsourcing.
- List the reasons organizations outsource functions and programs.
- Identify the advantages of outsourcing.
- Cite the risks and limitations of outsourcing.
- Develop the criteria necessary for managing the outsourcing relationship.

OUTSOURCING HR AT GM

In 2007, GM Service Technical College won the Optimas Award for Financial Impact for the amount of money they saved by outsourcing the training of service mechanics. The provider opened a new facility just for GM training and created a program that uses computer-assisted, television-broadcast, and classroom-based instruction to train GM mechanics. GM saved money because they no longer have to hire trainers or maintain 180 training facilities. The cost per hour to train a mechanic has been reduced from $140 to $10. Furthermore, 90 percent of all technicians are retrained annually, in contrast to 35 percent previously.[1]

Outsourcing

A contractual relationship for the provision of business services by an external provider

Outsourcing refers to a contractual relationship for the provision of business services by an external provider. In other words, a company pays another company to do some work for it. In HR, it means transferring high-volume transactional work from the HR department to an outside contractor. Currently, outsourcing is being promoted as one of the most powerful trends reshaping management. However, organizations have always outsourced some functions. For decades, most organizations hired firms to operate their cleaning or restaurant functions. One difference now is the scale. Firms are outsourcing everything from information technology management to entire functions such as human resources.

OUTSOURCING

Outsourcing occurs when an organization contracts with another organization to provide services or products of a major function or activity.

Work that is traditionally done internally is shifted to an external provider, and the employees of the original organization are often transferred to the service provider. Outsourcing differs from alliances, partnerships, and joint ventures in that the flow of resources is one-way, from the provider to the user. Typically, there is no profit sharing or mutual contribution.

The second difference is that much of the work that is being contracted out is being done offshore (i.e., outside of Canada) or outside the primary market. You have no doubt experienced this when you have called to get assistance with computer problems or credit questions. Now HR activities are being outsourced to India and other countries in order to lower costs and improve quality. This process is labelled *HRO* (*HR offshoring*)[2]. The impact of this trend in offshoring is described in HR Planning Today 13.1.

Outsourcing HR Functions

Surveys continue to show that nearly all organizations have outsourced parts of their HR functions.[3] In 2010, about 60 percent of all large Canadian organizations outsourced some HR services.[4] IBM outsourced its entire HR department, which was then called Workforce Solutions, a profit centre that produced gains in flexibility, accountability, competitiveness, and profitability. HR Planning Today 13.2 provides examples of other companies that outsourced parts of their HR functions.

HR Planning Today (13.1

The Impact of Offshoring in India

Many Western nations have outsourced activities to India because of the large English-speaking population, high levels of education (particularly in engineering and the sciences), the relatively calm political climate, an independent legal system that protects intellectual property, and cost efficiencies.

The scope of this activity has impacted the labour market in India. One growing trend is the reverse brain drain, in which Indian professionals, with foreign educational credentials and work experiences, are returning to work in newly created positions.

A second impact is the increase in wages, by approximately 10 to 15 percent. Turnover is high, contradicting the traditional view of Indian employees as loyal and deferential to authority.

These trends may impact the attractiveness of India for offfshoring. Coupled with this are the emerging competitors based in Eastern Europe. For example, Montreal-based Bombardier outsourced its accounting function to Romania. They compete not on wages, but on time zones and knowledge of many languages.

Source: Adapted from S. Gopalan and R. Herring III, "Managing Emerging Outsourcing Trends: The Indian Experience," *Allied Academies International Conference. Academy for Studies in International Business Proceedings*, Vol. 5, No. 2 (2005): 1–5; A. Seno, "Offshoring Island," Report on Business, *The Globe and Mail*, February 25, 2010, p. 26.

HR Planning Today (13.2

HR Outsourcing Examples

Many organizations outsource their HR functions. Here are some examples:

- TransCanada, a leading North American energy company with about 3,550 employees, has outsourced pension administration, savings plan administration, benefits administration, payroll, retirement planning, retiree benefits, pension payments, disability management, employee assistance program, relocation, career transition, and exit interviews.
- Gow Corp., a 90-employee Alberta organization that processes livestock for institutional and restaurant clients, teamed with its vertical partners (a distributor and a supplier) to outsource and share two HR professionals who would handle payroll, training, health and safety, and so on.
- The United Church of Canada outsourced job evaluation, recruitment, and compensation in order to tap a wealth of experience that was not available in-house. Pratt & Whitney Canada outsourced its training function to DDI (Development Dimensions International).
- Pratt & Whitney executives wanted a partner that could handle not only the tactical level in managing administrative tasks but also the strategic level in matching learning solutions to business needs.

Sources: Adapted from a presentation by D. Mackay and L. McKeown at the 2008 HRPAO Annual Conference, January 31, 2008; and A. Patel, "Vertical HR: Will the Experiment Work?" 14; L. McKibbin-Brown, "Who Is Outsourcing What?" 32; P.J. Labrie and J. Bedard, "Outsourcing Training at Pratt & Whitney Canada," 42—all from *HR Professional*, Vol. 10, No. 3 (June/July 2002).

What should an organization outsource? Activities most likely to be outsourced are:

- Rule based
- Repetitive
- Frequently undertaken
- Predictable
- Able to be fully or partly automated by technology
- Able to be delivered by remote sites[5]

In HR, the functions most likely to be outsourced are temporary staffing, payroll, training, recruiting, and benefits administration. HR Planning Notebook 13.1 lists the functions within HR that are likely to be outsourced. A new trend is to outsource absence management, because claims are complex, confidential, and require some degree of medical expertise.[6]

HR departments are under increasing pressure to produce deliverables, not just doables, and so are searching to determine which activities add value and who can best do these. Outsourcing is also a response to the demand from executives that HR reduce costs for its services. Outsourcing to service providers with international expertise also allows HR departments to harmonize employee packages for a global workforce, while complying with local laws.

HR Planning Notebook 13.1

HR FUNCTIONS THAT MAY BE OUTSOURCED

Compensation

- Payroll
- Benefits
- Compensation administration
- Pension

Training

- Program delivery
- Program design and development
- Training consulting to line departments
- Training needs analysis
- Program evaluation
- Strategic planning for training and development
- Administration
- Developing training policy

Recruitment and Selection

- Advertisements
- Screening of applications
- Testing
- Reference checking
- Preliminary interviews
- Salary negotiations at the executive level
- Exit interviews

Health and Safety

- Employee assistance programs
- Wellness programs

HR Planning Notebook 13.2

SMALL BUSINESS AND HR OUTSOURCING

Most businesses do not hire an HR professional until the employee numbers reach about 100, or even 400. But legislated HR functions, such as payroll and benefits, are necessary for every organization, regardless of size, so small businesses turn to other small businesses specializing in HR. The advantages are the following:

- Lessens the handling of routine, transactional HR work (payroll) by in-house staff
- Offers access to experts who may provide advice in atypical situations (employee fraud)

- Provides the management of one-off services (such as computer training)
- Ensures that the company is complying with current legislation
- Allows access to technology platforms that are too expensive to develop in-house

Outsourcing is not the same as using consultants who may provide assistance on a project-by-project basis. Small businesses are looking for a long-term relationship with a provider that understands small business in general and their business in particular.

While smaller firms might outsource all HR functions, most large firms retain the critical components. HR Planning Notebook 13.2 describes the reasons that small businesses outsource HR. Larger organizations rarely engage in 100 percent outsourcing for three reasons. First, as has been argued throughout this text, the HR function is so critical to the culture and strategic objectives of an organization that it must be closely managed by the organization itself. The functions that are deemed most critical, such as recruitment, selection, and performance management, are rarely outsourced. Second, situations arise that are impossible to predict, such as industrial relations disputes, and this unpredictability makes it difficult to develop a contractual arrangement with a vendor; timeliness of response is crucial. Third is the lack of providers of total HRM services. The field of outsourcing is replete with hundreds of small companies specializing in market niches. One company might do an excellent job of benefits counselling, and another might specialize in employee assistance, but few can do everything from training to managerial succession to payroll. These competencies have to reside within the firm.

THE RATIONALE FOR OUTSOURCING

Almost all organizations outsource, and the trend is growing. In a study conducted by Hewitt Associates, 94 percent of those surveyed said that they had outsourced one or more HR functions.[7] CIBC's decision to outsource is explained in HR Planning Today 13.3.

If the organization needs experts and cannot afford to hire or train them, outsourcing might be a solution. Most organizations want to achieve cost savings or improved services, or access to experts or technology, which serves as the basis for their decision to outsource. However, many managers approach outsourcing as a solution without first defining the problem.[8]

HR Planning Today 13.3

Outsourcing at CIBC

One of Canada's largest companies outsourced major portions of its HR functions. CIBC employs about 44,000 people, about 450 of those in HR. In 2001, CIBC outsourced payroll processing, benefits administration, a call centre for employment enquiries, occupational health and safety services, and HR technology to a company specializing in HR services, EDS, in a seven-year, $227 million deal. Two hundred CIBC HR employees were transferred to EDS, cutting the bank's HR department by nearly half. CIBC's vice-president of HR commented, "I don't think that in today's world, power is about the number of employees you have working for you. HR should get its power from how much it helps the business units meet their goals."

The reasons for outsourcing included the desire to improve service, to increase automation, and to have the HR department focus on the strategic issues of making a contribution to the company. CIBC does not add value by administering pension plans; EDS does. The HR department is freed from routine transactions and can focus on policy, providing advice and programs to move the business forward. The deal was made to help CIBC avoid capital expenses updating its computer systems and to take the guesswork out of the HR annual budget. It also allowed CIBC to standardize the quality of the service. For example, calls to the centre are now answered within 20 seconds 90 percent of the time, which is an improvement over service levels when CIBC managed this function.

The CIBC–EDS deal was unique as an outsourcing arrangement for several reasons. CIBC arranged with EDS to introduce best practices back into its organization and to update the bank on industry trends on a regular basis. CIBC searched for a vendor that would be a cultural fit with its organization. The main attribute the bank was looking for was "adapting to client needs." As the CIBC vice-president of strategic alliance management said, "You can't put everything in a contract, so it is important to choose a company you can work with. You should be as clear as possible in terms of defining roles and responsibilities, but you cannot possibly think of all eventualities upfront. . . . It is important to have a process built into the contract to manage these issues."

Sources: M. Rafter, "Promise Fulfilled," *Workforce Management*, Vol. 84, No. 9 (September 2005): 51–54; D. Brown, "CIBC HR Department Halved as Non-strategic Roles Outsourced," *Canadian HR Reporter*, Vol. 14, No. 11 (2001): 1, 6; S. Geary and G. Coffey-Lewis, "Are You Ready to Outsource HR?" *HR Professional*, June/July 2002: 26–29.

There are at least six major reasons that organizations outsource: financial savings, strategic focus, access to advanced technology, improved service levels, access to specialized expertise, and organizational politics.

Financial Savings

The first reason cited for the outsourcing decision is to save money. Organizations believe that costs can be reduced by outsourcing a function such as payroll. Economies of scale can be achieved when a provider, such as Ceridien, which specializes in benefits administration, concentrates on one area and provides this service to many corporations. Specialized vendors are more efficient, because they can spread the costs of training personnel and undertaking research and development across more users. Studies of outsourcing arrangements of at least two years' duration showed that outsourcing resulted in cost savings ranging from 10 to 20 percent, with an average of 15 percent.[9] About 50 percent of the firms believed that their cost savings objectives had been met, and that labour productivity had improved.

Related to the issue of saving money is cost control. Company users of a service might be more cautious when the contractor charges them for each service, as opposed to the "free" in-house service. Training is a good example. If in-house training is free and training provided by an external vendor costs $1,000 per day, then managers are more stringent about requiring employees to prove that the training is needed and that there will be measurable benefits. Sometimes when an organization is just starting to offer a service, such as fitness training for employees, it is cheaper to contract this out than to make the capital investments in a gym and specialized staff. This capital can then be redirected to other initiatives that have a higher rate of return. Outsourcing also makes sense when usage of a service is variable or unpredictable. An organization may recruit on an irregular basis for IT staff; in this case, retaining an in-house IT recruiter is not economically viable.

Strategic Focus

Employers recognize that they cannot pursue excellence in all areas. Theodore Levitt, an American economist, said over half a century ago that "not a single company can afford to even try and be the first in everything."[10] Therefore, they decide to focus on their core competency, such as customer service or innovation, and move secondary functions, such as benefits administration, to firms in which these functions are a core competency.

How is core defined? There are four meanings:[11]

- Activities traditionally performed internally
- Activities critical to business success—core work contributes directly to the bottom line; non-core work doesn't
- Activities creating current or potential competitive advantage
- Activities that will influence future growth or rejuvenation

Non-core work is transactional work that is routine and standard and can easily be duplicated and replicated; core work is transformational and adds value to employees or customers.[12] The notion of core competencies was created by Prahalad and Hamel, who argued that the real sources of competitive advantage were not products but management's ability to consolidate skills and technologies into competencies to adapt to changing circumstances.[13] A competency is a combination of technology, management, and collective learning. For Nike, that core competency is product design, and the company outsources nearly everything else.[14]

Executives will decide to concentrate on what the organization does best, and contract everything else out to vendors. Core functions that should not be outsourced are orientation, leadership development, employee relations, final selection, performance management, succession management, and organizational change, as these depend on an understanding of organizational culture, a long-term orientation, consistency, trust, and confidential information. For example, in high-tech firms, the speed of the changes in businesses means that vendors will not have the specialized skills in coaching to develop the next generation of leaders. Microsoft creates opportunities in a process that encourages employees to improve their coaching skills and develop relationships within the organization.[15]

By outsourcing non-core activities, managers hope to be able to focus on value-added roles. For example, CIBC outsourced the design of training programs and development and delivery, allowing the company to focus on planning, needs analyses, and coaching after program completion.[16] Companies that did outsource reported that they reduced administrative tasks by more than half and increased their strategic focus by 40 percent.[17] Avenor Inc. of Montreal outsourced all pensions, benefits, and payroll administration. As James Merchant, vice-president of HR at Avenor, explained:

> *Outsourcing allowed us to get out of low value-added administrative work and become more strategic. We now focus on health and safety, leadership development, total compensation, and employee and labour relations. Our department at head office has 12 staff today compared to 40 in 1994. But, with our change in focus, our performance within the organization has taken a quantum leap.*[18]

The best advice is to outsource transactions and insource transformations.[19]

Advanced Technology

Another driver of the outsourcing trend has been technology. Many functions are outsourced because organizations want to improve technical service, they cannot find technical talent, or they need quick and reliable access to new technologies.[20] Much of traditional HR service has involved answering employee inquiries about benefits or making changes to employee files. These kinds of tasks can be handled easily by interactive voice responses and managed by companies that specialize in this service. Technology also enables a company to reduce transaction time (the time it takes to handle a request).

Improved Service

Quality improvement is cited as another benefit of outsourcing. Performance standards can be written into the contract more tightly than may be possible with current and long-tenured employees. Managers can choose the "best-of-breed" vendors that have outstanding track records and more flexibility in hiring and rewarding their employees.

HR departments are often criticized for being overly bureaucratic. When using a service provider whose focus is service, clients of HR see a marked improvement in flexibility, response, and performance. Indeed, most HR directors value service accuracy and reliability more than cost savings.[21] Most firms gain control of their service levels because their outsourcing agreement can quantify deliverables in the contract.[22]

Confidentiality is also a good reason to outsource. An employee with a drinking problem, for example, is more likely to seek assistance from an external counsellor than an in-house employee assistance officer.

Specialized Expertise

Another reason cited by some companies for outsourcing is that they find the laws and regulations governing HR so complex that they decide to outsource to firms that have the specific expertise required. The motto is "Outsource when somebody can do it better than you." For example, some firms rarely conduct executive searches, so it makes sense to hire executive search consultants rather than employ a recruiter specialist.

Employees who are outsourced to the service provider may see opportunities for career development in their disciplines. In an organization specializing in training, for example, employees would have greater access to expert colleagues to use them as sounding boards, and to career paths and opportunities to upgrade their knowledge and skills.

The use of experts also reduces the risks and liabilities for organizations. Specialists know the legislation better than anyone and can assure the user organization that all their practices comply with legislation.

Access to leading practices is another motivator to outsource.

Organizational Politics

An outsourced function is not as visible as an in-house department performing the same tasks. Some organizations make the decision to outsource to get rid of a troublesome department, such as one where employees are underperforming. Outsourcing a function also reduces the head count. Head counts are important in the public sector; the fewer civil servants on payroll, the happier the tax-paying public. Organizations that outsource achieve a ratio of 1:231 (one HR person to 231 employees) in contrast to the traditional 1:100.[23] The contractor is often able to justify and negotiate technology improvements and other investments more easily than in-house managers. At United Kitchen, a company that outsourced all training, the goal was to buy an expert who could maintain an objective view and not get embroiled in office politics.[24]

RISKS AND LIMITATIONS OF OUTSOURCING

As with any major decision, there are positives and negatives to outsourcing. The decision to outsource carries risks and has limitations. Are the anticipated benefits realized? What are the risks to service levels? What is the effect on employee morale? Does outsourcing reduce the value of the organization? These four questions are discussed below.

Projected Benefits Versus Actual Benefits

For organizations with experience in outsourcing functions, there are hints that the process is not as cost-effective and problem-free as expected. Surveys have indicated that about half of the respondents found that it was more expensive to manage the outsourced activity than originally expected and that service levels were not as good as expected.[25] The extensive effort required by management to manage the outsourced activity is seen by some as the largest hidden cost of outsourcing.[26] According to one survey, about 80 percent of outsourced customer service agreements don't reduce overall costs.[27] About 40 percent reported problems with higher costs than forecasted. The reasons for the cost overrides include system incompatibilities and client demands outside the standard vendor package. Interestingly, one study found that about one-quarter of HR staff time was still spent on benefits administration, which had been outsourced (e.g., addressing problems that the outsourcing company could not handle or mishandled with employees). Worse, half of this routine work was being done by the wrong people: senior specialists and managers.[28] Outsourcing compares poorly to other processes designed to save costs. For example, re-engineering can generate cost savings over 50 percent; outsourcing savings seem to be, on average, 10 to 15 percent.[29] Over 30 percent of outsourcing arrangements were not renewed because the cost savings were not achieved.[30]

Service Risks

The vendor will provide services as specified in the contract. If the needs of the user organization change, contracts will have to change. The flexibility of adding new features or enhancing or reducing service is lessened, once the organization is totally dependent on the supplier, having lost all its organizational specialists.[31] Furthermore, it is possible that the vendor may enter the market and become a competitor. For example, Schwinn, a U.S. manufacturer of bicycles, outsourced the manufacture of its bicycle frames to a Taiwanese organization, Giant Manufacturing. A few years later, Giant entered the bicycle market and damaged Schwinn's business. Companies can lessen this risk by erecting strategic blocks—terms in the contract that limit the replication of certain competitive advantages, such as propriety technology—or spreading the outsourcing among many vendors. There might be problems too, with a disruption of service. A strike at Heathrow Airport that left 70,000 passengers stranded was a direct result of a labour relations problem with the outsourcing supplier that British Airways had contracted to do the catering. The public relations nightmare was for British Airways, not the catering company.[32]

An SHRM survey found that about 25 percent of respondents reported a decrease in customer service from the in-house service and a less personal relationship with its own employees.[33]

Employee Morale

One of the primary risks in outsourcing is the effect on employee morale and performance.[34] Outsourcing is a form of restructuring that always results in displaced employees. Organizations provide employees with a sense of identification and feelings of security and belonging. When these are disrupted, employees, as stakeholders, may feel resentful and retaliatory. About one-third of HR professionals resist outsourcing because they worry about the risk of losing their jobs, or about being forced to work for a vendor, and fear that management believes that outsiders are more competent.[35]

In an outsourcing arrangement, employees are transferred to the outsourcing firm, transferred internally to other functions, outplaced, and/or offered voluntary retirements. Despite all these options, redundancies and layoffs of staff do occur. In certain cases, the service provider employs the entire displaced workforce but may negotiate higher fees to accommodate what is perceived to be surplus or inefficient labour. Employees are resentful of these arrangements, with their connotations of "serfdom" in which the "serfs" are sold as capital equipment.[36]

Outsourcing can lead to the disintegration of an organization's culture. Instead of empowering and valuing employees, an outsourcing decision alienates and "de-skills" employees. The transferred employees will experience emotional loss and a change in culture. The outsourced function might have served as a developmental site for managers, and this is now lost unless arrangements can be made with the vendor.

In most cases, negotiated arrangements of pay and job security are not transferable. The vendor is able to offer cost savings because of reduced wages and increased work intensity.[37]

Organizations that attempt to outsource face a backlash. The City of Toronto endured a three-week strike by garbage workers over the issue of outsourcing. Citizens lived with rotting garbage on the streets during a heat wave while the strike was under way. Members of the Canadian Union of Public Employees (CUPE) were demanding job security ("lifelong employment") for employees, but the city won a public relations battle by saying that the demands were unreasonable because no working and tax-paying citizen enjoyed this right.

Once rumours of outsourcing arrangements are started, HR managers can expect talented employees to start job searches and all employees to suffer anxiety resulting in lost production. Managers will have to deal with the reactions of displaced employees and survivors and allow for a period of mourning.

Security Risks

There is always a risk of information being leaked. This is particularly important in software development generally for a company concerned with intellectual property rights. For HR, the major information risk is the loss of personnel information (employee confidential data).[38] Much of this information, such as performance and medical histories, is very sensitive.

Reduced Value

Extreme levels of outsourcing hollow out a company, leaving it a shell. There may be unintended consequences of outsourcing the organization's knowledge and skills to outsiders. The vendor may even sell the acquired knowhow and company secrets to a competitor. An organization can find that outsourcing employees' skills limits this organization's ability to learn and exploit changes. More troublesome is the emerging research which suggests that outsourcing an activity deemed to be routine and of low value did not result in the remaining HR staff becoming focusing on more "strategic" or higher-value work.[39]

The organization experiences a reduced capacity to generate profits or innovate. Even a non-core activity, such as IT, may be tightly linked to other functions such as HR, so outsourcing IT reduces the firm's capability for cross-functional synergies and creativity. The vendor cannot know your organization's special needs, nor can it distinguish your high-profile customer (the president of the company that outsourced the function) from any other customer. When HR functions are outsourced, the internal image of HR may deteriorate as there is less interaction with internal customers and less and less HR work is performed by the HR department.[40]

Even with these risks and limitations, it is estimated that only 1 to 20 percent of outsourced HR functions have been brought back in-house.[41]

MANAGEMENT OF OUTSOURCING

Managing the outsourcing well is critical. First, outsourcing must be subjected to a cost–benefit analysis. Can the contractor do a better job, faster, while maintaining service levels and meeting legislative requirements? How will this be measured? HR Planning Notebook 13.3 suggests a number of ways that organizations can prepare for outsourcing.

The following sections describe ways of selecting vendors, negotiating the contract, and monitoring the arrangement.

HR Planning Notebook 13.3
PREPARING FOR OUTSOURCING

In order to maximize the benefits from an outsourcing arrangement, some experts suggest that organizations complete the following tasks in preparation for moving to an outsourcing arrangement:

- *Develop meaningful benchmarks and data:* Unless you know the in-house costs of managing, for example, benefits administration, you will not know whether the vendor relationship will result in cost savings. Of course, service levels also have to be measured and quantified to provide a baseline for negotiations with the vendor to achieve service-level improvements. These two types of measures will enable you to develop a business case.
- *Develop change management skills:* Outsourcing any part of HR requires expertise in change management. Employee's lives will be transformed, and this transformation has to be carefully managed.
- *Develop contract and performance management skills:* Most HR departments have little experience with negotiating and

managing large contracts. There are two models for managing these outsourcing contracts. The first is to establish a dedicated vendor management unit. For example, the Development Bank of Singapore was managing 600 outsourcing contracts and found that this approach was inefficient. They established a centralized vendor management group, which developed the service agreements, compiled data, and monitored the vendor. Another model is to use a cross-functional team. The purchasing group might negotiate the contract while the HR group would manage the day-to-day monitoring. Basically, whatever model is used, subject matter expertise and supplier management skills are needed.
- *Develop communication channels and skills:* The quality of communication can determine the success or failure of an outsourcing arrangement. A study of 100 outsourcing deals suggests that face-to-face conversations were the most effective communication channel.

Sources: Adapted from Human Resource Outsourcing Association, "HR Service Delivery in the Federal Government: Are You Sourcing Ready?" www.hroassociation.org/file, retrieved on September 15, 2008; S. Khanna and J. Randolph, "An HR Planning Model for Outsourcing," *Human Resource Planning*, Vol. 28, No. 4 (December 2005): 37; N. Kasraie and N. Cline, "Communication as a Key to Success in Outsourcing: A Survey of the Top 100 Outsourcing Companies in the World," *World Journal of Social Sciences*, Vol. 1, No. 1 (March 2011): 200–211.

Selecting the Vendor

Once a decision is made to explore outsourcing a function, the organization should:

- Inform the staff of the affected function
- Prepare a **request for proposal (RFP)**
- Invite internal and external bids
- Establish a team to evaluate these bids

See HR Planning Notebook 13.4 for a summary of the key information that should be contained in a response to an RFP. If more than one HR activity is to be outsourced, the organization has to decide if they want one provider to undertake all the activities or work with specialized providers (best in class) for each activity. When asked in a survey, about 60 percent of HR managers polled preferred to work with one provider of multiple services.[42]

The point at which the staff should be informed about the potential outsourcing is hotly debated. If informed early in the process, the most talented and marketable employees might leave sooner rather than later, and the stress and anxiety among those remaining affect productivity from that point on. However, in any case employees will usually find out earlier than management might like, and it is far better to keep them in the loop; they might even play a vital role in the development of the RFP.

The items to be included in an RFP vary by the service to be outsourced. Typical details include activity levels, errors, response rates, deliverables, and goals.[43] Costs are never included.

Companies that have had successful outsourcing arrangements always started by comparing vendor bids against bids newly submitted by in-house functional experts.[44] The internal group might have had ideas all along to reduce costs or improve services, but might have been thwarted for any of a variety of

Request for proposal (RFP)
Describes the responsibilities to be outsourced and invites potential providers to present their proposal for carrying out the job

---

 HR Planning Notebook 13.4

RESPONSE REQUIREMENTS TO A REQUEST FOR PROPOSAL FOR OUTSOURCING

In a response to a request for proposal, the potential provider should do the following:

- Explain how the provider is uniquely qualified to accomplish the measurable objectives that are described in the request.
- Describe actual situations in which the provider is currently providing the services that are proposed for this operation.

- Identify the challenges that the provider expects to encounter while improving the operation.
- Explain how these challenges will be met and present a proposed timetable for meeting them.
- Describe the economic model that is proposed for the operation.
- Specify the fee that the provider believes to be reasonable compensation for its services.

Source: L. Moneta and W.L. Dillion, "Strategies for Effective Outsourcing," *New Directions for Student Services*, No. 96 (Winter 2001) (Malden, MA: John Wiley & Sons), p. 42. © 2002. Reprinted with permission of John Wiley & Sons, Inc.

HR Planning Today (13.4)

Criteria for Evaluating Potential Outsourcers

Companies look at the following criteria in their evaluations:

- HR process expertise
- Prior experience and track records
- Financial stability
- Service-level agreements in the contracts and compatibility of standardization

- Leading-edge technology and commitment to invest in more
- Cultural compatibility
- Readiness to invest in transition management

Sources: I. Hunter, "Outsourcing: The Business Model for the New Millennium," *Training Journal*, September 2007, pp. 26–32; K. Gurchiak, "Record Growth in Outsourcing of HR Functions," *HR Magazine*, Vol. 50, No. 6 (June 2005): 35–36; M. Milgate, *Alliances, Outsourcing, and the Lean Organization*, © 2001 Michael Milgate. Reproduced with permission of Greenwood Publishing Group Inc., Westport, CT

reasons. Once it is clear that outsourcing is the preferred route because the same service cannot be provided in-house, the organization can proceed with its outsourcing plans, assured that every avenue has been explored.

The evaluation team should include the technical experts, including a manager who will not be affected by the outcome, procurement officers who can qualify suppliers, and even customers who can check out the suppliers' track records and personnel.[45] This team sets the evaluation criteria, analyzes bids against the criteria, and chooses the vendor. The process should be as obsessive and detailed as the due diligence undertaken with mergers and acquisitions. Examples of evaluation criteria can be found in HR Planning Today 13.4.

Negotiating the Contract

Experts advise organizations looking to outsource not to work with the contract the vendor will offer, because these contracts typically do not include performance standards or penalty clauses if the vendor does not meet requirements.[46] Payment provisions in these standardized contracts also tend to favour the vendor. The vendor also has a tendency to want to start the service before the contract is signed and "take care of the details later." Anything not provided at the beginning is then subject to excess fees.

An essential first step that the user organization must undertake is the establishment of benchmark levels with current services. When managers with experience in outsourcing HR functions were asked what they would do differently, about half said that they would define service levels that aligned more clearly with business objectives.[47] The goal is to document baseline services currently being provided, using criteria such as response time, response cost, and customer satisfaction ratings. Thus, a performance standard might read that "90 percent of benefits enquiries must be answered within 24 hours." Of course, everyone forgets about the other 10 percent, so that too has to be specified (e.g., "The remaining 10 percent must be answered within three working days"). Economies of scale only work when the programs are standardized and have few exceptions. So the client must be ready to minimize exceptions that complicate or slow down the process.[48] Quality measures have to be included; for example,

HR Planning Today 13.5

Negotiating Service Outcomes

SaskCentral is a cooperative that supports credit unions in Saskatchewan. In deciding to outsource the payroll function, SaskCentral was looking for a supplier that would guarantee accuracy and be compliant with legislation governing compensation. Responsiveness was another critical criterion as SaskCentral's culture had always been customer oriented, and errors were fixed quickly by simply going to the HR specialist. Although cost savings and enabling HR personnel to focus more on strategic functions were important reasons to outsource, the outcomes of accuracy, currency with legislation, and responsiveness were the important deliverables.

Source: www.SaskCentral.com; Anonymous, "Thoughts on Outsourcing," *Canadian HR Reporter*, Vol. 23, No. 2 (January 25, 2010): 19–23.

"Clients rate the service satisfactory or excellent 98 percent of the time." The most common service-level agreements are transaction accuracy, data delivery, service availability, issue resolution, and client satisfaction.[49] Failure to meet these levels must result in penalties, such as reduction in the costs or payments to the user. On the other hand, if service is superior, incentives should be built into the contract. It might be necessary to include clauses for severe fluctuations in demand. Finally, any contract should include a termination clause.

The negotiations tend to be unbalanced, with the vendor having employed many technical and legal experts in order to prepare the agreement. The user organizations should do likewise and hire an expert to protect their interests. A technical expert can help develop performance standards, and a legal expert ensures that the customer's wishes are expressed in the contract. Read how SaskCentral built service requirements into their negotiations in HR Planning Today 13.5.

Monitoring the Arrangement

The most frequent causes of outsourcing problems, according to a study conducting by the Centre for Outsourcing Research and Education, are:[50]

- *Poor service definition:* The outsourced project or function must be clearly defined. If the terms are fuzzy, however, the contractor might be invited to brainstorm and help generate the guidelines and standards.[51] The work is managed by results—in other words, there are targets or objectives such as "All calls answered within 90 seconds"—not necessarily by time expended to generate the results.

- *Weak management processes:* A person needs to be assigned to monitor that the results are as expected; in complex arrangements, it might take a team, called the *stay-back team*, to do this monitoring.

A relationship with the firm must be established to ensure that the outsourcer acts in the firm's best interests and has knowledge of its unique needs. References have to be checked, just as when hiring any employee. Demand frequent and accurate reporting. In a United Kingdom survey on outsourcing, most HR managers were dissatisfied with the frequency and quality of the communication from the supplier.[52] Internal and external client satisfaction surveys should be conducted.

When outsourcing is managed according to these guidelines, organizations can maximize its benefits and mitigate the risks. The effective management of outsourced relationships, normally the role of the procurement department, is a skill set that HR departments need. It might be argued that organizations that invest in this skill set will have an advantage over their competitors.[53] Those with experience in this area find it easier to train HR professionals in supplier management than to train those in the procurement department in HR.[54]

SUMMARY

Outsourcing refers to the contractual arrangement wherein one organization provides services or products to another. There is a growing trend to outsource HR functions. The advantages of outsourcing include the reduction of costs; the increased energy and time to focus on an organization's core competencies; access to technology and specialized expertise, both of which result in increased levels of service; and the political advantages of removing a troublesome function or reducing headcount. But there are disadvantages: the anticipated benefits might not be realized; service levels might decrease; and employee morale and commitment, as well as the value of the organization, might decrease. Managing the contractual arrangement with the service provider is the key to optimizing the benefits and minimizing the risks.

Key Terms

outsourcing p. 352
request for proposal (RFP) p. 363

Web Links

The Human Resources Outsourcing Association (HROA) has information and tools to help with outsourcing issues:
www.hroassociation.org

The Centre for Outsourcing Research and Education has articles on various aspects of outsourcing, as does the Outsourcing Center:
www.core-outsourcing.org
www.outsourcing-canada.com

The Canadian HR Reporter has an online archive under the HR outsourcing icon, and reports on HR outsourcing deals signed by CIBC, BMO, and the Calgary Health Region:
www.hrreporter.com

Required Professional Capabilities (RPCs)

The following RPCs are relevant to material covered in this chapter. The RPC number represents the CCHRA number assigned to the RPC as presented on the CCHRA website. All of the RPCs can be found in the Body of Knowledge at www.chrp.ca/rpc/body-of-knowledge.

RPC 12 Develops business cases for HR initiatives and strategies

RPC 13 Sets clear goals, objectives, evaluation standards, and measures for HR programs and strategies

RPC 23 Develops budgets, and monitors expenditures and performance of outside HR contractors and other specialists

RPC 24 Develops RFPs and reviews submissions by third parties

RPC 28 Evaluates progress on deliverables

RPC 30 Advises on the status of dependent and independent contractors and determinants of employee status

RPC 48 Contributes to improvements in the organization's structures and work processes

RPC 86 Develops deployment procedures (e.g., transfers, secondments and reassignments)

Discussion Questions

1. Experts suggest that core functions should never be outsourced. Make a list of all the services and products that a large HR department in a large organization would provide. Prepare a definition of core functions. On a scale of 1 to 10, assign a weight to each HR service or product to assess whether it is core or non-core.

2. Canadians have experienced several strikes over outsourcing. Identify them and focus on the most recent strike. Analyze the media reports, and consult the employer and union websites to determine the perspectives of each on the issue of outsourcing. Have one team prepare the arguments against outsourcing from the union perspective; have another group prepare the arguments for outsourcing from the employer's perspective. Have each group write a two-page message to be given to the media.

3. Crowdsourcing is a novel approach to getting work done by people not employed in the organization. The term was coined by *Wired* magazine to refer to the fact that some people like to help organizations with a problem, or a provision of a service. It is an alternative form of staffing, in which monies might be paid only if the organization likes the solution. Is this a variation of outsourcing? How might crowdsourcing work for HR departments?

4. Martyn Hart, Chair of the National Outsourcing Association, has stated: "One of the most notable aspects of outsourcing is that people rarely like to talk about success stories. The truth is, thousands of companies outsource successfully each year, but it's worth remembering that each and every outsourcing deal is only as good as the planning that proceeds it."[55] Outline the steps that an organization should follow when the deciding to outsource an HR activity.

Exercise

1. Most of you reading this text are students at a community college or university. Using your educational institute's directory, make a list of all organizational functions. In groups, determine which functions are possible candidates for outsourcing. Choose one and establish a business case for the president to outsource the function. Identify one or two service providers, and consult with them about the benefits of outsourcing. Choose another function and establish a case for retaining the function internally.

Case   OUTSOURCING AT TEXAS INSTRUMENTS CANADA

Dawn McWhirter, CHRP, is the HR manager at Texas Instruments (TI) Canada. TI Canada outsourced its payroll function to a national provider but, faced with a large number of transaction errors, Dawn is crunching the numbers to determine whether it makes more sense to have payroll provided by staff internal to Texas Instruments.

The current external provider is paid $30,000 annually to prepare biweekly payroll inputs/changes, additions/terminations, ad hoc payments (such as commissions and bonuses), car allowances, mileage reimbursements, and so on, plus pay-slip printouts, tax remittances, and T4s. However, so many errors are made that Dawn has to pay an administrator $37,440 annually to correct mistakes and liaise with the provider. Additionally, the employees at headquarters in Dallas are also spending time correcting these errors for an additional cost of $12,000 annually. Dawn estimates that she is spending about 100 hours a year overseeing the errors and auditing quarterly reports for a cost of about $3,400.

To provide these same services internally, Dawn prepared the following estimates:

- *New national provider:* $4,000 annually for partial in-house—all biweekly payroll changes/additions would be input on-site using a secure web portal provided by the carrier; the new provider would only be responsible for printing pay slips, remitting taxes to government agencies, and preparing year-end filings such as T4 remittances.

- *Administrator:* $37,440.

- *Auditing:* $3,400.

Source: Correspondence with Dawn McWhirter, HR Manager, Texas Instruments Canada, October, 2008

Questions

1. If you were Dawn, what decision would you make and why?
2. What are the advantages and disadvantages of the decision that you made?

ENDNOTES

1. Smerd, J. "GM Service Technical College: Optimas Award Winner for Financial Impact." www.workforce.com, retrieved on October 9, 2008.

2. Pereira, V. and V. Anderson. (2011 in press). "A Longitudinal Examination of HRM in a Human Resources Offshoring (HRO) Organization Operating from India." *Journal of World Business*.

3. Gurchiek, K. 2005. "Record Growth in Outsourcing of HR Functions." *HR Magazine*, Vol. 50, No. 6: 35–36.

4. Potvin, J.F. 2010. "Out and About." *Benefits Canada*, Vol. 34, No. 11: 45–46.

5. Hunter, I. 2007. "Outsourcing: The Business Model for the New Millennium." *Training Journal*, September, 2007: 26–31.

6. Morandini, R., and V. La Fortune. 2010. "Outsourcing Absence Management." *Canadian HR Reporter*, Vol. 23, No. 16: 1.

7. Gurchiek, 2005.

8. McCauley, A. 2000. "Know the Benefits and Costs of Outsourcing Services." *Canadian HR Reporter*, Vol. 13, No. 17 (October 9): 18–19.

9. Adler, P.S. 2003. "Making the HR Outsourcing Decision." *MIT Sloan Management Review*, Vol. 45, No. 1: 53–60; Henneman, T. 2005. "Measuring the True Benefit of Human Resources Outsourcing." *Workforce Management*, Vol. 84, No. 7: 76–77; Oshima, M., T. Kao, and J. Tower. 2005. "Achieving Post-Outsourcing Success." *Human Resources Planning*, Vol. 28, No. 2: 7–12.

10. Shenkar, 0. 2011. "The Challenge of Innovation." *Ivey Business Journal Online*, retrieved on June 26, 2011 from AB/INFORM Global.

11. Alexander, M., and D. Young. 1996. "Strategic Outsourcing." *Long Range Planning*, Vol. 29, No. 1: 116–119.

12. Ulrich, D. "A New Mandate for Human Resources." *Harvard Business Review*, January/February 1998: 124–134.

13. Prahalad, C.K., and G. Hamel. 1990. "The Core Competence of the Corporation." *Harvard Business Review*, Vol. 68, No. 3: 79–91.

14. Leavy, B. 2005. "Nike, Ikea and IBM's Outsourcing and Business Strategies." *Human Resources Management International Digest*, Vol. 13, No. 3: 15–17.

15. Fulmer, R., and B. Hanson. 2010 "Developing Leaders in High Tech Firms—What's Different and What Works?" *People and Strategy*, Vol. 33, No. 3: 22–27.

16. Burn, D. 1998. "To Outsource Training or Not to Outsource Training: That Is the Question." *Human Resources Professional*, Vol. 15, No. 1(February/March): 18–23.

17. Oshima et al., 2005.

18. Burn, D. 1997. "Outsourcing: Transforming the Role of Human Resource Professionals." *HR Professional*, February/March: 26–33.

19. Vosbough, R.M. 2007. "HR." *Human Resource Planning*, Vol. 30, No. 3: 8.

20. LaCity, M.C., and R. Hirschheim. 1995. *Beyond the Information Systems Outsourcing Bandwagon*. Toronto: John Wiley & Sons.

21. Gray, R. 2009 "How Much Should You Give Up?" *Human Resources*, November 2009: 28–31.

22. Cooke, B. 2004. "HR/Benefits Outsourcing: Updating the Conventional Thinking." *Employee Benefit Plan Review*, Vol. 58, No. 8: 18–22.

23. Oshima et al., 2005.

24. Cooke, F.L., J. Shen, and A. McBride. 2005. "Outsourcing HR as a Competitive Strategy? A Literature Review and an Assessment of Implications." *Human Resource Management*, Vol. 44, No. 4 (Winter): 413–432.

25. Albertson, D. 2000. "Outsourcing Shows Limited Impact for Strategic HR." *Employee Benefit News*, Vol. 14, No. 10: 70.

26. Luvison, D., and M. Bendixen. 2010. "The Behavioural Consequences of Outsourcing: Looking Through the Lens of Paradox." *Journal of Applied Management and Entrepreneurship*, Vol. 15, No. 4 (December 2010): 28–52.

27. Anonymous. 2005. "Why Outsourcing Succeeds or Not." *HR Focus*, July, Vol. 82, No. 7: 1, 3.

28. Rison, R.P., and J. Tower. 2005. "How to Reduce the Cost of HR and Continue to Provide Value." *Human Resource Planning*, Vol. 28, No. 1: 14–18.

29. Bryce, D.J., and M. Useem. 1998. "The Impact of Corporate Outsourcing on Company Value." *European Management Journal*, Vol. 16, No. 6: 635–643.

30. Geary, S., and G. Coffey-Lewis. 2002. "Are You Ready to Outsource HR?" *HR Professional*, Vol. 19, No. 3 (June/July): 26–29.

31. Klass, B.S. 2008 "Outsourcing and the HR Function: An Examination of Trends and Developments Within North American Firms." *The International Journal of Human Resource Management*, Vol. 19, No. 8: 1500–1514.

32. Khanna, S., and J. Randolph. 2005. "An HR Planning Model for Outsourcing." *Human Resource Planning*, Vol. 28, No. 4 (December): 37.

33. Lilly, J.D., D.A. Gray, and M. Virick. 2005. "Outsourcing the Human Resources Function: Environmental and Organizational Characteristics That Affect HR Performance." *Journal of Business Strategies*, Vol. 22, No. 1: 55–74.

34. Elmuti, D., and Y. Kathawala. 2000. "The Effects of Global Outsourcing Strategies on Participants' Attitudes and Organizational Effectiveness." *International Journal of Manpower*, Vol. 21, No. 2: 112–128.

35. Babcock, P. 2004. "Slicing Off Pieces of HR." *HR Magazine*, Vol. 49, No. 7: 70–76; Sullivan, J. 2004. "The Case Against Outsourcing." *Canadian HR Reporter*, Vol. 17, No. 3: 15.

36. "Outsourcing and the Implications for Human Resource Development." *Journal of Management Development*, Vol. 19, No. 8 (2000): 694–699.

37. Bryce and Useem, 1998.

38. Khan, S., M. Niazi, and R. Ahmad. 2011. "Barriers in the Selection of Offshore Software Development Outsourcing Vendors: An Exploratory Study Using a Systematic Literature Review." *Information and Software Technology*, Vol. 53, No. 7: 693, retrieved on June 27, 2011 from ABI/INFORM Global.

39. Woodall, J., M. Gurney, T. Newham, and W. Scott-Jackson. 2009. "Making the Decision to Outsource Human Resources." *Personnel Review*, Vol. 38, No. 3: 236–248.

40. Sullivan, J. 2002. "The Case Against Outsourcing." *IHRIM Journal*, July: 38–41.

41. Gurchiek, 2005; Pollitt, D. 2004. "Outsourcing HR: The Contrasting Experiences of Amex and DuPont." *Human Resource Management*, Vol. 12, No. 6: 8–10.

42. Potvin, J.-F. 2010. "Out and About." *Benefits Canada*, Vol. 34, No. 11: 45–46.

43. The Economist Intelligence Unit. 1995. *New Directions in Finance: Strategic Outsourcing*. New York: The Economist Intelligence Unit.

44. LaCity and Hirschheim, 1995.

45. Laabs, J. 2000. "Are You Ready to Outsource Staffing?" *Workforce*, Vol. 70, No. 4: 56–60.

46. LaCity and Hirschheim, 1995.

47. Gray, R. 2009. "How Far Should Outsourcing Go?" *Human Resources*, July 2008: 33–36.

48. Anonymous. 2007. "How to Maximize Your Return on Outsourcing and Shared Services." *HR Focus*, April, Vol. 84, No. 4: S2.

49. Gurchiek, 2005.

50. Simke, J. 2007. "When Outsourcing Fails to Deliver." *Canadian HR Reporter*, Vol. 20, No. 9 (May 7): 19.

51. Petrick, A.E. 1996. "The Fine Art of Outsourcing." *Association Management*, December: 42–48.

52. Gray, R. 2009 "How Much Should You Give Up?" *Human Resources*, November 2009: 28–31.

53. Luvison and Bendixen, 2010.

54. Saunders, J. 2007. "After the Deal Is Done." *Personnel Today*, October 23, 2007, pp. 20–23.

55. Gray, R. 2010. "Great Expectations." *Human Resources*, November: 56–58.

CHAPTER
14

Evaluation of HR Programs and Policies

CHAPTER LEARNING OUTCOMES

After reading this chapter, you should be able to:

- Understand the importance of measuring the effectiveness of HRM activities.

- Outline five aspects of HRM that can be evaluated using the 5C model for measuring effectiveness: compliance with laws and regulations, client satisfaction, culture management to influence employee attitudes, cost control of the labour component of the budget, and the contribution of HR programs.

- Discuss methods of measurement, such as cost–benefit analysis, utility analysis, and auditing techniques.

- Identify the challenges in measuring HR activities.

KEEPING SCORE WITH THE SCORECARD

Jane Haberbusch, vice-president of HR for Enbridge Gas Distribution, is a keen supporter of the HR scorecard, which she discusses below:

The scorecard works like this: Motivated employees provide great customer service, which results in overall customer satisfaction, which is then correlated with reduced operating costs and increased net profit margins.

Our customer satisfaction ratings are the highest in our sector. We know that motivated and engaged employees provide the best levels of customer service. If you had a workforce that was highly motivated and actively engaged, what types of evidence would you see?

- *Low levels of employee turnover, especially of the "critical keepers"*
- *High levels of employee engagement and employee satisfaction (usually measured through employee feedback instruments)*
- *Low levels of absenteeism and "presenteeism" (showing up for work but not necessarily being productive)*
- *High levels of alignment to company goals and objectives*
- *Effective development of succession candidates to ensure leadership continuity*
- *Enhanced levels of innovation and creativity in response to business challenges*

Using these types of outcomes as measures and assigning stretch targets ensures focus and alignment of all HR-related initiatives. So, for example, before we introduce an HR practice such as a mentoring program for high potentials, we need to establish the connection or the "line of sight" to the company's overall goals.

Enbridge Gas Distribution's mission and goals can be found at www.egd.enbridge.com.[1]

Source: Courtesy of Jane Haberbusch

Aligning HRM programs and policies with organizational goals is the beginning of the strategic HR planning process. Assessing whether these policies and practices were effective is the end of one cycle in the planning process, because HR professionals need to know how their programs and policies are performing.

KEEPING SCORE

Corporate scorekeeping allows organizations to make the adjustments necessary to reach their goals. The scorecard, with its measures of key indicators, focuses managers' and employees' attention on what is important to the organization. Focusing on desired results increases the ability to attain the results. Measures allow us to make judgments about the relative effectiveness of various policies and practices, just as baseball scores and records allow fans to track the success of baseball teams. In business, the motivation to measure is driven by the need to improve results.

The model of strategic HRM planning outlined in Chapter 1 called for the measurement of the success of the plan. The tracking of customer satisfaction or absenteeism rates not only measures progress but also pinpoints weaknesses and identifies gaps. Just as organizations keep scorecards on their financial effectiveness, so too must the HR department track the effectiveness of its programs.

THE IMPORTANCE OF EVALUATING HRM

Over the past ten years, there has been a noticeable demand from executives for HR to take on a third role, that of strategic partner, and demonstrate its value in measurable terms.[2] This is an evolution from the service and administrative roles of the HR function previously. For example, an article in *Fortune* magazine called for the abolition of the HR function, arguing that HR managers are unable to describe their contribution to value except in trendy, unquantifiable, and "wannabe" terms.[3] The author also proposed that efficiencies could be increased by outsourcing legislated activities (such as payroll and equity) and returning "people" responsibilities to line managers. His exact words were "Blow up the HR department." Senior executives who read *Fortune* asked themselves, "Does HR make a difference? Does it add value?" Nearly a decade later, another journalist wrote an article called "Why We Hate HR," and said that HR practitioners did not have a seat at the table; they didn't even have a key to the boardroom.[4] Clearly, until HR managers can talk about the contribution and value of HR activities in the numbers language of business, the HR department and the HR profession will be vulnerable to destructive proposals such as those listed above. What is the numbers language of business? It means developing a case for any HR program along the lines of "If we implement this safety program, we will reduce lost-time injuries and accidents by 50 percent, saving $500,000 annually."

Increasingly, the HR department is being treated like other operational units—that is, it is subject to questions about its contribution to organizational performance. In the simplest terms, HRM must make a difference; if it doesn't, it will be abolished. Decision makers within organizations view HR activities, such as training courses, as expenses. They view results as value. The deliverables, not the doables such as training, are what make a difference to the organization. Measurement of the HR function is critical for improving both the credibility and the effectiveness of HR. If you cannot measure contribution, you cannot manage it or improve it. What gets measured gets managed and improved.

Business is a numbers game. Some surveys have shown that HR practitioners, while familiar with some numbers (such as the number of people employed in the organization), can't always recite other key numbers (such as the sales volumes, market share, profit levels, and rates of return for their organization). When asked to assess their contribution, most HR professionals describe it in such terms as "number of training courses" or "new hires." They do not provide numbers for outcomes. They say things such as "One hundred twenty people attended the training course," and rarely "The training courses resulted in a 15 percent improvement in customer satisfaction."

Resistance

Some HR managers resist measuring their work. Indeed, according to the 2008 IBM Global Human Capital Study, only 6 percent of those HR managers interviewed felt that they were very effective at using data to make decisions about the workforce. One reason for this low level is the lack of integration of human resources information systems (HRIS) with each other and with operational systems (finance, sales, and so on).[5] Another reason is that HR professionals have limited knowledge of measurement models and limited skills in measurement design. Even if consultants can be hired to do the measurement work,[6] HR professionals need to know how to understand, interpret, and explain the measures.

HR managers also argue that HR activities cannot be measured, because outcomes such as employee attitudes or managerial productivity are impossible to calibrate meaningfully or precisely. They assert that they cannot control the labour market. But the finance department cannot control the inflation rate, and the marketing department has little control over product quality, and yet each of these departments measures its activities and is accountable for results.

Measuring is expensive, but not as expensive as continuing an ineffective program. The main reason HR is not measured is that there is no standard way of measuring. Think of finance and accounting with their widely accepted principles of measurement.[7]

As the field of HR evolves, the analytic and data-based decision-making capability will develop.[8] There may evolve two types of HR, with one branch similar to sales and accounting transactions, and the other more like the marketing and finance strategic decision making.[9] For example, the necessary transactional work (similar to accounting) might be handled by a personnel department, and the strategic work by the HR department. The HR function needs to develop a set of analytic measures that can be used to describe, predict, and evaluate the quality and impact of HR practices.[10] The challenge is to not only develop measures, but also choose the measures that are important to the organization, not just the HR function. Boudreau describes business problems as often a case of "too much information and too few frameworks to interpret the information.[11]

Very few organizations measure the impact of HRM; about two-thirds of HR professionals in Fortune 500 companies measure HR productivity.[12] However, those that do measure are more likely to be treated as strategic partners.[13] Interest in measuring HR is growing slowly, fuelled by:

- Business improvement efforts across organizations

- Attempts to position HR as a strategic partner

- The need for objective indicators of success to accompany the analysis of HR activities

There are other pressures that make measurement a hot topic in HR. For example, *Sarbanes-Oxley* (American legislation that affects Canadian companies operating in the U.S.) requirements force HR to provide information about executive compensation, pension plans, and whistleblower protection. More HR professionals are now trained in the field of measurement and capable of developing HR scorecards and measuring human capital. There is an increased awareness among leaders that investments in HR can impact customers and then the bottom line.[14]

Rationale

Determining the quantitative impact of HR programs is so important that the Society for Human Resources Management, the largest HR association in the United States, has designated HRM impact as a top research priority and is funding research in this area.

There are nine compelling reasons for measuring HRM effectiveness:

1. Labour costs are most often a firm's largest controllable cost.
2. Managers recognize that employees make the difference between the success and failure of projects and organizations. Good performance can be rewarded objectively.
3. Organizations have legal responsibilities to ensure that they are in compliance with laws governing the employer–employee relationship.
4. Evaluations are needed to determine which HR practices are effective, because at this point managers and HR professionals cannot distinguish between a fad and a valid change program.[15] HR is often criticized for communicating with executives with PowerPoint (rhetoric), not Excel (results).[16] Professor Terry Wagar of St. Mary's University in Halifax has studied fads and determined that many of the practices are not integrated with other HR systems, and that they are fragile and do not survive.[17]

   For example, take a current fad: social media. There is little if any empirical evidence that social networking leads to better decision making in recruiting, staffing, and discipline or termination.[18] Social networking sites such as Facebook, MySpace, LinkedIn, and Twitter are starting to be used by HR practitioners. For example, SHRM (Society for HR Management, the national professional association in the U.S.), reported that 13 percent of HR departments use these sites for screening applicants, and 18 percent plan to use them in the future.[19] In a 2011 survey reported in the *National Post*, 45 percent of hiring managers used social media sites to check on job candidates.[20] Yet there is almost no evidence to suggest that the use of social media is a valid selection method. Many managers remain uncertain about the return on investment of social media to the organization.[21]

   The characteristics of fads are outlined in HR Planning Notebook 14.1.
5. Measuring and benchmarking HR activities will result in continuous improvements. Performance gaps can be identified and eliminated.
6. Audits will bring HR closer to the line functions of the organization. The practices must demonstrate that they enhance competitive advantage, not just that they are efficient or "best-in-class."[22]
7. Data will be available to support resource allocations.[23]
8. Investors want this information. Why? The market-to-book ratio suggests that for every $6 of market value, only $1 appears on the balance sheet. This money would represent tangible assets such as buildings and equipment, and financial assets such as cash and marketable securities. The remaining $5 represents intangible assets. For example, the market capitalization of Microsoft (i.e., the price per share times the number of shares outstanding) is $300 billion, while the total value of its tangible assets is only $20 billion. The $280 billion difference lies in its intangible assets such as brand equity and employee commitment. Likewise, Google has a market cap that was 2,500 percent greater than their equipment, property, and plant.[24] So when a metric such as employee commitment rises, investors can use this number to predict increases in customer satisfaction, retention, and sales.[25]

HR Planning Notebook 14.1

WHAT IS A FAD?

Over 100 magazines are devoted to business issues, 30,000 business books are in print, and 3,500 new ones are published every year. These books often contain contradictory advice: "the first-mover advantage" or "the second mouse gets the cheese." Fads, such as "emotional intelligence," become popular very quickly, and then undergo a steep decline.

A fad has a typical life cycle:

Stage 1: Ascendency:

- Such language as "Something new and revolutionary is here" and "Out with the old, in with the new"
- Descriptions and how-tos
- Great praise and high promise

Stage 2: Maturity:

- Exhortations to jump on the bandwagon
- Initial questions asking whether the technique is a fad
- Suggestions and pleas to look beyond the superficial

Stage 3: Decline:

- Problems, pitfalls, and failures
- Questions asking if there is anything worth saving

A fad can also be defined by these characteristics:

1. It is simple and claims to solve complex problems.
2. It claims to apply to and help anyone.

3. It is not anchored or related to any known and generally accepted theory.
4. Proponents hesitate to present it in academic settings or write about it in referred journals.
5. Proponents cannot tell you exactly how it works.
6. It is a "track" topic at 75 percent of the conferences that you have attended.
7. Its proponents claim that it has changed their lives and that it can change yours too.
8. Its greatest proponents are those with the least experience in the field.
9. It is just too good to be true.

Organizations often adopt a practice simply because others are doing it. This will occur if a large number of organizations are doing it (frequency-based mimicry), if large visible firms are doing it (trait-based mimicry), or if other firms seem to be successful by adopting a practice (outcome-based mimicry).

The solution for HR professionals when confronted with a consultant proposing "another fine idea"? Ask for evidence that it works. If you are tempted, implement the concept in one small unit, and measure the outcomes. For example, one might ask: What is the evidence that this concept will work in our organization, and what is the risk of implementing this practice?

Sources: A. Garman, "Shooting for the Moon: How Academicians Could Make Management Research Even Less Relevant," *Journal of Business and Psychology*, Vol. 26, No. 2 (2011): 129–133; B.S. Klass, "Outsourcing and the HR Function: An Examination of Trends and Developments Within North American Firms," *The International Journal of Human Resource Management*, Vol. 19, No. 8 (August 2008): 1500–1514; J. Pfeffer and R.I. Sutton, "Evidence-Based Management," *Harvard Business Review*, January 2006: 63–74; D. Miller, J. Hartwick, and I. le BretonMiller, "How to Detect a Management Fad and Distinguish It from a Classic," *Business Horizons*, Vol. 47 (July/August 2004): 7–16; D. Ulrich, *Human Resource Champions* (Boston, MA: Harvard Business School Press, 1997), p. 63.

9. HR managers are more likely to be welcome at the boardroom table, and to influence strategy, if they use measures to demonstrate the contribution of their function.[26]

The next section describes the areas in which HRM departments can be evaluated.

THE 5C MODEL OF HRM IMPACT

Executives, investors, customers, and HR professionals themselves make judgments in many ways about the effectiveness of the HR function. The numerous areas that are judged can be grouped into five clusters—the "5 C's" of evaluating HRM: compliance, client satisfaction, culture management, cost control, and contribution.[27]

Compliance

Senior management depends on HR expertise to ensure that organizational practices comply with the law, and many HR departments were started because of the need to record compliance with employment standards, such as hours worked and overtime payments. Legislation dealing with the employer–employee relationship is increasing, and the areas of safety, health, employment equity, and industrial relations are all highly regulated. Indeed, some people estimate that 20 to 30 percent of the increase in the salaries of HR professionals is due to the need to trust someone with the responsibility for compliance.

Highly publicized cases of safety violations in which board members of industrial organizations have been fined hundreds of thousands of dollars or threatened with jail time serve as another wakeup call. Other public cases that have cost organizations not only the expense of fines but also loss in business have occurred because managers have been held responsible for the sexual harassment of their subordinates. HR can make a difference by ensuring that managers and employees comply with the law, thus saving the company legal costs, fines, and damaging publicity.

Currently, HR is being asked to ensure not only that the organization complies with laws but also that it is ethical. This means the development of a code of conduct, protection for whistleblowers, and the redesign of orientation and training programs to include curriculum on ethics.

Client Satisfaction

Across Canada, many organizations are tracking their success by measuring customer satisfaction or soliciting input on client complaints and attitudes. These measures have been found to predict financial performance, on a lagged basis. This means that if employee morale drops, management can expect to see customer satisfaction levels drop in about six months.

Stakeholders, who include external and internal clients, are those people who can influence or must interact with the HR department. External clients of HR comprise candidates for positions, suppliers of HR services such as technology, and government regulators. Internal clients include employees grouped by occupation, union leaders, and managers. These stakeholder groups were discussed in Chapter 3.

Managers are turning to client or stakeholder perceptions of the HR department for input about the effectiveness of HR performance. This approach stems from earlier efforts in total quality management and tries to reconcile the gaps between client expectations and levels of satisfaction. The bigger the gap, the less effective the HR department. This qualitative approach surveys stakeholders about their perceptions of the effectiveness of the HR function. However, recent surveys have indicated that only one-half of managers and employees rate HR's overall performance as good.[28] "Keeping the clients happy" has important political repercussions for the HRM department, as "clients" such as the CEO control the purse strings and have the authority to approve HR policies and programs.

Advantages of Measuring Client Satisfaction

The advantages of measuring client satisfaction with the HR department include the following:[29]

- Measuring client satisfaction reminds the HR department that it is indeed a "service" that must deal with the expectations of its clients. The clients, in turn, use assessment criteria that are important to them, such as response time and helping them to meet their goals.

- Surveying clients about their unmet needs increases the credibility of the HR function.

- Initiating and managing change by surveying stakeholders before, during, and after a change program increases the possibility that the HR department will understand the clients' perceptions; identify resistance to change and overcome such resistance; and prove that the change program meets its goals.

Methods of Measuring Client Satisfaction

Information can be gathered from clients in several ways.

INFORMAL FEEDBACK   Stakeholder perceptions can be obtained informally, as part of the feedback process, whenever the HR professional is undertaking an assignment or completing a routine task such as filling a position. People can simply be asked if they are satisfied with the service.

Informal feedback is of limited use, however, for several reasons. Line managers might be reluctant to give honest feedback face to face; an individual HR officer might not be able to see patterns in the feedback because there is no method for measuring the frequency of problems; and HR professionals have little incentive to report negative feedback to superiors in the organizational hierarchy. For these reasons, a more systematic method must be developed to identify gaps in the performance of the HR department.

SURVEYS   Surveys can be used to solicit feedback confidentially, anonymously, and from a larger number of stakeholders. One approach is to list the HR activities, such as selection, and ask specific questions about them, such as questions about satisfaction with the time it takes to fill a vacant position and the satisfaction with a new employee's performance. Some questions that might be included in such a survey are:

- To what degree do you find the HR department cooperative?

- How would you rate the quality of service given?

- To what degree are HR employees available to deal with problems?

- Do you have confidence in HR advice?

HR Planning Notebook 14.2

HR ROLE ASSESSMENT SURVEY

The following is a sample of the type of survey clients can expect:

> Please rate your satisfaction with the HR department on the following items* (1 = low; = 5 high):
>
> HR helps the organization accomplish business goals.
>
> HR participates in the process of defining business strategies.

HR makes sure that HR strategies are aligned with business strategies.

HR is effective because it can measure how it helps make strategy happen.

HR is a business partner.

*The selected items measure the strategic role of HR.

- How would you rate the effectiveness of HR solutions?
- What is your opinion on processing time?
- To what extent does HR understand the needs of your department?
- Overall, how satisfied are you with the HR department?

Another survey, developed by Ulrich, asks managers to rate the quality of the various roles that HR plays in strategy formulation.[30] HR Planning Notebook 14.2 contains a sample of the questions used in this survey.

Managers might be asked to list the chief strengths and principal weaknesses of the HR department. Line managers might be asked questions about what the HR department has been doing particularly well or particularly poorly, what it should not be doing, how it might contribute more effectively, and so on.[31]

CRITICAL INCIDENT METHOD   In the critical incident method, clients are asked to describe a situation in which the HR department provided assistance that was particularly useful, the consequences of this help, and why it was seen as helpful. Similarly, they are asked to describe a situation in which the assistance was not at all useful, and why. Clients' responses help the HR department identify issues and services that affect unit effectiveness.

Problems with Measuring Client Satisfaction

Measuring client satisfaction is not without its weaknesses.

HIGH EXPECTATIONS OF CLIENTS   The goal of surveying clients is to identify gaps between their expectations and their satisfaction. If the clients in one business unit have extremely high expectations, their dissatisfaction scores will also be high, even though the level of HR service is constant across units. The temptation on the part of the HR department might be to promise or commit to less with regard to programs so as to appear to have performed better.

CONFLICTING EXPECTATIONS   Another problem occurs when different stakeholders have competing or conflicting expectations. The employee group might desire extensive counselling (a nurturing role) from the HR department, while senior managers might be concerned about maximizing productivity per employee (an efficiency goal). One group will be dissatisfied because it is difficult for the HR department to be both nurturing and efficient.

PROFESSIONAL AFFILIATIONS   Furthermore, gaps between expectations and performance might occur because HR professionals are more closely tied to the norms and values of their profession than to the norms of managers or line operators.[32] For example, line managers might value how fast a job is filled, while the HR professional might value the creation of a valid selection test. In other words, the HR professional might be trying to do what is right in the profession ("validate the selection test"), rather than what managers consider important ("just hire someone quickly").

Whatever the problems with the client satisfaction approach, the important message is that the viability of the HR function depends to a large extent on stakeholder perceptions of value and effectiveness. These must be measured and managed.

Culture Management

Highly effective organizations seek to influence employee attitudes through the development of an appropriate culture that will support optimum performance. (Remember that culture can be defined as the set of important beliefs that members of a community share—"the way we do things around here.") Executives carefully monitor cultural programs (such as that of empowerment) through attitude surveys of employees. The results of these surveys can then be linked to the objective results of the department.

The assumption underlying the culture management model is that HR practices can have a positive influence on employee attitudes, which in turn influence employee performance.

Attitudes

Perceptions or opinions about organizational characteristics

Attitudes, in an organizational context, can be defined as perceptions or opinions about organizational characteristics. Some examples include the attitudes expressed in these statements: "I think that management expects too much for the resources it gives me" or "I feel that I can talk to management about any problems I am experiencing."

The most frequently measured attitudes in the organization are job satisfaction and commitment. Surveys of satisfaction and commitment measure attitudes toward supervisors, colleagues, pay, promotions, and the work itself. The research supports the proposition that attitude affects behaviour. Highly committed employees will make personal sacrifices for the job, perform beyond normal expectations, work selflessly, and endure difficult times, and will not leave the organization for personal gain.[33] A Towers Perrin study of 40 global companies over three years showed that companies with employees with high engagement scores had more than 3 percent in net profit margin over those with low scores.[34] The study also showed that in Canada only about one-fourth of employees report high engagement, about the same as in the United States. A landmark

HR Planning Notebook 14.3

MEASURING EMPLOYEE ATTITUDES

Organizations use different terms in measuring employee attitudes:

- *Satisfaction:* This is a passive measure of employee contentment with little relationship to performance.
- *Motivation:* This measure probes whether employees feel stimulated in their role and are driven to meet work and organizational goals. Motivation is strongly related to productivity measures.
- *Commitment:* A measure of the alignment between the strategy, objectives, and values of the organization, commitment is strongly linked to employee loyalty and customer service excellence.
- *Advocacy:* This is a measure of whether employees will speak highly of the organization as an employer, and as an organization with products and service.

Advocacy is strongly linked to sales growth and employee attraction.

- *Engagement:* If an employee scores highly on motivation, commitment, and advocacy, then she would be classified as engaged. Engaged employees are more productive, deliver higher customer satisfaction levels, deliver the brand promise more effectively, create stronger growth, and generate higher profits.

Hewitt Associates describes the attitudes of an engaged employee in three simple ways:

- *Say:* Consistently speaks about the organization to co-workers, potential employees, and customers
- *Stay:* Has an intense desire to be a member of the organization
- *Strive:* Exerts extra effort and engages in behaviours that contribute to organizational success.

Sources: Adapted from A. Brown and S. Kelly, "Connecting Staff Research with Company Success," *Strategic HR Review*, Vol. 9, No. 1 (2006): 24–26; Hewitt Associates 2007 Best Employers in Canada Study.

study of 800 Sears stores demonstrated that for every 5 percent improvement in employee attitudes, customer satisfaction increased by 1.3 percent and corporate revenue rose by 0.5 percent.[35] Employees with the highest levels of commitment perform 20 percent better and are 87 percent less likely to leave the organization. Employees at Molson Coors, the beverage company, who reported high levels of engagement, were five times less likely to have a safety incident and seven times less likely to have a lost-time safety incident.[36]

HR Planning Notebook 14.3 examines the different terms that organizations may use when measuring employee attitudes.

Organizations should pay attention to employee attitudes and should attempt to manage the culture to improve individual and organizational performance. HR managers might want to ask the managers in their organizations about the effectiveness of the engagement surveys being used by asking questions such as:

1. Does the survey prompt discussions with your direct reports?
2. Does the survey help you identify actions that can be taken to improve the engagement scores?[37]

Cost Control

Traditional organizations continue to see personnel as an expense. The labour component of the production process in service organizations, such as universities and government departments, is an organization's single largest expense. This cost represents up to 85 percent of the expenses in white-collar organizations. The cost of employees consists of pay and benefits, the cost of absenteeism, and the cost of turnover. HR practices can reduce labour costs by reducing the workforce while attempting to get the same volume of work done with fewer employees. There are three ways to reduce labour expenses by reducing the size of the labour force:

- *Technology:* One of the most frequently used ways to cut labour costs is to increase the use of technology. Technology to process benefits claims and pursue e-learning has replaced HR staff, resulting in cost savings of about 30 percent.[38]

- *Outsourcing:* Firms are also outsourcing major activities in order to manage the costs of labour. However, there are detrimental effects of cutting costs in this way. Core talent may be lost and the capacity for innovation diminished.[39] See Chapter 13 for a more detailed discussion of outsourcing.

- *Downsizing:* Chapter 10 provides an analysis of the processes for restructuring.

Often, companies try to reduce the headcount in the HR department as part of a strategy to save costs. But the savings can be deceptive. For example, a financial services company cut its HR headcount by 30 percent (around 300 people). But then the line managers hired their own staff to handle the HR issues, and the shadow organization of HR specialists now numbers 150.[40]

HR departments can reduce expenses associated with employees in at least two other ways. The first is to increase the efficiencies of those working (i.e., achieve the same results at lower costs or faster speeds), and the second is to reduce the costs associated with behaviours such as absences or accidents that are, to some extent, under the control of the employee.

Increasing Efficiency

Efficiency

Results achieved compared to resource inputs

Efficiency is expressed in terms of the results achieved (outputs) in comparison to the resource inputs. Measures of efficiency include the following:

- Time (e.g., average time to fill an opening, process a benefits claim)

- Volume (e.g., number of people interviewed to fill a job, number of requests processed per employee)

- Cost (e.g., cost per training hour or per test).

HR managers should measure these resource inputs and then attempt to improve the measurements over time or across units. The use of benchmarks is critical in comparing one organization's efficiency ratios against the best in the field. Data revealing a cost per hire of $500 or turnover rates of 15 percent are meaningless without relevant comparison points. For example, a turnover rate of 15 percent among senior executives indicates a problem; a turnover rate of 15 percent in a fast-food restaurant is very low.

The ratios generated must be interpreted and analyzed by comparisons made over time, across departments, and against the benchmarks of best practices. These benchmarks allow the HR manager to make the following kinds of statements: "The cost per hire is $500, which is $50 less than last year and $60 less than another company. That shows we are doing a better job than we did last year and than other HR departments." HR Planning Notebook 14.4 provides examples of these measures.

These efficiency measures must be managed with effectiveness in mind. Conceptually, it is possible to reduce training costs to zero, but the performance of employees would suffer in the long run. Therefore, most companies add a qualifier to the ratio when judging efficiency. For example, lowering the cost per trainee would be acceptable only if job performance remained the same or improved.

Cost of Employee Behaviour

The costs of absenteeism, turnover, and occupational injuries and illnesses can all be measured, benchmarked, and managed. Any introductory textbook in HRM will describe how to measure these factors and will provide prescriptions for reducing the costs related to them. To control the expenses associated with employees, organizations should carefully track and compare the rates of absenteeism, turnover, and occupational injuries and illnesses. Here are some figures to think about: On average, each full-time employee missed 9.6 days over the year (7.8 for illness and 1.8 for personal or family demands).[41]

HR Planning Notebook 14.4
EXAMPLES OF EFFICIENCY MEASURES

Cost

Ratio of compensation expense to total operating expense

Benefit cost per employee covered

Ratio of benefits expense to total operating expense

Processing costs per benefit claim

Administration costs per benefit claim

Cost per training day

Cost per trainee per program

Volume

Number of training days

Number of interviews per selection

Ratio of filled positions to authorized positions

Percentage of employees with formal performance evaluations

Percentage of designated employees

Response Time

Time between requisition and filling of position

Time to process benefits

Time from identifying a training need to program implementation

Time to respond to requests by category

The costs of turnover, which include termination, replacement, loss of revenue when the position is vacant, and the learning time for new employees to become productive, are estimated at between 6 and 18 months of the employee's annual compensation. At Taco Bell, the stores with the lowest turnover yielded double the sales and 55 percent higher profits than stores with the highest turnover rates.[42] HR Planning Today 14.1 provides an example of how a smoking cessation program for employees can result in cost savings.

In keeping with the trend to view employees as investments, and not just as expenses, the next section examines how organizations measure the return on this investment.

Contribution

Unless HR can demonstrate its impact on the bottom line, it will continue to be seen as "overhead," as a department that grabs resources while contributing nothing. Many executives feel that it is time for the HR department to identify and evaluate its contribution, as other departments are expected to do.

The thesis underlying the contribution model is that HRM practices shape the behaviour of employees within an organization, and thus help the organization achieve its goals. In other words, the effective management of people makes a difference in how well an organization functions. Research has shown that HR practices can affect organizational performance in measurable ways. Studies have established that sophisticated and integrated HRM practices have a positive effect on employee performance: They increase knowledge, skills, and

HR Planning Today 14.1

The Costs of Smoking

Decades of research have established that smoking is addictive and that it is a health hazard. The costs to society of smoking include those associated with health care and income loss. The costs to organizations include those associated with absenteeism, medical care, morbidity and premature mortality, insurance, property damage and depreciation, maintenance, and passive-smoking effects.

It is estimated that about 35 minutes a day are lost to smoking, resulting in 18.2 lost days per year per employee. Smokers are absent three more days per year than non-smokers. Furthermore, each smoker increases by about one-fifth the expenses incurred by non-smokers (through involuntary smoke inhalation). The price tag is

$4,113 for each employee who smokes: $2,140 in lost productivity and $1,973 in excess medical expenses.

However, it may be illegal to prohibit smoking on company property. In a case involving Cominco Ltd. and the United Steelworkers of America, Locals 9705 and 480, the arbitrator ruled that nicotine addiction is a disability similar to alcoholism or drug addiction and that Cominco's policy of no smoking on company property discriminates against heavily addicted smokers. Under Section 13(1)(b) of British Columbia's *Human Rights Code*, discrimination in employment on the basis of physical or mental disability is prohibited. However, in a 2001 case, the court found that smoking and addiction to cigarettes is not a disability.

Sources: Adapted from W.F. Cascio, *Costing Human Resources: The Financial Impact of Behaviour in Organizations*, Kent Series in Human Resource Management, 3rd ed. (Boston: PWS Kent, 1991); T. Humber, "Snuffing Out Smoking," *Canadian HR Reporter*, April 11, 2005, p. 19.

abilities; improve motivation; reduce shirking; and increase retention of competent employees. These best practices have a direct and economically significant effect on a firm's financial performance.

HOW HR CONTRIBUTES TO ORGANIZATIONAL PERFORMANCE

Empirical studies have established some important findings:

- Organizations that used employee involvement practices (information sharing, rewards, skills training, and so on) reported a 66 percent higher return on sales, a 20 percent higher return on assets and investments, and a 13 percent higher return on equity.[43]

- Specific HR practices have been found to positively and significantly affect the financial performance of a company, causing as high as a 30 percent increase in shareholder value.[44] For example, flexible work arrangements are associated with a 3.5 percent gain in market value, while 360° feedback systems negatively affect market value by 5 percent.[45]

- Fifteen percent of a firm's relative profit can be attributed to HR strategy.[46]

- HR systems can affect a firm's market value by $15,000 to $45,000 per employee.[47]

- HR can affect the probability of survival of a new venture by as much as 22 percent.[48]

- HR can improve the knowledge, skills, and abilities of a firm's current and potential employees, increase their motivation, reduce shirking, and enhance retention of quality employees while encouraging non-performers to leave the firm.[49]

- An increase in sophisticated HR practices of one standard deviation raises sales per employee by an average of US$27,000 for one year, increases profits by US$3,814 per employee, and decreases turnover by 7 percent.[50] The advantages to employees of these high-performance firms may be higher wages and benefits and greater job security.

- Thirty key HR practices were associated with a 30 percent increase in market value. Superior human capital practices are a leading indicator of firm performance.[51]

- Strategic HR practices are positively related to knowledge management capacity which then has a positive effect on innovation.[52]

- Investments in HRM do pay off: Proactive firms that plan for future labour needs and make investments in recruitment and selection for the job at the outset are rewarded with higher labour productivity. Firms that systematically develop their employees receive a productivity payoff.[53]

The majority of published studies find an association between HR practices and firm performance.[54] HR matters. The basic causal model shows that HR practices impact collective commitment, operational performance, expenses, and profits.[55]

We will look now at two ways of measuring contribution: financial measures and measures of managerial perceptions of effectiveness.

Financial Measures

Survival

Private or for-profit organizations can measure a dramatic indicator of success: survival. This can be considered a zero-sum index. If the company survives—that is, does not go bankrupt or cease business—the organization is a success. Survival is the first measure of effectiveness, and the contributions of HRM practices should be judged against this life-or-death index.

When researchers tracked the survival rates over five years of new organizations listed on the stock exchange, they found that HR practices were associated with this ultimate measure of a firm's performance.[56]

This crude measure is not satisfying for most businesspeople, however, because it doesn't give relative measures of success. (Teachers who give a pass or fail, rather than an A, B, C, D, or F grade, leave the same sense of dissatisfaction among students.) Most employees desire a relative measure, and will even ask "How am I doing compared to the others?" at performance evaluation interviews. The most common measures of business success provide these points of comparison, which allow judgments to be made across divisions, companies, and even sectors. They are the bottom-line measures such as profits.

Profits or Return on Investments

ROI
Return on investment

ROE
Return on equity

All companies track sales, or revenues, return on investment (**ROI**), return on equity (**ROE**), expenses relative to sales, and other financial ratios. These indices measure the relative success of an organization in meeting its goals. Any HRM practice that contributes to these measurements likely would be endorsed by senior management. Measuring the impact of HRM investments in training or performance appraisal allows HR professionals to use the same language (e.g., basic costs, ROI) as other corporate units and provides a rational way of making decisions. HR Planning Today 14.2 illustrates how this might work.

There are some limitations to financial analyses, however; they capture certain immediate aspects of performance, but they do not capture managerial perceptions of effectiveness.

Measures of Managerial Perceptions of Effectiveness

Sometimes financial measures are not available to researchers who are studying privately owned organizations, and sometimes financial measures are not appropriate for public-sector organizations. It is meaningless to talk about government departments in relation to profits, for example. Therefore, other measures have been sought. One method is to ask managers to assess their organization's performance relative to the performance of sector competitors.[57] Despite the biases that might be introduced into such a measure, these perceptions have been found to correlate positively with objective measures of a firm's performance.[58] The principal advantage of using a perceptual measure such as this one is the ability to compare profit-seeking firms with public organizations.

HR Planning Today 14.2

Return on Investment Example: National Steel's Safety Incentive Program

National Steel was concerned about its safety record and was experiencing unacceptable accident frequency rates, accident severity rates, and total accident costs. A performance analysis indicated that the employees knew and understood safety guidelines and practices, so training was not the issue. The central safety committee felt that incentives were needed to motivate safe behaviour. The incentive plan was to offer each employee $75 cash (after taxes) for every six months without a medical treatment case. The committee established goals of reducing accident frequency from 60 to 20, and the disabling frequency rate from 18 to 0. The committee tracked the number of medical treatment cases, lost-time accidents, lost-time days, accident costs, hours worked, and incentive costs.

The costs over four years were as shown in the table below.

ROI Calculation

The cost of the annual incentive payout (two-year average) plus annual administrative plan cost was $72,172. The benefits were calculated as an annual improvement of $431,372 (accident costs for years 1 and 2 totalled $1,046,488, for an average of $523,244 annually; accident costs for years 3 and 4 averaged $90,872, for an annual improvement of $432,372).

An interesting twist in this case is that managers were asked what contributed to these improvements, and they estimated that 80 percent was due to the incentive program and 20 percent to their renewed managerial attention. So the calculations of benefits were revised to indicate that 80 percent of the annual improvement ($345,898) was due to the incentive program.

ROI of the safety incentive program

$$= \text{Net benefits} \div \text{Costs}$$
$$= (\$345,898 - \$72,172) \div \$72,172$$
$$= 3.79 \times 100 = 379\%$$

	Year 1 Before Plan	Year 2 Before Plan	Year 3 After Plan	Year 4 After Plan
Needs assessment costs	$1,200	$1,200	N/A	N/A
Plan administration/ evaluation	$1,600	$1,600	N/A	N/A
Safety incentive payouts	$58,013	$80,730	N/A	N/A
Cost of accidents	$468,360	$578,128	$18,058	$19,343
Total costs accidents + prevention	$468,360	$578,128	$78,871	$102,873

Source: From *Human Resources Scorecard* by Philips J., Stone, and P.P. Phillips, Copyright © 2001, Elsevier Science. Reproduced by permission of Taylor & Francis Books UK.

Templer and Cattaneo argue that organizational effectiveness is not easily defined.[59] Measures beyond survival and those discussed above might include the achievement of one group's political objectives at the expense of a competing interest group and the adaptation of an organization to its environment (which obviously contains an element of the survival measure).

The measure that supersedes all these might be one of goal optimization. Templer and Cattaneo combined these various perspectives to conclude that "an effective organization is one in which the behaviour of employees contributes towards the attainment of organizational goals and enables the long-term adaptation of the organization to its environment"—that is, survival and effectiveness.[60]

Which is the best measure of HRM performance? Managers will choose whichever of the 5C measures meets their needs for information. Some will require measurement of all the five C's; others will focus on one important indicator, such as cost control. Some companies are moving toward a balanced approach.

We have examined five areas in which HR practices and policies should be tracked. Now we turn to an examination of the various approaches to measuring the effectiveness of HR policies, practices, and programs.

APPROACHES TO MEASURING HRM PRACTICES

This section outlines a number of quantitative and qualitative approaches to measuring the impact of HRM policies and practices. Typical ways of measuring HR activities are:

- *Activity-based measures:* The number of employees completing training; the number of employees hired

- *Costing measures:* The cost of the training program, the cost per hire

- *Client satisfaction:* The manager has a problem solved; the HR department changed an employee's benefits information quickly

Most of these methods use numbers, which can measure the impact of HRM in the language of business: costs, days lost, complaints, and so on. But the question has to be asked: Where is the added value? See HR Planning Notebook 14.5 for a description of added value.

The next three approaches—cost–benefit analysis, utility analysis, and benchmarking—attempt to prove value.

▶ HR Planning Notebook 14.5
ADDED VALUE

What do we mean by added value? The following examples help explain this concept:

- An *activity* measure for an HR professional would be the number of people trained.
- A *performance* measure for an HR professional would be the number of trainees who passed the training test or rated the training courses as above average.

- An *added-value* measure for an HR professional would be the increase in profits, sales, or customer satisfaction, or decrease in complaints, errors, or defects, as a result of the skills learned in the training course.

Cost–Benefit Analysis

HRM activities, such as the process of selecting employees, cost money. Most organizations absorb the costs of these activities without conducting analyses to determine benefits. **Cost–benefit analysis** examines the relationship between the costs of a program and its benefits.

Costs included in these calculations are classified in several ways. **Direct costs** are those that are used to implement the program, such as the cost of selection tests or training materials. **Indirect costs** are those that an organization absorbs, such as the trainee's time away from work. Indirect costs often go unrecognized, and sometimes are not included in cost–benefit analyses. HR Planning Notebook 14.6 presents an example of a cost–benefit analysis.

Most programs can be subjected to a cost–benefit analysis if hard data are available, or the value of a program can be estimated from soft measures such as supervisors' estimates of productivity.

Cost–benefit analysis
The relationship between the costs of a program and its benefits

Direct costs
The hard costs that can be measured by expenditures

Indirect costs
The soft costs whose value can be estimated but not measured easily by financial expenditures

---

HR Planning Notebook 14.6

MEASURING THE CONTRIBUTION OF HRM PRACTICES

A wholesale produce company hired, and then fired, seven ineffective sales representatives over a two-year period. The company calculated the costs of these actions.

Costs

Training	$493,738
Recruiting	$30,100
Management time to train and terminate	$25,830
Lower profits and higher waste due to poor performance	$1,612,000
Total costs	$2,161,668

The HR department interviewed line managers to develop a profile of the ideal sales representative and identified 12 critical success factors. Then the company's HR department developed a solution involving three types of training:

- Behaviour-based interview training for managers

- A training program for newly hired sales representatives to accelerate performance readiness or weed out those who didn't meet the standards
- Performance counselling training for managers so that they could learn to discuss performance problems and ensure that trainees accepted responsibility for their own learning and performance.

The cost to implement these three programs was $15,400 (development and attendance costs).

The savings that resulted from this solution were then calculated.

Savings

Cost of the problem	$2,161,668
Cost of the solution	− $15,400
Total savings	$2,146,268

The cost–benefit ratio is as follows:

$$\$2,146,268 \div \$15,400 = 139{:}1$$

Source: Adapted from D.M. Burrows, "Increase HR's Contributions to Profits," *HR Magazine*, September 1996, pp. 103–110. Reprinted with the permission of *HR Magazine*, published by the Society for Human Resource Management (www.shrm.org) Alexandria, VA.

Utility Analysis

Senior managers are often faced with decisions about the most effective programs. For example, to motivate employees, should HR managers implement a leadership training program or a pay-for-performance program for new supervisors? To hire the best candidate, should HR managers use peer interviews or the new selection test? HR managers would have much to gain if they were able to estimate if program A provided a greater return than program B. The training director, for example, might argue that grouping 100 managers in a classroom for training is more expensive and less effective than e-learning.

Utility analysis

A method of determining the gain or loss that results from different approaches

A tool that calculates, in dollar terms, the costs and probable outcomes of decisions would assist HR managers in making choices among programs. **Utility analysis** is such a tool. It is a method of determining the gain or loss to the organization that results from different courses of action. Faced with a decision, managers use utility analysis to help them choose the strategy that produces the outcomes the organization is seeking.[61] This method measures the utilities (gains and losses) by using human resources accounting. Human resources accounting uses standard accounting practices to calculate and report an organization's human assets (or employees) in economic terms. The costs of recruiting, selecting, training, and retaining employees are calculated, and then these costs are amortized over the employees' working lives. Human resources (or asset) accounting is described in the Appendix. It seeks to quantify, in dollars, the value of improvements in HR activities, particularly selection. In utility analysis, which is an extension of cost–benefit analysis, the costs and benefits of alternative solutions to a problem are calculated and compared. The decision maker then can use the quantitative data that result from utility analysis to choose the alternative with the highest net value. HR Planning Notebook 14.7 provides an example of how utility analysis can be used to reach a decision.

HR Planning Notebook 14.7

AN EXAMPLE OF UTILITY ANALYSIS

Utility analysis is statistically complex, but it can be illustrated by the following simple example.

An organization has a choice between two types of selection procedures (or can use neither). The utility of a selection procedure is the degree to which it results in a better quality of candidate than would have been selected if the selection procedure had not been implemented. Quality can be measured by tenure (Did the employee selected using the selection procedure remain with the organization at least one year?) or performance (Did the new employee rate above average in performance after one year?)

or other objective outcomes (Did the employee sell more accounts or process more files?). The costs of using procedure one (an ability test), procedure two (peer interviews), or the usual selection method (or base rate) of managerial interviews are calculated. Then the benefits of the candidates chosen under each of the three methods are determined. If tests resulted in higher-performing candidates but cost more than the performance increase is worth, the tests have little utility. If peer reviews result in greater performance at no greater cost, peer reviews have great utility.

Source: M.L. Blum and J.C. Naylor, *Industrial Psychology: Its Theoretical and Social Foundations*, rev. ed., New York: Harper-Row, 1968.

Utility analyses have been used in various studies. Selection using assessment centres within the company instead of first-level management assessment was found to have a utility, over four years, of about US$12,000 in improved job performance per manager.[62] However, the computations involved are beyond the competencies of most managers.[63]

Auditing and Benchmarking

A plan needs an audit. An **audit** measures progress against goals. If the goal of the HR function is to train 100 managers, at some point data need to be gathered to determine if that goal was achieved. Audits keep the HR department on track and are the primary tool to assess current performance to develop action plans and future goals.[64] Audits can be done annually or quarterly, but a consistent checking against the plan ensures no year-end surprises and allows managers to take corrective action. For example, if the goal is to achieve 4 out of 5 on an employee satisfaction scale, and an audit shows pockets of low satisfaction, the HR department can target those areas for remedial action before year-end. Nevertheless, the audit is not the last step in the cycle of plan, execute, and measure.

Benchmarking is concerned with enhancing organizational performance by establishing standards against which processes, products, and performance can be compared and subsequently improved.[65] It is searching for the industry's best practices and then trying to achieve improved performance by adopting superior practices.[66] Benchmarking can be used to accomplish the following:

- stimulate an objective review of processes, practices, and systems;

- motivate employees to perform to a higher standard by providing a common target for improvement;

- provide objective comparative data with best-in-class organizations; and

- raise questions and stimulate discussions about better ways of operating.[67]

The process starts by targeting an area for improvement, such as university recruitment in the staffing function. Key measures are identified for comparison. In recruitment these might be cost per hire, quality of hire, processing times, and percentage of acceptances from first-choice candidates. The next step is to identify the best-practice organizations through publications, associations, experts, and awards ceremonies. There are four sources of benchmarking partners:

- Internal (e.g., compare university recruitment with high-tech recruitment, or compare previous year recruitment with this year's recruitment).

- Competitive (compare exact functions of a competitor).

- Sector (some conditions may differ for your organization)—some sector associations establish HR benchmarking subcommittees, which share information. There is a Human Resources Benchworking Network, which gathers data for health care, municipal governments, and not-for-profits. The BC HR association has a benchmarking service.

- Best-in-breed organizations (whose products, culture, and so on may not be comparable)—except for competitors, many organizations are willing to share this information if there is an incentive for them, such as a copy of the report, access to your metrics, and so on.

Audit
A measurement method that assesses progress against plan

Benchmarking
A tool that can enhance organizational performance by establishing standards against which processes, products, and performance can be compared and improved

Benchmarking can be done by either internal or external consultants. Internal consultants have the advantage of knowing more about the organization and being trusted by the staff supplying the information. However, external consultants might be more objective, have greater numbers of outside references or benchmarks, and be more likely to convey bad news to management. Sometimes an independent body, such as the Conference Board of Canada, will act as the project manager for the benchmarking study so that confidentiality is not an issue in data collection. This third-party intervention helps with the obvious question: Why would competitors want to reveal their best practices? And if they do so, is it because they have developed even more powerful processes that they do not share?[68] Obviously, the results obtained from audits can be compared with benchmarks obtained from previous years, with other organizational units, or with other companies.

After the data have been collected and compared, the differences will be obvious. The best organization might have metrics such as a six-week processing time, while your organization processes in twelve weeks. Interviews during or after the data collection might reveal the reasons for the speed—perhaps the entire processing is done on the Internet. The goal then becomes to match the best target for each of the indices.

For instance, the training function can be examined as a percentage of payroll spent on training, training dollars spent per employee, profits per employee, training costs per hour, and so on. The results of these examinations can be compared to comparable figures for other organizations. As an example, in Canada, organizations spend about $800 per employee on training, and each employee receives about seven hours of training a year.[69] These benchmark statistics can be used as guidelines. If statistics are available on the best-performing companies, organizations can attempt to match those figures.

Benchmarking is popular because the measures are easy to collect and the numbers have a superficial credibility, but there is no published research that supports a relationship between HR benchmarks and ultimate firm performance.[70] We all like to know benchmarks such as there is, on average, one HR person for every 100 employees, or that the profit per employee is about US$24,000.[71] But these numbers are relatively meaningless. For example, an organization can have one HR professional per 1,000 employees because it has outsourced most of the HR work. Knowing that your organization's cost per employee is higher than the sector benchmark does not provide you with anything of value, anything that would lead you to a cause and a solution. Finally, you cannot build competitive advantage by copying it, because the best capabilities (like the culture at Southwest Airlines) are complex and difficult to imitate. An organization has to create its own capabilities.[72]

The HR Scorecard

Balanced scorecard

A balanced set of measures to show contribution to organizational performance

Although the most popular way of measuring HR is benchmarking, the HR balanced scorecard is gaining momentum, with about one-third of companies using this method.[73] The **balanced scorecard** rests on the assumption that any successful business satisfies the requirements of investors (financial performance measures), customers (market share, customer commitment, and retention), and employees (employee satisfaction and organization commitment).[74]

The idea of a balanced scorecard arose from the idea that financial measures alone do not capture the true performance of an organization, and that these measures tend to reflect past performance and are not necessarily predictive. Other measures deemed of value to the analysis of a company included not only financial performance but also customer satisfaction and employee engagement. The balanced scorecard provides answers to these four basic questions:

1. How do customers see us? (The customer perspective)
2. What must we excel at? (The internal business perspective)
3. Can we continue to improve and create value? (Innovation and learning perspective)
4. How do we look to shareholders? (The financial perspective)[75]

The opening vignette about Enbridge Gas Distribution describes these relationships and the impact on HR practices.

The process starts with the organization's strategy and then HR looks for ways that the HR processes and practices can support that strategy. What can HR do to support the organization's goals, and how can this be measured? For example, the goal at a pipeline company was to increase revenues; one way to accomplish this was to reduce downtime for repairs. The HR goal in this case was to increase the amount of time devoted to preventive maintenance, by increasing employee skills sets in repairs, and to change the compensation system to include incentives to perform preventive maintenance.[76] This set of linkages is more fully described in Figure 14.1.

FIGURE 14.1

HR Deliverables Linked to Strategy

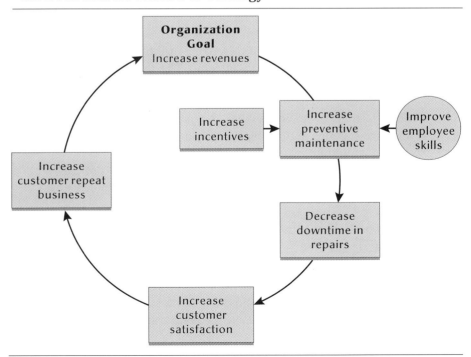

Measuring the Worth of Employees

Many company presidents say, "Employees are our greatest assets," or, as the president of Dofasco said, "Our product is steel; our strength is people." What do they mean? Human capital can refer to factors such as the employees' knowledge, skills, capabilities, and attitudes that impact performance.[77] Remember that it is not just the sum total of employee competencies, but also the application of these competencies in a way that has value to the organization, that provides the true measure of human capital.[78] There have been attempts to measure the worth of employees by counting them, and then attempting to put a number value on their knowledge. Those who want to measure the worth of employees to bring attention to the fact that human resources are of strategic and competitive importance. Another reason is that the value of these resources must be expressed in financial terms to bring credibility to the HR department.[79]

Assessing the worth of intellectual capital or human capital in an organization is incredibly complex; however, some methods are discussed in the Appendix. Our focus here is not on measuring the worth of employees, but on measuring the effect of organizational practices and policies.

Readers interested in a fuller description of measuring HR effectiveness should consult *Research, Measurement and Evaluation of Human Resources*.[80] The choice of measurement tool depends to a large extent on the organization's strategy and the stage of sophistication of its HR department. For example, an HR department that continues to focus on administration in a support role to employees and managers will measure efficiencies. Reports from HR will include statements such as "Processed 1,250 benefits questions; trained 10 percent more employees than last year." An HR department that is a business partner with line management will measure culture and employee productivity, and will establish direct links with organizational performance.

The measurement options available to HR professionals are summarized in Table 14.1. The first approach examines the efficiency of the HR operations. The second is an effectiveness measure, looking at the link between individual HR practices and a specific financial outcome. The third approach is the HR scorecard approach tying HR activities to business activities. The last approach is the cause-and-effect analysis, which focuses on measuring the links between HR programs, the links to employee links, and business outcomes.

The final two columns in the table list the advantages of each approach, and then expose the limitations by asking tough questions.

The measurement of HR effectiveness is not easy. The next section outlines some of the difficulties faced by those attempting to track HR effectiveness.

CHALLENGES IN MEASURING THE IMPACT OF HRM

Measuring the effectiveness of HRM practices has been widely viewed as a progressive step in the development of HRM as a profession and the positioning of HR as a strategic partner at the boardroom table. But in fact, most organizations do not undertake this evaluation because the measurement of HRM activities is

TABLE 14.1

Summary of HR Measurement Alternatives

Measurement Approach	Example Measures	Primary Appeal	Tough Questions
Efficiency of HRM operations	Cost-per-hire, time-to-fill, training costs, ratio of HR staff to total employees	Explicit currency-value calculations. Logic of cost savings is easy to relate to accounting. Standardization makes benchmarking comparisons easier.	"Wouldn't outsourcing cut costs even more?" "Do these cost savings come at the price of workforce value?" "Why should our costs be the same as the industry's?"
HR activity, "best practice" indices	Human capital benchmarks, human capital index	HR practices are associated with familiar financial outcomes. Data from many organizations lends credibility. Suggests there might be practices or combinations that generally raise profits or sales, and so on.	"What is the logic connecting these activities with such huge financial effects?" "Will the practices that worked in other organizations necessarily work in ours?" "Does having these practices mean they are implemented well?"
HR scorecard	How the organization or HR function meets goals of "customers, financial markets, operational excellence, and learning"	Vast array of HR measures can be categorized. "Balanced scorecard" concept is known to business leaders. Software allows users to customize analysis.	"Can this scorecard prove a connection between people and strategic outcomes?" "Which numbers and drilldowns are most critical to our success?"
Causal chain	Models linking employee attitudes to service behaviour to customer responses to profit	Useful logic linking employee variables to financial outcomes. Valuable for organizing and analyzing diverse data elements.	"Is this the best path from talent to profits?" "How do our HR practices work together?" "What logic can we use to find more connections like this?"

Source: From M. Effron, R. Gandossy, and M. Goldsmith, *HR Measurement Alternatives* (New York: John Wiley, 2003), p. 85. Reprinted with permission.

not easy (i.e., advanced skills are required) and the problems in measurement are difficult to resolve. Let us look at some of the problems that arise when we attempt to measure the impact of HRM practices.

Universality of Best Practices

No single best practice works in every situation. Some companies, such as banks, consist of many different companies, all with unique characteristics; in the case of banks, these companies include insurance companies, discount brokerages, and venture capital firms. The HRM policies and practices that benefit performance in the bank may hinder performance in the venture capital arm. The environment and culture of the parts of the larger company are very different. For example, the routine transaction work of the bank lends itself to compensation systems based largely on base salaries, while the entrepreneurial, risk-taking nature of the venture capital firm cries out for incentive-based pay.

Furthermore, organizations and businesses may have different strategic goals. The goal of the financial sector is to maximize ROE, while the goal of Citizenship and Immigration Canada might be to implement the government's immigration policy, which might include increasing the number of immigrants with certain skills. Within a single organization, the goals of one business unit might be to maximize market share (at the expense of profit), while another unit might be attempting to maximize profit. These differences lead to the conclusion that the impact of HRM must be measured against unit goals, not against some generality such as growth or profits. Moreover, some experts suggest that organizations not adopt best practices, but focus on fit. They argue that aligning HR practices with an organization's strategy (influenced by its environment) will result in greater performance than the method of copying other HR strategies (best practices and benchmarking).[81] This is described in Figure 14.2.

FIGURE 14.2

Two Approaches: Fit or Best Practice

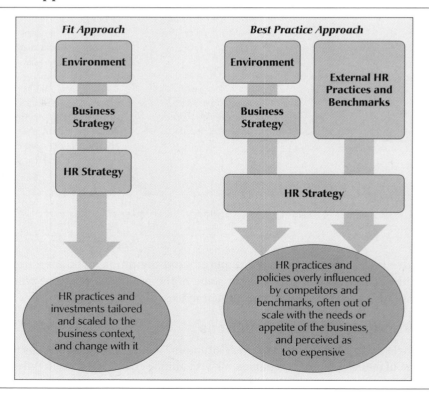

Source: Al-Karim Samani and Pardubyal Singh, *People and Strategy*, 34.1 (March 2011), p. 34

HR Planning Notebook 14.8

LEADING AND LAGGING INDICATORS

HR professionals need to be able to understand the link between HR activities and results. For example, is turnover a leading or a lagging indicator? A leading indicator anticipates, predicts, or affects the future. Higher employee turnover can precede outcomes such as lower customer satisfaction, which in turn can predict lower customer retention and sales. A lagging indicator represents information that results from an event or a change. The lagging indicators in the above example are the lower customer satisfaction, retention, and sales.

Source: Reprinted with permission from *People & Strategy: The Journal of the Human Resource Planning Society.* Adapted from the article, by N. Lockwood, which originally appeared in Issue 9, September 2006. Find out more about HRPS at www.hrps.org. All rights reserved.

Separation of Cause and Effect

The perennial problem in measuring the impact of HRM practices is separating cause and effect. For example, if a profitable company shares its profits with employees through bonuses, does the possibility of earning such a bonus make employees more productive and their companies more profitable? Research suggests that businesses that are profitable invest in HR practices and that this investment pays off in improved financial performance.[82] However, once a new HR practice is implemented, it may take years before its effects are observed. Experts have suggested that it takes two years to design and deliver an HR program and another two years before an organizational outcome can be measured.[83] Obviously, a leading indicator is more valuable for predicting future performance than a lagging indicator, as discussed in HR Planning Notebook 14.8 .

Associated with the lack of confidence in the explanation of causal links between specific HRM practices and organizational performance is the observation that the culture of an organization may explain more than a specific HRM practice. The day-to-day norms of an organization may influence employee behaviour more than any specific practice. For example, if an organization is deeply committed to valuing employees, the day-to-day actions of all managers have more powerful effects than a standalone program such as 360° feedback. Other challenges are outlined in HR Planning Notebook 14.9.

HR Planning Notebook 14.9

CHALLENGES OF EVALUATING HRM

- The work of assessing HR practices is costly; it can add 5 percent to the HR budget.
- HR professionals may not have the time or skills to evaluate.
- HR is not solely responsible for the behaviour of employees. A weak manager may influence productivity more than any HR practice.
- The numbers game—do the numbers reflect reality? Customers have been asked by service providers to give them a good rating when the evaluation agency phones, as their bonus depends on receiving a 10 out of 10.
- What if the result shows no impact of HR practices? How will this information be used? What is the risk to the HR professional's career?

HR Planning Today 14.3

Popular HR Measures

According to the Global Human Capital Study 2008, the most frequently reported measures are:

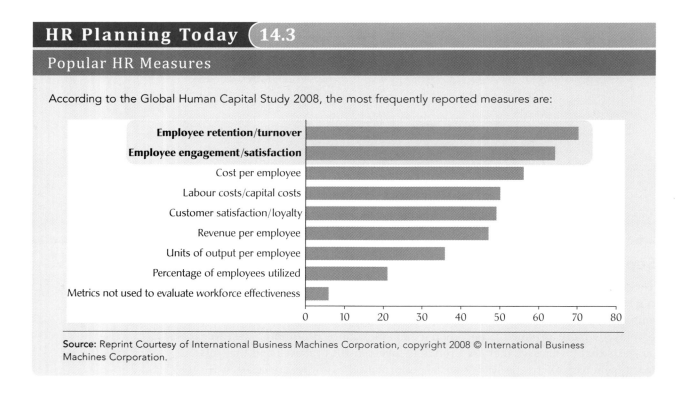

Source: Reprint Courtesy of International Business Machines Corporation, copyright 2008 © International Business Machines Corporation.

Successful Measurement

As you have just read, there are many ways to measure the contributions of the HR function. Organizations seem to focus on background, functional, and efficiency measure. According to a study of Canadian leaders, the most frequent measures are headcount and hires and terminations.[84] Other popular operational measures can be found in HR Planning Today 14.3.

Unlike the accounting profession, which has a set of accounting principles used and understood universally, the HR profession has yet to create a set of generic measures. A recent study identified three hurdles to the development of these HR metrics:

1. Identifying measures that are grounded in research and theory and are practical
2. Gaining acceptance of these measures by the stakeholders
3. Applying these measures consistently and over time[85]

There has been a tendency for HR practitioners to report isolated or averaged numbers, which are meaningless to managers. A meaningful measure is one that allows the managers to identify and solve the problems and report the results.[86]

Whatever measure you decide to use should have the following characteristics:

- *Alignment:* The measure and the potential results must offer some value to the strategy or goals of the organization. Measuring the ratio of HR professionals to the number of employees does not. Measuring the impact of the performance management system on customer satisfaction does. If your organization does not have clear goals, then choose metrics that are meaningful. Why measure cost per hire if you don't know if this number should be increased or decreased? Decreasing it might result in less qualified candidates who are easier to find, but ultimately result in poor quality work or increased turnover, thus increasing costs. In other words, the full cost of reducing or increasing these measures must be calculated.

- *Actionable:* As Albert Einstein said, "Not everything that can be counted counts, and not everything that counts can be counted." Choose only those measures that you can control. Why choose to measure work–life balance issues if your organization is not prepared to make substantial investments in changing working hours or options? Obtain metrics on things like employee commitment or turnover, items for which you can develop action plans.

- *Trackability:* A good metric must be trackable over time so that improvements, as a result of the introduction of solutions, can be assessed. Some measures, such as time to hire, should be tracked weekly for all positions; others, like employee engagement, may be tracked semiannually with a stratified sample.[87]

- *Comparability:* Try to choose measures that can be compared across units and even with best-in-world organizations. To obtain an employee engagement number of 4.5 is not helpful, unless you know that this is lower than in other departments, and much lower than, for example, that of the best employers.

- *Drill deep*: An average turnover figure of 10 percent is meaningless. You need to know that the turnover rate for new hires is 50 percent (a serious problem) while the turnover rate for key executives is 5 percent (not a problem). Employee engagement scores of 90 percent for the company may hide the fact that the operation in Jasper, Alberta is only at 15 percent.

- *Report and communicate a limited number of measures:* The availability of databases allows us to accumulate mountains of data, but very little meaningful information. Information overload is a more serious problem than not measuring at all. Decide on five to ten key measures, and report on these in the same way over time. This should be both historical (lag) and predictive (lead) measures. These key metrics almost always include indices of employee engagement, retention rates by occupational group and unit, absenteeism by occupational group and unit, productivity measures, and cost–benefit analyses for the introduction of any new program.

Another approach might be to listen to the questions being asked by line managers, such as "How can I improve the quality of our service?" and provide programs and then measure these programs to prove the increase in quality service.

All these measures can be arranged in a hierarchy:

Level 1: Basic data—headcounts, number of positions, etc.
Level 2: Operational data—training days, number of grievances, etc.
Level 3: Employee data—levels of engagement, absenteeism, turnover, etc.
Level 4: Organizational data—the correlations between turnover and sales; between engagement and unit performance,[88] etc.

Each of these levels is of interest to different levels in the organization, and would be provided to those managers. The reporting of measures may differ not only by level but by strategy. One study found that companies with a differentiation strategy preferred to receive measures of employee innovative capacities, while those with a cost leader strategy wanted measures of their employees' abilities to manage costs.[89] The lesson here is that the metrics provided have to be of value to the recipients.

The HR department can increase its credibility and power to help managers, and change the perception of the function from a cost centre to one that contributes to profits. HR professionals should continually identify instances of contribution such as "That executive search would have cost the organization $50,000, and we did it for $10,000"; "We have worked with the union and reduced grievances by 20 percent, saving 1,500 hours of managerial time"; and "We changed our benefits provider and saved the company 10 percent."[90]

At this time, metrics seem to inform strategy rather than drive it. Measurement is the key to the management of human capital, and the art of managing people is turning into the science of HRM. This trend will continue as more HR practitioners will be well educated in their discipline, certified and regulated, and adept at validating their profession through the measurement of its activities.

Reporting to Boards of Directors and Shareholders

Increasingly, external stakeholders want to know the human capital numbers, because they know that these are often linked to the future performance of the organization. For example, Aviva, the world's fifth-largest insurance group, provides the following information:

- Percentage of employees who consider that management supports diversity in the workplace

- Percentage of staff who feel that employees in the business are treated with respect

- Percentage of employees who participated in the Global Employee Climate Survey and rated us favourably on leadership index and engagement index[91]

We started this chapter with a description of some of the metrics used by Enbridge Gas Distribution. Enbridge reports on four "people" metrics under the heading "Develop a Healthy and Productive Workforce"—employee engagement, critical retention, attraction/recruitment effectiveness, and career learning opportunities. Executives and shareholders are now very interested in these measures, and HR professionals are increasingly able to supply them.

SUMMARY

This chapter attempts to close the loop in the strategic HR planning process by examining evaluation; when managers implement a plan, they need to know whether the plan was successful. In addition, it is important to measure the impact of HRM so as to prove the value of HR and to improve its performance. The 5C model for measuring HR effectiveness has five areas: compliance with laws and regulations, client satisfaction, culture management, cost control, and contribution. Methods to measure the impact of HRM include cost–benefit analysis, utility analysis, and audits. Benchmarking is a valuable tool that provides comparative data on key ideas and stimulates discussion about better ways to operate. However, there are challenges in measuring HR effectiveness: Overall organization goals might not be applicable to all branches or subsidiary companies; it is difficult to relate cause and effect; and some HR professionals do not see the benefit in such measuring.

Key Terms

attitudes p. 380
audit p. 391
balanced scorecard p. 392
benchmarking p. 391
cost–benefit analysis p. 389
direct costs p. 389

efficiency p. 382
indirect costs p. 389
ROE p. 386
ROI p. 386
utility analysis p. 390

Required Professional Capabilities (RPCs)

The following RPCs are relevant to material covered in this chapter. The RPC number represents the CCHRA number assigned to the RPC as presented on the CCHRA website. All of the RPCs can be found in the Body of Knowledge at www.chrp.ca/rpc/body-of-knowledge.

RPC 7   Audits existing HR programs to ensure that they are aligned with business objectives

RPC 8   Provides the information necessary for organizations to effectively manage people practices

RPC 9   Evaluates the effectiveness of HR strategies, applying various measurement and assessment programs

RPC 12 Develops business cases for HR initiatives and strategies

RPC 13 Sets clear goals, objectives, evaluation standards, and measures for HR programs and strategies

RPC 16 Provides the organization with timely and accurate HR information

RPC 55 Gathers and analyzes information on organizational context (climate, culture) in order to highlight key issues

RPC 64 Researches, analyzes, and reports on potential people issues affecting the organization

Discussion Questions

1. Your HR director has asked you to determine whether your organization (a group of about 50 non-unionized, full-time male managers and professionals working in scientific services in Alberta) has an absenteeism problem. You go to the Statistics Canada website and search for absenteeism data from the Labour Force Survey, where you are happy to discover that the average absenteeism rate in Canada (in 2010) is 8 days, and the employees in your organizations take an average of 8 days per year. Therefore, you do not have an absenteeism problem. Your manager tells you to "drill down." In other words, she wants data on the absenteeism rates by sector, by occupation, and so on. Does your organization have an absenteeism problem?

2. A company wishes to increase the sales performance of its staff. It has been determined that for each $15 product sold, the company makes $5 in profit. Currently, employees who are paid $20 an hour sell an average of four products an hour. A consultant is persuading the company to purchase a four-hour training course. The consultant guarantees that sales capacity will increase by 25 percent and that the effect will last one year (50 weeks of selling time, assuming an eight-hour day). The cost of the course is $400 per employee. Should the company buy the training course for its ten sales representatives? Conduct a cost–benefit analysis to determine the answer.

3. The Canada HR Centre provides a turnover calculator for estimating the costs of an employee quitting. In groups, choose a real job (for which you have compensation information) and calculate the cost of turnover for this position.

Exercises

1. You are the HR manager of a retail organization with 10,000 employees across Canada. The executive team and the board of directors want you to prepare an annual HR report. Choose ten measures that you want to include in the report. Explain why you chose these, how you will measure them, and why this information will be useful for the executives and directors to know.

2. The Government of Nova Scotia has published its HR strategic plan at http://gov.ns.ca/psc/about/overview. In groups, prepare a list of measures that will help the government leaders know if the strategic initiatives have been successful.

Case 1 MEASURING HR IMPACT AT CONVERGYS

Convergys, a global leader helping companies in 40 countries manage their payroll and pensions, was the 2005 winner of the Optimas Award for Financial Impact. The company was experiencing a serious turnover problem that affected their ability to provide excellent customer service. The attrition problem started in 1999, when the company went public and then doubled its workforce to 35,000 employees. The problem in 1999 was so serious that Convergys had to recruit 50,000 employees just to maintain a level of 35,000 employees!

The HR department tried many approaches to solve the problem, including pay raises that had little effect. They borrowed an approach from consumer marketing, in which the HR department held focus groups to determine what would make employees stay. On the basis of this analysis, they discovered which HR practices made a difference to employees. For example, employees said that they would stay longer if bonuses were given every six months, and if most of their requests for days off were granted. The result was a $57 million savings in recruitment and training costs.

Source: Mullich, J. "Attacking Attrition at Convergys," www.workforce.com

Question

1. This is an unusual approach to HR programs and practices. Employees were asked, "What would make you stay with the organization?" and then customized practices were implemented to satisfy their requests. What are the advantages and disadvantages? Though their efforts resulted in savings, what is missing from this case?

Case 2   MEASURING CULTURE TO SUPPORT GROWTH AT CMA

Certified Management Accountants of Ontario (CMAO) provides the CMA designation to certify professional accountants and resources to optimize enterprise performance. CMA of Ontario has approximately 25,000 members. CMA Ontario has 83 employees and has doubled in size from five years ago. Its annual revenue has also doubled from five years ago when a new strategic vision was adapted and propelled the not-for-profit organization to perform like a Fortune 500 company. Development at CMA has been fuelled by the need to offer members and prospects more value with an aggressive growth target of five per cent annually.

"If we are going to compete in today's marketplace, it's not enough to be a sleepy not-for-profit. We must operate similarly to our membership, many of whom are running successful Canadian businesses," says Christine Thrussell, Manager of Human Resources for CMA Ontario, who recalls the push for change when she first started with the organization. Ms. Thrussell made it her objective to be a designation of choice for employees in the not-for-profit sector. "To be competitive, we have to ensure we have the resources employees are looking for."

As part of having the necessary resources, CMA Ontario knew the importance of having a culture to support new work designs. As a result, it was important to the leadership to tap into how their employees valued their workplace. In combination with their balanced scorecard system, CMA Ontario implemented a culture audit assessing employee satisfaction with technology, training, benefits, etc.

At the beginning of Christine's career at CMA Ontario, the employee climate survey indicated they were at the bottom 10 percent of companies of similar size and revenue base. After four years of improvement and changes under the current leadership, CMAO reached the top 10 percent of the survey. For example, four years ago, 52 percent of employees believed they had the technology needed to support the business. Today, 88 percent indicate they have appropriate technology to do their work.

CMA Ontario reports back to employees on these improvements at quarterly town halls and senior leadership and management team meetings. "Employees are able to see the benefits. They've been able to draw a line of sight from what they *had* to what they have today," says Thrussell. "We have a different mindset now, where the focus is on a world-class customer service experience. It's all about implementing the strategy and doing it with discipline."

Source: Correspondence with Christine Thrussell, Human Resources Manager, CMA, June 2011.

Questions

1. If you were the manager of HR, how would you rationalize to your members investing in a culture audit?
2. What additional measures would you use to show the value of investing?

ENDNOTES

1. Courtesy of J. Haberbusch.
2. Lawler, E. and J. Boudreau. 2009. "What Makes HR a Strategic Partner?" *People and Strategy*, Vol. 32, No. 1: 14–22.
3. Stewart, J. 1996. "Blow Up the HR Department." *Fortune*, January 15.
4. Hammonds, K.H. 2005. "Why We Hate HR." *Fast Company*, 97 (August): 41–47.
5. IBM Global Services. "Unlocking the DNA of the Adaptable Workforce." *The Global Human Capital Study 2008*. Somers, NY: IBM Global Business Services. P. 42.
6. Tootell, B., M. Blackler, P. Toulson, and P. Dewe. 2009. "Metrics: HRM's Holy Grail? A New Zealand Case Study." *Human Resource Management Journal*, Vol. 19, No. 4: 375–392.
7. Toulson, P.K., and P. Dewe. 2004. "HR Accounting as a Measurement Tool." *Human Resource Management Journal*, Vol. 14, No. 2: 75–91.
8. Lawler, E.E., A.R. Levenson, and J.W. Boudreau. 2004. "HR Metrics and Analytics: Use and Impact." *Human Resource Planning*, Vol. 27, No. 4: 27–36.
9. Boudreau, J.W., and P.M. Ramstad. 2005. "Talentship and the New Paradigm for Human Resource Management: From Professional Practices to Strategic Talent Decision Science." *Human Resource Planning*, Vol. 28, No. 2: 17–27.
10. *The 2007–2008 Workplace Trends Report.* 2008. Washington, DC: Society for Human Resources Management.
11. Boudreau, J. W. 2010. *Retooling HR.* Boston: Harvard Business School Publishing. P. 127.
12. Corporate Leadership Council. 2001. *The Evolution of HR Metrics.* May, Cat. No. CLC13LNPC.

13. Lawler, Levenson, and Boudreau, 2004.

14. Anonymous. 2005. "Getting Real and Specific—With Measurements." *HR Focus*, Vol. 82, No. 1: 11–12.

15. Dolan, S.L., and A. Belout. 1997. "Assessing Human Resource Effectiveness: The Emergence of the Stakeholder Approach." *HRM Research Quarterly*, Vol. 1, No. 1 (Spring).

16. Hesketh, A. 2008 "Should It Stay or Should It Go?" *Strategic Outsourcing: An International Journal*, Vol. 1, No. 2 (2008): 154–172.

17. Wagar, T. 2002. "Seemed Like a Good Idea, but . . . The Survival (and Death) of High Involvement Work Practices." *HRM Research Quarterly*, Vol. 6, No. 1 (Spring).

18. Davison, H., C. Maraist, and M. Bing. 2011. "Friend or Foe? The Promise and Pitfalls of Using Social Networking Sites for HR Decisions." *Journal of Business and Psycholog*, Vol. 26, No. 2: 153–159.

19. Davison, Maraist, and Bing, 2011.

20. Hansen, D. 2011. "New Age, New Problems: Social Media No. 1 Concern for Employers." *National Post*, June 8, 2011. FP11.

21. Angel, R., and J. Sexsmith. 2011. "Social Networking: The Corporate Value Proposition." *Ivey Business Journal*, ABI/INFORM Global, retrieved on June 20, 2011.

22. Huselid, M.A. 1994. "Documenting HR's Effect on Company Performance." *HR Magazine*, Vol. 39, No. 1: 79–85; Boudreau, J.W., and P.M. Ramstad. 2003. "Strategic HRM Measurement in the 21st Century: From Justifying HR to Strategic Talent Leadership." In Goldsmith, M., R.P. Gandossy, and M.S. Effron, eds., *HRM in the 21st Century*. New York: John Wiley, 2003. Pp. 79–90.

23. Fitz-enz, J. 2000. *The ROI of Human Capital*. New York: AMACOM.

24. Schiemann, W. 2007. "Measuring and Managing the ROI of Human Capital." *Cost Management*, Vol. 21, No. 4: 5–15.

25. Cascio, W. F. 2011. "Becoming the Evidence Based Manager: Making the Science of Management Work for You." *Personnel Psychology*, Vol. 64, No. 1: 266–269.

26. Lawler, Levenson, and Boudreau, 2004.

27. Belcourt, M. 2001. "Measuring and Managing the HR Function: A Guide for Boards." *Ivey Business Journal*, January/February 2001: 35–39.

28. Pfau, B.N. "The State of HR." Presentation at Human Resources Planning Society Conference, April 27, 2004.

29. Tsui, A.S. 1987. "Defining the Activities and Effectiveness of the Human Resource Department: A Multiple Constituent Approach." *Human Resource Management*, Spring: 35–70; Dolan and Belout, 1997.

30. Ulrich, D. 1996. *Human Resource Champions*. Boston: Harvard Business School Press.

31. Rothwell, W.J., and H.C. Kazanas. 1988. *Strategic Human Resources Planning and Management*. Englewood Cliffs, NJ: Prentice Hall.

32. King, A.S., and T.R. Bishop. 1991. "Functional Requisites of Human Resources: Personnel Professionals' and Line Managers' Criteria for Effectiveness." *Public Personnel Management*, Vol. 20, No. 3 (Fall): 285–298.

33. Meyer, J.P., N.J. Allen, and C.A. Smith. 1993. "Commitment to Organizations and Occupations: Extent and Test of a Three Component Conceptualization." *Journal of Applied Psychology*, Vol. 78: 538–551.

34. TowersPerrin. 2008. *2007–2008 Global Workforce Study*, www.towersperrin.co, retrieved on June 15, 2010.

35. Kiger, P.J. 2002. "Why Customer Satisfaction Starts with HR." *Workforce*, Vol. 81, No. 5: 26–32.

36. Lockwood, N. 2007. "Leveraging Employee Engagement for Competitive Advantage: HR's Strategic Role." *HR Magazine*, Vol. 52, No. 3: S1.

37. Gable, S.Y. S. Chyung, A. Marker, and D. Winiecki. 2010. "How Should Organizational Leaders Use Employee Engagement Surveys? *Performance Improvement*, Vol. 49, No. 4: 17–25.

38. Caudron, S. 2001. "How HR Drives Profits." *Workforce*, Vol. 80, No. 12: 26–31.

39. Wright, P.M., and S.A. Snell. 2005. "Partner or Guardian? HR Challenges in Balancing Value and Values." *Human Resource Management*, Vol. 44, No. 2: 177–182.

40. Rison, R.P., and J. Tower. 2005. "How to Reduce the Cost of HR and Continue to Provide Value." *Human Resource Planning*, Vol. 28, No. 1: 14–18.

41. Anonymous. 2006. *Perspectives on Labour and Income*, Vol. 18, No. 3 (Summer): 58–62. Ottawa: Statistics Canada.

42. Fitz-ens, 2000.

43. Caudron, 2001.

44. Gerhart, B. 2005. "Human Resources and Business Performance: Findings, Unanswered Questions and an Alternate Approach." *Management Review*, Vol. 16, No. 2: 174–185.

45. www.watsonwyatt.com, retrieved on April 5, 2006.

46. Huselid, M.A. 1995. "The Impact of Human Resource Management Practices on Turnover, Productivity, and Corporate Financial Performance." *Academy of Management Journal*, Vol. 38: 635–672.

47. Davidson, W.N. III, D.L. Worrell, and J.B. Fox. 1996. "Early Retirement Programs and Firm Performances." *Academy of Management Journal*, Vol. 39, No. 4 (August): 970–984; Huselid, M.A., and B.E. Becker. 1995. "High Performance Work Systems and Organizational Performance." Academy of Management meeting, Vancouver; Huselid, M.A., and B.E. Becker. 1996. "Methodological Issues in Cross-Sectional and Panel Estimates of the HR–Firm Performance Link." *Industrial Relations*, Vol. 20: 245–259.

48. Welbourne, T.M., and A.O. Andrews. 1996. "Predicting the Performance of Initial Public Offerings: Should Human Resource Management Be an Equation?" *Academy of Management Journal*, Vol. 39, No. 4 (August): 891–919.

49. Jones, G.R., and P.M. Wright. 1992. "An Economic Approach to Conceptualizing the Utility of Human Resource Management Practices." In K. Rowland and G. Ferris, eds., *Research in Personnel and Human Resources Management*, Vol. 10. Greenwich, CT: JAI Press.

50. Huselid, 1995.

51. Warech, J., and J. Bruce Tracey. 2004. "Evaluating the Impact of Human Resources: Identifying What Matters." *Cornell Hotel and Restaurant Administration Quarterly*, Vol. 45, No. 4 (November 2004): 376–387.

52. Chen, C. and Collins, C. 2009. "Strategic Human Resource Practices and Innovation Performance." *Journal of Business Research*, Vol. 62, No. 1: 104–111.

53. Koch, M.J., and R. Gunther-McGrath. 1996. "Improving Labour Productivity: Human Resource Management Policies Do Matter." *Strategic Management Journal*, Vol. 17, No. 5 (May): 335–354.

54. Guest, D., J. Michie, M. Sheenan, and N. Conway. 2003. "A UK Study of the Relationship Between Human Resources Management and Corporate Performance." *British Journal of Industrial Relations*, Vol. 41: 291–314.

55. Wright, P.M., T.M. Gardner, L.M. Moynihan, and M.R. Allen. 2005. "The Relationship Between HR Practices and Firm Performance: Examining Causal Order." *Personnel Psychology*, Vol. 58, No. 2: 409–447.

56. Welbourne and Andrews, 1996.

57. Delaney, J.T., and M.A. Huselid. 1996. "The Impact of Human Resource Management Practices on the Perceptions of Organizational Performance." *Academy of Management Journal*, Vol. 39, No. 4: 949–969.

58. Powell, T.C. 1992. "Organizational Alignment as Competitive Advantage." *Strategic Management Journal*, Vol. 13: 119–134.

59. Templer, A., and R.J. Cattaneo. 1995. "A Model of Human Resource Management Effectiveness." *Canadian Journal of Administrative Studies*, Vol. 12, No. 1: 77–88.

60. Templer and Cattaneo, 1995: 79.

61. Brealey, R., and S. Meyers. 1991. *Principles of Corporate Finance*, 3rd ed. New York: McGraw-Hill.

62. Cascio, W.F., and R.A. Ramos. 1986. "Development and Application of a New Method for Assessing Job Performance in Behavioural/Economic Terms." *Journal of Applied Psychology*, Vol. 71: 20–28.

63. See A. Saks, *Research, Measurement and Evaluation of Human Resources* (Toronto: Thomson Nelson, 2000) for a detailed treatment of decision making using utility analysis.

64. Tyler, K. 2001. "Evaluate Your Next Move." *HR Magazine*, Vol. 46, No. 11: 66–71.

65. Pemberton, J.D., G.H. Stonehous, and D.J. Yarrow. 2001. "Benchmarking and the Role of Organizational Learning in Developing Competitive Advantage." *Knowledge and Process Management*, Vol. 8, No. 2: 123–135.

66. Moffett, S., K. Anderson-Gillespie, and R. McAdam. 2008. "Benchmarking and Performance Measurement: A Statistical Analysis." *Benchmarking: An International Journal*, Vol. 15, No. 4 (2008): 368–381.

67. Fitz-enz, 2000.

68. Maire, J.L., V. Bronet, and M. Pillet. 2005. "A Typology of Best Practices for a Benchmarking Process." *Benchmarking: An International Journal*, Vol. 12, No. 1: 45–60.

69. Thomlinson, A. 2002. "T & D Spending Up in US as Canada Lags Behind." *Canadian HR Reporter*, Vol. 15, No. 6 (March 25).

70. Becker, B., and M. Huselid. 2003. "Measuring HR?" *HR Magazine*, Vol. 48, No. 12: 56–66.

71. Davison, B. 2003. "Reviewing Corporate Financials Shows How HR Measures Up." *Employment Relations Today*, Vol. 30, No. 1: 7–17.

72. Woodcock C.P., and P.W. Beamish. 2003. *Concepts in Strategic Management,* 6th ed. Toronto: McGraw-Hill Ryerson.

73. Anonymous. 2005. *Strategic HR Review*.

74. Ulrich, D. 1997. "Measuring Human Resources: An Overview of Practice and a Prescription for Results." *Human Resource Management*, Vol. 36, No. 3 (Fall): 303–320.

75. Kaplan, R.S., and Norton, D.R. 2005. "The Balanced Scorecard: Measures That Drive Performance." Reprinted in *Harvard Business Review*, Vol. 83, No. 7: 1–10.

76. Becker, B., M.A. Huselid, and D. Ulrich. 2001. *The HR Scorecard: Linking People, Strategy and Performance*. Boston: Harvard Business School Press.

77. Chen, J., Z. Zhu, and H.Y. Xie. 2004. "Measuring Intellectual Capital: A New Model and Empirical Study." *Journal of Intellectual Capital*, Vol. 5, No. 1: 195–212.

78. Elias, J. 2004. "Evaluating Human Capital: An Exploratory Study of Management Practice." *Human Resource Management Journal*, Vol. 14, No. 4: 21–40.

79. Bullen, M., and K.A. Eyler, 2010. "Human Resource Accounting and international Development." *Journal of International Business and Cultural Studies*, Vol. 22, No. 1: 1–16.

80. Saks, A.M. 1999. *Research, Measurement and Evaluation of Human Resources*. Toronto: ITP Nelson.

81. Samnanai, A.K., and Singh, P. 2011 "Stop Chasing Best Practices: Focus on Fit for Your HR Function." *People and Strategy*, Vol. 34, No. 1.

82. Wright et al., 2005.

83. Van de Voorde, K., J. Paauwe, and M. Van Veldhoven. 2009. "Predicting Business Unit Performance Using Employee Surveys: Monitoring HRM Related Changes." *Human Resource Management Journal*, Vol. 20, No. 1: 44–63.

84. Uyen, V. 2003. "Finding the Right Numbers to Measure HR." *Canadian HR Reporter*, Vol. 16, No. 15: 1.

85. Tootell, B., M. Blackkler, P. Toulson, and P. Dewe. 2009. "Metrics: HR's Holy Grail?: A New Zealand Case Study." *Human Resource Management Journal*, Vol. 19, No. 4: 375–392.

86. Cook, I. 2011. "How Can HR Metrics Help Companies Grow?" *Canadian HR Reporter*, Vol. 24, No. 9 (May 26). ABI/INFORM Global, retrieved on June 20, 2011.

87. Anonymous. 2005. *Strategic HR Review*.

88. Robinson, D. 2009. "Human Capital Measurement: An Approach That Works." *Strategic HR Review* (Chicago), Vol. 8, No. 6: 5–13.

89. Gates, S., and P. Langevin. 2010. "Human Capital Measures, Strategy and Performance: HR Managers' Perceptions." *Accounting, Auditing, and Accountability Journal*, Vol. 23, No. 1: 111–132.

90. Cascio, W.F. 2000. *Costing Human Resources*. 4th ed. Cincinnati: South-Western College Printing.

91. *Aviva plc Corporate Social Responsibility Report 2008*, www.aviva.com/reports/csr08, retrieved on March 31, 2012.

APPENDIX

HR Accounting Methods

THE HUMAN ASSET ACCOUNTING APPROACH

The *human asset accounting approach* attempts to use accounting principles, such as those used to calculate the historical costs or replacement costs of assets, to put a value on the worth of an organization's human assets. The models used in this approach measure the investment made in employees, treating them as capitalized resources, in economic terms.

- *Historical costs model:* The historical costs model of accounting measures the investment in employees.[1] The investment consists of the costs of acquisition, training, orientation, informal coaching, and experience and development. These costs are amortized over the expected working lives of individuals. Those expenses incurred on behalf of employees who left the company (the un-amortized costs) are written off. This approach has the advantage of being relatively objective and consistent with the accounting treatment of other assets, thus allowing comparisons. Critics of this approach complain that this method is seriously flawed, because the assets are not saleable, and therefore there is no independent check of valuation. They say that estimating costs of informal training and experience is too subjective. In addition, allowances must be made for the changing value of the dollar. The main problem is that the process measures only costs and cannot distinguish between two employees; both may have cost the organization the same dollar amount in acquisition and training, but one may be an outstanding performer and the other a minimally effective worker.
- *Replacement costs model:* This model measures the cost of replacing an employee as an

estimate of market value. The cost includes recruitment, selection, compensation, training, and orientation.[2] This model is unsatisfactory for several reasons. Although substituting replacement cost for historical cost provides an updated valuation, the actual opportunities to do these calculations are limited. Most organizations have limited turnover, particularly at senior levels, and so building a complex human asset formula into the accounting system would not be worthwhile. Furthermore, a badly managed HR department that incurred abnormal expenses in recruiting or selection might overestimate the cost of replacing an employee.[3] A highly sophisticated system of staffing, orientation, and training would also generate high replacement costs, but the measure of the value added by exceptional employees would not be part of the accounting process.
- *Present value of future earnings model:* This model measures contributions, not costs. The organization tries to determine what an employee's future contribution is worth today by calculating future earnings, adjusted for the probability of an employee's death.[4] Contribution is calculated by the compensation paid to an employee. Probability of death is estimated using mortality tables. The problem with this model is that it assigns a value to the average worker, rather than to an individual. No investment in individual employees—for example, in training—is taken into account, and yet this training investment should have a payoff in future contributions.

These three models of human asset accounting value employee service at gross book value (the original investment expenses), net book value (the original investment minus depreciation), and economic value (the anticipated financial return on the investment).[5] These models, however, have not been accepted by HR professionals or by researchers for many reasons.

Limitations of Human Asset Accounting Models

As can be seen, the main problem with human asset accounting models is their failure to take into account employee effectiveness. They tend to measure only inputs, such as costs incurred in acquiring and training employees, and not outputs, such as employee productivity. Secondly, who is the best judge of employee worth—the employee, the manager, or the HR department? Another major problem is the cost and difficulty of obtaining these data. The focus seems to be on an industrialized economy rather than one that depends on knowledge management.[6]

The most recent trend is to measure the intellectual capital—the brainpower—of employees in the hope of measuring actual and potential contributions.

Intellectual or Human Capital Approach

The productivity of most organizations entering the 21st century is highly dependent on the intellectual capabilities of their employees. In this context, human capital refers to the knowledge, competencies, experience, and motivation of the employees.[7] The balance sheet cannot capture the value of this human capital. For example, the value of Microsoft was greater than that of General Motors, Ford, Boeing, Lockheed Martin, Deere, Caterpillar, Weyerhauser, Union Pacific, Kodak, Sears, Marriott, Safeway, and Kellogg combined![8] Yet a real source of Microsoft's value is the knowledge of its employees. An interesting observation is to note that that the market capitalization of Apple works out to $7.93 million for every one of its 46,600 employees.[9] The human capital approach is an attempt to quantify the economic value of employees in financial and management accounting terms.[10]

Intellectual capital can be thought of as intellectual material (knowledge) that can be formalized, captured, and leveraged to produce a higher-valued asset.[11] Intellectual capital can be seen as employee brainpower, some of which is described in skills inventories and patent lists.

Quinn and his colleagues described and ranked the importance of this intellectual capital:[12]

1. Cognitive knowledge ("know what")
2. Advanced skills ("know how")
3. System understanding and trained intuition ("know why")
4. Self-motivated creativity ("care why")

Employers will pay a premium for smart workers. In the United States, men with postgraduate degrees earn 130 percent more than men who never finished high school.[13] The pay gap between men with these different levels of education has doubled since 1980. Companies such as Scandia and Dow Chemical are struggling to identify, describe, and measure these intellectual assets in order to manage them. As one chief financial officer of a telecom company stated: "As a technology company, much of our ability to differentiate ourselves from our competitors depends on being able to market new product solutions more quickly than anyone else. For this, we rely on our intellectual capital."[14]

Intellectual assets have characteristics highly distinct from other assets. First, intellectual assets grow with use. Anyone who has gone back to school or completed a training course realizes that the learning of new knowledge, and its application, leads to even greater knowledge and a motivation to acquire more. Intellectual capital can be shared and cannot be depleted. Sharing it results in increased feedback, acquisition of new knowledge, and modifications and adjustments to current knowledge. Accenture links via email 82,000 employees in 360 offices in 76 countries, allowing the posting of problems on bulletin boards. Company management believes that this taps dormant capabilities of employees and expands energy and solutions to problems. However, there are also disadvantages to investing in intellectual assets. One is exclusivity. If you own a capital asset such as a building, you can prevent competitors from using it. However, a highly knowledgeable employee can moonlight, freelance, or subcontract for other companies or leave to work for a competitor.

Issues in Measuring Intellectual Capital

Experts in this nascent field estimate that the intellectual assets of an organization are worth three to four times the tangible book value. A common approach is to claim that the intellectual capital of a firm is equal to the difference between a firm's capitalized stock value and its book value. One study found that increases in employee capabilities directly influence financial results.[15] It is still very difficult to put a dollar value on the brain resources of employees. CIBC tries to do so by counting employee skills (e.g., the ability to manage a portfolio of clients), which can be used to build a competency inventory. But as skills change, the dynamics of measuring them become difficult. Furthermore, most of this asset is left idle: Observers and employees alike guess that only 20 percent of the knowledge available in their companies is used.[16] The role of HR programs in changing employee motivations cannot be underestimated. The on-time performance at Continental Airlines changed in one month from the bottom to the top of the industry, as a result of a new compensation system.[17] You can see when a factory is producing at a reduced capacity; you cannot always determine if your knowledge workers are working at capacity.

Educational and medical institutions have measured intellectual capital for decades, relying on peer reviews (and publication records) for decisions about the worth of the faculty or professionals. Thus, first measures of intellectual capital include peer review, although in some cases, it may be done by colleagues working together on projects. Some organizations add another review level, that of customer or client evaluations of outputs.[18] Customers are asked to rank team participants on professional knowledge and specific project contributions, and on overall satisfaction with results. To supplement these human evaluations,

some organizations add measures of efficiency and effectiveness, which normally are measured in business terms (e.g., costs, fulfillment time and accuracy, delivery times). Finally, some organizations track the intellectual assets created. CIBC charts the growth of intellectual capital by tracking the flow of knowledge among employees. The company counts, as indicators of intellectual capital, the number of new ideas generated, the number of new products created, and the percentage of income from new revenue streams.

The competitive advantage of intellectual capital is enormous. This asset cannot be traded or expropriated. Competitors fall farther behind because the top talent goes to organizations such as Microsoft to be part of a leading-edge organization.

Many researchers have tried and failed to come up with a single, limited criterion to measure the worth of an organization's human resources. Accountants cannot value intellectual capital, because there is no market for it—it cannot be bought and sold, and so valued. After reviewing the literature, researchers concluded that the search should be abandoned, despite its attraction for managers making internal management and external investment decisions.[19] But the start of the new century has seen a revival in attempts to measure human capital, driven by consulting companies and academics. The rationale for the search for the holy grail of human capital assessment is fuelled by the belief that these measures give a clearer indication of a firm's potential and future profitability than backward-looking accounting techniques.[20]

ENDNOTES

1. Cascio, W.F. 1991. *Costing Human Resources: The Financial Impact of Behavior in Organizations*, 3rd ed., Kent Series in Human Resource Management. Boston: PWS Kent.
2. Flamholtz, F.L.K., D.G. Searfoss, and R. Cof. 1988. "Developing Human Resource Accounting as a Decision Support System." *Accounting Horizon*, Vol. 2: 1–9.
3. Steffy, B.D., and S.D. Maurer. 1988. "Conceptualizing and Measuring the Economic Effectiveness of Human Resource Activities." *Academy of Management Review*, Vol. 13: 265–280.
4. Lev, B., and A. Schwartz. 1971. "On the Use of the Economic Concept of Human Capital in Financial Statements." *Accounting Review*, Vol. 46: 103–112.
5. Cascio, 1991.
6. Chen, J., Z. Zhu, and H. Y. Xie. 2004. "Measuring Intellectual Capital: A New Model and Empirical Study." *Journal of Intellectual Capital*, Vol. 5, No. 1: 195–212.

7. Gates, S., and P. Langevin. 2010. "Human Capital Measures, Strategy and Performance: HR Managers' Perceptions." *Accounting, Auditing, and Accountability Journal*, Vol. 23, No. 1: 111–132.

8. Lermusiaux, Y. 2002. "Managing Human Capital in a Downturn." *Ivey Business Journal*, Vol. 66, No. 4 (March/April): 14–16.

9. Akkad, O. 2011. "Apple's Familiar Act: Underplay; Overachieve." *The Globe and Mail*, July 20, 2011. B3.

10. Schwarz, J.L., and T.E. Murphy. 2008. "Human Capital Metrics: An Approach to Teaching Using Data and Metrics to Design and Evaluate Management Practices." *Journal of Management Education*, Vol. 32, No. 2: 164–182.

11. Stewart, T.A. 1994. "Intellectual Capital." *Fortune*, October 3, pp. 68–74.

12. Quinn, J.B., P. Anderson, and S. Finkelstein. 1996. "Leveraging Intellect." *Academy of Management Executive*, Vol. 10, No. 3: 7–28.

13. Quinn et al., 1996.

14. Edwards, S. 1997. "The Brain Gain." *CA Magazine*, April: 21–25.

15. Massingham, P. Nguyen, T. Massingham, R. 2011. "Using 360 Degree Peer Review to Validate Self-Reporting in Human Capital Measurement." *Journal of Intellectual Capital*, Vol. 12, No. 1: 43–60.

16. Edwards, 1997.

17. Wright, P. and G. McMahan. 2011. "Exploring Human Capital: Putting "Human" Back into Strategic Human Resource Management." *Human Resource Management Journal*, Vol. 21, No. 2: 93–104.

18. Wright and McMahan, 2011.

19. Scarpello, V., and H.A. Theeke. 1989. "Human Resource Accounting: A Measured Critique." *Journal of Accounting Literature*, Vol. 8: 265–280.

20. Toulson, P.K., and P. Dewe. 2004. "HR Accounting as a Measurement Tool." *Human Resources Management Journal*, Vol. 14, No. 2: 75–91.

INDEX

Page references with *b*, *f*, and *t* notations refer to a box, figure, and table on that page respectively